P. Carson Lantis
1964-

FREDERICK J. McDONALD

STANFORD UNIVERSITY

Illustrated by David Morgan

EDUCATIONAL

PSYCHOLOGY

EDUCATIONAL

PSYCHOLOGY

WADSWORTH PUBLISHING COMPANY, INC.

BELMONT, CALIFORNIA

EDUCATIONAL PSYCHOLOGY
Frederick J. McDonald

First printing, August 1959
Second printing, June 1960
Third printing,   May 1961
Fourth printing, June 1962
Fifth printing,   June 1963

Printed in the United States of America
L. C. Cat. Card No.: 59-11270

First published in Great Britain 1961

For Jan

FOREWORD

More than a quarter of a century ago, John Dewey concluded a Phi Delta Kappa lecture with the following statement:

> The sources of educational science are any portions of ascertained knowledge that enter into the heart, head and hands of educators, and which, by entering in, render the performance of the educational function more enlightened, more humane, more truly educational than it was before. But there is no way to discover what *is* "more truly educational" except by the continuation of the educational act itself. The discovery is never made; it is always making. It may conduce to immediate ease or monetary efficiency to seek an answer for questions outside of education, in some material which already has scientific prestige. But such a seeking is an abdication, a surrender. In the end, it only lessens the chances that education in actual operation will provide the materials for an improved science. It arrests growth; it prevents the thinking that is the final source of all progress. Education is by its nature an endless circle or spiral. It is an activity which *includes* science within itself. In its very process it sets more problems to be further studied, which then react into the educative process to change it still further, and thus demand more thought, more science, and so on, in everlasting sequence.[1]

This quotation aptly describes what I consider the most valuable characteristic of this book. Professor McDonald is quite apparently convinced that the teacher can and should see himself as engaged in

---

[1] John Dewey, *The Sources of a Science of Education*, New York, Liveright Publishing Company, 1929, pp. 76-77.

an uninterrupted cycle of inquiry, continuously generating and evaluating more adequate procedures, always tentative in his conclusions, and never permitted the luxury of dogma. The teacher's behavior is seen as the major source for his own improvement—the act of "teaching" is defined as an act of inquiry. Such a conception of the teaching role is neither new nor bold; it is, unfortunately, merely infrequent.

The equation of "teaching" with "inquiry" is explicitly used as a frame of reference in this book, and, in so doing, Professor McDonald is taking the position that a major function of educational psychology courses is that of helping prospective teachers learn the orientations and techniques that teaching requires. The reader is warned that psychological generalizations have only conditional and probable validity for any concrete situation. They cannot be viewed as propositions of certain validity; they are only starting points for the teacher's thinking.

If an educational psychology is to be consistent with the probabilistic nature of both teaching and psychology, a consideration of theoretical matters must be introduced frankly. This Professor McDonald does, and he demonstrates the necessity and usefulness of theoretical concepts in the analysis of "practical" educational problems. Consideration of theoretical concepts cannot be a "simple" affair. However, the atheoretical nature of most educational literature and discussions may predispose the reader initially to overestimate the complexity of the discussions in this book. A little patience and forebearance at this point will be rewarding.

It is believed that this text will appeal to all who agree that education is an ever-changing process which requires the teacher constantly to challenge his own procedures. This book is not filled with immediately usable recipes for teaching. Indeed, the thesis here is that such recipes for teaching are not admissible. Techniques of teaching must be the creative (and temporary) product of the teacher's intelligence as he moves from one learning context to another.

Arthur P. Coladarci
Stanford University

PREFACE

Writing a book requires one to select among ideas, generalizations and supporting data, and to emphasize some theoretical conceptions over others. This process of winnowing is inevitably influenced by the author's predilections and preferences. This being so, perhaps the student can profit from a statement of my conscious assumptions and preferences, as well as from a general statement of the possible and intended uses of this book.

This text was written in the light of an assumption about the nature of the teaching-learning process—that teaching activities are essentially professional. While teaching is commonly called a profession, the sense in which the word "profession" will be used here is not common, meaning "an avocation whose activities are subjected to theoretical analysis and are modified by theoretical conclusions derived from that analysis."[1] We are all aware that not every teacher views his work in terms of this definition. It is a major premise of this book, however, that teaching ought to be a profession in this sense of the word. This text has been written to demonstrate that teaching activities can be subjected to theoretical analysis and modified by that analysis.

In this respect, we can distinguish teaching from a "craft," which is "an avocation based upon customary activities and modified by the

[1] A. N. Whitehead, *Adventures of Ideas*, New York, The Macmillan Company, 1933, p. 72.

trial and error of individual practice."[2] Certainly, teaching is often conducted as if it were a craft, but we feel that many of the difficulties associated with modern education arise out of this conception of the nature of teaching activities. This "craft" conception of the nature of teaching activities is probably one of the reasons for the difficulty in preparing prospective teachers. We also suggest that this conception dominates much of public thinking about education and is what underlies the difficulties that educators have in initiating new practices and in defending rationally the practices they are using.

The conception of teaching as a profession, in the sense defined above, has dominated my thinking and has influenced the whole tone of the book. This book is not written to give teachers rules for good teaching. I firmly believe that there are no such rules, and that the preparation of teachers is hampered rather than enhanced by an attempt to create the impression that such rules do exist. For this reason the character of teaching activity is conceptualized essentially as a process of continual hypothesis-making and hypothesis-testing. The teacher is described as a decision-maker, who formulates his decisions as hypotheses to be tested rather than as rules to be applied.

The purpose of this book, therefore, is to help teachers become good hypothesis-makers. As a consequence, I have preferred to present the factual and theoretical content of educational psychology as tentative hypotheses about learning.

The teacher may also be conceptualized as a creator of learning environments. This means that the teacher organizes experiences likely to promote changes in pupils. Each act of a teacher in organizing learning experiences is seen as being essentially a hypothesis about events likely to promote changes in pupils. To be consistent with these conceptions, I have attempted to indicate the validity of the generalizations discussed and to identify the problems and difficulties in using these generalizations to create learning experiences. I have attempted to point out where we have reliable and relatively valid psychological knowledge at the present time. I have not hesitated to call the reader's attention to the fact that many of these generalizations and hypotheses have not been tested within typical classroom settings; these admissions of less than perfect knowledge should stimulate and encourage the teacher to participate in the process of hypothesis-making and hypothesis-testing. Consequently, the reader may be annoyed by the

---

[2]*Ibid.*, p. 73.

continual note of tentativeness in the discussions throughout this text. In one sense, this annoyance is precisely the effect desired. The effectiveness of this approach will be lost, however, if the reader fails to use the information in this book as a starting point for personal and creative theorizing about educational practice.

Another major conception in this book is that educational processes directly affect the development of the personality of the child. Although it is unnecessary to explain this conception at any length here, let me warn the reader that I am not thinking of "personality" in any narrow or crass sense. Personality is the totality of the child. The learning experiences provided by a teacher in a classroom affect the personalities of children in many different ways, and the curricula of schools are designed for the formation of personality in specified and desirable ways. Consequently, a model of personality processes and a description of personality in psychological terms is presented in the third chapter of this book. This theoretical conception of personality is introduced into this text in the hope of influencing students to develop a conceptual framework for analyzing teaching activities and evaluating their influence on the development of the personality of a child.

The student will find two major themes running throughout the text—the character of teaching activity and the character of personality development. These two themes will be interrelated consistently. The major hypotheses and generalizations will be statements about the relationship of learning experiences to changes in the personality of a child.

One other assumption has dominated the selection of materials for this text. I do not think that a textbook is the sole or perhaps even the primary educative device through which students learn. Neither do I believe that educational psychology should be a condensation of all psychology. This book will have failed in one of its purposes if students assume that they "know psychology" when they have finished reading it. This book is meant to be a starting point. I have attempted to provide a basic conceptual framework into which the student can integrate new psychological information, generalizations, hypotheses, and theories.

It also is my hope that both the approach and content of this book will provide a basis for additional study in professional education. Just as I do not believe that a text in educational psychology is a compendium of psychology, neither do I believe that it should be a compendium of professional education. This book is not an adequate substitute for rigorous professional training, either theoretical or applied. But I do hope that critical and thoughtful study of this textbook will enable the student to analyze recommendations for educational practice that he will receive in other courses and in his teaching career.

A recommendation for catching the tone and approach of this book may be helpful here. Many of the basic conceptions discussed throughout the book are summarized in the last chapter. A quick but thoughtful reading of this chapter should enrich systematic study of the other chapters. I would also urge that the student occasionally reread this chapter during his course in educational psychology.

To summarize, this book will not provide recipes, rules, or neat formulas guaranteed to make every teacher a success in the classroom. Instead, I have tried to encourage the teacher to analyze, criticize, and evaluate recommendations for educational practice in the light of theoretical conceptions and generalizations. This text and the course that accompanies it will introduce many new ideas, concepts, and generalizations. These should enable the student to find new ways of looking at human behavior, particularly the behavior of the child in the classroom. Knowledge of generalizations about human behavior should improve the teacher's ability to make predictions about and to explain the behavior he continually observes and attempts to influence in some ways. I hope that my emphasis on a critical, conceptual, hypothesis-making approach to the activities of educational practice will achieve one major purpose—to enable teachers to become thoughtful and critical generators and testers of hypotheses. I am urging this analytic approach not merely for the sake of theorizing, but because theorizing and hypothesizing are the essence of any critical evaluation of practice. Whitehead phrased this idea in the following way:

> Such criticism [of the activities of a profession] must be founded upon some understanding of the natures of the things involved in those activities, so that the results of action can be foreseen. Thus foresight based upon theory, and theory based upon understanding of the nature of things, are essential to a profession.[3]

This book is designed to contribute to an understanding of the psychological aspects of the educational process and to stimulate a

---

[3]*Ibid.*, p. 72.

theoretical and critical approach to the activities of educational practice.

I am grateful to Julian C. Stanley, University of Wisconsin, and Loh Seng Tsai, Tulane University, for their encouraging reviews of a portion of the early manuscript. I am also deeply appreciative of the frank and thorough evaluations of the entire manuscript provided by Shepard A. Insell, San Francisco State College, and Carson McGuire, University of Texas. Above all, I am indebted to Arthur P. Coladarci, Stanford University, for his challenging professional and personal encouragement and expert criticism throughout the writing of the book.

Many hands make a book. In particular I am indebted to Miss Rebecca Hayden, whose editorial assistance, skill, and patience contributed in innumerable ways to the development of this book; Mrs. Mary E. Warner, who was responsible for the numerous transcriptions of the manuscript, as well as a variety of journeyman tasks associated with its development; Dr. Elizabeth K. Bauer, whose superior quality of indexing has added to the usefulness of the book. Without this assistance the manuscript might still be in process.

Finally, my wife is particularly responsible for the development of this book. Her continual encouragement and interest provided the appropriate psychological climate.

Frederick J. McDonald
Palo Alto, California

CONTENTS

xvi

PART THREE

THE EVALUATION OF LEARNING

PART FOUR

THE SCHOOL AS A SOCIAL SYSTEM

PART ONE

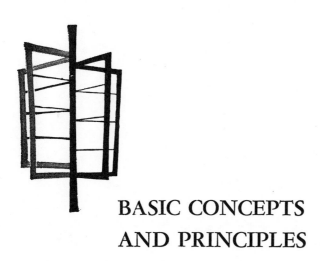

BASIC CONCEPTS
AND PRINCIPLES

THE EDUCATIVE
PROCESS

What does it mean to be educated? As a student you have spent many years in school, reading, listening, observing, talking with teachers and other students. You have acquired ideas and information, new tastes and interests. You have made plans for a career. You know more about yourself. In short, you have changed. You are in some degree different from what you were like a year ago, ten years ago, or even a month ago.

But, unlike Topsy, you have not "just grown." American society has provided a complex of educational institutions designed to foster this development in you. Direction has been given to this growth. Teachers have supervised the kinds of experiences you have had and have systematically attempted to promote changes in you. For example, you were encouraged to want to learn to read, and were given the opportunity to learn to read. This change and many others were planned for and fostered. You are what you are today in part because particular kinds of opportunities to learn have been provided for you.

In this chapter we will explain basic concepts and principles relevant to understanding the nature and function of the educational process. Essentially, we will be answering the question with which this chapter begins. Our answer will not describe one kind of educational "product," nor will the answer be in terms of specific kinds of schools or school systems, curricula, methods, students, or teachers. These concepts and principles will be equally applicable to any and all kinds of schools, students, and teachers. They will be applicable to any situation or institution which attempts to bring about desirable changes in people.

THE MEANING OF EDUCATION

DEFINITION OF EDUCATION. *Education, in the sense used here, is a process or an activity which is directed at producing desirable changes in the behavior of human beings.* By "behavior" we mean any response or action of a person, anything that a person does. Liking a teacher, talking to a fellow student, thinking through an algebra problem, reading a book, getting married, choosing a career—all of these are "behaviors," or "actions," or "responses" of a person. Note that some of these behaviors are directly observable, such as reading a book, while others, such as "liking a teacher," must be inferred from actions or behaviors that we observe.

The function of the educational process is to promote or facilitate *desirable* changes in behavior. A newborn child has only a limited number of responses that he can make, but over his entire life span he acquires new ways of behaving. The function of the kinds of experiences to which the child is systematically exposed is to produce specifiable and desirable changes in the kinds and number of responses that he can make. For example, the child learns the large number of responses required to compute accurately. "Computing behaviors" are behaviors that we can specify as desirable for an individual if he is to handle successfully a wide variety of problems. We devise experiences by which the child can acquire these responses. Any set of experiences designed to produce such changes is educational.

The product of this process at any given stage is a human personality. This personality is the complex system of behavior that an individual acquires. A change in the system of behavior is a change in personality. When Johnny has learned to read he has acquired a new set of behaviors. Johnny is now a somewhat different personality from what he was before he learned to read. His behavior system is more complex than it was. He acts differently than he did before he learned to read. As Johnny grows he will acquire many more behaviors, and will abandon others, such as crying when he cannot get what he wants. Each change is a modification of his personality to some degree. The essential elements in the educational process, then, are the human organism and a set of experiences that are intended to bring about changes in the personality of this organism.

VARIETY OF EDUCATIONAL EXPERIENCES. A little reflection will suggest that a wide variety of institutions and settings are involved in education. The "school" is only one of these. The puberty rites of a primitive tribe, the Komsomol activities of a Russian youth, and the school dance in an American high school are instances of potentially educational experiences. Each of these, in its cultural setting, represents an attempt to foster desired changes in behavior and, therefore, fits our definition of education as adequately as do "Algebra I," "French II," and "American History." Each, in its own way and for its own specific purposes, may contribute to desired changes in behavior and personality.

EDUCATION AND THE SOCIALIZATION PROCESS. Education also may be viewed as the socialization process: the process by which the child is inducted into the mores of the society in which he lives. The emerging personality of the child is in some measure defined by the behavior changes resulting from this process. Each institution in society and the experiences that a society provides contribute in varying degrees to the socialization of its members. The complexity of the task of socializing the child is such that it requires a division of responsibility among the institutions and the individuals who assume responsibility for the development of the child. Home, school, church, Boy Scouts, YMCA, football teams—these and many other institutions and organizations contribute to the socialization process. In principle, each attempts to influence the behavior of the child in such a way that his developing personality will become increasingly well adapted to the demands and aspirations of his society. The complex interaction of these diverse influences results in the child's development as a member of his society.

THE MEANING OF PERSONALITY

We have said that educational experiences contribute to the development of personality. Since there are a number of meanings attributed to the term "personality," it is important to distinguish between the common use of the term by the layman and the manner in which it is used by the psychologist. Note that the common, everyday meaning of the term "personality" embraces only some of the meaning included in this concept as we will use it.

COMMON MEANING. Personality is frequently thought of as something which people "have," some having more and some having less. Johnny is described as "having a lot of personality" and Mary, who is quiet and shy, "does not have much personality." The assumption in this conception appears to be that personality is "added to" the person, and some even speak of children who are born with or without this special quality. In this sense, we note that personality is something that is relatively independent of the person. From a psychological point of view, personality and person are not distinct; that is, when the psychologist speaks of personality, he is referring to the total person in all his characteristics and aspects.

PSYCHOLOGICAL DEFINITION OF PERSONALITY. *Personality is the unique, integrated, and organized system of all the behavior of a person.* This system of behavior includes such complex responses as the way a person looks at the world, his goals and interests, what he likes and dislikes, his ability to do or not to do something, the way he solves problems, how he feels about people, and what he wants out of life. All of his behavior, including both the behavior patterns that can be directly observed and behavior that is inferred, comprises this system of organized behavior that we call personality.

Each of these aspects of personality is not an element or trait that can be added to or subtracted from the person in some simple way. Nor does any one aspect in itself constitute the person's personality. The child who is happy, cooperative, and friendly may be described as a "cooperative" child. But his personality is not described in its totality by this single, relatively simple, trait description. Neither is the child who is called "shy" completely described by this term.

THE CHARACTERISTICS OF PERSONALITY DEVELOPMENT

CONTINUITY OF PERSONALITY DEVELOPMENT. *The development of personality continues throughout the entire life of the human organism,* and a remarkable persistence runs throughout this process of development. The accumulated learning from previous experience sets the stage for each new development in personality, and the person integrates each new learning into the pattern of his learned behavior. Johnny's apparently inexplicable outburst in class today is not, as it may appear to be, a singularly unique behavior unrelated to Johnny's previous experience. What the teacher, as the observer in this instance, may not see is that on some earlier occasion Johnny has learned to respond to frustrating conditions in this manner, although, up to this time, the classroom situation had not evoked such behavior from him. Present experiences take on meaning in the light of what has been previously learned. Johnny may find a certain situation frustrating today because similar conditions have been sources of frustration to him in the past.

UNIQUENESS OF PERSONALITY DEVELOPMENT. *The pattern of personality organization differs among individuals.* The society in which the child grows up sets certain limits on the development of personality, rewards the development of certain patterns of personality, and attempts to insure through the socialization process the development of the characteristics necessary for living in a particular society. However, despite the common characteristics that can be found among members of any society, the members themselves are somewhat different individuals. The differences lie not only in the specific patterns that are characteristic of a given person, but also in the manner in which all of the characteristics are organized into a total personality.

We frequently speak of the American as an "aggressive, achievement-oriented" type of person. While these characteristics are common to many members of our society, any two Americans will differ in the way they reveal these characteristics. For one person achievement-orientation will take the form of striving for success in the financial world; for another it will take the form of striving for success in intellectual activities. Two persons will differ in the manner in which they strive for achievement. One person perhaps may seek achievement as an end in itself—for example, one person must be "tops in everything"; the other person may seek achievement in one line of endeavor. We discover characteristics that are common to many different members of a given society, but at the same time we recognize particular emphases and different ways of organizing and integrating behavior that will result in uniqueness in each individual.

The study of personality requires that we seek both *commonalities* and *differences*. The teacher, for example, will find common characteristics among children of the same sex or children from the same social background. At the same time the teacher will observe many individual variations on the common theme.

DYNAMIC CHARACTERISTICS OF PERSONALITY DEVELOPMENT. Finally, *personality is dynamic—a personality is continually changing in many different ways.* The child develops physically, and his physical development makes it possible for him to do things and to acquire ways of behaving that effect changes in personality. Each child, as he grows, lives in an experiential world that is in varying degrees different from that of every other child, although the sets of experiences organized by society for the child are common experiences in some ways. All children go to school and have comparable kinds of experiences, yet these children will react to these experiences in different ways, will find different meanings in these experiences, and as a consequence will develop as somewhat different personalities. Children are taught to read in school and are given a wide variety of reading experiences. While these reading experiences are not identical, they have much in common. Yet surveys of reading interests of adults show a diversity of reading habits and interests.[1] Each child, as he learns to read, responds to the experience in a different way. Johnny finds biography more interesting than fiction, while Jane prefers dramatic works to novels. Johnny reads only occasionally and prefers a movie to a book, while Jane reads every chance she gets. Each has developed his own pattern of "reading behavior," though both have had comparable kinds of reading experiences.

Each child also brings to the world of experience a different hereditary endowment. The interaction of the child's native endowment—or potentialities—with his experiences results in the development of his personality. Table I gives data on the reading interests

---

[1]H. C. Link and H. A. Hopf, *People and Books,* New York, Book Manufacturers' Institute, 1946.

of "bright," "average," and "dull" children.[2] These children began life with different potentialities. They have had comparable but not

Per Cent Bright	Per Cent Average	Per Cent Dull
Adventure . . . 33.0	Mystery 23.4	Mystery 30.8
Mystery 19.7	Adventure . . . 22.1	Detective . . . 29.2
Detective . . . 14.2	Detective . . . 18.1	Adventure . . . 9.8
Science 10.4	History . . . 13.6	History 7.9
History 7.0	Invention . . . 8.2	Nature and Animal 7.9

Five Kinds of Books Liked Best by Bright, Average, and Dull Boys (From Lazar)

TABLE I

identical school experiences. Even when we study children in groups, as in this case, the effects of the interaction of ability and experiences are apparent; bright children differ in the order of their preferences. We can also discern commonalities in development; for example, "mystery" books rank high in the preferences of all three groups of children.

The personality of the child grows by a continuous process of reorganization and integration of new behavior in his total personality system. *Stability and consistency are frequently apparent in the course of development, but this development is an open-ended process.* The child who today knows only the world of his family, tomorrow knows the world of his teachers and schoolmates, and will someday move into the world of complex adult relationships. The child moving through these experiences is responding to his environment, learning new ways of behaving and new modes of responding, changing his perceptions of the world, altering his attitudes and feelings about the people and things in his environment, and integrating everything into his conception of himself and his environment.

PERSONALITY, HEREDITY, AND ENVIRONMENT

The complex system of behavior that we have called personality

---

[2]M. Lazar, *Reading Interests, Activities and Opportunities of Bright, Average and Dull Children,* New York, Bureau of Publications, Teachers College, Columbia University, 1937.

results from two major forces: (1) from the native endowment or potentialities of the organism; (2) from the learning opportunities provided by the experiences of the child. These two forces are inter-related in a complex manner, but considerable difference of opinion exists on the relative importance of each.[3] While this question cannot be resolved at the present time, certain principles are clear:

1. The native endowment of the human organism both provides a basis for and sets limits on the ultimate development of the personality.

2. Within the limits set by native endowment, the human organism is remarkably plastic and capable of diverse developments.

3. While the human organism is remarkably plastic, it is nevertheless dependent for its development on the experiences with which it is provided.

THE INFLUENCE OF HEREDITY. We do not expect the child who is physically or mentally handicapped to develop in the same way as the child who is not handicapped.[4] This is obvious, but the child who has no special handicaps also must develop within the limits set by his native capacity. We do not expect the child of average intelligence to become a theoretical physicist, nor do we expect the child with mediocre musical aptitude to develop into a concert artist. However, within the limits set by the endowment of the child, remarkable development is possible. The child somewhat below average in intelligence is capable of learning many things: he is capable of participating as a citizen in civic affairs; he is capable of supporting himself in a useful way; he is capable of developing hobbies and interests commensurate with his talents; he can lead a happy and productive life.

Native capacity, while it sets limits, also provides the potentialities for development. Capacity is the broad base on which an un-

---

[3]For a discussion of the problems of the influence of heredity and environment on behavior, see A. Anastasi, *Differential Psychology*, New York, The Macmillan Co., 1958, Chapter 3; also A. Anastasi, "Heredity, Environment, and the Question 'How?'" *Psychological Review*, 65 (1958), 197-208.

[4]R. G. Barker, B. A. Wright, L. Myerson, and M. R. Gonick, "Adjustment to Physical Handicap and Illness. A Survey of the Social Psychology of Physique and Disability," *Social Science Research Council Bulletin*, No. 55 (rev.), 1953.

limited number of personality structures can be built. The child of high intelligence may become a nuclear physicist, a novelist, a skilled craftsman, or any of a number of other things. But while native endowment sets limits and provides the essential base for development, it does not in any final sense determine the specific ways in which personality will develop. Variation, even within the limits of endowment, is for all practical purposes infinite.

THE INFLUENCE OF ENVIRONMENT. The infinite variations in personality result from the use that the human organism makes of its environmental opportunities, as well as from differences in native capacity. Two children within the same environment will learn different things,[5] as will two children who are in different environments.[6] We need only to look at the members of the same family to see that children growing up in comparatively the same environment will emerge as quite different personalities, even though we may recognize many common characteristics among these children. Even more obvious are the differences among children who grow up in entirely different environments. Neither native capacity nor environment alone can account for personality differences.

Each environment has unique features as well as characteristics common to other environments. The family that appears on the surface to comprise a relatively homogeneous environment is a complex of many different environmental situations. The family living conditions change in time as new possessions are acquired, and as the family moves from one house or community to another, as the parents acquire experience in raising their children and change their methods of child-rearing, or as new family members are added. The second child in a family does not have an environment that is identical to that of the first child. The younger child lives in a world that includes an older child. While we have similar curricula, methods, and materials for all the classes of the first grade in any school, still the environment within each classroom is remarkably different. Although we talk of the environment of the lower- or upper-class child, each

---

[5] S. C. Fisher, *Relationships in Attitudes, Opinions, and Values among Family Members*, Berkeley, University of California Press, 1948.

[6] Considerable data is available on this point. For representative studies, see: A. J. Brodbeck and O. C. Irwin, "The Speech Behavior of Infants without Families," *Child Development*, 17 (1946), 145-156; J. R. Wittenborn *et al.*, "A Study of Adoptive Children," *Psychological Monographs*, 70 (1956), Nos. 1, 2, and 3; E. A. Milner, "A Study of the Relationships between Reading Readiness in Grade One Children and Patterns of Parent-Child Interaction," *Child Development*, 22 (1951), 95-112.

child in a social class lives in a different environmental situation. Different environments foster the learning of different kinds of behavior patterns; the interaction of different patterns of native capacity and different learning experiences results in unique personalities.

THE NATURE OF ENVIRONMENTAL INFLUENCES

Jim and Joe are eighth grade students in the same school. Jim is taught by Mr. Ferris, and Joe by Miss Carrel. Jim's father is an engineer; Joe's father owns a grocery store. Jim has a sister and brother; Joe has a brother. Jim's father has a workshop that Jim uses. Joe's father does not have a workshop, but he and Joe share hunting and fishing equipment. Even from this brief description we can say that these two boys are growing up in different environments. We would expect that having fathers with different occupations and interests, having a different number of brothers and sisters, having different materials available to use, and having different teachers make a difference in what these boys learn.

CATEGORIES OF ENVIRONMENTAL INFLUENCES. What are the features of an environment that make a difference in what is learned in that environment? This question can have no final answer, but we can identify general features of environments which influence the kinds of behavior patterns that are acquired in those environments. These general features may be divided conveniently into two classes: (1) the cultural environment and (2) the interpersonal environment.

THE CULTURAL ENVIRONMENT. We include in the cultural environment anything that is relatively independent of the person, and that may be in some sense nonpersonal. The cultural environment includes distinctive physical objects such as the home in which a child lives, the furniture in this home, automobiles, pictures, the clothes he wears. The cultural environment also includes the mores and values of the society in which the child is growing up, as well as the language spoken in that society. The cultural environment is nonpersonal only in the sense that these objects, values, and customs can be viewed as being independent of a given person, and are acquired by the members of a society. The child in growing up acquires the language, the customs, and the values of his society, and they become integrated into his personality. People frequently speak about the cultural environment as being relatively independent of themselves, as when we talk about "our language," "our customs," "our American automobiles."

Cultural environments vary from society to society. A child growing up in the American society and going to an American school is confronted with a cultural environment that differs from that of a child in another society. For example, in learning his language, an American child learns only one word for the natural phenomenon that we call "snow," unless he is a ski enthusiast and then he will learn to qualify this noun in only a few ways. But the Eskimo child learns in effect a large variety of words for the equivalent of our word snow, that is, he learns to distinguish between wet snow, dry snow, old snow, new snow, and so on, using for each a different word.[7]

In his classroom the American child sees pictures of Washington and Lincoln on the walls rather than a picture of Lenin. He may go to and from school in an American car. His behavior is governed by the rules and customs for children in American society.

Even within a major social group there are different cultural environments. For example, some homes in American society have hi-fi sets. There are one- and two-car families. The differences in available objects in American homes reflect differences in cultural environments within the larger American culture. The smaller cultural environments exist within the framework of the total culture but, because of their distinctive features, provide a different setting for the development of personality.

The cultural environment in all its variety sets the stage within which the human being lives and responds as a personality. The cultural environment is a source of opportunities and limitations for the development of personality. For example, a city child, because he is living in a nonrural environment, may have difficulty in identifying farm animals. The rural child may be mystified by the complexities of transportation in a large metropolitan area. As the rural child and the urban child develop, each will have opportunities for changes in behavior that the other does not have. At the same time their environments will place limitations on the possibilities for personality development. The cultural environment determines the kinds of experiences that are likely to be provided for a child in that environment, and consequently will determine the kinds of experiences that he can

---

[7] O. Klineberg, *Social Psychology*, New York, Henry Holt & Co., 1940, p. 45.

understand and appreciate, and the kinds of behavior that he can interpret and learn.

THE INTERPERSONAL ENVIRONMENT. Still, are objects the really crucial elements in the environment of a child? In many ways we can see that other persons are much more important. Even accessibility to the physical and cultural objects is in many instances mediated through other people. Parents provide the objects of the home environment, and teachers provide the materials for the classroom. Furthermore, the attitude of the parent or the teacher toward the objects and toward the child himself is of crucial significance. The child who learns to value classical music does so at least in part because his parents or his teachers, in providing him with access to classical music, have indicated their appreciation of this kind of music. Similarly, the child who learns to value "bop" music in preference to classical music may do so because "significant other people" have shown preference for this kind of music.

The persons in the environment of a given child are not neutral, impersonal stimulus objects in the same sense that a table or words in a dictionary may be. All human beings are acting, responding organisms, and much of the activity of a human being originates in the context of his relationships with other people. A child in the presence of another person is aware that this person is responding to him and is acting on the basis of his reaction. This kind of interrelationship is called an interaction process. *Essentially an interaction process occurs when the behavior of one person serves as a stimulus to evoke responses from the other person and contrariwise.* A mother smiling at her child may serve as a stimulus that evokes from the child a smile or some other playful response. The teacher who calls for order in a classroom may evoke a response of silence from his pupils, and the pupil who does not respond with silence becomes a stimulus that evokes from the teacher further admonitions "to be quiet." Thus other people provide important stimulation to action on the part of a child. The child responds not only to physical and cultural objects but also to the people that are present in his environment. We see that any environmental situation is a complex of physical and social elements that act as stimulus events, or environmental events, which serve to *evoke, guide, punish,* and *reward* the behavior of the child.

CONTINUITY OF EXPERIENCE. Environmental situations are not discrete units except when we subdivide and categorize aspects of the environment for the purpose of analysis. The educational psychologist analyzes the classroom as an environment, the child psychologist analyzes the home situation as an environment, the social psychologist analyzes the factory work-group as an environment. For the individual, however, the environment is continuous in the sense that he is immersed in an experiential field to which he is continually responding.

The thread of continuity between different environments is provided by an individual's conception of himself as essentially the same person who is behaving in these environments. The child does not see himself as "Johnny in Miss Jones' class" and as an entirely different "Johnny who belongs to the Smith family." Rather he sees himself as Johnny who is in Miss Jones' class and as the same Johnny who belongs to the Smith family, who lives in a city, who has Mary and Bob as his friends. The stream of experience for the child, while differentiated in various aspects, is an integrated experience in which the central feature and focus is himself.

THE SCHOOL AS AN ENVIRONMENT

We have suggested two principles above which need to be interrelated at this point: (1) that the school is an institution which contributes to the total educational or socialization process directed to the development of the personality of the child; (2) that the school assumes certain responsibilities for specific aspects of this socialization process. The school is essentially a contrived environment, deliberately structured for the purpose of promoting desired changes in behavior of the child. These responsibilities are delegated to the school on the premise that the other institutions of society will assume other responsibilities in the socialization of the child, and that all of the experiences in which the child is immersed will be integrated and will lead to the fullest possible development of his personality.

The phases of the socialization process that the school shall be responsible for vary from time to time, from society to society, and from culture to culture. There are societies which have no formal schools and in which the socialization process is conducted entirely through the family or some other social unit.[8] There are also societies in which the school assumes most, if not all, of the responsibility for the socialization of the child.

The school, as a contrived environment for the development of the child, provides situations or experiences out of which the child will learn to behave in ways that are different from the ways he would behave if he did not take part in these experiences. When Johnny enters the first grade, he probably does not know the alphabet or how to read, he cannot write, he is not familiar with the formal aspects of language, he has very limited numerical concepts, he has no knowledge of the geography of his country, and he is unfamiliar with its history. Over a period of time he will acquire knowledge and skill in these and many other areas. While he is attending school, he will learn to interact with and respond to many more kinds of people than he would meet within the limited environment of his home or his neighborhood. The school condenses into a relatively short period of time the possibilities for learning many things that would take a lifetime to learn in a less structured and organized fashion, if they could be learned at all.

It hardly seems necessary to labor the point that the school provides an enormously rich experiential field which sets a stage for learning that could not be accomplished as easily or as surely in any other way. However, it is important to stress that the desired result of this process is the development of a person in a way that would not otherwise be developed. This learning is not something that is "tacked on to him," nor a luxury which he enjoys, nor a set of experiences that merely "broaden his mind," nor an intricate and expensive way of meeting other people. Rather the function of the school is to produce changes in the child in specifiable and desirable ways so that he will be able to take his place in adult society.

THE SCHOOL AND THE CULTURE

The school reflects the total culture of which it is a part;[9] it

---

[8]For an analysis of these differences and their relation to the development of personality, see M. Mead and M. Wolfenstein, *Childhood in Contemporary Cultures,* Chicago, University of Chicago Press, 1955. See also, J. W. M. Whiting and I. L. Child, *Child Training and Personality: A Cross-Cultural Study,* New Haven, Yale University Press, 1953.

[9]See A. B. Hollingshead, *Elmtown's Youth,* New York, John Wiley & Sons, 1949. See also, M. Mead, *The School in American Culture,* Cambridge, Harvard University Press, 1951.

transmits the dominant values, mores, attitudes, and ideas of society. The emphasis in American schools on learning the ways of democracy is an example of this principle of cultural transmission. Debate as we may about what our schools should be teaching and how they should be teaching it, there is nevertheless a general agreement that the schools should produce a citizen who is capable of living in and sharing the responsibilities of a democratic way of life. Other societies, in which democracy either is not the dominant mode of life or is conceived of in a different manner from what it is in American society, reflect in their schools emphases which suggest their own dominant cultural patterns.

Schools reflect the culture as it exists at a particular time. Our schools do not teach the churning of butter, or how to make shoes, or the essentials of log cabin building, but we do teach home economics, driver education, auto mechanics, and a variety of other specifics which, when they were introduced into the curriculum, were assumed to be necessary for at least some members of our society.

A comprehensive study of the educational process requires that we view the process in the cultural context in which it is taking place. From a psychological point of view, this sensitivity to the cultural context of education is necessary to sharpen our awareness of the kinds of experiences to which we will be exposing children, and to make us aware of alternative experiences and the kinds of personalities that the alternatives might produce. The school is not an independent, isolated institution, but is a part of a general cultural context which is reflected in the home, the school, small groups of one kind or another, and larger social institutions such as churches and clubs. As the child moves through these various environments, his personality is shaped and formed so that he will develop into a person who is capable of participating fully and responsibly in our society and the larger societies of which ours is a part.

SUMMARY

The purpose of this chapter has been to clarify the student's thinking about the psychological character of the educational process. From a psychological point of view, an educational experience is a process designed to promote desirable behavior change.

Behavior is any response—simple or complex—of a person. A person's organized system of behavior is his personality. This behavioral system embraces all that the person is. Consequently, the purpose of educational experiences can be thought of as the development of personality.

An individual has many educational experiences in the course of his life. These experiences are not confined to the school; they occur in many other institutional and non-institutional settings.

As an individual moves from one environment to another and as his capacities mature, his behavior changes. The result of these repeated modifications of behavior is a unique personality, and, typically, one that has developed consistently and continuously.

The school is a special environment designed to promote behavior changes which are consistent with the total development of the person as a member of his society. The school as one of the agencies of cultural transmission typically reflects the dominant mores and values of society.

The key concepts in this chapter are *behavior, personality, and environment. The school is an environment arranged to promote changes in behavior which result in the development of personality.*

The principal implication of this discussion for the teacher is that the concepts and general principles outlined here provide him with a new way of looking at the activities of classroom and school. The remainder of this book is an explication of what this new view implies. New views of familiar phenomena typically rekindle our interest, stir our imagination, and enlarge our comprehension. These concepts and principles are the foundation pieces for building an understanding of the psychological dimensions of the educational process.

STUDY AND DISCUSSION QUESTIONS

1. Describe several kinds of behavior change that the school attempts to promote. Specify the kinds of learning experiences provided to facilitate these changes. Be specific about both the desired change and the character of the learning experience likely to stimulate it.

2. List some organizations to which a child might belong. In what ways are these organizations educational? Specify the kinds of behavior changes that these organizations are likely to promote.

3. In what ways is a school dance an educational experience? In what ways might a history lesson and a school dance promote the same kinds of behavior changes?

4. Many people might think that a study of advanced mathematics bears little if any relation to socialization. In what ways may this kind of educational experience contribute to the socialization of a child?

5. What important cultural values might be learned in a history lesson; in an arithmetic lesson; at a school dance; at a work session of the school newspaper staff?

6. For what kinds of behavior change do the home and school share responsibility? What kinds of behavior change are assumed to be the specific responsibility of each institution? May the home and school attempt to promote behavior changes which are incompatible? In what ways?

7. Describe the neighborhood in which you grew up. In what ways did it differ from other neighborhoods with which you are familiar? Suggest some differences in personality development that may have been influenced by this environment.

8. Review the data in Table I. Suggest some environmental influences that may account for the differences in preferences among the three groups of boys. What assumption about environmental opportunity must we make before we can attribute the preference differences to the influence of an ability factor?

9. In what ways would a study of the reading interests of fraternal twins give us information about the relative effects of native endowment and environment? What assumptions would we make in analyzing the data from such a study?

RECOMMENDED READINGS

The following reading materials amplify the major ideas explored in this chapter. They also provide corroborative data for these ideas.

1. M. Mead and M. Wolfenstein, *Childhood in Contemporary Cultures*, Chicago, University of Chicago Press, 1955.

2. R. Linton, *The Cultural Background of Personality*, New York, Appleton-Century-Crofts, Inc., 1945.

3. A. Davis, "Socialization and the Adolescent Personality," *Forty-Third Yearbook of the National Society for the Study of Education, Part I*, 1944, Chicago, University of Chicago Press, pp. 198-211.

4. M. Mead, *The School in American Culture*, Cambridge, Harvard University Press, 1951.

5. A. B. Hollingshead, *Elmtown's Youth*, New York, John Wiley & Sons, 1949.

THE TEACHER AND THE EDUCATIVE PROCESS

In the previous chapter we discussed the school as a contrived, constructed environment designed to promote desirable changes in behavior. The school, however, is not a single homogeneous set of experiences, but rather a complex of many and varied experiences arranged throughout the entire span of schooling. The teacher has daily and direct responsibility for the organization of the immediate learning experience that the child is undergoing. State and local curriculum guides, textbooks and other available materials, and the training of the teacher create limits within which particular learning experiences are organized. Within these limits there is enormous variability in the kind of specific learning experiences, in terms of content, sequence, and scope, that can be provided for each child. The teacher has the responsibility for the day-by-day, minute-by-minute, experiential environment in which the child is placed.

In this chapter we analyze the relationship of the teacher to the educative process, and in the following chapter the relationship of the student or learner to this process. The

analysis is not limited to specific kinds of educational institutions or functions. The analysis is logical in character. It does not describe how particular teachers act in practice, but it is a description of how their activities may be analyzed in relation to the educational process, as we have described it.

THE EDUCATIVE ACT

The educational process is a sequence of particular events. The child does multiplication tables, recites spelling words, reads silently or orally, plays baseball, watches a film on India. The activities change by the hour and the day, and are different at various educational levels. But, essentially, each of these events is designed to promote behavior changes in students.

An *educative act* is an organized event in—an aspect or part of—the total educational process. Such an event or act may be simple in character and brief in duration, like memorizing a list of spelling words, or it may be more complex in character and of relatively long duration, like the successive discussions in a seminar. An educative act is what is done at a given time and place to produce desirable behavior changes in students. It is an element of the educational process.

The educative act has three aspects: (1) the formulation of educational objectives; (2) the organization of learning experiences; (3) the evaluation of learning. Logically, the educative act begins in a conception of a desired change in behavior. Experiences are organized to foster this change. Finally, a determination is made of the extent to which the change has taken place.

An elementary schoolteacher decides, for example, that the pupils in his fourth grade class are capable of learning what a sentence is. The teacher prepares illustrations of sentences and of groups of words which are not sentences. He presents these to the pupils and encourages them to discover the characteristics of a sentence. As they try this defining process, he provides more examples of sentences and other combinations against which they can check their provisional definitions. Eventually, the pupils appear to grasp the idea of a sentence, and the teacher summarizes this idea in a concise definition. To insure that the learning is adequate the teacher assigns exercises for homework which require the pupils to identify word combinations as sentences. He also asks each pupil to write ten sentences of his own. The following day the teacher checks the pupils' work, noting errors and pointing out correct responses.

This sequence of events is an educative act. From the viewpoint of the teacher this experience was designed to produce a specific behavior change. As a consequence of this experience, pupils presumably should be able to recognize and to identify sentences. The classroom activities, such as studying examples of sentences and attempting to formulate a definition of a sentence, are the experiences designed to produce this behavior change. The homework assignment is both an extension of the classroom learning experience and a means by which the teacher can identify what the pupils have learned. On the basis of this determination the teacher will plan new experiences (each of which is another educative act).

These three teacher processes are implicit in any educative act, even though a teacher may not actually plan his activities in terms of these processes. In the following section we discuss each of these processes in greater detail and emphasize their interrelations.

EDUCATIONAL OBJECTIVES. *An educational objective is a statement of a desired behavior change,* that is, it is a statement about the behavior that shall be acquired by the child.[1] If the child is central in the educational process, and if the educational process is to produce changes in behavior, educational objectives must be more than general statements of purpose, vague generalizations about what the school hopes to do, or descriptions of broad curricular areas.[2] It is not sufficient, for example, to state that "In the first grade Johnny will learn to read," unless we can also specify what behaviors shall be acquired by Johnny. Learning to read is a complex process that involves the acquisition of many behaviors ranging from learning to recognize the letters of the alphabet to being able to make a critical analysis of a novel. Each of these phases in the reading process is in itself a complex integration of skills, attitudes, and ways of thinking. Educational objectives should be formulated on the basis of the behavior that the learning experiences are expected to produce. Without a clear, com-

---

[1] For a comprehensive and detailed discussion of procedures for formulating behavioral statements of educational objectives, see Chapter Fourteen.

[2] Ideas for developing detailed and comprehensive statements of objectives can be found in the following sources: B. S. Bloom (ed.), *Taxonomy of Educational Objectives,* New York, Longmans, Green and Co., 1956; N. C. Kearney, *Elementary School Objectives,* New York, Russell Sage Foundation, 1953; W. French, *Behavioral Goals of General Education in the High School,* New York, Russell Sage Foundation, 1957.

prehensive, and fairly definite statement of expected changes, it is difficult to formulate and organize the learning experiences which are to produce these changes. An integral relationship exists between the kinds of behavior change desired, the learning experiences provided to produce these changes, and the process of evaluating whether these changes have taken place. Travers makes this point in the following terms:

> What is the teacher to conclude when he finds that he is unable to list specific behaviors as a means of defining a goal? The answer is simple: when the teacher does not know how the achievement of a particular goal affects the pupil's behavior, the goal is a meaningless thing. Unfortunately, many goals which seem to be worth-while on the surface turn out to be quite meaningless when they are subjected to the kind of analysis necessary for adequate definition.[3]

LEARNING EXPERIENCES. *Once the objectives have been formulated, the task of the teacher is to organize and arrange the learning environment.* A major portion of this book will be devoted to the principles of learning which must be taken into account in organizing learning experiences. At this point it is important to stress that the learning environment is organized and arranged to produce the specified behavior changes. The function of the psychology of learning is to determine the relationship between experiences and the behavior learned in response to these experiences. The teacher has the complex task of integrating what he knows about children and the learning process to create experiences that will produce the desired changes in behavior.

The activities of the teacher in organizing learning experiences are many and varied and embrace all aspects of his behavior and the physical and social environment in which he teaches. The text, the audio-visual aids he may have available, the materials the students will use, the arrangement of the classroom, the utilization of pupil activity, all of these must be organized into a complex of environmental events that will constitute experiences for the child out of which he will learn new behaviors.

From a psychological point of view, the learning environment has a three-fold function: (1) to elicit desired responses; (2) to rein-

---

[3]R. M. W. Travers, *How to Make Achievement Tests,* New York, The Odyssey Press, 1950, p. 20. By permission of the publisher.

force and strengthen responses so that they will occur easily and frequently in the future under the appropriate conditions; (3) to extinguish inappropriate or undesired responses. A child in the course of a day in a classroom makes literally thousands of responses, many of which are irrelevant to the desired learning experience. However, the function of the learning experience is to evoke the desirable responses, to strengthen these responses, and to hasten the weakening of undesirable responses. In describing the essential character of the learning experience as one of evoking and strengthening responses, it is not necessary to conceive of this process as a mechanical or a "push-button" type of process. The child enters each new learning experience with the accumulated effects of previous learnings. He brings to each new learning situation a complex integration of concepts, attitudes, and motor behavior, on the basis of which he will learn new ways of behaving. The function of the learning experience, which is a complex experiential field, is to bring about a reorganization of these concepts, attitudes, and motor responses, to facilitate new discriminations and differentiations, to acquire new modes of response, and to integrate the old and the new patterns into a more comprehensive system of behavior.

EVALUATION OF BEHAVIOR CHANGE. *The third phase in the educational act from the point of view of the teacher is evaluation of the learning.* In this phase the teacher systematically determines whether the expected and desired behavior changes have in fact taken place, that is, whether the student has acquired the new ways of responding that were specified as desired. The process of evaluation, like that of organizing learning experiences, is a complex process in itself.

To evaluate, there must be some method or way of measuring every behavior change that has been specified as desirable. Two errors are frequently made in this respect: (1) the teacher may fail to evaluate a behavior change that he has specified as desirable and for which he has provided learning experiences; or (2) the teacher may evaluate behavior without reference to the changes in behavior that have been specified as desirable. For example, if our fourth grade teacher, who explained the characteristics of a sentence, had not given exercises to determine whether the students understood what a sentence is, he would not know whether the desired changes had taken place. The second kind of error in evaluation procedures is exemplified by the college teacher who calls for critical thinking and creative expression on an examination after his lectures and assignments have emphasized the acquisition of facts. From the emphasis in the course, we would have inferred that the desired behavior change was the acquisition of facts. In either case the continuity between specified desirable changes, learning experiences designed to produce these changes, and the evaluation process to determine that the changes have taken place has been broken.

The process of evaluation is both varied and continuous. The evaluation process includes the tests constructed by the teacher to evaluate learning, standardized achievement tests, and the teacher's observations of the pupil's behavior in many contexts, such as in the classroom and on the playground. The teacher is, in effect, continually evaluating the behavior change of his pupils; Prescott makes this point when he says:

> Teachers interact with children an enormous number of times every hour of the day, no matter what they are teaching or what the grade level may be. Furthermore, everyone of these interactions is evaluative, requiring a judgment and a feeling about the situation. . . . During any single school day a teacher must make hundreds of decisions. . . . These accumulating decisions create the conditions under which the pupils live and learn at school.[4]

At almost any given moment of the day the teacher is evaluating the learning of the child, *and on the basis of his judgments about learning is revising the learning experiences provided for the child.* Periodic examinations are only more comprehensive and formalized evaluative procedures. The total evaluative process is a set of complex judgments made by the teacher about pupil learning. The teacher puts together all the information that he has accumulated about a given child, not merely for the sake of giving a grade or deciding upon promotion, but primarily to evaluate the pupil's learning. New learning experiences are provided on the basis of the judgment made in this evaluation.

EDUCATIONAL METHODOLOGY. The teacher is responsible for the over-all manipulation of the educative act, of which the child is the center and focus. The educative act is in no sense a mechanical process arranged in such a way that changes in behavior occur automatically if given kinds of environments are provided. The child is an active

---

[4]D. A. Prescott, *The Child in the Educative Process,* New York, McGraw-Hill Book Company, copyright 1957, p. 6. By permission of the publisher.

participant in the process and manipulates his own behavior to produce changes. The teacher attempts to stimulate and strengthen these changes by interacting with the child and by arranging the total learning environment. Systematic procedures for arranging learning experiences are called *educational methods*. What is the relation between educational methods and the educative act as it has been conceptualized here? *Educational methodology is the process by which the educative act is initiated and carried through.*

A common conception of educational methodology is one which views methodology as a routine, relatively mechanical process for organizing learning experiences. When we study and discuss educational methods, we sometimes assume that these methods are guaranteed devices for producing learning. At the present time there are no methods of this character. It is questionable whether there ever will be, particularly if the educative act is conceptualized in the manner discussed above. On the other hand, to say that educational methodology is not a routine set of devices for producing learnings does not imply that the educative act is essentially a haphazard process. Rather it emphasizes the essential characteristics of the educative act, namely, that it is dynamic, continuous, and adaptive.

THE TEACHER AS A DECISION-MAKER

If the teacher cannot routinely apply educational methods to pupils, how does he act in organizing learning experiences? *Essentially, the teacher is a decision-maker who, on the basis of his evaluation of pupils' readiness for learning or present status in learning, organizes a learning experience which will lead the child on to new differentiations and new integrations of behavior.* The teacher in making decisions is, in a general sense, manipulating and controlling the child's behavior. Implicitly he is also making predictions that, given a certain kind of learning experience, certain kinds of pupil behavior will be produced.

We are not here discussing an issue that has been formulated as "teacher-control" versus "pupil-control." The teacher's decisions are influenced by the goals, interests, and immediate behavior of the pupil. However, the teacher's decision-making processes set the limits within which pupil behavior occurs, and it is these decisions that give the learning environment its distinctive characteristics. Prescott has noted:

These accumulating decisions create the conditions under which the pupils live and learn at school. For example, they determine the freedom or restriction of movement, of speech, of access to materials, of spontaneous inquiries or comments, of choice of experiences. They profoundly influence the kinds of relationships the children are able to establish and maintain with adults in the school and with each other in the classroom, on the playground, and everywhere about the school. These decisions often determine the actual learning experiences to which the children are exposed, the content upon which attention is focused, and the food for mental, social, and spiritual growth that is offered each child. They determine the aspects of life and the world with which the pupils are brought into contact, and they evoke or fail to evoke the various steps of the reasoning process, and encourage or discourage curiosity and imagination. They promote certain codes of conduct and imply the validity of certain attitudes and values for living in our times and in our society. These judgments permit some adjustment processes and mechanisms to operate and discourage others. They emphasize certain meanings as valid and condemn others as untrue and unacceptable.[5]

An example perhaps will make clear the point being discussed. A fourth grade teacher was introducing a unit on "Pioneer Life." He asked the students what they wanted to study about "Pioneer Life" and what kinds of questions they should raise concerning the subject. As the discussion proceeded the children suggested the usual categories for studying a history unit, namely the pioneers' food, shelter, and clothing.

One child mentioned that he had seen a western movie recently and that, in the movie, a man who was accused of horse-stealing was hanged. This comment on the movie evoked considerable interest in the group and one of the children asked why the man had been hanged right away. The teacher discussed this question by saying that it was not relevant to a discussion of pioneer life. The teacher's decision to utilize or not utilize this question in effect sets the stage for the kinds of things that the pupils will talk about in studying pioneer life. Had the teacher chosen to capitalize upon this question, topics concerning pioneer conceptions of justice, concepts of due process of law, the function of law-enforcing bodies, and the validity of citizens' arrests could have been developed. These topics did not emerge in the ensuing discussion nor were they included as relevant points in the outline of topics to be studied under the heading of "Pioneer Life." The teacher had at this point made a decision which determined the

_____
[5]*Ibid.*, pp. 6-7.

character of the learning experience that was provided for the children he was teaching.

DECISIONS AS HYPOTHESES. *Each of the decisions that a teacher makes in the course of conducting the educative act is in effect a hypothesis about learning.* While the teacher does not speak in this kind of language, what he does can be formulated in propositions something like this: "If I introduce these words into the vocabulary lesson, then the pupils will have more words available to read Scott's *The Lady of the Lake.*" These hypotheses, simple or complex, are in effect predictions about the behavior that will result from certain kinds of learning experiences. In principle, such hypotheses have varying degrees of probable validity.

Coladarci points up the essential characteristics of this kind of thinking:

> Intelligent hypotheses are not chosen randomly nor are they found full-blown. An intelligent hypothesizer thinks along the lines of the following model: "*On the basis of what I know now* about individual differences and the reading process, I hypothesize that this kind of grouping-for-reading will lead to the kind of pupil-progress in reading that I would like to bring about."[6]

FACTORS INFLUENCING THE TEACHER'S DECISIONS. Three general factors influence the particular decisions that the teacher makes in the organization and construction of learning experiences: (1) cultural factors; (2) professional factors; (3) scientific factors.[7] The teacher's decision-making processes have been influenced by the whole course of his own life and training. The teacher grows up in American society and acquires the patterns of behavior, the values, and the attitudes of members of American society. Each teacher has been influenced by his family, the general social milieu, the schools he has attended, the community in which he lives, and the school in which he teaches. He also maintains comparatively wide professional contacts, both within his school and in the teaching profession. He

---

[6]A. P. Coladarci, "The Relevancy of Educational Psychology," *Educational Leadership,* 18 (1956), No. 8, 489-92. For a comprehensive discussion of the teacher as a hypothesis-maker, see also A. P. Coladarci, "The Teacher as Hypothesis-Maker," *California Journal for Instructional Improvement,* 2 (1959), 3-6.

[7]For a comprehensive discussion of these factors and their relation to the character of the teacher's decisions, see Prescott, *op. cit.,* Chapter I.

has also studied the educational process as a part of his professional training, and presumably has acquired a body of reliable knowledge which, in part, forms a basis for his educational practice.

Any particular decision a teacher may make at a given time in a classroom will be influenced in varying degrees by each and all of these factors. In some instances a decision will be influenced primarily by the kind of person the teacher has become as a result of growing up in our culture. For example, the teacher of English will be influenced both in his choice of reading selections and in what he emphasizes in these readings by his philosophy of life and his standards of "good" literature. The kinds of pupil behavior he encourages and discourages will be a function of what he regards as the appropriate kind of behavior for a pupil.

In other decision-making situations the teacher's judgment will be influenced by his professional contacts. He has read or heard that a certain technique for teaching reading is valuable because one of his colleagues has found it effective. How he feels about a pupil may be strongly influenced by what he has learned about the pupil from another teacher. His conception of the role of the teacher in his school will be in part influenced by the conceptions of his fellow-teachers.

Finally, the body of scientific knowledge that exists about the educational process will in some way shape the judgments of the teacher. While this body of knowledge is by no means definitive, most teachers in the course of their professional training will have read about experiments in education, will have received suggestions for teaching procedures based upon research, and will have some familiarity with the research literature of education.

The act of hypothesis-making is a creative act. The teacher pulls together many sources of information, reactions to stimuli in his environment, previous experiences, and combines these to formulate a hypothesis about what is needed in the present learning situation. Ordinarily the teaching process is sufficiently complicated without requiring that teachers specify in advance the rationale for every procedure that they devise. Ultimately a science of teaching would require the development of such rationales and a systematic investigation of them.

RESEARCH AND THE EDUCATIVE ACT

In what sense is the educative act susceptible to scientific investigation? If teaching procedures are hypotheses about learning, these hypotheses are in principle testable. Given appropriate research procedures we can determine whether the predicted effects did occur. By a continuous process of critical inquiry we can determine the validity of our procedures, revising them when the evidence indicates that our predictions were not substantiated. A vast body of educational literature is a testimonial to the fact that such investigations can be conducted. That such research has tended to be unsystematic and far from definitive is hardly arguable. The remedy for this situation, however, is not to abandon educational research but to improve it.

THE TEACHER AND THE IMPROVEMENT OF PRACTICE. Furthermore, the teacher himself must be a continual inquirer into the validity and reliability of the procedures that he is using. Corey emphasizes this point:

> Most of the study of what should be kept in the schools and what should go and what should be added must be done in hundreds of thousands of classrooms and thousands of American communities. The studies must be undertaken by those who may have to change the way they do things as the result of the studies. Our schools cannot keep up with the life they are supposed to sustain and improve unless teachers, pupils, supervisors, administrators, and school patrons continuously examine what they are doing. Singly and in groups, they must use their imaginations creatively and constructively to identify the practices that must be changed to meet the needs and demands of modern life, courageously try out those practices that give better promise, and methodically and systematically gather evidence to test their worth.[8]

At the moment when the teacher decides what is the appropriate educational procedure to utilize, teaching is essentially creative. Teaching procedures are, however, susceptible to scientific investigation. Creativity in hypothesis-making combined with careful and systematic research will develop a sound body of knowledge about effective learning experiences. The teacher, as a practitioner, participates in this critical inquiry by continually evaluating and criticizing his own activities, and utilizing his knowledge for the revision of educational practice.

---

[8]S. M. Corey, *Action Research to Improve School Practices*, New York, Bureau of Publications, Teachers College, Columbia University, 1953, p. viii.

EDUCATIONAL SCIENCE. The development of a comprehensive educational science has hardly begun. The development of such a science will take the combined efforts of many people, both teachers and research workers. The teacher's contribution to this development consists essentially in providing suggestions for hypotheses that can be rigorously tested by experimental means. But we cannot wait for the flowering of such a science if we are to conduct the day-by-day work of the schools.

Teaching as it is presently practiced is largely a practical art in the sense that procedures are revised and changed in a trial and error manner. The main objection to a trial and error methodology is that it tends to be unsystematic. Practices are revised consequent to "errors." The consequences of educational procedures are not always predicted or predictable. New ideas are not generated out of theoretical conceptions or previous research. Change in procedures depends too frequently on unexpected consequences, feelings, hunches, or opinion.

In criticizing the trial and error approach to educational practice, we are not referring to the way a beginning teacher learns the practice of his profession. A teacher, like any learner, must learn "to do" the act of teaching, to make appropriate responses under given conditions, to acquire "teaching behaviors." We are criticizing the attempt to develop a body of knowledge about teaching procedures merely from a "let's try this to see if it works" or a "I wonder what I should do now that that didn't work" approach to educational methodology.

As new concepts and theories develop, the teaching process will be governed less by the trial and error method of testing procedures and more and more by the results of careful and systematic investigation. If the history of science repeats itself in education, we can hope that in time the educational process will appear less mysterious, will demand for its operation less and less trial and error methodology, and, with more comprehensive theoretical conceptions, will improve rapidly and consistently. Such a development in educational science will not be forthcoming unless there is widespread conviction among educational workers that educational research is potentially productive in the improvement of educational practice. While such a conviction at present requires a relatively large degree of optimism, to abandon any hope of improvement through careful investigation would consign the educational process to the limbo of the most naive kind of practical approach.

THE ROLE OF PSYCHOLOGY IN EDUCATION

PRESENT STATE OF EDUCATIONAL THEORY. While we have discussed the relationship of theoretical analysis and science to the improvement of educational practice, the student may well raise the question about the role that educational psychology—the proper subject of this text—has to play both in the development of an educational science and in the practice of education. The practice of any art begins to improve with the development of new ways of viewing the activities that comprise it. New concepts and new theories enable us to give meaning to the activity in which we are engaged, to increase our understanding of this activity, and to predict and control the course of the activity. Ideally the underlying science of the activity should provide the basis for this understanding and control; however, we have no general and comprehensive educational theory or science. As a consequence, educational theory has drawn largely on those theories and sciences which seem to be most relevant to the educational process. Among these are, of course, the behavioral sciences and, in particular, psychology.

Psychologists have always taken a great interest in the educational process and educational psychologists have had considerable influence on educational practice. E. L. Thorndike, with his conception of learning as a set of stimulus-response bonds or connections, is one outstanding example of an educational psychologist whose theory of learning greatly influenced the practices of the American school.[9] The mental test movement is another example of the contribution of psychologists to educational practice.

These are some of the comparatively specific contributions. It should be equally obvious that the general subject matter of psychological investigation is of relevance to educational practice. The psychologist investigates the learning process, the development of personality, the interrelations between children and their environments, and a host of other problems—all of which are related to educational problems. Psychology is the science of behavior change

[9]See "Thorndike's Connectionism" in E. R. Hilgard, *Theories of Learning*, 2nd ed., New York, Appleton-Century-Crofts, Inc., 1956, Chapter 2.

and the function of the educational process is to promote desirable behavior changes.

RELEVANCE OF PSYCHOLOGY. However, to note that the psychologist studies events which are relevant to the kinds of activities in which teachers are engaged is not to suggest that everything the psychologist has to say is immediately usable by the educational practitioner. Educators have complained frequently that many investigations in learning, for example, are not immediately applicable to the classroom situation.

> The psychological laboratory, because of its rigid control and accuracy, has set a standard worthy of emulation by anyone interested in the scientific study of schoolroom learning. Laboratory experimentation is characterized by specific practice upon functions to be improved, definite time limits, control of irrelevant influences, awareness of success and error, and maximum motivation. Under such conditions, improvement is always secured. The materials, methods, and measures of learning which contribute toward improvement in the laboratory are the very factors which restrict their applicability for schoolroom use.[10]

The teacher studying psychology should not expect to find simple answers to his questions. The psychologist will probably ignore the question about what to do specifically when Johnny throws spitballs. For as much as psychologists do know about learning, only an uncautiously brave, and perhaps foolhardy, psychologist would describe specific teaching procedures that would be universally applicable.

If psychology does not provide simple recipes for teaching, of what value is the study of psychology for the educator? Psychology contributes to the development of the teacher in three ways: (1) by providing the teacher with a set of concepts and principles that will enable him to view human behavior more critically and to increase his understanding of this behavior; (2) by providing the teacher with skills that are directly related to the educational process, such as ways of interpreting intelligence test and achievement test scores; and (3) by introducing the teacher to the elements of the logic and methods of research in human behavior.

---

[10]R. A. Davis, "Applicability of Applications of Psychology with Particular Reference to Schoolroom Learning," *Journal of Educational Research*, 37 (1943), 22. Also in A. P. Coladarci, *Educational Psychology: A Book of Readings*, New York, The Dryden Press, 1955, p. 34.

UTILITY OF PSYCHOLOGICAL CONCEPTS. Psychology, as a science, assumes that human behavior is lawful, that is, that it is predictable and explainable. In order to explain and predict the phenomenon that a science studies, scientific investigators utilize concepts and theories which improve their ability to explain and predict. Psychology as a science of human behavior has introduced new ways of looking at human behavior. From a study of psychology the student will acquire new ways of analyzing human behavior and will find this behavior more intelligible and more predictable.

Specifically for teachers this means learning new ways of "seeing" children and how children learn. Fifty years ago deficiencies in learning could be attributed to "a bad will" or "a weak mind." As a result of considerable scientific investigation, we no longer accept such simple explanations of behavior. The teacher today who wishes to explain why Johnny is not learning to read will be aware that there are many contributing factors, and that probably no single factor will explain his deficiency. He knows that, whatever the reasons for Johnny's deficiencies, they cannot be attributed to some vague idea, such as "a bad will."

A psychological study of the educational process familiarizes the teacher with concepts and theories which form the basis for making hypotheses about educational deficiencies or educational achievements. A poor reader may be working out his frustrations by refusing to learn to read, or he may have defects of vision which are handicapping him in learning to read, or his experiential background may be impoverished. Formulating these potential explanations for a reading deficiency suggests that the teacher is seeking the cause of the deficiency, that he views this behavior as multicaused, and that he has a set of concepts and relationships that interrelate many aspects of the child's behavior. In somewhat simpler words, we expect that a teacher who has studied psychology in relation to education no longer views behavior as something that "just happens." He sees that behavior in some sense is determined, and he continually analyzes behavior to ferret out these determinants.

UTILITY OF PSYCHOLOGICAL SKILLS. A teacher who studies psychology will also learn a number of principles and procedures relevant to *some* educational practices. For example, we have suggested that an integral part of the educative act is the process of evaluating behavior change. This process of evaluation, if it is to be systematic, must be consistent with basic principles of measurement. An evaluation would be inadequate if a teacher gave an arithmetic test consisting of one relatively simple problem, or based his judgment of a student's attitude towards his fellow students on one instance of an outburst of temper. Our criticism of a teacher who would operate in this manner would be based upon our awareness that, in evaluating, we must obtain an adequate sample of the student's behavior. This is a simple example of the use of a fundamental principle of measurement. It is this kind of a principle that the teacher studies in educational psychology.

In addition, the teacher will learn many specific things about tests, such as how to interpret IQ tests and achievement test scores. He will learn how to utilize the principles of measurement in developing marking and grading systems, and in systematizing his observations of children.

UTILITY OF PSYCHOLOGICAL RESEARCH. Finally, educational psychology contributes to the development of the teacher by familiarizing him with the procedures of scientific investigation as these are utilized in the study of human behavior. We have stressed that, if education is to improve, the teacher must become a constant inquirer into the validity of his own procedures. This process of investigating the validity of one's own procedures can be conducted either formally or informally. Under the press of multiple duties it is not likely that the classroom teacher will conduct many formal educational experiments in the course of his teaching career. But, whether the investigation of one's teaching procedures be conducted formally or informally, there are certain canons of scientific logic that must be observed. A study of educational research, particularly of a psychological nature, should familiarize the prospective teacher with these principles of scientific logic.

The teacher needs to know what factors will delimit the usefulness of any educational procedure he adopts. He also needs techniques for quantifying whatever data he gathers about his procedures. For example, it is not sufficient to say that one has an impression that students have improved when method X has been used to teach reading. Measurements of reading behavior, when analyzed, will validate or invalidate this impression. A study of *the literature of educational psychology* will familiarize the teacher with the methods and problems of data gathering—how to analyze data, how to draw inferences from these data, and how to generalize conclusions that are consistent with the data.

A single course in educational psychology will not train a teacher to become a proficient research worker. At best such a course can expose the teacher to the principles of research and suggest the relevance of this research to the kinds of judgments that teachers are continually making about educational procedures that they use. The scientific approach to educational problems can impress upon the teacher the idea that conclusions about educational methods need to be based upon something more than hunches or impressions or feelings. The teacher can thus gain some insight into what is meant by the scientific investigation of educational procedures. At the same time familiarity with the scientific study of human behavior will prepare the teacher to read critically the literature of educational research. A teacher cannot read educational research intelligently unless he has some conception of what is meant by research and what constitutes good research. A course in educational psychology will expose the teacher to good educational research and at the same time familiarize him with the way this research is conducted.

Thus educational psychology makes the same kind of contribution to the development of the teacher that the study of any science does to students of that science. The study of a science enlarges the vision of the student, gives him new ways of seeing the world or the events that this science studies. It provides him with new concepts and understandings of relationships between events, and enables him to give meaning to events which before were largely meaningless or unpredictable. In addition, the science acquaints him with the methods of its investigations so that if he chooses he may utilize these methods.

Psychology, however, as distinct from physics, is concerned with events of a kind that the teacher himself deals with in his daily work. Psychology studies people and their relationship to their environment, and it is with people, particularly children and their environments, that the teacher is continuously concerned. The major contribution of a course in educational psychology should be to change a teacher's conception of the nature of the learning process, and in particular of the processes by which children learn, grow, and develop into mature personalities.

SUMMARY

This chapter has introduced two major ideas. We have defined the educative act as a specific organized learning experience. This act has three aspects: (1) formulation of conceptions of desired behavior changes, called educational objectives; (2) the organization of learning experiences to produce these changes; and (3) the utilization of evaluation procedures to determine the extent and character of behavior change. The teacher is responsible for the character of individual educative acts.

The organization and facilitation of an educative act requires that the teacher make decisions continually. Each of these decisions is a hypothesis about the relation between a learning experience and an expected behavior change.

With these two conceptions, a rationale for the relevancy of educational psychology can be established. Educational psychology provides concepts, principles, and theories that can be utilized to make hypotheses about learning. A study of educational psychology familiarizes the teacher with scientific procedures used in investigating behavior change. The study of educational psychology fosters the development of the teacher as a continual and critical inquirer into the validity of his educational practices. This study also prepares the teacher to participate intelligently in the processes requisite to the development of an educational science.

The implication of this discussion is to restructure teachers' conceptions of their function in the educational process. This conception of the character of educational practice professionalizes teaching activities.

STUDY AND DISCUSSION QUESTIONS

1. Consider the following statement of an educational objective: "The educated person uses his native language effectively." What kinds of behavior change are implicit in this statement?

2. Statements of this kind have been criticized for their vagueness. Why is such a statement vague? How will clarification of the meaning of this statement help teachers organize learning experiences?

3. What might be the objectives of the following experiences: visiting a science museum; producing a class play; participating in varsity athletics; reading one of Dickens' novels?

4. In what ways might the purposes of students differ from the proposed objectives of these learning experiences? Specify what some of these purposes might be and indicate how they may or may not be inconsistent with the objectives of the learning experience.

5. Many educators argue that the purposes of an educational experience should arise out of pupils' interests. What hypotheses are implicit in this argument?

6. Does the process of clarifying the objectives of a learning experience presuppose that all objectives are teacher-made? How might a teacher utilize pupils' interests in clarifying the objectives of a learning experience?

7. Some teachers use daily quizzes in their classes. What hypotheses about behavior changes are implicit in this practice?

8. A fifth-grade teacher encourages his pupils to make scrapbooks of pictures of different parts of the United States. What hypotheses might this teacher be making about behavior change?

9. A history teacher asks a local judge to discuss civil rights with his class. Formulate several hypotheses relating this practice to behavior change.

10. Some educators argue that psychological experiments do not duplicate classroom conditions. Present a defensible argument to demonstrate that such experimentation might be helpful in organizing learning experiences.

11. How do you account for the fact that many apparently "successful" teachers may know very little psychology? How do you explain the fact that some teachers who have studied psychology are not "successful" in the classroom?

12. Some educators argue that a teacher's personality is the most important determinant of his success in the classroom. What hypotheses about behavior change are implicit in this argument? Does this argument contradict the point of view presented in this chapter?

13. Some people maintain that teaching is an art. In what sense might this point of view be supported by the ideas presented in this chapter?

14. Is an "art of teaching" incompatible with a "science of education"?

RECOMMENDED READINGS

The first two readings in the list below discuss the conception of the teacher as a hypothesis-maker. The readings from Dewey explore in greater detail the meaning of critical inquiry, particularly in relation to educational thought. The last two readings discuss the relation of psychology to education in substantially the same terms as in this chapter; however, a reading of these presentations may suggest some additional insights.

1. A. P. Coladarci, "The Relevancy of Educational Psychology," *Educational Leadership*, 13 (1956), 489-92, and "The Teacher as Hypothesis-Maker," *California Journal for Instructional Improvement*, 2 (1959), 3-6.

2. J. Dewey, *The Sources of a Science of Education*, New York, Liveright Publishing Corp., 1929.

3. J. Dewey, *How We Think*, Boston, D. C. Heath & Co., 1933, Chapter 7.

4. J. M. Stephens, *Educational Psychology* (Rev. Ed.), New York, Henry Holt & Co., Inc., 1956, Chapter 1.

5. L. J. Cronbach, *Educational Psychology*, New York, Harcourt, Brace & Co., 1954, Chapter 1.

THE LEARNER AND THE EDUCATIVE PROCESS

In the previous chapter the role of the teacher as a hypothesis-maker was discussed. We suggested that one of the major purposes in studying educational psychology is to develop information and ideas that can be used by the teacher for hypothesis formation. The purpose of this chapter is to introduce the student to the psychological view of human behavior and to provide a systematic description of basic concepts used by psychologists to analyze, describe, and explain human behavior. This chapter, frankly, will be theoretical and perhaps somewhat difficult. However, if the student begins his study of educational psychology with an understanding of what this science is attempting to describe and explain, he should be able to organize his knowledge systematically and to develop greater insight into human behavior.

SCIENTIFIC CHARACTERISTICS OF PSYCHOLOGY

A science begins with observations of events in the phenomenal world. The function of any science is to describe and explain the events of the phenomenal world (the world as perceived) that are in its area of concern and study. Each science has marked off for itself, as it were, sets of observable events that are the object of study in that science. Physics, for example, describes and explains the relationships between matter and energy.

SUBJECT MATTER OF PSYCHOLOGY. Psychology, as a science, *has as the object of its study the observable behavior of organisms*. The function of psychological science is to describe and explain this observable behavior. A psychologist inquires into why human organisms behave as they do, as well as into the conditions in environments or the relationships among organisms that lead to specific kinds of behavior. The following are some of the questions asked by the psychologist: What conditions in the life of a child bring about "aggressive" actions or behaviors? What kinds of experiences enable a child to learn to read or to write? Why do people choose the occupations they enter? Why do some people seem to be better at problem-solving than are others?

EXPLANATION IN PSYCHOLOGY. What do we mean when we say that the psychologist attempts to explain behavior that he has observed? The psychologist attempts to relate the observed behavior to sets of antecedent environmental conditions, or experiences and states of the person whose behavior he has observed. Many of us, in the course of everyday life, attempt to do exactly the same thing. We wonder why a friend has not spoken to us in the last few days, or we are curious about why the teacher seemed annoyed when we asked that last question.

It is probably safe to say that everybody has his own psychology of behavior, somewhat unsystematic, probably oversimplified, and usually based on rather limited, casual observations. The difference between the psychologist and the non-psychologist is that the psychologist systematizes his observations and attempts to develop more comprehensive explanations than most of us develop in everyday relationships with other people.

SCIENTIFIC AND COMMON-SENSE EXPLANATIONS. The method of explaining behavior used by psychologists is essentially that used by any scientist. A given kind of behavior is observed and an attempt is made to relate this behavior to other observable factors. This is substantially what we do in everyday life when we attempt to explain the behavior of other people. For example, teachers and students alike feel that performance on tests in various courses depends upon factors other than knowledge of the subject being tested. We often hear an explanation such as, "Johnny did poorly on this test because he wasn't feeling well." This statement about the relationship of Johnny's feelings to his test performance is an attempt to formulate an explanation for the observed behavior. But we must raise a question here as we do about all explanations: Is the explanation a valid one? We can answer this only by systematic observation of the behavior of many people.

Also, we must be sure that, in analyzing the relationship between test performance and the way Johnny feels, we have not overlooked other factors which may account for his test performance. Perhaps Johnny's inability to understand the test directions is related more to his test performance than "how he feels" at the time of the test. In other words, we are attempting to determine how likely it is that the way Johnny feels will affect his test performance. Only when we know whether or not feeling states tend to influence test performance can we assign the explanation of Johnny's test performance to this factor.

PRACTICAL APPLICATION OF SCIENTIFIC KNOWLEDGE. The teacher in this example has a twofold problem—that of knowing what factors are likely to affect the test performance and that of determining which of these factors actually are influencing this test performance. The second problem depends upon the first. Since the teacher usually makes decisions related to the second, it seems obvious that without a background of knowledge about human behavior, the teacher's decision-making processes will at best be fortuitous and at worst be poor, perhaps even harmful, guesses. Practical decision-making should be based upon sound knowledge about the behavior that is being observed and about which decisions are being made.

Whether the teacher is operating on the basis of a common-sense psychology or is systematically using well-established principles of psychological science, the body of knowledge which underpins his decision-making is arrived at by relating behavior to other events or conditions. The teacher and the psychologist continually seek to answer the question: What factors are related to this observed behavior?

THE METHOD OF ANALYSIS IN THE STUDY OF BEHAVIOR

THE CONCEPT OF VARIABLES. A science attempts to relate one set of observable events to another set of observable events. In more technical language the behavior and the factors related to this behavior are called *variables*. More specifically, the behavior that is the object of study and investigation is referred to as the *dependent variable*. The factors which are related to this behavior, and on the basis of which we can explain or predict the behavior, are of two kinds: (1) independent variables and (2) mediating variables.

DEFINITION OF INDEPENDENT VARIABLES. *Independent variables are factors that are measurably distinct from the behavior being studied as the dependent variable.* Assume that we were studying children's spelling ability. Our problem is to account for differences in spelling ability. Any factor which can be measured independently of spelling ability is a potential independent variable, such as the intelligence of the children, their attitude toward spelling, and their visual and auditory acuity.[1] Note that independent variables may be behavior, such as attitude toward spelling, but the measure of attitude toward spelling is not a measure of spelling ability as such. We use a spelling test to measure spelling ability. To measure children's attitudes toward spelling we determine how well they like spelling.

Many factors measured as independent variables are objectively discriminative aspects of the environment of the behaving person. For example, if we wanted to determine the factors which affect academic performance, we would probably consider variables such as the home conditions of children, the characteristics of the children's teachers, and specific conditions in classroom situations such as the lighting, the arrangement of desks, the materials and books available. We would also consider such factors as the general social and economic background of the students and their previous academic training. All of these conditions are related to the environment in which learning is taking place. Obviously these vary from school to school, class to class, and teacher to teacher. A list of factors that could be investigated in relation to pupil behavior would be infinite, but the function of research in psychology and education is to

---

[1] D. H. Russell, "Characteristics of Good and Poor Spellers," *Teachers College Contributions to Education*, No. 727, New York, Columbia University Press, 1937.

determine the factors most highly related to specific kinds of pupil behavior.

We can also study certain objective properties of the human organism itself and relate these to the behavior of the organism. When we attempt to relate factors such as age, sex, intelligence level,[2] and basic metabolic rate to behavior,[3] we are relating a set of independent variables, which are characteristics of the organism itself, to the behavior of the organism.

A common investigation is one which relates age to behavior—for example, the relation between age and vocabulary development.[4] In Figure 1 is a graph demonstrating the relation between these two variables. From these data we learn that a child's spoken vocabulary increases at the rate of about five hundred words a year after the second year. The rate of change is uniform. The six-year-old child has a fairly large vocabulary when he enters the first grade. These data can be applied in organizing learning experiences. One of the reasons that "sight" reading is recommended for beginning readers is that they can learn to read stories composed of familiar words. Using familiar words simplifies the learning experience for the beginning reader.

While the number of variables that can be discriminated and measured objectively depends upon the imagination and skill of investigators, the process of sorting these variables out in terms of their relative importance is necessarily a time-consuming one. Many teachers feel that they cannot wait for the results of educational research before they make practical decisions about the learning

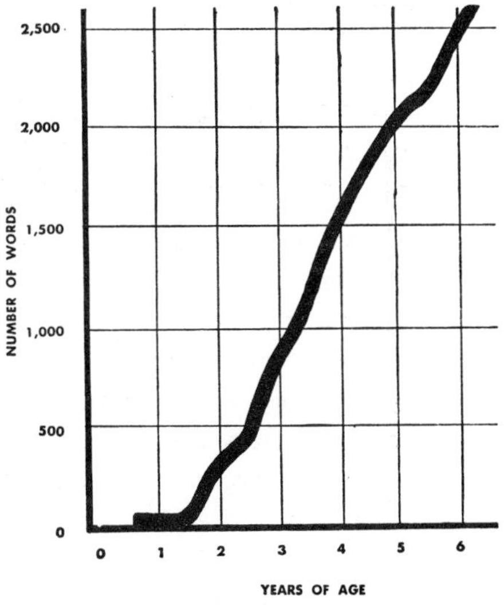

Increase in spoken vocabulary in the first six years. (From Smith)

FIGURE 1

[2] D. G. Shaw, "A Study of the Relationships between Thurstone Primary Mental Abilities and High School Achievement," *Journal of Educational Psychology*, 40 (1949), 239-49.

[3] M. E. Yarbrough and H. G. McCurdy, "A Further Note on Basal Metabolism and Academic Performance," *Journal of Educational Psychology*, 49 (1958), 20-22.

[4] M. E. Smith, "An Investigation of the Development of the Sentence and the Extent of Vocabulary in Young Children," *University of Iowa Studies in Child Welfare*, 3 (1926), No. 5.

experiences they must plan for their classes. This objection is a valid one, but practical decision-making cannot be divorced from systematic investigation of human behavior. The teacher acts on the best information he has available, and revises his procedures as new knowledge is developed. The teacher and the psychologist are both asking the same kinds of questions, and the answers affect the kinds of decisions that are made in practical situations.

DEFINITION OF MEDIATING VARIABLES. We have mentioned another class of variables called *mediating variables*. On the one hand, we have a set of variables, the independent variables, which typically represent discriminative objective characteristics of environments and organisms; on the other hand, we have observable behavior. Our fundamental problem is to relate the independent variables to the dependent variable. Frequently, it is not possible to relate them directly without assuming that there are processes within the human organism that are related to both.

An example will make this point clear. Suppose that we find, as one investigator did,[5] that human beings may learn even when correct responses are punished and that, in some cases, learning is as effective when the correct responses are punished as when they are rewarded.

Because of previous experimentation[6] on the effects of reward, we do not expect organisms to learn as well when punished as when they are rewarded. The apparent inconsistency can be resolved by assuming that the rewards and punishments used in the experimentation have different "meanings" for different subjects. If one subject obtains information from a punishment experience which enables him to make the correct responses, but another subject obtains the same kind of information from a reward experience, then the interpretation the subject makes of the objective situation is presumably an important variable that influences his behavior.

Teachers are quite frequently confronted by similar situations in the classroom. In the classroom the teacher "punishes" (responds in some negative fashion) undesirable behavior and an effect similar

---

[5] K. F. Muenzinger *et al.*, "Motivation in Learning, I: Electric Shock for Correct Response in the Visual Discrimination Habit," *Journal of Comparative Psychology*, 17 (1934), 266-77. Also see by the same authors, "Motivation in Learning, II: The Function of Electric Shock for Right and Wrong Responses in Human Subjects," *Journal of Experimental Psychology*, 17 (1934), 439-48.

[6] E. L. Thorndike, *The Fundamentals of Learning*, New York, Teachers College, Columbia University, 1932.

to that in the experiment is frequently obtained. The punishment is supposed to stop an undesired response, such as "talking out in class"; but repeated remonstrances to a student appear to have no effect on changing his behavior. This failure to stop the undesired behavior appears to be inexplicable since we assume that reprimanding a student is "punishing." Perhaps, however, it is only when he is reprimanded that this student obtains any attention from the teacher. If a student is seeking the teacher's attention, inappropriate classroom behavior may be strengthened because the supposed punishment is a reward for attention-getting behavior. The objective feature of the environment, namely, reprimand from the teacher, means one thing to one student and something entirely different to another student.

To develop his explanatory and descriptive system, therefore, a psychologist will postulate certain processes operating within the human organism. These postulated processes are called *mediating variables;* they are intermediaries between the independent variables and the dependent variables and are used in statements describing and explaining behavior. For example: when a teacher reprimands a pupil (independent variable), the pupil will continue to make disruptive responses (observed behavior) if he interprets the teacher's reaction as special attention (mediating variable). Ideally, when psychological science reaches some maturity, laws will be available which will interrelate independent variables, such as the immediate environmental conditions, the processes within the organism, and the observable behavior.

Another example will illustrate the use of mediating variables in psychological explanation. Bruner and Goodman studied the relationship between the social class position of boys and their ability to estimate coin sizes.[7] In this study the investigators found that "poor boys" differed significantly from "rich boys" in their estimation of coin sizes, the former tending to overestimate the coin sizes more frequently than did the latter. The authors of this study argued that the social class position of the boys was related to their need system,[8] the former being an independent variable of the kind discussed above and the latter a mediating variable. Poor boys, having stronger needs

---

[7] J. S. Bruner and C. C. Goodman, "Value and Need as Organizing Factors in Perception," *Journal of Abnormal and Social Psychology*, 42 (1947), 33-44.

[8] Need is used here in the sense of "want" or "desire." It is not used in the sense of "required" or "desirable." The "desires" of boys differ; hence they have different "need" systems. A more detailed and precise definition of this concept is discussed in Chapter Four.

that can be satisfied by obtaining money, perceived even the objective stimulus of the coins differently from the boys of a higher social class presumably because the need systems of the two groups were different. Note that a higher and more generalized level of explanation may be reached when the objective independent variable can be related to functional characteristics of the organism. The explanation seems to "make sense" when the mediating variable of differential needs is introduced into the explanation. This "making sense" does not, of course, validate the explanation itself. But this relationship, if systematically tested, may enable us to explain this phenomenon and many others of a similar nature. For example, a teacher may act consistently from day to day in his classroom. But one child will see the teacher as friendly and another will see him as threatening. We know that children's perceptions of teachers' behavior varies with social class.[9] We would hypothesize that these differential perceptions are influenced by differences in needs.

The choice of the particular mediating process used in the explanation may be disputed. Other variables may prove to be more useful in explaining this phenomenon.[10] A systematic science like psychology continually examines and re-examines functional relationships of this kind. But the relationships developed interrelate independent variables, mediating variables, and observed behavior.

SIMILARITIES TO COMMON-SENSE EXPLANATIONS. Recall that the process the psychologist is using systematically and formally is similar to the kind of thinking that we employ in our daily life. Oliver Goldsmith noted the relationship between behavior and objective properties of the environment in his famous line, "Well the boding tremblers [pupils] learn to trace the day's disaster in his [the teacher's] morning face." Teachers and parents have learned to dread the rainy season because of the somewhat less than pleasant effects upon child behavior. We generally assume a relationship between class size and the success of the teaching enterprise. Teachers sometimes maintain that girls are better behaved in class than boys. In all of these instances we are relating independent variables—properties of the organism such as being a boy or girl, or characteristics of the environment such

---

[9] P. H. Sorensen, *Some Correlates of Pupils' Perceptions of Teaching Behavior* (unpublished doctoral dissertation), Stanford, Calif., Stanford University, 1957.

[10] G. S. Klein, H. J. Schlesinger, and D. E. Meister, "The Effect of Personal Values on Perception: An Experimental Critique," *Psychological Review*, 58 (1951), 96-112.

as the weather, class size, or the appearance of the teacher's face—to the behavior of students.

Similarly we make numerous inferences about processes operating within individuals. We frequently refer to the "attitudes" of other people and relate their behavior to these attitudes. Words, such as "like," "dislike," "want," "desire," are commonly used to describe states or processes within people presumably related to their behavior. Suppose that Johnny's behavior in class today is particularly disruptive. We might "explain" this in two ways: (1) by noting the fact that Johnny had an inadequate breakfast and ascribing his behavior to lack of an adequate breakfast; (2) by assuming that Johnny is in a "bad mood" and accounting for his behavior in terms of his mood. In the first instance, we are relating the independent variable of food intake or diet to the observed behavior; in the second case, we are relating an inferred state or mood to the observed behavior. We can go even further and say that when Johnny has not had an adequate breakfast he is tense, nervous, and irritable, and therefore "acts up" in class. This kind of explanation is essentially of the same character as the kind of explanation that the psychologist is attempting to develop. Again we emphasize that the difference between a psychologist's and a non-psychologist's explanation of this behavior is not in the character of the propositions, but in their validity and reliability, their comprehensiveness, and their power in explaining and relating many instances of behavior. We are not implying that the common-sense kind of psychology that most people employ is as valid as the more scientific psychology that a systematic investigator is attempting to develop. But these explanations of behavior are of the same general logical character. They are statements about interrelations between variables.

BASIC PRINCIPLES OF BEHAVIOR CHANGE

We have suggested above that any systematic explanation of human behavior will interrelate several classes of variables. The function of this systematic explanation is to interrelate these variables in valid and reliable propositions. The next step is to be more specific about the kinds of variables with which psychologists and educators will be concerned and to specify general relationships between them. Each science attempts to couch its explanations in propositions of the kind we have been discussing. Sciences are distinguished from one another by the kinds of variables studied. A psychologist and a geneticist, for example, are both interested in heredity. The geneticist studies the gene; the psychologist, behavior. The geneticist wants to know what factors influence the transmission of genes. The psychologist wants to know what behavior is influenced by the transmission of genes.[11]

Later in this chapter we will present a descriptive model, to outline the kinds of variables that we will study in describing the learning processes and the development of personality. Before we outline the elements in the model, let us first discuss two instances of behavior and note the common features in both cases.

ROBERT BUILDS A MODEL AIRPLANE

Mrs. Jones, the second grade teacher in the Garfield Elementary School, has set aside a portion of each day during which the children engage in construction activities. During this time they are free to build objects of their own choice. Materials and tools are available for this activity. Mrs. Jones supervises the activity, moving from child to child, making suggestions and offering help where it is necessary.

Robert, a typical second grader, has decided that he wants to build a small model airplane. He is interested in airplanes because he has seen many kinds of airplanes on television programs. He has a book at home in which there are pictures of airplanes, and his father has taken frequent business trips by airplane. He also lives near a Naval air base and jets frequently fly over his home.

Robert begins his work by seeing that wood and tools are available for building a plane. The class has tools such as a hammer, a saw, nails, and several kinds of wood in various sizes and shapes. Robert knows that the plane has two main parts, the body and the wings, and he begins to scout through the woodpile for pieces of wood which could be used for these parts. He finds a long and comparatively thick piece of wood which he can use for the body and a somewhat shorter and thinner piece of wood which can be used as a wing.

His next problem is to decide on the shape of the wing and the body. He decides that he needs to cut off the corners on the piece of wood that he is going to use for the wing. He then goes to the tool chest and selects a saw and begins the process of shaping the wing and the body of the plane.

When he has finished, his next task is to attach the wing to the plane. This he does by again going to the tool chest, selecting a hammer and nails, and nailing the wing to the body.

---

[11]The distinctions between sciences in terms of variables studied are arbitrary. Sciences frequently overlap as new knowledge develops.

He is still somewhat dissatisfied with his product because it lacks a tail piece. He goes back to the wood supply and picks out a small piece of wood which he can attach to the body to resemble a tail. Again he goes through the process of shaping the piece and attempting to attach it to the fuselage. He soon finds, however, that he cannot attach the tail piece as easily as he did the wing structure, and he begins to try a number of alternatives. At first he attempts to nail it to the body of the plane, but this fails. He then inquires from Mrs. Jones whether some glue is available so that he can glue on the tail piece. Mrs. Jones provides him with some wood glue, and he makes the attempt but thinks that even when the glue dries the tail piece will not be stable.

Robert then seeks advice from Mrs. Jones. She suggests that he saw a small slot, insert the tail piece in this slot, and tighten the whole structure with glue. This he does. When he has finished he proudly displays his relatively crude model of an airplane.

Several of his classmates take an interest in his project and ask questions about it. One boy remarks that it does not look much like an airplane since it does not have motors and propellers. At this point Robert decides that the addition of a propeller is a task beyond him and sets the plane aside as the construction period comes to an end. Briefly, before returning to his seat in the classroom, he plays with the plane and puts it through imaginary maneuvers.

JANE WRITES AN ARTICLE FOR THE SCHOOL PAPER

Jane, a junior in Lincoln High School, has been on the school paper staff during the past school year. The editor and the faculty adviser both have requested that she write a feature article for this paper. Jane is happy to accept this assignment because she has been wanting for some time to write an article that will distinguish her from the general staff of reporters.

She decides that she will write an article about Mr. Bradford, who is a science teacher and who has spent the summer traveling in Europe. She believes that other students would be interested in reading about European students, and she plans to ask Mr. Bradford to compare American and European students. So Jane arranges a time for an interview. She obtains from Mr. Bradford as much information as she can about the characteristics of European students and in what ways they are like and in what ways they are different from American students.

When she has all the necessary information, she spends several hours digesting it and presenting it in a readable and interesting form. She realizes that if she can emphasize some startling differences between American and European students, she will catch the eyes of her readers. In this way she will attract more attention to the article and consequently to herself as the writer of the article. She decides that her major point will be the difference in the amount of time spent in classroom activities by European and American students. She also decides to emphasize the differences between the activity programs of European and American students. She builds her article around these differences and also develops the similarities between the students as a concluding point.

Having typed her article, she presents it to the editor and adviser, both of whom find it interesting and appealing and indicate that it will be published in the next issue of the paper. Several days later the paper is published with Jane's article prominently featured in it. She is happy to note that a large number of her fellow students read the article and talk to her about it. Her English teacher also comments favorably on her writing style and suggests that Jane continue to develop her interest in journalism.

COMMON ELEMENTS. As we read through the above examples, we find that several elements are apparent in each case. These common features are elements which characterize all instances of behavior change.

1. *The behavior is motivated*. By this we mean that the person wants to do something, there is some goal that the person is attempting to achieve, there is some action that he intends to accomplish. Robert wanted to construct an airplane; Jane, to write an article for the school paper.

Robert was interested in airplanes and had seen airplanes, and this aroused in him a desire to want to build a model airplane. He may have been motivated by a need for the praise that his teacher would give him when he had completed the project, or by a need for the interest and attention that his fellow students would show in the project when he had completed it. No matter how complex the combination of specific needs that were influencing Robert's behavior, these coalesced to arouse in him the desire to build a model airplane.

In other words, Robert was in a state of psychological tension of a limited kind that could be resolved or reduced by constructing the airplane. His tension would be still unrelieved if he had failed to construct the airplane. If he had constructed the airplane to attract the attention of his teacher or his fellow classmates and they had failed to notice it, he would have been left in a state of dissatisfaction or tension.

Similarly, Jane wanted the attention and praise that she would receive when her article appeared in the school newspaper. Again, if her article had not been included in the paper or if it had not been noticed when published or if she had been severely criticized for it, her original need for approval would not have been satisfied. She would have been left in a state of dissatisfaction and unrelieved tension.

The examples illustrate a fundamental principle. _Behavior change begins in a motivated state of the organism, and this motivated state arises out of the needs of the organism._ In the next chapter we will discuss in detail the concept of motivation and needs, but it is important at this point to realize that behavior occurs on the basis of motivation. A person makes specific responses to try to bring about a reduction in the tension caused by his need state.

The complexity of the needs of human organisms is great. The needs of individuals vary considerably from time to time within one individual and between various individuals. A need state may be intense and felt by the organism in obvious kinds of ways, or the need state may be a relatively mild state of tension. Furthermore, the person may be consciously aware of his particular needs or his behavior may be motivated by unconscious strivings. Ignoring for the moment the complexity of the need system of the human organism, we can see that it is necessary to understand the motivating conditions of behavior if we are to explain, predict, and control this behavior in some way.

2. _Motivated behavior is goal-seeking behavior._ Jane wanted to attract the attention and esteem of her fellow students. She could have done this in a number of ways. She might have chosen to become a cheer leader, or she might have relied on her academic ability to win esteem. In this instance she chose to write a feature article as a way of obtaining what was a _goal_ for her, namely, winning the approval of her classmates.

Thus we can see that motivation has a double aspect: first, the presence of a state of tension, or dissatisfaction, in the person; second, an awareness of a goal whose attainment will reduce the state of tension. _The function of the attainment of the goal is a reduction in the tension in the need state of the person._

If Robert and Jane knew their goals could not satisfy their needs, they would choose other goals. If they had found that these goals were not satisfying their needs, they would then have gone on to other activities which presumably would have satisfied their needs.

The relationship of the need system of an individual to the goals that he seeks in order to satisfy this need system is a complex psychological problem—and discussion will again be deferred. However, it is important to note at this point that goals are chosen or sought after in relationship to their potentiality for satisfying particular needs. The individual is not always correct in his choice of satisfying goals. The goal is not necessarily a fixed and immutable end. The goal need not be clearly foreseen by the individual. But in the process of striving for need satisfaction the individual is seeking goal objects, whose function will be to reduce his state of need.

3. *The goal which the person is actually striving for influences the behavior which a person adopts to attain the goal.* As a consequence motivated behavior is *selective* and *regulative* in character. The human organism chooses those responses which are more likely to lead to the attainment of the goal that will satisfy its needs.

Robert's desire to build an airplane influenced the kinds of behavior responses that he made. For example, he sought out appropriate materials and tools, he sought advice on construction techniques, he tried particular types of construction activities.

Once Jane had decided to write a feature article, she immediately engaged in activities which would enable her to write the article. She did not go out on regular reporting assignments, nor did she spend time in editing copy and in doing paste-ups for the next edition. Inappropriate behaviors or responses were discarded.

As Jane wrote her article she wanted to create vivid contrasts between European and American students. In attempting to do this she made many tries or responses. When she found that a particular way of writing the article did not seem to give her the desired vividness, she rewrote the article.

Again, remember that Jane chose to write a feature article as a way of satisfying her need for esteem and approval from her fellow students. Had this general response or behavior proved unsatisfactory, she would be unlikely to attempt this kind of behavior again to attain her goal. It is not the goal as such that produces these behavior changes. Rather it is the person who manipulates his behavior in relationship to attainment of the goal.

4. *The environment provides opportunities for and sets limits on the behavior of the organism.* The environment acts as a context that determines the likelihood of occurrence of certain responses. Robert could not have constructed his airplane if time and materials were not available for the construction activity. Jane could not have satisfied her need for approval by writing a feature article for the paper if there were no school paper or if the editor had decided that he would not accept a feature article from Jane.

The environments of both Robert and Jane did provide opportunities for the satisfaction of their needs, but limited the satisfaction of these needs in fairly specific ways. For example, Robert was limited in the kind of a plane that he could construct with the materials and tools available. Jane was limited in the number and kinds of feature articles that she could write by the availability of interesting material for feature writing.

The environment also acts as a complex stimulus situation which serves to evoke particular kinds of responses. Behavior is shaped in part by the context in which the behavior occurs. When Robert went to the woodbox to choose materials, the kinds of wood that were available served as stimuli which evoked a specific choosing response on Robert's part. The presence of many different kinds of wood made this choice-response possible. Had there been only one kind of wood in the box, Robert probably would have selected it.

5. *Behavior is influenced by processes within the organism.* Both Robert and Jane retain the effects of previous experience. They

have ways of looking at the world and attitudes towards their environment.

On the basis of past experience, Robert knows that the easiest way to attach the wing to the body of the plane is to use nails for this purpose. He has also learned how to use a hammer and a saw. He utilizes his perceptions of how planes look in constructing his own model.

Jane has learned that a feature article with a by-line represents a significant contribution to a newspaper. She has learned that success in newspaper activities brings rewards in terms of esteem and praise. She also has specific knowledge about how to write a feature article. Sharp contrast and vividness of detail, she knows, will make her writing style more interesting and appealing.

Robert and Jane both chose specific responses to attain their goals partly on the basis of their conception of and attitude toward specific aspects of their environment.

6. *Behavior is determined by the capacities of the human organism.* Robert's ability to construct an airplane is determined, in part, by his capacities. He is probably too young to be able to construct a complex, detailed model. He is limited by his intelligence and abilities. If Robert is bright and skillful, this construction activity will present little difficulty for him. If he is not, either he will not engage in this activity, or he will not do it well.

Jane's feature article is partly determined by her capacities. Again, if Jane is not very intelligent, her choice of subject and the manner in which she writes about it will reflect the limitations placed on her by her comparative lack of intelligence. The article will also reflect particular aptitudes that she may have.

What the organism brings to a particular situation will, in part, determine the kinds of responses that the organism will make. Each person in a given situation is influenced by his capacities and present stage of development. For example, we do not expect very young children to learn to read or to write simply because this behavior is beyond their abilities at their present stage of development. Even when children reach the stage of development at which most children are capable of reading and writing, some will read and write better than others because of differences in their capacity to learn.

CONCEPT OF REINFORCEMENT. The behavior that we have been observing, such as building an airplane or writing a feature article, is a complex of many specific kinds of behavior which are integrated into the total response. The total response is behavior which achieves the attainment of a specific goal for the organism. For Jane the goal was the attainment of the esteem and approval of her classmates, and the writing of the feature article was the behavior leading to the attainment of this particular goal.

When a behavior is successful in leading to the attainment of a goal, the behavior is reinforced, or strengthened, or stabilized, because the goal brings about need reduction, or satisfaction of the need which motivated the behavior. On future occasions, if Jane wants to win the esteem and approval of her classmates, it is likely that she will again attempt to write a feature article because in the past this response has been successful in the attainment of a goal which satisfied her needs.

SUMMARY. We have presented a fundamental set of concepts and generalizations that can be used to analyze the behavior of any organism in any context. When we observe behavior, we find that it is initiated in a motivated state of the organism; that is, the organism has some need that it is attempting to satisfy. The behavior that we are observing is behavior which leads to the attainment of a goal, whose attainment is likely to reduce the need tension of the organism. The person selects specific behaviors to lead to the attainment of this goal. These behaviors are chosen on the basis both of what the environment provides in the way of opportunities for response and of the organism's interpretations of this environment. Specific responses are selected in terms of their consequences, namely, whether or not they lead to the attainment of the goal.

A DESCRIPTIVE MODEL OF MAJOR VARIABLES USED IN THE ANALYSIS OF BEHAVIOR CHANGE

Earlier in this chapter we discussed the manner in which a psychologist analyzes behavior in terms of independent variables, mediating variables, and the dependent variable. We then analyzed two instances of behavior and noted the factors related to these behaviors. At this point we will combine these two analyses into a general model for analyzing and describing human behavior. This model will enable us to analyze particular instances of behavior or the total behavior system of the individual.

The factors that we discussed above are variables, and some of these can be classified as *independent variables,* such as the intelligence of the child or the age of the child. Others we will classify as *mediating variables*, such as the need system of each child, the way each child views the environmental situation, and the child's attitudes towards the environmental situation. In both our examples and in our general model, our *dependent variable* is and will be the behavior that we are studying. This model is presented in Figure 2.

CATEGORIES OF INDEPENDENT VARIABLES. Note the three categories of independent variables:

a.   *Heredity, age, sex:* These are variables which characterize and differentiate organisms; on the basis of these variables, we can make objective discriminations among organisms. For example, we can ask questions about the relationship of age, sex, intelligence—which have a basis in heredity—to the processes within the organism and the behavior of the organism.

b.   *Conditions of drive:* The organism at any given moment is in a state of satisfaction or dissatisfaction which presumably has some type of physical basis. Changes in this neurophysiological base are the source of the organic energy that leads to behavior change. An increase in this organic energy is a *drive state.* The physical basis for some kinds of needs is fairly obvious. For example, the hunger need is usually related to physical changes within the organism. More complex needs, such as the need for approval, are also presumed to have some neurophysiological base, though this base at present is unknown. As changes take place in this neurophysiological system, presumably changes will also take place in the need system of the organism.

c.   *Stimulus situation:* This is the environmental context which the person is in at any given moment. The environmental context includes not only physical objects but also other persons, as we noted in Chapter One.

CATEGORIES OF MEDIATING VARIABLES. The mediating variables, it will be recalled, are processes within the organism. These variables are as follows:

a.   *Capacities and abilities:* By virtue of its inherited endowment the organism has capacities and abilities, on the basis of which its behavior system will develop.

b.   *The need system:* Each organism has its own need system which is the basis for its activity. *A need is a state of psychological tension which is manifested in goal-seeking behavior.* The organism wants something which, when attained, reduces or relieves this state of psychological tension. For example, Jane wanted the approval of her classmates, and her need for approval was satisfied or partially relieved when she obtained this approval. *The need system is the motivational system of the organism.*

c.   *The cognitive-attitudinal-value system:* The organism brings to each situation a way of looking at the world, feelings about its environmental context, and a system of values that it places upon objects and persons in this context. This complex process of thinking, feeling, and evaluating influences behavior, as we noted in the examples above.

d.   *Behavior space and the behaving self:* Each organism has a generalized perception of the context in which it is placed and a perception of itself as a person in this context. This process embraces the organism's perceptions of the relationships between itself and its environment. *It is an integration of the organism's beliefs, attitudes, and values about aspects of its environment, and its perceptions of the objective characteristics of the environment.* On the basis of the organism's perception of itself and its relationship to its environment, the organism then acts or behaves.

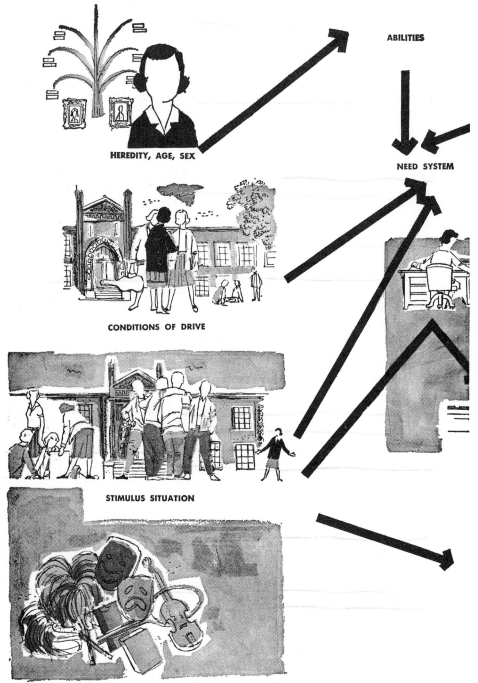

HEREDITY, AGE, SEX

ABILITIES

NEED SYSTEM

CONDITIONS OF DRIVE

STIMULUS SITUATION

FIGURE 2: *Descriptive Model of Personality and Behavior Analysis*

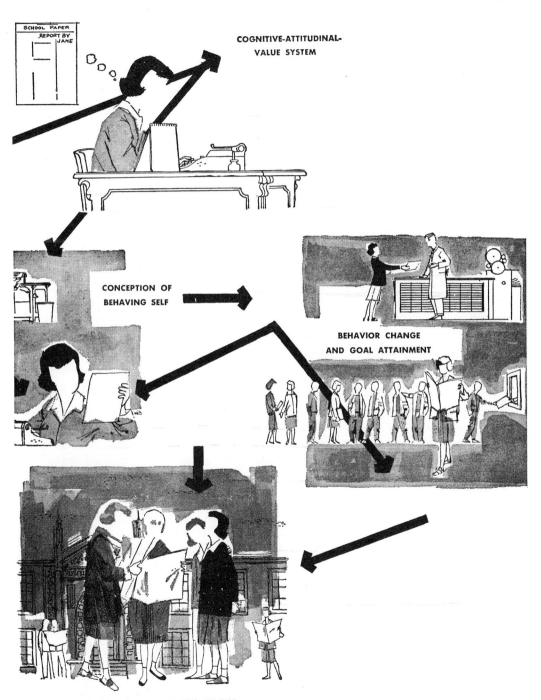

COGNITIVE-ATTITUDINAL-
VALUE SYSTEM

CONCEPTION OF
BEHAVING SELF

BEHAVIOR CHANGE
AND GOAL ATTAINMENT

RESTRUCTURED CONCEPTION OF SELF

61

Let us again analyze the example of Jane's behavior in terms of the above model. In terms of the independent variables, Jane was placed in an environmental context which can be described on the basis of its principal features, such as the school in which she was studying, the newspaper of which she was a staff member, the presence in the school of a teacher who had observed European students, and the kinds of students who were her classmates. We also know Jane's age and general level of maturation. We know nothing about the physiological basis for her need for approval and can only infer that changes take place in her drive states.

The specific need influencing Jane's behavior is her desire for the esteem and approval of her classmates. We also know that she sees the writing of a feature article as a means for attaining the goal which will satisfy her needs. Jane has attitudes about writing feature articles, attitudes about her classmates, and attitudes about the importance of being esteemed by one's fellows. As a consequence, Jane probably has a perception of herself as a person who is capable of and interested in writing this article and as someone who is able to win the esteem of her fellow students. Furthermore, she sees herself in a situation which provides her with the opportunity of achieving the goal that she is seeking.

On the basis of the environmental situation she is in and her present status as a person—the independent variables—and on the basis of certain processes presumed to be operating in her personality structure, such as her particular need, her way of viewing the situation, and her conception of herself, Jane behaves in specified ways which lead to the attainment of her goal.

RELATIONSHIPS AMONG VARIABLES. In Figure 2, arrows have been drawn between the various categories of the independent and mediating variables. These arrows represent some of the principal relationships among the variables.

1. *The stimulus situation and the need system are related.* The environmental situation acts as a stimulus for the arousal of certain kinds of needs.[12] The fact that Jane is working on a

---

[12]An example of a study of this kind of relationship: J. L. Gewirtz, "Three Determinants of Attention-Seeking in Young Children," *Monographs of the Society for Research in Child Development*, 19 (1954), No. 2.

school newspaper, whose editor encourages her to write a feature article, acts as a stimulus which may arouse her need for approval. We see many examples in everyday life of this kind of relationship; for example, the presence of certain kinds of foods will arouse the hunger need of a person even though before he had seen these foods he had not felt hungry. In general, then, the environmental context can operate as a source of stimulation to arouse given kinds of needs.

2. *The stimulus situation and the cognitive-attitudinal-value system are interrelated.* People learn to conceptualize their environments in certain ways, to have attitudes about objects in this environment, and to place values on these objects.[18] Robert knows that hammers are used for pounding nails. Jane knows that people who have had interesting experiences are good material for feature articles. Jane has placed a high value on receiving the approval of her classmates. Robert has positive attitudes about airplanes. All of these ways of conceptualizing the environment, these attitudes toward and values placed upon objects in the environment are the result of previous learning. They affect the person's present conception of and attitude toward the environment.

3. *The stimulus situation influences the person's conception of the behavior space and of himself (the behaving self).* The person sees himself as placed in an environment which he perceives in a given way. He sees himself in relationship to that environment. Jane sees herself as a high school student. A few years from now she will see herself as a college student, and still later she will see herself as a mother. In each of these instances, the environmental context determines, in part, Jane's perception of herself and the particular context which she is in.

4. *The drive state of the person influences his need system.* The general physiological conditions of the organism affect its need state. This is most obvious in the case of needs for which

---

[18]An example of a study of this problem: J. S. Bruner, L. Postman, and J. Rodrigues, "Expectation and the Perception of Color," *American Journal of Psychology,* 64 (1951), 216-27.

there is a known physiological basis. For example, when certain physiological changes take place, the hunger need is stimulated. However, at the present time, the neurophysical changes related to more complex needs are unknown but are assumed to exist.

5.   *Heredity, age, and sex are related to capacity and ability.* The capacities of the organism are determined by its native endowment. The present operating level of these capacities is a function of the stage of development of the organism. Jane and Robert have certain abilities in part because of capacities that they have on the basis of their hereditary endowment. This endowment is the organic base which sets the limits for learning and personality development.

6.   *The need system and the cognitive-attitudinal-value system are interrelated.* Our needs, in part, shape our way of viewing the world, and our way of viewing the world influences our needs. This point will be discussed in detail in the chapter on motivation, but an example here will make the point. A high level of hunger need will influence our perceptions of what are edible foods. An extremely hungry man will see as edible, foods which in less intense states of hunger need he would not consider edible. Contrariwise, as we develop new ways of looking at the world and new attitudes and values, we also develop new needs. As we develop new ideas and new tastes, these in turn stimulate needs in us, which can be satisfied only by attaining goal objects relating to these new ideas and tastes. As we grow up, for example, we learn that there are many pleasant and enjoyable things that we can obtain from other people, such as their affection, interest, and esteem. As we find these relations with other people satisfying, we develop needs for affection and approval from other people.

7.   *The cognitive-attitudinal-value system influences the perception of the behavior space and the behaving self.* The person in a given context perceiving his environment in particular kinds of ways integrates these perceptions into a more general perception of the immediate environment and of himself in

this environment. We view a given context on the basis of our unique conceptions of this environment. Jane, for example, sees herself as a student who is capable of writing a feature article, and also realizes that the environment provides her with the opportunity for doing this. Her generalized perception in the immediate environment is related to a host of more specific conceptions about feature articles, their character, their utility for getting one's name in by-lines, and about the value of the experiences of one of her teachers as material for this article.

8.   *A change in behavior leads to a restructuring of the behavior space and to the concept of the behaving self.* As Robert and Jane try out responses which might lead them to their goal, their perceptions of themselves and of their immediate environment change. Robert sees the environment somewhat differently at the time that he has his plane partially constructed than he did at the time he was just beginning the process. He has hopes of success. He also knows the difficulties confronting him and can estimate the probability of his ultimate success or failure. When he has finished the plane he is, in effect, in a modified and new environment. He is no longer Robert-who-is-about-to-build-a-plane, but is now Robert-who-has-constructed-a-plane. The consequences of having behaved change his perception of his environment and of himself.

Similarly, when Jane has completed her feature article and it has been read and praised by her fellow students, she sees herself in a new and modified environment. She also is now Jane-who-has-written-a-successful-feature-article, as distinct from Jane-who-wanted-to-write such an article. As the organism acquires new behaviors, its perception of itself and its relationship to its environment continually change.

The model that we are proposing here has a dynamic aspect to it. It can be used to analyze any particular sequence or unit of behavior, such as writing a feature article to win approval. Furthermore, it provides us with a scheme for analyzing the effects of behavior change on the total personality. Successful completion of a sequence of action leads to reorganization and new integrations within the personality structure; this is represented by the part of the diagram which has been labeled *Restructured Conception of Self.* Jane now sees herself and her relations with her classmates in a different light. Her behavioral environment has changed.

THE DESCRIPTIVE MODEL AND THE STUDY OF EDUCATIONAL PSYCHOLOGY

The model that has been presented here provides us with a way of conceptualizing the variables and the relationships that we will study in educational psychology. Our study of educational psychology will be focused around these variables and their interrelationships. All of the interrelationships that we have outlined in the model suggest a host of psychological questions that must be answered if we wish to improve our understanding of human behavior.

An important problem for teachers is motivating students to learn. Therefore, one of the problems that we will study is the relationship between environmental conditions and the need systems of individuals. We can ask questions like these: Does providing approval for work well done encourage better work? Does approval arouse the needs of pupils so that they will do better work to satisfy these needs? We will want to know what principles will govern our manipulation of the environment in order to arouse the needs of students and thereby motivate them to learn.

We will also want to know something about the relationship of need systems to learning. Some needs can be satisfied within the context of the learning situations provided by the school; others cannot. Some needs can be capitalized on to enhance learning; others will interfere with learning. A need for approval, for example, might lead to behavior appropriate for attaining a teacher's approval. But a strong need to be encouraged or supported might interfere with learning independent and self-reliant behavior.

We will study how students acquire their ways of looking at the world, and how they acquire their attitudes and values. Why does one child distrust foreigners when another does not? A question of this kind is a question about how children learn concepts and attitudes. We will want to know what kinds of learning experiences will produce changes in the conceptual-attitudinal-value system of our students. For example, can teachers provide learning experiences which change prejudices? Furthermore, we will be concerned with how the need system and the cognitive-attitudinal-value system of the student influence his conception of himself. We will also want to know the relationship of the learning experiences of students to their conceptions of themselves. How do learning experiences change one's concept of himself?

In other words the model provides us with a way of conceptualizing behavior and a guide for our study of educational psychology. As we study the relationships among these variables we will be developing generalizations and hypotheses about behavior which will enable us to understand behavior in the educational context. This understanding should improve our hypothesis-making when we are working with students and attempting to change behavior in desirable directions.

We will, perhaps, find it profitable to refer back to the model from time to time to place the principles and generalizations that we are studying in the framework of the model. In this way the many details and the many principles that we will be assimilating can be organized in a meaningful pattern.

SUMMARY

In Chapter Two we discussed the nature of the educative act, and in this chapter we have discussed basic principles governing the acquisition of behavior. We have presented the general features of both of these conceptions. Our problem is now to interrelate these two conceptions and to suggest how we will further our understanding of these concepts and relationships.

We have stated that the first aspect of the educative act is a clear conception of the objectives of the educational process. We specify in behavioral terms what a person is to be like when he has been exposed to a given educational experience. *The process of specifying educational objectives is a process of being concerned about the dependent variable in our model of behavior change.*

We have also said the teacher organizes a learning experience— the function of which is to bring about the specified behavior changes. The teacher enters the model of behavior under the heading of *stimulus situation*. The teacher along with the physical and social context, is the stimulus situation to which the person responds. This particular environmental context is an aspect of a larger environmental context which also influences the behavior of the person. The environmental context includes the persons who are being educated; we can therefore describe these people in terms of the other independent variables, such as heredity, age, and sex. The combination of the environmental context provided by the teacher and the school and the kinds of students who are in this context constitute the sources of the independent variables that influence behavior change.

Furthermore, the individual students will have their own need systems, their own conceptual-attitudinal-value orientations, and their own perceptions of the environment and of themselves. The interaction between these processes within the student and the environmental context will produce changes both in the need systems and in the cognitive-attitudinal-value systems. These changes lead to behavior which is consonant with the specified objectives of the educative act. Refer again to the example of Robert: Mrs. Jones, her classroom, the activities permitted and encouraged in this classroom, the relationship among the pupils, the materials and tools provided, are all aspects of the environmental situation. Robert with his capacities, abilities, and temperament is in this environmental situation. Robert brings to this situation needs and values, attitudes, and ways of looking at the world. Mrs. Jones utilizes the need system of Robert to evoke behavior which she regards as desirable. Robert utilizes his conceptions of the environment to select and regulate his behavior leading to the attainment of his desired goal. In this process his ways of viewing the environment are changed, and his attitudes and values are modified.

Finally, as we noted earlier, when a particular educative experience has terminated, the teacher must assess the extent to which the desired behaviors have been acquired by her students. In Robert's case, his teacher was probably concerned with the attainment of more complex behavior, such as independent creative activity, than with the construction of an airplane. The function of the evaluative devices that Mrs. Jones will use is to determine whether constructing an airplane is an adequate measure of independent creative activity. By assessing Robert's behavior, she can determine whether the desired change has occurred.

As you acquire generalizations, concepts, and principles, you will be acquiring materials for hypothesizing about educational experiences. Examine your hunches and opinions, as well as educational precepts and folklore in the light of these generalizations, concepts, and principles. Answer systematically the question: Do my ideas about educational experiences make sense in the light of what is known about behavior change?

STUDY AND DISCUSSION QUESTIONS

1. Literary men often show great insight in describing human behavior. Why is a science of psychology necessary as long as we have these other observations of human behavior? Might not the same argument be made for the observations of an experienced teacher?

2. Suggest some explanations for the following observed events:

   a. John reads any book on the Middle East that he can find.

   b. Rick quit the basketball team after it lost its last game.

   c. Jim collects butterflies and stamps.

   d. Joe is usually late for class.

3. Review your explanations for the above events and analyze the origins or sources of your explanations. Which of these explanations were based on your observations; which were derivations from some general psychological principles you hold?

4. Critically evaluate your explanations by attempting to determine what observations influenced them. How many observations did you make before formulating the principles you used? Were these observations systematically made, or did they "just happen"? What factors may have influenced your judgments of what you observed?

5. Below are a number of statements about behavior change and such factors as teaching procedures, home influences, and personality characteristics. These statements may have varying degrees of validity; they are presented mainly for critical analysis. (1) Identify the independent, mediating, and dependent variables in these statements. What behavior would you observe to determine whether changes in these variables had occurred? (2) Locate the variables identified in the model of personality presented in this chapter. (3) Formulate each of these statements as hypotheses about behavior change. (4) Identify the assumptions about personality and behavior change implicit in these statements. Clarify, refine, and improve these statements in any way that will make their meaning clear. Suggest ways in which you might make observations to test these hypotheses.

   a. Pupils learn better with frequent tests.

   b. Bright students are frequently bored in class.

c. Girls are better than boys at English.

d. Children should be taught number concepts by having them manipulate objects in various combinations.

e. Spelling is learned more efficiently if taught as needed.

f. Geography is more interesting if realistic models of terrain and other physical objects are used.

g. Students of plane geometry should do considerable construction work with ruler and compass so that they will learn geometric principles.

h. Geometry can be learned better when students build objects requiring an application of geometric principles.

i. The way a child feels about another child depends on the kind of home in which he is being raised.

j. Cooperation among children is improved when children work on projects together.

k. Students are more likely to be interested in school work when it is related to their problems.

l. The best-liked teachers are friendly and helpful.

RECOMMENDED READINGS

The first of the readings describes the requirements for validating our ideas. The second reading is a description of the procedures used in child study. It presents an overview of basic methodology and the problems involved in the study of children. The third reading is a discussion of the scientific character of modern psychology, and is a comprehensive discussion of the general principles of psychological investigation.

1. H. A. Larrabee, *Reliable Knowledge,* Boston, Houghton Mifflin Co., 1945.

2. J. E. Anderson, "Methods of Child Psychology," in L. Carmichael (ed.), *Manual of Child Psychology* (2nd ed.), New York, John Wiley & Sons, 1954, Chapter 1.

3. C. C. Pratt, *The Logic of Modern Psychology,* New York, The Macmillan Co., 1939.

PART TWO

LEARNING AND
THE DEVELOPMENT
OF PERSONALITY

MOTIVATION
AND LEARNING

Teachers are very much aware of the importance of motivation in facilitating learning, and they use a variety of techniques to induce pupil motivation. Such devices as grades, honor rolls, gold stars, achievement medals, praise and blame, have been used, rightly or wrongly, as devices for encouraging pupils to want to learn. Attempts to motivate human beings so that they will change their behavior in desired ways is not confined to the schools. The parent who gives a child a piece of candy for learning correct table manners, or the management group that institutes a new incentive plan to increase production, is attempting to motivate changes in behavior. The business world invests large sums of money each year in advertising to motivate people to buy and use commercial products.

In this chapter we will describe what is meant by motivation, and the relationships between motivation and learning. We will also describe the process by which teachers can assess the motivational processes of their students. You will not be given specific techniques guaranteed to produce motivation for learning in any and all students. The problem of motivating students is an extremely complex one for which there are no simple rules. A study of motivation should make the teacher sensitive to the complexity of this problem and aware of motivational principles that can guide his educational practices, although there are as yet no infallible specific guides to action. As Hilgard and Russell have observed, there is "no panacea for all the ills of indifference, dislike, and rebellion encountered in children placed in unsuitable school environments. If there is any conclusion from recent research of which a teacher may be sure, it is that there is no known formula or infallible set of procedures to motivate all pupils at all times. . . . The evidence seems rather clear, too, that motivation is not something applied apart from the learning situation but is an intrinsic part of it."[1]

WHAT IS MOTIVATION?

As a basis for developing an understanding of the concept of motivation, consider the following example:

John and Bill are members of the Junior Class at Lincoln High School, and both are enrolled in the physics course. Both have been "A" students and are among the students obtaining the best grades on each of the tests given by Mr. Richards, the physics instructor. Mr. Richards has announced a test for next week on the topic "Electricity." Both boys study intensively for this test, and both receive high grades.

1. John is quite concerned about his grade, a 91, and sees Mr. Richards about his paper. He wants to discuss his paper with Mr. Richards because he feels that he should be given a few more points. John points out that he would like to get a 92 or a 93 because this grade will affect his over-all average which is important to him because he wants to be considered for an officership in the ROTC unit at the school. Grade average is a criterion used in the selection of students for the ranks of officer in this unit. Mr. Richards points out that John's answers do not justify changing his mark. The discussion becomes somewhat heated, and John is obviously upset when he realizes that his grade will not be changed. After his discussion with Mr. Richards, he complains to several of his fellow students that he doesn't think he is being treated fairly and that Mr. Richards is too demanding in what he expects.

---

[1] E. R. Hilgard and D. H. Russell, "Motivation in School Learning," *Forty-ninth Yearbook of the National Society for the Study of Education, Part I, p. 37.*

2. Bill, who is interested in becoming an engineer, also goes to Mr. Richards about his paper. He is quite concerned because he has missed questions, but the basis of his concern is the inadequacies of his own knowledge. He spends some time discussing with Mr. Richards the questions that he missed. When he finishes his discussion with Mr. Richards he feels satisfied that he now knows the subject matter of the test better than he did before. His comments to his classmates are remarkably different from those of John. Bill sees Mr. Richards as a helpful teacher, one who is interested in seeing that his students learn. Bill states that he likes having teachers who expect you to perform at your best because he feels that this is the best preparation for the kind of career that he is planning.

In the above example, note that the behavior of the two boys is in many respects substantially the same. Each has studied intensively for the test; each has performed at about the same level on the test; each has gone to the teacher to discuss his paper with him. But it is obvious that the reasons for their behavior are radically different. John is interested in obtaining good grades, because they are means for securing an officer rank in the ROTC unit. John is working for this rank, and grades in his classes are means to this goal. Bill, on the other hand, is interested in becoming an engineer and knowledge of physics is important to him. He is concerned with his mistakes because faulty or inadequate knowledge will eventually hamper him in his preparation for his career. Bill's goal is engineering, and knowledge of physics is a means to attaining this goal.

INFERRING MOTIVATION FROM BEHAVIOR. The differences between these two boys are differences in motivation. How do we know that their motives for obtaining good grades are different? We cannot observe motivation directly, all that we can observe is the behavior of the person. On the basis of this behavior, we make inferences about what it is that the person seeks in engaging in a particular activity. Inferring that John is motivated by a desire to become an officer in the ROTC unit, we can say, "John wants good grades so that he will have the necessary average to be selected for officer rank." Inferring that Bill is interested in physics because he wants to become an engineer, we can say, "Bill wants good grades in physics because they tell him how much he knows about the subject."

This distinction between *observed behavior* and *inferred processes* is important, and one that is frequently overlooked in our common-sense explanations of behavior. We talk about motives as if they were directly observable and forget or ignore the fact that we are making inferences, the accuracy of which depends upon the reliability of our observation.

A teacher, for example, had a student in her second grade class who would not follow directions. After many futile attempts to get this student to do as directed, the teacher in desperation called in the principal and demanded that the pupil be removed from her class. At this time the principal told her that the child was partially deaf; the child's apparent indifference to the teacher's directions was probably the result of not hearing what the teacher was saying. In this case the teacher lacked adequate data and consequently made a faulty inference.

RELIABLE INFERENCES ABOUT MOTIVATION. Before we can conclude reliably about the the motives underlying the behavior that we observe, we should have adequate samples of the person's behavior. Furthermore, the inferences that we make must be checked by observing other behavior that is consistent with the assumed motive. John's motivation to attain a high officer rank will probably be apparent in many other kinds of behavior. The teacher can check the correctness of this inference by observing John's behavior in other situations and determining whether this new sample of behavior is reasonably consistent with the inference about John's motives. For example, does John assume leadership with his companions? Does he participate actively in ROTC drills?

Two important principles are apparent in the above discussion of motivation:

1. Motivation is a process within the individual. Knowledge of this process helps us to explain the behavior we observe and to predict other behaviors of the person.

2. We determine the character of this process by inferences from observable behavior. The accuracy of these inferences depends upon the reliability of our observations. The validity of these inferences is established by their usefulness in enabling us to predict and to explain other instances of behavior.

A DEFINITION OF MOTIVATION. It is not sufficient to describe motivation as a process that we infer from observable behavior. Other processes are also inferred from observable behavior, such as the thinking and evaluating processes. Motivation can be distinguished from these other processes. *Motivation is an energy change within the person characterized by affective arousal and anticipatory goal reactions.* This definition contains three elements:

1. *Motivation begins in an energy change in the person.* We assume that all changes in motivation arise out of some energy change in the neurophysiological system of the human organism. For many motives the exact organic nature of this energy change is unknown. The organic basis of Jane's desire to win the esteem and approval of her fellow students cannot be described, but we assume that some energy change is the basis for Jane's behavior. Similarly, the organic base of John's and Bill's motives is unknown. The organic base is known for some other energy changes. The hunger motive typically originates out of physiological changes in the digestive system of the person.

2. *Motivation is characterized by affective arousal.* A number of terms have been used to describe this "feeling" state. Previously we have referred to it as a state of psychological tension. Subjectively this state may be characterized as "emotion." When a child tells us that he was "mad" when he struck a companion, he is describing the feeling state accompanying this motivated behavior. We may know what his motive is when we determine what this act accomplished for him.

It is not necessary that this affective arousal be intense, nor even that the person be conscious of a change in his affective state. Intense affective arousal is frequently obvious from behavior. A student engaged in a discussion in which he is intensely interested argues heatedly, his voice rises, he gesticulates more frequently, and the words flow freely and rapidly. A person may cry, laugh, swear, sweat, breathe more heavily, raise and lower his voice, wave his arms, appear to be intensely occupied. On the other hand, the evidence of affective arousal may be minimal, and we may have difficulty in inferring that the person is concerned or involved in some new process. The student working quietly at his desk gives very few, if any, manifestations of affective arousal, except the intentness with which he appears to be working. But we infer that this very intentness is a manifestation of the psychological change that has occurred within him.

3. *Motivation is characterized by anticipatory goal reactions.* The motivated person makes responses which lead him to a goal, the function of which is to reduce the tension created by the energy change in him. Motivation, in other words, leads to goal-seeking responses. In our example of Jane, we noted that she wanted the praise and approval of her classmates. At some point when her need for approval became sufficiently strong, Jane began making responses which would lead to a goal that would satisfy her need. Each of her responses was a step along the way to her goal. But the goal was not reached until the article was published and had won for Jane the ap-

proval of her classmates. *The responses leading to this goal were anticipatory*, in that they were presumably leading to the attainment of her goal. We *infer* that Jane anticipated achieving this goal on the basis of responses that she made.

ELEMENTS OF MOTIVATION. Motivation has an inner and an outer component. The *inner component* is the change that takes place in the person, the state of dissatisfaction, or psychological tension. The *outer component* is what the person wants, the *goal* towards which his behavior is directed. We can assume Jane had a fairly general need for praise and approval (the inner component) which could have been satisfied in a variety of ways (goals, or outer components). She chose to satisfy her need (inner component) through writing a feature article which she anticipated would win for her the approval of her classmates (the outer component).

GOALS AND MOTIVATED STATES. We have deliberately simplified the relationship between the motivated state of the person and his goal-seeking behavior. We have assumed, first of all, that the person was capable of making the responses necessary to lead to the goal which would reduce his psychological tension. In many instances, the person may seek ways of satisfying his needs by selecting unattainable goals. If Jane lacked the skill to write an interesting feature article, she could not have won the approval of her classmates by this means. If she had no other way of winning this approval, she could not satisfy her need for approval from fellow-students.

Secondly, we have been assuming that the goal when attained is satisfying to the individual. If Jane had not won the approval of her classmates when her article was published, her need for approval would remain unsatisfied, and she would have had to find other ways in which to satisfy this need. The person estimates the potentiality of a goal for satisfying his needs, and this estimate may be more or less correct.

NEED-SATISFACTION AND REINFORCEMENT OF BEHAVIOR. It is also important to note the effects of the attainment of the goal on the behavior of the individual. *Behavior which has led to satisfaction of needs tends to be repeated when the needs are aroused.* Jane has learned that writing a feature article has won her classmates' approval. When she is motivated again to seek approval she will probably try this means a second time. The behavior which has led to the goal is *reinforced* and *strengthened; that is, when the person is again motivated in the same way, the behavior is likely to occur.* Jane may look for interesting people to write about, she may use some of the same techniques in writing that she used the first time.

From the teacher's point of view, many instances of classroom behavior are inexplicable and difficult to eradicate simply because they have been strongly reinforced through need-satisfaction. The child who is continually talking in class, answering out of turn, and generally disruptive of classroom procedures may be attempting to satisfy a strong need for attention. Since his behavior is obviously attention-getting, angry outbursts and reprimands on the part of the teacher produce the very effect that the behavior is designed to stimulate.

Even in situations which are presumably rewarding to a child, deviant kinds of behavior may be learned because the needs of the child are being met in other ways. The following example may make this point clear:

> In the first instance (2/28/56) we are at a seed distribution. Every year, in this area, children go from door to door in the neighborhood selling seeds to raise money for incidental expenses of the school. The children buy the seeds in school from ten to twenty cents a pack and sell them. The fact that no package is less than a dime is generally well known to the children. Nevertheless we will see that Bobby tries to buy a package for a nickel. He says to the teacher: "Any for five cents?" And the teacher says, "No, *dear*, they're all at least a dime. You just need one more nickel, don't you?" And Bobby says, "I'll get it tomorrow."
>
> Bobby was the only child in the class to make this mistake. In correcting him the teacher gently called him "dear," and gave him another chance in close contact with her by having him bring the extra nickel the next day. No other child got a second try at teacher. Thus, Bobby's erratic behavior was inadvertently reinforced by the teacher.[2]

Bobby has learned that deviant behaviors bring him the attention that he wants. The more attention that he receives, the more likely he is to be disruptive.

---

[2]J. Henry, "Working Paper on Creativity," *Harvard Educational Review*, 27 (1957), 152.

MOTIVES, NEEDS, DRIVES

We have discussed the general idea of motivation, indicating that when we are talking about motivation we are describing a process with certain characteristics. Psychologists have used many terms to refer to the motivational state, such as motives, needs, drives, wants, interests, desires. While these terms are sometimes used interchangeably, some distinctions can be made among them for the sake of clarity.

DEFINITION OF NEED. What is a need? We have noted that a motivated state arises out of a change within the person. *Needs describe the relatively permanent tendencies in persons to be motivated in specific ways, and we infer them from the commonalities among the goals that the person appears to be seeking.* Needs are aroused or activated either by internal changes within the organism, or by stimulus events in the environment of the organism. Once the internal change has taken place, the energy basis for goal-seeking behavior is available. To make this clear, let us refer again to Jane. As observers, we noted certain specific kinds of behavior, such as Jane's gathering of information for an article, writing the article, and some behavioral manifestations of satisfaction when this article was praised. On the basis of this behavior, we inferred that Jane was motivated by a need for approval which she obtained through writing the feature article for her school paper. Jane's activity began in a change in her need system. Jane wanted something and wanted it with sufficient strength to seek a given goal.

Before we can infer that Jane has a need for approval we will have to observe additional samples of approval-seeking behavior. We cannot conclude on the basis of one or two instances of approval-seeking behavior that Jane has a relatively permanent tendency to seek approval. Individual instances of motivated behavior are the basis from which we infer needs.

EXPERIMENTAL EVIDENCE FOR NEED-AROUSAL. What evidence do we have that such changes take place, since they are not observable? The evidence for the existence of internal changes in Jane's psychological need system is based upon knowledge of what happens when goal-seeking behavior is interrupted or frustrated. We could be reasonably certain that a change of sufficient strength was operating if a person persisted in attempts to attain a goal.

An interesting experiment demonstrated this point. Ovsiankina[3] set up a laboratory situation in which she had students work on a variety of tasks, such as solving puzzles and modeling animals in clay. The tasks were presumably interesting, but of no personal importance to the students. However, when a student became interested in the tasks, the experimenter interrupted and asked the student to move on to a new task. The student was allowed to complete the second task and then was free for a short period after he had completed this task. Two results were apparent. First, the students resisted the initial interruption and took on the second task only with persuasion. Second, without prompting from the experimenter, the students frequently returned to finish the interrupted task; seventy-nine per cent of the interrupted tasks were resumed spontaneously by the students.[4] In explaining these data, we may infer a tension which is reduced only by completion of the task.

A similar kind of effect was produced under entirely different experimental conditions. Zeigarnik[5] gave her experimental subjects a series of twenty simple but varied tasks, each requiring a few minutes of work. Half of these were interrupted and half were not. At the end of the work period the subjects were asked to recall as many as possible of the twenty tasks. Sixty-eight per cent of the uncompleted tasks were recalled, whereas only forty-three per cent of the completed tasks were recalled.

In these experiments the subject's tendency to return to an incomplete task cannot be explained by immediate environmental influences. The experimenter neither required nor urged the subjects to finish all tasks. We infer that the persistency in completing tasks is related to the strength of some need to finish the task. Experimental evidence suggests that the character of the need involved may be quite complex.[6] We could postulate several specific needs as the probable bases for motivation. The experimentation demonstrates that

---

[3] N. Ovsiankina, "The Resumption of Interrupted Tasks," *Psychologische Forschung*, 11 (128), 302-379.

[4] A similar result was obtained with nursery school children. See E. Katz, "Some Factors Affecting Resumption of Interrupted Activities by Pre-school Children," *Institute of Child Welfare Monograph Series*, No. 16, Minneapolis, University of Minnesota Press, 1938.

[5] B. Zeigarnik, "Uben das Behalten von erledigten and unerledigten Handlungen," *Psychologische Forschung*, 9 (1927), 1-85.

[6] For a review of these studies see W. C. H. Prentice, "The Interruption of Tasks," *Psychological Review*, 51 (1944), 329-40; for a critical analysis of experimentation, see G. W. Boguslavsky, "Interruption and Learning," *Psychological Review*, 58 (1951), 248-55.

under the influence of an internal process, called *motivation,* the individual's behavior persists until a goal has been reached. The goal in these experiments was the completion of the tasks. On attainment of the goal the behavior leading to the attainment of the goal subsides.

We see many instances of the effects of need-arousal in everyday life. The student who wants to be a physician enters willingly on a long career of preparation, during which he foregoes many immediate satisfactions and pleasures to attain his long-term goal. The teacher who has trouble getting Johnny to do his school work is sometimes surprised at the long hours of arduous practice that Johnny will put in on the baseball field. For the motivated learner difficulties and problems are met willingly, and seemingly unpleasant tasks no longer have the flavor of being chores.

DEFINITION OF DRIVE. What is a drive? In Figure 2 we depicted drive conditions as independent variables which influence behavior change. *A drive is an initiating neurophysiological condition, that is, a change in the neurophysiological structure of the person which is the organic basis for the energy change we call "motivation."* That neurophysiological changes provide a basis for motivation is apparent in the case of some needs, such as the hunger need and the thirst need. Needs of this character have fairly obvious physiological bases, and changes in the physiological structures of the organism initiate conditions which lead to need-arousal.[7] However, there are some needs

---

[7] See C. T. Morgan and E. Stellar, *Physiological Psychology,* New York, McGraw-Hill Book Co., 1950, Chapter 18.

for which there is no known physiological base. We would be hard put to describe the changes in the neurophysiological system that either preceded or accompanied the arousal of a need for status, for example. However, in a complete description of behavior we must allow for the effects of neurophysiological changes on the motivation of behavior.[8] At the present time we must be satisfied with assuming that need-arousal is accompanied by changes in the neurophysiological structure of the organism without being able to specify what these changes are, and without being able to manipulate them in any way.[9]

NEEDS AND MOTIVES. What is a *motive?* We will use this term in describing instances of goal-seeking behavior. A child's motive in striking a playmate is the goal he is seeking by that action. He may be striking his companion to demonstrate that he is bigger and stronger. He may be relieving his hostile feelings. Jane's motive in writing a feature article is to win approval. Bill's motive in talking with Mr. Richards is to correct his mistakes. Bobby's typical motive is to get the teacher's attention.

From motives we infer needs. We use many instances of motivated behavior to determine needs. Motives arise out of needs. When a person is motivated specifically, he is attempting to satisfy some underlying need. At this point we have described the *motivation process.* A *motive* is an instance of motivated behavior, an instance of goal-seeking behavior. From similarities among motives we infer *needs*, or stable tendencies to be motivated in specific ways.

Throughout this chapter we will be amplifying our concept of the need system and its relation to behavior change.

THE NEED SYSTEM

Are there needs common to all individuals? Or does each individual have his own unique pattern of needs? Is the need system of a person highly stable and unchangeable? Questions like these have great practical importance for educators. If we could specify the common needs of children, we could organize their environment so

---

[8]For an account of new developments in this field and their implications for motivational concepts, see N. E. Miller, "Central Stimulation and Other New Approaches to Motivation and Reward," *The American Psychologist*, 13 (1958), 100-108.

[9]For a critical analysis of the concept of drives see B. R. Bugelski, *The Psychology of Learning*, New York, Henry Holt and Co., 1956, Chapter IX.

that their needs would be satisfied, and we could utilize these needs to bring about desirable kinds of learning. A basic principle of a current curriculum theory is that the curriculum must meet the needs of the child. Such a principle presupposes the existence of definable and observable needs in children, and probably also assumes some commonalties among the needs of individual children. The questions that we are raising here have, therefore, both theoretical and practical importance.

CLASSIFICATION OF NEEDS. The attempt to classify the common needs of human beings has been largely ineffective. There are probably as many lists of needs as there are psychologists who have attempted to formulate these lists. As yet there is comparatively little experimental evidence to support these speculations.[10] The reasons for this difficulty in formulating any comprehensive list of needs is that human adaptability and the variability of human behavior are so great that need satisfaction takes many different forms. One student strives for excellence in academic activities, another for excellence in athletic activities. Are these students motivated by different needs, or is it that each is motivated in essentially the same way but has learned that different goals satisfy his common needs? This is essentially the problem the psychologist faces when he attempts to classify and to organize the goal-seeking behaviors of human beings.

PRINCIPLES OF CLASSIFICATION. We will not attempt a new classification nor will we adopt some standard list of needs. It is probably more profitable for the prospective teacher to be familiar with the processes of inference involved in identifying the needs of an individual than it is for him to memorize some relatively arbitrary list of needs. Table II provides several lists developed by psychologists. You will notice in these lists some agreement and considerable differences among the needs cataloged. The lists differ both in number of needs included and the kinds and definitions of needs. Our decision not to repeat this cataloging process does not imply that everybody's opinion is equally good in the matter of defining needs. Rather, we wish to emphasize the process by which needs are identified and the importance of the need concept as an element in behavior and personality change.

---

[10] For a discussion of this and related problems see S. Koch, "The Current Status of Motivational Psychology," *Psychological Review*, 58 (1951), 147-56.

The following are some of the principles relevant to the determination of common needs:

1. *There is a set of basic needs;* that is, physiological conditions for these needs are common to all men, and the environment is sufficiently stable to provide conditions for satisfying these needs. An example is the need for food. Changes in the physiological condition of the organism lead to changes in the state of the hunger drive of the person. Furthermore, the environment provides conditions by which the need can be met, though not the same under all environmental conditions.

TABLE OF NEEDS AND NEED SYSTEMS

Psychologists define systems of needs consistent with their assumptions about personality and their interpretations of experimental and clinical evidence. Some psychologists define these needs in detail and attempt to distinguish them from each other; Murray's list below is one such example. Others develop a list of needs which are generally defined but appear to have relevance for interpreting behavior. Cronbach's list is of this character. Still others suggest an organizational principle for a system of needs, as does Maslow's. Maslow has developed an integrated system of needs arranged in a hierarchical order based on the relative importance of the satisfaction of the needs. Higher-order needs do not develop until lower-order needs are minimally satisfied, according to Maslow.

Murray's List[1]

Abasement. To surrender. To comply and accept punishment. To apologize, confess, atone. Self-depreciation. Masochism.

Achievement. To overcome obstacles. To exercise power. To strive to do something difficult as well and as quickly as possible.

Acquisition. To gain possessions and property. To grasp, snatch or steal things. To bargain or gamble. To work for money or goods.

Affiliation. To form friendships and associations. To greet, join, and live with others. To cooperate and converse sociably with others. To love. To join groups.

Aggression. To assault or injure. To belittle, harm, blame, accuse or maliciously ridicule a person. To punish severely. Sadism.

Autonomy. To resist influence or coercion. To defy an authority or seek freedom in a new place. To strive for independence.

Blamavoidance. To avoid blame, ostracism or punishment by inhibiting asocial or unconventional impulses. To be well-behaved and obey the law.

Counteraction. Proudly to refuse admission of defeat by restriving and retaliating. To select the hardest tasks. To defend one's honour in action.

Cognizance. To explore. To ask questions. To satisfy curiosity. To look, listen, inspect. To read and seek knowledge.

Construction. To organize and build.

Deference. To admire and willingly follow a superior. To co-operate with a leader. To serve gladly.

Defendance. To defend oneself against blame or belittlement. To justify one's actions. To offer extenuations, explanations and excuses. To resist 'probing.'

Dominance. To influence or control others. To persuade, prohibit, dictate. To lead and di-

These drive states and their associated needs are intimately related to human survival and, as we suggested earlier, the physiological basis for these needs is known. Included in this set of needs are needs for food, air, elimination, activity, rest, and probably a few others.

2. *Some needs are characteristically acquired within cultural contexts.* A need for success, or a need for achievement, characterizes many members of American society. Other societies reward achievement and excellence so infrequently that the need for achievement does not characterize the members of that society. Among the Alorese, for example, "strength does

---

rect. To restrain. To organize the behaviour of a group.

Exhibition. To attract attention to one's person. To excite, amuse, stir, shock, thrill others. Self-dramatization.

Exposition. To point and demonstrate. To relate facts. To give information, explain, interpret, lecture.

Harmavoidance. To avoid pain, physical injury, illness and death. To escape from a dangerous situation. To take precautionary measures.

Infavoidance. To avoid failure, shame, humiliation, ridicule. To refrain from attempting to do something that is beyond one's powers. To conceal a disfigurement.

Nurturance. To nourish, aid or protect the helpless. To express sympathy. To 'mother' a child.

Order. To arrange, organize, put away objects. To be tidy and clean. To be scrupulously precise.

Play. To relax, amuse oneself, seek diversion and entertainment. To 'have fun,' to play games. To laugh, joke and be merry. To avoid serious tension.

Rejection. To snub, ignore or exclude. To remain aloof and indifferent. To be discriminating.

Retention. To retain possession of things. To refuse to give or lend. To hoard. To be frugal, economical and miserly.

Sentience. To seek and enjoy sensuous impressions.

Sex. To form and further an erotic relationship. To have sexual intercourse.

Succorance. To seek aid, protection or sympathy. To cry for help. To plead for mercy. To adhere to an affectionate, nurturant parent. To be dependent.

Superiority. This need is considered to be a composite of achievement and recognition.

Understanding. To analyze experience, to abstract, to discriminate among concepts, to define relations, to synthesize ideas.

Cronbach's List[2]

Affection
Approval from Authority-Figures
Approval by Peers
Independence
Self-Respect

Maslow's List[3]

Physiological needs
Safety needs
Love and belonging needs
Esteem needs (needs for achievement and recognition)
Self-actualization needs
Desires to know and understand.

TABLE II

[1]From H. A. Murray, *Explorations in Personality*, New York, Oxford University Press, 1938.
[2]From L. J. Cronbach, *Educational Psychology*, New York, Harcourt, Brace and Co., 1954.
[3]From A. H. Maslow, "A Theory of Human Motivation," *Psychological Review*, 50 (1943), 370-96; also, from A. H. Maslow, "Some Theoretical Consequences of Basic Need Gratifications," *Journal of Personality*, 16 (1948), 402-16.

not rate very high; neither does skill; nor are these qualities greatly admired. They have no skilled artisans who take pride in achievement and special talent, which, even if it did exist, would get no special esteem."[11]

Stability in the patterns of reward and in the goals that an environment provides influence the consistency with which needs are acquired by members of a given cultural or subcultural group. The variability in environments suggests that the need systems of children will vary considerably, even though we may be able to identify some commonalities in needs among children.

3. *The need system of individuals is dependent in part on their state of development*. Since children in growing up are progressively exposed to more varied environments, the influence of these environments on their need system will depend on their stage of development.

These three principles imply a hierarchy of needs.[12] First, there are some needs common to men irrespective of their cultural environments. Second, some needs will be common to members of the same society, but will vary from one society to another. Third, needs will develop as the individual's experience expands. Commonality in needs among individuals results from common experiences, and variability from differences in experience.[13]

DEVELOPMENT OF THE NEED SYSTEM. Presumably the child begins life with a limited system of needs, and as he develops into a mature person, his need system becomes elaborated and differentiated. The young child under the close supervision of his parents may have acquired comparatively strong dependency needs, which he manifests by such behaviors as seeking help from his parents, continually questioning them, staying close to them, holding his parent's hand when

---

[11]A. Kardiner, *Psychological Frontiers of Society*, New York, Columbia University Press, 1945, p. 235.

[12]For one writer's conception of this hierarchy, see A. H. Maslow, "A Theory of Human Motivation," *Psychological Review*, 50 (1943), 370-96, and A. H. Maslow, " 'Higher' and 'Lower' Needs," *Journal of Psychology*, 25 (1948), 433-36.

[13]For an analysis of one aspect of this problem, see R. R. Sears, J. W. M. Whiting, V. Nowlis, and P. S. Sears, "Some Child-Rearing Antecedents of Aggression and Dependency in Young Children," *Genetic Psychology Monographs*, 47 (1953), No. 2, 135-234.

he crosses the street, and wanting to know where his mother is. As he develops and becomes increasingly able to handle his own affairs without the assistance of adults, his dependency need tends to diminish, a change which we infer from the fact that his help-seeking behaviors become fewer and fewer.[14] We now may notice behaviors which we could classify as evidences of a need for independence. At a later age the child may even prefer to be left alone to make decisions on his own. The extent to which changes in needs take place and the particular forms that these changes assume is a function of many factors, such as the way the child's needs at any stage of his life are met, changes in available goal objects for satisfying his needs, and demands made upon him by his environment.[15]

IDENTIFICATION OF NEEDS

Every time that we infer that a person wants something we are making an inference from his behavior about his needs. In attempting to describe the need system of a child we may be looking for the motivational basis of his behavior in a particular instance; for example, we may be attempting to determine why a child is crying at this moment, or is annoying another pupil, or picks a science book from the library shelf. Or we may be interested in determining the need system which underlies most of the child's behavior; for example, we may want to find out whether a child is motivated by a need to achieve, a need for affection, or a need for status. Whether we are attempting to determine a motive or a need, the process of inference is essentially the same.

METHOD OF INFERRING NEEDS. *The inference about motivation and the need system is made from the persistency and direction that may be observed in behavior.* This inference may be made in two ways: (1) by observing goal objects for which the individual appears to be continually striving; (2) by observing the effects that occur when what appear to be goal objects are denied the individual. If we are applying the first principle, we infer the character of the need from

---

[14]This relationship between independence and dependence needs has been simplified in this discussion. Recent experimental work suggests the complexity of this relationship; see E. K. Bellar, "Dependency and Independency in Young Children," *Journal of Genetic Psychology,* 87 (1955), 25-36.

[15]For a comprehensive study of relationships of this kind, see R. R. Sears, E. E. Maccoby, and H. Levin, *Patterns of Child Rearing,* Evanston, Illinois, Row, Peterson and Co., 1957.

the kind of goal object sought. We assume the existence of the need from the fact that goal objects of a given kind are persistently striven for. For example, we would infer that a child was motivated by a need for prestige if he seemed to be interested in positions and activities that carried prestige. In the second instance, we infer the presence of a need from the fact that the person may continue to seek a goal object even when it has been removed. For example, if a student lost an election to a club presidency, but tried for this officership again, we would infer that he is motivated by a need for the goal that the officership represents to him.

Assume that we observe that a student in one of our classes is a persistent worker, who completes all assignments on time and who does his work carefully. Assume also that on several occasions this student has inquired about the exact nature of an assignment, has attempted to determine whether he has done the work correctly, and has shown interest in the grades he has received on his assignments and tests. We would use this observed behavior as evidence of motivation, and assume that the student was attempting to satisfy some needs by these activities. We would infer that he is motivated to do well in academic work. But this statement tells us comparatively little about what goals he is seeking and what needs he is attempting to satisfy by striving to succeed in his school work. If the student told us that he wanted to be on the honor roll or to win a scholarship or a prize for academic achievement, we would have additional evidence to support our inference that the goal the student was striving for was success in his school work. However, only if we observe the student striving for other goals will we be able to make inferences about an underlying need that motivates much of this student's behavior. For example, does he go out for varsity sports because he wants to win a letter, or enter the debating contest in an attempt to win prizes? If we observe that he attempts to be best in whatever he does, we have additional evidence for an inference about an underlying need.

POSSIBLE ERRORS IN INFERENCE. The above example illustrates the difficulty in making inferences about needs from the character of the goal for which the pupil is striving. Shall we say that this student is striving for academic success? Does he want to achieve success irrespective of the nature of the activity? Or is it the prestige that goes with the obtaining of a prize that he is seeking? We can arrive at a reliable inference about needs only by careful observation of the student in many situations. It is all too easy to misjudge the character of the motivation because of inadequate observation of the child.

We may also make faulty inferences about needs by generalizing from particular instances of goal-seeking behavior to general patterns of goal-seeking behavior. We may infer that the student who is striving for academic success has a need to achieve, and then assume that this need can be satisfied by achieving in many different ways. However, the student may satisfy his need for achievement simply through striving for academic success, and may be indifferent to other kinds of achievement.

We may also be misled by inferring a commonality among goal objects, which the person whom we are observing does not see. The student who strives for academic success and wants to win a varsity letter in football, may be satisfying different needs in each case. Academic success may satisfy his need for achievement and winning a varsity letter his need for prestige and status. While we will make inferences about needs from the goals that individuals appear to be seeking, our inferences about needs should be checked against new observations of goal-seeking behavior.

CHECKING INFERENCES BY PREDICTING BEHAVIOR. The teacher, once he has assumed that a child is motivated by a given need, should make predictions about what kinds of behavior would be expected if a child were motivated by such a need. These predictions can then be tested by observing the behavior of the child. If we inferred that a student was motivated by a need for achievement, we would predict that this student would attempt to do his best in situations that offered an opportunity to excel. If we observe persistent attempts to excel in a variety of situations, we have evidence that our hypothesis about the need system of this student is probably true.

AN INVESTIGATION OF THE RELATIONS BETWEEN NEEDS AND BEHAVIOR. The problem of the relationship between behavior and motivation requires extensive scientific investigation. A scientific investigation of this relationship formalizes and refines inferential processes of a kind that we have suggested the teacher will be using. One study,[16] which attacked this problem directly, illustrates this refinement of observation. It also exemplifies that relationships between specific behaviors and needs are not obvious and straightforward.

---

[16]E. Frenkel-Brunswik, "Motivation and Behavior," *Genetic Psychology Monographs*, 26 (1942), 121-265.

Adolescents were rated on the strength of their need systems, and the ratings were related to behaviors of the adolescents. The children had been observed over a long period of time, from the fifth grade to the end of high school, and extensive observational and test data had been gathered.

The investigator utilized, with some refinement, a list of needs assumed to be characteristic of most adolescents, making an assumption that these needs are common to adolescents. Table III lists the needs that were inferred from observations and the behaviors on which data had been gathered. Judges independently rated the children on the strength of their needs and on the degree to which the children manifested these behaviors in social situations. For example, an adolescent rated high on grooming activity had been observed to spend a great deal of time in grooming activity. An adolescent rated high on energy output had been observed to be highly active "practically all the time." Ratings were available for each adolescent in the study on the strength of needs, such as the need for recognition or for social ties, and on the extent to which he manifested behaviors, such as grooming activity, energy output, and interaction with the opposite

---

NEEDS

1. *Need for Autonomy:* Striving for independence and freedom; desire to be free from social ties, to shake off influence, coercion, and restraint; relatively little care for conventions and group ideology; tendency to act as one pleases.

2. *Need for Social Ties, Social Acceptance:* Desire to be generally well-liked; to conform to custom, to join groups, to live sociably, to be accepted by a group in any form, to make contacts.

3. *Need for Achievement:* Desire to attain a high standard of objective accomplishments; to increase self-regard by successful exercise of talent, to select hard tasks; high aspiration level.

4. *Need for Recognition:* Desire to excite praise and commendation; to demand respect, social approval and prestige, honors and fame.

5. *Need for Abasement:* Tendency to self-depreciation, self-blame or belittlement; to submit passively to external forces, to accept injury, blame, criticism, punishment; tendency to become resigned to fate, to admit inferiority and defeat, to confess, to

seek punishment and misfortune; masochistic tendency.

6. *Need for Aggression:* Desire to deprive others by belittling, attacking, ridiculing, depreciating.

7. *Need for Succorance:* Desire for support from outside; from people, institutions, or supernatural agencies.

8. *Need for Control (Dominance):* Desire to control one's human environment, by suggestion, by persuasion or command.

9. *Need for Escape:* Tendency to escape all unpleasant situations; to avoid blame, hardship, etc.; to project own failures on others or on circumstances; to gain immediate pleasure with inability to postpone pleasure; use of fantasy, etc.

BEHAVIOR RATINGS

Attractive Appearance: Attractiveness and pleasantness of appearance, including coloring, features, proportion of body, carriage cleanliness, facial expression, becoming clothes, distribution of fat.

Grooming Activity: Obviously spends a great deal of time in grooming self. Frequently arranges or combs hair, brushes off clothes, puts on make-up.

Energy Output: Overtly active practically all the time, including gross movements and aggressive contacts with physical environment; eager, animated, bodily movements.

Interest in Opposite Sex: Continually initiates contacts with and takes every opportunity to attract attention of members of opposite sex, for activities in which sexes are mixed.

Reference to Opposite Sex: When none of opposite sex are present: frequently talks about members of opposite sex; tries out techniques usually successful with, or in anticipation of, future contacts with opposite sex.

Social Participations: Takes every opportunity for social contact allowed by the nature of the situation. Continually directs attention toward others, talks to them and participates in activities with them.

Seeking of Adult Company: Seeks out adults in preference to children in a group. Hangs around adults making frequent bids for attention. Identifies self with adults. Very cordial to adults.

Resistance to Authority: Deliberately breaks rules. Refuses to comply with requests of person in charge. Subtly resists authority; evasive, sly, two-faced, smooth, in contrast to: Eager to comply with adults' wishes; anticipates what adults must want; asks adult assistance in enforcing regulations; extremely suggestible with adults.

Social Self-Confidence: Very assured behavior with both adults and children. Takes failure in matter-of-fact way. Invites new situations requiring poise and confidence.

Attention-Seeking: Constantly seeks to put self in a conspicuous position; bluffing, showing off. Exerts strenuous efforts to gain recognition of associates.

Affectation: Markedly affected speech, mannerisms, or gestures; simulation of modesty or wistfulness.

Social Stimulus Value: Frequently stimulates others by his presence. Attracts and keeps their attention

Popularity with Same Sex: Generally approved and admired by others. Efforts repeatedly made by others to attract his attention. A preferred partner in activities; his company sought by many.

Popularity with Opposite Sex· (Definition same as above.)

Self - Assertion: Monopolizes conversation with, or interferes with activities of others. Continually giving directions and ordering others about.

Sensitivity and Dependence on Approval: Excessively concerned about the sort of impression he makes on his associates. Very sensitive and easily "hurt." Reacts strongly to praise or blame. Constantly leaning on others for approval of his actions, or help in his decisions.

Leadership: Highly successful in influencing the group either directly or by indirect suggestion. Competent in organizing and handling group activities. Comments or suggestions welcomed by the group and readily accepted.

Group Interest vs. Self-Interest: Quickly adapts himself and buoyantly carries the load of enthusiasm for group interests and activities, or, quickly adapts and devotes himself unreservedly to the interests of the group. Enthusiastically encourages activities in which most of the group are interested.

Talkativeness as contrasted with Quiet.

Dissatisfied as contrasted with Content.

Exuberant as contrasted with Gloomy.

Excitedness as contrasted with Calmness.

Irritability as contrasted with Good-naturedness.

Tenseness as contrasted with Relaxed.

Impulsiveness as contrasted with Deliberative.

Anxiety as contrasted with Carefree.

Frequent Mood Swings as contrasted with Constancy of Mood.

Selfishness as contrasted with Cooperative.

Irresponsible as contrasted with Responsible.

Exploitive, demanding of others as contrasted with non-exploitive, undemanding.

Well Adjusted Socially as contrasted with Poorly Adjusted Socially.

Predominantly Oriented toward Opposite Sex as contrasted with predominantly Oriented toward Same Sex.

Smooth Social Functioning, i.e., without emotional interference as contrasted with Blocked in Social Situation, frequent emotional interference.

Needs on Which Groups of Adolescent Students Were Rated and Behavior Ratings on Which Data Were Gathered (From Frenkel-Brunswik)

TABLE III

sex. The raters had known these children for a long period of time, and the agreement among raters was sufficiently high. The function of the statistical analysis in the study was to relate ratings on needs to the ratings on observed behavior.

What was the relationship between any particular inferred need and the behavior description? Let us use the need for recognition for illustrative purposes. No relationship between the strength of the need for recognition and attractive appearance was found; that is, children with a high need for recognition were neither more nor less attractive than those children who had a low need for recognition. However, there was a comparatively high relationship between the need for recognition and grooming activity; that is, children who had a high need for recognition were also rated as spending more time in grooming activities. There was also a significant relationship between the need for recognition and energy output. Other significant rela-

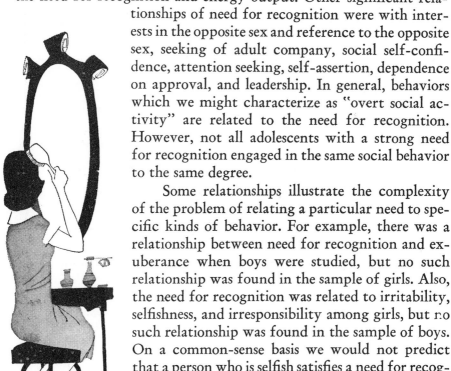

tionships of need for recognition were with interests in the opposite sex and reference to the opposite sex, seeking of adult company, social self-confidence, attention seeking, self-assertion, dependence on approval, and leadership. In general, behaviors which we might characterize as "overt social activity" are related to the need for recognition. However, not all adolescents with a strong need for recognition engaged in the same social behavior to the same degree.

Some relationships illustrate the complexity of the problem of relating a particular need to specific kinds of behavior. For example, there was a relationship between need for recognition and exuberance when boys were studied, but no such relationship was found in the sample of girls. Also, the need for recognition was related to irritability, selfishness, and irresponsibility among girls, but no such relationship was found in the sample of boys. On a common-sense basis we would not predict that a person who is selfish satisfies a need for recognition through his selfish behavior. But the data in this study suggest the possibility of such a relationship, at least for girls who have a high need for recognition. On a common-sense basis we might also have predicted that either a boy or girl with a strong need for recognition would be exuberant, but the data do not support this prediction.

The data from this study illustrate that need-satisfaction may take a variety of forms. We may assume that the needs measured are independent but that they are being satisfied in a variety of ways, some of which are similar. Both the need for recognition and the need for aggression were related to behavior items in the category "Overt Social Activity." A child with a strong need for recognition may be satisfying it in the same way as a child who has a strong need for aggression, or each of these needs may be satisfied in distinctive ways.

The complexity of the interrelationship between motivation and behavior is further illustrated in Figures 3 and 4. Figure 3 relates need strength to the emotional adjustment and social success of students. The investigator has separated four groups out of the total sample on the basis of their social success and emotional adjustment, and then plotted the average strengths of the needs of these children. Note that there are some differences in strength of need between groups whose general patterns of behavior are similar. For example, compare the two socially successful groups. If the children are rated as socially successful but differ in emotional adjustment, the general level of need strength is somewhat lower for the emotionally adjusted than the level of need strength for children who are emotionally maladjusted. The same kind of relationship differentiates the socially successful and unsuccessful.

Figure 4 further illustrates the relationship between need and behavior. The investigator has formed four small groups of boys on the basis of the relationship of the strength of their need for abasement and their need for aggression. Note that the behavior profiles differ considerably when two needs are taken in combination. This kind of relationship suggests another problem, that of the interrelationships between needs. The children who are high on need for aggression and low on need for abasement are rated higher on their dependency behavior. We would hypothesize that dependency behavior is related to some interaction between the needs rather than to either need itself.

The data from this investigation illustrate the complexity of the relationship of motivation to observed behavior. In everyday life we frequently make inferences about the motives of students and other people, but long experience with children does not guarantee

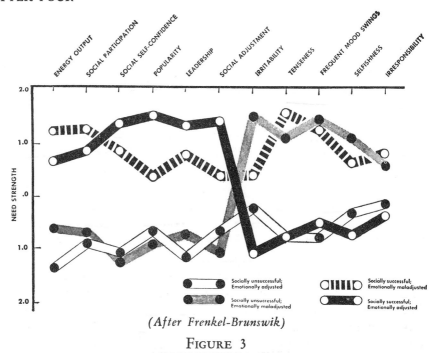

(After Frenkel-Brunswik)

FIGURE 3

that our inferences will be reliable. The teacher who expects to have accurate knowledge about the need systems of children should, in the first place, have extensive behavior data about these children. The somewhat casual observations of the classroom are a poor substitute for systematic and extended observation. Furthermore, the teacher must continually check his inferences by making predictions about behavior to be expected, assuming the presence of a specific need disposition in the personality of a child. These inferences must be revised continually and checked as the teacher acquires more information about the child.

INFERRING NEEDS FROM BEHAVIOR IN FRUSTRATING EXPERIENCES. A more reliable test of the existence of a need is what the individual does when a presumed need is frustrated in some way. If we removed some goal object that we had inferred a person was striving for, and the individual gave up striving for the goal, we would infer that the need motivating the goal-seeking behavior was not a strong one. While laboratory situations can be devised in which needs are frustrated in a limited way, the practical requirements of everyday life and the value standards that we generally accept do not permit us to frustrate the needs of other individuals extensively. However,

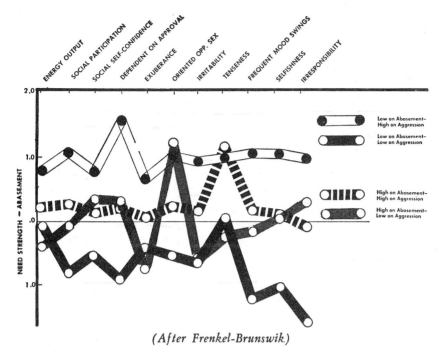

(*After Frenkel-Brunswik*)

FIGURE 4

in the ordinary course of circumstances the needs of individuals will be frustrated, and from the behavior that we observe at these times, we may make inferences about the presence of needs in the motivational system of an individual. A child who is striving for academic success may not achieve this success or may not achieve it to the degree that he has desired. At such a time we can observe the effects of this frustrating condition upon him. If he becomes highly disturbed or makes renewed efforts to achieve success, or if he criticizes the teacher for failure to give him a good grade, we may infer that his need for success is a strong motivating force in his personality.

Mildly frustrating conditions can be established in experimental situations to study the effects of frustration on motivation. Hartup[17] studied the effects of withdrawing social approval for a task children were performing. Two groups of children were given approval by adults while they were working. One group of children continuously received the approval of an adult while they worked; a second group of children worked for a short period during which they received

---

[17]W. W. Hartup, "Nurturance and Nurturance-Withdrawal in Relation to the Dependency Behavior of Pre-School Children," *Child Development*, 29 (1958), 190-201.

approval, and then for a period during which they did not receive the approval of an adult. Both groups of children were then
asked to learn two simple tasks. Children in the second group, the
group which was deprived of adult approval preceding the learning
period, took fewer trials to learn the task and made fewer errors in
the process. The results supported the hypothesis that withdrawal of
approval stimulated learning to a greater extent than did providing approval. The children in the second group had experienced
mild frustration of their need for approval; as a consequence, the
strength of this need became greater and motivated the learning behavior. The children in the first group did not have to work so hard
because their needs for approval were being met, whereas the children
in the second group worked harder in order to get adult approval and
satisfy their needs.

When a frustrating situation leads to problem-solving behavior
and where there is evidence of increasing striving, we can infer the
existence of a need-disposition which the person is attempting to
satisfy by goal-seeking behavior.[18] In more technical terms, *the facilitation of performance is a function of the strength of the motivation.*
We infer the strength of the motivation from the degree and extent
to which behavior changes. As we noted earlier, social conditions will
frequently produce frustrating situations, and the teacher, on occasion, inadvertently may deprive children of goals that they are seeking. The teacher who is sensitive to the relationship between frustrating circumstances and the strength of motivation should be able
to infer the particular needs of a child from the effect of the frustrating situations on the behavior of the child.

NEEDS AND GOALS. We have defined a goal as that which, when
attained, will satisfy the needs of a person. But we have also noted
that there is no necessary correspondence between a given set of needs
and specific kinds of goals. In our earlier example, Jane satisfied a
need for approval by writing a feature article for her school newspaper and that, in turn, led to the goal of receiving approval from her
classmates. We would expect that many of the boys and girls in Jane's
class had some need for approval, but not all of these children will
seek the same goals to satisfy this need. One child in the class perhaps
attempts to satisfy his need for approval by winning the praise of his

---

[18]A person does not always respond with adaptive behavior in frustrating circumstances.
Other modes of response are discussed in Chapter Ten.

teacher; another child, by being an outstanding athlete and winning the praise of his classmates and the adults in the community.

The relationship between a need and a goal object which satisfies that need is something that an individual must learn. One person differs from another in the strengths and kinds of his needs, and in the manner in which he learns to satisfy them.

SOCIAL INFLUENCES ON THE ACQUISITION OF NEEDS

The human organism is born with a comparatively simple system of needs based on the primary drives. The primary drives are related to physiological changes which occur with relative constancy in all human organisms. People become hungry in part because of physiological changes in their organic systems. However, we assume that such needs as the need for approval, the need for status, the need for achievement, the need for affection are not inborn.[19] Needs of this kind presumably are acquired or learned as the individual interacts with other persons in his environment.[20] The environment in which a child is raised is a complex system which provides a child with opportunities for specific kinds of learnings and which rewards this learning. The process of inducing behavior change by rewarding certain kinds of behaviors and not rewarding or punishing other kinds is the *process of socialization.* Socialization practices vary in different societies and subsocieties. The American child is socialized in somewhat different ways, depending upon the social class in which he is being raised. Sociologists and psychologists discriminate layers or strata of American society by the level of occupation that characterizes the members of these strata, the amount of income, the level

---

[19]Psychologists differ on what needs are learned and the manner in which they are learned. For a discussion of this problem, see J. Deese, *The Psychology of Learning,* New York, McGraw-Hill Book Co., 1958. pp. 108-14.

[20]For experimental evidence that needs can be acquired, see N. E. Miller, "Studies of Fear as an Acquirable Drive: I. Fear as Motivation and Fear-Reduction as Reinforcement in the Learning of New Responses," *Journal of Experimental Psychology,* 38 (1949), 89-101. For a discussion of learned motives, see N. E. Miller, "Learnable Drives and Rewards," in S. S. Stevens, ed., *Handbook of Experimental Psychology,* New York, John Wiley & Sons, 1951.

of education, and other objective criteria of this kind.[21] The objectively differentiated classes have been shown to differ in child-rearing practices.[22] The differential patterns in child-rearing tend to reinforce the learning of differential needs and goal expectations.

SOCIAL CLASS AND NEED ACQUISITION. The social class of a person is that group of individuals with whom a person is most likely to associate on a more or less intimate basis and who share common ideals, values, attitudes, and ways of behaving. This social milieu creates a learning environment for the growing child. The environment provides him with available goals for which he may work and rewards him for striving for these goals.

> Within each of these participation levels, with their cultural environments, a child learns characteristic behavior and values concerning family members, sexual and aggressive acts, work, education, and a career. A child of middle status, that is, acquires different social goals, different needs, different codes of right and wrong, and he experiences different psychological rewards and punishments from those learned by a child of either upper or lower status.[23]

The home is an important influence on the pattern of needs acquired by a child. Home influences are related to the social status of the family and to specific child-rearing practices within any home. Children of homes of a given social status are likely to have a common pattern of needs and a relatively common set of goal expectations. But within any social class we will find differences among children, depending upon the kind of child-rearing practices emphasized in the home.

CHILD-REARING PRACTICES AND NEED ACQUISITION. Winterbottom[24] has studied the relationship between the demands made by parents on their children and the achievement needs of the children. In this study mothers were interviewed to obtain information on the

---

[21]W. L. Warner, et al., Social Class in America, Chicago, Science Research, 1949.

[22]A. Davis and R. J. Havighurst, "Social Class and Color Differences in Child Rearing," American Sociological Review, 11 (1946), 698-710. Also, E. Maccoby, et al., "Methods of Child Rearing in Two Social Classes," in A. P. Coladarci, Educational Psychology: A Book of Readings, New York, The Dryden Press, 1955, pp. 97-121.

[23]A. Davis, "Socialization and Adolescent Personality," Forty-third Yearbook of the National Society for the Study of Education, Part I, 1944, p. 203.

[24]M. R. Winterbottom, "The Relation of Childhood Training in Independence to Achievement Motivation," cited in D. McClelland et al., The Achievement Motive, New York, Appleton-Century-Crofts, 1953, pp. 297-306.

demands that they made of their children and the age at which they made these demands. Then the children were tested to determine the strength of their need for achievement. As Figure 5 illustrates, children with high achievement needs, up to about age nine, are children from homes in which the mothers make greater demands. The demands reflected emphasis on independent achievement at an early age. For example, the mothers of children with high achieve-

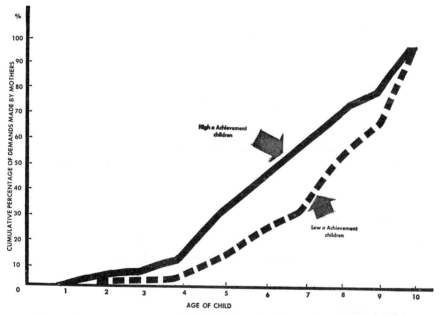

Cumulative curves showing the proportion of total demands made up to each age level as reported by mothers of children scoring high and low on n Achievement. (From Winterbottom)

FIGURE 5

ment needs expected their children to know their way around the city, to try new things for themselves, to do well in competition, and to make their own friends. McClelland *et al.* state:

> The mother of a son with high *n* Achievement [need for achievement] is interested in her son's developing away from her, in urging him to master things on his own, whereas the mother of a son with low *n* Achievement is willing to let such things slide and let him remain somewhat more de-

pendent on her. . . . Achievement motivation in boys is associated with stress on independence training by their mothers.[25]

The same study investigated the relationship between the kind of reward provided for achievement and the strength of the child's achievement need. The mothers were asked in what manner they rewarded a child when he did something that they wanted him to do. The data indicate that "mothers who used physical rewards for fulfillment of achievement demands have sons whose average *n* Achievement score is twice that of mothers who use more attenuated means of affective arousal."[26] The data in this study illustrate that the strength of needs varies with the goals which children are encouraged to strive for and the rewards which are given for striving for these goals.

HOME INFLUENCE AND GOAL ORIENTATION. A study by Kahl[27] demonstrates the relationship between the social status of a family, as measured by the father's occupation, and the educational and occupational aspirations of the boys in the family. In Table IV the boys have been classified on the basis of their fathers' occupation and their levels of intelligence. As the data in the Table indicate, the largest

| | IQ Quintile | | | | | All Quintiles |
| | (Low) 1 | 2 | 3 | 4 | (High) 5 | |
Father's Occupation						
Major White Collar	56%	72%	79%	82%	89%	80%
Middle White Collar	28	36	47	53	76	52
Minor White Collar	12	20	22	29	55	26
Skilled Labor & Service	4	15	19	22	40	19
Other Labor & Service	9	6	10	14	29	12
All Occupations	11	17	24	30	52	27

Percentage of Boys Who Expect to Go to College, by IQ and Father's Occupation (3348 Cases) (From Kahl)

TABLE IV

---

[25] D. C. McClelland, J. W. Atkinson, R. A. Clark, and E. L. Lowell, *The Achievement Motive,* New York, Appleton-Century-Crofts, Inc., 1953, pp. 303-304.

[26] *Ibid.,* p. 306.

[27] J. A. Kahl, "Educational and Occupational Aspirations of 'Common Man' Boys," *Harvard Educational Review,* 23 (1953), 186-203.

percentage of boys who expect to go to college are those who have both the highest intelligence and whose father's occupation is of the highest level. However, among all of the boys who fall into the highest intelligence category, the percentage that expect to go to college decreases as we move down the scale of occupations.

In this same study, Kahl interviewed 24 boys intensively. All of these boys had sufficient intelligence to go to college, but half of them planned to go to college and half did not. All of them came from working class homes, and had done satisfactorily in school. Kahl was interested in determining the extent to which parents encouraged these boys to go to college. The data in Figure 6 suggest a strong relationship between the amount of parental pressure toward college and the son's aspiration to go to college. As is evident from these data, practically all of the boys who were not aspiring to go to college were also living in homes in which there was no parental pressure to go to college. The majority of boys who expected to go to college were living in homes in which there was parental pressure to go to college.

On the basis of extensive interviewing with the parents, real differences in attitudes and expectations could be found among these homes. The homes in which there was little pressure to improve one's lot by going to college were described as follows:

> . . . concerned with balancing the budget each week, with living for the moment in a smooth manner. They looked neither to the past nor to the future. The father wanted a job which offered congenial workmates, an easy boss, a regular pay check. . . . The children were told to stay in high school because the diploma was pretty important in getting jobs nowadays, but they were allowed to pick their own curriculum according to taste. The value "doing what you like to do" was applied to school work, to part-time jobs, and to career aspirations. Rarely was the possibility of a college education seriously considered: "we can't afford such things," or "we aren't very bright in school." Indeed, their perception of college and the kinds of jobs college-trained people held were exceedingly vague. . . . In some, they

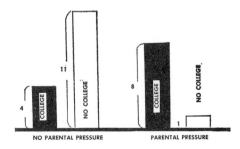

Relation between parental pressure and son's aspiration for college (24 boys). (After Kahl)

FIGURE 6

felt that common people like themselves were lucky to have a regular job, that the sons would be as the fathers, that such was life and why think about it.[28]

On the other hand, the homes in which there was considerable pressure for advanced education were described as remarkably different in their attitudes:

> . . . the parents who believed in "getting ahead" were more sensitive to social hierarchies and thought more about the subject than those who were satisfied with their lot. They used the middle class as a reference group that was close enough to have meaning, though far enough away to be different. They kept thinking: "There, but for a few small difficulties, go I." The difficulty they usually referred to was lack of education. These people spoke with monotonous regularity about their handicap of poor education. Sometimes they blame themselves for not taking advantage of their opportunities when young; they said that they did not realize when they still had time how important it was to get advanced training. . . . They saw an occupational world stratified according to the basic principle of education, and education was something you got when you were young.[29]

The differences in these homes illustrate the differences in the kinds of environment that lead to differential goal expectations and needs in children. The various social strata in American society may be differentiated on the basis of differences in attitudes and values, in goal expectations, and in rewards provided for appropriate goal striving.[30] The middle-class family, for example, places greater emphasis upon *attainment* and striving for success. The middle-class family typically emphasizes independence training, which is begun earlier than in lower status families. Success and striving for success are highly rewarded in such families, with the consequent development of strong needs for achievement in children of middle-class families. However, while middle-class families have many characteristics in common, the environment created within each of these families is not identical. Every child of a middle-class family will not be motivated to achieve to the same degree as every other middle-

---

[28]*Ibid.*, p. 192-93.

[29]*Ibid.*, p. 193.

[30]For interesting descriptions of such differences consult the following: A. B. Hollingshead, *Elmtown's Youth*, New York, John Wiley & Sons, 1949; W. L. Warner *et al.*, *Who Shall be Educated?*, New York, Harper & Brothers, 1944; W. L. Warner and P. S. Lunt, *The Social Life of a Modern Community*, New Haven, Yale University Press, 1941.

class child. However, middle-class children as a group are more likely to be motivated by achievement needs than are children coming from lower status families.

APPLICATION TO STUDYING THE CHILD. These distinctions have important implications for the teacher who must attempt to assess the motivations of his students. Generally, children from different status levels in society will be characterized by different motivational systems, will have different goal expectancies, and will be motivated by different kinds of rewards. Since the American school typically has children from practically all levels of society, the teacher is faced with the complex problem of motivating children who have different need systems. One of the major problems of the American school is motivating children from lower status homes. The child who has not learned to value education or the goals to which it leads is not likely to be motivated to participate actively in school work. Whatever the teacher does to motivate lower status children will probably involve a substantial reorganization of their need systems and goal expectancies. Recall the general principle cited earlier in this chapter that the relationship between goals and need-satisfaction is learned. New needs and goal expectations will have to be acquired by a child who does not expect to find satisfaction in the goals achieved through formal education.[31]

While differences of the kind described here characterize the various strata of American society, the teacher studying the individual child cannot be certain that every middle-class child is highly motivated to achieve and every lower-class child is not motivated to achieve. As we have suggested, the learning of these needs depends upon the characteristics of each family. As the study of working class boys (see Figure 6) suggests, even within the strata of a society which would be classified as lower status, there are families in which there is considerable pressure for achievement and in which the goal expectations are similar to those of middle status families. The problem for the teacher always resolves itself into a determination of the need systems of a particular child. The teacher must ask such questions as "What is it that this child wants? What is it that this child is willing to work for?"

---

[31] The suggestion has been made that school experiences be reorganized to meet the needs of lower-class children. In this suggestion the term "needs" is being used differently from what it is here. A discussion of this other use of the term is presented in the latter part of this chapter.

What the teacher can learn from this discussion of the influence of environment on the acquisition of needs is that differences in environment tend to produce differences in the motivational systems of children. The child who comes to school has already begun to learn that certain goals are important. He will have begun to develop a system of needs that will be continually reinforced by his home and community associations. In some instances the goals and needs of children will not be consonant with the goals that are held up as desirable and the rewards that are provided by the school. In other cases the child will have learned that the goals held up as desirable by the school are important for him, and will be strongly motivated to achieve them. Where there are discrepancies between goals generally held desirable by educators and those held desirable by children's families, the teacher's problem is essentially that of attempting to broaden the children's conceptions of what are desirable goals, to encourage them to develop new expectancies with respect to goals, and to induce needs which will motivate them to strive for these goals. To bring about this reorganization in the motivational system of the child, the teacher can capitalize on the needs that characterize the child at this point in his development. For example, if a child is strongly motivated by a need for affection and adult approval the teacher can build on this in motivating the child to strive for goals that he will find satisfying and rewarding when attained. As the child strives for new goals to satisfy his need for affection he learns that these goals have reward characteristics. Eventually he can learn to strive for these goals independently of attaining the approval and love of his teacher.

GOAL-SETTING BEHAVIOR

Most individuals have complex need systems which are satisfied by a wide range and variety of goals. Jane, in our earlier example, is not motivated solely by a need for approval. She may also have needs for achievement, for affection, for status—each of which is satisfied in one special way at one time in her life and in another way at other times in her life. Bill, who wants to be an engineer, has other goals—some of which lead to his goal of being an engineer, others of which are more or less related to it. Eventually he will probably want to get married and raise a family. When he becomes an engineer he will seek new goals within his chosen profession. In the process of development the individual's need system becomes more diversified and more complicated, and the number of goals and the kinds of goals which will satisfy his needs also change.

The goal of a need is an *expectation* about something which will satisfy the need when attained.[32] The goal in a behavior sequence is something that is psychologically distant from the individual, some goals being more distant than others. The student beginning his high school career who wants to be an engineer has immediate goals which will lead him further toward his goal of being an engineer. We have seen that an individual must learn that a given goal is likely to satisfy his needs.

In the process of development an individual acquires experience both in goal-setting and goal attainment. One child will seem to be remarkably clear about what it is that he wants, and will appear to be confident of attaining his goals. Another child will seem to be confused and uncertain about what it is that he should strive for, and will be uncertain about his capacities for attaining his goals. Differences of this kind develop out of the person's experience in goal-seeking activities.

LEVEL OF ASPIRATION. A person's expectation of how he will perform a task is called his *level of aspiration.* Suppose that we have been teaching fractions in arithmetic to a group of children. They have worked a number of problems and have had the basic processes explained to them. We present the children with ten problems and ask each child how many he expects to get correct. On the basis of their previous experience with problems of this kind the children will make various statements about how well they expect to do. One child will expect to get all of the problems correct because during the learning experiences he has been repeatedly successful with problems of this kind. Another child will state that he expects to get only a few problems correct because he has been experiencing difficulty with this kind of a problem. Each child has an estimate of his own abilities based on his experience with an activity or task. On the basis of this estimate of his own ability, he predicts how he thinks he will do.

Statements from children on their expectations of success in a task performance are not accurate estimates of the goals for which

---

[32]For a theoretical discussion of the relation between motive, expectation, and rewards provided by the environment, see J. W. Atkinson, "Motivational Determinants of Risk-Taking Behavior," *Psychological Review,* 64 (1957), 359-372.

they are working.[33] Some children will set expectations for themselves considerably beyond a level that they could reasonably be expected to achieve. Other children will set their *level of aspiration* below what can be achieved. However, by studying the factors which influence the level of aspiration, we obtain an estimate of the factors which are likely to influence a child's goal expectations.[34]

SUCCESS AND FAILURE AND LEVEL OF ASPIRATION. As we suggested above, success and failure in previous experiences influence a person's willingness to work for a goal. A relationship between success and failure and the level of aspiration has been demonstrated in a number of experimental studies.[35] In some of these studies the child had little or no experience with the kind of task that he was asked to perform in the experiment, and success and failure experiences were fabricated by the experimenter. In other studies the effects of long-term success and failure on the level of aspiration in tasks with which the child was familiar have been studied. The general conclusion from both kinds of studies is substantially the same—that success tends to raise the level of aspiration, and failure tends to depress it. However, the relationships between previous experience and immediate success or failure are complex, and a study by Sears has demonstrated the effects of these variables on the level of aspiration.[36]

In her study, Sears chose three groups of children who were in the fourth, fifth, and sixth grades. The first group, called the "success" group, were children who had experienced success in school, as evidenced by their grades, and who felt that they had been successful. A "failure" group was composed of children who, by the same criteria—school grades and how they felt about their school experience—had experienced failure. A mixed group, called the "differential" group, was made up of children who had successful experiences in reading

---

[33]P. S. Sears, "Levels of Aspiration in Academically Successful and Unsuccessful Children," *Journal of Abnormal and Social Psychology*, 35 (1940), 498-536. For a critique of the relevance of level of aspiration studies to educational practice, see D. Sivertsen, "Goal Setting, Level of Aspiration, and Social Norms," *Acta Psychologia*, 13 (1957), 54-60.

[34]P. S. Sears, "Levels of Aspiration in Relation to Some Variables of Personality: Clinical Studies," *Journal of Social Psychology*, 14 (1941), 311-36. See also H. M. Schroder and D. E. Hunt, "Failure-Avoidance in Situational Interpretation and Problem Solving," *Psychological Monographs*, No. 342, 1957.

[35]A review of these studies and a critical analysis can be found in K. Lewin, *et al.*, "Level of Aspiration," in J. McV. Hunt (ed.), *Personality and the Behavior Disorders*, New York, Ronald Press Co., (1944), pp. 333-78.

[36]Sears, *op. cit.*, 1940.

and unsuccessful experiences in arithmetic. The three groups were comparable in age, intelligence, and the number of boys and girls in each group.

Each group of children was given tasks under what were called "neutral" conditions. These were reading and arithmetic tasks of the type that children usually do in elementary school and on which they are frequently tested. The children were administered a series of these tasks, and after each one the child was asked to estimate his time on the succeeding task. During this session with the children, the experimenter made no comment to indicate whether the child was successful or unsuccessful at the tasks. In this "neutral" condition we have a measure of each child's level of aspiration as he moves from one reading task to another, and from one arithmetic task to another.

If we compare the levels of aspiration in these groups of children, we have some estimate of the relationship between previous success or failure in reading and arithmetic and the level of aspiration that the child sets for himself in a situation which is non-threatening. Figure 7 illustrates the differences between the three groups. As is apparent from the diagram, the children who had previous experiences of failure were more variable in setting levels of aspiration for themselves on these tasks. The children who had experienced some success appeared to be more realistic in setting their level of aspiration.

EFFECTS OF SUCCESS AND FAILURE UNDER THREAT. After this initial experience the children in each group were called back to perform on tasks similar to the ones they had performed under "neutral" conditions. However, half the children in each group were told that they had been highly successful in their performance under the "neutral" conditions, and half the group were told that they had done very poorly on the tasks in the initial testing. Figure 8 gives the data for the groups after the experience of success and failure.

The effects of immediate success and failure are similar to the effects of long-term success and failure. Under success conditions the level of aspiration tends to correspond realistically to the performance level of the child. Under failure conditions there are large discrepancies between performance and level of aspiration. In general, the children under failure conditions are more variable in their estimates of their expected performance than are the children under success conditions.

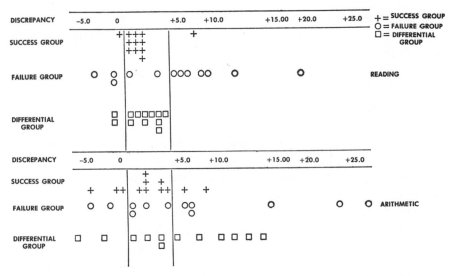

Comparison of groups: discrepancy scores, neutral condition, of groups varying in past experience of success or failure. (From Sears)

FIGURE 7

MEANINGS OF GOAL-SETTING BEHAVIOR. The data presented suggest the general relationships between success and failure and the individual's level of aspiration. Sears explored the meaning of setting an expected goal for one's self in greater detail by comparing three groups of children: (1) a group in which there was a small discrepancy between the level of aspiration and actual performance, (2) a group that had a high discrepancy between level of aspiration and performance, (3) a group that consistently set the level of aspiration below their performance level. For example, children's performance and level of aspiration would follow a pattern similar to this:

	High Positive Discrepancy	Low Positive Discrepancy	Negative Discrepancy
Performance Level, Last Task	3 Problems Correct	3 Problems Correct	3 Problems Correct
Level of Aspiration, Next Task	10 Problems Correct	4 Problems Correct	2 Problems Correct

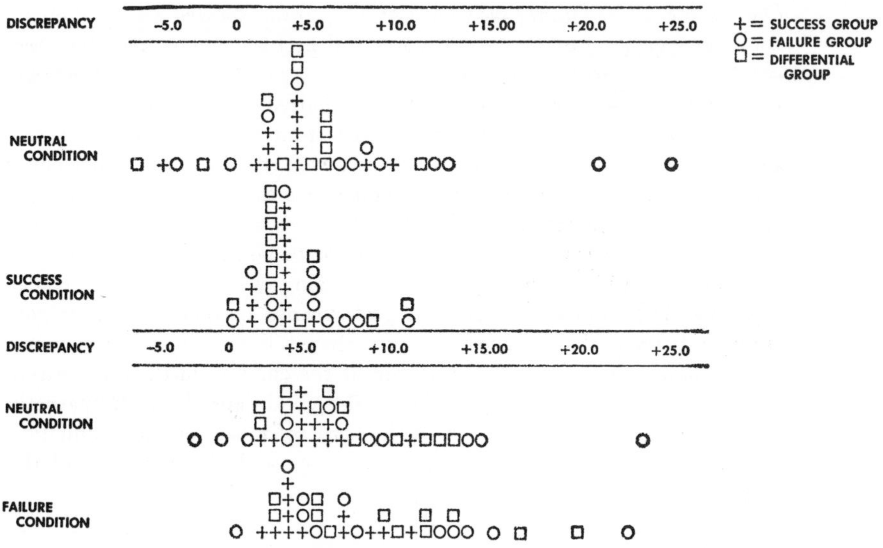

Comparison of conditions: discrepancy scores under conditions of experimentally induced success and failure. Three groups and two tasks combined. (From Sears)

FIGURE 8

In comparing these three groups it seemed apparent that the behavior of setting a goal had different meanings for each of these three groups:

1. *The Low Positive Discrepancy Group:* This is a group that consistently sets the level of aspiration above performance level on the last task. *For these children the discrepancy measure was usually smaller after success and larger after failure.* The level of aspiration seems to be affected by immediate performance: "In addition, these subjects showed marked goal directiveness toward the stated level of aspiration under all the experimental conditions employed. They take account in a practical way of their previous good and bad performances as reported and showed little conflict over the placement of their aspiration level. They react rather strongly to success and failure in terms of general behavior, but they do not change the level of aspiration a great deal under such conditions. . . . The levels of aspiration of this group might be described as closely tied to a (for them) satisfactory reality, with a goal for achievement usually just ahead of present accomplishment but easily modified in response to a change in the reported performance."[37]

---

[37]*Ibid.*, pp. 522-23.

2. *The High Positive Discrepancy Group:* This group showed a large discrepancy between level of aspiration scores and performance scores. *For these children high positive discrepancy scores decrease under success and increase under failure conditions:* "Frequently the children of this group set initially a level of aspiration which is far removed from their performance scores and they maintain this level almost rigidly, even if their performance never approaches it in excellence. If the performance should approach the level of aspiration, the latter is immediately raised so that a large discrepancy continues to be present. These subjects seem to be inwardly compelled to do so, as if they never felt that they were doing well enough. . . . Under experimentally induced success, the performance becomes markedly goal directed. If the goal is achieved, however, there is is no such satisfaction and relaxation of tension as is characteristic of the children in the low positive discrepancy group. . . . Under the failure conditions sluggish, apathetic behavior sometimes appears, as if the limit of tolerance for the assimilation of failure had been reached and escape must be sought by 'going out of the field.' "[38]

3. *The Negative Discrepancy Group:* This is the group of children who persistently set their level of aspiration below their performance scores. *Under both success and failure the discrepancy between the level of aspiration and performance was increased:* "In responsiveness and flexibility the members of this group resemble the low positive discrepancy children, but the end toward which this behavior is directed may be seen to differ; in the low positive group the subjects are responsible and flexible in terms of a stated goal which is ahead of their performance; in the negative discrepancy group the responsiveness and flexibility are directed toward avoiding the failure of a performance *worse* than that prescribed by the level of aspiration. Subjects of the negative discrepancy group take only indirect account of their previous good and bad performance scores in the placement of the level of aspiration. Their aim is to be always on the safe side—an aim which seems to them most probable of achievement when the level of aspiration is placed just equal to or lower than the performance immediately previous."[39]

PROVIDING SUCCESS EXPERIENCES. The data from the Sears' study clearly indicate the relationship between previous experience and the level of performance or goals that an individual is willing to set for himself. Out of his past experience the individual develops a conception of what he is likely to be able to do and adjusts his standards accordingly. The child who has experienced failure to some degree in his previous experience with a task may not expect to do well when confronted with the task again. But apparently some children with

---

[38]*Ibid.,* pp. 523-24.
[39]*Ibid.,* pp. 524-25.

failure experiences set unrealistic goals, as if they wished to perform at this unrealistic level even though they may not expect to do so. Even providing success experiences for children who have had failure experiences in the past does not guarantee that they will become more realistic in their conceptions of their goals. It is frequently recommended that every child should have some experience of success in some activity. While this is probably sound advice, the teacher should not assume that a few success experiences can immediately offset the effects of previous experiences with failure. A child who has learned that he does not do well in reading is not likely to change his conception of himself nor of his goals by a few experiences of success with reading tasks. To offset the effects of a relatively long history of failure, a correspondingly long sequence of success experiences must be provided.

The nature of the task and the general expectations about what constitutes success and failure in this task influence the levels of performance that an individual will set for himself. A child who has learned to read materials at the second grade level is not likely to feel that he is a failure because he cannot read materials at the fifth or sixth grade level. The child has learned that there is a range of acceptable performance, and has corresponding feelings of success or failure with respect to this range of performance. The child in the second grade who is reading well below the level of second graders is not likely to feel successful because he can read better than children in the kindergarten. A child's expectation or goal for his own performance in a task is influenced by the generally accepted levels of performance for children with his experience and of his age level. The practical import of this fact is that it is probably impossible to induce motivation by raising the standard of success above a level which most children would consider realistic for themselves. However, as long as the standard is within the acceptable range for children at a given age level or grade level, successive elevations of the success standard may motivate students to set higher standards for themselves, provided that the students have had success in meeting the previously established standards.

INFLUENCE OF THE GROUP
ON GOAL-SETTING BEHAVIOR

Experimental evidence has demonstrated the influence both of a child's previous experience and of his immediate experience upon his goal-setting behavior. Is a child likely to be influenced by the group with which he is working, or does he set his standards solely in terms of what he knows about himself and his abilities? Does the bright child adjust his standards of performance to the class average, and would he raise his standards of performance if he were placed in a group which had high standards? Will the child who has not been performing successfully set higher standards for himself if he is placed in a group whose average performance is above his own? Obviously, these are important practical questions related to the psychology of motivation. Experimental data do suggest that the child's level of aspiration is influenced by the standard of performance within his own group.

KNOWLEDGE OF PERFORMANCE AND LEVEL OF ASPIRATION. Anderson and Brandt[40] conducted an experiment to answer some of the questions raised above. These investigators set up two groups, an experimental and a control group, and attempted to motivate the children in the two groups in different ways. Both groups were given a simple cancellation task to perform. On successive days the children in the experimental group were given their relative standing in class, whereas the children in the control group were not provided with such information. Each child in the experimental group knew where he stood with respect to the group, and was asked to set a standard for himself on the task The experimental group was significantly superior to the control group in achievement on the task. We infer that the motivation produced by knowledge of where one stood in the group was related to this difference in achievement. This conclusion is consistent with data from other studies which indicate that knowledge of how one is doing tends to enhance performance and motivation for improvement.[41]

This study also produced important data on the goal-setting behavior of the children in the experimental group. Recall that these children knew what their relative position in the group was each time

---

[40]H. H. Anderson and H. F. Brandt, "Study of Motivation Involving Self-Announced Goals of Fifth Grade Children and the Concept of the Level of Aspiration," *Journal of Social Psychology*, 10 (1939), 209-32.

[41]Experimental data on this point are reviewed in R. S. Woodworth and H. Schlosberg, *Experimental Psychology*, New York, Henry Holt and Co. (1954), pp. 686-88. See also, L. Plowman and J. B. Stroud, "The Effect of Informing Pupils of the Correctness of Their Responses to Objective Test Questions," *Journal of Educational Research*, 36 (1942), 16-20. For a more recent study, see E. B. Page, "Teacher Comments and Student Performance: A Seventy-Four Classroom Experiment in School Motivation," *Journal of Educational Psychology*, 49 (1958), 173-81.

they were asked to set a new standard for themselves. Children who were in the lowest ranks of actual achievement consistently set goals considerably above their past achievements, whereas those in the upper ranks consistently set goals considerably below their preceding achievement (see Figure 9). There appears to be some type of group standard toward which the children are tending. This group standard represents a wished for or hoped for level of achievement for the child who is not doing well. Apparently the child who is achieving well above this standard can maintain his feeling of success even by lowering his own goals in the direction of the level of the group average.[42]

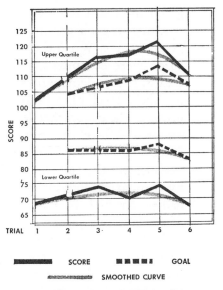

Mean achievement scores and mean goals by trials for upper and lower quartiles of achievement. (From Anderson and Brandt)

FIGURE 9

EFFECT OF KNOWLEDGE OF OTHER GROUPS' PERFORMANCES. Does a group tend to establish its standard by reference to the standards of other groups? For instance, will a group of freshmen algebra students establish a standard of performance relative to the performance of other freshmen students taking algebra courses, or will each group be influenced principally by its own previous experience? This question was investigated by Chapman and Volkmann.[43] A group of college students was divided into four groups, and were told that they were to take a test of literary ability. The first group was given instructions about the nature of the test; the second group was given, in addition to the instructions, the mean score obtained on this test by a group of literary experts; the third group was given the mean score of a group of college students on the test; and the fourth group was

---

[42]For comparable results with a group of college students, see E. R. Hilgard, E. M. Sait, and and G. A. Magaret, "Level of Aspiration as Affected by Relative Standing in An Experimental Social Group," *Journal of Experimental Psychology*, 27 (1940), 411-21, and M. Hertzman and L. Festinger, "Shifts in Explicit Goals in a Level of Aspiration Experiment," *Journal of Experimental Psychology*, 27 (1940), 439-52.

[43]D. W. Chapman and J. Volkmann, "A Social Determinant of the Level of Aspiration," *Journal of Abnormal and Social Psychology*, 34 (1939), 225-38.

given the mean score of a group of WPA workers on the test. The students in each group were then asked to estimate their expected performance. When the mean estimates of how the students expected to do were computed, the investigators found the second group—that is, the students who knew the average score of literary experts—set their level of aspiration much lower than any of the other groups. The group that was told the performance of the WPA workers set their level of aspiration higher than that of any of the groups. Since none of the students in these groups knew how he would actually perform on the test, he was presumably estimating his performance by comparing himself with what he knew about how other groups had performed. In a second part of the experiment, another group of students was given similar instructions, but not until after they had taken a first form of the test. Under these conditions the students estimated their expected performance more in terms of their own previous performance than in terms of the known performance of the other groups.

CLASSROOM PROBLEMS. The level of aspiration of a child is influenced by his knowledge of how his group performs, how other groups perform, and his own experience with a task. Teachers are frequently urged to encourage a child to set his standards in relation to his own abilities. However, a child's conception of his ability is determined in part by the effect that the performances of others had on his conception of himself. A child who is relatively unsuccessful in reading or arithmetic has learned to judge his performance by what he has seen of the performances of his fellow students. As long as the child is able to determine where he stands with respect to other children, his feelings of success and failure and his consequent goal-setting behavior will be influenced by his knowledge of his place in the group.

Frequently teachers will divide a class up into several groups of differing ability levels and encourage each of these groups to work at its own pace. Whether this is an effective technique for producing feelings of success is not known. The likelihood of this technique being successful would depend upon the children's information about the relative standings of the three groups. Common-sense observation suggests that children would easily learn the status differences between the three groups. A child can recognize that the teacher spends considerable time with one of the groups while permitting another group to work independently. Even the most cursory inspection of the materials being used will tell a child that there are differences in the complexities of these materials. It is not difficult for a child to determine that he is in the "low group," even though the group may never be labeled as such. Consequently, the possibility of developing a personal standard of excellence or achievement in ignorance of the standards set by a group does not seem likely.

Furthermore, since each group sets its own standards, a child is more likely to regulate himself by the standard of his own group. This standard, if the group is a low group, would inevitably be a lower standard. The teacher is left with a dilemma. Should he place poor students in groups in which the level of performance is considerably above that of the poorer students, or should he construct groups in which the level of the performance is not radically different from that of most of the members of the group? If he chooses the former alternative, he may induce continued feelings of failure on the part of the poorer students. If he chooses the second alternative, the group standard may be sufficiently easy to meet so that a student will not be motivated to achieve higher standards. In order to insure that a child will always have some feelings of success, the experienced teacher tends to use both kinds of arrangements while at the same time encouraging him to strive for higher goals. By placing him in groups of children with the same level of ability, the teacher can encourage the child to work up to his capacities and maximize the probability of his having successful experiences. By his membership in many groups of varying ability levels, the child will be able to form a realistic conception of his own ability. But he will have had sufficient success experiences to minimize the relative failure he may experience when working with students of higher ability.

INCENTIVES AND MOTIVATION

School environments typically provide many kinds of rewards for successful performance, such as grades, prizes, teacher approval, and the approval of classmates. The use of such devices rests on the assumption that students are willing to work for these rewards. These rewards are also called *incentives* because we assume that they will motivate students to work harder and to perform better. What is the relationship of these incentives to the concepts of motivation that we have been discussing, such as needs and goals?

INCENTIVES AND GOALS. Is there a difference between an incentive and a goal? A goal is an object or state of affairs which when attained will satisfy the needs of an individual, whereas an incentive may or may not satisfy his needs. Some incentives are obviously related to need-satisfaction, and for ordinary purposes a distinction between such incentives and goals is unnecessary. A hungry child is motivated by a need which can be satisfied by food, and food is an incentive for a hungry child. In this case the incentive and the goal are identical. However, in more complex kinds of motivations, the relationship between the need and the goal depends upon what the child has learned to expect as satisfiers. For example, the need for approval or for achievement may be satisfied in a variety of ways, for there are many goals which will satisfy them. A teacher introducing an incentive on the assumption that it is a goal which will meet the needs of an individual may or may not be correct.

GRADES AS INCENTIVES. Grades are an example of a standard incentive introduced into practically all learning environments in schools. As motivational devices, grades are useful incentives only insofar as children's needs will be satisfied by attaining high grades. As every experienced teacher is aware, there are many children for whom grades do not serve as an incentive. What this means psychologically is that these children are motivated by needs that are not satisfied by attaining high grades. Children will work for grades in order to satisfy a variety of needs, as our example of John and Bill illustrated. A child who receives praise and approval from his parents for receiving high grades has different expectations about the value of grades than does a child whose parents ignore or minimize the value of high grades.[44]

Since grades give a student information on his performance, we would then expect them to influence a student's level of aspiration. Treat[45] studied the relations of grading practices to students' performances and levels of aspiration. In one class, grades were distributed on a normal curve—that is, the percentage of each letter grade was fixed. In another class, the grading system varied with performance, so that higher grades were given if performance improved.

---

[44]T. R. Ford, "Social Factors Affecting Academic Performance," *School Review*, 65 (1957), 415-22. Also, J. J. Kurtz and E. J. Swenson, "Factors Related to Over-Achievement and Under-Achievement in School," *School Review*, 59 (1951), 472-80.

[45]W. C. Treat, "Motivational Effects of an Ascending Grade Scale" (unpublished doctoral dissertation), Stanford, Calif., Stanford University, 1950.

Treat found improved performance and more realistic levels of aspiration in the class in which the ascending grade scale was used. The students in this group were like the children in Sears' "low positive discrepancy" group. In the class in which a fixed grade system was used, performance did not improve systematically, and the level of aspiration was less realistic. Achieving good grades is a success experience, so motivation and performance improved when grades were administered to create a success experience.

In this experiment, the investigator manipulated incentives to provide success experiences. The incentive could be obtained if the student wanted to work for it. *Incentives must have goal-properties if they are to be motivating*. But the incentive must be available or within the student's reach if it is to motivate behavior. It does not make sense to urge a "C" student to work for higher grades if he cannot obtain a higher grade. The conclusion should not be drawn that "good" grades should be given indiscriminately. A grade is a measure of achievement, but these measures can be used to influence motivation. Unfortunately, the amount of research on grading and motivation is meager.

CLASSROOM USE OF INCENTIVES. Teachers and the school environment provide incentives which may or may not be related to the goals that a child is seeking. *The goal is what the child is seeking; the incentive is what the teacher provides*. These may or may not be related. The teacher is limited in the number of incentives that he can provide. For example, money is rarely used as an incentive in school situations. Actually, the kinds of status symbols that can be provided are relatively meager and temporary.

What the teacher cannot assume is that any incentive will invariably motivate all children. Most children are motivated to some extent by a need for approval, but not all children are motivated by a need for either adult approval or the approval of teachers specifically. A child who has grown up in a home in which he has received comparatively little approval from his parents for expected behavior is not necessarily a child who is going to be strongly motivated to seek the approval of teachers. What is more likely is that this child has learned that adults are not sources of approval, and he will not be strongly motivated to seek approval from adult figures. A child who has consistently received approval for his behavior from adults cannot be motivated indefinitely by more and more approval. As long as he is receiving approval from parents or from teachers the mere addition of more and more units of approval in the form of praise or recognition may not continue to motivate him, because his needs are being satisfied. For a child, a temporary withdrawal of approval may act as more of an incentive than additional approval.

The teacher must learn to use incentives in a variety of ways and to expect different results with different pupils as he uses these incentives. No incentive will be indefinitely valuable for motivating all pupils.[46] Here again the teacher hypothesizes about what incentives are likely to motivate a particular student and continually revises his estimates of the value of incentives on the basis of the performance of students when these incentives are provided. Hilgard and Russell have pointed out:

> The proper motivation of learning is one of the basic essentials of any set of educational experiences. Learning seems to be more complete and more efficient when it is energized and directed by strong motivational factors. Accordingly, a large part of the teacher's task is to understand the motives of children and to use them in stimulating desirable learnings.
>
> Motivation must be considered, not as a temporary device to stimulate interest, but as a complex of the needs of the child in the social situation in which he lives. As such, motivational factors are continually shifting as the child develops and as new elements enter the home-school-community pattern. The teacher, accordingly, is alert to the dynamic qualities of motivation and to shifts in patterns affecting behavior and learning.
>
> Because of the large number of factors comprising a motivational pattern, the teacher can never expect a single teaching device or a larger group of procedures to stimulate different children or adolescents in the same way. In general, that teacher is most successful who can provide a variety of purposes and satisfactions in the learning process. Directing interests and activities towards social approval, or esthetic satisfaction, stimulating mental curiosity relating to both immediate and more remote goals, capitalizing on a variety of interests—all these and other procedures are needed in a well-motivated school program.[47]

---

[46]See, for example, G. G. Thompson and C. W. Hunnicutt, "The Effect of Praise or Blame on the Work Achievement of 'Introverts' and 'Extroverts'," *Journal of Educational Psychology*, 35 (1944), 257-66.

[47]E. R. Hilgard and D. H. Russell, "Motivation in School Learning," *Forty-ninth Yearbook of the National Society for the Study of Education, Part I*, 1950. pp. 66-67.

NEEDS OF THE CHILD
AND EDUCATIONAL OBJECTIVES

Educational objectives are statements of desired behavior changes. From the viewpoint of the teacher, educational objectives represents goals for which students should strive. What is the relationship of these goals to the needs of students? Does the attainment of the goals represented by educational objectives guarantee that the needs of students will be satisfied? Or must the student acquire new needs in order to attain these goals?

Most statements of educational objectives represent long-range goals.[48] For example, a statement such as, "the educated person can work and play with others," or, "the educated person appreciates the family as a social institution,"[49] represent long-range accomplishments for the individual. "Appreciating the family as a social institution" is a complex behavior which takes many different forms, develops over a long period of time in its more complex forms, and may undergo change and variation throughout a lifetime. The organization of the curriculum would reflect this goal in the kinds of specific goals that are set up for children and the kinds of learning experiences that are organized to motivate children to attain it. Progressive behavior change leading to successive goal attainments facilitates the development of the child in the directions reflected in the statement of objectives.

A child or even an adolescent does not have a time perspective which would enable him to look into the future and visualize with any great clarity the kind of a person that he is likely to be. He is immersed in present activities and immediate goals. The goals of the moment are the goals that are important to the child. The teacher must interrelate these specific goals with the long-term goal if it is to be achieved. The specific goal in the second grade classroom may be that of getting along with one's classmates. The attainment of this goal will be part of a process which will eventually lead to the long-range goal of appreciating the value of other people, respecting their rights, and recognizing the importance of institutions such as the family.

The second grade child may study the relationship of his family to the community, and may be concerned with such specific things

---

[48]See *The Purposes of Education in American Democracy*, Educational Policies Commission, National Education Association, 1938.

[49]*Ibid.*

as how the family contributes to the community and how the community in turn supports and maintains the family. In these activities he presumably is motivated by specific goals which can be attained within a relatively short period of time. But each of these goals may be part of a general structure of goals which lead to the abstract goal represented in the statement of educational objectives. The first problem, therefore, in organizing learning experiences in terms of goals is to organize these experiences on the basis of fairly specific and attainable goals, which are related to the more general goals represented in the usual statement of educational objectives.

The question still remains whether or not the goals of education, as they are reflected in statements of educational objectives, are in fact the goals that will satisfy children's needs. Modern educators have attempted to solve this problem by constructing curricula which relate the needs of children to educational objectives. The principle has been frequently cited that the curriculum must be built upon the needs of children.[50] When educators speak of building a curriculum related to the "needs of children," are they using the term "needs" as it has been used in this chapter? Most curriculum conceptions built upon the needs of children begin with an analysis of present society and then proceed to a statement of what children need in order to adjust to this society. However, *what children need to adjust to this society is not necessarily what children desire or want.* Wright makes this point in the following statement:

> Children need optimum health; they need vocational preparation. Here we are talking about what, in the opinion of adults, children ought to have, but seldom if ever strive to get. Children need recreation; they need rewarding social contacts. Now, we are talking about what, in their own living, children very often strive to get, whether adults like it or not.[51]

NORMATIVE AND PSYCHOLOGICAL NEEDS. In the above discussion, we have made a distinction between two ways in which the concept of need is used. For the sake of convenience, the two categories of needs embraced in this distinction may be called *normative* needs and *psychological* needs. *Normative needs* represent adult expecta-

---

[50]For a discussion of the relationship of the needs of children to the organization of the curriculum, see V. T. Fair, C. Zachry, and R. Kotinsky, *Reorganizing Secondary Education,* New York, Appleton-Century-Crofts, Inc., 1939.

[51]H. F. Wright, "How the Psychology of Motivation is Related to Curriculum Development," *Journal of Educational Psychology,* 39 (1948), 149-56.

tions of what a child *should* need—whether he knows it or not. A *psychological need*, on the other hand, is a state of tension within the child; it is the basis for the child's striving for particular kinds of goals. Psychological needs provide motive power, whereas normative needs do not. Psychological needs become linked to goals in the environment, and the child strives for these goals because he expects that attainment of these goals will satisfy his needs. Normative needs are conceptions of what a person ought to be like, and are not necessarily goals which are actively striven for, unless there is an interrelating of psychological needs to the goals represented by normative needs. The goals represented by educational objectives are statements of the normative needs of children. The goals may or may not actually be sought by children. Psychological needs, on the other hand, influence children to seek specific goals which may or may not be related to the goals reflected in statements of educational objectives.[52]

Starting with statements of educational objectives which represent goals that the educated person will have attained, the teacher must utilize the actual motives and goals of children in such a way that they will strive for goals which will result in behavior stated as desirable. This is the problem that we have been discussing throughout this chapter—the problem of how to utilize the need systems of children to motivate them to seek goals which are regarded as desirable by the society at large.

Curriculum organization has profited from the conception of basing the curriculum on the needs of children. Much subject matter which is no longer useful in any sense has been eliminated from the curriculum, and a broader and more realistic conception of education has resulted. Modern educators have built a curriculum derived from conceptions of what the majority of children will need in order to be adjusted members of society, with provisions for the needs of particular groups of children. This reorganization of the curriculum has not simplified or resolved the problem that has always confronted teachers—the problem of motivating students to work for specific goals. The teacher faces children with varying needs and learned goal expectations. The teacher's task is to broaden children's conceptions of their goals, foster the acquisition of new needs, and through this process enhance the total development of the child.

---

[52]For a comprehensive discussion of the concept of need and its relations to educational theory, see R. D. Archambault, "The Concept of Need and its Relation to Certain Aspects of Educational Theory," *Harvard Educational Review*, 27 (1957), 38-62.

As a final note, we might point out that in the process of determining the motives and needs of children, and in the process of devising procedures for motivating children, the teacher again acts as a hypothesis-maker. Each statement about the particular needs of a child represents a hypothesis that such a need is, in effect, a characteristic of this child's personality. The use of motivating devices, such as incentives, are also, in principle, hypotheses that if such incentives are used children will be motivated in specific kinds of ways. We have deliberately emphasized the complexity of the problem of motivation in order to impress upon the teacher that there are no simple recipes for motivating children to learn. On the other hand, a sensitivity to the complexity of this problem can lead to improved procedures, both for determining children's motives and for devising ways of motivating them. Essentially, the concepts and principles in this chapter should clarify for the teacher the characteristics of human motivation and their implication for behavior change.

SUMMARY

In this chapter we have discussed the concept of motivation and its influence on behavior. The following were the main ideas presented in this discussion:

1. Motivation is an inferred process, one of the processes which we have referred to as a mediating variable. Motivation, as such, is not directly observed, but is inferred from observed behavior. We use the concept of motivation to explain the energy base for changes in behavior.

2. We define motivation as an energy change which is characterized by affective arousal and anticipatory goal reactions. Because the human being seeks goals, we can infer that an energy change, which provides the power for this goal-seeking behavior, has taken place within the organism.

3. When attained, the goal sought by the person in a motivated state will reduce the state of motivation. The person seeking the goal acts on the assumption that the goal will prove satisfying to him when attained, and he may be more or less correct in his

estimate of the goal's potentialities for satisfying his motivavational states.

4.   An important effect follows when the goal has been attained and reduces the motivational state of the person. Behavior which has been successful in leading to goal attainment is reinforced, that is, made stronger. This same behavior is likely to reoccur when the person seeks the goal to satisfy his motivational states.

5.   We have made a distinction between motives and needs. Motives are specific instances of the motivational process, whereas needs are the underlying states out of which particular instances of motivation arise. Needs are stabilized potentialities to be motivated in specific ways. The presence of a need in the personality of a person implies that the person is likely to be motivated in specific kinds of ways.

6.   A variety of factors influences the kinds of needs systems that the person develops. Some needs arise out of basic physiological conditions of the organism, such as the hunger need. Other needs are acquired under environmental influences. The home, the social class in which the person lives, various groups to which the individual belongs, all influence the kinds of goals that he regards as desirable. These groups also provide rewards and punishments for specific kinds of goal-seeking behavior. Goal-seeking behavior which is persistently rewarded leads to the development of stabilized needs.

7.   We have noted that a number of other factors influence goal-setting behavior. Success and failure in attaining goals, the standards set by the groups to which an individual belongs, an individual's knowledge of his attainment of goals, are all factors which influence the kinds of goals for which a person is willing to work.

Throughout this chapter we have emphasized the role of the teacher in assessing the need systems and motives of the children that he is teaching. We have stressed that the process of determining these needs and motives is essentially an inferential process based on the observed behavior of the children. We have not formulated a system of needs which characterize any and all children, but have chosen to indicate the process by which a determination of the need system of a child is made.

The teacher's problem is to utilize the motives and needs of children to encourage them to work for goals that are regarded as educationally desirable. In the process of seeking these desirable goals behavior changes will take place. Educational experiences are designed to promote these behavior changes. The task of the teacher is, therefore, to motivate children to work for desirable goals and, in the process, to acquire desirable behaviors.

We have pointed out that educational objectives are statements of desirable behavior changes, but have emphasized that these desired changes reflect desirable goals as seen by society. We have used the term *normative needs* to describe statements about what children require if they are to become adjusted members of their society. We have noted that these normative needs are not necessarily *psychological needs;* that is, children may or may not be motivated to seek the goals reflected in statements of educational objectives. The problem of the classroom teacher is to interrelate the psychological needs of children with the normative needs reflected in the educational objectives.

Teachers frequently use *incentives* to motivate children to seek desirable goals. Incentives, whatever their nature may be, are useful only insofar as they represent goals which will satisfy the psychological needs of children. As a consequence, the teacher must be creative and imaginative in devising incentives to motivate children to seek desirable goals.

STUDY AND DISCUSSION QUESTIONS

1. Refer to the example of John and Bill presented in the first part of this chapter. Describe the *motives* of each of these boys in the situation described. What *needs* would you infer from these motives? What predictions would you make about other motives that you would expect these boys to have if your inference is accurate?

2. A student participates quite actively in class discussions. What motives might underlie this behavior? What needs would you infer from these motives?

3. Suggest several motives for each of the following instances of behavior:

    a. A student pushes another student as they stand in line.

    b. A student insists on rewriting his papers when they are corrected.

    c A student joins the debate team and the student newspaper.

    d. A child collects stamps and rocks.

    e. A student does not attend school dances.

    f. A student signs up for the French course.

4. Using the motives you suggested in the above examples, describe the needs that may underlie these motives. Predict the kinds of behavior you would expect to observe if the students were motivated by these needs.

5 What needs might be satisfied by a boy who is interested in working on automobiles? How might these activities be learned as a source of need-satisfaction?

6 Some students are intensely interested in interscholastic athletic activities even though they are not members of the varsity teams. What needs might be satisfied by attending games and "rooting" for the team? Suggest some ways in which these sources of need-satisfaction may have been learned.

7. How do you account for the fact that some students do not find intellectual activities a source of need-satisfaction? How might such activities be learned as sources of need-satisfaction?

8. In the Ovsiankina experiment cited earlier, the students were interested in tasks of no apparent relevance to their usual activities. How do you account for this fact? In what ways might this situation be similar to some of the kinds of learning experiences provided for children in school? Can you expect interest to develop in a comparable manner in these learning experiences? If not, why not?

9. Define each of the following kinds of needs in terms of the behavior from which you would infer the need. Describe the behaviors specifically, and the situations in which you would expect the behaviors to occur.

    a. A need for approval.

    b. A need for affection.

    c. A need for independence.

10 What differences in goals and needs would you predict might characterize the following children? Describe the kinds of behavior you would look for to check your predictions.

    a. A boy whose father is an engineer.

    b. A boy whose father is a steelworker.

    c. A girl whose father is an engineer.

    d. A girl whose father is a steelworker.

11. Dependency needs characterize many young children. In what ways might a dependency need be manifested in the behavior of an older child and an adult? If you observed behavior from which you inferred a need for independence, may you conclude that the person has no dependency needs or that a dependency need was not a motivating force in his behavior at some earlier period in life? In what ways may these two kinds of needs be related?

12. How do you explain the fact that girls with strong needs for recognition were characteristically more irritable and selfish? May we assume that girls with this kind of need are more likely to be irritable and selfish?

13. Under what conditions would you use withdrawal of social approval as a means to increase motivation in a learning experience? What kinds of children might not be motivated by such a procedure? If this procedure did not achieve the desired effect, what explanation would you offer?

14. What kind of behavior in learning experiences would you predict would characterize a child whose mother urged him to be independent? Assume that you observed him to be particularly dependent in school, how would you account for his behavior?

15. Two children are doing poorly in arithmetic. One, however, is achieving below what you would expect in terms of his ability. The other is achieving consistently with his ability. What hypotheses would you offer about the relationship of their "failure" experiences to the kinds of goals they set for themselves? Would they be equally "unrealistic" in their estimates of future success? Would you attempt to provide "success" experiences for the child who is achieving below his ability? What hypotheses are implicit in the procedures you would use with this child?

16. Some people argue that "failure" experiences are necessary since children will have to meet such experiences "in life." Evaluate this argument in the light of the experimental evidence presented in this chapter.

17. A child is achieving below what would be expected in terms of his ability. Would you place him in a group of students of comparable ability or lesser ability? Formulate the hypotheses implicit in the procedure you recommend.

18. Some people argue that "gifted" students should be grouped together. They maintain that these students will work harder since they will be in a group for which the expectations will be higher. Does the evidence presented in this chapter support this argument? Would you expect this procedure to achieve its purpose for all gifted students? What other factors might influence motivation in this kind of a situation?

19. Some students claim that they are interested in learning, but not in grades.

What needs might characterize such a student? In what ways might he be motivated differently from a student who "works for grades."

20. Below are several *normative* needs. How might a child with a strong need for independence be motivated to strive for the goals involved in these needs?

    a. Children need to compute accurately.

    b. Children need to know how to read.

    c. Children need a knowledge of their country's history.

21. Some people argue that the needs of children are better provided for in the activity program of the school than in the classroom. Would such an argument be valid if the "needs" referred to are normative needs? Psychological needs?

RECOMMENDED READINGS

The first, fourth, and fifth readings below provide theoretical discussions and research evidence on the problems discussed in this chapter. The second reading discusses the problem of motivation in relation to learning in school. The third reading presents an interesting discussion of particular problems of motivation in the classroom. The evidence is mainly clinical in character, and the suggestions should be evaluated against the experimental evidence provided.

1. R. D. Archambault, "The Concept of Need and Its Relation to Certain Aspects of Educational Theory," *Harvard Educational Review*, 27 (1957), 38-62.

2. E. R. Hilgard and D. H. Russell, "Motivation in School Learning," *Forty-ninth Yearbook of the National Society for the Study of Education, Part I, Learning and Instruction*, Chicago, University of Chicago Press, 1950, pp. 36-68.

3. R. Dreikurs, *Psychology in the Classroom*, New York, Harper & Brothers, 1957.

4. D. C. McClelland, *Studies in Motivation*, New York, Appleton-Century-Crofts, Inc., 1955.

5. N. E. Miller, "Learnable Drives and Rewards," in S. S. Stevens (ed.), *Handbook of Experimental Psychology*, New York, John Wiley & Sons, 1951, pp. 435-72.

LEARNING AND THE
COGNITIVE PROCESSES–I

In Chapter Three we identified and discussed the behavior variables that we would consider throughout this text. One set was called *mediating variables,* which are processes that we assume operate within the individual and that enable us to explain human behavior. The "need system," one group of mediating variables, was discussed in the preceding chapter. In this and following chapters, we will consider another group of mediating variables, which we will call the *cognitive-attitudinal-value processes.*

The cognitive-attitudinal-value processes are essentially orienting functions of the human organism. We know that people have ways of "looking at" themselves and the world around them. People have ways of thinking about and feeling about the phenomena that they perceive—which tend to become stabilized as the person develops. These relatively systematic and stable ways of viewing the environment enable the individual to interpret his environment and to react to it with consistency and assuredness.

THE COGNITIVE PROCESSES

In this and the next chapter we will direct our attention to the cognitive aspects of this complex set of processes; in the following chapters the attitudinal and evaluative components will be considered. This division is an arbitrary one and should not lead the student to conclude that the cognitive, attitudinal, and evaluative processes are independent of each other. Many of our ways of thinking are clothed with feelings, and our feelings and emotional reactions have cognitive aspects.

THE SCHOOL AND THE COGNITIVE PROCESSES. A major task of the school is the development of concepts and generalizations that either may not be learned outside of school, or may be learned more efficiently and systematically in school. The high school student studying chemistry learns such complex concepts as valence, electron, chemical reaction, electrochemical series, which he would not learn if he were not exposed to them systematically. A fifth grade child may hear something about the battle at the Alamo from his family. Few children, however, would understand the significance of this event in American history were we to leave the teaching of this, or any other aspect of history, to the casual experiences of the child.

COGNITIVE PROCESSES AND PERSONALITY DEVELOPMENT. The concepts, generalizations, and principles a child is learning become integrated into his personality, resulting in a personality quite different from that which would develop had he been exposed to other concepts and generalizations. These differences in personality structure resulting from different kinds of concept formation vary among cultures and societies and even within the same culture. They also vary from individual to individual within the same society.[1] Every child, for example, learns a concept of "my country." The child living in the eastern part of the United States, however, differs some-

---

[1]Cultural differences in concept formation are reflected in the generalized "images" people hold about each other's countries. The following studies will be of particular interest to American college students in this connection since they suggest the "images" of America held by college students from foreign lands: C. P. Loomis and E. A. Schuler, "Acculturation of Foreign Students in the United States," *Applied Anthropology*, 7 (1948), 17-34; R. B. Zajonc, "Aggressive Attitudes of the 'Stranger' as a Function of Conformity Pressures," *Human Relations*, 5 (1952), 205-216; W. H. Sewell, R. T. Morris, and O. M. Davidson, "Scandinavian Students' Images of the United States: A Study in Cross-Cultural Education," *The Annals of the American Academy of Political and Social Science*, 295 (1954), 126-135.

what in his concept of "my country" from a child living in the Southwest. The American child, the French child, and the Russian child have different meanings for the concept "native country," because the relevant experiences differ in their own countries. These and other concepts are integrated into a complex orientation to environment. As these concepts become stabilized, they become difficult to change and become an integral aspect of personality.[2]

The process of concept formation is intimately tied in with the total development of the child's personality. The child who is beginning school has already developed a system of concepts and characteristic ways of perceiving and organizing the stimuli from his environment. Learning experiences extend, diversify, and reorganize this conceptual system. As this conceptual system changes, the child's personality changes.

In this chapter we will discuss principally the learning of *formal* concepts. By formal concepts we mean the concepts that the school systematically inculcates, such as electron, photosynthesis, equalitarianism, rationalism, the expanding frontier, States' rights, compound sentence. Each of these and many others are concepts used to interpret the subject matter of different areas of knowledge.

Children are continually forming concepts informally and haphazardly as they interact with their environment. Since some of these concepts are related to the concepts that the school is attempting to form, another function of the school is to expand, revise, and clarify these concepts. In this chapter we will be concerned with this latter process, rather than with the process by which children acquire concepts informally. These formal concepts differ from those the child acquires informally in that the meanings of the concepts have generally been clarified to some extent, and the meanings are shared and communicable, whereas the concepts the child acquires informally may be highly subjective and personal.

WHAT IS A CONCEPT?

A third grade class is studying a unit on "Ships, Harbors, and Cargoes." In this unit the children are to learn what a "harbor" is. The teacher describes a harbor as a "sheltered body of water having

[2]J. Watson and R. Lippitt, "Cross-Cultural Learning: A Study Among a Group of German Leaders," *Institute of International Education News Bulletin*, 30 (1955), 2-5.

piers." Some teachers might be satisfied if the children were able merely to repeat this description of a harbor. However, if the teacher wants the child to acquire the *concept* of "harbor," a much more complicated process of learning is involved. The formation of a concept is distinguished from the rote memorization of the verbal definition of a concept in the following ways:

1. *A discrimination is required:* The child must be able to distinguish what a harbor is. He must be able to distinguish a harbor from other geographical formations, particularly other bodies of water, such as rivers, lakes, seas, oceans.

2. *A generalization is required:* The child must be able to utilize the description of a harbor to identify many examples of harbors. The concept of a harbor is a categorization or a grouping which applies to many different kinds of harbors, each of which is characterized by a sheltered body of water and piers.[8]

DEFINITION OF A CONCEPT. *A concept,* such as that of "a harbor," *is a classification or systematic organization of stimuli, characteristics, or events which have common characteristics.* The concept is not the event itself, nor the stimulus itself, nor even the stimulus experience itself, but a *classification* of certain stimuli, events, or characteristics. A child in using the concept "harbor" may be thinking in terms of harbors he has seen, or he may be thinking of the only harbor with which he has had any experience. But the concept is formed when this classification can be extended beyond this single experience or event. Thus, two processes are involved in learning a concept: first, the child

---

[8]The teacher in this example has restricted the definition of a harbor to include only those sheltered bodies of water which are used for transportation purposes. The restriction of meaning is consistent with the purpose of the unit. The psychological problem would be whether or not the learning of the concept in this form at this time would inhibit or facilitate the learning of a more generalized definition.

makes discriminations by which he distinguishes one concept from another; second, he *generalizes* the concept to other examples of it.

One of the common errors in teaching is to assume that a child who utilizes a class or category name has an appropriate concept for that category or class. The process of learning concepts consists of more than memorizing the definitions for class names. In one sense a concept is never completely learned since new experiences with the concept will develop new meanings and new associations for that concept.

Many concepts learned in and out of school are difficult to define in any precise way and, consequently, the processes of discrimination and generalization required to learn these concepts are not easily promoted. Consider, for instance, the teacher's attempt to teach the principles of democracy and the importance of "democratic" behavior in political, social, economic, and interpersonal affairs; "democratic" behavior is not easily defined. Even within a given society, the meaning of the concept may shift. Court decisions, for example, redefine what behavior is consistent with democratic principles. A concept of this kind is both highly generalized and nonspecific. Furthermore, such concepts are revised as the child grows up; the meaning of the concept shifts with new associations as the child's field of experience broadens.

RELATION OF CONCEPTS TO BEHAVIOR. Whether the concepts that the child learns are sharply defined or vaguely defined, whether he acquires them formally through organized school experiences or informally by organizing his varied experiences, they enable him to interpret his experiences. The observable behavior of the person will vary with the kind of conceptual interpretations he makes of his environment. The child whose concept of a teacher is defined by such evaluations as harsh, demanding, overbearing, punitive, and unsympathetic, will behave differently from the child who sees the teacher as helpful, kind, sympathetic, and rewarding.[4]

Man invents categories necessary to interpret his environment and to deepen and broaden his understanding of the phenomena that he perceives. The principles discussed here have been summarized as follows:

---

[4] H. H. Anderson and J. E. Brewer, "Studies of Teachers' Classroom Personalities, II: Effects of Teachers' Dominative and Integrative Contacts on Children's Classroom Behavior," *Applied Psychology Monographs*, No. 8, 1946.

We begin with what seems a paradox. The world of experience of any normal man is composed of a tremendous array of discriminably different objects, events, people, impressions. There are estimated to be more than 7,000,000 discriminable colors alone, and in the course of a week or two we come in contact with a fair proportion of them. No two people we see have an identical appearance and even objects that we judged to be the same object over a period of time change appearance from moment to moment with alterations in light or in the position of the viewer. All of these differences we are capable of seeing, for human beings have an exquisite capacity for making distinctions.

But were we to utilize fully our capacity for registering the differences in things and to respond to each event encountered as unique, we would soon be overwhelmed by the complexity of our environment. Consider only the linguistic task of acquiring a vocabulary fully adequate to cope with a world of color differences! The resolution of this seeming paradox—the existence of discrimination capacities which, if fully used, would make us slaves to the particular—is achieved by man's capacity to categorize. *To categorize is to render discriminably different things equivalent, to group the objects and events and people around us into classes, and to respond to them in terms of their class membership rather than their uniqueness.* [Italics added.] Our refined discriminative activity is reserved only for those segments of the environment with which we are specially concerned. For the rest, we respond by rather crude forms of categorical placement.[5]

THE PROCESS OF CONCEPT FORMATION

Concept formation is a process in which a person interacts with his environment and organizes the mass of stimuli that he is experiencing. From this organization he interprets the environment and acts on the basis of this interpretation. The generalizations discussed on the following pages are pertinent to an adequate understanding of this complex process.

CONCEPT FORMATION AND APPROPRIATE EXPERIENCE. *Concepts cannot be learned without some relevant experience with the phenomena which are to be conceptualized.* The third graders studying the concept of "a harbor" can be provided with a variety of experiences which would enable them to identify a harbor. They may study harbor formations on maps and distinguish these configurations from

[5]J. S. Bruner, J. J. Goodnow, and G. A. Austin, *A Study of Thinking*, New York, John Wiley & Sons, 1956, p. 1. Reprinted by permission of the publisher.

other configurations as they are illustrated on maps; they may visit a harbor and observe the harbor formation directly; they may watch a film on harbors of the world which illustrates the essential characteristics of a harbor.

Experience enables the child to make the necessary discriminations. The range of these experiences will vary from those which are direct and immediate to experiences which are more or less remote from the direct sensory experience of the phenomenon being conceptualized. The child studying harbor formations on maps is having a direct sensory experience of maps, but not of harbor formations.

The essential task of the teacher is to predict the experiences which are most likely to facilitate the processes of discrimination and generalization necessary to learn the concept. There is little experimental evidence on what kinds of experiences facilitate the formation of particular kinds of concepts.[6] The teacher, here again, acts as the hypothesis-maker. He tries out various kinds of experiences and notes the effects of these experiences in terms of the ease with which children grasp the concepts and their ability to identify new instances of the concept. The educational process could undoubtedly be improved if we had clear-cut empirical evidence on the kinds of experiences that would maximize the learning of particular concepts. Until we have such evidence, each teacher must use and examine a variety of techniques for providing presumably relevant experiences. Teachers will continue to use field trips, movies, books, and verbal descriptions on the assumption that each of these is contributing to the development of a particular concept.

CONCEPT FORMATION AND THE INFERENTIAL PROCESS. *To acquire a concept a person must abstract or infer from sensory data and his experiences*. If we take a child to see a harbor, he perceives literally thousands of events and phenomena. If the child is to learn the concept of a harbor, however, many of these events must be ignored, and he must focus his attention on others. For example, the size of the harbor is irrelevant to the concept, as is the color of the water. The number of piers, the construction of the piers, the kind of men employed on the piers, the details of loading and unloading cargo—all must be ignored in acquiring a concept of a harbor. The child must focus on

---

[6] For a critical review of research on this problem, see A. M. Broenig, "General Methods of Teaching," *Review of Educational Research*, 9 (1939), 295-302.

specific features—the sheltered body of water and the piers—and must recognize these as the essential characteristics of a harbor. Thus, the process of abstraction or inference in concept formation is essentially one of focusing on the relevant characteristics of the concept.

Failures to discriminate lead to misconceptions and consequently to incorrect interpretations. Such errors in discrimination can be made in two ways: (1) by omitting essential features or (2) by including features which are not essential to the concept. If a child noticed that the harbor which he was observing had a lighthouse located on the shore, and assumed that lighthouses were characteristic features of harbors, he could err in either of the two ways. He could identify any formation which had a lighthouse as a harbor, or he could fail to identify as harbors those which did not include a lighthouse.

Failures in discrimination lead also to errors in generalizing the concept to other examples of it. This phenomenon is quite apparent in very young children whose concept formation is necessarily limited by experience. The small child who calls every man "daddy" has focused on certain features of his father which are characteristic of other men, but which do not distinguish his father from these other men. Failure in discrimination in this instance leads to overgeneralization.

CONCEPT FORMATION AND THE CHARACTER OF EXPERIENCE. *The kinds of concepts children develop will be limited by the kinds of experiences that are available to them.*[7] Some kinds of experiences cannot be provided for children because they have not reached the stage of development which permits them to participate in the appropriate activity.[8] The primary grade child does not study international affairs because he does not have sufficient experience with any form of social organization beyond that of his own family. We familiarize him with the concepts of local government, and gradually proceed to concepts of national and international organization when he has experiences from which he can formulate these concepts, or when he can be easily introduced to the relevant experiences.

---

[7] J. M. Deutsche, *The Development of Children's Concepts of Causal Relations*, University of Minnesota Institute of Child Welfare Monographs, 1937; G. M. Peterson, "An Empirical Study of the Ability to Generalize," *Journal of General Psychology*, 6 (1932), 90-114.

[8] Age differences have been consistently found in concept formation: See L. A. Welch, "A Preliminary Investigation of Some Aspects of the Hierarchical Development of Concepts," *Journal of Genetic Psychology*, 22 (1940), 359-78; M. G. Colby and J. B. Robertson, "Genetic Studies in Abstraction," *Journal of Comparative Psychology*, 33 (1942), 385-401.

Social and family conditions provide the child with a set of experiences from which concepts are developed.[9] One of the difficulties in developing geographical concepts, and such concepts as time and distance, may be the relative immobility of the child and his family. A child who has not traveled beyond his own neighborhood, who has never flown in an airplane, who has not traversed large sections of this country, forms his concepts of distance, transportation time, and location from abstract and indirect experiences. It may not be necessary for a child to traverse time zones to develop an understanding of the concept of time zones; many people have a basic understanding of time zones without ever leaving their local community. But many concepts may be difficult for a child to understand because his home, community, and school cannot provide him with the requisite experiences for developing them adequately.

The author had occasion to visit a small school in a farming community. In one of the classrooms visited, the teacher was discussing "white-collar workers." The teacher was trying to convey some idea of what was meant by the "white-collar worker," the conditions of his work and life, and his general social position. In the course of discussion, the author happened to look out a window and noticed a group of men in front of a feed store across the street. The men in this community were obviously not white-collar workers and probably wore white collars, literally speaking, only on Sundays. In this community the child would probably have difficulty in grasping the concept of a "white-collar worker." He has had no direct exposure to "white-collar workers," to the kinds of communities they live in, or to the kinds of jobs that they perform. In situations like this, the teacher decides, first, what kinds of experiences are likely to generate the concept and, second, whether these experiences can be provided with sufficient ease to justify the consideration of the concept at this time. In some cases, the learning of a concept may be so important that the teacher is willing to use less appropriate experiences, which will help the children to gain at least some understanding of the concept.

CONCEPT FORMATION AND FORMAL AND INFORMAL EXPERIENCES. *Concepts are learned both through organized experiences and from casual, everyday experience.* Children come to school with a

---

[9]H. Ordan, *Social Concepts and the Child Mind*, New York, King's Crown Press, 1945.

system of concepts. One of the first tasks for the teacher is to determine the present stage of concept development of the child and its significance to the acquisition of new concepts. Most "reading readiness" tests given to kindergarteners and first graders are essentially tests of concept formation. From these tests the teacher may estimate whether the child has an adequate grasp of concepts for which he will be learning the word symbols. The child entering the primary grade has acquired concepts of many kinds; he has concepts for most of the objects in his environment, such as the persons in his family, his home, the family car, and the utensils he uses. He has also developed relational concepts, such as "inside of," "outside of," "from," "to," "up," "down."[10] He may have only the vaguest grasp of some other kinds of concepts, such as "smaller than" or "larger than."[11]

At any level of education there will be varying degrees of concept formation within any group of children.[12] Even the concepts introduced in school in a systematic manner will be influenced by the kinds of experiences that a child may have out of school. History books frequently emphasize the concept of America as a land of opportunity. A child growing up in the slums and one coming from a better section of the city will not have the same experiences for forming this concept. To the child from the slums the concept of "opportunity" may very well be no more than a word. He may have no experiential base for the concept symbolized by the word.

INFLUENCE OF PREVIOUS LEARNING ON CONCEPT FORMATION. *The child's interpretations of new concepts will be influenced strongly by the concepts he has already developed, both formally and informally.*[13] The concept of fractions, for example, is introduced after the concept of a whole number; the child is taught addition of fractions after he has learned the concept of addition of whole numbers. Logical arrangements of this kind are perhaps most satisfactory where the out-of-school experience of the child is not likely to be related to the concepts he is being taught in school, and where the concepts are not

---

[10]L. B. Ames, "The Development of Verbalized Space in the Young Child," *Journal of Genetic Psychology,* 72 (1948), 63-84.

[11]For a review of the literature on children's number concepts, see W. E. Martin, "Quantitative Expression in Young Children," *Genetic Psychology Monographs,* 44 (1951), 147-219.

[12]For one discussion of this problem, see W. A. Brownell, "Readiness and the Arithmetic Curriculum," *Elementary School Journal,* 38 (1938), 344-54.

[13]M. E. Oakes, "Children's Explanations of Natural Phenomena," *Teachers College Contributions to Education,* No. 926, New York, Columbia University Press, 1947.

likely to have personal and social meanings. When concepts relate to experiences that a child may be having out of school, these concepts may be clothed in emotional and imaginative meanings.

This point may be illustrated by the following experiences of a group of sixth graders. The students were working on a unit on India. The teacher invited a university student from India to speak to the children and to describe his country for them. After the talk

the teacher asked the children to write down their impressions of India. During the talk the speaker had illustrated his points with slides, showing pictures of various scenes in India. In this situation the child was exposed to a wide variety of events relating to "India" in a fairly unsystematic fashion. He responded in terms of the concepts that he had already developed. Here are some of the impressions of "India" reported by the children after the visitor's remarks:

Wayne: I'm thinking of the sweeping beauty of a temple, its semi-precious stones gleaming in the morning mist, remains of a ruined Buddha in the age-old temple, the creeping vines growing up through the crack in the ancient rock, it's huge bulk a monument to the ancient ones who built it.

Ruth: A village home with oxen screeching and stamping up and down the walks.

Sandy: The Taj Mahal with its beauty and luster. The Black Pagoda, cold, black and sinister. The Red Forts worn with battle but still beautiful. The palaces and the temples all symbolize the want for beauty of the Indian people.

Layne: The people on the boardwalk seemed so natural, the way they were just sitting there, thinking and talking, with children playing. Everything they did was just so natural.

Scott: Drinking water where the cows take a bath seems like eating mud.

Bryan: It was interesting how the man put a cobra and a mongoose together and let them fight. It seemed sort of stupid because he sat with his legs crossed and let the two fight right in front of him. If the cobra struck at the mongoose and missed he would be bit. Also, the cobra might turn on him.

This rich variety of impressions is all the more striking when we recall that each of these children heard the same words and saw the same pictures. The children had essentially the same stimulus experience, but each child interpreted and selected from the stimuli in terms of his own conceptual system and his attitudes and feelings. One child responds to the beauty of the temples; another, to the awesome sight of a cobra and a mongoose fighting. Another child sees the personal habits of the people as repulsive; still another sees the people as natural and as human as the people he knows.

These children will probably develop concepts about India which have common characteristics. They will remember the Taj Mahal as a large, white, beautiful building. They will know the details of dress and the personal habits of the people of India. In these respects their concepts will be fundamentally alike, but each concept will still have a different meaning for each child. The total system of concepts of each child will be unique because common concepts will have different associations, that is, meanings, feelings, and emotions associated with them.

These variations in the conceptual systems among children influence the learning of any given concept. Too frequently we assume that the mere presentation of a learning experience guarantees that each child will learn concepts in identically the same fashion. The child who sees the habits of the people as repulsive and the child who sees the people as "natural and human" will make different interpretations about the significance of life in India. The school influences concept formation by controlling the experiences to which children are exposed. While the teacher has little control, if any, over the out-of-school experiences, the teacher may influence the development of concepts by the kinds of experiences he provides for the child in the process of learning a concept.

ORGANIZING LEARNING EXPERIENCES TO TEACH CONCEPTS

MEANING OF EXAMPLES OF A CONCEPT. The process by which the concept "harbor" is acquired, as distinct from memorizing the definition of "harbor," consists in presenting the student with both examples and non-examples of harbors. With each presentation the student must identify or discriminate the features which characterize a harbor, and on the basis of this discrimination classify a geographical formation as either a harbor or a non-harbor. The examples of the concept are referred to as "positive instances," and the non-examples are referred to as "negative instances," or "positive" and "negative" examples.

A positive example or instance is a stimulus complex which contains the characteristics of the concept. A negative example is a stimulus complex which does not have any or all of the appropriate characteristics of a given concept. Negative examples of harbors would be other geographical formations. Some of these formations quite obviously have none of the characteristics of harbors—for example, mountains or a peninsular formation. Other bodies of water would also be non-examples of harbors, but would have some of the characteristics of a harbor; for example, a lake is a body of water, but it may or may not be sheltered, and may or may not have piers. If a concept is ambiguously defined, or if it shares many characteristics in common with other concepts, the process of discriminating this concept from others, even for the person who has learned the concept, may be a difficult task.

What is the relationship of the examples used to illustrate a concept to the learning of the concept? Would it be possible for a student to learn what a harbor is if we presented him with examples of non-harbors only? Or should we present him with examples of harbors only? Or should we give him both examples and non-examples of harbors? In what order should these examples and non-examples, if we use both, be presented? Should we present all the examples simultaneously, or should we present them one at a time, waiting until the student has acquired all the necessary information for a particular example? Will the third grader understand the concept of a harbor better if we take him out and show him a harbor, or will he understand the concept better if we present him with a series of simplified pictorial representations of harbors? These kinds of questions are psychological questions which can be and have been investigated, and experimental literature provides us with some answers to these questions.

Essentially, the presentation of an example or a non-example of a concept is information-giving. Some of the information is relevant to what is to be learned, and some is not. The learner is confronted with a complex sorting task. The problem for the teacher is to present him with sufficient information to facilitate the learning of the concept. The psychological question here is how much relevant information is necessary to learn a concept and how much irrelevant information impedes the learning. The experimental data available indicate that the conclusions presented in this section are tenable.

SEQUENCE AND KIND OF EXAMPLE USED. Experimental data indicate that a sequence of positive instances, or a mixture of positive and negative instances, does not appreciably influence the accuracy of learning. We cannot say that to teach a concept we must present only positive instances, or only negative instances, or a mixture of positive and negative instances. Students differ in their ability to profit from these kinds of series; however, more students tend to prefer a mixture of positive and negative instances.[14] If negative instances are presented early in the learning sequence, they apparently confuse some students. The student does not have a sufficiently adequate grasp of the essential characteristics of the concept to be helped by the addition of a negative instance. Negative instances have a corrective value, however, and can serve as a checking device once

---

[14]See K. L. Smoke, "An Objective Study of Concept Formation," *Psychological Monographs*, No. 191, 1932; K. L. Smoke, "Negative Instances in Concept Learning," *Journal of Experimental Psychology*, 16 (1933), 583-88; K. L. Smoke, "Experimental Approach to Concept Learning," *Psychological Review*, 42 (1935), 274-79.

the student has a reasonably adequate grasp of the basic dimensions of the concept. The introduction of negative examples, examples of what the concept is not, tends to increase accuracy in discrimination.

Suppose that we wanted to teach a second grader the concept "cow." In principle, the child could learn this concept from examples of "cow" and non-examples of "cow." Using non-examples, the child could learn what a cow is not; a cow is not a horse, a sheep, a mule, a pig. With a large number of non-examples the child theoretically might conceptualize "cow." This is patently inefficient. The process of sorting non-examples is more complex, and concept acquisition takes longer. Using examples of the concept "cow" speeds up the process of acquiring the concept, although it does not necessarily improve the accuracy of the child's concept. Non-examples provide relevant information and can be used to check the accuracy of a concept.

This discussion may seem artificial unless we remember that there are typically more non-examples of any concept than examples. We do not know at the present time the sequences of examples and non-examples that facilitate the learning of a concept. For example, if we are teaching the concept of "prime number" to an algebra class, should we start with a series of examples, such as 3, 5, 7, 11, 13, or should we intersperse non-examples, such as 4, 6, 8? How many examples and non-examples should we use, and in what order? These questions cannot be answered for all cases. Again, acting as a hypothesis-maker, the teacher must experiment with various sequences for a given situation.

One general principle of sequence arrangements can be given. If students learn a concept by using examples, they are typically better at recognizing examples than non-examples. If they practice on non-examples, they are better at recognizing non-examples than examples.[15] In learning with positive instances or examples, the learner is making discriminations of the appropriate characteristics of the concept. However, non-examples provide him with information also, since they expose him to phenomena which have none or only some of the characteristics of the concept. Two kinds of discrimination are required to learn a concept: (1) discrimination of the appropriate characteristics; (2) discrimination of the inappropriate charac-

---

[15] A. H. Buss, "A Study of Concept Formation as a Function of Reinforcement and Stimulus Generalization," *Journal of Experimental Psychology*, 40 (1950), 494-503.

teristics. More experience with either kind of discrimination produces greater facility in making that kind of discrimination.

The fact that some students tend to prefer positive instances and others prefer mixtures of positive and negative instances suggests that the manner in which students learn concepts tends to be individualized. There are probably some students who can learn better from the presentation of positive instances of a concept; others, from a mixture; still others, from a large proportion of negative instances in a series. The teacher arranges the presentations of the examples for a group, and usually does not know which student is likely to profit from a particular kind of sequence. Under these conditions a larger proportion of positive instances probably should be used in initial phases of learning a concept. As the learning progresses, negative instances may be introduced to insure accuracy by facilitating the student's checking the correctness of his concept.

COMPLEXITY OF STIMULUS SITUATION. Experimental data also indicate that when the student is presented with a stimulus complex, any feature of which accentuates the essential characteristics of the concept, learning is facilitated.[16] This conclusion is congruent with our common-sense notions, but its application frequently may be overlooked in educational practice. Quite frequently students are exposed to experiences which are enormously complex so far as information is concerned. If we take students to a harbor with little or no introduction to the concept of "a harbor," and then expect them to learn what a harbor is, we are presenting the students with a complex problem in discrimination. The student has an extremely difficult task in sorting out the many stimuli and determining the essential characteristics of the concept. The problem can be simplified by accentuating the essential characteristics of the concept; experimental evidence suggests that this may facilitate concept learning.

The third grade teacher, for example, could begin a discussion of harbors with a brief descriptive statement used as a definition. Then, using diagrams and pictures, he could give examples and non-examples of harbors. Finally, on a visit to the harbor, the teacher could point out the essential characteristics. At each step the teacher is focusing the child's attention on the essential characteristics of a

---

[16]See C. L. Hull, "Quantitative Aspects of the Evolution of Concepts," *Psychological Monographs*, No. 123, 1920. Also, Z. Y. Kuo, "A Behavioristic Experiment on Inductive Inference," *Journal of Experimental Psychology*, 6 (1923), 247-93.

harbor The teacher can also use the children's questions to keep the essential characteristics in focus. If a child asks, "Do harbors have lighthouses?" the teacher can point out that this is not an essential characteristic of a harbor.

A recent experiment[17] illustrates the utility of accentuating essential characteristics. Two groups of biology students were to learn how to identify the parts of flowers. One group was given "real" flowers and was taught the parts with the real flowers as examples. The second group was presented with a large and simplified diagram of the parts of a flower, from which the parts were to be learned. Since the first group was working with "real" flowers, it might be assumed that they would learn the parts of a flower more quickly and easily; however, the results of the experiment indicated that the group using the diagram learned the parts of a flower more accurately and easily. They also were able to generalize their knowledge to real flowers better than the first group. For the group using the diagram there were no other stimuli to interfere with attention to the crucial features of the flowers which had to be learned.

Some educators will argue that simplifying the examples of concepts deprives the student of contact with the richness and variety of the phenomena being studied. The issue here is not whether the child is deprived of richness and meaning, but at what point in the learning sequence the child should be exposed to all the shadings and meanings that may be associated with a concept. The experimental evidence suggests that in the *initial* phases of concept learning, simplicity and clarity in the examples used will facilitate the learning of the concept. Once the differentiating characteristics of the concept have been grasped adequately, variety in meaning and association may be introduced. The child who has some concept of what a harbor is has already enriched his knowledge, and is able to cope with the complexities of a "real" harbor. He can develop a wealth of associations and interpretations, and can interpret his environment much more easily and efficiently if he has had a systematic understanding of the characteristics essential to the concepts.

The issue is not between learning from textbooks and learning from "real life experiences." We do not know as yet what experiences are most likely to facilitate learning of many concepts. The teacher will

---

[17]G. W. Boguslavsky, "Psychological Research in Soviet Education," *Science*, 125 (1957), 915-918.

undoubtedly use a variety of experiences, but the whole experience must be simplified so that the essential characteristics of a concept can be determined easily by the child.

REALISTIC EXPERIENCES AND CONCEPT ACQUISITION. *Initial* learning of concepts in "real life" situations may complicate learning because of the threatening nature of some real life situations. Marks and Ramond[18] performed an experiment in which concepts were evoked in two different situations, described as "real life" and "textbook." The subjects in the experiment were to form a complex size-position concept from a series of stimuli presented on cards. In the "real life" situation, the subject performed the task with the cards by himself. In the "textbook" situation, the experimental subject was asked to help a person described to him as performing the task in a real life situation. The concept formation task was essentially the same for both groups, except that the subjects in the "real life" situation actually performed the task themselves by manipulating the cards. The "textbook" group produced significantly more correct solutions at a significantly higher rate than did the "real life" group. Marks and Ramond suggest that the "real life" situation may inhibit the subjects. The "real life" situation may be so complex that it is threatening to the subject; consequently, it may inhibit him in making analyses so that he does not adequately form the concept.

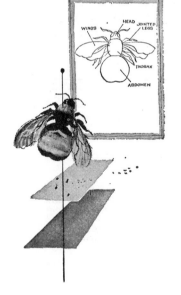

The educational implication from these data is cautionary rather than prescriptive. The data do not suggest that we should not expose students to "real life" situations. The appropriate conclusion is that complex learning environments may be so threatening that they inhibit concept acquisition. Some preparatory introduction to the nature of the concept should familiarize the student with the situation so that the inhibiting effects of some real life situations might be reduced.

Lifelike experiences have other advan-

---

[18]M. R. Marks and C. Ramond, "A New Technique for Observing Concept Evocation," *Journal of Experimental Psychology*, 42 (1951), 424-29.

tages that should not be overlooked. A visit to a harbor may be more motivating, and stimulate greater interest in the concepts to be learned, than would merely pictorial or graphic representations of harbors. The teacher can weigh the advantages to be gained, in motivation and interest, against those to be gained by simplicity and clarity of presentation of a concept. Here, again, the teacher operates as a hypothesis-maker. Rather than utilize one kind or set of experiences, he can manipulate the experiences of the students so that the advantages of the various kinds of experiences may be maximized in the total learning. One set of experiences may produce motivation and interest, while another set of experiences may facilitate accuracy and ease in learning. A judicious combination and integration of experiences will produce the greatest amount of learning.

SIMPLE AND COMPLEX CONCEPTS. School practice typically builds from simpler to more complex concepts. The definition of a harbor given to the third grade class presupposed that the third graders had already learned the meaning of such concepts as "sheltered," "body of water," and "piers." The concept "harbor" is a complex concept which can be understood only by understanding the concepts used to define "harbor." Assume that third graders did not know what is meant by the concepts "sheltered," "body of water," and piers." Could they have learned the concept of harbor as easily or as quickly as a group that had adequate meanings for these other concepts? Common sense suggests that understanding more complex concepts could not be achieved without first understanding the concepts used to define the complex concepts.

Experimental evidence partially corroborates this common-sense notion. Kendler and Vineberg[19] used three groups of college students to study the acquisition of a complex concept. The first group learned both of the simple concepts which made up the complex concept that was to be learned. The second group learned one of the simple concepts, and the third group learned neither. Then all three groups were tested on their ability to learn the complex concept. The group that had learned the two elements of the compound concept learned the compound concept fastest, the group that had learned one element was next in speed, and the group that had learned neither of the simple concepts was the slowest. This experiment demonstrates

---

[19] H. Kendler and R. Vineberg, "The Acquisition of Compound Concepts as a Function of Previous Training," *Journal of Experimental Psychology*, 48 (1954), 252-58.

that the compound concept can be learned, even though the elementary concepts have not been previously learned, but the learning process is less efficient. The greater time spent in learning a compound concept—without previous experience with the concepts composing the compound concept—does not result in greater accuracy of learning.

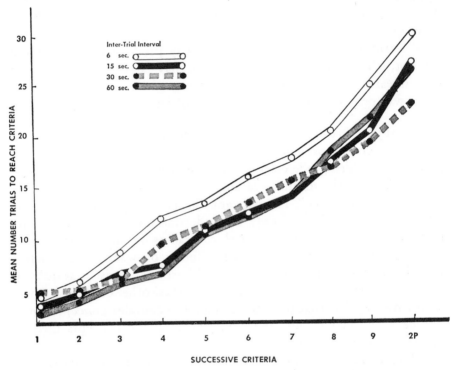

Trials-to-learning curves for the four conditions.
(From Oseas and Underwood)

FIGURE 10

PRACTICE AND CONCEPT ACQUISITION. Quite frequently, in learning situations, concepts are not introduced one at a time, but many concepts are introduced more or less simultaneously. The sixth grade class that heard the talk on India was exposed to a large number of concepts. We would expect that the newer concepts would not be easily assimilated without additional learning experiences.

In learning concepts, would the learning be better promoted by working intensively on the acquisition of the concepts, or by spreading the learning out over a period of time? Oseas and Underwood[20] tested the effects of *massed* (that is, concentrated) practice versus *distributed* practice on learning concepts. Distributed practice produced faster learning than did massed practice, although retention of the concept was high under both sets of conditions (see Figure 10). In later discussions on the effects of practice, the student will note that this conclusion is appropriate for practice in other kinds of learning.

The experimental data suggest that concept formation will be facilitated by repeated study of a concept over periods of time. Concepts will be learned accurately and easily if they are repeatedly used as new learning is taken up. Too frequently the concepts taught are treated as discrete units which may never be used again. Repeated use of concepts enhances learning.

One way to insure repeated use of concepts is to organize the curriculum around basic concepts. A proposal for organizing the social studies curriculum[21] divides human social activities into eight categories (see Figure 11). Each of these categories is a complex concept for interpreting social activity. These categories are used throughout the social studies program as particular societies are studied. For example: the first grade child studies the family; the second grade child, the school; the third grade child, the community. They also analyze the activities of these various communities in terms of the basic concepts. As these concepts are used again and again, concept learning is strengthened. Also, new meanings and associations are developed for the concepts.

Such a curriculum arrangement incorporates a number of principles discussed above. The child learns the concept from his present experiences; the experiences are progressively more complex, but built on previous learning; the concepts are not mere memorized abstractions, but rather are ways of interpreting the environment.[22]

REINFORCEMENT AND CONCEPT ACQUISITION. Reinforcement has a significant effect upon the learning of concepts. In an experi-

---

[20]L. Oseas and B. J. Underwood, "Studies of Distributive Practice: V. Learning and Retention of Concepts," *Journal of Experimental Psychology*, 43 (1952), 143-48.

[21]P. R. Hanna, "Society—Child—Curriculum," in C. W. Hunnicutt (ed.), *Education 2000 AD*, Syracuse, New York, Syracuse University Press, 1956.

[22]A comparable proposal has been made for reorganizing the science curriculum; see *General Report of the Physical Science Study Committee*, Massachusetts Institute of Technology, 1957.

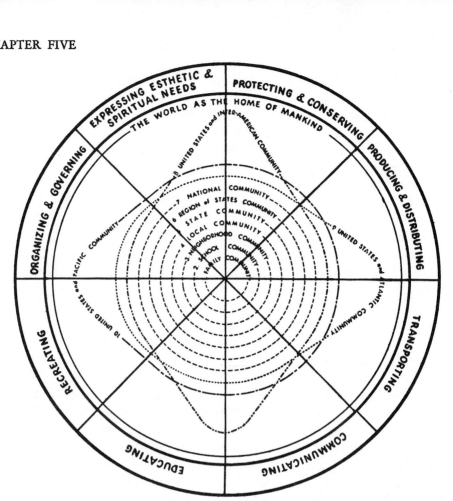

A social studies curriculum design. (From Hanna)

FIGURE 11

mental situation, a <u>reinforcement is an operation, arranged by the</u>
<u>experimenter, that "rewards" a correct response.</u> The experimenter,
for instance, might reward a response by saying "that's right."

Carpenter[23] studied the effects of reinforcement on the learning
of concepts. He formed four groups of students and had them learn
a set of concepts, using simple materials. The reinforcement used in
this experiment was the experimenter's statements, "That's right"
or "That's wrong." In the first group, the experimenter reinforced a
correct response, that is, a correct identification of an example of the

---

[23]F. Carpenter, "Conceptualization as a Function of Differential Reinforcement," *Science Education*, 38 (1954), 284-94.

concept, every fourth time. In the second group, every other correct choice was reinforced; in the third group, every correct choice was reinforced; in the fourth group, every correct choice was reinforced and every incorrect choice was reinforced by the experimenter saying "that's wrong." Table V shows the percentage of trials reinforced for each of the four groups.

Group	No. Ss	Percent of correct trials reinforced	Percent of incorrect trials reinforced
I	23	25	
II	23	50	
III	23	100	
IV	23	100	100

(From Carpenter)

TABLE V

What is the effect of reinforcement on the learning of concepts? Does the fourth group, which is being told which responses are correct and incorrect, learn more quickly and easily than does the first group whose correct responses are being reinforced much less frequently? The results of this experiment indicated that the group that was most frequently reinforced was also the group which learned the concept in the fewest number of trials and in the shortest amount of time. These results are shown graphically in Figures 12 and 13.

The foregoing experiment indicates the importance of reinforcement for the learning of concepts. The student should not conclude that for the learning of every concept complete positive and negative reinforcement must be given for every correct and incorrect use of the concept. We do not know what schedules of reinforcement will produce the most efficient learning for any and every kind of concept. However, the experimental data do suggest that frequent reinforcement is an important factor in the learning of concepts. Carpenter concluded:

This study suggests together with what is already known that the teacher may find profit in: (1) Being certain that the desired response is performed before assuming that learning has occurred. (Far too often teachers seem to operate on the assumption of osmosis and that this absorption of knowl-

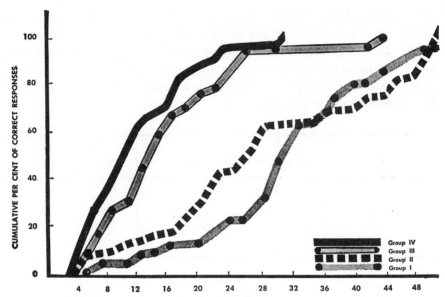

Cumulative per cent of subjects reaching criterion by groups as a function of the number of trials. (From Carpenter)

FIGURE 12

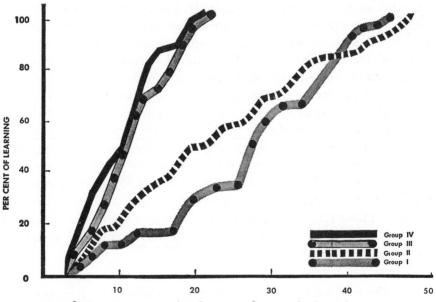

Cumulative per cent of subjects who reached criterion as a function of time in minutes. (From Carpenter)

FIGURE 13

edge will guarantee sufficient transfer to the level of application.) (2) Noting the various responses that compose a skill, act, or complex behavior, and making sure that ample reinforcement is contiguous with them instead of rewarding only end results. This suggests that *we focus attention upon the behavioral processes instead of only products.* [Italics added.][24]

VERBALIZATION AND CONCEPT ACQUISITION. Carpenter's experiment also provided evidence on another important aspect of conceptual learning. We frequently assume that, unless a child can verbalize a concept, the concept has not been acquired. In Carpenter's experiment, even though 72 of his subjects were able to operate with the materials in a manner indicating that they had learned the concepts, only 18 per cent of these were able to verbalize the defining characteristics of the concepts. Other experimenters have observed the same phenomenon.[25]

The assumption that the child does not understand unless he can verbalize is consistent with the emphasis placed upon the defining and memorizing of definitions that characterize much school learning. As experimental evidence indicates, however, and as common-sense observations of children suggest, a child is capable of responding to his environment conceptually without being able to define in verbal symbols the characteristics of the discriminations that he is making. An important psychological and educational problem is to explain why subjects who apparently have mastered the concept cannot define it. Carpenter suggests an explanation:

> . . . that the non-verbal learning required establishment of different responses than the verbal learning and that it is not necessary to expect 100% transfer from one to the other. Also, there was no systematic reinforcement of verbalization during learning. But it is quite possible that Ss verbalized implicitly such that reinforcement was "sometimes" associated with the correct responses. Since S was told to seek for the identifying characteristics of each class, it may have been that much implicit verbalization accompanied the overt movements.[26]

In the less artificial atmosphere of the classroom, the teacher who expects the child both to acquire the concept and to be able to define the characteristics of the concept must teach for both kinds of re-

---

[24]*Ibid.,* p. 293.
[25]Hull, *op. cit.,* Smoke, *op. cit.*
[26]Carpenter, *op. cit.,* p. 292.

sponses. Reinforcement also will be beneficial in the learning of the verbalization.

SUMMARY. If concept formation is to be facilitated, students will need a variety of examples of the concept. Accentuation of the important defining characteristics of the concept, simplification of the stimulus, focusing the student's attention on the important features, preparation by training on basic concepts, and reinforcement of correct responses made in learning concepts tend to enhance the learning of concepts. The process, as well as the end result of learning concepts, is important. Reinforcement should not be postponed until the concept can be correctly defined, or even correctly used, but should be applied throughout the learning process to facilitate learning. Errors in concept formation are opportunities for learning, rather than mistakes to be dismissed or merely punished. An error in the process of acquiring a concept is an opportunity for revising the student's understanding of the characteristics of the concept.

In the process of concept formation, the child is performing as a hypothesis-maker. The child formulates hypotheses about what he thinks the concept is. He then tests these by applying the concept correctly or incorrectly to examples and non-examples of it. Concept formation is an active process on the part of the learner. Concepts are much more efficiently acquired when the child is active (that is, formulating hypotheses about the nature of the concept and testing them) than if he acts merely as a passive recipient of stimuli.[27]

CONCEPTS AND PERSONALITY

In the first part of this chapter we pointed out that the cognitive processes are an important aspect of personality. Concepts are not learned in isolation; they are not discrete entities attached to the personality of the child. Each concept learned by the child becomes for the child a way of interpreting his environment, a way of meeting the world, which influences his behavior.

Consider the concepts that are used in classifying people. An individual who has two classifications for the people whom he meets —friends and enemies—has an extremely narrow and rigid conceptual

---

[27] G. M. Della Piana, "Searching Orientation and Concept Learning," *Journal of Educational Psychology*, 48 (1957), 245-253.

scheme for interpreting the behavior of other people. The fact that this kind of an individual classifies people into only two categories necessarily limits the kinds of relationships that he is likely to have with people.

DEFINITION OF A STEREOTYPE. In one sense concepts are "pictures in our heads"; they are impressions, visualizations, representations of phenomena that actually have been observed or about which we know something even though we have not actually observed the person, the place, or the event which we have conceptualized.

Concepts of people, places, or events, which have not been formed on the basis of adequate experience with events, are called *stereotypes.* A stereotype is a "fixed impression, which . . . results from our defining first and observing second."[28] Stereotyping occurs when there is "a tendency to attribute generalized and simplified characteristics to a group of people in the form of a verbal label."[29] An individual cannot observe every phenomenon about which he has some concept. Frequently, he must rely on sources of information which may be unreliable or inadequate. A child may have a concept of Negroes, Jews, Russians, Germans, or Turks without ever having seen individuals who belong to these racial, ethnic, and national groups. What associations occur to you when you hear the words "hillbilly," "foreigner," "hick," "dude"? Many of these stereotypes arouse strong emotional feelings. Stereotypes are developed because the individual does not think critically, does not observe, does not analyze.

> There seems to be a real difference between analytical, differentiated, and directed thinking or reasoning on the one hand, and the autistic, emotional, uncritical, memory and recognition thinking of stereotyping on the other. In stereotyping it almost seems as though the individual either judges not at all, or does so only via well-worn, dependable, swiftly traversable channels which require a bare minimum of defining, distinguishing, inducing, weighing of evidence, or any of the so-called higher mental processes.[30]

CONCEPTS AND STEREOTYPES. An important aspect of stereotyping is the character of the concepts embedded in the stereotype. Table

---

[28]D. Katz and K. W. Braly, "Racial Stereotypes of One Hundred College Students," *Journal of Abnormal and Social Psychology,* 28 (1933), 287.

[29]W. E. Vinacke, "Explorations in the Dynamic Processes of Stereotyping," *Journal of Social Psychology,* 43 (1956), 105.

[30]J. Fishman, "An Examination of the Process and Function of Social Stereotyping," *Journal of Social Psychology,* 43 (1956), 34-35.

Traits checked, rank order	No.	Per cent	Traits checked, rank order	No.	Per cent
GERMANS			**NEGROES**		
Industrious	65	65	Superstitious	84	84
Stolid	44	44	Lazy	75	75
Intelligent	32	32	Happy-go-lucky	38	38
Scientifically-minded	78	78	Ignorant	38	38
Methodical	31	31	Musical	26	26
Extremely nationalistic	24	24	Ostentatious	26	26
Progressive	16	16	Very religious	24	24
Efficient	16	16	Stupid	22	22
Jovial	15	15	Physically dirty	17	17
Musical	13	13	Naive	14	14
Persistent	11	11	Slovenly	13	13
Practical	11	11	Unreliable	12	12
ITALIANS			**IRISH**		
Artistic	53	53	Pugnacious	45	45
Impulsive	44	44	Quick-tempered	39	39
Passionate	37	37	Witty	38	38
Quick-tempered	35	35	Honest	32	32
Musical	32	32	Very religious	29	29
Imaginative	30	30	Industrious	21	21
Very religious	21	21	Extremely nationalistic	21	21
Talkative	21	21	Superstitious	18	18
Revengeful	17	17	Quarrelsome	14	14
Physically dirty	13	13	Imaginative	13	13
Lazy	12	12	Aggressive	13	13
Unreliable	11	11	Stubborn	13	13
ENGLISH			**CHINESE**		
Sportsmanlike	53	53	Superstitious	34	35
Intelligent	46	46	Sly	29	30
Conventional	34	34	Conservative	29	30
Tradition-loving	31	31	Tradition-loving	26	27
Conservative	30	30	Loyal to family ties	22	23
Reserved	29	29	Industrious	18	19
Sophisticated	27	27	Meditative	18	19
Courteous	21	21	Reserved	17	17
Honest	20	20	Very religious	15	15
Industrious	18	18	Ignorant	15	15
Extremely nationalistic	18	18	Deceitful	14	14
Humorless	17	17	Quiet	13	13
JEWS			**JAPANESE**		
Shrewd	79	79	Intelligent	45	48
Mercenary	49	49	Industrious	43	46
Industrious	48	48	Progressive	24	25
Grasping	34	34	Shrewd	22	23
Intelligent	29	29	Sly	20	21
Ambitious	21	21	Quiet	19	20
Sly	20	20	Imitative	17	18
Loyal to family ties	15	15	Alert	16	17
Persistent	13	13	Suave	16	17
Talkative	13	13	Neat	16	17
Aggressive	12	12	Treacherous	13	14
Very religious	12	12	Aggressive	13	14
AMERICANS			**TURKS**		
Industrious	48	48	Cruel	47	54
Intelligent	47	47	Very religious	26	30
Materialistic	33	33	Treacherous	21	24
Ambitious	33	33	Sensual	20	23
Progressive	27	27	Ignorant	15	17
Pleasure-loving	26	26	Physically dirty	15	17
Alert	23	23	Deceitful	13	15
Efficient	21	21	Sly	12	14
Aggressive	20	20	Quarrelsome	12	14
Straightforward	19	19	Revengeful	12	14
Practical	19	19	Conservative	12	14
Sportsmanlike	19	19	Superstitious	11	13

The Twelve Traits Most Frequently Assigned to Each of Various Racial and National Groups by 100 Princeton Students (From Katz and Braly)
TABLE VI

VI indicates descriptions of national groups according to traits attributed to these groups by college students. Certainly not all the individuals in each of these national groups has each of the characteristics listed by the students in the study. Not all Negroes are superstitious and lazy, nor are all Chinese superstitious and sly, nor are all Englishmen sportsmanlike and intelligent. Most of the traits attributed to these national and racial groups reflect a vague, undifferentiated, socially shared picture of each of these groups. The concepts involved in these pictures are obviously inadequate and overgeneralized.

In this study there was a close relationship between preference for association with these groups and the desirability of the traits attributed to them. Our preferences for association with people or groups of people, our prejudices, and our feelings about people and events, are strongly involved in our concepts of them. A child who has had no experience with members of other ethnic or national groups but who has a picture of them which is unfavorable, will probably also have prejudiced feelings and unpleasant emotional reactions to these people.[31]

Stereotypes represent inadequate conceptualizations, and one of the responsibilities of the educational system is to develop adequate concepts of people, places, and events. The process of changing an individual's prejudices toward a particular group is not simply an intellectual process. Many children's concepts of people and events have developed in a haphazard manner. Other people's ideas and concepts have been accepted uncritically, and the child has had limited opportunity to be exposed to the necessary observation and information to develop adequate concepts.[32] The school serves an important social function by providing children with the experiences necessary to revise their concepts about other racial and national groups, and about individuals, places, and events with which they have had limited, if any, experience.

The conceptual system of the child is one of his interpretative processes, as we have noted continually throughout this chapter. The school's responsibility is to develop this conceptual system, to enlarge it, refine it. By encouraging careful discriminations and generaliza-

---

[31]M. Radke and J. Sutherland, "Children's Concepts and Attitudes about Minority and Majority American Groups," *Journal of Educational Psychology*, 40 (1949), 449-68.
[32]E. L. Horowitz, "The Development of Attitude toward the Negro," *Archives of Psychology*, No. 194, 1936.

tions, and by providing the experience necessary for the development of a concept, the school, through its teachers, encourages the development of a conceptual scheme which will enable the child to interpret his environment adequately and make the necessary behavioral adjustments to it.

SUMMARY

In this chapter the following concepts and principles have been considered:

1. The cognitive processes have been defined as processes by which the person interprets his environment. We have noted that one of the major functions of the school is to communicate certain kinds of concepts to children. The development of personality is influenced by the kinds of concepts that children acquire.

2. The process of forming a concept requires a discrimination of the appropriate characteristics of the concept, and a generalization of the characteristics to many examples of the concept. A concept is a classification or a systematic organization of stimuli, characteristics, or events that have common characteristics.

3. The process of concept formation requires that the learner have extensive experience with the phenomena to be conceptualized. This experience may be either direct sensory experience of the phenomena or indirect mediated experience. One of the functions of the teacher is to determine the most appropriate kinds of experiences to teach particular concepts. The character of children's concepts is influenced by the kinds of experiences they have.

4. In organizing learning experiences to teach concepts, the teacher will use examples and non-examples of the concept. An example is an instance of the concept that contains all of the characteristics of the concept. A non-example is some phenomenon which contains either none or only some of the characteristics of the concept.

5. Little is known at the present time about the sequence of examples and non-examples that may facilitate the learning of many different kinds of concepts. In general, examples, rather than non-examples, probably should be used in the early phases of learning a concept. Non-examples are most useful for checking the accuracy of a student's knowledge of the characteristics of a concept.

6. Concepts are learned more efficiently when the essential characteristics of a concept are emphasized in the examples from which a child learns the characteristics of the concept.

7. The learning of simple concepts facilitates the learning of more complex concepts; however, this facilitation is mainly in terms of speed of learning, rather than in accuracy of learning.

8. Distributed practice during concept learning produces faster concept acquisition than does massed practice. Both kinds of practice seem to be equally efficient in strengthening retention of the concept.

9. The learning of a concept and the ability to verbalize the characteristics of a concept are not necessarily correlative. A child may acquire a concept without being able to verbalize the nature of the concept. Learning experiences which reinforce the acquisition of the verbalization response, as well as the acquisition of the concept, must be organized.

We discussed one comprehensive kind of concept, namely, the stereotype. Stereotypes are fixed and uncritical impressions of events, places, or people. Stereotypes are frequently formed without adequate information and represent inadequate conceptualizations, frequently clothed in prejudiced feelings and negative emotional reactions.

Throughout this chapter we have emphasized the importance of concept formation in the development of personality. By means of concepts, the child interprets the world around him. The kinds of interpretations that he makes depend upon the kinds of concepts that he has acquired. Since these concepts will influence his behavior, the kind of personality he is will depend in part upon the kinds of concepts that he has developed. One of the responsibilities of the school is to teach certain kinds of concepts, particularly those related to the structure of knowledge that the school is attempting to communicate. We have also stressed the difference between memorization of the characteristics of a concept and the acquisition of a concept as such. The principles outlined in this chapter describe learning processes designed to facilitate the acquisition of concepts.

STUDY AND DISCUSSION QUESTIONS

1. List the major concepts in some course or subject you are likely to teach. Describe the defining characteristics of these concepts. What kinds of examples of these concepts would you use?

2. Analyze this list and the accompanying descriptions to determine to what extent the learning of any one concept is likely to facilitate the learning of other concepts. Explain in what way the learning of one of these concepts is likely to facilitate the learning of another concept. What hypotheses about concept formation are implicit in your stated relations?

3. Teachers frequently encourage learning of the concepts associated with cooperative behavior. How would you define "cooperation"? What kinds of experiences are likely to facilitate learning the discriminations and generalizations required to learn this concept? How would you determine that a child had acquired the concept of cooperation? If a child is cooperative, may you assume that he has learned the concept? Would you make a distinction between "being cooperative" and understanding the concept of cooperation?

4. Suggest some kinds of experiences from which children might infer the characteristics of the following concepts. What features of the stimulus events that you describe will have to be ignored? Do not recommend such undefined kinds of experiences as "take a field trip." Be specific about the character of the experience.

   a. Equal rights.

   b. Sportsmanship.

   c. "Hard work."

5. Describe some kinds of experiences that might have influenced a child's idea of these concepts. In what way might these previous associations interfere with or facilitate the learning of these concepts?

6. List some negative examples of the above concepts. What information is a child likely to acquire by learning that these are negative examples of the concepts?

7. Suggest some negative examples of the following concepts. Describe some ways in which they may be used to facilitate learning of these concepts:

    a. odd number

    b. circular

    c. flat

    d. into

8. Experimental evidence suggests that some students find concept learning easier with positive examples than with negative examples. What factors in their previous experience might account for this preference?

9. Assume that a child is developing a concept of "fair play." He is exposed, in the course of events, to quite a few negative instances of the concept, but fewer positive instances. How might these experiences influence the learning of other concepts in addition to that of "fair play"?

10. What kinds of experiences may have influenced a child to see members of some national or racial group as "sly," "superstitious," and "dirty"?

11. Under what conditions is information which contradicts a person's stereotypical thinking likely to influence a change in his thinking?

12. Is there a stereotype of the teacher? What factors might influence acquisition of such a stereotype by students?

RECOMMENDED READINGS

    The first of the readings is a general discussion of basic principles related to concept formation with particular application to the school situation. The second reading reviews theory and research on concept formation in children. The third reading is a critical review of experimentation in concept formation and a summary of present thinking on this process.

1. W. A. Brownell and G. Hendrickson, "How Children Learn Information, Concepts, and Generalizations," *Forty-ninth Yearbook of the National Society for the Study of Education, Part I, Learning and Instruction,* Chicago, University of Chicago Press, 1950, pp. 92-128.

2. D. H. Russell, *Children's Thinking,* Boston, Ginn & Co., 1956, Chapters 5 and 8.

3. R. Leeper, "Cognitive Processes," in S. S. Stevens (ed.), *Handbook of Experimental Psychology,* New York, John Wiley & Sons, 1951, Chapter 19.

CHAPTER SIX

LEARNING AND THE
COGNITIVE PROCESSES—II

In Chapter Five we discussed concept formation as one kind of cognitive process. We assume that concept formation is an essential ingredient in the development of cognitive processes. However, concepts are not discrete units stored in a child's head in some kind of mental filing system. Concepts are used to facilitate the kinds of cognitive processes that we will describe in this chapter. Some of the other processes are reasoning, critical thinking, the acquisition and use of genereralizations or principles, and associative kinds of thinking.

These processes, like concept formation, enable a person to interpret his environment. A child who has learned that the evaporation of a liquid increases directly with the temperature of the liquid has acquired a principle he can use to understand such diverse phenomena as the drop in level of boiling water and the drying of creek beds in summertime. Such simple associations as "a red light means stop" prepare him to cross streets on his own. Here we will again be concerned with the variables in learning environments which influence the development of these cognitive processes.

THE ACQUISITION OF GENERALIZATIONS

Children are continually acquiring generalizations by making inferences from their experiences. A child who is warned repeatedly "not to speak out in class" may formulate the principle that "speaking out in class will be punished." He may, however, formulate another principle: "expressing one's thoughts or feelings is undesirable." Irrespective of the appropriateness of either of these generalizations, the child has carried out essentially the same process in arriving at each of them. He has observed a number of events, he has conceptualized or categorized them, and he has related these sets of events to each other. The first principle states a relationship between a concept called "speaking out" and another concept called "being punished." The second principle is of the same general character.

DEFINITION OF A GENERALIZATION. *A generalization is a statement of relationship between two or more concepts.* The statement that "particles with charges of opposite sign attract each other" states a relationship between charged particles of opposite sign. Another example is the well-known generalization: "the force of attraction between two bodies is directly proportional to the product of their masses and inversely proportional to the square of the distance between them." Three concepts—force, mass, and distance—are utilized in this generalization, and the relationship between them is a functional one stated in terms of proportionality.

A generalization is meant to be applied to more than a single event. The concepts included in the generalization refer to categories, and the statement of relationship between these categories is meant to be a relationship that applies to all particular instances of the concepts. For example, the generalization that the volume of a gas varies directly with the temperature of the gas applies to all particular instances of volume changes and temperature changes and to any gaseous substance. The child who has inferred that "good boys get good marks" will apply this generalization to different examples of "good boys" and many kinds of "good marks."

LEVELS OF UNDERSTANDING GENERALIZATIONS. A generalization can be learned simply by memorizing it. A student can memorize that "democracy flourishes when a free press is maintained." Many generalizations are learned in this way. The psychological process involved in acquiring principles at this level is essentially that of remembering. However, we wish to emphasize *the distinction between remembering a statement of a principle and understanding the principle*. The student's ability to repeat a generalization is not an adequate measure of his understanding of the generalization.

When understood, a principle can be applied in many instances. For example, the child who has learned that the volume and the temperature of a gas vary directly understands this generalization when he can use it to explain the increase in pressure in a tire on an automobile that has been driven for several hours. Similarly, a student understands principles about the relationships between wages and prices when he can explain the phenomenon of inflation by using these principles. The generalization that "democracy flourishes when a free press is maintained" is meaningless unless the student can use this principle to explain the relationship between the rise of a dictatorship and suppression of a free press. The important psychological question for the teacher is—"How can learning experiences be organized to facilitate the acquisition of generalizations at this level of understanding?"

ACQUIRING GENERALIZATIONS BY DEDUCTION AND INDUCTION. When a child learns a generalization, he organizes his experience into patterns which enable him "to make sense" of this experience. In our earlier example involving Jane, we noted that she had learned a generalization about feature articles, namely, that articles about the experiences of interesting people are likely to attract attention. Jane may have learned this generalization simply by taking her teacher's word for this statement, or she may have learned this generalization by observing the reactions of people to articles of this kind. In either case, Jane did begin to organize the events that she had perceived into meaningful relationships.

Generalizations can be developed in two ways: (1) by deductions from other generalizations; (2) by induction from observations. The kind of reasoning used in geometry is a good example of the first process. Using such generalizations or assumptions as "things equal to the same thing are equal to each other," other generalizations, such as "equal central angles subtend equal arcs on the circumference of a circle," can be developed. The cognitive process used in such derivations is that of logical reasoning, in which a person begins with a generalization and by logical reasoning arrives at other conclusions, which are themselves generalizations.

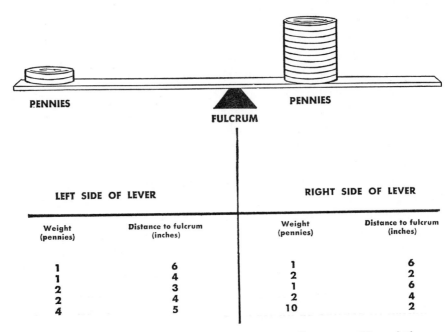

Weight (pennies)	Distance to fulcrum (inches)	Weight (pennies)	Distance to fulcrum (inches)
1	6	1	6
1	4	2	2
2	3	1	6
2	4	2	4
4	5	10	2

From the specific measurements, can you generalize a quantitive relationship which is true for any condition?

Can you check the generalization with another example and observation? What degree of confidence do you have in making predictions from your generalization?

FIGURE 14

In the induction process a person begins with a set of observations and, on the basis of the observations, develops a generalization which appears either to explain or to predict the pattern of relationships that he has observed. Suppose that a teacher wants the children to learn the principles of the lever. The following simple procedure could be used: He could begin by placing a board on a fulcrum; then he could place objects of different weight on each side of the fulcrum and balance the board by moving the objects to or away from the fulcrum until the board balances (see Figure 14). Such a demonstration could be carried out easily with pennies as weights, since the weight on each side of the fulcrum could be manipulated by adding or subtracting pennies. The teacher could have the children record the weight of pennies used on each side and the distance of the stack of pennies from the fulcrum (see Figure 14). The child now has a set of observations from which it is possible to infer a general principle about levers. The child might note that the lever balances when the heavier stack of pennies is moved closer to the fulcrum. The teacher now may develop the idea that the products of each weight times its distance from the fulcrum are equal. He could point out, for example, that "one times four equals two times two," using the data from the second observation.

As another example, assume that a teacher wishes to have students learn the generalization "adjectives modify nouns." Notice that this statement is definitional in character, describing what is meant by an "adjective." This definition may be used as a generalization or principle, and the learning of this definition can be thought of either as a process of concept formation or the learning of a generalization. If the teacher presents a series of examples of words modifying nouns and then asks the children to *infer* the definition of an adjective, the children will be encouraged to use inductive processes to arrive at this definition. On the other hand, the teacher could define what is meant by an adjective, and then have children identify examples of adjectives. The second procedure encourages children to use deduction to develop an understanding of the principle. The method of stating definitions or generalizations and then requiring students to find examples or to check examples and non-examples of the generalizations is a fairly common teaching method. An important psychological question is, "Which of these two processes, induction or deduction, is likely to develop a clearer understanding of the generalization?"

In an early study, Winch compared learning under conditions that encouraged inductive thinking and under conditions that encouraged deductive thinking.[1] The study did not demonstrate the general superiority of either method. Children taught by the deductive method did better when they were tested on the kinds of materials that they had used in learning the generalization by the deductive process. However, the inductive method proved superior when children were tested on new but related materials. When children had learned a generalization by induction, they were able to use the generalization to interpret new material.

RELATIVE EFFECTIVENESS OF INDUCTIVE AND DEDUCTIVE PROCESSES. The effects of using deductive or inductive processes in learning

---

[1] W. H. Winch, *Inductive versus Deductive Methods of Teaching: An Experimental Research,* Baltimore, Warwick and York, 1913.

generalizations have not been adequately explored. A related problem that has been explored is the relationship between "rote learning" and "meaningful learning." Brownell and Moser compared learning by meaningful versus learning by mechanical procedures in a study of subtraction.[2] Brownell and Moser were interested in comparing the effectiveness of two methods of subtracting: the decomposition and equal additions methods. Both methods were taught in two different ways to forty-one experimental classes. Some students were taught to use the methods mechanically. Other students were taught "meaningfully"; subtraction was explained to them and they learned *why* the method led to correct results. We are not interested here in the superiority of either of the subtraction methods for learning subtraction procedures, but in the effects of the meaningful and mechanical learning. On tests of accuracy given at the end of the learning experience, as well as six weeks later, groups that had learned by the "meaningful method" were superior in subtraction processes to groups that had learned by the mechanical method.

However, one interesting conclusion from this study illustrates that the differences in performance cannot be explained solely in terms of meaningful versus mechanical learning. The students had learned the two methods, subtracting by decomposition or by equal additions, using two digit numbers. They also were given a test which required them to subtract three digit numbers. Those who had learned by the decomposition method were superior in applying their knowledge in this new task, for which they had not been specifically trained. In other words, although methods which emphasize understanding generally produce better results, some methods or approaches to content are more comprehensible than others. Processes which are taught meaningfully so that students are likely to understand them contribute to the development of superior performances. While research evidence generally supports the hypothesis that teaching "for meaning" is superior to teaching by rote methods, the teacher should distinguish between a process which may be explained by the teacher and a process which, when explained, is likely to be understood by students.[3] A process is meaningful to the degree that students' understanding of the process is increased.

---

[2] W. A. Brownell and A. G. Moser, "Meaningful versus Mechanical Learning: A Study in Grade Three Subtraction," *Duke University Research Studies in Education*, No. 8, 1949.

[3] See, also, C. L. Thiele, "The Contribution of Generalization to the Learning of the Addition Facts," *Teachers College Contributions to Education*, No. 763, New York, Columbia University Press, 1939.

The sense in which we have been using the term "deductive learning" is not meant to include rote learning. The distinction between the two processes can be made clear by an example. Suppose that a teacher wishes to teach a child the formula for the area of a plane figure, such as the area of a rectangle. He might begin by presenting a series of rectangles of varying sizes. The children could then be asked to measure the areas by breaking up the areas into squares. After the children had carried out this process on a number of rectangles, they would probably be able to formulate the generalization that the length times the height of the rectangle yields the area of the rectangle. In this case, the children would be learning by an inductive process.

The teacher could also introduce the formula for the area of a rectangle and have the children apply this formula to a variety of rectangles. In this case, the children would learn by a deductive process —if the teacher explained why the formula yielded the area of a rectangle and the relevance of the formula to the examples. Deductive learning would also be fostered by having the children work on problems for which the application of the formula was not immediately apparent. On the basis of the Winch experiment, we would predict that children learning by either the inductive or deductive method would understand the generalization, but that the children who learned by inductive processes would be more likely to generalize the rule to other kinds of problems in which it could be used. In any case, we would predict that if the children learned to apply the rule in a rote manner, their performance on these kinds of problems would be somewhat inferior to that of children who had learned by more "meaningful" methods; they would be handicapped in generalizing the rule to new problems.

THE ROLE OF DISCOVERY IN LEARNING GENERALIZATIONS. The deductive and inductive processes can be distinguished in the following way. In the deductive process, the child is given the rule or generalization and must discover for himself many of the instances to which the rule or generalization applies. In the inductive process, the child discovers for himself the generalization as well as the instances to which the rule applies. To what extent do factors fostering discovery of a generalization influence the learning of this generalization and transfer of it to new instances?

Kirsch experimented with the effects of independent discovery as compared to direction in discovery of a generalization;[4] he theorized that the superiority of meaningful learning depended upon the extent to which the learner developed his own generalizations. He reasoned as follows: "If meaningful learning is the key concept, it should make no difference whether learning occurs with or without direction, so long as the learner becomes cognizant of the essential relationships. However, it is very likely that some procedures of learning may be superior to others simply because they are more likely to cause the learner to become cognizant of the relationships."[5]

Kirsch set up three experimental groups. The groups were to work on a series of problems involving arithmetical and geometrical relationships. The first group, called a "no-help" group, was required to discover the rules for working the problems without any assistance from the experimenter. The second group, called the "direct-reference" group, was given some direction in the form of visual aids that would help to clarify the problems and verbal instructions that directed their attention to the visual aids. The members of the third group, called the "rule-given" group, were told the rules directly and were given practice in applying the rules without attempting to understand the arithmetical or geometrical relationships involved in the problems. In this experiment, notice that the first two groups were to learn by inductive processes and were distinguished from each other by the amount of help given for discovering the generalization. The third group was to learn in a mechanical or rote way.

The results of the experiment suggest that the group called the "direct-reference" group, the group which received some direction in discovery, did understand the relationships involved somewhat better than did the other groups. The "no-help" group was, however, superior to the "rule-given" group. The experiment confirms that a procedure which facilitates meaningful learning is superior to rote learning. The results also suggested that transfer of learning to new situations was facilitated by independent discovery.

While these results are consistent with other experimental data, the experiment provides data which clarify the influence of the variables involved in the learning process. Kirsch gathered data on students' motivation for the tasks at hand. After the experiment, the students were asked questions about why they worked problems in certain

---

[4]B. Y. Kirsch, "The Adequacy of 'Meaning' as an Explanation for the Superiority of Learning by Independent Discovery," *Journal of Educational Psychology*, 49 (1958), 282-92.

[5]*Ibid.*, p. 282.

ways, why they were unable to recall rules or generalizations when working on new problems, and how they felt about the learning situation. Kirsch concluded that the students in the "no-help" group appeared to be better motivated to continue working on the problems than were students in the other groups. While all students were motivated by external kinds of reward, such as the approval of the experimenter, the students in the "no-help" group developed an interest in the problems as such. One student in the "no-help" group reported that he was so intrigued with his success in discovering the rules that he told his friends of his experiences and tried out the problems on them. Other students in the "no-help" group went to the library in an effort to find formulas that would be useful in working the problems.

This experiment calls our attention to some of the problems associated with deciding on appropriate processes to facilitate the learning of generalizations. We may hypothesize that learning by independent discovery is likely to facilitate more comprehensive understanding; however, we must realize that not all students in the "no-help" group were able to discover the generalization unaided within the time provided. Two factors may influence the probabilities of students discovering generalizations without help: (1) their general level of intelligence and (2) the amount of time provided for attempts at discovery. In general, learning through inductive processes appears to take longer than learning the applications of a given rule or generalization.

We can say, however, that the processes of independent discovery appear to facilitate increased motivation. The students are likely to become more involved in the task, to work on it for longer periods of time, and to seek out new sources of information to improve their understanding. If these kinds of effects were consistently obtained, the inductive method would have powerful advantages for stimulating student learning. Both the increased motivation and the additional time spent in attempts to acquire the generalization would probably, in the long run, produce superior understanding. We would also hypothesize that students learning generalizations inductively would "learn how to learn." By working independently, students may discover procedures for developing generalizations which are useful in a variety of situations.

We can summarize the above discussion by formulating the following hypotheses: (1) long-term retention and transfer of generalizations to relevant new situations are facilitated by processes which encourage independent discovery of the generalization; (2) immediate acquisition of the generalization can be facilitated by providing procedures that aid discovery, but probably with some loss in long-term retention and ability to transfer the generalization; (3) procedures that facilitate independent discovery are more likely to motivate students to become interested in the learning of the generalization and are likely to encourage students to spend additional time and effort in attempting to discover the generalization; (4) procedures that emphasize understanding, rather than rote learning, are more likely to facilitate the learning of a generalization in a manner in which it can be used in a wide variety of situations. In general, processes that facilitate independent discovery are likely to require more time before students will learn the generalization. Furthermore, this kind of procedure probably is not equally effective for all students. There is some evidence to suggest that students of lower ability are more likely to profit from the direct-rule-giving kind of approach.[6]

In organizing learning experiences, the teacher will need to decide what kinds of behavior changes he wishes to foster. In part, his decision will be influenced by the character of the generalization to be learned, for considerable time could be spent acquiring generalizations of relatively little importance. In other words, the teacher must have a clear conception of the kind of behavior change that he is attempting to foster, and then decide on the learning experience most likely to foster this change.

OTHER FACTORS INFLUENCING THE LEARNING OF GENERALIZA-TIONS. An important factor that appears to influence the ease with which generalizations are acquired is familiarity with materials from which the generalization is formed. *Familiarity* appears to be one of the factors in previous learning that may facilitate new learning. In the previous chapter we pointed out that compound concepts could be learned more quickly if the simple concepts involved in the compound concepts were already known.[7] Recall, however, that students who learned the compound concepts without knowledge of the

---

[6]B. Corman, "The Effect of Varying Amounts and Kinds of Information as Guidance in Problem Solving," *Psychological Monographs*, No. 2, 1957, 1-21.

[7]See Chapter Five, p. 149.

simple concepts eventually learned the concept to the same degree as students who had knowledge of the simpler concepts.

Brownell and Stretch performed an experiment which demonstrates the relevance of the variable of "familiarity."[8] Children were given the same problems in four different forms. In Form A, the problems were written in terms familiar to children. In Form B, relatively less familiar terms were used. In Form C, the terms used were not familiar to children, and Form D employed artificial terms. The children were tested on the problems written in each form. The percentages of problems worked correctly for each of the forms are given below:

Form A	Form B	Form C	Form D
64	58	57	51

While these differences are not large, they were statistically significant and suggest the influence of the variable of familiarity in understanding and using generalizations.

In another kind of experiment, Wilkins presented students with syllogisms in familiar and unfamiliar terms.[9] For example, the same syllogistic form would be presented in the following three ways:

1. No dogs are cats	2. No blits are spuken	3. No X's are Y's
No cats are men	No spuken are lichts	No Y's are Z's
Therefore, no men	Therefore, no lichts	Therefore, no Z's
are dogs.	are blits.	are X's.

Wilkins found that syllogisms written in familiar terms were somewhat easier for college students than were syllogisms written in unfamiliar terms or symbols, as in columns 2 and 3.

USING FAMILIAR MATERIALS IN ORGANIZING LEARNING EXPERIENCES. While the above data support our common-sense notions, we should not overlook the fact that materials may be more familiar to some students than they are to others. Furthermore, some material may be so abstract that the likelihood of a student being familiar with

---

[8] W. A. Brownell and L. B. Stretch, "The Effect of Unfamiliar Settings on Problem Solving," *Duke University Research Studies in Education*, No. 1, 1931.

[9] M. C. Wilkins, "The Effects of Changed Material on Ability to do Formal Syllogistic Reasoning," *Archives of Psychology*, No. 102, 1928.

concepts or events relevant to the generalization is extremely low. Obviously common-sense kinds of empirical referents cannot be found easily for all concepts and generalizations. In discussing the theory of relativity, for example, we may use physical models to clarify the abstract concept. Such models provide an approximation to the ideas in the theory, but a comprehensive understanding of the theory would require a student to acquire the concepts and generalizations in their abstract form.

The recommendation that the materials used should be familiar to students has been made so frequently that we may easily overlook the fact that familiarity is only one of the variables in learning a principle; furthermore, familiarity may inhibit as well as facilitate learning. Teachers may use events in students' lives to aid in the understanding of a historical period. Such a practice would be consistent with the hypothesis that familiar materials will facilitate the learning of a generalization, but if students assumed that Roman family life was not different from American family life, the procedure would produce an undesirable effect. We also noted in the previous chapter that some "familiar materials" may be anxiety-inducing.[10] When familiar materials or problems are anxiety-inducing, learning is inhibited.

When students must learn generalizations for which they have not had relevant previous experiences, we may use what might be called a "pre-induction period" in which we familiarize the students with the materials from which they will formulate generalizations. Many teachers use what they call "exploratory periods" in which the child is allowed to play with or manipulate new materials to familiarize himself with them. For example, a fifth grade teacher introduced a unit on "The Space Age" by placing models of rockets and pictures of the moon and stellar constellations around the room. The children began to ask questions about the materials, and the teacher used these questions to develop concepts and generalizations about space.

Finally, it is well to remember that our conception of what is familiar to a student is, in effect, a hypothesis about the effects of previous learning, and this hypothesis may not be valid. We may overlook materials which are familiar to students, or we may incorrectly assume that they are familiar with the materials available.

From this discussion we may formulate several hypotheses rele-

---

[10]See Chapter Five, p. 148.

vant to organizing learning experiences to aid the acquisition of a generalization. The learning of a generalization is likely to be fostered if the materials from which the generalization is to be learned are familiar to the student. Further, such familiarity is likely to be produced by exposing students to the materials and allowing them to explore and manipulate the materials. There is some evidence to suggest that in such exploratory periods an individual can "learn how to learn"; he may be "practicing" observation of events and the testing of consequences.[11] He learns what is associated with what and what follows from what. However, familiarity with the materials from which a generalization is to be learned may inhibit learning if these materials are anxiety-inducing, or if students erroneously assume that what is to be learned is exactly like something previously learned.[12]

THE DEVELOPMENT OF CRITICAL THINKING

One of the objectives commonly agreed upon for the modern school is the development of ability to think critically. As attractive as such an objective may sound, we must be clear about what we mean by critical thinking, and we must raise the question about whether learning experiences can be organized to foster critical thinking. Pingry has pointed out that studies of critical thinking conducted in schools have used at least five different meanings for the term "critical thinking." According to Pingry, critical thinking has been defined as: (1) collecting data, organizing data, and formulating hypotheses from data; (2) use of correct principles of logic and understanding the nature of proof; (3) criticism of thinking; (4) understanding the psychology of propaganda and advertising techniques; (5) synon-

---

[11]The data to support this hypothesis have been based largely on teachers' observations only. The experimental evidence available is based on infrahuman organisms. See, for example, H. F. Harlow, "The Formation of Learning Sets," *Psychological Review*, 56 (1949), 51-65; "Learning and Satiation of Response in Intrinsically Motivated Complex Puzzle Performance by Monkeys," *Journal of Comparative and Physiological Psychology*, 43 (1950), 289-94; "Analysis of Discrimination Learning by Monkeys," *Journal of Experimental Psychology*, 40 (1950), 26-39. Data from experiments in concept formation may be generalized as further support for this hypothesis. Davidon found that subjects allowed to manipulate materials in a concept formation experiment did better in acquiring the concepts than those who were not permitted to manipulate the materials. See R. S. Davidon, "The Effects of Symbols, Shift, and Manipulation upon the Number of Concepts Attained," *Journal of Experimental Psychology*, 44 (1952), 70-79.

[12]Literature on the familiarity and personal relevance of a problem on efficiency in problem-solving, in one area, is discussed in G. M. Wilson, "Arithmetic," in *Encyclopedia of Educational Research*, W. S. Monroe (ed.), New York, The Macmillan Co., 1950.

ymous with problem-solving.[18] We probably will find that teachers also conceptualize what they mean by critical thinking in these different ways. For our present purposes, it is not necessary to agree that any one of these definitions shall be the sole acceptable definition of critical thinking. The school attempts to foster all of these processes and, for our purposes, we will agree that in the ensuing discussion critical thinking can be defined as any and all of these processes. A discussion of problem-solving is reserved for Chapter Ten; the student should relate principles discussed in that chapter to the development of critical thinking.

THE MEANING OF CRITICAL THINKING. The above statement of different conceptions of critical thinking suggests the elements involved in this kind of process. Critical thinking involves an *attitude* about problems and ideas within one's experience. This attitude has sometimes been called "the attitude of suspended judgment" or "the attitude of systematic doubt." Such an attitude predisposes a person to analyze and evaluate his experience, to question its meaning and significance.

Critical thinking also requires that a person be able to think logically and be able to gather and use data. When an individual has this combination of attitudes and skills and is predisposed to use these skills in a continual process of analysis and evaluation of his experience, we say that he can think critically.

We will find it convenient to conceptualize critical thinking as a process in which a person utilizes the cognitive processes that we have been discussing, such as his concepts and generalizations, his ability to reason, his ability to think inductively in a complex manner and in relationship to the analysis of his own experience.

A student has improved in his ability to think critically when he no longer accepts generalizations merely on the word of the teacher, but systematically analyzes the evidence that purports to support these generalizations. He can think critically when he is willing to ask questions and seek answers to these questions by formulating hypotheses and gathering data to test these hypotheses. He can think critically when he revises his concepts and generalizations on the basis of new data. In each of these processes, an individual is acting in a

---

[18]R. E. Pingry, "Critical Thinking: What is It?" *Mathematics Teacher*, 44 (1951), 466-70.

complex way in which he utilizes the concepts, generalizations, the patterns of thinking, and attitudes and values that he has acquired.

We are not suggesting that the student who can think critically is hostile and aggressive in his attitudes toward his teachers or toward other adults who may know more about some subject than he does. Neither are we suggesting that a person who thinks critically holds no ideas with conviction. Rather, we are describing a process, which we hope to foster, that enables a child to develop rational grounds for his convictions and that eventually will enable him to come to conclusions about his experience without the continual direction and supervision of an adult.

Since critical thinking is not a unitary kind of process, but rather a complex integration of many processes, we would expect that the course of development of this ability would be influenced by a wide variety of factors. The ability to think critically is probably learned gradually over a period of time and, as we will suggest in the following sections, some kinds of experiences are more likely to foster the development of this ability.[14] Critical thinking does not occur in a vacuum; a person thinks critically *about his experience.* We are not surprised to find a range of differences in people's ability to think critically in many different areas of human experience. We are all probably familiar with the specialist who is capable of critical analysis of the theories and data in his field of specialty, but who thinks unintelligently and uncritically about other subjects. An important psychological question is, then, what factors in learning experiences stimulate the development of the ability to think critically?

CONTENT AND PROCESS IN CRITICAL THINKING. A common assumption is that some types of material or subject matter lend themselves to the development of thinking ability. Some people will argue, for example, that plane geometry with its emphasis on careful definition of terms, specification of assumptions, and rigorous deductive logic improves the ability to think critically. The early form of this point of view was called "the theory of formal discipline." This theory held that mind was composed of discrete faculties that could be strengthened by exercise and, the more difficult the material on which a person practiced, the greater would be the strength of a faculty used in the practice.

---

[14]For one conception of the developmental aspects of this process, see J. Piaget, *Judgment and Reasoning in the Child,* New York, Harcourt, Brace & Co., 1928.

An early set of experiments demonstrated that the theory of formal discipline was not tenable in the form in which it was stated.[15] The theory of "identical elements" was developed to explain the results found in these experiments. According to this theory, training or learning in one content area is likely to be beneficial in learning in a new or different content area in the degree to which the two areas share common elements. Another way of stating the idea in this theory is to say that, in any two situations requiring the same set of responses, the learning of responses in one situation will transfer to the new situation in the degree to which the situations are similar.

This theory has had its critics. In many of these early studies,[16] evidence was found that, under certain conditions, what was learned in one situation would carry over or transfer to learning in a new situation. When the *processes* being learned were the central focus in the learning experience, transfer of these processes to new learning situations was increased. On the basis of his experimentation, Judd formulated the principle that training in one situation is likely to be beneficial in a new situation if *processes and principles* learned in the first situation could be used in the new experience.[17] A modern version of this experiment is discussed in Chapter Ten.

Both of these explanations of the phenomenon of transfer are useful for developing hypotheses about the transfer value of concepts and generalizations. A concept or a generalization is learned because of its utility for interpreting a wide variety of situations. In accordance with Judd's theory, we would predict that new learning would be facilitated by previously acquired concepts and generalizations relevant to the new learning experience. However, a child who has learned a concept or generalization is likely to be able to apply it more easily in situations similar to the situations in which the concept or generalization was learned. Additional experience will be required with situations less similar to the original learning situation if the

---

[15]These early experiments are largely of historical interest only; however, they have had considerable influence on theories of education. See E. L. Thorndike and R. S. Woodworth, "The Influence and Improvement in One Mental Function upon the Efficiency of Other Functions," *Psychological Review*, 8 (1901), 247-67, 384-95, 553-64; also, E. L. Thorndike, "The Influence of First Year Latin upon the Ability to Read English," *School and Society*, 17 (1923), 165-68; E. L. Thorndike, "Mental Discipline in High School Studies," *Journal of Educational Psychology*, 15 (1924), 1-22, 83-98.

[16]For instance, A. A. Hamblen, "The Extent to Which the Effect of the Study of Latin Upon a Knowledge of English Derivations Can be Increased" (doctoral dissertation), Philadelphia, University of Pennsylvania, 1925.

[17]C. H. Judd, "The Relation of Special Training to General Intelligence," *Educational Review*, 36 (1908), 28-42.

concept or generalization is to be used in a wide variety of situations. The child who has learned the principle of product moments in connection with the lever will probably have little difficulty applying this principle to the use of the teeter-totter on the playground or in balancing a scale. However, the child may not be able to see the relevance of the principle in the more complex examples of levers found in the human skeleton.

This discussion of the general principles of transfer is relevant to our discussion of critical thinking. We would predict that no particular subject matter, as such, has unique value in the development of critical thinking. If, however, the processes of critical thinking are taught in relationship to subject matter, we would predict that the development of critical thinking would be facilitated. It is probable that learning to think critically with respect to a subject area or problem does not guarantee that a child can think critically with other materials.

An experiment by Ulmer demonstrated that emphasis on the principles of logical reasoning facilitated the development of logical thinking about geometric and non-geometric content when children were taught these principles in connection with the study of geometry.[18] Ulmer used three groups of high school students in his study. One group of students was taught geometry by the traditional methods. The second group was taught geometry through a method that emphasized the principles of logical reasoning and that encouraged critical thinking both on geometrical and non-geometrical problems. The third group served as a control group and was not exposed to either program of training. From tests of syllogistic reasoning and the detailed records that the teacher kept, the evidence indicated that the second group was superior to the other groups in the ability to use principles of reasoning both on geometric and non-geometric materials. This study does not demonstrate that children who have learned the principles of reasoning invariably use them in all situations in their lives. It does illustrate the importance of emphasizing the process of critical thinking and of providing the student with opportunities to use the principles of logical thinking in as many different situations as possible.

While we have noted that studying a subject that is logically

---

[18]G. Ulmer, "Teaching Geometry to Cultivate Reflective Thinking: An Experimental Study with One Thousand Two Hundred and Thirty-Nine High School Pupils," *Journal of Experimental Education*, 8 (1939), 18-25.

organized does not guarantee that a person will learn logical reasoning, some subjects, such as mathematics and science, may lend themselves more easily to procedures designed to develop critical thinking. Nonetheless, even subjects, such as science and mathematics, which are logically organized and which require students to use critical thinking to learn them adequately, do not foster the development of critical thinking unless the emphasis in learning the content of these subjects is on critical thinking.[19] Many educators maintain that critical thinking can be taught in any subject area when emphasis is placed on the learning of critical thinking. While this hypothesis has not been tested extensively, it is consistent with the experimentation to date.

CRITICAL THINKING AND THE ANALYSIS OF PROPAGANDA. One of the common methods used to encourage critical thinking is to teach children to analyze propaganda. Experimental studies have demonstrated that children can be taught to identify illogical arguments and misleading statements in newspapers, magazines, and other media of communication.[20] While such studies have demonstrated that children can learn to detect propaganda devices, our concern is with the extent to which such training contributes to the development of critical thinking.

A study by Osborn indirectly supports the conclusion discussed above. Unless the emphasis in such teaching is on learning processes rather than content, the learning experiences are not likely to be effective for a comprehensive development of critical thinking processes. In Osborn's study, students were presented with a unit of instruction called "Public Opinion and Propaganda."[21] After four weeks of study, the students' attitudes toward capital punishment were assessed by giving them a test of knowledge concerning capital punishment and a propaganda selection on "Why Capital Punishment is Necessary." Two weeks later the students were given another test of attitudes toward capital punishment. On the basis of data obtained, Osborn concluded that the students had learned to detect specific propaganda devices, but that this learning did not protect

---

[19]For additional evidence to support this point of view, see H. P. Fawcett, "The Nature of Proof," *The Thirteenth Yearbook*, National Council of Teachers of Mathematics, 1938.

[20]For examples of such teaching procedures, see W. C. Armstrong and L. Wood, "Analyzing Propaganda," *Social Education*, 4 (1940), 331-37; also, F. A. Gage, "A Unit on Propaganda Analysis," *Social Education*, 4 (1940), 483-88.

[21]W. W. Osborn, "An Experiment in Teaching Resistance to Propaganda," *Journal of Experimental Education*, 8 (1939), 1-17.

them against the effects of propaganda appeals. Osborn had made the assumption that if students were taught the forms of propaganda they would be better able to resist propaganda. The data, however, did not support this assumption. Osborn suggested that students' attitudes can be affected by propaganda even after they have learned to detect propaganda devices. As we noted above, teaching procedures designed to foster critical thinking in students apparently are most likely to be effective when the emphasis in teaching is on critical thinking, and when students are given an opportunity to utilize what they have learned about critical thinking in a wide variety of situations.

FACTORS INHIBITING CRITICAL THINKING. Among the major factors influencing an individual's ability to think critically are his attitudes and values. Some attitudes interfere with critical thinking. Prejudices and stereotypes, which are products of uncritical thinking, inhibit critical analysis. We will explore the development of attitudes and their influence on behavior in greater detail in the following chapter. We may note at this point, however, that logical reasoning, the willingness to seek for facts, and the careful testing of hypotheses are behaviors that presuppose an attitude of relative detachment and a willingness to change one's ideas.

A variety of personal and social factors are likely to interfere with the development of this attitude. People's opinions are swayed by the dominant opinion of people in groups to which they belong.[22] The greater the influence of prevalent opinion on an individual, the less likely he will be to analyze his conceptions and principles.[23]

The significance of the way in which a person thinks or acts can be understood only when we know what meaning this behavior has for him. For example, a person who holds a stereotype of some minority group finds the use of this particular concept rewarding. The generalizations that he holds about this minority group have meaning in satisfying his needs. An individual is unlikely to change his concepts or generalizations until a need for re-evaluation of his way of thinking is stimulated. Earlier in this chapter we noted that a

---

[22]This point is documented and discussed in detail in Chapters Eight and Ten.

[23]The following study illustrates how concepts and attitudes are formed under the influence of prevalent opinion: K. B. Clark and M. K. Clark, "The Development of Consciousness of Self and the Emergence of Racial Identification in Negro Pre-school Children," *Journal of Social Psychology*, 10 (1939), 591-99.

child might learn that not speaking in class is a way of avoiding punishment. Such a child has learned a generalization which enables him to interpret his environment successfully, that is, enables him to satisfy his needs. Unless the child is motivated by the strength of other needs, he is not likely to unlearn or give up this generalization. If we are interested in fostering the development of critical thinking, we need to be aware that other processes in personality influence the cognitive processes. Critical thinking involves the total personality of an individual, and is not likely to be developed if we ignore the influence of needs, attitudes, and values on thinking processes.

Any lack of skill in logical reasoning or in the techniques of data-gathering and hypothesis-testing will probably interfere with critical thinking. A child's opinion of capital punishment is likely to be influenced by the kinds of data that he uses in forming his opinion. If he gathers data unsystematically, if he does not recognize valid and reliable information, if he does not know the sources of appropriate information, his opinions will reflect the inadequacies of the data.

We can summarize this discussion of factors inhibiting critical thinking by calling attention again to the fact that critical thinking is a process that involves the total organism. Inadequate attitudes or deficiencies in skills necessary for critical thinking will presumably interfere with learning to think critically. Because of the complexity of the process that we are attempting to foster, it is not likely that critical thinking will be learned in one course or in a few units in a social studies program. Neither is it likely that mere exposure to subject matter which ordinarily requires critical thinking will, in itself, guarantee the development of the process.

THE SCHOOL AND THE DEVELOPMENT OF CRITICAL THINKING. Glaser, who conducted an experiment to determine the extent to which children can be taught to think critically, comments in the following way on the characteristics required for a program designed to develop critical thinking in students:

> The efficacy of given training to think critically and the amount and quality of transfer which occurs will be greatly influenced by: (1) the method of presentation, (2) the degree to which self-activity and personal experience are induced, (3) the means of furnishing precision, definiteness, and stability to the course of this activity, (4) the extent to which the desired outcomes are set up as definite goals of instruction, (5) the extent to which the processes of reasoning and guiding principles are made clear

to the students, (6) the degree of relationship or similarity between specific elements in the training and their existence in the new situation to which transfer is desired.[24]

The school, by organizing learning experiences, provides opportunities to learn to think critically. Some of these learning experiences may be designed to teach specific skills related to and necessary for the development of critical thinking. In science classes, for example, we teach students the methods for gathering data from which to develop generalizations about physical events. In social studies we may teach students the procedures and requirements for adequate data-gathering. One of the functions of the experiment in science classes is to teach students appropriate experimental techniques. As we have noted, however, learning these skills and techniques does not in itself guarantee the development of critical thinking. Emphasis on thinking critically is probably equally important in the teaching of specific skills. Further, the school must provide a wide range of opportunities to think critically. As we have noted before, and will note frequently throughout this book, behavior which is rewarded is behavior which is most likely to be learned. Children will learn to think critically to the extent that thinking critically is a rewarding activity.

ASSOCIATIVE THINKING

If you were asked what street you live on, you would probably be able to respond immediately and correctly. You probably learned this response originally by associating the name of the street with simple cues. One of these cues was the question, "What street do you live on?" for which the appropriate response is the name of the street. We teach children their own proper names, their house numbers and streets, and the names of many common objects through a process of associating these names and numbers with appropriate stimuli. *Associations are developed by attaching responses to certain stimuli, called cues, so that when the cues or stimuli occur the appropriate response to them is made easily and quickly.* This kind of cognitive process is somewhat simpler than deductive and inductive thinking,

---

[24] E. M. Glaser, "An Experiment in the Development of Critical Thinking," *Teachers College Contributions to Education*, No. 843, New York, Bureau of Publications, Columbia University, 1941, p. 71.

or acquiring concepts and generalizations. However, much thinking is of this character and, like the other cognitive processes that we have studied, it enables an individual to make appropriate interpretations of his environment. Imagine the difficulties that would be involved if we had to reason out the name of every person whom we met or the name of every common object.

The educational significance of associative thinking is that desired behavior changes require the learning of associations. While we want children to understand the process of multiplication, we also wish them to learn the associations required in a multiplication table. When a child is given the stimulus "two times two equals," we want him to be able to respond "four" easily and quickly. Other examples of associations that we encourage children to learn are formulas of various kinds, foreign language vocabulary, dates of historical events, and such conventions as, "Capitalize the first word in a sentence."

THE MEANINGFULNESS OF ASSOCIATIONS. Some of the associations that we encourage children to learn can be given meaning when the principle underlying the association is explained or discovered. A child can understand why "two times two is four," when he understands the principles of combinations by multiplication. Many modern texts in arithmetic are designed to foster this understanding of arithmetic processes; for the sake of efficiency, we also encourage the child to remember the associations in the multiplication table. We will discuss at a later point in this chapter the relation between understanding and remembering.

Many of the associations to be learned in school are essentially meaningless. Statements such as "Sacramento is the capital of California," have to be learned even though we can give no rational meaning to the association between the term "Sacramento" and the place of the capital of California. Contrast the meaning that can be given to "two times two equals four." We may be able to explain how the capital of California came to be called Sacramento, but such an explanation gives no intrinsic meaning to the association. Another example of an essentially meaningless kind of association is the association between "red light" and "stop." The convention governing traffic signals is an arbitrary one, but before a person can observe traffic rules he must learn this association. It would be impossible to explain to a child why a red light means stop—other than to say that this is a matter of agreement.

Considerable emphasis in modern education is placed on making learning "meaningful." A distinction should be made at this point between giving meaning to learning a task and the meaning inherent in the character of the task. We may make the task of learning that Sacramento is the capital of California a meaningful task by relating the task to important concepts or generalizations that the child will have to learn in order to satisfy his needs. For example, children studying the history and government of their state need to understand geographical concepts and place orientations. They must be able to give the location of many governmental agencies, and to do this must learn the name of the state capital. Learning the name of the capital "makes sense" or has meaning in this larger context of learning. Note, however, that we have given meaning to the task of learning but have not added any intrinsic meaning to the association to be learned.

Associations, whether they are meaningful or not, depend heavily upon memory. An individual must retain an association if he is to use it. A child who cannot remember the multiplication tables is slow and inefficient in computational tasks. A discussion of associative thinking requires an understanding of factors that influence remembering and forgetting—so that learning experiences may be organized to facilitate the acquisition of these associations.

MEMORY AS AN INFERRED PROCESS. The experience of "remembering" is so obvious that we may overlook the fact that the process is not directly observable. We account for certain observations of human behavior by postulating a process called "memory." The behavior from which we infer the memory process may take any one of three forms. If a person has studied a poem and can recite the poem at some time after he has studied it, the behavior that we observe is *recall behavior*. Another kind of behavior from which we infer the influence of memory processes is that of recognizing an association previously learned. An individual may identify the correct date for the Declaration of Independence from a list of dates, even though he might not have been able to recall this date without having the list in front of him. This kind of behavior is called *recognition behavior*. Another kind of behavior from which we can infer the influence of memory processes is facility in relearning a task that has originally been learned. If a child has memorized a list of vocabulary words, he will forget some of these words over a period of time. If he studies the list a second time, he probably will be able to learn the list much more quickly than he did the first time. We account for this phenomenon of rapid *relearning* by inferring that not all of the responses involved in the original learning had been forgotten and that those not forgotten were used in the relearning.

The behavior phenomenon that we observe in all these cases is that of *retention*. Memory is the process we use to account for the observed behavior called retention. What variables influence retention? That a knowledge of these factors is important for teachers is obvious, since learning experiences are typically designed to facilitate behavior change which is retained.

REORGANIZATION AND RETENTION. When a person meets a situation which is unfamiliar to him, he apparently strives to reorganize his impressions of the situation in terms of his previous experience.

This attempt at reorganization enables a person to interpret a new experience and at the same time probably increases his retention of what is learned in the new experience. Deese provides an interesting example of this tendency to organize the unfamiliar. Figure 15 gives a sample of the kind of picture that Deese presented to a group of subjects in an experiment.[25] The subjects in this experiment were to remember a series of forms of this

(After Deese)

FIGURE 15

[25]J. Deese, "Complexity of Contour in the Recognition of Visual Form," *WADC Technical Report*, No. 56-60, 1956.

kind that were given to them. Deese found that his subjects typically applied some label to the forms; for example, the most frequent name assigned to the form in Figure 15 was "dog's head." These familiar labels presumably facilitated retention of the forms.

Bartlett has also demonstrated the tendency to restructure as a way of organizing experience. Bartlett presented his experimental subjects with a series of pictures, and at a later time asked them to reproduce these pictures from memory. Figure 16 shows one such reproduction. Notice the sequence from a drawing fairly similar to

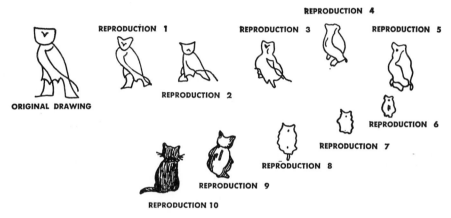

A form reproduced from memory. The form is altered at each reproduction. The influence of labeling as a coding device is seen in the change from a conventional Egyptian symbol for an owl to a picture of a cat. (After Bartlett)

FIGURE 16

the original to one which is radically different from the original but which preserves some of the basic features of the original. What is apparent in this reproduction is that the memory of the original drawing apparently has been recoded in terms of a more familiar object.[26]

The reproduction of the Egyptian owl as a cat illustrates that this reorganization process has disadvantages as well as advantages. The subject who recalled the original drawing as a cat, while he has

---

[26]F. C. Bartlett, *Remembering: A Study in Experimental and Social Psychology,* Cambridge, England, Cambridge University Press, 1932.

REPRODUCED FIGURES	WORD LIST I	STIMULUS FIGURES	WORD LIST II	REPRODUCED FIGURES

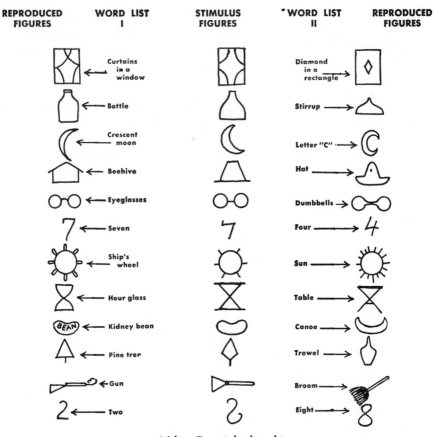

(After Carmichael et al.)

FIGURE 17

retained some of the features of the original drawing, has apparently forgotten considerable detail.

An experiment by Carmichael[27] demonstrates that this process of reorganizing can be influenced. He presented a series of stimulus pictures to two groups of subjects. A stimulus word was given with each of the pictures; however, two different lists of stimulus words were used with two groups of subjects. After the subjects had seen the stimulus pictures and a set of associated words, they were asked to draw the pictures from memory. Figure 17 shows the changes in

[27]L. Carmichael, H. P. Hogan, and A. A. Walter, "An Experimental Study of the Effect of Language on the Reproduction of Visually Perceived Form," *Journal of Experimental Psychology,* 15 (1932), 73-86.

the reproduced figure associated with the kind of stimulus word that was used with the picture. You will notice that the original figure has been changed in the direction of a figure more consistent with the stimulus word.

An important qualification needs to be made on the data from the experiments cited. We cannot tell to what extent the reproduction of a figure has been influenced by original inaccuracies of perception. The factor of inaccurate perception would account in part for distortions in the reproductions. However, the systematization of the successive reproductions, as in Bartlett's experiments, suggests the influence of a coding process.

All of the possibly influential factors in the recoding process have not been explored adequately. The variable of familiarity appears to influence the recoding process and, consequently, the retention of what is learned.[28]

Three major processes appear to be involved in this system of reorganization: (1) a *leveling process* in which irregularities or asymmetrical features are removed; (2) a *sharpening process* in which striking or unusual features are accentuated; (3) an *assimilation process* in which what is retained is changed in the direction of something more common and familiar to the individual—the cat in the earlier illustration, for example.

What we do not know at the present time are the factors that are more likely to initiate one of these processes than another. Experimental evidence suggests that the selection and recoding process appears to be strongly influenced by individual factors. Bartlett showed his experimental subjects a set of pictures and described the people in the pictures in conventional terms. For example, a pictured young man might be described as clean-cut, energetic, dynamic, and good-humored. The subjects' recall of the pictures appears to be strongly influenced by the attitude that the picture or description aroused. In Chapter Four, we cited Zeigarnik's experiment in which individuals remembered more uncompleted tasks than completed tasks. Here we were provided with an example of the influence of motivational factors on what is remembered.

UNDERSTANDING AND RETENTION. The hypothesis that individuals try to "make sense" out of what they are experiencing would

---

[28]M. D. Arnoult, "Familiarity and Recognition of Nonsense Shapes," *Journal of Experimental Psychology,* 51 (1956), 269-76.

suggest a hypothesis that the introduction of an organizing principle into the study of new material would be likely to facilitate both learning and remembering this material. This hypothesis has been supported in a number of experimental studies. An example from Katona will demonstrate the difference between the effects of what has been called "rote" learning and "meaningful" learning; that is, learning with and without organizing principles that give meaning to what is being learned.[29] Katona used two groups of experimental subjects, each of which was to learn the following series of numbers:

$$5 \; 8 \; 1 \; 2 \; 1 \; 5 \; 1 \; 9 \; 2 \; 2 \; 2 \; 6$$
$$2 \; 9 \; 3 \; 3 \; 3 \; 6 \; 4 \; 0 \; 4 \; 3 \; 4 \; 7$$

The first group was told that a principle underlay the arrangement of the numbers. Most of the subjects soon discovered that the principle consisted of alternately adding 3 and then 4; for example, 5 plus 3 equals 8, 8 plus 4 equals 12, 12 plus 3 equals 15, and so on. The second group was to learn the numbers by rote. The experimenter suggested that the best method to use would be a rhythmical grouping of the numbers; for example, 2 9 3, 3 3 6, and so on. The subjects in this experiment were tested shortly after the experiment and at a period three weeks later. The results of these tests are summarized in Table VII. The data in the Table suggest there was little difference

	Subjects who reproduced correctly		Subjects who made 19 or more errors	
	CLASS I ("understanding")	CLASS II ("rote")	CLASS I ("understanding")	CLASS II ("rote")
Half-hour after learning	38%	33%	10%	7%
Three weeks later	23%	0%	15%	74%

Retention of Number Sequences Learned with Understanding and Learned by Rote (From Katona)*

TABLE VII

*There were 29 subjects in Class I and 30 in Class II for the original tests. Of these, 26 and 23 were available for the retests.

[29]G. Katona, *Organizing and Memorizing*, New York, Columbia University Press, 1940.

between the two groups in original learning. Three weeks later, however, a substantial proportion of the subjects who had learned with understanding had retained what they had learned.

A study by Tyler demonstrates that knowledge of principles and generalizations is more likely to be retained than is knowledge of less meaningful material, such as terminology.[30] Tyler studied how much course content was retained after one year, using the terms learned in biology and zoology courses, knowledge of principles, and ability to interpret new experiments. The latter two kinds of processes depend heavily upon understanding, whereas the first process depends

Type of Examination Exercises	Mean Scores at:			Per cent of the Gain made in the Course which was lost by June, 1932
	Beginning of Course	Time of Course Examinations	June, 1932	
1. Naming animal structures pictured in diagrams	22.2	61.8	31.4	76.8
2. Identifying technical terms	19.7	83.1	66.5	26.2
3. Recalling information a. Structures performing functions in type forms	13.3	39.3	33.9	20.8
b. Other facts	21.4	62.6	54.1	20.6
4. Applying principles to new situations	35 2	64.9	65.1	Gain 0.7
5. Interpreting new experiments	30.3	57.3	64.0	Gain 24.8
Average for all exercises in the examination	23.7	74.4	63.3	21.9

Comparison of the Results of the Course Examinations, the Test in June, 1932, and the Standing of Students at the Beginning of the Zoology Course (From Tyler)

TABLE VIII

[30] R. Tyler, "Some Findings from Studies in the Field of College Biology," *Science Education,* 18 (1934), 133-42.

more typically on association. The results from this study are presented in Table VIII. As the results indicate, much of the terminology is forgotten, but the principles and experiments are retained. The data suggest that the latter are known even better a year after the termination of the course. This retention of material which requires understanding may result from additional practice, if the students continued to use these principles in other contexts or if they were restudied in other courses. While this possibility may account for some of the retention, it is not likely that it accounts for all of it.

These experiments demonstrate the utility of understanding and organization in facilitating retention. We would hypothesize that if a teacher organizes material to be retained in terms of generalizations and principles, students are likely to retain this material longer. We must face the problem, however, that many things that are to be learned cannot be made meaningful. For example, we would want to know to what extent the students in Tyler's experiment needed to recall terminology in their future work. If this terminology were not important for future study, we would question the reason for having to learn it at all. But, in these and other courses, a knowledge of the special vocabulary is necessary if the student is to develop an understanding of the subject. Consequently, we must be concerned with factors likely to facilitate the retention of materials which are essentially meaningless or to which comparatively little meaning can be given.

OVERLEARNING AND RETENTION. Assume that a student is required to learn a list of twenty French vocabulary words. We will have him study these by going through the list. Each time he has gone through this list we will ask him to recall as many French equivalents as he can. Each of these steps is a "trial." We can determine how many trials are required before the student can give us all of the equivalents correctly. Assume, for the purposes of discussion, that he has mastered all of the words after twenty such trials. We will refer to this level of retention as "bare mastery," that is, after twenty trials the student is able to give all of the French equivalents for the words in the list. At this point we may say that the student has learned the equivalents. If the student continues to practice on the list, beyond the point of "bare mastery," he is "overlearning" the words in the list.

What effect does overlearning have on retention? At the end of twenty trials the student has learned the list to the point where he can recall all of the words in the list. Will he be able to retain this knowledge better if he continues to study the list? Common sense suggests that this is likely, and experimental data support this common-sense hunch.

Figure 18 indicates the learning curves for different degrees of overlearning taken from a study by Krueger.[31] One hundred and fifty per cent overlearning means that the subjects in this experiment use half again as many trials in practice as they used on the original learning; and two hundred per cent overlearning means that the subjects used twice again as many trials in practice as in the original learning. Based on our example, the level of "bare mastery" would be twenty trials; one hundred and fifty per cent overlearning would be thirty trials, and two hundred per cent overlearning would be forty trials. As the curve suggests, the amount retained is proportional to the amount of overlearning, even though all subjects gradually forget more and more of what they originally learned.

The teacher may organize learning experiences so that students overlearn what they have originally barely mastered. If learning experiences are organized in such a way that a student must continually

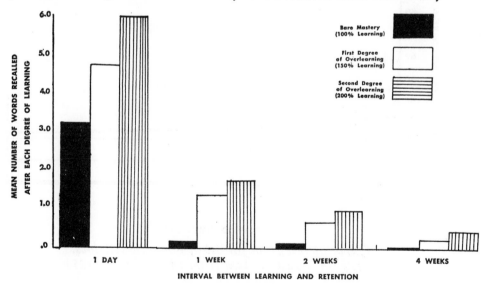

*Effects of two degrees of overlearning on retention.
(After Krueger)*

FIGURE 18

[31]W. C. F. Krueger, "The Effect of Over-learning and Retention," *Journal of Experimental Psychology*, 12 (1929), 71-78.

re-use what he has already learned, he is overlearning. That is, he is continuing to practice on the material. In learning a foreign language, for instance, we may organize the writing and speaking exercises in such a way that a student continually re-uses words that he has already learned. Perhaps the students in Tyler's study quickly forgot terminology because they had little opportunity to overlearn words that they had "barely mastered."[32]

REVIEWING AND RETENTION. Teachers frequently introduce review periods into learning sequences. A review is an opportunity for relearning and a way of implementing overlearning. How can such reviews be arranged to facilitate retention? To understand adequately some of the general principles relevant to this question, we must know what the general course of forgetting is. Figure 19 reveals a curve of forgetting consistent with the data usually obtained in memory experiments.[33] As the figure illustrates, the greatest amount of for-

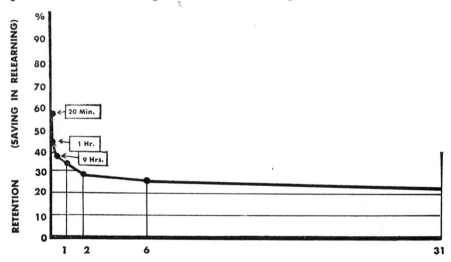

ELAPSED TIME — DAYS

Curve of retention for list of nonsense syllables.
(Hilgard, based on data from Ebbinghaus, 1885)

FIGURE 19

[32]For additional data on this point, see H. F. Spitzer, "Studies in Retention," *Journal of Educational Psychology*, 30 (1939), 641-56.

[33]E. R. Hilgard, *Introduction to General Psychology*, Harcourt, Brace and Co., 1953, p. 262, based on data from H. Ebbinghaus, *Memory*, translated by H. A. Ruger and C. E. Bussenius, New York, Bureau of Publications, Teachers College, Columbia University, 1913.

getting occurs relatively soon after the initial learning has taken place. On the basis of the characteristics of this curve, we would hypothesize that overlearning or relearning in the form of review is most likely to be effective immediately after the original learning; however, some reviewing probably must also be done at other periods after the initial learning period. Experimental evidence suggests that more frequent reviews immediately after the initial learning, followed by relatively widely spaced reviews over a period of time, is more likely to be effective in reducing forgetting.[34]

We cannot prescribe the exact number of days to allow between periods of review; still, we can state some general principles relevant to making decisions of this kind. The teacher will have to take into account four factors in deciding upon the appropriateness of the timing of review sessions: (1) the amount of overlearning at the time of initial learning; (2) the fact that the greatest amount of forgetting takes place immediately after learning; (3) the extent to which the original learned material is used in new learning; (4) the meaningfulness of the material originally learned. We have seen that three of these factors contribute directly to the amount of material retained. When little time has been spent on overlearning, reviews probably will have to be more frequent. When material is not continually re-used, greater frequency of reviews will probably facilitate retention. The teacher may gather data on pupils' retention by systematically questioning students about material previously learned. From such data the teacher may make inferences about the extent of forgetting and plan appropriate reviews.

The word "review" may have two meanings. We have been using it here in the sense of "going over" previously learned material. Review may also be used to refer to a learning experience in which what has been learned previously is integrated with new material; new relationships between the old and the new are developed. After students have learned a number of concepts or generalizations in a course of instruction, the whole sequence of the material used to that point may be looked at in the light of these concepts and generalizations. This kind of review involves more than repeating previously learned responses. In any case, the process of review probably does not comprise a mere exact *repetition* of what has been learned. Since the stu-

---

[34]See L. Tsai, "The Relations of Retention to the Distribution of Relearning," *Journal of Experimental Psychology*, 10 (1927), 30-39.

dent has been learning continuously between review periods, he will probably do some reorganizing and reintegrating of new material with old material. Since this continual reorganization and reinterpretation facilitates understanding, we would predict that it will also facilitate retention.

RECITATION AND RETENTION. Assume again that a student is memorizing a list of words. One of the ways in which he can memorize this list is by reading and rereading this list to himself. He may also cover the list as he studies and attempt to recite the words to himself, or he may participate with another student in a mutual testing of knowledge of the list. Each of these possibilities suggests different levels of active participation in the process of remembering. Reading and rereading is a fairly passive kind of process, while self-recitation or reciting to another person requires greater involvement of the individual in the task. Experimental evidence suggests that the latter kinds of processes facilitate retention. Active recall tends to improve retention. Figure 20 plots the per cent of material retained in relationship to the per cent of time devoted to self-recitation.[35] At numerous points in this text we will point out that learning experiences which require the learner to participate more actively in the learning experience facilitate learning. The teacher may encourage students to use methods of self-recitation or mutual recitation in studying. The teacher may also organize learning experiences which require active recall. We would predict, for example, that the

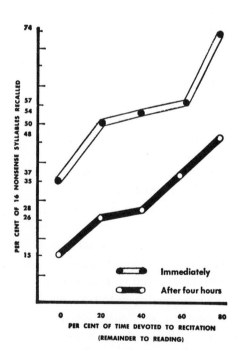

The value of self-recitation in memorizing. (After Gates)

FIGURE 20

[35] A. I Gates, "Recitation as a Factor in Memorizing," *Archives of Psychology*, No. 40, 1917. For additional evidence on the same point, see G. Forlano, "School Learning with Various Methods of Practice and Rewards," *Teachers College Contributions to Education*, New York, Columbia University Press, No. 688, 1936; also, L. C. Seibert, "A Series of Experiments on the Learning of French Vocabulary," *Johns Hopkins University Studies in Education*, No. 18, 1932.

periods of recitation used by teachers in vocabulary lessons will improve retention.

INTERFERENCE THEORY OF FORGETTING. Learning experiences are units or sequences of activity. As a learner moves from one learning experience to another, he encounters new activities, problems, and materials. Assume that a student has learned twenty words of French vocabulary today. Tomorrow he learns twenty more, and the next

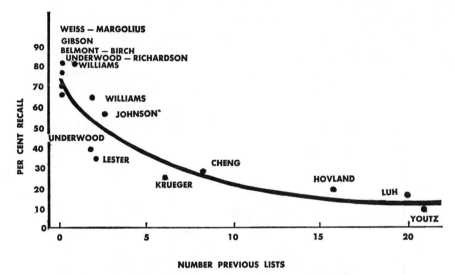

Recall as a function of previous lists of similar material learned by the subjects. This curve was obtained by combining the data of a number of different investigators. The authors of the separate studies are indicated by the names beside the circles. (From Underwood)

FIGURE 21

day twenty more. What are the effects of these learning activities on successive attempts at learning vocabulary? Figure 21 shows the results from several studies based on this question. The curve shows the relationship between the amount recalled and the number of previous lists of similar material that subjects had to learn. It is clear that the greater the amount of similar material to be retained, the less the amount of material actually retained.[36]

---

[36]B. J. Underwood, "Interference and Forgetting," *Psychological Review*, 64 (1957), 49-60.

Data of this kind have been used to support what is called the "interference theory" of forgetting. According to this theory, forgetting occurs because a person learns new responses between the time that he has originally learned a response and the time that he again is called upon to use it. Applying this conception to memory, we would say that between the time that a student learns a list of words and the time that he is called upon to use these words, he may have learned many more words. The more similar the intervening material, the more likely it is to interfere with the originally learned material when the student is required to recall it.

This hypothesis about factors influencing forgetting can be used as a basis for making decisions about organizing learning experiences. In general, the teacher would expect students to have difficulty retaining highly similar materials which are learned in close proximity to each other. However, any factor which strengthens retention of the original learning is likely to reduce the effects of interference.

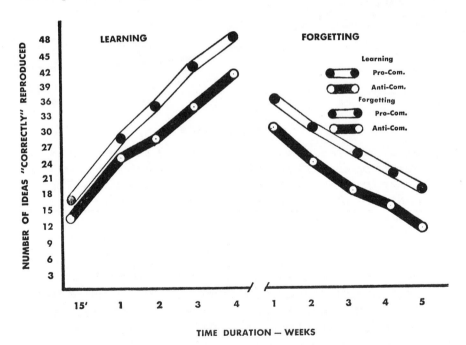

Learning and forgetting curves for "correct" responses for pro-communist and anti-communist groups of the pro-Soviet Union selection. (After Levine and Murphy)

FIGURE 22

In other words, something that is well learned is likely to be retained, even though the person learns something else similar to the original learning, in either form or content.

INFLUENCE OF PERSONAL FACTORS ON FORGETTING. Personal factors play an important part in forgetting. There is some experimental evidence to suggest that pleasant associations are more likely to be recalled than unpleasant associations.[37]

An individual's attitudes and values tend to influence what he will recall. This process has been called "selective forgetting." By selective forgetting we mean that an individual, because of certain attitudes or feelings, is predisposed to forget some of the material he has presumably learned. A study by Levine and Murphy demonstrates

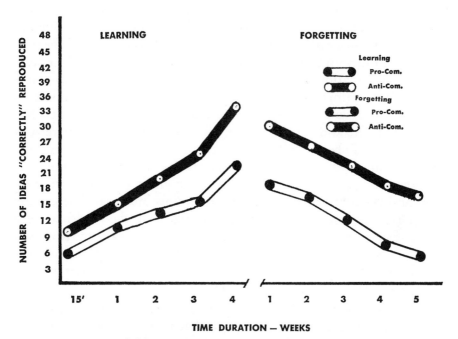

Learning and forgetting curves for "correct" responses for pro-communist and anti-communist groups of the anti-Soviet Union selection. (After Levine and Murphy)

FIGURE 23

---

[37]See H. Meltzer, "Individual Differences in Forgetting Pleasant and Unpleasant Experiences," *Journal of Educational Psychology*, 21 (1930), 399-409; also, R. H. Thomson, "Experimental Study of Memory as Influenced by Feeling Tone," *Journal of Experimental Psychology*, 13 (1930), 462-67.

this phenomenon.[38] In this experiment students' attitudes toward communism were determined. The students were then given both pro-communist and anti-communist selections to read, and their recall of the material in the selections was tested immediately after the reading. This process was repeated for three successive weeks and recall tests were given for five weeks after this. The results of this investigation are given in Figures 22 and 23. As the figures indicate, anti-communists remembered more anti-communist material than did pro-communists, and pro-communists remembered more pro-communist material than did anti-communists. These differences were maintained over a relatively long period of time.

The term "selective forgetting" may suggest to some readers that the person *chooses* what he will forget. Understanding of the phenomenon might be improved if we thought of the process involved as *selective perception and remembering*. In the Levine and Murphy study, we would suspect that a person's initial perceptions of the material are influenced by his attitudes; that is, he is more likely to notice items of information or points of view consistent with his own. As a consequence, he may ignore points contradicting his own point of view. What he would remember would be in part a function of what he had observed, and, consequently, what he retains would be related to what he had observed. That this selective perception does not entirely explain the data is apparent from the fact that pro-communists, for example, do remember some anti-communist material and anti-communists do remember some pro-communist material. The process of reading and rereading probably insured that the students were aware of some information and generalizations contrary to their own point of view. However, the process of selective perception and selective remembering determines the extent to which material consistent with one's own attitudes is retained.

This discussion of the causes of forgetting suggests some of the reasons why children do not retain all that they originally learned in school. The teacher is limited in the extent to which he can eliminate forgetting. As we have seen, much forgetting can be accounted for by the effects of interpolated activities on recall. The teacher does have some control over the arrangement of learning experiences and, through this control, can influence the extent to which the students

---

[38]J. M. Levine and G. Murphy, "The Learning and Forgetting of Controversial Material," *Journal of Abnormal and Social Psychology*, 38 (1943), 507-17.

are likely to retain what they have learned. Where attitudes, feelings, and emotions affect what is being retained, the teacher is less able to influence effectively what is retained. In the following chapter we will discuss the learning of attitudes and values; after reading these chapters, the student will have a more comprehensive view of personality factors which influence learning. We may note at this point, however, that in some cases retention of learning is inhibited by an individual's reactions to what is being learned. Obviously, the teacher will not always be able to arrange learning experiences so that students are not exposed to materials that are unpleasant to them or which contradict their attitudes and values. To encourage behavior change in desirable directions, more fundamental reorganizations of attitudes and values will have to be attempted.

SUMMARY

In this chapter we have extended our discussion of the cognitive processes to include a consideration of the learning of generalizations, critical thinking, and associative thinking. An individual learns generalizations, as well as concepts, as ways of organizing and interpreting his experience. An individual categorizes the phenomena of his experience by means of concepts. His generalizations express the relations among these concepts. The following are some principles and hypotheses about the process of learning or acquiring generalizations:

1. Generalizations are learned ways of organizing and giving meaning to experience. An individual must participate in relevant experiences from which he can develop these relationships between concepts that we call generalizations. In schools, we provide the kinds of experiences appropriate to encouraging the process of formulating generalizations.

2. A generalization can be acquired in a rote manner, that is, by remembering a stated generalization. When a generalization is learned in this manner, an individual probably does not understand the meaning of the generalization in any effective way; he is limited in the use that he can make of it in interpreting his experience.

3. Generalizations may also be learned by deduction from other generalizations or by induction from experience. Some generalizations may be learned in either way. Learning generalizations either by induction or by deduction tends to improve understanding and retention of the generalization.

4. Learning experiences may be organized in such a way that students will acquire generalizations by inductive or deductive thinking. Teaching procedures which foster inductive or deductive thinking tend to produce different effects. Inductive processes probably require more time for initial learning of the generalization, but the generalization tends to be retained longer and to be more likely to transfer to new learning. Learning experiences which encourage induction may stimulate greater interest and more active participation in the learning experience.

5. Generalizations are usually meant to interpret a wide variety of phenomena. In learning a generalization a student will typically have experience with a limited number of instances of the phenomena to which the generalization applies. Consideration must be given to factors which will facilitate the transfer of the generalization to new experiences for which it is appropriate. Transfer is promoted when the new and original learning experiences are similar. Transfer is also facilitated by demonstrating the application of the generalization to new situations.

Critical thinking is a process in which an individual evaluates and analyzes his own experience. Critical thinking is not a single process but an integration of many cognitive processes in thinking about the meaning of one's own experience. The modern school is interested in fostering the development of critical thinking in students. An important psychological question is: To what extent can critical thinking be taught?

6. Since critical thinking is a complex process, it is not likely that it can be taught in one course or one year in school. Critical thinking is a process that must be rewarded consistently if it is to be learned.

7. In order to think critically a student will have to develop an attitude that predisposes him to analyze his experience, to re-evaluate it continually, and to make judgments tentatively. In addition to this general attitude, a student will have to acquire skills in logical thinking and empirical inquiry.

8. Many people have assumed that some subject matters lend themselves to the development of critical thinking. Research evidence, however, tends to support the hypothesis that emphasis on the process of critical thinking, rather than on logically organized content as such, is more likely to encourage the development of critical thinking.

Cognitive processes are strongly influenced by associative thinking. An association is an established relationship between a response and a cue, such that when the cue occurs the response follows easily and quickly. Some of these associations are meaningful in that they can be understood rationally; that is, they "make sense." Other associations are relatively meaningless; they involve conventions or agreements, such as "red light means stop," or "capitalize the first word in a sentence." The retention of these kinds of cognitive associations depends heavily on memory. The following hypotheses are relevant to the improvement of retention:

9. Understanding tends to improve retention. Meaningful material is more likely to be remembered than non-meaningful material. The retention of essentially meaningless material can probably be improved by relating such associations to meaningful contexts.

10. Retention is improved by overlearning—by continued practice on material after it has been "barely mastered."

11. An efficient form of overlearning can be implemented by arranging learning experiences so that students continually re-use what they have learned. Review periods are also useful in re-establishing original learning, and are most likely to be useful if they are scheduled soon after the original learning period and are spaced over a period of time.

12. Retention tends to be reduced when new material being learned is highly similar to the original material. However, with more thorough original learning, the interference effect of new and similar material is reduced.

In this and the previous chapter we have noted that an individual's attitudes and values influence his cognitive processes. Attitudes and values tend to influence both what is originally learned and what is retained. In the following chapter we will discuss the attitudinal-evaluative processes in detail. At this point the prospective teacher should be aware that such processes play an important part in the development of the cognitive processes. When attitudes and values interfere with desired behavior changes in the cognitive processes, a learning experience probably will have to be organized to evoke changes in attitudes and values. The possibilities for success when such learning experiences are organized will be discussed in the following chapters.

STUDY AND DISCUSSION QUESTIONS

1. List the most important generalizations to be learned in one of the following areas:

   a. Some course in your major field.

   b. Some course or subject that you are teaching or may teach.

   c. The content of the preceding chapter.

   Identify the concepts that are part of these generalizations and describe the relationships between these concepts.

2. In what sense is a concept a generalization? What may be the difference between the process of generalization by which a concept is applied to many instances of a concept and the description of a generalization provided in this chapter?

3. Below are several generalizations. Describe how each of these generalizations might be learned by inductive and deductive processes. Be specific about the kinds of experiences that would be used as examples of the generalizations, or as instances from which the generalization would be inferred.

   a. A cooperative effort was necessary on the American frontier to preserve the American way of life.

   b. Trial by jury is necessary to preserve individual freedom.

c. Radioactive fall-out increases the concentration of strontium 90 in the bone structure of the body.

4. The above generalizations may require some modification or qualification. In what way would an individual learning these generalizations test their relative validity? Is a generalization tested when you find examples of it?

5. Some people argue that rote learning is necessary if the learning is to be retained. They cite as an example the necessity of memorizing the multiplication tables, or the parts of speech, or vocabulary in a foreign language. Evaluate this argument in the light of the discussion presented in this chapter on "meaningful" learning. What is the relationship between "meaningful" learning and retention?

6. Recall Kirsch's experiment on the role of discovery in learning generalizations. Under what conditions would you expect a discovery group, that is, a "no-help" group, not to become interested in the problem situation, or to be less motivated toward problem solution than students who received help in problem solution?

7. How do you account for the consistent results obtained in experimental studies to the effect that students who acquire generalization through understanding are better able to use these generalizations in new situations where they are appropriate? What might the student be learning in the process of attempting to understand these generalizations which facilitates this transfer?

8. What kinds of "familiar materials" could you use to stimulate students to learn the following generalizations?

   a. Equals added to equals yield equals.

   b. To every reaction there is an opposite and equal reaction.

   c. In the United States the scope of governmental power depends upon the consent of the governed.

9. Is critical thinking as important in the study of mathematics and foreign languages as it is in the study of history, economics, and social science? How would you describe critical thinking in the study of mathematics or foreign languages?

10. Assume that you are an English teacher discussing your interpretation of a passage from one of Thomas Hardy's novels. How will you be able to identify the students who are thinking critically about the passage and your interpretation of it? If the students seem to accept your interpretation, would you infer that they are not thinking critically?

11. How would you organize the study of the following topics with a view to improving critical thinking?

   a. A study of the procedures used in introducing a bill into Congress.

   b. A study of the voting records in city elections.

    c. A translation of a passage from a French essay.

    d. A discussion of a new technique for teaching reading.

12. Some teachers use mnemonic devices to facilitate students' retention of material that is to be memorized. For example, teachers may suggest remembering the word "face" to recall the notes in the spaces of the C clef. In what ways may such devices facilitate retention and in what ways may they inhibit retention?

13. In what ways could learning experiences be organized so that long-term retention of the following materials would be improved?

    a. A vocabulary list in a foreign language.

    b. A list of spelling words.

    c. A multiplication table.

    d. The dates of important events in the American Revolution.

Explain in what ways you are using the principles discussed in this chapter in your suggested organizations of learning experiences.

14. Suggest ways in which review of materials in the previous question may be organized to improve retention. Again, explain the ways in which you are applying the psychological principles relevant to efficacy of review.

15. Students in high schools and colleges study many different subjects during the course of each day. Would you predict that this arrangement of courses would tend to reduce retention of what is being learned?

RECOMMENDED READINGS

    The first reading suggested below describes basic principles and their relevance to learning experiences organized in schools. The second reading is an analysis and review of experimentation on critical thinking, with particular emphasis on experiments conducted in school situations. The third and fourth readings review and analyze the experimental literature on the learning of generalizations and retention. The fifth and sixth readings are reports of original experimental work and theoretical conceptions that have been developed on the basis of this experimental work. The seventh reading is an interesting analysis of the processes of inference, particularly as they are exemplified in mathematical thinking.

1. W. A. Brownell and G. Hendrickson, "How Children Learn Information, Concepts, and Generalizations," *Forty-ninth Yearbook of the National Society for the Study of Education, Part I, Learning and Instruction*, Chicago, University of Chicago Press, 1950, pp. 92-128.

2. D. H. Russell, *Children's Thinking*, Boston, Ginn & Co., 1956, Chapter 10.

3. R. Leeper, "Cognitive Processes," in S. S. Stevens (ed.), *Handbook of Experimental Psychology,* New York, John Wiley & Sons, 1951, Chapter 19.

4. C. I. Hovland, "Human Learning and Retention," in S. S. Stevens (ed.), *Handbook of Experimental Psychology.*

5. F. Bartlett, *Thinking: An Experimental and Social Study,* New York, Basic Books, Inc., 1958.

6. F. Bartlett, *Remembering: A Study in Experimental and Social Psychology,* Cambridge, England, Cambridge University Press, 1932.

7. G. Polya, *Mathematics and Plausible Reasoning,* Princeton, Princeton University Press, 1954.

LEARNING AND THE
ATTITUDINAL PROCESSES—I

In this chapter we will discuss the nature of attitudes and how attitudes are acquired. The modern school has accepted some responsibility for the development of a wide range of attitudes. American schools have always attempted to influence attitudes to some extent. The little red schoolhouse was interested in teaching students the basic principles of American democracy, and in arousing positive feelings about American democracy and the American way of life. The modern school differs from its antecedents only in the range of attitudes that it attempts to develop. For example, we now want students to have appropriate attitudes toward sanitation and hygiene, toward safe driving, toward active participation in the affairs of government, toward ethnic, racial, and religious groups. The task is not a simple one. Because man is a thinking and feeling organism, we cannot assume that merely exposing students to a variety of formal concepts and principles will guarantee the development of appropriate attitudes.

In a high school civics course, the teacher had spent a considerable amount of time emphasizing appro-

priate attitudes toward government and participation in the affairs of government. He particularly emphasized "respect for property" as one of the requirements of good citizenship. One of the students in this class climbed the flagpole in the school yard during after-school hours, hauled down the flag, and started a fire at the base of the flagpole. This student had been receiving "A" grades in his civics course. The teacher was deeply disturbed by the student's behavior because it so clearly indicated that many of the attitudes that the teacher was attempting to develop had obviously not been acquired by this student. Whatever the reasons for his behavior, it does not appear that the student had learned the appropriate attitude toward property.

In this case, the student had presumably developed abstract concepts related to law and order and the processes of government. He had not acquired appropriate *attitudes* about law and order and government. We are not suggesting that it is the sole responsibility of the school to develop attitudes like these, nor even that the school can be held accountable for the failure of the student to acquire them. The important point is that appropriate concepts and attitudes must be developed if desirable behaviors are to be acquired. A school cannot develop responsible citizens merely by teaching verbal abstractions about government, law, and justice. If students are to be law-abiding and intelligent participants in the processes of democracy, they must acquire adequate concepts of government and positive attitudes toward the processes and symbols of government.

WHAT IS AN ATTITUDE?

In 1956 the Purdue Opinion Panel polled a nation-wide sample of high school students on their ideas and feelings about science and scientists. Some of the facts that came out were as follows:

Twenty-five per cent of high school students think scientists as a group are "more than a little bit odd."

Twenty-seven per cent feel that scientists are willing to sacrifice the welfare of others to further their own interests.

Twenty-eight per cent believe that scientists don't have time to enjoy life.

Thirty per cent declare that one can't raise a normal family and become a scientist.

Thirty-five per cent believe that it is necessary to be a genius to be a good scientist.[1]

Must a scientist be a genius? Do scientists lead such unusual lives that they cannot lead a normal family life? Will scientists sacrifice the welfare of others to further their investigations? An objective evaluation of the work and life of scientists would show that many scientists are not geniuses,[2] that many raise families and lead a normal home life, and that many of them are deeply concerned about the effects of their scientific investigations on the welfare of humanity.[3] How can we account for this discrepancy between the views of students and the realities of the life of a scientist?

The students sampled in this survey have some concepts of the scientist and his life. We also see that the opinions of the students not only involve formal concepts but also include *feelings* about the life of a scientist. Many of the students have negative feelings towards the career of a scientist. They do not want to be scientists; they regard the life of the scientist as dull, boring, and perhaps potentially immoral. Many of these students have had little or no experience with a scientist; some have never met a scientist or observed one working. Yet they have strong feelings about what scientists are like. They have attitudes toward scientists.

The same students were asked how they felt about such subjects as religion, ethics, dating, parents, and teachers. The students' answers to these questions indicate *attitudes* that are based on complex psychological processes which are combinations or integrations of ideas, feelings, and impressions. What a person *thinks and feels* about Russians, Communists, Republicans, Democrats, the Constitution, his next door neighbor, his closest friend, a book he has read, the color of a person's hair, colonialism, Picasso's art, the Yankees, or school integration, depends on the attitudes that he has toward these subjects. Whether or not an individual's attitudes are based upon accurate or adequate concepts, whether or not his attitudes are appropriate to

---

[1]H. H. Remmers and D. H. Radler, *The American Teenager,* Indianapolis-New York, Bobbs-Merrill Co., copyright 1957, p. 164, used by special permission of the publisher.

[2]C. G. Wrenn, "Potential Research Talent in the Sciences Based on Intelligence Quotients of Ph.D.'s," *Educational Record,* 30 (1949), 5-22.

[3]For studies of the characteristics of scientists, see A. Roe, "A Psychologist Examines 64 Eminent Scientists," *Scientific American,* 187 (1952), 21-25; L. M. Terman, "Scientists and Non-Scientists in a Group of 800 Gifted Men," *Psychological Monographs,* No. 7, 1954; A. Roe, "A Psychological Study of Physical Scientists," *Genetic Psychology Monographs,* 43 (1951), 121-39; L. M. Terman, "Are Scientists Different?" *Scientific American,* 192 (1955), No. 1, 25-30

the subject toward which they are directed, does not concern us here. People do have attitudes, and these complex mediating processes influence almost all aspects of behavior. These processes, like the cognitive processes, are mediating variables that may describe and explain behavior (see Chapter Three).

DEFINITION OF AN ATTITUDE. *An attitude is a predisposition to action, a state of readiness to act in a particular way.* Attitudes are generalized states of the individual, which lead to or result in a wide variety of particular ways of behaving. In a classroom many students have positive attitudes toward the teacher. These students like their teachers, their school work, and think that most teachers are friendly and helpful people; however, they do not act in exactly the same way. One student will be quiet, retiring, respectful in the presence of the teacher; another will be open, inquisitive, perhaps argumentative. While the behaviors of these two students are quite different, each kind of behavior is consistent with the attitude of the student toward the teacher. On the other hand, the student who is hostile toward teachers will manifest his attitude in quite different behavior. For example, a student who will argue with the teacher in a classroom may or may not have a positive attitude toward the teacher. For the student with a positive attitude, arguing does not represent an attack upon the teacher, whereas it may for the student with a hostile attitude toward the teacher.

ATTITUDES AS ORIENTATION PROCESSES. Attitudes are sets of processes assumed to be operative within the individual; these processes influence his behavior in specifiable ways. *Attitudes,* like concepts, are *orientation processes,* that is, they are processes which enable a person to interact selectively with his environment. An attitude involves *direction* and *selectivity.* If I don't like Negroes, or think that Jews are untrustworthy, I have an orientation towards Negroes and Jews. I have a way of seeing and feeling about Negroes and Jews which is different from any number of other ways that I could think and feel about these people. The fact that I think and feel in this specific manner means that I am *predisposed* to see Negroes and Jews in certain kinds of ways. I am not neutral or indifferent about Negroes and Jews. I am *set, prepared, predisposed,* to think and feel in certain ways, and I tend to act in ways consistent with the way I think and feel. If I don't like Negroes, I probably will not want to live in the same neighborhood with them; I may not want to go to school with them; I will limit my contacts with them. On the other hand, if I have a positive attitude towards Negroes, if I feel that they have the same rights as all other human beings, I will be predisposed to act consistently with this way of thinking and feeling. I will be for school integration and for integrated living areas; I will not hesitate to have Negroes among my friends or invite them into my home.

ATTITUDES AS INFERRED PROCESSES. This relationship between the predisposition to action and particular ways of behaving is an important one. An attitude is a process that cannot be observed directly. In our model of variables of personality (see Chapter Three, Figure 2) we have placed attitudes, as well as concepts and needs, in the class of variables called mediating variables. We know that these variables cannot be observed directly; they are inferred from behavior. Observed behavior is the basis for an inference about an attitude, but the observed behavior is not the attitude itself. If I want to know what American teenagers think about science or scientists, I must observe some behavior of these students that is related to science and scientists. I can look at the statistics on the number of students enrolled in science courses and make an inference about the attitudes of the students toward science. My inference may be more or less correct, but the behavior of taking science courses is assumed to be related in some way to an attitude toward science. Certainly I would demand more evidence than merely the number of students enrolled in science courses before I drew conclusions about students' attitudes toward science.

The investigators in the study quoted earlier asked the students a series of questions relating to how they felt about science.[4] When a student says he agrees with the proposition that "there is something evil about scientists," and when he also agrees with the statement "scientific work is too boring for me," we may infer that this student's attitude toward science is a negative one. We know that he does not find science interesting and that he is somewhat suspicious of the intentions of scientists. From these behaviors and other responses we make an inference about his attitude toward science and scientists. The greater consistency that we find among various behaviors, the more likely our inference is to be accurate. If this same student does

---

[4]One method to determine students' attitudes toward science used written essays on this subject. See M. Mead and R. Metraux, "Image of the Scientist Among High School Students," *Science*, 126 (1957), 384-90.

not enroll in science courses, never watches a science program on television, makes disparaging remarks about science students, we have more confidence that our inference about his attitude is correct.

This distinction between the observed behavior and the underlying attitude has practical significance for the teacher. The teacher is continually making inferences about the attitudes of his students on a wide variety of subjects. Teachers commonly make inferences about the attitudes of students toward school and the subject the teacher is teaching. "Mary is interested only in boys; school is just a way of meeting boys for her." "Rudy's only interest is athletics; school is a bore for him." "Jane's attitude toward school work is positive; you can't give her too much work to do." These kinds of comments are continually made by teachers; they appear in discussions of students, in interviews with parents, in the records of students. Each is an inference about the attitudes of students toward school and school work, and presumably is based upon the observations of the teacher. As we noted when discussing the motives of students, inferences about either motives or attitudes must be based on reliable observations; further, an inference must be checked continually against new observations. If the teacher remembers that the observed behavior is not the attitude itself but used only as an indicator of a presumed attitude, he can be more cautious and systematic in his judgments about students' attitudes.

ATTITUDES AND MOTIVES. Motives and attitudes are alike in that we infer the presence of an attitude or a motive from consistencies and directions in behavior. However, attitudes and motives differ in important ways:

1. An *attitude* is a state or condition of the organism which predisposes the individual to be motivated in specific ways, but it is not an existing motive. For example, a student who has a positive, constructive attitude toward school work will be predisposed to be motivated by assignments given by the teacher. If the teacher announces a test for the following day, the student with the positive, constructive attitude will be motivated to study hard. A student with a negative attitude toward school work is less likely to be motivated in this way. The student who hates school work either will not study at all or will study poorly. Similarly, the student who likes school work

is more likely to be motivated to achieve the awards given for a superior performance than is the student who feels negatively toward school work.[5]

2. A *motive* is generally more specific than an attitude. A motivated student is working toward a particular goal, and is energized at the moment to achieve that goal. The student with a positive attitude toward school work will be motivated in many different but related ways, such as working for a high grade on a test, doing extra readings, studying his notes thoroughly. In each of these cases the student is working toward a particular goal, and common to all of these goals is a positive attitude toward school work. *The general, persistent attitude underlies the specific motives.* The specific ways in which the student may be motivated, because of the attitude that he holds, are almost unlimited. When we have correctly inferred what the student's more general attitude is, we have a basis for explaining the specific kinds of motives that we inferred from our observations of the student's behavior.

CHARACTERISTICS OF ATTITUDES

An attitude has been defined as a predisposition or a state of readiness. An attitude may also be characterized as one kind of an anticipatory response. Not all anticipatory responses are attitudes. A child of three or four can anticipate his mother's displeasure if he drags mud into the house, but it is unlikely that the child has an attitude about dragging mud into the house. If we are driving a car, we make numerous anticipatory responses, such as anticipating a change in lights or a sudden swerving of a driver in an adjoining lane. While we have attitudes about driving and other drivers, these attitudes may not be related to specific anticipatory responses. The following characteristics differentiate attitudes from other kinds of states of readiness:

1. *Attitudes imply a subject-object relation.* Attitudes are related to objects, people, places, events, abstract ideas and concepts

---

[5]We are not concerned here with the complex personality reaction in which the individual may do that which he hates; our interest is with the more general case in which attitudes predispose to motivations consistent with the attitudes.

in the environment of the person. Anything that the person can distinguish as psychologically separate from himself can be an attitude-object. We have attitudes toward groups of people, toward institutions, about particular people; we have attitudes toward physical objects, such as our home, our desk, our favorite book. An individual differentiates himself from some aspect of his environment, and this differentiation is the basis for the subject-object relationship. When the individual has feelings about this object, he has an attitude toward this object.

An individual may have attitudes toward himself, and in this respect the individual is psychologically distinguishing some aspects of himself toward which he has attitudes. An adolescent may have an attitude toward his body; the fact that he talks about his physical make-up as "his body" indicates that, to him, his body is an attitude-object.

We have attitudes toward "things," though what is an attitude-object varies from person to person and from time to time for the same person.

2.   *Attitudes have direction.* Attitudes are directional orientations toward objects, whether the objects are persons, places, or abstract ideas. We are "for" or "against" something, we prefer one group to another group, we like and dislike. All these ways of describing psychological movement toward or away from something suggest the directional character of an attitude. A person who has an attitude is not neutral toward the attitude-object.[6]

3.   *Attitudes are characterized by an intensity factor.* Two people with the same attitude toward science feel more or less strongly about science and scientists. One student may agree that scientific work is boring, but may not feel very strongly about how boring this work is. Another student may feel very strongly about the boring character of scientific work.

---

[6]In attitude studies, some individuals are identified as in a neutral position on an attitude continuum, that is, somewhere between the positive and the negative side of an attitude dimension. It would be equally correct to describe these people as having "no attitude," or to say that they have an attitude which falls midway between the extremes of the attitude. The neutral point has meaning only with reference to the extreme positions on the continuum of the attitude scale.

Psychologists who study attitudes construct scales in such a way that an individual can strongly agree or just agree, or strongly disagree or just disagree with some attitude statement. For example, most people have some kind of attitude toward war and the inevitability of war. If we present a group of people with a statement, "War is inevitable," and ask them to respond with *yes* or *no* to this statement, we would not detect the range of agreement or disagreement with this statement. However, if we allow them to indicate whether they strongly agree, agree, are undecided, disagree, or strongly disagree with this statement, we obtain some indication of the strength of their feelings about this statement.

In describing people's attitudes, we can conceive of them as having varying degrees of strength or intensity. If a person's attitude is relatively weak, if he does not feel strongly about Negroes, or Jews, or school, or baseball, we would predict that his observable behavior will not be greatly influenced by his attitude toward these subjects. On the other hand, if a person feels very strongly, either positively or negatively, about Negroes or Jews or baseball, we would predict that his observable behavior would be correspondingly more influenced by these attitudes.

4   *Attitudes are acquired.* A child is not born with a set of attitudes toward his environment. As we noted above, attitudes are orientations; they are ways of interpreting the environment and reacting to environmental stimuli. These ways of interpreting and reacting require a discrimination and a generalization over many similar kinds of objects.[7] An individual may or may not have an attitude toward a particular Negro, a particular Jew, or a particular Boy Scout group. But if he has an attitude toward Negroes, Jews, or Boy Scouts, he has generalized his attitude to embrace any of the particular individuals who fall into these categories. A Negro, a Jew, or a Boy Scout will influence this individual to respond in a way in which he has responded to other Negroes, Jews, and Boy Scouts. Through the processes of discrimination and generali-

---

[7] A theoretical discussion of this relationship can be found in R. J. Rhine, "A Concept-Formation Approach to Attitude Acquisition," *Psychological Review,* 65 (1958), 362-70.

zation, the individual develops a generalized pattern of response which we call an attitude.

One startling, unusual, or traumatic experience can influence an individual's attitude for the rest of his life.[8] Other attitudes are built up over a period of time; the individual has new experiences and interprets these and integrates them into his ways of thinking and feeling. A child of two or three may have no strong attitudes toward school because he has had little experience with school or with teachers. When he starts kindergarten, he begins to react to the environment of the school, he forms clearer impressions and develops stronger feelings about school, he develops some general orientations toward schooling. As he progresses through school, some of these reactions to school are strengthened and reinforced. His reaction to one teacher may be generalized to other teachers. Eventually he reaches a point in his development where we can say with some assurance that he has a definite attitude toward school and teachers. The modern school emphasizes the importance of initial and continuing pleasant and rewarding school experiences for the child. The modern teacher is encouraged to be warm, pleasant, and friendly so that children may develop correspondingly positive attitudes toward the teacher.

The process of acquiring an attitude, such as a positive attitude toward school, is complex. We cannot be sure that a pleasant kindergarten teacher or a pleasant kindergarten experience, or even a few years of a rewarding and agreeable school environment will result invariably in the acquisition of a positive attitude toward school. A pleasant school environment may or may not offset the influence of a parent who continually rewards expressions of his own negative school attitude. Since attitudes are sets to respond to one's environment, the stimuli to which one is responding during attitude development are important determinants of the attitude that is learned.

---

[8] The evidence for this statement is largely clinical in character. Case histories of psychotherapists report the effects of such incidents on the development of personality. Experimentation on this problem is necessarily limited for ethical reasons. Studies on reaction to and adaptation to unpleasant stimuli supply some relevant evidence. See, for example, N. W. Shock and C. H. Coombs, "Changes in Skin Resistance and Affective Tone," *American Journal of Psychology*, 49 (1937), 611-20.

5. *Attitudes are characterized by stability and consistency.* While attitudes may have varying levels of specificity, that is, while we may have an attitude toward the boy at the desk across the aisle or our next door neighbor, we do not speak of our feelings about these persons as attitudes unless there is some consistency in our reactions. An attitude is said to exist when the individual has acquired a stabilized, consistent way of interpreting and responding to his environment.

The teacher can err in inferring what the attitudes of his students are if he interprets momentary or spontaneous reactions as indicators of a stabilized attitude. Shifts in mood or feeling, or the effects of a disaster on the playground, should not be interpreted as indicative of attitudes toward either the teacher or the school. If the teacher remembers that attitudes are stabilized patterns of behavior and not momentary and spontaneous sets, he can avoid incorrect inferences about students' attitudes.

THE ACQUISITION OF ATTITUDES AND NEED-SATISFACTION

We have stressed the importance of the relationship between experience and attitude formation and development. The child acquires ways of responding to the set of stimuli or environmental events which form the pattern of his experience. The child who says, "Negroes are lazy" or "School isn't any fun," has learned a way of interpreting and responding to his environment.

Attitudes are responses, and acquiring an attitude is a behavior change, though this behavior change is not directly observable. The general principles that explain behavior change apply to attitudes as well as to other kinds of behavior phenomena.

Behavior change begins in a motivated state of the organism. The need system of the person is aroused or energized, and the person makes responses, the function of which is to reduce the state of need. Attitudes, as responses, must be need-satisfying, or must lead to responses which themselves are directly satisfying. Since attitudes are not directly open to observation, the relationship of attitudes as complex sets of responses to the need system of the organism is not obvious.

Nonetheless, we can frequently trace the relationship of an acquired attitude to the satisfaction of a need.

REWARDS FOR LEARNING ATTITUDES. A child usually has a need for affection and love from his parents. To satisfy this need, the child learns to behave in ways which are pleasing to the parents, because when he behaves in these ways he receives love and affection. He notices that his parents have certain ways of talking and acting when the subject of Negroes comes up, or he observes his parents in contact with Negroes. He hears his father making derogatory remarks about the living habits of Negroes and "detrimental effects that Negroes have on a neighborhood." He hears his mother's suspicions about the Negro employees at a local department store. If the child wants to maintain the love and affection of his parents, he may act in ways that are pleasing to them. He may have learned that when he acts as his parents do, he receives strong approval and demonstrations of affection. If the child makes unkind remarks about a Negro playmate, he is not punished for them, but is rewarded for making these remarks by subtle demonstrations of approval or affection. This child may quickly learn that these particular responses and the implied ways of thinking and feeling, when expressed openly and verbally, bring reward and not punishment. Adult approval and rewards for behavior resulting from a given attitude serve as the mechanism by which the child learns that a given kind of attitude is likely to satisfy his needs.

Since interpersonal relationships are the situations in which many of our social needs are satisfied, we would expect individuals to learn attitudes which maintain satisfying interpersonal relations. Many of the child's basic attitudes are learned in the context of the family where the behaviors associated with these attitudes are consistently rewarded and intimately tied in with the child's needs for satisfaction. If a child wants to be loved and valued by his teachers, his classmates, parents, and neighborhood friends, he will probably acquire the attitudes which guarantee the maintenance of these friendly and satisfying relations.

CONFLICT IN ATTITUDES. A child may be in conflict over the appropriate attitudes to adopt because he may be striving for two or more goals, both of which are desirable but which cannot be attained at the same time. For example, a child may want the approval of both his parents and his classmates. In some cases attaining the approval of both is incompatible. The child is in conflict because as he strives for the goal of parent approval, he also wishes to avoid the undesirable aspects of winning parent approval, namely, giving up the approval of his peers. As he strives for student approval, he wishes to avoid the

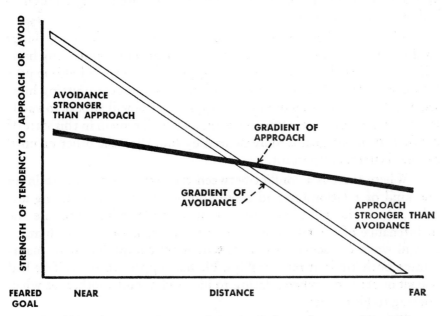

Simple graphic representation of an approach-avoidance conflict. The tendency to approach is the stronger of the two tendencies far from the goal, while the tendency to avoid is the stronger of the two near to the goal. Therefore, when far from the goal, the subject should tend to approach part way and then stop. In short, he should tend to remain in the region where the two gradients intersect.

It is only for the sake of simplicity that the gradients are represented by straight lines in these diagrams. Similar deductions could be made on the basis of any curves that have a continuous negative slope that is steeper for avoidance than for approach at each point above the abscissa. (From Dollard and Miller)

FIGURE 24

undesirable aspects of winning student approval, namely, giving up parent approval. One aspect of this kind of conflict can be diagramed as in Figure 24.[9] As the child approaches one desirable goal, feelings

---

[9]From J. Dollard and N. Miller, *Personality and Psychotherapy*, New York, McGraw-Hill Book Co., 1950, p. 356. By permission of the publisher.

of avoidance also arise. When the feelings of avoidance are strong enough, he withdraws from striving for the first desirable goal and returns to a point where his feelings of approach and avoidance balance each other. He then may strive for the second desirable goal, but the same process of approach and avoidance is repeated. He will approach this goal until his avoidance feelings are strong enough to pull him away from it.

We would expect to find the child in our example doing things to obtain parental approval but at the same time not committing himself wholeheartedly to winning this approval. We would also expect him seeking to win student approval but, again, not committing himself wholeheartedly to winning this approval. He will appear to vacillate or be in conflict over what he wants. He will remain in this state of conflict until one goal is more desired by him than the other or until neither becomes important.

Where there is a conflict between the attitudes for maintaining one kind of relationship and those appropriate for maintaining another, the child will choose the set of attitudes which promise the maintenance of the relationship which is more important to him, or he will work out sets of attitudes which are compatible with maintaining both kinds of relationships. He may appear to act as if he had one set of attitudes when relating to his teacher and another set when relating to his parents.

The diversity and conflicting nature of many special attitudes in our society frequently leave children in a state of indecision about what attitudes are most appropriate. This problem seems to be particularly acute as the child's world of social relations expands, and it becomes important for him to "get along with" a wide variety of people who hold divergent attitudes. As one teenager put the problem,

It's pretty hard to know what to think. Mostly kids in our school think that going steady is the thing to do. But my parents keep telling me that I shouldn't be tied down to one boy, that I'm too young to decide now about a boy. They want me to go to college, and keep saying that I shouldn't be thinking about marriage at my age. But if I don't go steady with a boy, I'll be left out of things around here. A girl who hasn't a steady is just a nobody. The other kids seem to think that there's something wrong with you if you can't tie a boy to you.[10]

---

[10]Remmers and Radler, *op. cit.*, p. 164.

This teenager is undecided and in conflict over discrepant attitudes toward dating. How she will resolve the conflict will depend upon what attitudes will ultimately lead to the greatest satisfaction of her needs. For the time being she vacillates between accepting the attitudes of her parents and those of her fellow students, a situation which is not entirely satisfactory to her and gives her only temporary relief from her uneasiness and self-doubt. Whatever attitude she develops, either momentarily or more permanently, will be a function of her needs and of the behavior that leads to the satisfaction of these needs.

THE IDENTIFICATION PROCESS AND THE ACQUISITION OF ATTITUDES

We have emphasized the function of attitudes as a way of satisfying needs. The learning of appropriate attitudes and responses is not merely a trial and error process. Some attitudes are probably acquired through trial and error, but attitude acquisition is often facilitated by the more general processes of *imitation* and *identification*. Everyone has observed a small child at one time or another imitating or copying his mother and father or his brothers and sisters. The fact that human beings imitate each other is undeniable. What is not always apparent is that imitation is rewarding for the imitator.

IMITATIVE BEHAVIOR. By *imitation* we mean *copying*—a process in which one person acquires the behavior patterns of another by copying his patterns. All kinds of particular behaviors are acquired in this manner—gestures, ways of speaking, ways of dressing, ways of walking. In the processes of imitation, one person serves as a stimulus or cue for the behavior of a second person. Dad hitches his pants up a certain way, Johnny sees this stimulus event and attempts the same kinds of responses. Eventually Johnny reaches the point where he can copy exactly the behavior of his father and can perform this behavior without his father being present. In the early stages of the imitative process the imitator needs a model that he can perceive in some way in order to learn the pattern of responses being performed by the model. Eventually the imitator can perform these responses so efficiently on his own that the model need not be present.

The imitative behavior becomes stabilized only if it is rewarded. Johnny's father and mother laugh and pat Johnny on the head when he imitates Dad. The models stimulate and encourage the copying process. Johnny is told to act like Dad, to hold a fork like Dad, to comb his hair like Dad. One adolescent serves as a model for another, but is imitated only if the imitator's behavior is rewarded in some way. The fads that periodically sweep the ranks of adolescents are examples of imitative behavior. A teenager is just not one of the gang if he does not cut his hair a certain way, hitch his pants at a certain height, slouch

to the left or to the right in the appropriate manner. Failure to imitate the current fads or fashions can often cause social ostracism. The behavior pattern which he observes becomes a part of his own repertoire of behavior if he is rewarded for this imitation.

THE IDENTIFICATION PROCESS. If the reward value of being like another person is sufficiently great, the process of imitation converges into the process of identification. *Identification is a process in which one individual becomes psychologically involved in and assumes the behavior patterns of another person.* When one individual *identifies* with another, he sees himself *as* this other person and takes on not only this person's way of walking, talking, gesturing, but also begins to think and feel as he assumes the other does. The boy who has been imitating his father may eventually identify with his father, if the rewards for being like his father are sufficiently need-satisfying. Because the child has had a relatively long exposure to his father's ways of thinking and feeling and acting, he develops a fairly clear picture of how the parent would probably respond in a variety of situations. If he attempts to respond as he thinks his father would respond, the child is identifying with the parent. Identification is a step beyond simple imitation because, when the individual has identified, he acts independently of the model, but his behavior is consistent with his conception of how the model would act. Attitudes, as well as other behaviors, are acquired through the processes of imitation and identification.

MODELS IN THE IDENTIFICATION PROCESS. The child is exposed to the attitudes of a variety of people. If he imitates, and more particularly if he identifies with these people, he will tend to take on their ways of thinking and feeling. A child can identify with any number of models. However, he will not identify with other persons if there are no rewards or need-satisfactions attached to the process of identifying with these individuals. A boy may identify with a male teacher, a coach, the best athlete in the class, the best student in the class, the class rebel, the class hero, baseball players, jet pilots, movie stars, singers. Some of these identifications are temporary and affect the behavior of the child only in minor ways. The five-year-old who imitates and identifies with a western hero and the fourteen-year-old who identifies with the latest popular singer temporarily assume the behaviors and attitudes of their respective heroes. At this particular time, the identifications have some reward value; the identifications are abandoned when they no longer have reward value or when other identifications have greater reward value.

As the word *model* suggests, the person who is imitated or with whom the child identifies must be observable by the child. The model need not be immediately present, but the child must have some way of knowing how this person would act and feel. Historical figures cannot be directly observed by the child, but the child acquires information about these individuals through books, moving pictures, and television programs so that he has some image of the person who is to be imitated. A child can read in school the speeches of Abraham Lincoln and may even memorize the Gettysburg Address. In this way he infers something about the way Lincoln thought and felt on important problems. Whether or not the child identifies with Mr. Lincoln depends upon other factors, but if he is to identify at all with Mr. Lincoln or any other person, he must have knowledge of the person's behavior.

THE IDENTIFICATION PROCESS AND THE SCHOOL. Since a child acquires many of his attitudes through identification with other individuals, the kinds of persons with whom the child is identifying are of crucial educational significance. A child's attitudes toward school and the attitudes that he brings to school will have been strongly influenced by his identifications within his own family. The following comment, taken from notes of a counselor, illustrates this point:

Tom was enrolled as a freshman in a pre-engineering program. He first came to the counseling bureau because he was academically deficient. Tom was having difficulty in applying himself to studying. Tom's interests were consistent with his plans, and he had sufficient ability to follow the pre-engineering program successfully. Why was he doing poorly in his academic work? Tom frequently referred to his eminently successful father. Tom's image of his father was that of a man who was largely self-made. Tom's father had not gone to college. He was a highly successful insurance sales-man, and Tom enjoyed many of the benefits that resulted from his family's superior economic position. Tom thought highly of his father and admired his success. As he discussed his goals and his academic problems, he frequently expressed the idea that he could be as successful as his father had been with-out pushing himself through a demanding academic program. Tom ques-tioned whether it was worth his while to put off the rewards of success in business to go to college.

A short time later Tom's father came in to discuss Tom's academic prob-lems. The father made it quite clear during the course of conversation that, while he thought college was important for Tom, he himself had been a success even though he had not had the opportunities for a college educa-tion. He subtly disparaged the values of a college education. Assuming that he spoke in this manner in Tom's presence, at least occasionally, it is highly probable that Tom's basic attitude toward the importance of college had been largely shaped by his father. If Tom wanted to be like his father, and he did, then he would think and act as his father did. This meant taking a deprecating attitude toward the values of college and feeling that the important thing was to get into business and push himself to success as his father had done before him.

This example, one of many that can be cited by almost every teacher, shows how the child's attitude toward school, as well as many of his other attitudes, has been shaped by his identification with his parents or other family members. Attitudes developed through identi-fication with family members are not easily changed because of the rewards attached to holding these attitudes. When these attitudes are not consistent with the attitudes the school is attempting to develop in the child, the likelihood of the school having any influence is not great. Where the attitudes learned in the home are consistent with those learned in school, the attitudes are reinforced and strengthened.

The Bennington College study[11] provides interesting examples of this kind of conflict. Attitudes toward public affairs of the girls at Bennington College were studied over a four-year period. Bennington had opened during the Depression, and the formative years of the college coincided with the period of the "New Deal." One of the im-

---

[11] The complete details of the Bennington study appear in T. M. Newcomb, *Personality and Social Change*, New York, Dryden Press, 1943. Summaries and condensations appear in T. M. New-comb and E. L. Hartley (eds.), *Readings in Social Psychology*, New York, Henry Holt and Co., 1947, pp. 345-57; T. M. Newcomb, "Attitude Development as a Function of Reference Groups: The Bennington Study," in E. E. Maccoby, T. M. Newcomb, and E. L. Hartley (eds.), *Readings in Social Psychology*, 3rd Edition, New York, Henry Holt and Co., 1958, pp. 265-75.

portant characteristics of the college was "the conviction on the part of the faculty that one of the foremost duties of the college was to acquaint its somewhat oversheltered students with the nature of their contemporaries' social world." Many of the girls held conservative social and political attitudes. On the other hand, the faculty of the college strongly advocated a more liberal point of view and encouraged an active interest in public affairs. One of the major questions the study sought to answer was whether the Bennington atmosphere produced a substantial change in the attitudes of the girls who had spent several years there. Cited below are comments made by some of the most conservative girls; that is, girls whose attitudes had changed the least in their stay at Bennington. Included also are comments from girls who were the most liberal; that is, girls whose attitudes had changed the most during their stay at Bennington.

CONSERVATIVE GIRLS:

F32: *Family against faculty has been my struggle here.* As soon as I felt really secure here I decided not to let the college atmosphere affect me too much. Every time I have tried to rebel against my family I found out how terribly wrong I am, and so I have naturally kept to my parents' attitudes.

D22: I would like to think like the college leaders, but I'm not bold enough and I don't know enough. So the college trend means little to me; I don't even realize how much more conservative I am than the others. *I guess my family influence has been strong enough to counterbalance the college influence.*

M12: It isn't that I have been resisting any pressure to become liberal. The influences here didn't matter enough to resist, I guess. *All that's really important that has happened to me occurred outside of college,* and so I never became very susceptible to college influences.

NONCONSERVATIVE GIRLS:

H32: I accepted liberal attitudes here because *I had always secretly felt that my family was narrow and intolerant, because such attitudes had prestige value.* It was all part of my generally expanding personality —I had really never been part of anything before.

Q43: It didn't take me long to see that liberal attitudes had prestige value. But all the time I felt inwardly superior to persons who wanted public acclaim. Once I had arrived at a feeling of personal security, I could see that it wasn't important—it wasn't enough. *So many people have no security at all. I became liberal at first because of its prestige value.*

Qx: Every influence I felt tended to push me in the liberal direction: My underdog complex, *my need to be independent of my parents, and my anxiousness to be a leader here.*

Q63: *I came to college to get away from my family,* who never had any respect for my mind. Becoming a radical meant thinking for myself and, figuratively, thumbing my nose at my family. *It also meant intellectual identification with the faculty and students that I most wanted to be like.*

As the above comments illustrate, the problem of identification may be central to changes in attitude. The girls most strongly identified with their families were also the girls whose attitudes changed the least; the girls who wished to break off their ties with their families or who wanted the reward of prestige approval were the girls who became most identified with the Bennington community and, consequently, changed their attitudes to the greatest extent. As the data from this study suggest, schools can influence attitudes. But the extent to which a school will influence an attitude development will be dependent upon the nature of the identifications of the students. Attitudes built on strong identifications are not easily modified.

While in school, a student may work out a number of solutions to a conflict between attitudes held by persons with whom he has strongly identified and the attitudes that the school is attempting to communicate. His attitudes may change temporarily in some respects while in school, and then change again when he returns to his home. A student may work out a kind of temporary psychological isolation so that he is secure in school without radically changing his attitudes.

EMINENT PERSONS AS IDENTIFICATION FIGURES. The school typically provides a wide variety of models in hopes that these will be identification models for the students. There are three principal kinds of potential identification figures present in the school environment: (1) historical personages, prominent individuals in contemporary society, idealized conceptions of men and women; (2) the teachers themselves; (3) fellow students.

Heroes of history are typical figures held up to students as models for appropriate attitudes and behavior. Many of these people are comparatively remote from the life of the students. The differences in social conditions from one era to another, the unusual dramatic lives led by these people, suggest to the student that they are models for admiration or copying but not for identification The "Horatio Alger" myth is probably an unrealistic model for success in American society at the present time. The American school boy, born in a hospital and reared in a large city, who attends elementary school and high school without ever having to worry about obtaining a basic education, would probably have some difficulties identifying with the Lincoln of the log cabin, who studied by firelight.

TEACHERS AS IDENTIFYING FIGURES. The teachers in a school are also potential identification figures. Some students identify with their teachers, even to adopting the teachers' ways of speaking and mannerisms.[12] While there are many different personalities among teachers, teachers as a group do not present a wide range of identification models. Teaching historically has been largely a female occupation; only recently have large numbers of men entered the teaching profession. As a consequence, the likelihood of boys identifying with female teachers is not great simply because the rewards for male identification are far greater than for female identification. Even for girls, the teacher presents a rather limited range of identification figures. The stereotype of the teacher in modern society has been that of a middle-aged female, frequently unmarried, relatively restricted in her social life by community conventions and mores. The elementary and high school teacher has not even been thought of as a member of an intellectual elite.

> But when the American hears the words "school teacher"—to the extent that he fills it in in a general way and not merely with an image of Miss Jones of the fourth grade, to whom he took flowers or who caught him smuggling worms into class—the image will be something like this. He will think of a grade-school teacher who teaches perhaps the third or fourth grade; this teacher will be a woman of somewhat indeterminate age, perhaps in the middle thirties, neither young nor old, of the middle class, and committed to the ethics and manners of a middle-class world. In the emotional tone which accompanies the image there will be respect, a little fear, perhaps more than a little affection, an expectation that she will reward his efforts and struggles to learn and conform, and a spate of de-

---

[12]At present, experimental evidence is lacking on the extent to which students identify with teachers and the factors which influence such identification. It is generally assumed that some students do identify with some teachers.

lighted memories of those occasions when he himself perpetrated feats of undetected mischief. She stands in his mind on the borderline of childhood, urging, beckoning, exhorting, patiently teaching, impatiently rebuking a child in whom the impulse is strong to escape the narrow bounds of the school room into the outdoors where birds are nesting, or the sun-lit pavements are waiting for marbles.[13]

Certainly not all American teachers fit this stereotype, yet this stereotype may dominate our thinking of what a teacher is like.[14] In many homes this is the kind of teacher for which children are prepared. The child may be prepared to see only those aspects of the teacher which conform to this stereotype and to ignore those which do not fit. The role of the teacher in American culture is not highly valued except in the panegyrics that accompany the retirement of a teacher who is finishing fifty years of service. "Teachers" tend to be associations with childhood, not models for life. Practically speaking, these facts suggest that the likelihood of pupils identifying with their teachers is not great. Insofar as the teacher represents something more than the stereotyped image of the typical American school teacher, the possibility exists that students will identify with their teachers.

As a matter of practical consequence, the faculty of any school should probably include a wide variety of personality types, both male and female, who represent a range of inferred attitudes and observable behavior patterns. An important but at present unanswered question is this: What is the probability that students will acquire the attitudes fostered by the school if they do not identify with some of their teachers?

The school, more than any other social institution, is responsible for encouraging and stimulating intellectual attitudes. In the

[13]M. Mead, *The School in American Culture*, The Inglis Lecture (1950), Cambridge, Harvard University Press, 1951, p. 5.
[14]An interesting description of this stereotype, as it appears in literature, can be found in A. Foff, "Scholars and Scapegoats," *The English Journal*, 47 (1958), 118-26.

school students develop an attitude toward the pursuit of learning; they learn to value critical thinking, the incessant search for facts, and the value of logical argument and careful experimentation. The school provides rewards for problem-solving, and responsible social behavior is encouraged and systematically taught. Critical tastes and refined feelings are developed, and the emotional and affective life of the child is enriched. The attitudes which will facilitate the development of these changes in behavior are not likely to be learned through identification processes if students regard teachers as dull, boring, spinsterish, and socially useless.

A recent experimental study illustrates the relationship we have been discussing.[15] The experimenter measured the extent to which teachers' behavior was seen as warm and friendly by students. He also measured the amount of required work done by students and the amount of work that students initiated on their own. Significant positive relationships were found between the extent to which the students described the teacher as friendly and warm and the amount of self-initiated and required work that they did. While this study does not directly demonstrate the relationship between identification with teachers and change in pupil behavior, the experimenter suggested that the identification process could account for the relationship found. Teachers frequently advocate "working on one's own." However, the extent to which a student works on his own is a measure of the relationship between his attitudes and those of the teacher. The pupil works on his own because in identifying with the teacher he has taken on the teacher's values about the importance of self-initiated work.

Other hypotheses could be generated to explain this relationship. However, other studies have indicated that the identification process is fostered when the identification figure is warm and friendly.[16] Further experimental work will be necessary before we can say that changes of the kind studied in this experiment are mediated by the identification process.

---

[15]M. L. Cogan, "The Relation of the Behavior of Teachers to the Productive Behavior of Their Pupils" (unpublished Ed.D. dissertation), Harvard University, 1954. A brief account of this study can be found in H. Levin, T. L. Hilton, and G. F. Liederman, "Studies of Teacher Behavior," *Journal of Experimental Education*, 26 (1957), 81-91.

[16]"Warmth" may be related to identification, but recent experimental work suggests the importance of other variables in facilitating this relationship. For a discussion of this problem, see R. R. Sears, E. E. Maccoby, and H. Levin, *Patterns of Child Rearing*, Evanston, Illinois, Row, Peterson and Co., 1957. A comparable discussion can be found in A. Bandura and R. H. Walters, *Adolescent Aggression*, New York, Ronald Press, 1959.

The school is not entirely responsible for the image of the teacher that is so common in American society, but the school can do something about invalidating this image in choosing the teachers that are employed to staff our schools. Providing the kinds of teachers with whom students will identify is not simply a matter of having a faculty of young teachers or of married teachers, but of having a faculty of teachers who are sensitive to the world in which they and the children are living. The teacher must be the kind of person whose behavior has meaning and relevance for his students, as the principles discussed suggest. The students do not have to want to be teachers in order to want to be like their teacher. The student can admire the critical, inquiring attitude of the teacher and recognize that this kind of attitude will be rewarding to adopt. Being like the teacher in some ways will have its rewards in enabling the student to interpret his own environment and to adjust to it successfully.

INFLUENCE OF GROUPS ON THE ACQUISITION OF ATTITUDES

We have been discussing the influence of one individual on the formation of attitudes in another person. People have group relationships as well as person-to-person relationships, and these groups influence the attitudes of their members. Members of any given political party, religious group, fraternal organization, or social club have relatively common attitudes. Membership in one of these groups presupposes that the individuals who are in or wish to join the group have attitudes similar to those held by the group. This commonality of attitudes, interests, and values characterizes both the groups which have a formal organization and those which are informally organized. We tend to associate with people who share our point of view on a wide variety of subjects.

Individuals identify with groups as well as with other individuals. When a person identifies with a group he sees himself as a member of that group. He thinks of himself as having the attitudes of the members of this group. As in the case of identification with individuals, the person is influenced by the prevalent attitudes of the groups to which he belongs.

MEMBERSHIP AND REFERENCE GROUPS. Not everyone who belongs to a group necessarily shares the attitudes and values of the group, nor identifies with the group. We can distinguish between *membership* groups and *reference* groups. *A membership group is a group in which an individual is formally enrolled or a group of which he is regarded as being a member. A reference group is a group which influences the attitudes of an individual because he identifies with the group even though he may not be formally a member of this group.* At Bennington College, in the study referred to above, all of the girls were formally enrolled in the college organization. Bennington was the membership group for all of these girls. However, for some of these girls Bennington was not a reference group; the college group had comparatively little influence on their attitudes. The girl who said that the main influence on her life was her home, is a member of two groups—her family and the Bennington College group—but only the family is her reference group.

This distinction between membership group and reference group behavior explains a wide variety of behavior that can be observed in almost any school. Every student is a member of a school, of classes in the school, and frequently of other groups within the school. Teachers and administrators are often puzzled by the lack of influence of the school, or of particular groups within it, on the behavior of some pupils. These discrepancies are easily explained when we realize that formal group membership does not guarantee that the psychological processes of group identification will be initiated. In almost every class there are "outsiders," students whose interests seem to lie primarily outside of the school and who have no close ties with any of the groups within the school. In other cases, students' identification with groups preclude the influence that the school is capable of having on their attitudes. A student who joins the "Dirty Dozen," a group which is primarily interested in being known as the "beer drinkers" and whose dominant attitude is that school is a place for having fun, is not likely to be strongly influenced by the more academic groups nor is he likely to be appropriately affected by the experiences which the school provides for the purpose of encouraging particular kinds of attitude development.

NEED-SATISFACTIONS PROVIDED BY GROUPS. How does a group influence the attitudes of its members? People join groups for a variety of reasons related to the satisfaction of their basic needs. Some people join a group because the project the group is working on is one in which they are interested. These individuals will obtain their satisfactions from the achievements of the group. Others will join a group because they like people and the social interaction resulting from group membership provides satisfaction.

Groups are also sources of prestige and status. The prestige of the group spreads to its members. In a complex organization like the school there are many groups, and a hierarchy of prestige can be found among them. Gordon studied the social organization of a high school and found the following groups among the students:[17]

1. *Athletic Crowd:*

> The athletic clique contained five varsity football members. . . . They were known as the "beer drinking crowd, who go over to the westside

[17]C. W. Gordon, *The Social System of the High School*, Glencoe, Illinois, The Free Press, 1957, p. 120.

sometimes for sexual experimentation. . . . They have cars, dates, money, and usually liquor, and are highly clothing-oriented.

2. *Music and Club Activity Crowd:*

The music clique concentrated on intramural and second-line prestige sports. They were more grade-oriented than the athletic group.

3. *Dating Crowd:*

The dating clique concentrated slavishly on dress, intramural sports, and less prestige varsity sports. They were all "steady dates." They were not considered "big wheels" by cliques 1 and 2. They considered themselves "big wheels." Their major focus was on spending money in the proper manner, playing the social game, and religious adherence to dress.

4. *The "Brainy" Crowd:*

The "brainy" clique's major focus was on scholastic achievement. Four members were elected to the National Honor Society. They combined participation in organizations of various kinds with extreme emphasis on scholarship. . . . Conformity on dress and dating was much more casual.

5. *The Hunting and Fishing Crowd:*

The hunting and fishing clique "rated" with the "people who didn't rate." Out-of-school-oriented, they were members of the Outdoor Club, a low prestige organization. They were not as conforming to dress and dating as the other four cliques. There were several nonresident students among them.

The above ranking of these groups represents the order of prestige of the groups in the school. Each of these groups provides special kinds of rewards and satisfactions for their members. A student who belongs to the athletic crowd can satisfy his needs for high social prestige and prominence in the school. A student who belongs to the hunting and fishing crowd can satisfy his needs for outdoor activities, but he could not satisfy a need for social prestige. Such cliques control a wide variety of social behavior within the school; even the dating-behavior of these students may be group-controlled to some extent.

That the groups provide rewards for their members is apparent in the following sample of statements by clique members.[18]

The clique you belong to has a definite bearing on your prestige. If you belong to a fast moving athletic clique, you are usually the same and this

---

[18]*Ibid.,* pp. 106-108.

tends to build up your prestige outside of school and in dating more than would the other organizations of the school.

When you are in a good clique I think it helps your dating. For instance Mary Sands just recently started going around with us. It wasn't planned, but it just sort of happened. When she started going around with us she automatically got more dates.

These kinds of groups provide even more subtle rewards and satisfactions. The contemporary secondary school system in the United States is essentially grade-oriented. One of the functions of the cliques in a school is to provide security for members, even when their school achievement is not entirely satisfactory. If one belongs to the "athletic crowd," poor achievement may not be important, and many compensations are provided for failure to achieve successfully in school. These groups also provide status for the individual; they open ways for acquiring things that must be competed for, such as dates and school offices. They provide the individual with a sense of adequacy and security, and they set the standards for behavior which, if maintained by group members, bring with them the rewards and satisfactions that the group can provide.

Frequency of Choice	Freshmen		Sophomores		Juniors-Seniors		Entire College	
	N	Mean	N	Mean	N	Mean	N	Mean
40-89	—	—	3	60.3	5	50.4	8	54.1
12-39	—	—	5	65.6	15	57.6	20	59.7
5-11	—	—	5	65.3	18	62.2	23	62.7
2-4	10	64.6	18	68.6	19	61.6	47	65.3
1	12	63.4	17	68.6	15	62.1	44	65.0
0	61	72.8	39	71.3	14	69.0	114	71.7
Total	83	70.5	87	69.2	86	61.5	256	67.1

Mean PEP Scores, Classified According to Frequency of Being Chosen as Representative, 1938 (From Newcomb)

TABLE IX

Table IX summarizes data on the relationship between prestige and attitude change for the girls in the Bennington study.[19] The PEP scores are on a scale of "political and economic progressivism." Low scores on this test indicate nonconservatism, which was the prevalent attitude at Bennington. High scores represented conservatism. The students were asked to nominate the five students "most worthy to

---

[19] T. M. Newcomb, *Personality and Social Change*, p. 55.

represent the college" at an intercollegiate gathering. As the data in the Table indicate, students most frequently chosen were those having the lowest scores on the test of political and economic attitudes. The students whose attitudes were most consistent with the dominant attitudes at Bennington were also accorded the most prestige by their fellow students. This relationship was consistent in all four college classes. While these data do not prove that the nonconservatives changed attitudes in order to achieve prestige, they do demonstrate the relationship between learning the prevalent group attitudes and achieving the consequent rewards.

GROUP PRESSURES TO CONFORMITY AND ATTITUDE CHANGE. The power of the group to influence the attitudes of its members results in part from the pressures that the group sets up to encourage conformity. When an individual joins a group, he is made aware of the standards and values of that group in both obvious and subtle ways.[20] Deviation from the accepted attitudes and values is punished by the group with rejection, exclusion, ignoring of the deviant member, and deprivation of the rewards that the group can provide.

> By the time you are a senior, you should know when to wear heels, earrings, etc., and when to wear flats. People that would wear earrings to school or flats to the American theater naturally don't know anything. . . . Of course, you wouldn't wear saddles with hose or black suede flats with bobby socks. That would be unforgivable.

> Vance keeps everyone else in line on dress. He is always making fun of someone else's clothes. He'll say, "Look at that guy's socks. Is he 'fruit!' You gradually get on to what to wear."[21]

The influence of the group on opinions of individuals has been demonstrated experimentally by Asch,[22] who used a simple experimental task, that of matching a line of given length with one of three unequal lines. In this experiment the subject asked to do the matching

---

[20]L. Berkowitz, "Group Norms Among Bomber Crews: Patterns of Perceived Crew Attitudes, 'Actual' Crew Attitudes, and Crew Liking Related to Aircrew Effectiveness in Far Eastern Combat," *Sociometry*, 19 (1956), 141-53.

[21]Gordon, *op. cit.*, p. 117-18, 120.

[22]S. E. Asch, "Effects of Group Pressure upon the Modification and Distortion of Judgments," in E. E. Maccoby, T. M. Newcomb, and E. L. Hartley (eds.), *Readings in Social Psychology*, New York, Henry Holt and Co., 1958, pp. 174-83. The same data are also reported in S. E. Asch, "Effects of Group Pressure upon the Modification and Distortion of Judgments," in H. Guetzkow (ed.), *Group Leadership and Men*, Pittsburgh, Carnegie Press, 1951.

did so in a group. The other members of the group had been instructed by the experimenter to make errors deliberately in the matching. The subject was confronted with a situation in which the opinions of the group members flatly contradicted his own observations. Some of the "errors" made by the other members of the group were obviously large. What was the effect of the majority opinion on the judgment of these subjects? The following results were obtained:[23]

1. There was a marked movement toward the majority. One third of all the estimates in the critical group were errors identical with or in the direction of the distorted estimates of the majority. The significance of this finding becomes clear in the light of the virtual absence of errors in the control group, the members of which recorded their estimates in writing (see Table X).

Number of critical errors	Critical group* (N=50)	Control group (N=37)
	F	F
0	13	35
1	4	1
2	5	1
3	6	
4	3	
5	4	
6	1	
7	2	
8	5	
9	3	
10	3	
11	1	
12	0	
Total	50	37
Mean	3.84	0.08

Distribution of Errors in Experimental and Control Groups (From Asch)

TABLE X

*All errors in the critical group were in the direction of the majority estimates.

[23]*Ibid.*, pp. 176-77.

2. At the same time the effect of the majority was far from complete. The preponderance of estimates in the critical group (68%) was correct despite the pressure of the majority.

3. We found evidence of extreme individual differences. There were in the critical group subjects who remained independent without exception, and there were those who went nearly all the time with the majority. . . . One fourth of the critical subjects was completely independent; at the other extreme, one third of the group displaced the estimates toward the majority in one half or more of the trials.

These laboratory groups were artificial groups since the subjects were assigned to the groups in a random manner. The group members associated with each other as a group only in the experimental situation. The evidence from this experiment is all the more striking when we recall that the task required the subjects to use the evidence provided by their own observations. There was little ambiguity, little room for opinion, in the essential nature of the task. We would expect that the influence of the majority would be even greater where there is room for differences of opinion. A group of high school students deciding on appropriate dress would be such a situation. The rules for proper dress are comparatively arbitrary. The group is free to set up its own standards, and the individuals in the group have no clear criteria for deciding what is appropriate, other than the group standard. In such situations we would predict that the influence of the majority opinion would be all the more marked.

In the above experiment a large percentage of subjects was not strongly influenced, or was not influenced at all, by the opinions of the group. This result can be explained in the following ways: (1) There were probably some individuals in the group who felt it to be important to maintain an independence from majority opinion. (2) There were probably some individuals who were withdrawn from the group activity, and who reacted to the experimental task as an individual problem. (3) There were probably some individuals in the group committed to performing the task as well as they could irrespective of other people's judgments. These individuals probably had not formed identifications with their groups.

We would expect to find people in formally organized groups for whom these groups are merely membership groups, not reference groups. When this kind of a relationship exists between an individual and a group to which he belongs, the influence of the group on his opinion is relatively small. But when an individual is strongly identified with a group, and particularly in those areas of group concern for which there are no clear-cut criteria, the individual is likely to be influenced by the prevalent opinion in his group.

CONFORMITY PRESSURES AND PATTERNS OF COMMUNICATION. In another experimental situation, Schachter[24] set up groups which were to decide on the disposition of a problem in human relations. He introduced three members into each group, one of whom agreed with the majority opinion, another of whom deviated slightly from the majority opinion, and a third member who deviated considerably from the majority opinion. Schachter then studied the acceptance of these individuals in the group and the patterns of communication directed toward them. He found that the largest number of communications were addressed to the most deviant member, particularly when group members were highly interested in the group activity. The group member who agreed with the majority had no more communications addressed to him than did any other member of the group. The slightly deviant member had some communications addressed to him until he shifted to a position of agreement with the group. These data suggest the pattern of pressures verbally transmitted to the members of a group.

At the end of the experimental session the members were asked to nominate individuals to committees; one, an executive committee which had high prestige and the other, a correspondence committee which had low prestige. The deviates were nominated much more frequently for the correspondence committee than were any other members and were undernominated for the executive committee. This experimental study illustrates group pressures for conformity, even in groups which are artificially and temporarily formed.

A group communicates its standards, its prevalent attitudes and values, to its members both openly, through verbal communication, and subtly, through suggestions and hints. One can identify the rewarding of conforming behavior and the punishing of nonconforming behavior. The student who shows up at school in dress which does not conform to the pattern for his group is told, either directly or indirectly, that his dress is inappropriate. When the group is highly

---

[24] S. Schachter, "Deviation, Rejection, and Communication," *Journal of Abnormal and Social Psychology*, 46 (1951), 190-207. Also in D. Cartwright and A. Zander, *Group Dynamics: Research and Theory*, Evanston, Illinois, Row, Peterson and Co., 1953, pp. 223-48.

attractive to the student, when he expects to obtain rewards by being a member of the group, when it is important for him in any way to belong to the group, these pressures will tend to produce conformity to the group standard. If the student does not conform, if he is not interested in the group, if the group is merely a membership group and not a reference group for him, he will tend to be isolated and cut off from the group. If he is free to leave, he may join another group that will provide rewards for him.

SUMMARY

Let us review at this point the basic concepts and principles that are relevant to the learning of attitudes.

1. Attitudes are hypothesized as acquired patterns of responses. These responses are inferred from observable behavior, but cannot be directly observed themselves. Attitudes are sets which predispose a person to act in specific ways and to be motivated in specific ways.

2. Those attitudes are acquired which produce or lead to need-satisfaction.

3. The learning of attitudes is facilitated by the identification process. The identification process is initiated within an individual when he begins to see himself as being like another person, or when he sees himself as being like the members of a group. In this process the person begins to think and feel like the person or group with whom he is identifying.

4. An *identification figure,* or a group, influences attitude formation because the identification figure or the group is a source of need-satisfaction. By identifying with a person or a group an individual obtains rewards which lead to need-satisfaction, but these rewards can be obtained only by acquiring the attitudes of the identification figure or group.

5. Identification figures and groups also exert pressures to conformity by punishing behavior which is not consistent with the attitudes of the identification figure or group.

6.   Before a pupil can learn an attitude the teacher desires him to learn, he must have an opportunity to observe the behavior relevant to the appropriate attitude. He must know the attitudes of the identification figure or group.

Because this identification process is of central importance in the formation of attitudes, we cannot assume that attitudes are easily changed. If a child's attitudes are to be influenced by the teacher, the teacher in some degree will need to be an identification figure for the child. Before any individual can be an identification figure for another, two conditions must be satisfied: (1) the identification figure must have sufficient prestige so that adopting his attitudes will be rewarding for the person; (2) a unique relationship must be established between the identification figure and the person. At present, all the factors influencing the establishment of this unique relationship are not known, but this kind of a relationship seems to be fostered when the identification figure is a warm, friendly, understanding person.

The school-age child is influenced by many people. As a consequence, his attitudes are being changed because of interaction with individuals other than his teachers. When a child enters school, some attitudes have already been formed, and others are in the process of being developed. The school, as a social institution, attempts to encourage desirable attitudes in children. Learning experiences are provided to promote behavior changes of this kind. An important question for education is—What characteristics of learning experiences are likely to facilitate attitude formation or attitude change? In the next chapter we will discuss additional specific factors which influence attitude change. One important conclusion that we will draw is that no single factor in itself is sufficient to produce attitude changes in all individuals. We will also see that some factors that people have commonly assumed to be influential in producing attitude change probably have comparatively little influence. When the teacher has studied the factors influencing attitude change, he will have information that can be utilized to formulate hypotheses regarding the organization of learning experiences. We emphasize here the complexity of the problem of attitude formation and change, to impress upon the teacher the need for thought and imagination in organizing learning experiences that most probably will result in the attitude development of concern to the school.

STUDY AND DISCUSSION QUESTIONS

1. Review the description of the opinions held by students who seem to have a negative attitude toward scientists. What factors in these students' lives may have influenced the development of their attitudes toward scientists? What kinds of need-satisfactions might a student obtain by holding such attitudes? Would you argue that these students were merely uninformed about the lives of scientists?

2. From what behaviors that you could observe, would you infer that a student—

    a. did not like teachers?

    b. felt that students from lower socio-economic groups were inferior to him?

    c. thought the study of history was valuable?

    e. felt that participation in athletic competition was childish?

3. You infer that a student has a positive attitude toward achievement in school; in what ways would you predict that he would be specifically motivated?

4. You infer that a student feels strongly that it is important to get along with other people; again, predict the ways in which this student is likely to be motivated.

5. What attitudes would you infer from the following instances of motivated behavior?

    a. A student works hard for a scholarship.

    b. A student tries hard to win a place on a varsity team.

    c. A student works actively on the student newspaper.

6. In responding to Question No. 5, have you suggested only one attitude that may be inferred from each of these instances of motivated behavior? Review your list of inferred attitudes and predict other instances of motivated behavior that you would expect to observe if the student held these attitudes.

7. Below is a list of activities that may be goal objects for a student. Suggest some conflicting attitudes that a student may hold relevant to these goal objects. Explain what factors may influence a conflict in attitudes relevant to these goal objects.

    a. Going to college.

    b. Using the family car.

    c. Steady dating.

    d. Being a top student.

8. Suggest the need-satisfactions that may be attained by a student who identifies with the following people:

   a. Mother or father.

   b. A teacher.

   c. A popular classmate.

9. What models do you think parents would suggest a boy imitate if he is to learn his masculine sex role? What models probably would be suggested to girls if they are to learn their feminine sex role?

10. Small children may be observed to imitate Western heroes whom they watch on TV. What is the probability that these children identify with these heroes? What factors may influence identification?

11. Some people argue that TV programs and movies that portray the lives of criminals have a bad influence on children. Evaluate this argument in the light of the discussion of the identification process presented in this chapter.

12. What factors in the Bennington environment may have increased the probability that girls attending Bennington would identify with the Bennington community? What differences between Bennington and other colleges and universities might account for the fact that students at other institutions may identify to a lesser degree with their respective college communities? What factors associated with attending a high school may inhibit strong identification with the high school community?

13. Some people argue that boys in the elementary schools have difficulty in assimilating the attitudes teachers try to develop in students because the teachers are frequently women. Evaluate this argument by relating the concept of identification to these attitude changes.

14. Are there some student attitudes that teachers are less likely to influence? If you think so, explain what factors would account for the fact that these attitudes are not likely to be changed.

15. Describe some student organizations with which you are familiar in terms of the dominant group attitudes of these organizations as you perceive them. What pressures to conformity are typically exerted by the members of these groups?

16. Groups may be more or less attractive to their members. What prediction would you make about the relationship between the attractiveness of a group to its members and the pressures to conformity in these groups? Check your predictions by reading Schachter's study of this relationship.

17. What kinds of need-satisfactions may be obtained by a group member who adheres to the group standards for behavior?

18. You observe that a student does not seem to have any group associations in your school. What hypotheses would you offer to explain this observed behavior? How could you determine whether this student had been "rejected" by other students?

RECOMMENDED READINGS

The first reading reviews basic principles relative to attitude formation and their application to the organization of learning experiences. The second reading is a review and analysis of experimental data and theories on children's attitudes. The third reading is the report of an extensive study on the attitudes of American teenagers. The fourth reading is an analysis of the basic principles and concepts relevant to a theory of the psychology of attitudes. The last two readings are more extended discussions of many of the topics treated in this chapter.

1. D. B. Harris, "How Children Learn Interests, Motives, and Attitudes," *Forty-ninth Yearbook of the National Society for the Study of Education, Part I, Learning and Instruction*, Chicago, University of Chicago Press, 1950, Chapter 5.

2. D. H. Russell, *Children's Thinking*, Boston, Ginn & Co., 1956, Chapter 6.

3. H. H. Remmers and D. H. Radler, *The American Teenager*, Indianapolis-New York, Bobbs-Merrill Co., 1957.

4. M. Sherif and H. Cantril, "The Psychology of 'Attitudes'," *Psychological Review*, 52 (1945), Part I, 295-323.

5. T. M. Newcomb, *Social Psychology*, New York, The Dryden Press, 1950, Chapters 4, 6, 7.

6. S. E. Asch, *Social Psychology*, New York, Prentice-Hall, Inc., 1952, Chapters 16, 18, 19.

LEARNING AND THE
ATTITUDINAL PROCESSES—II

In the preceding chapter we discussed the general processes by which attitudes are learned. We have stressed that the interpersonal relationship called the identification process is an important determinant in attitude change. We have observed, however, that even in the identification process, an individual must have an opportunity to observe the behavior of his identification figure. He must know what the attitudes of the identification figure are. A communication process by which an individual learns the content of an attitude is required.

The content of the attitude can be communicated in a variety of ways. Much of this information is assimilated casually and informally as children observe adults. In other cases, we systematically attempt to communicate appropriate attitude content; for example, a teacher discussing attitudes toward the forms of democratic government is conveying information about the content of the appropriate attitudes. He is saying, in effect, that a student who has a desirable attitude toward democratic government thinks and feels in certain ways.

The communication process can be organized so that the content of the communication is more persuasive. This chapter is devoted to a discussion of factors in the communication process which are likely to influence attitude change. In the latter part of the chapter the evaluative processes will also be discussed.

FACTORS INFLUENCING ATTITUDE CHANGE

Attitudes arise from experience; if attitudes are to be changed, the individual must have new experiences relevant to the desired attitude change. If we want Johnny to think that whites and Negroes have the same rights and are to be treated in comparable ways, then Johnny must have a set of experiences in which he finds adopting this attitude rewarding. We attempt to encourage attitude change through communication and by creating rewarding conditions.

When we say that we attempt to change attitudes through communication, we mean that a teacher, a parent, or another individual attempts, through communicating with a person, to persuade him to change his way of thinking and feeling. In this section we will study the relation of the communication process to attitude change.

Considerable experimental evidence indicates that attitudes, and their reflection in opinions, can be changed.[1] The degree to which an attitude is changed depends upon a wide variety of factors. As an introduction to this topic we will discuss a communication experiment on attitude change, conducted in an ordinary classroom. The experimental techniques resemble typical classroom procedures.

One hundred and sixty-two high school students participated in this experiment.[2] Initially, the students were tested to determine the extent to which their attitudes reflected prejudice toward groups of people other than their own racial, ethnic, or religious group. The students were then divided into three groups. The first group was shown a film on prejudice, and the members participated in a discussion of the film after the showing. The second group only saw the film. The third group did not see the film nor did they discuss the subject of prejudice; they merely were tested for prejudice. The film,

---

[1]For a survey of results obtained in studies of intergroup attitudes and a critical analysis of research in this area, see R. Williams, *The Resolution of Intergroup Tensions,* New York, Social Science Research Council, 1948. Another but less critical survey of a selected area of studies can be found in P. E. Jacob, *Changing Values in College,* New Haven, Edward W. Hazen Foundation, 1957.

[2]L. L. Mitnick and E. McGinnies, "Influencing Ethnocentrism in Small Discussion Groups through a Film Communication," *The Journal of Abnormal and Social Psychology,* 56 (1958), 82-90.

The High Wall, treats group prejudice as a "communicable disease" and traces its origins in the family and community. After the first group had completed its discussion of the film, all three groups of students took the same tests they had taken before the film. An information test on the content of the film was also given to the groups that had seen the film at that time. The initial testing showed that in all three groups there were students who had high, low, or intermediate degrees of prejudice.

In this experiment a typical pattern of communications was used. The students saw a film that presented a point of view and that had the purpose of persuading the viewers that prejudice was a disease that should be uprooted and destroyed. Does this kind of a communication influence the attitudes of students? Does the predisposition of the student have any influence on whether or not his attitudes will be changed? Will the student who is highly prejudiced be less prejudiced after seeing this film? Does the experimental treatment—that is, whether a student saw the film with or without discussion—affect attitude change?

The results of this experiment were as follows: (1) Significant reductions in prejudice as measured by the test were produced in both experimental groups, that is, the groups that had seen the film. The reduction in prejudice was not related to the predisposition of the students, however, but to the kind of experimental treatment. (2) When the students were tested at a period one month later, students who had participated in discussion maintained the greatest change over that period of time. As Figure 25 indicates, the groups that had seen the film showed a significant shift in attitude immediately after the film, but there was a gradual change back to the original attitude. The least amount of change back to the original attitude was found in the groups that discussed the film after they had seen it (see Figure 26). (3) The amount of information learned from the film was related to the initial attitude of the students. Those individuals who were low in prejudice learned more factual information from the film than did those who were high in prejudice (see Figure 27).

These experimental results suggest the problems associated with organizing experiences to produce an attitude change. The film produced significant shifts of varying degrees in attitudes among all the people who saw the film. However, because of intervening experiences and the effects of initial learning of attitudes, the change in attitude is not maintained to the same extent by all the viewers. The regression to the original attitude apparently is minimized if students participate actively in a discussion in which the learning from the film is reinforced.

This experiment has not been discussed to suggest a methodology for changing attitudes. What this experiment illustrates is the variety of factors that influence attitude change and that must be taken into account in any methodology the teacher may devise. Let us summarize what these factors are: (1) The predisposition of the student—the attitude that he brings to the learning situation—influences the amount of factual content that he will learn from the film. He may not even get his facts straight and he may not remember them if he is negatively predisposed to the subject presented. (2) Some of the general principles of learning also apply. The film conveys a mass of concepts, ideas, principles and facts that are difficult for students to assimilate. One of the contributions of the discussion period after the film is probably clarification of ideas. We can only speculate on other

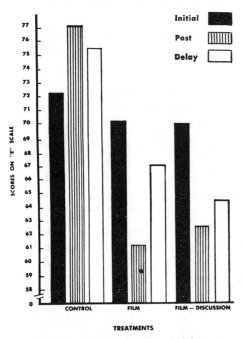

Initial, posttreatment, and delay scores on the "E" scale for each treatment. (After Mitnick and McGinnies)

FIGURE 25

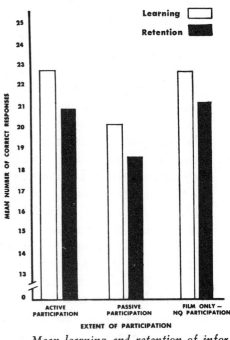

Mean learning and retention of information scores for each level of participation. (After Mitnick and McGinnies)

FIGURE 26

values of the discussion, such as the opportunity to express feelings that can be clarified by being brought out into the open and the opportunity to discover that other people take the same position. (3) The extent to which a student participates actively in the discussion is related to the amount of attitude change (see Figure 28). We do not know what personality variables determine the extent to which a student will participate in the discussion. These unknown variables may be the crucial factors that are likely to produce attitude change.

There are several important factors which are not taken into account in this experiment. For example, suppose that discussion groups, instead of being organized with subjects of varying degrees of prejudice in each group, were organized so that all subjects with the same degrees of prejudice were in the same group. We would have groups with high prejudice members and other groups with low prejudice members. Would the discussion now make a difference? We would predict that, when group members discovered that there

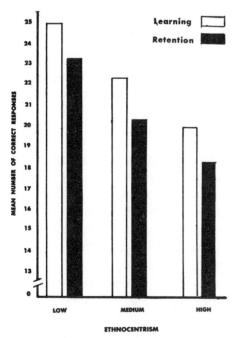

Mean scores on the learning and retention test for each predisposition group. (After Mitnick and McGinnies)

FIGURE 27

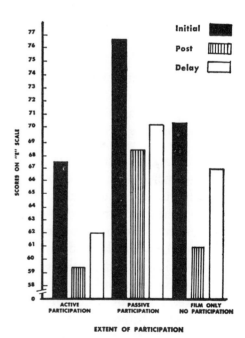

Initial, posttreatment, and delay scores on the "E" scale for each level of participation. (After Mitnick and McGinnies)

FIGURE 28

was a common group norm, the original attitude would be strengthened and the amount of attitude change would be correspondingly affected. In this case the predisposition of the students would probably make a difference. When we put similarly prejudiced people together and ask them to discuss a communication that is contrary to what they believe and feel, we would expect them to strengthen each other's attitudes and to reject as a group the attitudes supported by the communication. In the above experimental communication, only one side of the issue was presented. What would have been the effects if both sides had been presented simultaneously or one after the other? As we have noted so frequently before, psychological research has suggested many factors which must be taken into account in devising an educational methodology. We raise these questions to point out that other factors relevant to the character of the communication may influence attitude change.

We cannot lay down specific rules to tell the teacher how and in what way he must arrange educational experiences in order to produce attitude change. What the psychological literature does provide is a knowledge of the factors that are crucial in the development of any methodology. What are these factors? Recall again that one of the major devices in attempting to produce attitude change is to establish a communication of some kind, to provide information, to make persuasive statements. In the following sections we will discuss the characteristics of communications that influence attitude change.

INFLUENCE OF THE PRESTIGE AND CREDIBILITY OF THE COMMUNICATOR. One of the important factors influencing the extent to which a communication, as we are using the term here, will affect an attitude change is the prestige and credibility of the source of the communication. The communicator who has prestige with his audience, or whom his audience regards as trustworthy, will effect changes in attitudes and opinions in the direction that he advocates.

Kelman and Hovland[3] used an identical communication with three different kinds of communicators. High school seniors were asked to listen to a recording of an educational program, ostensibly to judge its educational value The guest speaker was introduced in three different ways to three different groups of students. The first speaker was identified as a judge of a juvenile court, a highly trained

---

[3]H. C. Kelman and C. I. Hovland, "Reinstatement of the Communicator in Delayed Measurement of Opinion Change," *Journal of Abnormal and Social Psychology*, 48 (1953), 327-35.

and experienced authority. The second communicator was identified as a member of the studio audience chosen at random. The third communicator was presented as if selected from the audience, but an introductory interview with him revealed that he had been a delinquent as a youth and that he was currently on bail after being arrested on a charge of dope peddling. Each communicator gave exactly the same communication, a statement advocating extreme leniency toward juvenile delinquents. What was the effect of the source of communication on attitude change? As the data in Tables XI and XII indicate, a large percentage of students thought that the judge, the

	Source of the Communication		
	Judge	Audience Member	Juvenile Delinquent
Judgment	N=110	N=60	N=102
Per cent of each group judging him as giving a "completely fair" or "fair" presentation	73%	63%	29%

For positive vs. negative $p < .001$

Audience Evaluation of the Same Talk on Juvenile Delinquency When Delivered by Positive, Neutral, and Negative Communicators (After Kelman and Hovland)

TABLE XI

Group	N*	Mean†
Judge	97	46.7
Audience Member	56	45.7
Juvenile Delinquent	91	42.8

Immediate Effects of Different Communicators on Opinion Scores. (After Kelman and Hovland)

TABLE XII

*A high score represents the position of leniency advocated in the communication.

†t pos. −neg. $=4.11$ $p < .001$
t pos. −neutr.$=0.79$ $p=.21$
t neutr.−neg. $=2.36$ $p < .01$

positive communicator, was completely fair in his presentation, whereas the former juvenile delinquent was regarded by only a small percentage of students as being fair in his presentation. Furthermore, the largest amount of attitude change occurred in the group that heard the communication from the judge. In other words, the communicator of a message has a definite effect upon the attitude change of the individuals who hear his message.

The situation is not so simple as this conclusion seems to indicate, however. Kelman and Hovland found that when they studied the attitudes of these students three weeks later the differences in attitudes had disappeared and that the three groups of students, each of whom had heard a different communicator, had now substantially the same attitudes. However, when at this later date some of the students were reminded of the source of the communication, the original changes in attitude were reproduced. For those students who were not reminded of the original sources of communication, the attitude changes disappeared. The major conclusion seems to be that the prestige and authority of the communicator has its greatest effect on immediate opinion change and that whatever changes in attitude are effected at this time can be maintained only by a continual association of the communicator with his message.

An important factor affecting the listener's evaluation of the source of the communication is the listener's perception of the trustworthiness and prestige of the communicator.[4] If the source of the communication is suspect in any way, if the listener feels that the communicator personally has something to gain by persuading people, his prestige and authority is diminished. A communicator has only relative prestige; the prestige of a person speaking on a subject on which he is presumed to know little has comparatively little effect in producing attitude change. If we want to know something about the effects of atomic testing on genetics, we are likely to be influenced by the opinions and attitudes of scientists who are most informed on this subject. We will probably tend to disregard the attitudes and opinions of people whose training and experience are in fields completely unrelated to this subject.

Some individuals have so much prestige that they can influence attitudes and opinions on a wide variety of subjects, including those

---

[4] C. I. Hovland and W. Mandell, "An Experimental Comparison of Conclusion-Drawing by the Communicator and by the Audience," *Journal of Abnormal and Social Psychology*, 47 (1952), 581-88.

on which they are not experts. Also, some social roles represent sufficient prestige that the ideas and opinions of individuals in these roles carry great weight. A recent study illustrates this latter point.[5] Two groups of high school students heard a recorded communication. This communication made no cognitive sense. The communication was a set of sentences logically unrelated to each other, or to any underlying theme. One group of students was told that this was a communication from a college president; the other, that it was a communication from a PTA member. In both cases the same voice and content was involved. The students were asked to indicate whether they understood the communication. They were also asked to indicate the sense of the communication if they thought they understood it, or to explain why they did not understand it if they had indicated that they did not. Students who heard the communication as though it were given by a college president tended to "understand" the communication; students who heard the same communication "from a PTA member" tended to "not understand." The former group more frequently attempted to make sense out of the communication than did the latter, which characteristically recognized that the communication did not make sense. In other words, even a communication that is nonsense is treated as if it were important when the communication source carries prestige.

At the present time we do not know all the social roles or individuals who have sufficient prestige to influence attitudes and opinions on a wide variety of subjects. The influence of some prestige figures can be attributed to the fact that people can easily identify with them. Many heroes of adolescence are influential in forming attitudes because adolescents can identify easily with them. In cases such as this, the crucial determinant of attitude change is probably the identification factor. In other cases, the prestige factor will be an important determinant, even though identification with the prestige figure may be limited.

Using a positive communication source is probably one of the commonest devices of teachers to promote attitude changes. The mottoes and maxims of great men adorn many classrooms. The argument from authority is one of the commonest arguments used in attempting to prove a point. The likelihood of students being influenced

---

[5] A. P. Coladarci, E. Elson, and K. Finis, "The Effect of Prestige Symbols in 'Critical Listening'," *California Journal of Educational Research*, 5 (1954), 202-08.

by credibility sources is not great if this is the only factor that is manipulated in presenting students with communications designed to change their attitudes. This method of persuasion even contradicts one objective that schools attempt to achieve, namely, the critical evaluation of information, opinions, and principles in the light of objective evidence rather than on the basis of authority for the statements. Practically speaking, the use of credibility sources is not likely to produce drastic changes unless the child identifies with the communication source and unless the authority figure remains imaginatively present so that his influence on the communication can be maintained.

THE TEACHER AS A CREDIBILITY SOURCE. While we have no experimental evidence on the credibility of the teacher, the possibility that the teacher has high credibility is important. Little can be said by way of experimental evidence to suggest in what ways the teacher's influence is likely to be crucial in producing attitude change. The fact that "teacher says so" may be influential in determining attitude change in younger children, but the teacher's prestige as such probably has comparatively little influence on attitude change.[6] In American culture the teacher is not a high prestige figure.

Practically speaking, the use of prestige figures to communicate attitudes is a useful device, but its effectiveness in promoting permanent attitude changes is apparently limited. The authority figures that are used must be regarded as trustworthy and must have prestige with the students. The heroes of adults are not necessarily the heroes of children. Anyone, children included, must learn who the experts in a given field or on a given subject are before he is likely to be influenced by the attitudes and opinions of these experts. Furthermore, a device of this kind, even though it has limited effectiveness, probably should not be used at the expense of critical thinking on the part of students. When students can get the facts for themselves or when they can arrive at a solution to a problem by their own efforts, it probably is advisable to avoid a process in which they are rewarded for accepting answers on the basis of what somebody else says.

---

[6]Since the problem has not been studied adequately, this conclusion must be held tentatively. Frequently there are considerable prestige differentials among teachers in colleges and universities. An interesting study could be developed to compare the influence of teachers with more prestige than that of teachers with less prestige. On the basis of present knowledge, we would predict that in general the greater the prestige of the teacher, the greater his influence.

INFLUENCE OF FEAR-AROUSING APPEALS. The use of an emotional appeal couched in vivid imagery is one of the oldest devices for attempting to change human behavior. Teachers frequently use strongly worded and emotional appeals in endeavoring to change attitudes of children particularly when teaching younger children. How effective are such presentations? If a teacher is trying to develop positive attitudes toward dental hygiene and wants his pupils to brush their teeth regularly, should he give a coldly dispassionate presentation of the facts of dental hygiene, or should he enliven the presentation with dramatic pictures of the harmful effects of improper dental care? If you are teaching the facts of conservation and the importance of a positive attitude toward preserving natural resources, should you give the "cold facts" about the effects of poor conservation practices on our natural resources, or would your arguments be more effective if you presented films of raging forest fires, depleted farms, and migrants from the dust bowls?

Experimental data indicate that when a persuasive communication is designed to create sustained preferences or attitudes, a strong emotional appeal, based on *arousal of fear,* is not so effective as a minimal emotional appeal. Janis and Feshbach[7] studied the effects of fear-arousing communications on changes in attitudes. The dental hygiene practices of a group of high school students were surveyed. The group was then exposed to a fifteen-minute illustrated lecture on the causes of tooth decay which contained a series of recommendations about proper oral hygiene. Three forms of the talk were presented to three different groups of children: Form *1* contained a strong appeal pointing out the consequences of diseased gums, tooth decay, and all the other defects that result from improper dental hygiene; Form *2* presented a milder and more factual description of essentially the same information; Form *3* presented a minimal appeal in which the consequences of tooth neglect were referred to infrequently. The experimenters found that the greatest amount of worry and concern about dental hygiene practices was aroused in the group which had the strongest emotional appeal. But, as the data in Table XIII indicate, the greatest amount of change in the direction of conformity to dental practices occurred in the group which was subjected to the least emotional appeal. At a later date the experimenters intro-

---

[7] I. L. Janis and S. Feshbach, "Effects of Fear-Arousing Communications," *Journal of Abnormal and Social Psychology,* 48 (1953), 78-92.

Type of Change Group:	Strong (N = 50)	Moderate (N = 50)	Minimal (N = 50)	Control (N = 50)
Increased conformity	28%	44%	50%	22%
Decreased conformity	20	22	14	22
No change	52	34	36	56
Total	100	100	100	100
Net change in conformity	+8%	+22%	+36%	0%

Effect of the Illustrated Talk on Conformity to Dental Hygiene Recommendations (From Janis and Feshbach)

TABLE XIII

duced another communication which contradicted the original communication in at least one important feature. When the attitudes were studied after this countercommunication, the group given the minimal amount of appeal was again the group that was most resistant to the countercommunication (see Table XIV).

Strongly worded appeals and fear-producing pictures and words arouse strong tensions within the individual which he must handle in some way. There are several ways in which the anxiety-producing effects of a strong emotional appeal can be minimized. The students in the study, for example, can "stop listening" by ignoring the content

Type of Change Group:	Strong (N = 50)	Moderate (N = 50)	Minimal (N = 50)	Control (N = 50)
More agreement	30%	28%	14%	44%
Less agreement	38	42	54	24
No change	32	30	32	32
Total	100	100	100	100
Net change	-8%	-14%	-40%	+20%
Net effect (experimental minus control)	-28%	-34%	-60%	

Effect of the Illustrated Talk on Reactions to Subsequent Counterpropaganda: Net Percentage of Each Group Who Changed in the Direction of Agreeing with the Statement That "It Does Not Matter What Kind of Toothbrush a Person Uses" (From Janis and Feshbach)

TABLE XIV

of the message being conveyed. Or they can direct their anxiety against the communicator of the message. The person focuses his attention on his own anxiety and tensions rather than on the content of the message or his attitudes relevant to the content of the message. Threats, warnings, and vivid descriptions of evil consequences to follow have comparatively little effect in producing desired long-term attitude change. Threats of this kind may be effective as a temporary restraining technique but their effectiveness for producing long-term attitudinal changes is probably minimal. It is important not to overgeneralize the above study, even though other experimental evidence is consistent with the data from this study. For some topics and for some age groups, a strong emotional appeal may be more effective than a minimal appeal.[8] However, the weight of evidence at the present time suggests that extreme appeals are not likely to be highly effective in producing the attitude changes in which the school is interested.

INFLUENCE OF LOGICAL ARGUMENTS. The above study suggests that perhaps logical argument and careful presentation of factual evidence is more likely to influence attitude change. Common sense would suggest that simply presenting facts in a cold, logical manner is not likely to be highly effective in promoting attitude change. There are many ways in which facts can be presented. We can present the facts on only one side of an issue or on both sides. We can present the attitude-supporting facts first, followed by the attitude-contradicting facts; or, we can present the facts and arguments against an attitude position first, followed by the arguments for it. The effects of the kinds of presentations will vary depending upon the initial attitude position of the individuals listening to the arguments. A comprehensive study of these factors was conducted during World War II, and the results of these experiments have implications for teaching.[9]

---

[8]For example, the experimental data on the effects of punishment and the effects of success and failure are consistent with the above conclusion, if we assume that punishment and failure arouse anxiety. Recent experimental studies have determined the predisposition of children to be influenced by anxiety-evoking stimuli and have related this predisposition to behavior change in an anxiety-producing situation. The results indicate that subjects who become highly anxious in learning situations do not learn easily and efficiently. See, for example, R. R. Waite, S. B. Sarason, F. E. Lighthall, and K. S. Davidson, "A Study of Anxiety and Learning in Children," *Journal of Abnormal and Social Psychology*, 57 (1958), 267-70. See also I. E. Farber and K. W. Spence, "Complex Learning and Conditioning as a Function of Anxiety," *Journal of Experimental Psychology*, 45 (1953), 120-25. A theoretical discussion of the relation of anxiety to motivation and a comprehensive bibliography can be found in J. A. Taylor, "Drive Theory and Manifest Anxiety," *Psychological Bulletin*, 53 (1956), 303-20.

[9]C. I. Hovland, A. A. Lumsdaine, and F. D. Sheffield, *Experiments in Mass Communication. Studies in Social Psychology in World War II*, Vol 3, Princeton, Princeton University Press, 1949.

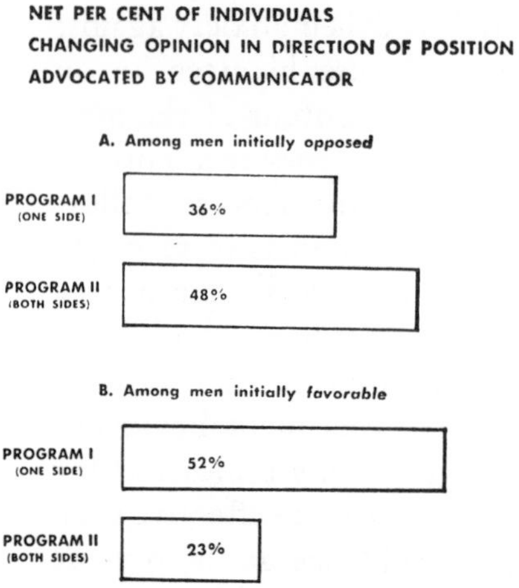

NET PER CENT OF INDIVIDUALS
CHANGING OPINION IN DIRECTION OF POSITION
ADVOCATED BY COMMUNICATOR

A. Among men initially opposed

PROGRAM I
(ONE SIDE)   36%

PROGRAM II
(BOTH SIDES)   48%

B. Among men initially favorable

PROGRAM I
(ONE SIDE)   52%

PROGRAM II
(BOTH SIDES)   23%

Effects of a one-sided vs. a two-sided presentation on beliefs. (After Hovland, Lumsdaine, and Sheffield)

FIGURE 29

What are the effects of presenting either one side or both sides of an issue on which people already have attitudes and opinions? If a person is initially opposed to the position advocated by the teacher, he is more likely to be influenced by a presentation which shows both sides of the argument. However, if a person is initially favorable to the position that is being advocated, he is more likely to be influenced by a presentation of arguments on the favorable side (see Figure 29). If the audience as a whole was studied, without considering the initial position of the listeners, probably no advantage would be found for either kind of presentation. The effect of giving both sides of an argument to those opposed is to weaken their position; when only one side is given to a person who already favors a position, obviously the arguments strengthen this position.

In the same experiments the effects of the educational level of the audience were studied. The two-sided argument was more effective with individuals who had more education. When both education and initial attitude position were studied, the communication which gave both sides proved to be most effective among those who were better educated irrespective of their initial stand. As might be expected, the one-sided presentation was mainly effective with those who were already convinced, among the less well-educated group. The more capable a person is of thinking critically, the more likely he is to evaluate the evidence for himself. A teacher in a classroom, discussing an issue on which the students already have attitudes and opinions, probably should present both sides of the issue. We would expect that the students who are most capable of thinking for themselves will most likely be influenced by the arguments for the position advocated when they have had an opportunity to evaluate both sides (assuming that the weight of evidence is on the side of the position advocated).

Teachers discuss many issues on which there are numerous points of view. In such subjects as social studies, art, and literature, a range of opinions and attitudes is possible on a wide variety of subjects. On some of these issues the weight of evidence will be on one side rather than the other, but on other issues the teacher's presentation probably will be influenced by his own opinions. If a teacher is discussing modern art, or the works of Faulkner, or even such tried and true classics as the works of Dickens or Scott, students' attitudes and opinions may differ considerably from those of the teacher. Probably the best presentation and discussion of such comparatively controversial subjects would be one in which a variety of opinions are presented, and in which the students are allowed to express freely their own reactions, attitudes, and opinions. If the teacher, at the same time, strongly encourages critical thinking and intelligent evaluation based upon careful gathering of facts and logical argument, the students are more likely to accept an attitude or an opinion when the weight of evidence favors this attitude or opinion. Haranguing students about what they

	Present All Sides	Prejudiced	Undecided
	%	%	%
Total	60	23	17
Boys	59	26	15
Girls	62	20	18
Grade 9	58	17	25
Grade 10	55	28	17
Grade 11	62	22	16
Grade 12	63	22	15
East	57	28	15
Midwest	62	20	18
South	63	20	17
Mountain-Pacific	58	22	20
Population to 2,500	63	19	18
2,500 to 25,000	56	29	15
25,000 to 250,000	63	19	18
Over 250,000	58	26	16
Low income	60	21	19
High income	61	25	14

In Discussing Controversial Topics, Do Your Teachers Usually Present All Sides of the Question Fairly or Do They Tend to Present a Prejudicial Viewpoint? (From Remmers and Radler)

TABLE XV

ought to think or feel is not likely to be effective. Presenting only one side of an issue is likely to be convincing only to those who already agree with the position.

Students do not uniformly agree that teachers characteristically present all sides of an argument, although the majority of them feel that teachers are fair in their presentation of controversial subjects (see Table XV). Students also agree that teachers should express their personal opinions and judgments about the material that they are teaching (see Table XVI).[10] A teacher has a reasonable certainty that

	On Art			On History and Government			On Present Political and Economic System of the U.S.			On Science like Biology and Chemistry		
	Yes %	No %	? %	Yes %	No %	? %	Yes %	No %	? %	Yes %	No %	? %
Total	73	15	12	58	34	7	53	35	11	71	16	9
Boys	69	18	13	59	33	7	51	35	11	71	18	8
Girls	78	12	10	57	34	8	54	34	11	72	15	9
Grade 10	71	15	14	55	35	9	48	38	12	72	16	9
Grade 11	71	17	12	59	33	7	54	33	13	73	14	9
Grade 12	78	13	9	61	32	5	57	33	8	70	19	8
Rural	69	17	14	57	33	9	54	32	13	71	16	10
Urban	77	13	10	58	34	7	52	37	10	72	17	8
East	75	15	11	55	36	8	53	34	11	75	15	8
Midwest	76	14	10	57	35	8	49	38	12	69	18	9
South	68	18	14	64	28	7	57	31	10	71	16	8
West	76	13	11	57	36	6	52	35	10	72	15	10

Should a Teacher Express Personal Opinions and Judgments in the Classroom About the Material He is Teaching? (From Remmers and Radler)

TABLE XVI

if he is fair in his presentation and if he advocates a point of view while presenting all sides of an argument, students will not resent his personal advocacy. Some students probably will resent an opposite point of view to their own, and will be antagonistic to attitudes different from theirs. The likelihood of influencing these students is not great with the means that are typically available to the classroom teacher.

[10]H. H. Remmers and D. H. Radler, *The American Teenager*, Indianapolis-New York, Bobbs-Merrill Co., copyright 1957, p. 132 (Table XV) and p. 136 (Table XVI). Used by special permission of the publisher.

As we have suggested above, attitudes are learned because they produce need-satisfaction. The teacher does not have complete control over the rewards and satisfactions which are reinforcing all of the attitudes of his students.

INFLUENCE OF GROUP MEMBERSHIP. We have discussed the effects of group membership on the formation of attitudes. What happens when we attempt to change the attitudes of a group? Does the group attitude preclude attitude change? We would predict that members who have strong ties with the group, those for whom the group is a reference group, will be least influenced by an attempt to change attitudes on which the group sets standards.

Kelley and Volkart[11] studied this problem with a group of Boy

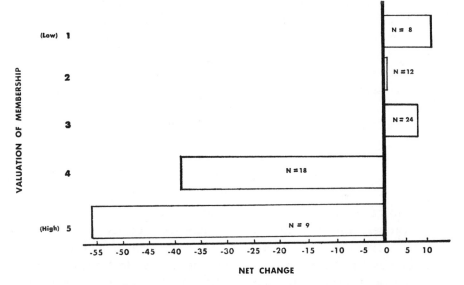

Opinion change in response to counternorm communication for Scouts with various degrees of valuation of membership* *("private" samples only). (From Kelley and Volkart)*

FIGURE 30

*Combining categories 1, 2, and 3 and comparing them (in terms of net change) with 4 and 5 combined, p < .02 using one-tailed test. Net change equals the per cent change in direction advocated by the communication minus the per cent changing in the opposite direction.

[11]H. H. Kelley and E. H. Volkart, "The Resistance to Change of Group-Anchored Attitudes," *American Sociological Review*, 17 (1952), 453-65.

Scouts. The experimenters first determined how closely each Boy Scout in twelve Boy Scout groups valued the scouting program. A week later an adult appeared before the troops and gave a talk in which he criticized many of the activities in which Scouts engage. He suggested that modern boys would profit more from learning about their cities than from studying the outdoors. The experimenters retested the attitudes of the Scouts on Scouting after this communication. The results showed that Scouts who highly valued Scouting were least influenced by the communication from the adult and those who valued it least were the most influenced (see Figure 30).

These data have implications for teaching. Attacking a group or directing persuasive arguments against the dominant attitudes of a group are devices likely to have little desired effect upon the group members for whom the group has the highest value. On the other hand, one of the most powerful means of influencing attitudes is by developing strong group identifications. This technique has been used consistently by teachers. Teachers urge students who are not doing well in school "to get in with" a group of students actively interested in school, who are leading in activities and generally doing well in school. This technique is not uniformly successful because the group may not accept the proposed member; but when a student can be inducted into a group of this kind, startling changes in attitudes are frequently observed. If a student already has some attitudes he shares in common with members of a group which he is being encouraged to join, the rewards of group membership will strengthen these attitudes and facilitate the learning and adoption of new attitudes.

Teachers also attempt to minimize the negative influence of groups by encouraging students to leave these groups. This technique would be useful if the student who is encouraged to leave one group can enter other groups that will provide satisfactions and rewards for him. Encouraging a student to leave a group whose attitudes are interfering with the student's success in school will only isolate the student and leave him without the satisfactions that he was seeking to obtain by belonging to the group in the first place.

In the Kelley and Volkart study the attitudes of the boys who strongly valued Scouting were even stronger after the communication against Scouting. This effect has been observed by teachers many times, although administrators and teachers still persist in openly criticizing groups that they feel are not helping their student members to achieve success in school. A teacher can acquire sensitivity to the formative effect that groups have on the attitudes of students. He can learn to use the effects of group identification to develop attitudes that are consistent with the objectives of the school and which foster the adjustment and development of the student in socially desirable ways.

INFLUENCE OF PERSONAL INVOLVEMENT. We have noted above that emotional appeals are not entirely successful in producing attitude change, nor is the mere presentation of logical arguments and reliable facts. Such presentations are effective, but under limited kinds of conditions. There is one factor that does seem to be especially effective in changing attitudes—namely, *active participation* in the processes being used to effect attitude change. By active participation we mean that, in the process of producing attitude change, the individuals whose attitudes we are attempting to influence are involved in the appeals.

King and Janis[12] presented groups of college students with a persuasive communication about the prospects of military service. The communication argued that over 90 per cent of college students would be drafted within one year after graduation and that the length of military service required of the majority of college students would be at least three years. All of the subjects in the experiment were college students of draft age and were not deferrable. The students were divided into two major groups. In the first group all the students read the communication, but read it aloud and into a tape recorder. The second group read the communication silently. The students in the first group were then told that their speaking ability was to be assessed. Some of these students were asked to read a prepared script based on the communication as if they were giving a talk. The remainder of the students in this group were asked to improvise a talk based on the communication.

In this experiment we have three levels of participation, or personal involvement, in the communication. All students read the communication; one group, however, read the communication into a tape recorder and then made a talk on the basis of this communication (improvisation group); a second group read the communication and a script based upon the communication (oral reading group); and

[12]B. T. King and I. L. Janis, "Comparison of the Effectiveness of Improvised versus Non-Improvised Role-Playing in Producing Opinion Changes," cited in C. I. Hovland, I. L. Janis, and H. H. Kelley, *Communication and Persuasion,* New Haven, Yale University Press, 1953, pp. 222-25.

the third group merely read the communication. Before the experiment the students were tested on their attitudes toward military service. The test was repeated after the experiment. Table XVII presents the changes in opinion that took place under these experimental operations. As is apparent from this table, the students who were most involved in the communication process itself were also the students whose attitudes changed to the greatest extent.[18]

Opinion Items	Improvisation Group A (N = 32)	Oral Reading Group B (N = 23)	Silent Reading Control Group (N = 20)
	Net Percentage Who Changed in the Direction Advocated by the Communication		
1. Estimates of required length of service for draftees	41	27	5
2. Estimates of percentage of college students who will be deferred	44	26	25
3. Estimates of percentage of college students who will become officers	70	47	45
4. Personal expectations of length of military service	59	46	50
5. Personal expectation of being drafted	50	26	55
6. Combined index: per cent influenced on three or more of the five opinion items	87½	54½	65
	p = .01		
	p = .03		

Effect of Role-Playing on Opinion Changes Following Exposure to a Communication Concerning the Prospects of Military Service for College Students
(From King and Janis)

Table XVII

The degree of active participation provided in this experiment was limited. The students merely gave a talk based upon information presented to them by somebody else. However, as the student gave the talk, he was playing a *role*, he was acting as the communicator of the information. As he attempted to communicate the information and

---

[18]For additional evidence on the effects of active participation, see I. L. Janis and B. T. King, "Influence of Role-Playing on Opinion Change," *Journal of Abnormal and Social Psychology*, 49 (1954), 211-18. Also discussed in C. I. Hovland, I. L. Janis, and H. H. Kelley, *Communication and Persuasion*, pp. 219-21.

arguments realistically, he began to think and feel as the "real" communicator would think and feel. He became involved in the role, he began to take on the attitudes and feelings of the person who ordinarily lived this role.

Role-playing is a device that has been used to bring about attitude changes. In any role-playing technique the participants are asked to portray as realistically as possible the life, the behavior, the feelings, the emotions, the attitudes, the opinions of some other person. One of the major effects of role-playing seems to be illustrated in the foregoing experiment: the individual playing the role begins to think like the other person. He begins to understand how a person living this role would think, and his attitudes may change in the direction of those held by the person whose role he is playing. Certainly the person who understands racial segregation better than anyone else is the person who has to live a life in which he has been segregated because of his race. If we have had no experience of this kind of life, our feelings about it are likely to be highly intellectualized. Through role-playing we do not actually live the life, but we approach it; by approaching the experience of another person, we may take on the attitudes and feelings of that person.

At the present time there is little experimental evidence on the effects of role-playing in educational settings.[14] Role-playing has been widely advocated and extensively used.[15] Experimental evidence does suggest that active involvement in a role does influence attitudes. We can hope that by utilizing role-playing techniques in our classrooms that we can produce attitude changes which would not be produced by other methods, such as emotional appeals or even logical arguments.[16] Here again, the teacher must devise methods and procedures experimentally until the time when more clear-cut formal experimental evidence is available. Some role-playing procedures that a

---

[14]A critical analysis of experimental research on role-playing can be found in J H. Mann, "Experimental Evaluations of Role-Playing," *Psychological Bulletin*, 53 (1956), 227-34.

[15]S. M. Corey, "Role-Playing as Training in Learned Behavior," *Nation's Schools*, 53 (1954), 52. Also, H. H. Jennings, "Sociodrama as an Educative Process," *Fostering Mental Health in Our Schools*, Washington, D. C., NEA Yearbook of the Association for Supervision and Curriculum Development, 1950; J. L. Moreno, *The Theatre of Spontaneity*, New York, Beacon House, 1947.

[16]The following studies contain descriptions of classroom experiments on the use of role-playing techniques: B. Hansen, "Sociodrama—A Methodology for Democratic Action," *Sociatry*, I (1948-49), 347-63; B. Hansen, "Sociodrama in the Classroom," *Sociatry*, I (1947), 334-50; A. Kaminsky, " 'You Are There' in the Social Studies Classroom," *High Points*, 36 (1954), 43-45; F. B. Moreno, "Sociodrama in the Sociology Classroom," *Sociatry*, I (1948-49), 404-13.

teacher may try will not be effective in producing attitude changes.[17] Rather than abandon role-playing procedures, the teacher ought to devise new ways of implementing active participation, personal involvement in a role and in the thoughts, feelings, and attitudes of individuals who live those roles.

THE IDENTIFICATION PROCESS AND COMMUNICATION. Throughout this discussion on factors influencing attitude change we have emphasized both the advantages and disadvantages, the possibilities and limitations, of various devices for promoting attitude change. At this point we will discuss another experiment that included many of the factors that we have been discussing. The experiment also supplies us with an opportunity to relate the concept of identification to the factors that we have been discussing. While this experiment was conducted in a military setting, the general procedures used approximate educational methods.

In this experiment[18] an attempt was made to influence trainees to eat a ration which was not particularly appetizing. This attempt to change attitudes was part of a training program for 427 air crewmen undergoing survival training. For experimental purposes the trainees were divided into six groups, each of which received a different approach to the problem of persuading the men to eat this ration. The experimental operations used in the six different groups were as follows:

1. In this group the instructors were briefed to make no effort to influence the trainees to accept the ration. They were instructed to say as little as possible about it, but were cautioned to avoid any impression of personal dislike for the ration.

2. In this group the instructors also were briefed to make attempts to influence the trainees to accept the ration. They were instructed to set a good example for the men by eating the ration themselves and casually expressing favorable reactions to it.

3. In this group the instructors were asked to give information about the value of the ration for emergency purposes and about ways of preparing

---

[17]That the results in role-playing are not always positive is indicated by the following author, who also discusses factors influencing role-playing activities: W. Coleman, "Role-Playing as an Instructional Aid," *Journal of Educational Psychology*, 39 (1948), 429-35.

[18]E. P. Torrance and R. Mason, "Instructor Effort to Influence: An Experimental Evaluation of Six Approaches," *Journal of Educational Psychology*, 49 (1958), 211-18.

it. The presentation was objective and factual, and given in a "take-it-or-leave-it" manner.

4. In this group, in addition to giving facts about the value of the ration and ways of preparing it, the instructors were asked to emphasize psychological factors which might influence the men in accepting the ration. This group, in other words, received information about the ration and factors which might influence them to accept or reject it.

5. In this group essentially the same experimental operations were used as in Group 4, except the procedures were carried out on an individual basis, rather than on a group basis.

6. The instructors were told to use mildly coercive techniques in the form of "grading down" the trainees if they did not "really" try the ration.

Let us note the way a number of factors that we have discussed above were worked into the experimental procedures. For example, in several of the groups an attempt was made to persuade the trainees by using logical arguments and factual information. In other groups attempts were made to influence the trainees by setting an example that could be imitated and by using an anxiety-arousing technique, namely that of "grading down."

Data were gathered on the extent to which trainees accepted the attempts to persuade. Records were kept of the amount of the ration that was eaten, and data were gathered on the trainees' reactions to the ration. With these data, the experimenters could rank each trainee on the degree to which he accepted or rejected the ration.

The greatest amount of change was produced in Group 6; the group in which mildly coercive techniques were used. We can relate the effects here to a principle cited earlier—namely, that attitudes are learned when rewards are produced for learning these attitudes and when the learning of attitudes leads to need-satisfactions. Positive results were also obtained in experimental Group 3 in which the information concerning the ration was presented in an objective and factual manner, and in Group 4 in which the same information and general explanations of personal factors were given. In this experiment logical arguments were effective.

In Groups 2 and 5, where personal influences of the instructors were used, negative results were obtained; the trainees were more opposed to the ration at the end of the experiment than they were when it began. The authors suggest that an explanation for this might be that the trainees saw themselves as quite different from the instructor;

they not only did not adopt his attitudes, but they also took attitudes widely different from, and even opposing, his. This phenomenon has been called *negative identification*. In this experiment the instructor was not a member of an air crew, as were the trainees; furthermore, he was a woodsman, comfortable in the out-of-doors. The instructors were also frequently young and in outstanding physical condition, whereas the trainees were older and in comparatively poorer physical condition. Consequently, there appears to be a basis for the phenomenon of negative identification.

This experiment further illustrates the complexity of arranging learning experiences to produce attitude changes. In the first place, we note that the role of the teacher, as an identification figure, is an important factor. In this experiment the instructors apparently were not identification figures for the trainees. When procedures for changing attitudes depended heavily upon identification with the instructor, an effect opposite to the one desired was obtained. In this experiment, objective evidence and logical argument were influential in producing some change. This interesting effect may have been obtained because of the relative maturity of the trainees, or because they did not have strong emotional predispositions for rejecting the attitude change. Finally, the greatest influence was exerted when a system of rewards and punishments was established for learning the desired attitude. Earlier we noted that anxiety-arousing appeals are not highly successful in producing attitude change. The difference between the experiment cited earlier on this point and this experiment is that in the latter a system of rewards and punishments was provided. The possibility of punishment, while being anxiety-arousing, also carried with it the possibility of avoiding punishment by taking on the desired attitude. In the earlier experiment, while the advantages and disadvantages of dental hygiene were emphasized, the application of reward and punishment was not as immediate. In that experiment the students were required to visualize the possibilities with which they may have had no previous experience.

SUMMARY. The prospective teacher reading this discussion may be somewhat pessimistic about the possibilities for producing attitude change. Such is not our intent, although we wish to suggest the complexity of the problem facing the teacher. For too long we have probably assumed that attitudes are easily changed, and we have been somewhat naive in our assumptions about the methods which are likely to produce attitude change. The schools have not fully explored the possibilities for producing attitude change; they have tended to rely upon what have been assumed to be the effective methods of the past, principally emotional appeals and logical arguments.

The factors which influence attitude change are complex, and attitudes are formed in a variety of environments, some of which provide greater rewards for the students than does the school. Attitude change is possible, but the teacher must be creative and imaginative in formulating procedures for producing these attitude changes.

We have stressed the importance of certain factors which must be taken into account when any procedure is improvised for producing an attitude change. We know that the prestige and trustworthiness of the communicator is an important factor. We know that emotional appeal has a desirable effect if it is not violent and extreme. We know that logical arguments are most likely to be effective when both sides of the arguments are presented. But we know we will not influence everybody, either by the emotional appeals or by the logical arguments. We have also stressed the importance of group identifications on the formation of attitudes. We have strongly urged caution in attempting to change the attitudes of a group, or of individuals in a group, by attacking openly the attitudes on which the group sets standards. But we have also emphasized how groups can be used to develop attitudes by encouraging students to enter groups with attitudes that are consistent with wholesome social, emotional, and intellectual development. Finally, we have stressed that probably the most crucial factor in any procedure used to produce attitude change is insuring active participation of the students in the processes being used. In the Mitnick and McGinnies study we have noticed that attitude change was influenced by discussion, and in the Janis and King studies we have noted that where the students were called upon to play an active role, attitude change was greater. Whatever the form that participation takes, the more personal involvement that it requires on the part of the student, the more likely it is that attitude changes will be produced.

INFLUENCE OF THE SCHOOL
ON ATTITUDE CHANGE

In the preceding section we discussed factors influencing attitude change. In this section we will discuss programs for attitude change in school. Both within classes and in schools as a whole, a number of procedures have been experimented with to produce specific kinds of attitude changes. We will also be concerned with the general question of whether going to school produces attitude changes.

INFLUENCE OF INFORMATION ON ATTITUDE CHANGE. In the learning experiences provided by schools, considerable information is given to students on subjects toward which they have attitudes. For example, questions of racial differences will be raised and answered in a sociology or an anthropology course. Information about the characteristics of racial groups is typically provided. Such information is frequently introduced into high school courses in civics and social studies. Do these courses produce changes in attitudes? The evidence for attitude change is inconclusive.

EFFECT OF INFORMATION PROVIDED IN COURSES. Apparently mere exposure to the content of a course does not guarantee that students' attitudes will change on the topics being studied.[19] The inconclusiveness of these data should not surprise us when we consider that typical classroom procedures may include all or some of the factors that we have discussed as relevant to producing attitude change.

When classroom procedures are systematically used to influence attitude change, such changes are more likely to occur. A classroom experiment will illustrate how carefully organized learning experiences, using some of the principles previously discussed, successfully influenced attitudes.

Bond[20] used the materials of a genetics course to attempt to influence attitude change toward national groups, races, and imperialism. The course was built to emphasize generalizations about people from the subject matter of genetics. The instructor emphasized problem-solving and critical thinking rather than merely giving information to be absorbed by the students. The students were encouraged to draw their own generalizations based upon the available evidence. Other groups of students taking genetics were taught the course in a traditional manner, which emphasized providing informa-

---

[19] A summary of some of these studies can be found in R. Williams, *The Resolution of Intergroup Tensions, op. cit.* See also J. C. Lagey, "Does Teaching Change Students' Attitudes?" *Journal of Educational Research,* 50 (1956), 307-11; C. M. Stevenson, "Effect of a Course in Minority Group Relations on the Attitudes of College Students," *Progressive Education,* 32 (1955), 19-21.

[20] A. Bond, "An Experiment in the Teaching of Genetics," *Teachers College Contributions to Education,* No. 797, New York, Columbia University Press, 1940.

tion and generalizations for the students. Bond found that the experimental technique produced greater understanding of the generalizations and also induced positive attitude changes toward national groups, races, and imperialism.

In this study we do not have information on a variety of factors which may be influential in producing attitude change. We can speculate, in line with data cited earlier, that the process of requiring students to think critically and solve problems induces greater personal involvement in the problems being studied. The students apparently think about the material and relate it to their own ideas and conceptions. In a traditional course, the students need not become personally involved in the material as long as they can remember it well enough to pass an examination.

Other studies also suggest that when procedures are used that require greater personal involvement, attitude changes are more likely.[21] A common feature in many of these studies is student participation in discussion about the attitude problem. We can speculate that the discussion process provides a student with an opportunity to express his feelings and to clarify his thinking. Again, we must warn that the factors in the discussion method which influence attitude change are not presently clear.

In general, the relationship between information obtained and attitude change has not been adequately clarified. The common assumption at the present time is that if attitudes have not been strongly formed, information relative to the attitude object will be influential in affecting formation and change of attitudes. However, Grace[22] tested students' attitudes toward ten countries and also the amount of knowledge they had of these countries. Grace found two kinds of relationships. One group of persons was most intense in like and dislike for those nations about which they knew the most, and were neutral about those they knew the least. A second group of persons liked best the nations about which they knew the most, and liked least those about which they knew the least. Twice as many students were in the first group as in the second. As suggested by these data, knowledge in itself does not guarantee that attitudes will be favorable.

---

[21]D. S. Laird and C. F. Cumbree, "Experiment in Modifying Ethnic Attitudes of College Students," *Journal of Educational Sociology*, 25 (1952), 401-409.

[22]H. A. Grace, "Information and Social Distance as Predictors of Hostility Towards Nations," *Journal of Abnormal and Social Psychology*, 47 (1952), 540-45.

EXPOSURE TO ATTITUDE OBJECT. Another aspect of the information problem is the effect of increased familiarity with the attitude object. Teachers frequently invite speakers from foreign countries or minority groups into their classes to discuss the problems of these people. Another common procedure is to invite members of national or racial groups to participate in discussions of intergroup problems. One of the assumptions underlying the use of such procedures is that contact with and exposure to members of these groups will tend to reduce negative attitudes and will increase positive attitudes. Again, the evidence is not conclusive that such procedures are uniformly successful. In an early study, Horowitz[23] surveyed attitudes of children living in the north and the south toward Negroes. Horowitz also

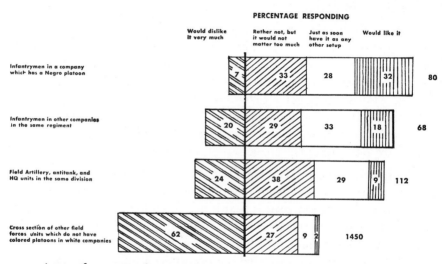

Attitudes toward serving in a company containing Negro and white platoons among men who have done so and men who have not (Europe, June, 1945). The numbers following the bars are the number of cases on which percentages are based. (From Stouffer)

FIGURE 31

compared the attitudes toward the Negro of children in segregated and unsegregated schools in New York City. He found no significant differences in attitude toward the Negroes among these groups of

---

[23]E. L. Horowitz, "The Development of Attitude Toward the Negro," *Archives of Psychology*, 28 (1936), No. 194.

children and concluded that familiarity with or contact with Negroes was not an important determinant of the children's attitudes. The important determiner seemed to be the children's contact with the prevalent social attitude toward the Negro. Children living in New York City, who had little or no exposure to Negroes, formed their attitudes on the basis of what adults in their environment thought about the Negro. This conclusion is consistent with our previous discussion of the influence of adults on the attitude formation of children, where we pointed out that adults provide rewards for adopting adult attitudes.

As we noted above, the evidence on this point is not always in the same direction. Since World War II, service units of white and Negro soldiers have been progressively integrated. A study has been made of the attitudes of white soldiers toward the integration process.[24] Some of the data from this study are recorded in Figure 31. As the data suggest, soldiers in mixed companies are more favorable to integration than are soldiers who are not in mixed companies. This kind of

Meeting place	Integrated interracial projects		Segregated biracial projects	
	Koaltown*	Sacktown*	Bakerville*	Frankville*
As neighbors in the building	60	53	0	0
Through laundry facilities located in or near building	13	17	0	0
Outside on benches	46	64	7	21
In office, etc.	2	1	7	17
At tenant meetings	2	17	28	28
Shopping in stores, in the streets around project	12	13	81	60
Through the children's schools	1	3	14	0
Total cases†	102	86	43	42

Percentages of Housewives Indicating Their Most Likely Contacts with Negro People (From Deutsch and Collins)

TABLE XVIII

*The project names are pseudonyms.
†Only the people who responded "yes" or "uncertain" to the question of getting to know Negro people are included. The percentage figures add up to more than 100 because many people named more than one place.

[24]S. A. Stouffer *et al.*, *The American Soldier: Studies in Social Psychology in World War II*, Vol. 1, Princeton, Princeton University Press, 1949.

study does not permit us to make definitive statements about cause and effect relationships. We cannot say that placing soldiers in mixed companies produces a favorable attitude toward Negroes; however, the relationship suggests the possibility that exposure to Negroes tends to reduce hostility toward them.

Comparable kinds of results were obtained in a study of integrated and segregated housing projects.[25] The data in Table XVIII illustrate the relationship between integrated and segregated housing and the extent to which Negroes are in contact with people in the projects. Other data suggest Negroes are fairly well known by whites when the opportunity for contacts between Negroes and whites is increased. Again, cause-and-effect relationships cannot be definitively established. We do not know, for example, if initial attitude disposition is a factor that determines which kinds of people will live in an integrated housing situation. If only individuals with neutral or positive attitudes toward Negroes enter such housing projects, then increased knowledge about Negroes would be expected. Furthermore, there is evidence in this study to suggest that the group norm in the integrated housing project is quite different from that in the segregated housing project. Housewives in the integrated project expect to be rewarded for contacts with Negroes, whereas housewives in the segregated housing expect to be ostracized if they are friendly toward Negroes.

Exposure to the attitude object occasionally has an effect opposite to that desired. For example, Smith[26] studied the effect of intercultural experiences on students' attitudes toward different national groups. The students in this study were 183 high school and college students who had spent some time in Europe in an experiment in international living. One of Smith's findings was that students who were exceptionally nationalistic in their attitudes tend to become more so after exposure to other national ways of living.

This study also provided an opportunity to compare two different kinds of intercultural experiences. Some of the students participated in an experiment in international living in which they lived with members of different national groups. Others lived in a camp

[25]M. Deutsch and M. E. Collins, *Interracial Housing. A Psychological Evaluation of a Social Experiment*, Minneapolis, University of Minnesota Press, 1951.

[26]H. P. Smith, "Do Intercultural Experiences Affect Attitudes?" *Journal of Abnormal and Social Psychology*, 51 (1955), 469-77.

composed mainly of American students. Greater changes took place in the second group of students than in the first.

From the above discussion, two conclusions can be drawn. First, exposure to or information about attitude objects in itself does not guarantee attitude change. However, if the process of gathering data about the attitude object requires a student to become actively involved in the process, acquisition of information and generalizations and familiarity with the attitude object is likely to be related to attitude change. Second, initial predisposition of the student appears to be an important factor. Where student attitudes have not been formed, information and evidence are likely to be influential in forming attitudes. Where strong attitudes have been formed, evidence that contradicts the attitude held is not likely to have an effect in producing attitude change.

COMPREHENSIVE SCHOOL PROGRAMS. A number of school systems have initiated comprehensive programs to bring about attitude changes. Most of these have been concerned with influencing attitudes toward minority groups.[27] Because of the comprehensiveness of these programs, reliable experimental data are occasionally lacking. In general, reports on these programs suggest that positive results have been obtained with the procedures. Because a variety of procedures have been used, it is not possible to determine which factors were most influential in producing the observed changes.

A survey of these programs suggests that they have incorporated, in one way or another, many of the factors that we have indicated as important determinants of attitude change. In the first place, the programs were set up to influence the attitudes of parents and teachers, as well as those of students. Many of the experimenters recognized that attempts to influence students' attitudes toward minority groups would be unlikely to succeed if these attitudes were not reinforced in the home and community environment. Second, most of the programs included procedures for bringing the various groups together on a basis of equality. These groups then discussed and worked on

[27] A. Halligan, "A Community's Total War Against Prejudice," *Journal of Educational Sociology*, 16 (1943), 374-78; H. E. Amerman, "Perspective for Evaluating Intergroup Relations in a Public School System," *Journal of Negro Education*, 26 (1957), 108-20; F. T. Smith, *An Experiment in Modifying Attitudes Towards The Negro*, New York, Teachers College, Columbia University, 1943; H. H. Cummings, *Improving Human Relations*, National Council for the Social Studies Bulletin, No. 25, 1949; M. Levine, "The Changing School Community," *Social Education*, 10 (1946), 348-50; S. E. Dimond, "The Detroit Citizenship Study," *Social Education*, 12 (1948), 356-58.

common problems. Third, members of minority groups chosen to participate in these programs of discussion and problem-solving were frequently individuals of high prestige within their own group, or in the larger community. Fourth, the school programs and administrative procedures were revised to implement democratic principles. Fifth, many of these programs began with the elementary school child because children at this age are more likely to be influenced than older children.

In these programs the experimenters usually report that the individuals involved obtain greater insight into their own feelings and attitudes—particularly teachers and parents who apparently had not realized the extent to which their attitudes were being manifested in subtle ways. An obvious but important conclusion from the programs used in these studies is that attitude change can be produced, but that attitude change must be planned for and systematically implemented. When a school engages in a comprehensive program to foster attitude change, we would expect the rewards for such changes to become increasingly greater. This factor, combined with the other factors that we have noted, probably insures some success for such programs in producing the desired changes.

THE EVALUATIVE PROCESS AND THE LEARNING OF VALUES

A distinction is sometimes made between attitudes and values, or between the attitudinal and the evaluative processes. This distinction is not always clear, and it is difficult to maintain. We will suggest a definition of values and the evaluative process, but the teacher should remember that the two terms are used interchangeably in this text. At the present time, there is no reason to believe that different psychological processes are involved in the acquisition of attitudes and values, or that the attitudinal and evaluative processes are psychologically distinguishable.

DEFINITION OF A VALUE. *A value is a preference based upon a conception of what is desirable.* Values, like attitudes, are orientation processes by which the person is prepared to respond to his environment in predetermined ways. Values, also, are states of readiness, or predispositions to act and to be motivated in specific kinds of ways. Attitudes and values are alike in that both represent preferences of the person; however, values are preferences based upon conceptions of what is desirable, whereas attitudes need not be based upon such conceptions.

Attitudes are reflected in such words as "like" and "dislike." Values are reflected in such words as "good" and "bad." A child may say, for example, that he likes swimming and thinks that stealing is wrong. In the first case he is expressing a preference which may not reflect any conception of the rightness or wrongness of his preference. In the second case he has indicated his conception of what is desirable. However, this conception of desirability may be unrelated to personal preferences.

The suggestion that values are based upon some conception of the desirable does not imply that evaluative processes do not have an emotional component. Values, like attitudes, have an intensity factor, and an individual may feel more or less strongly about a particular value that he holds. One child may be cognitively aware that stealing is wrong and hold this proposition as a value. Another child may have the same value but feel very strongly about the "badness" of stealing.

HOW VALUES ARE LEARNED. Values, like attitudes, are presumably learned as ways of obtaining need-satisfaction. As we have stressed in previous chapters, the socialization process of a child insures the learning of certain behaviors by the application of rewards and punishments. Out of this process the child learns what is regarded by society as desirable and undesirable behavior. From these conceptions he forms his value standards. A child, for example, cannot learn that stealing is wrong, unless he is exposed to adults who, in effect, teach him this value and reinforce its learning by rewarding behavior consonant with this value.

Similarly, the identification process appears to be crucial in the development of a value system.[28] The identification process, it will be recalled, describes the way in which a child internalizes the attitudes and values of another individual. One of the psychological problems discussed in personality development is the acquisition of social control. We have chosen to describe this process of development as essentially a process of interiorizing attitudes and values of society as they are communicated to children through cultural agents, such

---

[28]See R. R. Sears et al., Patterns of Child Rearing, Evanston, Illinois, Row, Peterson and Co., 1957, Chapter 10.

as parents and teachers. From a psychological point of view, social control, or "conscience," is a process in which behavior is governed by processes within the individual. These processes within the individual we have called the attitudinal-evaluative processes, and have suggested how socially desirable values and cultural attitudes are internalized through the identification process. Consequently, it is not necessary to repeat our description of how values are learned through the identification process. The process is presumed to be the same for attitudes and values. The result of the identification process, whether identification be with individuals or groups, is an individual who has an integrated system of attitudes and values. This system of attitudes and values is a determinant of specific behaviors, and influences the ways in which an individual can be motivated.

INFLUENCES ON VALUE ACQUISITION. Again, the experimental evidence suggests that the same kinds of influences affect the acquisition of values as affect the acquisition of attitudes. For example, home influences seem to be a major determinant in the acquisition of values. In a classical study, Hartshorne, May, and Shuttleworth,[29] correlated children's ideas of right and wrong with the ideas of their parents, friends, club leaders, day school teachers, and Sunday school teachers. These experimenters found the highest relationship between children's ideas and those of their parents. Interestingly enough, the lowest relationship was found between children's ideas and those of their Sunday school teachers. The low relationship with the ideas of right and wrong of Sunday school teachers does not suggest that children are not influenced by their Sunday school teachers. Here, again, we meet the problem of describing the influence of any teacher on the attitudinal and evaluative processes of children. The relationship with parents is likely to be the strongest because parents exercise a primary and initial influence on the development of children's values, and because the identification process between parents and children tends to be fostered.

However, the development of a value system is not as simple as the above description suggests. Obviously, not all children acquire values that their parents try to transmit to them. For example, some children learn antisocial behavior, perhaps of an aggressive and hostile

---

[29] H. Hartshorne, M. A. May, and F. K. Shuttleworth, *Studies in the Organization of Character*, New York, Macmillan Co., 1930.

nature, in homes in which there is considerable punishment for such behavior. Recent studies have thrown light on the characteristics of the parent-child relationship which influence the development and internalization of acceptable social values.

VALUES AND THE PARENT-CHILD RELATIONSHIP. The child's initial relations with his parents are dependent in character. The infant, of necessity, relies upon his mother to provide him with the requisites for the sustenance of life. Obviously, the child cannot be independent in satisfying his own biological needs. Out of this dependency relationship with the mother the child typically acquires a dependency need, that is, he finds relying on his mother a source of need-satisfaction. With increasing age, the child must also develop independence needs so that he can acquire the behavior which will free him of dependency on his parents.

Complicating this relationship is the necessity for the child to acquire his proper sex role. The male child must establish male identification achieved through identification with the father. Thus, a male child comes to depend upon his father as a source of rewards for typically masculine behavior. Consequently, satisfaction of the dependency need takes many different forms at different stages in the child's life. But the dependency need, because of the nature of the parent-child relationship, tends to be a prevalent and strong need in children.

Parents may reward or punish dependency behavior. Typically, the very young child is rewarded for dependency behavior, but as the child grows older dependency behaviors are less frequently rewarded. The child is encouraged to think and act for himself within the limits set by the parents. In this process, repeated punishment for dependency behavior as the child grows older can lead to frustration of the child's dependency needs. Consequently, the manner in which the child's dependency needs are handled by the parents becomes crucial in determining the development of the identification process of the child. The identification process presupposes that the child rely in some way on the parents as a source of rewards, a relationship fostered by his dependency needs. If the dependency need is persistently punished, however, the identification process may itself be inhibited. As a consequence, the child in not identifying with the parents does not learn the attitudes and values necessary for social control, or the development of "conscience." One result of the frustration of dependency needs appears to be the development of aggressive behavior.[30]

Bandura and Walters[31] studied the relationship between antisocial behavior of adolescent boys and the parent-child relationship. In this study the investigators chose a sample of boys who had a record of antisocial behavior and carefully matched them with a sample of boys of comparable age and social status who had not manifested antisocial behavior. Through a series of personal interviews with the parents of both groups of boys and with the boys themselves, the investigators determined the relationships between the character of the parent-child interaction and the presence or absence of antisocial behavior in the boys' behavior patterns.

One of the major findings was that the parent-child relationship for aggressive boys was frequently characterized by a lack of warmth and affection. The aggressive group of boys manifested little overt emotional dependency on either their mothers or their fathers. The mothers of these boys, while encouraging the dependency relationship, discouraged it at the same time. The consequence was that the aggressive boys generally tended to inhibit their dependency relations with their parents and other adults. Furthermore, the parents of the aggressive group tended to control their children principally by physical means. Again, and presumably as a consequence, a minimal social control resulted from fear of parental punishment rather than from identification with parental values.

The establishment of male identification for these boys depended upon a rewarding relationship with their fathers. The fathers of the aggressive boys had not established affectionate relationships with their sons, had spent little time with them, showed little warmth, acceptance, or esteem for the boys, and were more punitive than the fathers of the nonaggressive boys. In other words, the parents of these children did not provide rewards for identification with the male parent.

These data suggest the complexity of the relationships between parents and children and the influence of these relationships on the development of the value system. In the homes of the aggressive boys, value standards were upheld, but the manner in which they were upheld emphasized forms of punishment that tended to cut the boys off

---

[30] R. R. Sears, J. W. M. Whiting, V. Nowlis, and P. S. Sears, "Some Child Rearing Antecedents of Aggression and Dependency in Young Children," *Genetic Psychology Monographs*, 47 (1953), 135-234.

[31] A. Bandura and R. Walters, *Adolescent Aggression*, New York, Ronald Press, 1959.

from identification with their parents. Recall that this study compared two groups of boys, one of which represented little social sensitivity and "conscience" development. The pattern of parent-child interaction is markedly different for these two groups of boys. The data from this study tend to support the hypothesis that, if the identification process is not fostered, values will not be internalized. But the identification process itself depends heavily upon the character of the child's relations with his parents and is fostered when the parents, in addition to indicating what is right and wrong, become a source of rewards for the child.

INFLUENCE OF SCHOOL ON DEVELOPMENT OF A VALUE SYSTEM. The problems that we have discussed concerning the school and the development of attitudes are the same problems that characterize the relationship of the school to the development of a value system. If a child has not learned to identify with adult figures, and has found relationships with these adult figures to be punishing and frustrating, the likelihood of his identifying with a teacher probably is not great. We do not know at the present time to what extent failure to identify with the principal adults in a child's life will generalize to other adults. We cannot say definitively that if a child does not identify with his parents he will of necessity not identify with one or more of his teachers. On the other hand, neither do we know the factors that are likely to facilitate identification with some other adult if the identification process has not been fostered in the home.

We have discussed the problem of conflict and attitudes, and the principles that we cited in that discussion are applicable to conflict and values. The school, through teachers, tends to reinforce the general value standards of society. The teacher's relationship with the child is similar to that of the parents, in that both parent and teacher are sources of reward and punishment for desirable behavior. We can again hypothesize that identification with teachers and the teachers' value systems will be facilitated by the same kind of relationship that facilitates identification with parents. We would predict that using ridicule, deprivation of privileges, and, in extreme cases, physical punishment, and a cold and harsh manner would suggest to a child that the teacher is rejecting him as a person. The child will learn, as with his parents, that his dependency needs cannot be satisfied by identification with the teacher. In such cases we would expect the teacher to have comparatively little influence on the development of the child's value systems.

On the other hand, where children have established identifications with parental figures, identifications with teachers probably depend on similarities between teachers and parents. If the child is treated by the teacher in the same way that he is by his parents, and if the value standards of teacher and parents are similar, we would expect the teacher to have influence in reinforcing and strengthening the learning of values.

Again, we have suggested the complexity of the problem of value standards. We have emphasized that the psychological processes for the acquisition of values are similar to those for the acquisition of attitudes. The same general principles of learning and the same variables appear to be crucial in the development of both attitudes and values. The major factor in the development of a value system appears to be the identification process. The identification process is fostered and facilitated when an adult figure is a source of rewards, and when adopting the adult's behavior is need-satisfying. We have hypothesized that, as in the case of the parent-child relationship, the identification process will be fostered if the teacher's relationships with the child are characterized by warmth, acceptance, and esteem.

INFLUENCE OF THE ATTITUDINAL-EVALUATIVE PROCESSES ON THE COGNITIVE PROCESSES

We have emphasized that the attitudinal-evaluative processes orient the person to his environment. This orientation is essentially a selective process by which the person focuses his attention on some aspects of his environment and ignores others. In this section we will explore the influence of the attitudinal-evaluative processes on the cognitive processes. An experimental study will illustrate the general character of this relationship.[32]

EXPERIMENTAL EVIDENCE. In this experiment the experimental subjects were exposed to words that can have value orientations. In Table XIX are lists of words used and their categorization into some major value dimensions. Each of the subjects took a test to determine

---

[32]L. Postman, J. S. Bruner, and E. McGinnies, "Personal Values and Selective Factors in Perception," *Journal of Abnormal and Social Psychology*, 43 (1948), 142-54.

his pattern of values. These values were classified as theoretical, economic, aesthetic, social, political, and religious. For example, a person whose dominant value system is theoretical is a person whose major interests lie in the "discovery of truth." A person whose dominant value is economic is primarily interested in "usefulness and practical-

Theoretical	Economic	Aesthetic	Social	Political	Religious
theory	income	beauty	loving	govern	prayer
verify	useful	artist	kindly	famous	sacred
science	wealthy	poetry	devoted	compete	worship
logical	finance	elegant	helpful	citizen	blessed
research	economic	literary	friendly	politics	religion
analysis	commerce	graceful	sociable	dominate	reverent

Stimulus Words Representing Six Value Categories
(From Postman, Bruner, and McGinnies)

TABLE XIX

ity." A person whose dominant value is aesthetic emphasizes "form and harmony." Social values reflect love of people and sympathy; political values represent an interest in power relations; religious values denote a dominant interest in identifying with a larger and more comprehensive totality.[33]

The words associated with each of the value dimensions were exposed on a tachistoscope, a device which permits the experimenter to expose the words at varying speeds. A word that is rapidly exposed is difficult to recognize. Each subject in this experiment was requested to give his idea of what the exposed word was. The experimenters were attempting to determine whether there was any relationship between the value system of the subject and the kinds of words he could recognize quickly and easily.

The experimenters determined the recognition time for each of the words. When these times were plotted and related to the subject's dominant value system, the data indicated a significant relationship between the kinds of words quickly recognized and the dominant value system of the subject. This relationship is demonstrated in Figure

---

[33]A more precise meaning is given to each of these value systems by the constellation of items checked on the test used to measure the dominant value systems. The test used was G. W. Allport and P. E. Vernon, *A Study of Values*, Boston, Houghton Mifflin Co., 1931.

32. In this figure note that words corresponding to the principal value of a subject, as represented by a value rank of 1, were words which were most quickly recognized.

In a further analysis of the data the experimenters studied the kinds of words the subjects offered as answers before they correctly recognized the word on the tachistoscope. Some of these words were consistent with the major value dimensions of the subject. For example, if the word on the tachistoscope was "sacred," and the subject said that he saw the word "sacrifice," he supplied a word which has a value connotation relevant to that of the word on the tachistoscope

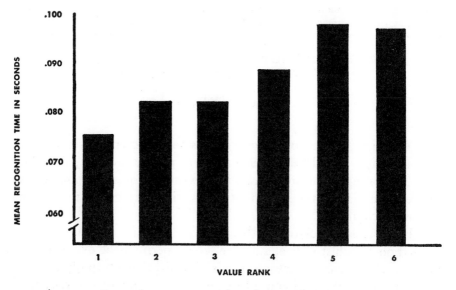

Average time of recognition for the words representing the six values of the Allport-Vernon study, arranged in rank order. (From Postman, Bruner, and McGinnies)

FIGURE 32

(called "covaluant" words by the experimenters). Other words offered by subjects had opposite value connotations to the words on the tachistoscope. For example, if the subject said "scornful" and the word was "helpful," or "revenge" when the word was "blessed," the word he has supplied has a value connotation opposite to that of the exposed word (called "contravaluant" words). Finally, two other kinds of prerecognition responses were identified. One of these was a nonsense-kind of response; for example, "linone" for "income." Another kind of response, which the experimenters called "structural," consisted of words which had some of the characteristics of the exposed words. For example, "mowing" or "lowing" for "loving." The subjects who made such responses typically arrived at the correct response.

Another purpose of the experiment was to find out whether there was any relationship between the kinds of prerecognition responses the subjects gave and their dominant value systems. The results of the analysis are shown in Figure 33. As the bar graph illustrates, the subjects gave more covaluant and structural responses to exposed words that were consistent with the value system of the subject. The subjects also gave more nonsense and contravaluant responses to exposed words which were not consistent with their dominant values.

The data in this study suggest the influence of the attitude and value systems of a person on what he perceives. The data here suggest

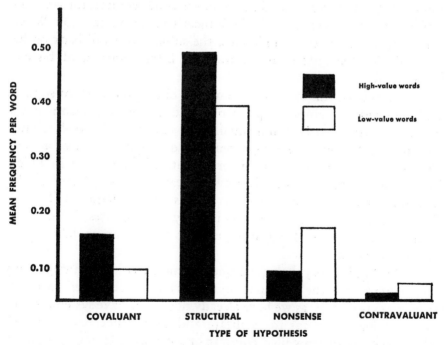

Mean frequency with which various types of prerecognition hypotheses were given in response to high-value and low-value words. (From Postman, Bruner, and McGinnies)

FIGURE 33

that an individual in a simple task, such as recognizing words, apparently will be influenced by his dominant value system. He quickly recognizes words that are consistent with his value system, and even his prerecognition responses are consistent with this value system. Words that are not consistent with his value system are not easily recognized, and he makes prerecognition responses to them which are either nonsensical or contravaluant.

FORMS OF INFLUENCE. The attitude and value system of a person influences his cognitive processes in three ways: (1) The person does not respond as quickly to stimuli which are inconsistent with or contradictory to his attitudinal-value system. This kind of relationship was apparent in the data provided in the above experiment when subjects were slower in recognizing words inconsistent with their value system. (2) A person recognizes and assimilates more quickly stimuli which are consistent with his attitudinal-value system. This kind of relationship appeared in the lower time required for recognition of words consistent with the subject's value system. (3) When the stimulus situation is ambiguous, the subject will fall back on his attitudinal-value system to facilitate his interpretations of his environment.

The data in this experiment and the discussion of them suggest an important psychological principle. The human organism is not a response system that responds equally and unselectively to all stimuli that impinge upon it. A person tends to organize and select among the stimuli. One of the major determinants of the manner in which he recognizes and selects is his previous learnings, as reflected in the concepts, attitudes, and values that he has already acquired. The influence of these previous learnings is likely to be greatest in environmental situations which are ambiguous to the person or difficult for him to interpret.

This kind of psychological phenomenon has its advantages and disadvantages for the organization of learning experiences. In many learning experiences, as we have already noted, we have systematically used previous learnings to facilitate and to enhance new learning. This process has been called *transfer of learning*. However, in other learning situations, previously learned concepts, attitudes, and values will make it difficult for a person to see things "in a new way." If a concept, attitude, or value has been particularly useful to the person in interpreting his environment, and has provided him with persistent need-satisfaction, the likelihood of producing a changed "point of view" is not great without extensive reorganization of his conceptual-attitudinal-value system.

COMPLEX SYSTEMS OF ATTITUDES AND VALUES. Those integrations of attitudes and values which have persistently been reinforced apparently tend to produce stable and consistent trends in personality. Some psychological research has been devoted to determining what these major systems of attitudes and values may be. One of the purposes of the test devised by Allport and Vernon, which was used in the experiment cited above, is to determine to what extent individuals have developed dominant attitudinal-value patterns. One of the most comprehensive studies of this kind was concerned with a personality type called *the authoritarian personality*.[34] A major finding of this study was the complexity of the attitude-value system of individuals and its influence on behavior. The investigators began their research by studying fairly specific attitudes, such as attitudes toward Negroes and Jews. As their research progressed, they found that these more specific attitudes appeared to be embedded in a general attitudinal-value orientation which resulted in a fairly specific kind of personality type, which they later called "the authoritarian personality." The authoritarian personality is a prejudiced person. His prejudice takes the form of being submissive and respectful to members of what is called the in-group, that is, the group with which he identifies, and of being aggressive, hostile, and punitive to members of the out-group. Thus, the authoritarian personality can be found in any social group, whether or not it is a minority group.

The researchers found that this basic attitude-value orientation was related to and integrated with a wide variety of other specific attitudinal-value orientations. Else Frenkel-Brunswik, in a study of prejudiced children, observed the following characteristics which are also the characteristics attributed to the authoritarian personality:[35]

1. The ethnocentric child (that is, a child prejudiced toward out-groups and strongly attached to the in-groups) tends to have a stereotyped, rigid,

---

[34] A complete discussion of the original research on this subject can be found in T. W. Adorno, E. Frenkel-Brunswik, D. J. Levinson, R. N. Sanford *et al.*, *The Authoritarian Personality*, New York, Harper & Brothers, 1950.

[35] E. Frenkel-Brunswik, "A Study of Prejudice in Children," *Human Relations*, 1 (1948), 259-306.

and glorified concept of himself and the in-group to which he belongs. Furthermore, he tends to reject the minority and out-group, perhaps with open aggression and hostility.

2. He rejects all that is "weak" and "indifferent."

3 His rejection of "weakness" is related to an admiration of the "strong," "tough," and "powerful."

4. He emphasizes the dichotomy of sex, and the opposite sex tends to become an out-group.

5. His admiration for success, power, and prestige appears to be related to a submission to authority based on fear of punishment.

6. He tends to give approval on the basis of external moral values, frequently including such values as "cleanliness" and "politeness." He also values conformity to accepted social standards.

7. He is intolerant, inflexible, rigid, and incapable of facing ambiguous situations.

8. He has a more fearful and catastrophic conception of the world and tends to be more superstitious.

Note the complexity in the attitudinal-value system of the ethnocentric child. He is not simply a child who likes people in his own group and dislikes people outside of it. He has a basic attitudinal-value orientation which includes his relationships with his own group and the out-group, and a wide variety of other subjects. His attitudinal-value system tends to be inflexible and rigid, with the consequence that he falls back on his basic values to interpret the world around him. He likes the strong and dislikes the weak. He admires success, power, prestige. At the same time, he is submissive to authority and conforms to approved social values.

The development of an attitudinal-value system of this kind of personality occurs over a long period of time. Children are not born with these characteristics. Specific kinds of attitudes are integrated into more complex attitudes and values, which set a pattern of personality development. Consistent with our discussion above on the influence of attitudes and values on the cognitive processes, we note that ethnocentric children tend to prefer sharply defined situations rather than ambiguous ones. In ambiguous situations, these children tend to redefine the environment in terms of sharply defined and rigid categories of what is right and wrong.

At the present time, the determinants of a personality development of this kind are not completely known.[36] Research evidence suggests that this kind of a personality develops out of a specific kind of parent-child interaction. These children typically come from homes in which there is considerable emphasis on conformity and submission to authority, usually accompanied by strongly coercive systems of punishment. We can speculate that children develop authoritarian personalities by identifying with adults with this kind of personality, who reward them for identification.

We have discussed the concept of the authoritarian personality to illustrate the complex ways in which attitudes and values become integrated into personality systems. At the present time, psychological research has not progressed to the point where we can describe well-defined personality types and the attitudinal-value systems which particularly characterize them. The significant point here is that attitudes, values, concepts and generalizations are not held in isolation, but are interrelated and integrated into complex systems for interpreting and responding to the environment. The more highly integrated the system, the more predictable the individual's behavior.

SUMMARY

In this chapter we have discussed factors influencing attitude change. We have noted the following major points:

1. Attempts to change attitudes consist essentially in communications designed to persuade individuals to adopt a new attitude position. The influence of these communications is enhanced by such factors as the prestige and credibility of the communicator.

2. The effect of these communications is varied when the form of the communication emphasizes logical argument or emotional appeal. These factors, in addition to the prestige of the communicator, have varying degrees of influence in producing attitude change.

---

[36]There is disagreement as to whether the characteristics of the ethnocentric person constitute a personality *type* as such. For a critical review of research in this area, see R. Christie and M. Jahoda, *Studies in the Scope and Method of "The Authoritarian Personality,"* Glencoe, Illinois, The Free Press, 1954.

3. An important determinant of the extent of attitude change is the predisposition of the person whose attitude is being influenced. Logical argument is most likely to be effective in producing attitude change if the individual does not have a sharply defined attitude, or if he is already somewhat favorably disposed toward the attitude position advocated. An emotional appeal is less likely to be effective if it is anxiety-arousing.

4. We have noted that the major determinant of attitude formation is the identification process. Any factor that facilitates identification, either with an individual or with a group, tends to enhance attitude change. For the same reason, attitude communications contrary to attitudes based upon strong identifications are not likely to be effective.

5. Procedures used to influence attitude change, in general, are most likely to be effective the more the individual is actively involved in the process itself. Active participation probably enhances identification with the role of the communicator of the attitude and tends to bring about attitude change.

6. We have noted that values and attitudes have many characteristics in common. Insofar as values are distinguished from attitudes, the distinction is made on the basis that values imply some conception of what is desirable.

7   We have suggested that the processes by which values are acquired are similar to the processes by which attitudes are acquired. We have discussed the influence of the parent-child relationship in the formation of conscience and the value system. If the parent-child relationship, and presumably any other adult-child relationship, is characterized by mutual warmth, acceptance, and esteem, the identification process is likely to be enhanced. The result of this enhancement is that the individual assimilates and internalizes the values of the identification figure.

8. We have stressed throughout the last four chapters the interrelationships of attitudes, values, and concepts. We have noted that the attitude-value system influences the individual's interaction with his environment by predisposing him to see

this environment in given kinds of ways. The attitude-value system acts as a selection device which orients the individual to aspects of the environment that are consistent with his attitude-value system.

9.　　Finally, we have noted that attitudes and values tend to become integrated into complex systems which, in some cases, evolve into marked personality types.

The school is necessarily involved in attempting to influence attitudes and values of the students. The school as a social agency reinforces the dominant attitudes and values of society. The school also acts as an agency to promote desirable changes in attitudes and values. The process of bringing about these attitude changes is complex. The teacher who organizes learning experiences designed to produce these changes again must act as a hypothesis-maker, taking into account the factors discussed in this chapter. The concepts and principles presented in this chapter provide a basis for making hypotheses about learning experiences likely to produce changes in attitudes and values.

STUDY AND DISCUSSION QUESTIONS

1. Refer to the Mitnick and McGinnies study presented at the beginning of this chapter. What hypotheses about attitude change would you offer if the experimental conditions had been arranged so that the discussion of the problem treated in the film took place before the film was shown? What predictions would you make about attitude changes in students who discussed the problem treated in the film but did not see the film?

2. Assume that in a situation of the kind described in the Mitnick and McGinnies study the students could infer from the teacher's behavior that his attitude was at variance with the attitude advocated in the communication presented in the film. Suggest hypotheses that predict the effect on attitude change of the teacher's behavior in this context. Under what conditions might the teacher's behavior have little, if any, influence? Under what conditions might the teacher's behavior have more influence than the film communication?

3. Assume that you are teaching a class in which some of the students have a negative attitude toward members of racial groups other than their own. You find through questioning that the students view the members of these racial groups in terms of the typical stereotypes associated with such groups. You present information to demonstrate that the stereotypes are inappropriate.

Formulate hypotheses about the effects of this procedure on attitude change. What variables need to be considered in making these predictions about attitude change?

4. Suggest some prestige figures that may influence the attitudes of students on these subjects:

    a. Attitudes toward drinking alcoholic beverages.

    b. Attitudes toward participation in the affairs of civic government.

    c. Attitudes toward athletics.

    In each case describe the group whose attitudes you are trying to influence and suggest your reasons for believing that these individuals will be prestige figures for these groups.

5. How do you explain the fact that the influence of a prestige figure on attitude change is relatively impermanent? Suggest ways in which you may test the hypotheses that comprise your explanation.

6. Review the discussion on critical thinking in Chapter Six. Is the use of prestige figures to influence attitude change likely to inhibit the development of critical thinking? Would you make a distinction between the "expert" and "prestige" figures?

7. In this chapter it has been suggested that younger children may regard the teacher as a prestige figure and a source of credible statements. Assuming that this may be the case, what factors would account for this fact? What factors would explain the fact that older children may be less likely to regard the teacher as a prestige figure and credible commentator?

8. Assume that you are trying to influence students' attitudes toward maintaining a healthy regimen of eating and sleeping. Assume also that you portray the beneficial effects of such a regimen rather than the harmful effects of not following healthy practices in this respect. Suggest some hypotheses about attitude changes under these conditions. Would a minimal emotional appeal of this kind be more effective than a strong emotional appeal?

9. Many people feel that a positive appeal is more likely to produce attitude changes than a negative approach to fostering the same kinds of changes. Offer some hypotheses that would support this point of view.

10. Suppose that you wish to persuade students that the use of the atomic bomb in World War II was a commendable action. Predict the effects of using logical argument, of fear-arousing communications portraying the effects likely to have occurred if the bomb had not been used, and of the authoritative opinions of the President and military experts.

11. Assume that you have a group of students in your class who have a negative

attitude toward the subject you are teaching. Suggest some procedures that you might use which might influence them to change their attitude to a more positive one. Predict the probability that any of these procedures is likely to effect a change. Explain the limitations of the procedures that you suggest and the factors that are likely to reduce the effectiveness of these procedures. What information would you need about these students before you could decide on appropriate procedures?

12. The American school typically holds as one of its objectives the promotion of behavior changes in attitudes toward the American way of life. What learning experiences do schools typically use to produce positive attitudes toward the American way of life? Which of the variables that we have discussed in this chapter seem to be operative in these activities? Suggest the limitations of these activities for effecting this attitude change.

13. Some people argue that the extracurricular program of the school fosters attitude changes which interfere with the development of positive attitudes toward "more intellectual" activities. Evaluate this argument.

14. Some people argue that the extracurricular program of the school has greater influence on producing desirable attitude changes than do many classroom activities. Assume that this statement is correct. What factors in the activity program may account for this relatively greater influence?

15. Refer to the Kelley and Volkart study discussed in this chapter. Assume that the communicator had praised the activities of scouting and strongly favored them. What effects would you predict that this kind of a communication would have on the scouts who were the least interested in scouting? Assume that the communicator presented both sides of the question on the value of scouting. What effects would you predict this kind of a communication would have had on the attitudes of the most interested and least interested scouts?

16. A teacher wishes to influence students to acquire a more positive attitude toward the United States' participation in the United Nations. He organizes the students into a mock UN Assembly. What difficulties might be involved in stimulating the students to play the roles of UN members? Assume that one of the students had a negative attitude toward the United States' participation in the UN. What is the probability that this role-playing procedure will influence attitude change in this student?

17. Review the experiment on attempts to influence air crewmen to eat a survival ration. How do you account for the fact that in this experiment the presentation of information in an objective manner influenced behavior change? Relate the results in this respect to the discussion of the influence of logical argument presented earlier in the chapter. In what ways are the procedures used in this experiment similar to the ones cited earlier? In what ways are they different?

18. Some people argue that students need to know the facts of American history

if they are to develop patriotic attitudes. Evaluate this argument in the light of the principles discussed in this chapter.

19. We have suggested that "warmth" in relations between parents and children, or teachers and children, may influence the child to identify with these adults. Can a teacher be both "warm" and "strict"?

20. Describe the behavior patterns that you would expect to characterize a teacher who "rejects" a student. How could you determine whether the teacher's behavior is seen as "rejecting" by the student?

21. Is the teacher likely to influence the students' values even though the students may not identify with the teacher?

22. What are the criteria for determining that a child has internalized the values which his parents and teachers have encouraged him to learn?

23. Assume that you observe a student who apparently conforms to the principal attitudes and values of a group to which he belongs. How could you determine whether the student has internalized the attitudes and values? In general, how could you distinguish public conformity without internalizing values from genuine internalization of attitudes and values?

24. Suggest some of the specific behaviors that you might observe from which you could infer that a child had the characteristics described as associated with the authoritarian personality. Refer to the list of characteristics presented in this chapter. What kinds of need-satisfactions would a child with these characteristics be likely to be obtaining with the attitudes that he has acquired?

RECOMMENDED READINGS

The first two readings present a review of experimental literature and a critical analysis of the influence of communication variables on attitude change. The third reading presents a critical analysis of some procedures used in changing attitudes of group members. The fourth reading is an analysis of attitude change and the resolution of social conflict. These readings may contribute in varying ways to an understanding of the complexity of the problem of attitude change. While some of the experiments discussed in these readings have been conducted in settings other than the classroom and the school, the teacher may analyze for himself the relevance of the variables investigated to the kinds of learning experiences that may be organized in the school setting.

1. C. I. Hovland, I. L. Janis, and H. H. Kelley, *Communication and Persuasion,* New Haven, Yale University Press, 1953.

2. C. I. Hovland, A. A. Lumsdaine, and F. D. Sheffield, *Experiments in Mass*

Communication: Studies in Social Psychology in World War II, Vol. 3, Princeton, Princeton University Press, 1949.

3. R. Williams, *The Resolution of Intergroup Tensions,* New York, Social Science Research Council, 1948.

4. K. Lewin, *Resolving Social Conflicts,* New York, Harper & Brothers, 1948.

LEARNING OF SKILL PERFORMANCES

In the preceding chapters we discussed aspects of personality that are inferred from observable behavior. In this chapter we temporarily interrupt our discussion of specific aspects of personality to analyze the learning of certain complex patterns of responses. These patterns are integrations of the processes we have been discussing and of the observable responses.

Jane's behavior in writing a feature article (see Chapter Three) illustrates the kind of behavior patterns we will be studying. When Jane sat down at her desk to write the feature article, she performed a large number of responses, some of which were directly observable and some of which were not. In writing the article she had to think about the subject of the essay, formulate ideas on the subject, clarify her concepts related to the subject, and express in words her thoughts and feelings about the subject of the essay. When she wrote, however, she was performing another set of responses which could be directly observed. She held a pencil or pen, wrote out the letters, and varied the amount of pressure on the pen or

pencil. That complex set of responses called "writing" is called a "performance."

To write her article, Jane had to be able to carry out a sequence of responses called "writing." If she had chosen to type her article, she would have had to carry out a sequence of responses called "typing." In other words, Jane had to learn concepts, attitudes, and manipulative behaviors to carry out the "performance" of writing a feature article.

In this chapter we will discuss the organization of learning experiences to facilitate the acquisition of the *manipulative* aspects of performance behaviors. The term *performance behavior* is not common. Usually, the material to be discussed in this chapter is treated under the heading of "motor skills," or "skills." We have departed from this fairly standard practice because many of the "skills" that the school attempts to teach students are not simple motor behaviors. A course in driver education, for example, attempts to teach much more than the motor behaviors required to manipulate an automobile. We attempt to teach a "performance" called "driving a car," a performance which requires the learning of a sequence of manipulative or motor behaviors and the learning of appropriate concepts, generalizations, attitudes, and values.

THE LEARNING OF PERFORMANCES

"Performances" cannot be defined as distinctive aspects of personality. Rather, performances are integrations of response patterns. A highly integrated response pattern seems to be a single, unitary response to an observer. Words and phrases, such as "typing," "walking," "singing," "playing the piano," and "playing football," reflect our tendency to conceptualize these response patterns as unitary responses. Usually, learning experiences are designed to achieve this integration, and we do not consider that the performance has been acquired until some minimal integration of responses has been achieved. A student has not learned to "type" or "play the piano" if he can make only the basic finger movements.

THE COMPLEXITY OF PERFORMANCES. To learn a performance an individual must acquire the specific responses involved in the performance and the integrated sequence that forms the pattern of performance. As we have indicated, some of these responses are overt and observable, and are motor or manipulative in character. We can observe the person "doing something," and we assess his facility in performance from this observed behavior. For example, we judge a person's facility in driving a car or playing a piano from the responses that we can observe. If a driver grinds gears or does not brake the car properly, or if a pianist makes errors in striking the keys, we make inferences about his facility in these performances.

These errors may arise from the learner's failure to acquire appropriate concepts or attitudes, or the manipulative behaviors themselves. The extent to which the learning of any one specific response sequence influences the learning of another sequence depends upon the character of the total performance being learned. When we talk about a performance called "playing the piano," we usually imply that a person must be able to play musical compositions. A child can learn the basic manipulative behavior required to play fairly complex compositions; however, the child must also learn how to read music and acquire concepts such as phrasing, rhythm, and tempo which he can express in his piano playing. The child may not have to acquire these formal concepts to express such qualities in his piano playing. This possibility suggests an important theoretical problem, namely, can the manipulative aspects of a performance be learned directly? An attempt to answer this question can be made if we have a clearer conception of the character of manipulative behavior.

MANIPULATIVE BEHAVIOR. Manipulative behavior is the pattern of observable responses which has been acquired as an integrated sequence of movement. Manipulative behaviors are "movement responses," by which a person "moves" himself, as in walking, or "moves" some environmental object, as in playing a piano, hitting a baseball, or typing a letter. Such responses can be attached to internal or external stimuli, called cues, so that, when the stimuli occur, the appropriate response follows. For example, a person can learn to shift the gears in a car by responding to the "feel" of the gear lever as it is moved from one position to another. In a typing class, students are taught to position their hands on the keys of the typewriter by "feel." A player attempting to hit a pitched ball responds to external stimuli, such as the position of the ball, and to internal stimuli from muscle movements.

If responses can be learned directly by association with stimuli, the manipulative aspects of a performance can be acquired directly.

For example, a person can learn to shift gears without understanding the pattern of movement required. An important question is—Can such learning be facilitated by understanding the movement pattern? A clear-cut and definitive answer cannot be given to this question. This kind of question needs to be investigated for each of the performances we attempt to teach. In the latter part of this chapter we will outline some general principles governing this relationship between understanding and manipulative behavior. At this point, however, we will distinguish among cognitive processes, which might facilitate the learning of a manipulative sequence, and cognitive, attitudinal, and evaluative processes, which are an integral part of a total performance. For example, concepts and attitudes relevant to safe driving are integral aspects of the performance of driving a car. The performance is not adequately learned if these concepts and attitudes are not acquired.

The essential characteristics of a performance are a matter of definition and description. When we decide what constitutes a performance pattern, we can determine what concepts, attitudes, and manipulative behaviors must be perfected to learn the total performance.

SKILL PERFORMANCES. Performances are frequently called "skilled behaviors," because many of these processes are perfected so that the performance occurs easily and efficiently. A performance can be acquired unsystematically to a high level of skill without any formally organized learning experience, as when a child learns to walk. In school, however, we attempt to organize learning experiences to teach certain kinds of performances to a fairly high level of skill. A performance has more utility for a person if he can carry out the performance almost automatically. A musician, for example, learns the basic performance involved in playing his instrument. This basic performance is repeatable whenever he plays his instrument. Adaptations and variations in performance can be learned quickly and easily with the response patterns already learned. He does not have to relearn the basic performance if he has acquired this performance to a high level of skill.

We have chosen to use the term *skill performance* rather than the word "skills" to emphasize an important distinction. The word "skill," as it is used in everyday speech, generally applies to any activity that is conducted with a high level of facility. We speak of skill in playing football, in playing the violin, in typing, in vocabulary, in English usage, in playing chess. From a psychological point of view, playing football or chess, or using a typewriter or the English language correctly demands complex sets of responses, some of which are cognitive, some of which are attitudinal, and some of which are manipulative. For example, "skill" in playing baseball requires that the baseball player be able to perform sets of responses with ease, quickness, and economy of motion. A baseball player must be able to hit, throw, and catch a baseball, and be able to do each of these under a variety of conditions. But the baseball player must also *understand* the strategy of the game. The player who can throw accurately but does not know which base to throw to or how to hold a runner on base is not a skilled baseball player. This player is not lacking manipulative facility, but he fails to understand the concepts and generalizations about the strategy of the game. The player must also have attitudes about the game. He must like to play the game and find playing the game satisfying. He must have attitudes about sportsmanship and winning. The total performance that we observe when we watch this player is a complex set of processes—cognitive, attitudinal, and manipulative. This complex integration of processes is what we usually mean when we refer to "skill in playing baseball."

LEARNING EXPERIENCES AND SKILL PERFORMANCES. We emphasize the distinction between manipulative and other aspects of a performance because the variables that affect the learning of concepts, of attitudes, and of manipulative behaviors may differ. We have stressed the importance of identification in the learning of attitudes. The baseball player's interest in the game and his desire to become a successful major leaguer is frequently assimilated from his father or a coach whose attitudes and values he has taken on through the process of identification. But assimilating his father's attitude toward baseball will not guarantee that he can actually perform all the responses necessary to be a successful player. He must also acquire manipulative facility.

Failure to make the above distinction can lead to inappropriate organization of learning experiences. For example, if children are required to practice number combinations, they will acquire facility in associating answers to combinations of numbers. We want children to be able to respond quickly and correctly to stimuli like "two times two equals ———" and "twelve times four equals ————." However, facility in making this kind of response, necessary as it may be, does not guarantee that the child has an adequate understanding of the number concepts or number relations involved. When we use the terms "arithmetic skill" and "mathematical skill," we ordinarily imply facility in both understanding and making verbal responses. The total learning experience should be designed to produce facility in the total performance. Because certain variables influence the development of understanding and other variables influence the acquisition of manipulative facility, learning experiences must provide for both kinds of variables. The teacher should remember that many of the complex behaviors he will be teaching will require the learning of concepts, generalizations, attitudes, and values.

PERSONALITY AND PERFORMANCE BEHAVIORS. The kind of behavior patterns that a person acquires will affect the kind of personality that he develops. As we noted in Chapter One, personality is the totality of a person's behavior patterns. By acquiring performance patterns, a person can interact efficiently and easily with his environment. Skill performances facilitate the acquisition of goals that will satisfy needs. If a child wants approval from his companions, he can acquire this approval by becoming a skilled pianist. He is invited to parties because he can entertain. He can join the school orchestra and share the approval orchestral performances win. In other words, new ways of satisfying his needs are available to him because he can carry out certain skill performances.

Failure to acquire certain skill performances may also influence the development of his personality because of the way in which he is treated for this failure. If a teacher ridicules a child for poor writing, spelling, or oral reading, the child's concept of himself—his attitudes toward these activities and the values that he places on them—will be influenced. Because he has learned different concepts, attitudes, and values about reading, his personality will be somewhat different from that of a child who has more positive attitudes toward writing, spelling, and reading.[1]

Some skill performances should be acquired because they are universally shared in a particular culture. We expect children to learn how to use eating utensils, but we do not expect every child to

[1]One respect in which his personality will differ from that of other children will be in his conception of himself. See, for example, A. M. Walsh, *Self-Concepts of Bright Boys with Learning Difficulties*, New York, Bureau of Publications, Teachers College, Columbia University, 1956.

be a skilled tennis player. Some performance processes are important at one time in life but not at a later period. Athletics may be socially important during the period of schooling because of the rewards attached to skilled performances in athletics, but skilled athletic performance is generally less important in adult life. A child must acquire skill performances, during the period of his development, that are essential for manipulating his environment and learning his roles in society. Strong rewards are attached to the acquisition of these skills, and society fosters the acquisition of the needs which will motivate the learning of these skill performances.[2] Failure to acquire skill performances of this character will interfere with a child's adaptation to society. Personality development will be correspondingly affected, since the child cannot obtain the rewards society provides for the acquisition of these performances.[3]

CHARACTERISTICS OF SKILLED PERFORMANCES

Performance behaviors are generally acquired for their instrumental value, that is, their utility for attaining goals. Walking is one of the performance behaviors acquired early in life. Generally, walking is acquired as a means of moving about in one's environment and for obtaining positions and objects in the environment that will satisfy his needs. By walking the child can reach objects more easily and quickly than he can by crawling.[4] The violinist who wants to perform a musical score must acquire response patterns such as fingering and bowing. The baseball player learns to hit, throw, and catch a baseball, to run the bases, and to slide in order to be able to participate in the game and consequently to achieve the goals and satisfactions with which playing baseball provide him.

The more skillful a performance, the greater the instrumental value of the performance behavior. Many students can type with

---

[2] A more comprehensive discussion of this point can be found in Chapter Eleven under the heading "Developmental Tasks."

[3] From our previous discussion on motivation, it should be apparent that the acquisition of a performance process may be important to an individual as a means of need-satisfaction even though there may be no social pressure to acquire this performance behavior. The acquisition of the behavior would affect personality development in this case, as does the acquisition of any behavior related to attaining need-satisfaction.

[4] We are not suggesting that there is a teleological purpose involved in learning to walk, or that the child himself is conscious of any purpose in acquiring walking behavior. The acquisition of walking responses is instrumental to the attainment of goals and consequent need-satisfactions.

some skill, but the value of the ability to type increases with the level of skill developed.

What are the characteristics of a skilled performance? The fan sitting in the stadium can quickly distinguish the good players from the poor. An executive can easily determine the level of typing skill of his secretary. Parents attending the school's musical concert have little trouble in identifying the skilled musicians. What distinguishes the skilled performance and the skilled performer from the less skilled performance and performer?

ACCURACY AND SKILL PERFORMANCE. The skilled performer makes relatively few errors and seldom repeats those that he has made. The sour note, the dropped pass, the misspelled word, all indicate a lack of skill. The errors may be apparent either in the performance itself or the product of the performance. We can observe an incorrect movement; for example, we can tell that a golfer is not moving back far enough on his back swing. We also can observe the effects of an error when a football player drops a pass, or when we find that a woodworker's chair falls apart when it is sat upon. Minimization of error is an essential characteristic of a skilled performance.

COORDINATION AND SKILL PERFORMANCE. *Coordination is another characteristic of a skill performance.* By coordination we mean the integration of the specific responses required in the performance. The skilled performer has so integrated the responses in his performance that they appear to be one continuous movement. In hitting a golf ball, a complex series of specific responses are required. The golfer must hold the club correctly, must move through the back swing. then through the arc, the face of the club must strike the ball at the proper angle, and the golfer must follow through. While performing all of these responses, the golfer is also shifting his hips and has already positioned his feet even before he begins the swing. The beginner at golf consciously attends to as many of these specific responses as he can. The skilled golfer moves with ease through these responses as if they were one continuous response. His movement is characterized by grace and ease; there is no hesitancy, no abrupt shifting of movement, once the sequence has begun.

The unskilled performer, or the person who is just learning the skill, makes many responses which are unnecessary and occasionally conflicting. In Figure 34 is a picture of the performance of an op-

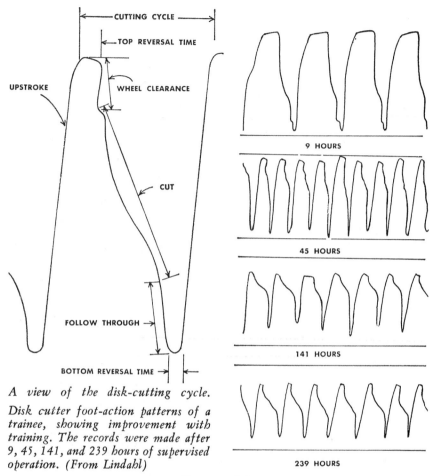

A *view of the disk-cutting cycle.*

Disk cutter foot-action patterns of a trainee, showing improvement with training. The records were made after 9, 45, 141, and 239 hours of supervised operation. (From Lindahl)

FIGURE 34

erator being trained on a machine. The operation requires a sequence of responses which is successful if the operator has acquired the proper speed, form, rhythm, and pressure pattern in a complex hand and foot action.[5] The diagrams in Figure 34 are paper tape recordings of the foot movements of an operator as he practices the movement over a long period of time. As the diagrams suggest, the operator has added some responses over this period of time and has dropped others. Also, the sequence of movement is smoother in the latter stages of practice than in the earlier stages.

---

[5]See L. G. Lindahl, "Movement Analysis as an Industrial Training Method," *Journal of Applied Psychology*, 29 (1945), 420-36.

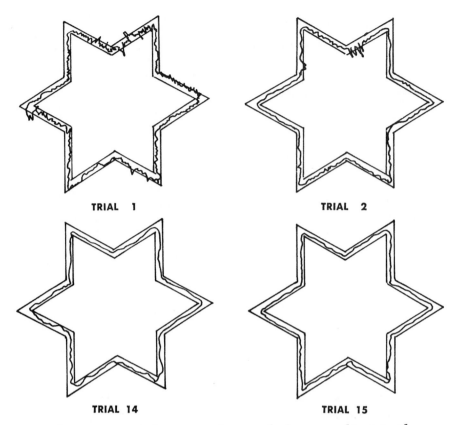

TRIAL 1   TRIAL 2

TRIAL 14   TRIAL 15

The tracings of the star outline made by one subject in the mirror-drawing experiment. The drawings for the first two and the last two of fifteen trials are shown. The stars were five inches from tip to opposite tip, and the distance between the lines was one eighth of an inch. (From Kingsley)

FIGURE 35

A simple laboratory experiment illustrates the characteristics of skill performance that we have outlined here.[6] In this experiment the subject is placed in front of a mirror and a star pattern is placed on a sheet of paper in front of the subject. He cannot see the star pattern except in the mirror and must trace this star pattern between the lines on the pattern by looking in the mirror. Because of mirror

---

[6]H. L. Kingsley, *The Nature and Conditions of Learning*, 2nd ed., Englewood Cliffs, N. J., Prentice-Hall, Inc., copyright 1946, 1957, pp. 304-05. Reproduced by permission.

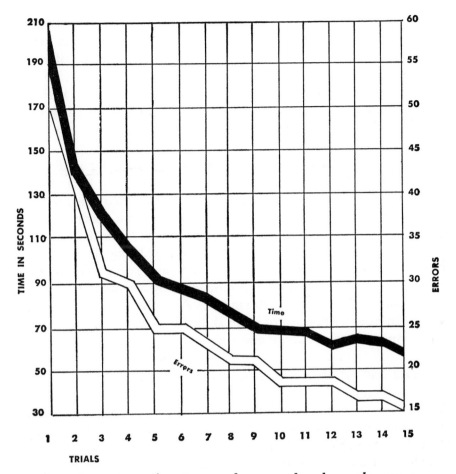

Learning curves for time and errors, based on the mean scores of fifty subjects in the mirror-drawing experiment. (After Kingsley)

FIGURE 36

reversal the subject must learn to move in directions opposite to the way he appears to be moving in the mirror. A complex set of responses requiring integration of what he sees and of his hand movements is necessary if this subject is to perform the task at all. In this experiment an error is defined as touching either of the boundary lines of the star. In Figure 35 are pictures of the tracings on a series of trials, two at the early stages of the acquisition of the performance and two at the later stages. As these diagrams illustrate, the subject makes fewer and fewer errors as he becomes more skillful. His pattern of movement, as reflected in the line that he is drawing, becomes smoother and more integrated. Figure 36 shows the reduction in both number of errors and the time required in making a tracing over fifteen trials. By trial fifteen, the subject has acquired a certain degree of skill, which is demonstrated by the fact that he can perform the tracing much more quickly and make fewer errors while doing so.

SPEED AND SKILL PERFORMANCE. Accuracy and coordination characterize skill performances. Speed may or may not be a characteristic of a skilled performance. A behavior can be performed rapidly, but not skillfully. The first student who finishes a task does not always receive the highest grade for accuracy. Johnny, who fills out the answers to the multiplication tables quickly, may make a large number of errors. Where speed is a recognized component of a skill performance, the acquisition of speed, accompanied by a reduction in error, is an indicator of skilled performance. A typist who can type ten words a minute without error is not skilled because this skill performance requires both accuracy and speed.

THE USE OF CUES AND SKILL PERFORMANCE. The skilled performer is distinguished from the unskilled performer in another way. As a performer moves through the behavior pattern, he is continually responding to stimuli originating both internally and externally. As the golfer swings the club, he responds to internal stimuli from his muscles and adjusts his movements accordingly. As he begins his back swing he responds to internal stimuli which tell him whether he has reached the appropriate point to start his forward motion. As he swings, he also responds to external stimuli—the image of the ball in relationship to the club, the distance from the ball to the green, and the position of the tee in relation to the green. The process of learning a skilled behavior involves learning appropriate responses to stimuli. The beginner must learn which cues to respond to and which to ignore. As the skilled performer learns the cues to respond to, he also learns to respond to fewer cues. A beginning typist may watch his hands on the keys and may look at the letters on the keys, but he is taught to touch the keys without having to look at the letters on them. A skilled typist can place his fingers in the correct position and move them without looking at his hands or the letters that he is typing.

The skilled performer also responds to subtler cues than does the beginner. The batter standing at the plate notices movements of the pitcher which "telegraph" the kind of pitch that he is going to throw. To the beginning golfer, all greens look alike; the professional is sensitive to the slope of the green and even to the texture of the grass. The skilled performer's greater sensitivity to cues enables him to anticipate potential errors and to avoid them.

Although we have described the characteristics of a skilled performance and a skilled performer, the description alone does not help us organize learning experiences. The important educational question is how learning experiences should be organized so that skill performances can be developed. The common-sense notion of skilled behavior is that it is essentially an automatic performance and that this automatic act is developed by continual practice. Does practice alone produce a skilled performance, and by "practice" do we mean merely the repetition of a response sequence? What are the effects of motivation on the acquisition of skilled behavior? What effect does fatigue have on the acquisition of a skill? Can a skill, such as swimming, be learned at any age, or does the stage of physical and mental development of the learner determine the optimum time for learning a skilled behavior? These are the important psychological questions that have a direct bearing upon the kinds of educational experiences that can be organized to develop skilled performances.

THE ACQUISITION OF SKILL PERFORMANCES

In this section we will study two general classes of variables that influence the acquisition of skill behaviors: (1) *task variables*, which are factors in the learning situation that facilitate the acquisition of a skilled behavior; (2) *individual variables*, which are characteristics of the learner that facilitate the acquisition of skilled behavior.

INFLUENCE OF DEMONSTRATION. Performance behaviors are observable. For this reason, the manipulative aspects of a skilled performance can be demonstrated. A teacher can illustrate by his own actions the responses which characterize the skilled behavior.

An important variable affecting the facility with which a skilled behavior is acquired is the *amount of guidance* provided in the learning experience. Experiments requiring the learning of fairly simple skilled behavior illustrate this principle.[7] The experimental task was to learn to run a maze with a progressive reduction in number of trials and errors so as to achieve a criterion level of improvement; varying amounts of guidance were provided. The analysis of the data relates the amount of guidance to reduction in error and in number of trials required for learning. As the graphs indicate (Figures 37 and 38), the amount of guidance is related to improvement in skilled performance, with some qualifications. In these experiments the amount of guidance facilitated the acquisition of the skilled performance, if an

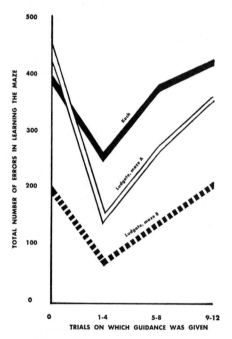

Effect of location of four guided trials on the number of errors made in learning a maze. In all three studies, guidance given on trials 1 to 4 resulted in fewer errors than when no guidance was given and fewer than when guidance was introduced later in the series. (After Koch, Ludgate)

FIGURE 37

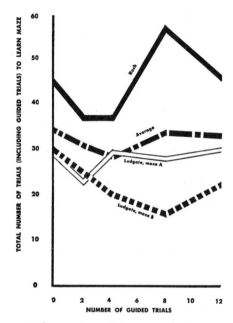

Effects of guidance on number of trials required to learn a maze. In general, two or four guided trials given at the beginning of training decreased the total number of trials required to master the maze. (After Koch, Ludgate)

FIGURE 38

[7]H. L. Koch, "The Influence of Mechanical Guidance Upon Maze Learning," *Psychological Monographs*, No. 5, 1923; K. E. Ludgate, "The Effect of Manual Guidance Upon Maze Learning," *Psychological Monographs*, No. 1, 1923.

adequate amount of guidance was given at the right time—usually early in the learning series.

When a student is beginning the process of learning a performance behavior, he has at best only hazy ideas of the responses required. At this point careful demonstration enables him to interpret the situation in which he is performing the behavior and to clarify his conception of the required responses. Once the learner has clarified the character of the response required and is able to make interpretations of the learning situation, additional guidance may only confuse him. He may be given more information than he can assimilate at the time, or he may not yet be able to integrate new responses into the pattern that he has already learned. The student reaches points in learning a complex sequence of responses where he must integrate sets of responses and assimilate the information that has already been provided. Until this process of assimilation and integration is completed, addition of new information, or the demonstration of new responses, interferes with the assimilation and integration process.

Unfortunately no rules are available so that the teacher can know just how much information to provide at any stage of the learning of a skilled behavior. If the teacher is himself a skilled performer, he is likely to overlook the complexity of the responses involved in the skilled behavior. As a skilled performer he has long since integrated the complex sequence into an organized, integrated pattern of response, and may have forgotten the details of the particular responses involved in the skilled behavior. The teacher may give the student too much information simply because he is thinking in terms of the total pattern of the skilled behavior, rather than in terms of the particular response, or segments of responses, that the learner is acquiring at this time in the learning process.

Guidance and demonstration are most effective initially because the learner knows so little at this time; however, as he acquires information and some skill in making specific responses, additional information given too soon may interfere with the acquisition of further skill. If we are teaching a child to play a musical instrument, we first familiarize him with the instrument, showing him the various parts of the instrument, the way it is to be held, and the basic movements. Once he has acquired the basic movements, we teach him the refinements of these movements and the more complex aspects of the skill. Guidance at any phase of learning is beneficial, provided the learner

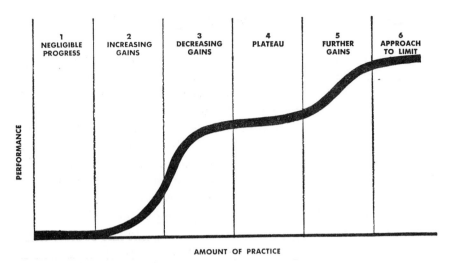

| 1 NEGLIGIBLE PROGRESS | 2 INCREASING GAINS | 3 DECREASING GAINS | 4 PLATEAU | 5 FURTHER GAINS | 6 APPROACH TO LIMIT |

PERFORMANCE

AMOUNT OF PRACTICE

A general learning curve.

FIGURE 39

is ready to assimilate the additional information that the guidance or demonstration provides.

THE SEQUENCE OF LEARNING. Figure 39 is a graph of a typical learning curve. Although this pattern of learning is not applicable to the acquisition of all kinds of skill performances, this type of curve is frequently obtained when we plot the acquisition of responses against some measure of learning progress. Note that the curve is characterized by the following phases:

1. A period of a slow progress, during which there is very little improvement in performance.

2. A period during which the rate of learning increases fairly rapidly.

3. A period when the learning appears to slow down.

4. A period during which there is no apparent improvement, called a "plateau."

5. A period of gradual improvement.

6.   A period during which there is again a decrease in rate of improvement.

The learning curve is a theoretical picture of the course of learning a skill performance. Learning curves plotted for particular skill performances vary considerably with the kind of behavior being acquired and with the variety of conditions under which the learning could take place.

There are a number of reasons for the changes in the learning progress that are illustrated in Figure 39. A study of this highly generalized pattern of learning can sensitize the teacher to kinds of changes in learning that may occur in acquiring a skilled performance.

The rate of learning does not follow a straight line course; there are periods of rapid progress and periods of slow progress, as well as periods in which there is no apparent progress. During the periods of no apparent progress, the student may be assimilating new information and organizing and integrating the responses that he has already learned.[8] Introduction of new information and new demonstrations of appropriate responses at this phase of learning would probably interfere with this process. We can be reasonably certain that guidance in the initial phases of learning is beneficial, and we can probably say that guidance is helpful during the period in which the student is making fairly rapid progress.

KINDS OF DEMONSTRATION. We have been using the word "guidance" in this section in the sense of *demonstration*. There are many ways in which responses can be demonstrated. The teacher can explain verbally what the response ought to be; he can show the student by his own behavior what the appropriate responses can be; he can even move the student through the response, literally taking him by the hand. When teaching a child to write, we can guide or demonstrate the appropriate responses in several ways. The child could trace the letters; the teacher could hold the child's hand and help him to make the appropriate movements; a film demonstrating the appropriate movements could be shown to the class.

---

[8]There is a difference of opinion among psychologists on whether plateaus in learning invariably occur. There is experimental evidence to suggest that such plateaus are not invariably found. For a discussion of this problem and a review of relevant research, see D. W. Taylor, "Learning Telegraphic Code," *Psychological Bulletin*, 40 (1943), 461-87.

Gates and Taylor[9] performed an experiment in which they tested the values of copying and tracing letters in learning to write. One group of children was given the letters *a, b, c, d,* and *e,* and they traced them through tissue paper. A second group, of comparable ability, age, and intelligence, copied the letters from models during the learning period. When the children were given a copying test, the group that had practiced copying the letters did twice as well as the group that had traced the original letters. When the children were called upon to copy letters that they had neither copied nor traced previously, the copying group still maintained their superiority, even though both groups did not do well on the test of copying new letters. The test called for a skill that had been practiced by the copying group, and this accounts, at least in part, for the superiority of this group. Two methods of demonstration or guidance were used in this experiment, and the evidence suggests that the copying method in this case was superior. The superiority of the copying method is related to the kinds of responses that the children developed and the relationship of these responses to the manner in which the children were later called upon to use them.

---

[9]A. I. Gates and G. A. Taylor, "The Acquisition of Motor Control and Writing by Pre-School Children," *Teachers College Record,* 24 (1923), 459-68.

A method of guidance is useful if it clarifies the manner in which a response is to be made. Extensive guidance may actually inhibit improvement by limiting the amount of time that the student may spend actively attempting the responses himself. A demonstration method that requires the student to participate actively will generally be superior to a method that requires less active participation by the student.[10]

Films, film-strips, and slides are frequently used to demonstrate skilled behavior. One of the major advantages of the movie or film-strip is an administrative one; that is, a large number of students can conveniently observe the demonstration at the same time. From a learning point of view, however, the value of a movie demonstration will depend upon the factors that we have discussed above. In the first place, if the film attempts to teach too much, the student will receive more information than he can assimilate. Second, the film may provide so much guidance at one time that the student does not have adequate opportunity to attempt the responses on his own. Third, the film may not require him to attempt the response in the manner in which he will eventually have to make the response. The movie observer usually is limited to verbal and imaginative rehearsal of what is to be done. This kind of behavior is not an adequate substitute for attempting the performance responses.

EFFECT OF KNOWLEDGE OF RESULTS. In the Gates and Taylor experiment, the children who had the opportunity to make mistakes by copying performed better than the children who had limited opportunities for making errors in the same kinds of movements and responses. The learner must have an opportunity to attempt the response; however, attempting a skilled behavior does not guarantee that the behavior will be acquired. In a learning sequence in which the learner has to attempt a large number of responses, he must receive information about the correctness of each of the responses that he makes. Experimental evidence clearly indicates that knowledge of correct performance or performance errors rapidly improves the learning of a performance pattern.

Figure 40 shows the results of an experiment conducted in train-

---

[10]This conclusion has been noted in our discussion of memory, and concept and attitude acquisition. For additional evidence, see A. K. Kurtz, J. S. Walter, and H. Brenner, "The Effects of Inserted Questions and Statements on Film Learning," *Pennsylvania State College Technical Reports*, SDC—297—16, 1950.

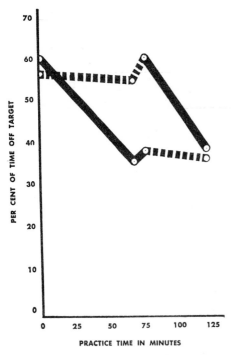

Effect of knowledge of results in learning tracking. The solid lines represent practice given with knowledge of results (a buzzer sounding whenever the tracker was off target); the dashed lines represent practice given without knowledge of results. (After Biel et al.)

FIGURE 40

ing men to use army gun directors.[11] The instructor, who used a check sight to determine whether or not the men were accurately sighting the target, sounded an electric buzzer to indicate when the tracker was off target. The group which received immediate information about the correctness of their responses improved rapidly. When the second group, which had not been receiving this information, were given the additional information, improvement was marked and immediate. Neither group showed any improvement in tracking when knowledge of the results was withheld. [12]

As the learner attempts responses, he can revise his performance only on the basis of information about its accuracy. Without this information he may continue to make the same error over and over again. Even with the information, he may continue to make errors, but he cannot correct the errors without the information.

In learning performance patterns, feedback information can be obtained in two ways: (1) In some cases, the learner knows immediately whether he has made an error. A musician blows a flat note; the ball player misses the ball; the golfer slices into the woods. In each of these situations the effect of error is immediately apparent to the learner. (2) In other situations, the learner cannot determine the accuracy of his response unless this informa-

[11]W. C. Biel, G. E. Brown, R. M. Gottsdanker, and R. C. Hall, *The Effectiveness of a Check Sight Technique for Training 40-mm Gun Pointers*, OSRD Report 4054, Tufts University, 1944.

[12]For additional experimental evidence, see J. L. Elwell and G. C. Grindley, "The Effect of Knowledge of Results on Learning and Performance," *British Journal of Psychology*, 29 (1938), 39-53 Also, see S. J. MacPherson, V. Dees, and G. C. Grindley, "The Effect of Knowledge of Results on Learning and Performance. II. Some Characteristics of Very Simple Skills," *Quarterly Journal of Experimental Psychology*, 1 (1948), 68-78.

tion is provided by some other person or a mechanical device. A child attempting a multiplication problem cannot tell whether he has made a mistake unless the teacher checks the correctness of his answer. Usually, a third grader can tell whether he has made the letter "a" correctly, but he may not know whether he has spelled "house" correctly. In any learning sequence, the learner must know the correctness or incorrectness of his responses.

EFFECT OF REINFORCEMENT. An operation that indicates to the learner the correctness of his response is called a *reinforcement*. When a golfer drives a ball straight down the fairway, he tries to carry out his swing in the same way the next time he drives. If a violinist who is attempting to learn how to change positions accurately finds that a particular wrist movement results in rapid and accurate finding of new positions, he tends to repeat this wrist movement.

If the consequences of making responses also lead to need-satisfaction, the reinforcement of the response pattern is even greater. The batter who knocks out a home run receives reinforcement from many different kinds of consequences of hitting this home run. The home run reinforces the pattern of batting responses; in addition, the batter receives reinforcement through need-satisfaction from the prestige that he receives for performing a socially valued action. If the consequences of a response have *reward* value, either by indicating to the learner that he is making the correct response or by obtaining need-satisfaction for the person, the response pattern is strengthened, and it is likely to occur more frequently the next time the response pattern is attempted.

Even a punishing consequence, when it indicates a right response, may have the same effect. Jones[18] required a group of thirteen- and fourteen-year-old boys and girls to learn to operate a punchboard maze. In order to find the correct solution, the learner had to make choices, some of which were correct and some incorrect. Under one experimental condition a pattern of lights, an agreeable stimulus, was flashed on when the child made a correct choice. Under another experimental condition a disagreeable vibration in the subject's stylus was set up when he made a correct choice. There was no difference in learning under these two conditions (see Figure 41). In this experiment, punishment, as well as reward, was used to indicate correctness

---

[18]H. E. Jones, "Trial and Error Learning with Differential Cues," *Journal of Experimental Psychology*, 35 (1945), 31-45.

of responses, assuming that the stimulus patterns were punishing and rewarding for the students. As long as the learner is receiving information about the correctness of his response, he may tolerate and even be "rewarded" by mild punishment.

Responses that are not reinforced are usually dropped. Through the selective application of reinforcement, a performer can learn to discriminate between desirable and undesirable, or correct and incorrect responses. A mother may reward the correct behavior of a small child by smiles, pats on the head, and affectionate gestures. The child

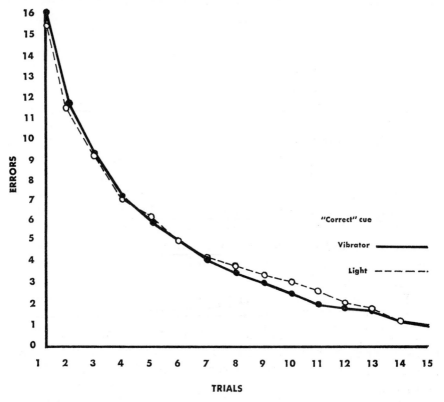

Learning curves with "right" indicated by agreeable or by disagreeable stimuli. The subjects were 114 junior high school students, who learned two maze patterns in which the right choice was indicated by a pleasing light pattern in one and by a disagreeable vibration in the other. (After Jones)

FIGURE 41

can learn to distinguish between the responses for which he will receive rewards and those for which he will not. The unrewarded responses will tend to disappear from his behavior, and the rewarded responses will be strengthened.[14]

Two problems face the teacher who attempts to utilize these principles of reinforcement in organizing learning experiences. The first is that the child must be motivated to learn. A child must attempt the response before the teacher can arrange conditions that may reinforce the correct responses. The second problem is one of management. A child makes thousands of responses in the school situation. It is inevitable, therefore, that he will make many responses which are not reinforced by the conditions created by the teacher. If children are working on multiplication problems and only the answers are checked, every response that has been made to obtain the answer tends to be strengthened by the reinforcement given for the answer.

One solution to the problem of providing comprehensive reinforcements has been the use of mechanical devices designed to provide reinforcement for responses as they are made.[15] Problems are arranged in a machine in such a way that a child cannot move on to the successive steps in working an arithmetic problem until he has performed each step correctly. It is argued that since each child is receiving reinforcement for correct responses as he makes them, the learning of correct responses is greatly facilitated. Devices of this kind promise to solve some of the problems associated with providing adequate reinforcements for learning, but their use is limited at present and comprehensive research is not yet available.

The teacher is limited in the kinds of reinforcements he can utilize. Many reinforcements are verbal or gestural in nature, such as saying "that's right" or "that's wrong," or smiling. The teacher needs to be imaginative in devising consequences that are rewarding to students. We may assume that a given consequence is not rewarding when the learner does not see the consequence as rewarding. Teachers permit students to do library reading when they have completed an assignment in a workbook. For some of the students in the class this

---

[14] For an experimental demonstration of the effects of reinforcement and non-reinforcement on a learned behavior, see E. R. Hilgard, R. K. Campbell, and W. N. Sears, "Condition Discrimination: The Effect of Knowledge of Stimulus-Relationships," *American Journal of Psychology*, 51 (1938), 498-506.

[15] For an interesting discussion on the use of mechanical devices in teaching, see B. F. Skinner, "The Science of Learning and the Art of Teaching," *Harvard Educational Review*, 24 (1954), 86-97.

consequence is rewarding; for other students it is not, since the library reading may require additional work that they do not want to do.

TIMING OF REINFORCEMENT. In general, reinforcements must be given promptly if the consequences of making correct responses are to have a facilitating effect upon the acquisition of behavior. Attempting responses is necessary if the learner is to acquire the correct response pattern. However, the student who is required to make responses when he is unable to evaluate their correctness is not in an efficient learning situation. Prompt and frequent reinforcement while the learner is attempting responses shortens the learning time by strengthening the appropriate responses.

At present we do not know the optimum time required between attempted response and reinforcement. We do know that different schedules of reinforcement have varying effects on performance. If reinforcements are given at fixed intervals, say every five minutes, the rate of responding is initially slow but increases as the time for reinforcement approaches. Teachers have observed this phenomenon in their classrooms. Assume that a teacher has assigned a typing exercise, and has told the students that the papers will be corrected every ten minutes. We would expect to find students working more intensely near the end of the ten-minute period than at the beginning. This effect may not be invariably found in all students since other factors affect performance, but this kind of an effect will frequently be produced by scheduling reinforcements in this manner.[16]

A suggestion is often made in methods textbooks that students be given ample opportunity to try a response before any evaluation is provided. For example, in teaching students to speak a foreign language, the teacher is counseled to let the student speak at some length before correcting his errors. Is this an efficient application of reinforcement? In the absence of clear-cut experimental evidence on this point we can only speculate about its validity. The "response" in this example is so complex that the student requires considerable time and effort merely to attempt it. When students are attempting responses of this complexity, immediate reinforcement of specific responses

---

[16]A discussion of reinforcement and learning and the problems suggested here can be found in J. Deese, *The Psychology of Learning*, New York, McGraw-Hill Book Co., 1958, Chapters 2 & 3. Original research on these problems is presented in—B. F. Skinner, *The Behavior of Organisms*, New York, Appleton-Century-Crofts, Inc., 1938; B. F. Skinner, *Verbal Behavior*, New York, Appleton-Century-Crofts, Inc., 1957; C. B. Ferster and B. F. Skinner, *Schedules of Reinforcement*, New York, Appleton-Century-Crofts, Inc., 1957.

probably interferes with trying out the total response. This total response probably should not be attempted until the student has mastered some of the specific responses. Efficiency in performance could probably be improved by breaking the complex response down into these specific responses, with adequate and immediate reinforcement for learning the specific responses. The responses requiring integration can then be attempted and reinforced as a whole. Reinforcement would then be applied for the integration rather than for the specific responses.

Assume, however, that we are interested in encouraging the students to try to speak in the language. In this case, the response to be reinforced is the "trying" response. Rewarding precision or punishing errors in grammar or sentence structure may seem to indicate that our primary concern is formal correctness rather than the attempt to speak the language. An anecdote will illustrate this point. A young child had seen her first circus. When she came home, she rushed to her mother and said, "You should have seen them clowns!" The mother replied, "*Those* clowns." The girl repeated the original statement, and her mother again corrected her. At this point, the girl said, "I don't think you're interested in what I want to tell you." The *desired* response is the response that must be reinforced.[17]

STAGE OF DEVELOPMENT OF THE LEARNER. We have stressed the importance of the factors over which the teacher has direct control in the acquisition of skilled behavior—guidance and reinforcement. The capacity and the stage of development of the learner are also important factors. Some skilled performances are beyond the capacities of children and the teaching of these behaviors must wait until the child has reached an enabling maturational level. A one-year-old child probably cannot hold or manipulate a fork, and elaborate training is

[17]Most of the research on reinforcement has been done on subhuman species; however, the following studies have been conducted in classroom settings with children: D. Auble and E. V. Mech, "Quantitative Studies of Verbal Reinforcement in Classroom Situations: I, Differential Reinforcement Related to the Frequency of Error and Correct Responses," *Journal of Psychology*, 35 (1953), 307-12; D. Auble and E. V. Mech, "Partial Verbal Reinforcement Related to Distributed Practice in a Classroom Situation," *Journal of Psychology*, 36 (1953), 165-86; D. Auble and E. V. Mech, "Response Strength in a Classroom Task Related to a 'Forward' Delay in Reinforcement," *Journal of Educational Psychology*, 45 (1954), 175-81; E. Kapos, E. V. Mech, and W. H. Fox, *Schoolroom Motivation: I, Two Studies of Quantity and Pattern of Verbal Reinforcement as Related to Performance on a Routine Task*, Bulletin of the School of Education, Indiana University, No. 1, 1957; E. Kapos, E. V. Mech, and W. H. Fox, *Schoolroom Motivation: II, Two Studies of Quantity and Pattern of Verbal Reinforcement as Related to a Measure of Drive on a Routine Task*, Bulletin of the School of Education, Indiana University, No. 2, 1957.

not likely to facilitate his acquisition of this behavior at this age. Sports requiring complex hand and eye coordination cannot be learned until the child has developed sufficiently to be able to acquire the coordinations. A boy cannot play baseball if he is not strong enough to lift the bat. Printing is taught before cursive writing because in learning to print the child will develop muscular skill and coordination that will facilitate his learning to write cursively. Improvement of skills in children is a function of their experience, growth, and development.

The relationship between experience and maturation was demonstrated in an experiment conducted by Josephine Hilgard.[18] In this

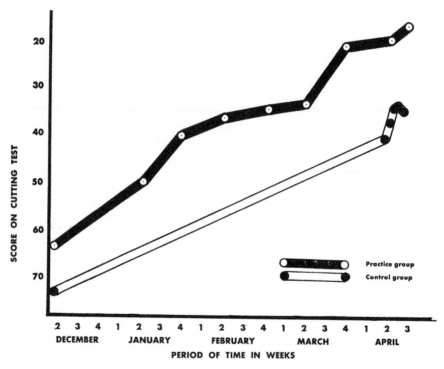

Mean learning curves for two groups in cutting (10 subjects in each group). The practice group trained for 12 weeks; the control group trained for one week. (After Hilgard)

FIGURE 42

[18]J. R. Hilgard, "Learning and Maturation in Pre-School Children," *Journal of Genetic Psychology*, 41 (1932), 36-56.

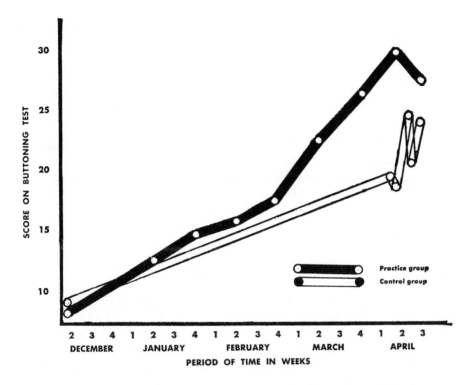

Mean learning curves for two groups in buttoning (9 subjects in each group). The practice group trained for 12 weeks; the control group trained for one week. (After Hilgard)

FIGURE 43

experiment two groups of fifteen children each were matched by chronological and mental age, sex, and initial ability in three skills—buttoning, cutting with scissors, and climbing. One group, the *practice group,* received intensive training in these skills for twelve weeks; a second group, the *control group,* received no training until the four days immediately following the twelve-week period. Tests were given in each of these skills at the beginning and end of the twelve-week period, and at the end of the four-day period following the twelve-week period. The data produced in this experiment are plotted in Figures 42 and 43. The curves indicate:

1.   Both groups steadily improved over the twelve-week period.

2. The control group showed marked improvement immediately after the twelve-week period and the four-day training session.

3. The practice group showed increased acceleration in learning near the end of the twelve-week period. Both groups improved even though one group was not practicing.

This effect presumably can be attributed to maturation. As the children developed, they were ready to acquire the skill and showed increasing improvement in the skill behaviors. The practice group was consistently better than the control group, however, and this difference can be attributed to the effects of the training that this group was receiving. When the control group received intensive training, the children were at a point in development where they could profit quickly by the practice, and a rapid increase in their performance ability took place.

Progress in learning a skill depends upon the maturation of the learner, as well as the kinds of experiences that he has had. If a child is too immature for learning a particular performance skill, it is largely a waste of time to attempt to teach him the behavior. The effects of training are most beneficial when they are introduced at a point where the learner has reached a sufficient level of development to profit quickly and easily from the training.

A child may have sufficient physical growth to learn a complex skill, but he may lack the mental growth necessary for learning the skill. A child must be able to read and interpret the music if he is to learn to play a musical instrument.

The skill behaviors that are systematically taught in schools have not been studied extensively enough to determine the optimum time for teaching these skills. Nonetheless, most curricula are arranged on the assumption that the experiential background and maturational stage of the pupil are adequate for acquiring the performance skills at the grade level involved. Some skill behaviors could probably be taught to children earlier in their schooling than is now the case, but there are probably few performance processes being taught too soon for the children to learn them. Some complex skills can be simplified, so that children can learn the basic response patterns without having to learn the complete skill performance until a later point in their schooling. For example, children are continually practicing performance processes, such as running, jumping, and climbing, which will later be integrated into more complex performances. A graded sequence of performance processes that parallel the child's growth and development insures that children will not be required to learn a skill until they have the experiential or physical basis for learning the skill. At the same time the learning process can be simplified by gradually introducing more complex patterns of response.

THE EFFECTS OF PRACTICE

A performance process is ordinarily acquired over a relatively long period of time. During this time period the learner's progress varies considerably. A learner works at a skill during limited periods of time. Football practice lasts two or three hours; we have baseball practice sessions, music practice sessions, typing practice, all of which are times during which the learner works on the acquisition of a skilled behavior. What is the most efficient arrangement of these practice sessions? In learning to play a piano, should the student practice intensively for an hour, leave his piano for a short period of time, and then come back for another hour of intensive practice? Would his performance improve if he practiced fifteen minutes at a time and rested and then practiced for another fifteen minutes? Should he practice every day, every other day, or only once a week?

There are other important questions about practice and its effect upon the acquisition of a skill. If a skill, such as typewriting, is made up of a variety of responses that must be integrated, should the learner practice each separate response, or should he attempt the whole response without practicing the individual movements? Should a golf player start swinging at a ball at the beginning of practice, or should he practice holding the club and then move into a backswing, and, when he is sufficiently proficient in these movements, should he then go on to practice the other parts of the swing? In typing, is it better to learn how to strike individual letters with the appropriate finger, or should the student learn to type words immediately? These are important questions relevant to organizing learning experiences for the acquisition of skill behaviors. Enough research evidence is available on these problems to allow the statement of some general principles.

DEFINITION OF MASSED AND SPACED PRACTICE. The issue of how much time should be spent during a practice session has been described as the problem of *massed versus spaced practice*. By *massed practice* we mean intensive practice without rest between the practice trials. For example, if a boy is learning to punt a football, massed practice would be a session in which he punted the ball one time after another with little or no pausing between punts. *Spaced practice* provides for rest periods between the trial periods. If a boy punting a football rests for fifteen seconds between each punt, this arrangement would be spaced practice.

The terms *massed* and *spaced* are relative terms. No one can practice for an indefinite period of time. The essential question is this: During a training session where successive trials in the skilled behavior can be made, how much time should be provided between each of these attempts?

In analyzing the arrangement of time in practice sessions, we first must define what we mean by a *trial* and decide on a length of time for the trial. What constitutes a trial is a function of the response that the learner is attempting to make. If by a trial we mean practicing a twenty-page piece of music which takes roughly an hour to play, then the response that is being practiced is that of playing the entire piece, and the trial time is one hour. If we define the response sequence as practicing a scale, an exercise which takes ten seconds, then the trial time is ten seconds, and the trial consists of playing the scale once. Football and baseball practice sessions are not single trials, but are arrangements of many trials of many different responses. A football player may practice punting for part of the football practice session, tackling for another part, blocking for another part. The issue of how to arrange practice time must be related to the particular set of trials with which we are concerned, the punting practice, the tackling practice, or the blocking practice.

EFFECTS OF MASSED AND SPACED PRACTICE. The problem of the arrangement of practice time is important because of a very simple and obvious phenomenon. The player's performance drops off between practice sessions[19] (see Figure 44). The longer the period of time between trials or practice sessions, the greater the loss of performance skill. Athletes refer to the negative effects of "laying off" during the off-season. One of the purposes of spring training is to bring an athlete's skills back up to the performance level of the regular

---

[19]S. J. MacPherson, V. Dees, and G. C. Grindley, "The Effect of Knowledge of Results on Learning and Performance: III, The Influence of the Time Interval Between Trials," *Quarterly Journal of Experimental Psychology*, 1 (1949), 167-74.

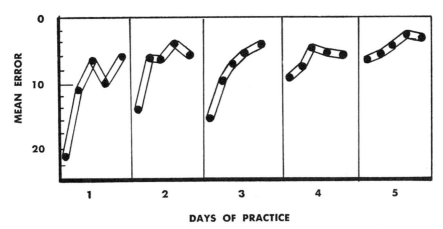

MEAN ERROR

DAYS OF PRACTICE

Learning to depress a Morse key for a duration of .7 seconds. The approach to the "bull's-eye" was shown after each attempt; i.e. the practice was with prompt "knowledge of results." The 10 daily trials were at 12-second intervals and each data point shows the mean error for 10 operators, two successive trials by each operator. The loss at the beginning of days belongs under the head of forgetting. The error reported is in arbitrary units measured on the galvanometer scale. The figure is so drawn as to make a rise in mean improvement. (After MacPherson, Dees, and Grindley)

FIGURE 44

season. Sometimes the decrement in performance results from loss of warm-up or the adjustment to the requirements of the skill being learned. The pianist, for instance, needs a period in which he "loosens up his fingers."

We might conclude that if practice sessions are spaced closely together, that is, massed, possible decrement in performance will be reduced to a minimum. While the massing of practice trials, grouping them closely and allowing for no rest between trials or only a minimal rest between trials, may prevent a drop-off in performance, massing of practice may have other effects that are not desirable. The longer a person practices, the more likely he is to become fatigued or bored, and with fatigue or boredom his performance may deteriorate. *Experimental evidence strongly favors the conclusion that spaced practice is more beneficial than massed practice for the learning of skilled performance.* The results of an experiment comparing massed and spaced practice are presented in Figure 45. In this experiment[20] two

---

[20]G. A. Kimble and R. B. Shatel, "The Relationship Between Two Kinds of Inhibition and the Amount of Practice," *Journal of Experimental Psychology*, 44 (1952), 355-59.

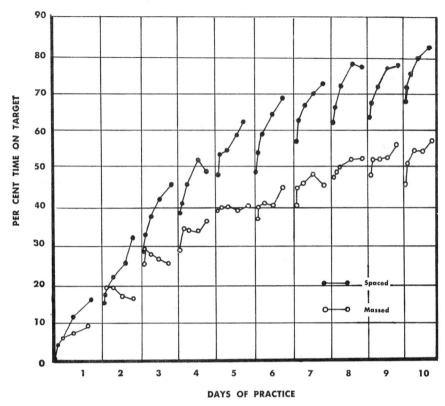

PER CENT TIME ON TARGET

DAYS OF PRACTICE

Massed and spaced practice on a pursuit rotor which turned at the rate of 78 revolutions per minute. The curves are smoothed within each day, except for the first, second, and last trials of the day. (After Kimble and Shatel)

FIGURE 45

groups of college students practiced a simple motor skill. Each group practiced the skill for fifteen trials a day for ten days, and the trial time was thirty seconds. The massed group had a five- to ten-second rest between trials, but the spaced group had a sixty-five to seventy-second rest between trials. Figure 45 shows the curves for each day. Several features are apparent in these curves that are consistently found in experiments on massed and spaced practice:

1. The over-all superiority of the spaced group is apparent. This group after the second day of practice is consistently superior to the massed practice group.

2.   For both groups there is an improvement between the first and second trials for each day's practice. This improvement is the result of warming up, during which the level of performance is generally raised to what it had been on the previous day.

3.   After the warm-up the massed group frequently declines in performance.

4.   Both groups show a drop in performance on the first trial of each succeeding day.

LENGTH OF INTERTRIAL PERIODS. While experimental evidence consistently favors spaced practice over massed practice, a crucial question often arises as to the time that should be allowed between trials. In the experiment cited above a short rest period was given the massed practice group. There appears to be an optimal intertrial rest period for each particular skill performance. However, for many of the skills with which teachers are concerned, the optimum time between trials is unknown. Experimental data[21] (see Figure 46) indicate that for a particular skilled behavior there is a certain length of time for rest between trials which maximizes the learning. In experiments on massed versus spaced practice the time between trials is exceedingly short, probably so short that the effects produced by a rest period cannot be reliably established. Consequently, spaced practice in which the interval is relatively longer usually results in an increase in learning which is greater than that for massed practice.

While some time between trials facilitates the learning of a skill performance, too much time between trials will interfere with learning. There are also a limited number of situations in which massed practice seems to be more beneficial than spaced practice. When the task to be learned is simple, and the time required to learn it is comparatively short, massed practice is usually more beneficial than spaced practice.[22] When the learning task requires considerable exploration to discover the correct responses, massed practice appears to be more beneficial than spaced practice because the learner must devote suffi-

---

[21]M. J. Kientzle, "Properties of Learning Curves under Varied Distributions of Practice," *Journal of Experimental Psychology*, 36 (1946), 187-211.
[22]D. O. Lyon, *Memory and the Learning Process*, Baltimore, Warwick & York, 1917.

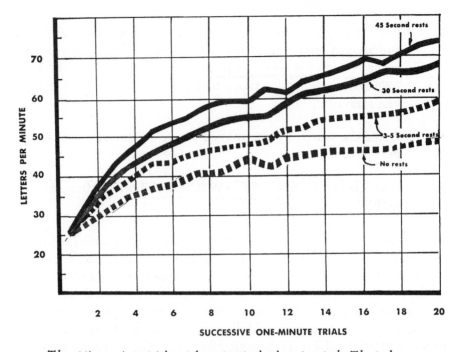

The optimum intertrial rest for a particular learning task. The task was to print the capital letters upside down from right to left in each line so that if the page were inverted, the letters would appear right side up and in alphabetical order. Time was called at the end of each minute's work and a rest was given before the next trial except in the case of the massed group. The lowest curve shows the successive mean scores of the 91 students in the massed group. There were 115 students who had either 3 or 5 seconds per rest period, 56 who had 30 seconds, 42 who had 45 seconds. There were still other groups. With 10 or 15 seconds of rest the curves fell in due order between the curve for 3-5 seconds and that for 30 seconds, but with rests of more than 45 seconds (up to seven days) there was no further gain. In rotary pursuit practice, with work periods of 22 seconds, rest periods of 1-2 minutes were better than either shorter or longer ones. (After Kientzle)

FIGURE 46

cient time within any given trial or set of trials to discovering what the correct responses are.

APPLICATION TO TEACHING PROCEDURES. The practical implication of these principles for teaching skill performances is that the teacher, in arranging learning sessions, should take into account the length of time required to complete the pattern of responses and adjust the number of trials and time between trials in order to maximize performance over a period of time. If a teacher notices that performance begins to drop off after a series of trials, he can hypothesize that because he is not allowing enough time between trials, the effects of fatigue and boredom have produced lower performance. If a skill is to be developed to a high level, the teacher should also provide practice sessions that are frequent enough to prevent the decrement in performance from becoming too great between sessions.

In discussing the amount and arrangement of time to be devoted to practice, we noted that the teacher must decide on how much of a response sequence or pattern is to be practiced in any one session or during any one trial. Because performance processes are complexes of responses it is not always possible to learn the entire pattern of responses during one learning or one practice session. If we are learning a complex skill, such as playing golf, we must acquire a number of complex patterns of responses, each of which is a skill performance in itself. Some golfers are good with woods; others have good iron shots; others are good putters. Each of these aspects of playing golf is a skill performance, and a golfer has developed a total skill when he has integrated all of these into a performance skill, which he can demonstrate by playing a game of golf. The learner will not be a skilled golfer until he has integrated each of these units into a total skill performance. He can, however, learn each of these independently, and the learning of the total skill is simplified by breaking it up into convenient practice units. Similarly, a pianist learning to play a twenty-page concerto will probably be more efficient if he breaks the concerto up into convenient units which are "wholes" that can be practiced as units.[23]

If a comparatively simple performance process is broken down too finely into units, the efficiency of learning may be reduced. If a pattern is broken up into discrete responses to be practiced separately, the individual responses may be practiced in a way in which they will never be used. In learning to type, for example, practicing with one finger at a time teaches certain basic movements. Considerable practice on these basic movements probably is a waste of time because the typist will never have to type with his first finger, and then with his second finger, and then with his third finger. Instead, he must make

---

[23]R. M. Gagné and H. Foster, "Transfer of Training From Practice on Components in a Motor Skill," *Journal of Experimental Psychology*, 39 (1949), 47-68.

a series of movements that are integrations of each of the individual movements and involve coordination between hands.

Another danger in breaking up a response sequence into the smallest responses is that the learner may never see the importance of integrating these responses. A pianist who can play scales beautifully and efficiently, but never learns to play a piece of music, has limited technical competence.

REALISTIC PRACTICE. The discussion of how much to practice at one session suggests the importance of practicing under conditions as similar as possible to those under which the skill will be used. Realistic practice is ultimately the most beneficial and efficient kind of practice. At some point the golfer must leave the putting green and the driving range and get out on the course. The batter must leave the batting cage and show his skill in a game. The musician must eventually abandon his exercises for musical compositions. Simplified practice conditions are beneficial in the initial phases of learning a skill. But as the response pattern becomes stabilized and the learner becomes more proficient in the skill performance, he must have the opportunity to practice it under a wide variety of circumstances. While the skill performance is repeated in essentially the same way each time, nevertheless, subtle variations and changes are required by changes in conditions. Not every pitcher throws a baseball to the batter in identically the same way. Variations in pitching style and the circumstances under which pitches are thrown require continual adjustments on the part of the batter. The performer must learn to respond to the appropriate cues in the environment and adjust his skill behavior to the cues presented in changing conditions.

The school is limited in providing realistic practice conditions for the learning of some kinds of skills. Only a limited number of musical performances can be staged during a school year. The students learning typing for vocational purposes will probably not be using their typing in business tasks until sometime after they have acquired the basic responses of the skill. However, training devices can be utilized to approximate realistic conditions. The Link trainer used in the training of pilots is an example of a device which simulates as closely as possible the conditions under which a pilot will actually be flying. Performing in a Link trainer is not flying, but the conditions are sufficiently similar so that the student pilot can practice many of the responses that he will be called upon to perform in identically the same way while flying. If the typing class is composed of students who are training to be secretaries, the typing exercises should provide practice exercises on business letters. Once an elementary school child has learned basic letter formations in writing, the greater portion of his practice time ought to be devoted to writing words rather than writing single letters or artificial combinations of letters. Modern practice in learning a musical instrument favors moving quickly to the playing of simple pieces rather than practicing exercises endlessly.

Throughout this chapter we have discussed the factors influencing the acquisition of skilled performances. Again, we have not spelled out methodologies for the teaching of every kind of skilled performance that schools attempt to develop in students. But the general principles are clear and well established. Inadequacies in skilled performance learning can usually be traced to failure to incorporate these principles into educational procedures. Students are permitted to practice large blocks of complex responses with little or no reinforcement of correct responses. Students are permitted to waste valuable time in attempting to determine what is the correct pattern of response when this pattern could easily be demonstrated for the student during the initial phases of learning the skill performance. A systematic organization that maximizes the acquisition of a complex skill performance would include: units that can be practiced with ease, careful distribution of practice time, adequate guidance, and consistent reinforcement of correct responses.

The acquisition of a skill performance has potential reward value in itself. As the student becomes proficient at dancing, public speaking, or athletics, his opportunities for manipulating his environment and for interacting with other people are maximized. He obtains rewards for success in an endeavor that is valued and socially important. The acquisition of these skill performances gives the student confidence in his ability to handle himself and his environment and facilitates the development of his total personality.

SUMMARY

In this chapter the following points have been discussed as relevant to the performance processes:

1. A "performance" is a complex integration of behavior patterns. These response systems are integrations of cognitive,

attitudinal, evaluative, and manipulative behaviors. We infer the acquisition of these complex patterns from their overt aspects, that is, the manipulative behavior that we can observe.

2. The behavior patterns included in a performance pattern are a matter of definition and description. When the elements of the performance are known, different kinds of learning experiences can be organized to facilitate learning of these elements and their integration.

3. Throughout this chapter we have used the term *skill performance* to refer to performance behaviors that have been developed to the point where they can be carried out easily and efficiently. We have indicated that the term "skill" is used in everyday language to describe complex organizations of behavior which include cognitive, attitudinal, evaluative, and performance processes.

4. Skill performances, that is, performance patterns which have been learned to a relatively high degree of efficiency, have the following characteristics: (1) A skill performance is characterized by accuracy; that is, few errors are made in carrying out the appropriate behaviors. (2) Skill performances require coordination of responses into a smooth pattern of performance. Speed may or may not be a characteristic of a skill performance. We have also noted that the skilled performer is sensitive to more cues, and subtler ones, than is the unskilled performer.

5. Two kinds of variables are relevant to the acquisition of skill performances: (1) task variables—factors in the learning situation which facilitate the acquisition of the skilled behavior; (2) individual variables—characteristics of the learner which facilitate the acquisition of skilled behavior.

6. The major task variables which influence the acquisition of a skilled performance are: (1) demonstrations of the appropriate responses; (2) reinforcement of the appropriate responses; (3) practice on the appropriate responses.

7. A teaching procedure designed to demonstrate responses is

most efficient when the procedure requires the learner to participate actively in the process. Demonstration facilitates learning when the appropriate responses are clearly indicated and described, and when the response being demonstrated is not too complex for the learner.

8. Reinforcement strengthens appropriate responses and is most useful in facilitating learning when applied frequently and promptly.

9. Spaced practice that provides sufficient time for the learners to attempt responses is more efficient in facilitating learning than is massed practice, except under some special conditions.

10. One of the most important individual variables is the learner's stage of development. Unless the learner has a background of experience and a level of maturity adequate for the performance process, it is uneconomical to attempt to teach this skill. When the learner has reached the stage of development required for the skill performance, it will be learned more rapidly than at an earlier time.

11. Another important individual variable is the motivation of the learner, a fact that we have not discussed in detail in this chapter, since all learning assumes a motivated state of the organism.

12. We have also noted that the course of learning typically follows a sequence characterized by an initial period of small progress, a period of fairly rapid improvement, followed by a period in which learning appears to slow down, then a period of gradual improvement. Throughout this sequence there may be plateaus —periods in which there is no apparent progress. We have hypothesized that during these periods the learner may be reorganizing and integrating his responses. Typically, the pattern of learning is characterized by periods of relatively slow improvement followed by periods of rapid improvement. In general, learning does not occur in regular increments or a straight line course.

As in previous chapters, we have pointed out general principles relevant to the organization of learning experiences. We have noted a number of points on which we do not have clear-cut experimental evidence of immediate and direct use to the teacher. Such factors as the amount and timing of reinforcement and the period of rest between trials in spaced practice have not been sufficiently explored to permit clear and specific directions for the teaching of the many skill performances the school attempts to teach. Here again, the teacher must act as a hypothesis-maker, formulating hypotheses on the basis of these general principles and his experience.

Throughout this chapter we have emphasized the relationship of the acquisition of skill performances to the development of personality. Insofar as a performance pattern is culturally and socially important, acquisition of this process directly influences personality, particularly the child's concept of himself as a person. The school provides opportunities to learn many skill performances which are socially or occupationally useful, and in this way fosters the development of the child's personality.

STUDY AND DISCUSSION QUESTIONS

1. Describe the patterns of specific responses involved in the following performances:

    a. Driving a car under ordinary driving conditions.

    b. Writing a letter of thanks for a gift.

    c. Singing a solo in a musical production.

    d. Giving a talk on student problems before a student assembly.

2. For each of the above performances, describe the requirements of a skill performance. What kinds of errors in performance would be regarded as evidence of a lack of skill?

3. Describe the concepts, generalizations, and attitudes that must be learned as part of the pattern of performance for each of these performances.

4. What environmental interactions are facilitated by skill in each of the following performances:

    a. Typing.

    b. Arithmetical computing.

    c. Giving a talk.

    d. Playing tennis.

5. As we have seen, guidance may be most beneficial in the early phases of learning. Under what conditions is guidance likely to facilitate improvement of performance in the later stages of acquiring a skill performance?

6. Describe the kinds of demonstrations that might be provided to facilitate learning the following performances:

    a. Using the card catalogue in the library.

    b. Using a laboratory scale to weigh chemicals.

    c. Wiring an electric bell in a simple circuit.

7. For each of the kinds of demonstrations that you have suggested for the skill performances in Question No. 6, predict the relative effects of each in terms of facilitation of learning. How would you explain the assumed relative superiority of some of these methods of demonstration?

8. How is "feed-back" information obtained in the learning of each of the following performances?

    a. Typing.

    b. Using correct grammar.

    c. Translating a foreign language passage correctly.

    d. Giving a class talk.

9. Review the learning curves from the Hilgard experiment. How do you account for the fact that the control group showed a steady improvement in performance without practice?

10. For each of the following performances, specify the specific patterns of response that need to be acquired to learn the total performance. Analyze these patterns and specify the responses to be practiced in successive trials. Estimate, where possible, the length of time to be allotted a trial for each of these responses, and suggest arrangements of practice time that may facilitate the learning of these responses.

    a. Dialing a telephone number.

    b. Jumping rope.

    c. Playing checkers.

    d. Throwing a baseball.

11. Suggest some realistic practice situations for the learning of the following performances:

a. Using English grammar correctly.

b. Spelling.

c. Working percentage problems in arithmetic.

d. Using a slide rule.

RECOMMENDED READINGS

The first of the readings is a general discussion of the principles of learning skill performances in school. The other three readings are detailed analyses of experimental data on the learning of skill performances.

1. C. E. Ragsdale, "How Children Learn the Motor Types of Activities," *Forty-ninth Yearbook of the National Society for the Study of Education, Part I, Learning and Instruction,* Chicago, University of Chicago Press, 1950, pp. 69-91.

2. D. Wolfle, "Training," in S. S. Stevens (ed.), *Handbook of Experimental Psychology,* New York, John Wiley & Sons, 1951, Chapter 34.

3. R. H. Seashore, "Work and Motor Performance," in S. S. Stevens, (ed.), *Handbook of Experimental Psychology,* Chapter 36.

4. N. L. Munn, "Learning in Children," in L. Carmichael (ed.), *Manual of Child Psychology,* 2nd Ed., New York, John Wiley & Sons, 1954, pp. 387-407.

PROBLEM-SOLVING PROCESSES

In the five preceding chapters we have discussed how a person learns such basic behaviors as concepts, attitudes, values, and skill performances. We have treated each of these behaviors as a relatively discrete process in personality; we have emphasized, however, that as the person meets each new aspect of his experience he reacts as a totality. If the person finds familiar features in the new experience, he tends to use previously learned responses in the adaptation process. If he recognizes that the previously learned responses are not now adaptive, he knows he must learn new modes of response or acquire new integrations of learned responses.

Here we will study the complex process called problem-solving, by which the person interacts with the *novel* aspects of his experience. In problem-solving the person reacts as a totality, using his concepts, attitudes, values, and skill performances in a situation in which previous learning cannot be used easily and readily in adapting to the situation.

Problem-solving is an inferred process—classified in the category of mediating variables listed in our

model of personality in Chapter Three. We observe a person in some kind of situation; he is striving for a goal that is not readily attainable in that context. We observe his hesitancies in selecting the means to goal attainment and his modifications of response patterns as he attempts to attain the goal. Both the goal and obstacles to it may be observable aspects of the environmental context, or the goal and sources of difficulty in attaining it may also be inferred. In either case, we observe modifications of attempts to attain the goal and infer that problem-solving processes are influencing the individual's behavior.

Problem-solving is not an isolated, unitary kind of process. It is an integration of many particular processes, and it may take many different specific forms. In any case, problem-solving behavior is likely to appear when the person finds himself in a problem situation.

WHAT IS A PROBLEM SITUATION?

In Chapter Five we described a class studying a unit on India. The children were exposed to many new and unusual experiences. They were placed in a problem-solving situation in which they needed to learn in various ways—to assimilate the new material, to interpret it, and to learn adaptive responses. For what would children ordinarily know about Indian culture or what should they think or feel about the manners and customs of the Indian people? One purpose of the teacher in introducing this unit was to develop an understanding of the Indian culture. The process of achieving the goal—in this instance, an exceedingly complex goal involving understandings, attitudes, and acquisition of information—required that the child acquire complex sets of responses that would enable him to attain an understanding of another culture. If the child knew what he had to do, what he had to think and feel, and if he were able to respond immediately in a way that indicated he understood the Indian culture, he would have no problem.

Earlier we discussed Jane, a girl who wanted to achieve the approval and esteem of her classmates. If Jane had had to try different ways of attaining her goal and had not been sure in advance that a particular way would work successfully for her, she would then have been confronted with a problem. If there had been no school newspaper for which Jane could write an article, the means to her goal would not have been available and she would have had to choose another alternative. Or if the feature article had not been a successful means for obtaining her goal, she would have had to try some other means.

DEFINITION OF A PROBLEM SITUATION. The children studying India and Jane writing a feature article are in problem situations. *A problem exists when there is a goal to be attained, but the individual sees no well-defined, well-established means of attaining it, or when the goal is so vaguely defined or unclear to the person that he cannot determine what are relevant means for attaining it*. If Jane has consistently attained her goal of winning prestige and approval by her writing activities, she has no problem in deciding on a means to attain this goal. If a child in the sixth grade class studying India has already learned that he can understand other people by acquiring information about their customs and history, he knows that he will probably attain his goal of understanding the Indian culture if he studies Indian history and customs. Sometimes, however, a "goal" such as understanding the Indian culture may be so meaningless for a child that he cannot determine whether the responses he is making are appropriate to its attainment.

Problem situations vary from person to person. A problem situation cannot exist for a child unless there is a goal that he wishes to attain. If a child in the sixth grade class is not motivated to want to understand Indian culture and history, understanding the Indian people is not a problem for this child. Even though he is not interested in understanding the Indian culture, he may have other problems, such as how to maintain his standing in class or how to keep out of trouble while working in a situation in which he is not interested. The attainment of these goals constitutes a problem for the child.

Similarly, a problem does not exist for a child when he knows the means by which he can attain the goal. One of the major functions of the educational process is to teach children how to solve problems that they will meet frequently in the course of their development. Getting along with other people, for example, is a general problem. If we want to enable children to solve this problem under many and varied conditions, we introduce children to experiences that require them to solve this kind of problem frequently. We place them in groups in which they will interact with fellow students and adults. In all of these situations, we attempt to facilitate the child's learning about how to interact with a wide range of people. As he has more and more experience, and as he profits from his experience by adapting to interactions with other people, he becomes more confident of his ability to get along with other people. He has available a wide variety of means which he knows are successful for attaining this general goal. When he is placed in a new interpersonal situation, he is prepared to analyze it and to decide on the likeliest means of attaining the goal.

In a course in driver education, students solve the typical kinds of problems that they will meet when driving. In learning sports, the class or team devotes time to analyzing and planning plays for meeting common problem situations that will arise. Students thereby learn the most likely means for attaining specific goals when they are confronted with the problem situation.

THE SCHOOL AND PROBLEM-SOLVING. Because the schools cannot reproduce in the curriculum every situation that children will meet, it is essential that children learn how to become effective problem-solvers. The function of school experience is twofold: (1) to prepare the child for the general kinds of problems he is likely to meet; (2) to develop the child's ability to solve problems that cannot be anticipated in the course of his formal education. Many learning experiences are arranged so that students solve problems similar to the kinds of problems they are likely to meet in later life. In an English class, for example, a student learns how to solve problems such as organizing facts and arguments into a clear exposition of his ideas. He learns to use the library and reference works for gathering information. He learns the techniques of effective writing. He tries to solve the problem of presenting his ideas clearly by writing themes and reports and by giving talks to his class. In these ways, he is prepared to solve the general problem of presenting his ideas clearly. At the same time we attempt to develop students' abilities to attack problems by providing them with concepts, attitudes, information, and methods of solution for problems that cannot be anticipated.

The development of students as problem solvers is one of the most important functions of the school. Unless a child develops his problem-solving ability, he will be limited in his ability to interact efficiently and satisfactorily with his environment. In a complex and rapidly changing society such as ours, the need for the development of this ability is great. Culture changes so rapidly in modern society that many of the techniques for solving problems, as well as many of the current problems, are no longer meaningful to the student by the time he has completed his formal education. Children in school today may eventually be faced with problems that we cannot even imagine at the present time. By developing their ability to meet and solve problems, children will be able to face these unimagined problems.

In this chapter we will study the variables that influence successful problem-solving. We will be answering two basic questions: How are problems solved? What factors influence problem-solving?

HOW PROBLEMS ARE SOLVED

Although the processes of problem-solving have not been so completely investigated that we can state clearly and definitely their exact nature, experimental evidence suggests the principal features of problem-solving processes.[1] Investigations have attempted to determine what steps are required for successful solution of problems. One kind of methodology used in past experiments consisted of presenting people with situations in which they discussed their approach to the problems, thus permitting the investigator to obtain a record of their methods of problem-solving.

Investigators have classified the steps or processes apparent in observed attempts to solve problems in a variety of ways.[2] Differences result in part from the kinds of responses evoked by the problems the investigator used and from the manner in which he classified his data. Nonetheless, at least two processes appear to be common in all these analyses; these are illustrated in the following records from one of the experiments.

ESSENTIAL ELEMENTS IN THE PROBLEM-SOLVING PROCESS. Duncker[3] confronted experimental subjects with a variety of problems and asked them to "think aloud" as they attempted to solve the problems. He concluded that the two most important phases of problem-solving were *analysis of the goal* and *analysis of the situation*. To make clear what is meant by these two phases, we will use one of Duncker's problems and a solution provided by one of his subjects.

---

[1]Comprehensive reviews and analyses of the experimental literature can be found in D. M. Johnson, *The Psychology of Thought and Judgment*, New York, Harper & Brothers, 1955; W. E. Vinacke, *The Psychology of Thinking*, New York, McGraw-Hill Book Co., 1952.

[2]See, for example, H. E. Durkin, "Trial and Error, Gradual Analysis, and Sudden Reorganization: An Experimental Study of Problem-Solving," *Archives of Psychology*, No. 210, 1937; S. S. Sargent, "Thinking Processes at Various Levels of Difficulty: A Quantitative and Qualitative Study of Individual Differences," *Archives of Psychology*, No. 249, 1940.

[3]K. Duncker, "On Problem-Solving," *Psychological Monographs*, No. 270, 1945.

The problem was this: Given a human being with an inoperable stomach tumor and rays that can, at sufficient intensity, destroy organic tissue, how can one use the rays to free him of the tumor but avoid destroying the healthy tissue which surrounds it? This problem is not solved unless steps can be taken to attain the goal: the destruction of the tumor without the destruction of the healthy tissue. Usually the schematic sketch shown in Figure 47 was given to the

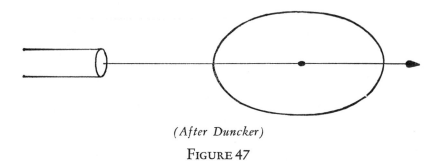

(After Duncker)

FIGURE 47

subject along with the problem. Below is the protocol of responses made by one subject. (The letter *E* prefixes comments made by the experimenter.)

PROTOCOL

1. Send rays through the esophagus.
2. Desensitize the healthy tissue by means of a chemical injection.
3. Expose the tumor by operating.
4. One ought to decrease the intensity of the rays on their way: For example —would this work?—Turn the rays on at full strength only after the tumor has been reached. *(E: False analogy; no injection is in question.)*
5. One should swallow something inorganic (which would not allow passage of the rays) to protect the healthy stomach-walls. *(E: It is not merely the stomach-walls which are to be protected.)*
6. Either the rays must enter the body or the tumor must come out. Perhaps one could alter the location of the tumor—but how? Through pressure? No.
7. Introduce a cannula.—*(E: What, in general, does one do when, with any agent, one wishes to produce in a specific place an effect which he wishes to avoid on the way to that place?)*
8. (Reply:) One neutralizes the effect on the way. But that is what I have been attempting all the time.
9. Move the tumor toward the exterior. (Compare 6.) (The *E* repeats the

problem and emphasizes, ". . . which destroy at *sufficient intensity.*")

10. The intensity ought to be variable. (Compare 4.)

11. Adaptation of the healthy tissues by previous weak application of the rays. *(E: How can it be brought about that the rays destroy only the region of the tumor?)*

12. (Reply:) I see no more than two possibilities: Either to protect the body or to make the rays harmless. *(E: How could one decrease the intensity of the rays en route? [Compare 4.])*

13. (Reply:) Some divert . . . diffuse rays . . . disperse . . . stop! Send a broad and weak bundle of rays through a lens in such a way that the tumor lies at the focal point and thus receives intensive radiation. (Total duration about half an hour.) [4]

How did the subject arrive at a solution to the problem? Did it just "pop" into his head? Did he flounder around until he hit upon a plausible solution without understanding why it was the correct solution until after he had hit upon it? On the basis of an analysis of this protocol and others like it, Duncker concluded that the two elements noted earlier must appear in a problem-solving process: *analysis of the goal* and *analysis of the situation.*

ANALYSIS OF THE GOAL. In the foregoing problem, the subject had to keep clearly in view the character of the goal to be attained. The tumor was inoperable. The tumor had to be destroyed, if at all, by using rays. But the rays could not be permitted to destroy healthy tissue. The goal was to destroy the tumor by using the rays, but at the same time preserving the healthy tissue. The subject had to ask himself what could and could not be done. Before he had a relatively clear conception of the goal to be attained, the subject suggested solutions that were impractical or unrealistic (see items 4, 5, 6 in Protocol). When he proposed an operation for the tumor and an application of the rays without provision for protection, he apparently did not understand the goal.

MOTIVATION AND PROBLEM SOLUTION. The person in a problem situation must have more than a clear conception of the goal; he must be motivated to work toward attaining it. The sixth grade children working to attain the goal of understanding the Indian culture should have as clear a conception of that goal as possible, and they should also

[4]*Ibid.*, pp. 2-3.

be willing to work for that goal. The child who is motivated only to keep out of the teacher's way, or to stay out of trouble, or to obtain approval by giving correct answers, is not involved in the problem situation of understanding Indian culture. If the other goals are incompatible with attainment of the goal in the problem situation, the problem is not likely to be solved by the students working for the other goals. We would predict that if the goals of a problem situation are relevant to the satisfaction of a child's needs, he is more likely to become involved in attempts to solve the problem. Since the goals of some problem situations may be relatively remote from the psychological needs of children, we hypothesize that children will not become interested in such problems or in making the responses necessary to solve them.

Some of the problem situations in which we place children are so complex that the goal to be obtained is difficult to define; children have only a hazy conception of the goal. A teacher conducting a civics course, with a goal of developing citizenship, will have difficulty in enabling the children to solve the problem of becoming citizens if their conception of this goal is nebulous. Highly abstract goals of this kind probably can be obtained by encouraging children to work for sub-goals which, when accomplished, lead to the attainment of the over-all goal. In the civics class, for example, we may teach pupils how to conduct meetings according to the rules of parliamentary procedure—the goal being to conduct meetings in an orderly fashion. They also may solve problems to attain other goals, such as maintaining effective working relations in groups and compromising differences of opinion to attain common goals. When they have attained a wide variety of sub-goals of this kind, they will have progressed toward the attainment of the more general goal of "being a good citizen."

ANALYSIS OF THE SITUATION. The problem-solving process also requires an analysis of the problem situation. The person attempting to solve a problem must first analyze the *conflicting elements in the problem.* In the earlier problem we saw that rays could be used to destroy the tumor, but that the rays could also destroy healthy tissue. Several of the proposed solutions to the problem attempted to resolve this conflict. The subject suggested desensitizing the healthy tissues, turning the rays on at full strength only after the tumor had been reached, and neutralizing the effect of the rays on the way to the tumor. When the subject became aware that he must neutralize the the rays in some way en route to the tumor, he came closer to resolving the conflict. If he had not been aware of this conflict at all, it would have been impossible for him to solve the problem.

Another way a person analyzes the problem situation is by determining the materials that are available for the solution of the problem. These materials may be either present in the situation or obtainable. In the above problem, the subject had first to formulate a principle: the rays had to be kept weak until they were in the locale of the tumor. After that, he had to use relevant information to answer the question of how the rays could be strengthened once they reached this locale. Knowing that lenses focus rays, the subject had only to suggest the use of a lens, and he had arrived at the basic elements in the solution of the problem. In some problem situations, the solution will require adaptation or utilization of materials already present in the situation. In other situations, the problem solver will have to call upon his general knowledge and experience in order to introduce into the situation available material that will facilitate the solution of the problem.

While these two phases, analysis of the goal and analysis of the situation, appear in the problem-solving process, they are not simple, discrete steps which guarantee the solution of a problem. The subject analyzing the above problem needed information and concepts that would enable him to attack the analysis of the situation and the goal. He had to be able to analyze the relation between a proposed solution and the consequence of carrying out that solution. When the subject suggested exposing the tumor by operating, he had clearly forgotten an important condition in the problem—that the tumor was inoperable. He could not solve the problem satisfactorily unless he remembered that fact. As the problem solver attempts to solve a problem, he proposes hypotheses and tests them either actually or imaginatively. The process of hypothesis formation presupposes a critical analysis of the problem.

Logical analyses of the problem-solving process usually suggest a series of four or five steps in the process,[5] but experiments in problem-solving indicate that the problem solver does not necessarily go through these steps in a systematic order. One of the steps is hypothe-

---

[5] See J. Dewey, *How We Think*, Boston, D. C. Heath and Co., 1933. This author warns that logical analyses of problem-solving do not describe the way in which individuals attack problems.

sis-making. Before the problem solver can make reasonable hypotheses, he must have analyzed the goal and the situation. His first hypothesis may be highly inaccurate. When Duncker's subject suggested exposing the tumor, he had forgotten an important element in the problem situation. To abandon this hypothesis he needed only to remember this fact. But some of his hypotheses were untestable, such as the suggestion that "something" should be swallowed to protect the healthy stomach-walls. Some hypotheses may be little more than wild guesses, while others may be developed by logical reasoning from assumptions. In the process of hypothesizing solutions, a person probably relies heavily on his previous experience. He will also be influenced by his prejudices, biases, and stereotypical thinking. The testing of hypotheses and their subsequent revision also may be somewhat haphazard and unsystematic. Logical analyses of problem-solving are useful in calling our attention to the requirements of a logically satisfactory problem solution, but they do not describe how people actually solve problems. Merely knowing what steps are likely to lead to probable solutions does not guarantee that the steps can or must be followed in a precise, systematic, and definite fashion, or that following them will produce the qualitatively "best" solution.

Problem-solving is a complex process in which the person analyzes and evaluates the problem situation, utilizes information and concepts that he has previously learned, and formulates hypotheses and tests them. Since these processes seldom occur in any systematic and automatic fashion, we would expect a variety of reactions to the problem situation. Not everyone can solve a problem successfully. Some individuals can only approximate a solution, while others are quite successful in solving a problem. An individual may become bored with a problem, frustrated by it, angry at the problem situation, or annoyed with people in the problem environment.

REACTIONS OF THE INDIVIDUAL
IN THE PROBLEM-SOLVING SITUATION

The reactions that we will discuss here are modes of adapting to the problem situation in which the individual psychologically leaves the problem or changes it to one that he can solve. In some problem situations, the individual is "blocked" from obtaining a goal by an obstacle on a standard route to a goal, and sometimes because the goal is not foreseen clearly enough to choose appropriate means for reaching it. If Jane (see Chapter Three) does not obtain the approval of her classmates by writing a feature article, she will not attain her goal and will feel frustrated and annoyed by her failure to do so. If she tries other means of attaining this same goal, such as being attractive to her classmates, being friendly, or being helpful, and if none of these means is effective in attaining the goal, her feelings of frustration and annoyance will increase. Jane can keep trying new ways of attaining her goal, give up the goal entirely, attempt to relieve her feelings of frustration by being hostile to her classmates, or decide that some other goal is more important than this goal.

Within the context of a particular problem, solutions which lead to the attainment of the goal are adaptive; attempted solutions which fail to lead to the attainment of the goal are maladaptive. An effective solution may, none the less, be maladaptive in a more general sense because it may be inconsistent with accepted value standards for appropriate solutions or may interfere with the attainment of other desired goals. The class "bully" may resolve problems by force, but the method of solution is regarded as inappropriate and may interfere with the attainment of such desired goals as making friends. Some reactions in the problem situations we are discussing are maladaptive in both a specific and a general sense, such as aggressive attacks on objects and people. Other reactions are maladaptive only in the sense that they do not lead to the attainment of a specific goal; however, they are not necessarily maladaptive in the more general sense because they may be adaptive ways of satisfying needs, even though particular goals cannot be obtained. Consider the premedical student who wishes to become a doctor but fails in chemistry; the attainment of his goal then becomes very unlikely. If there are no other means by which he can still continue in his premedical course, he will have to be satisfied with substituting some alternative goal that will satisfy his needs. If he wanted to become a doctor because of his desire to help people, for instance, he can probably satisfy his needs in another profession that involves working with people.

REPETITION OF INAPPROPRIATE RESPONSES. One reaction to frustration in attaining a goal is to persist in making inappropriate responses. Compare the reactions of the two students to difficulties in the following problem situation. The first graders were working on building activities, and Cris and Allen had both decided to build a small boat. The first step required sawing pieces of wood to a manageable size. Allen placed a piece of wood in a clamp and began sawing. As he sawed, the wood slipped because he had not adjusted the wood so that he could cut off the length he needed. Allen looked around the class and then went back to his sawing. He continued sawing with great difficulty and finally managed to obtain a piece of wood that was much larger than what he wanted. The bell terminated his building activity. Cris began in exactly the same way, by placing a board in a clamp. As he sawed, he also ran into difficulties, because he too had not adjusted the wood to obtain the size that he wanted. Cris stopped work, opened the clamp, readjusted the piece of wood, tightened the clamp, and began the work over again. His sawing was easily completed, and when he was finished, he had a piece of wood of the size he desired. He was able to finish the boat within the allotted time.

We can see, in the Cris and Allen example, the difference between persisting in making a response that does not lead to the goal and changing to responses which lead to the goal. Why did Allen persist in sawing in a way that prevented him from doing what he wanted to do? He may not have known what changes should be made in order to saw correctly. People are prevented from changing their problem-solving methods by inadequate information and faulty concepts.[6] A person also may lack the necessary skill to change his attempts at problem-solving. A student who does not know how to use the logarithm tables cannot use logarithms for quicker and simpler solutions of problems. A chemistry student who cannot operate a balance correctly will be handicapped in solving some kinds of chemical problems.

Sometimes the problem solver *persists* in using a method of solution because he feels secure with this method of attacking a problem and has found it successful in the past.[7] The "old way" of doing things may be preferred because the person is afraid to try a new method or a new approach, even though the method that he has been using is

---

[6]A number of studies have demonstrated that inadequate vocabulary development and reading difficulties are correlated with lack of success in problem-solving. While such correlations do not prove that inadequate vocabulary "causes" poor problem-solving, a hypothesized relation of this kind is reasonable. Reviews of studies in this area can be found in the following: E. Eagle, "The Relationship of Certain Reading Abilities to Success in Mathematics," *The Mathematics Teacher*, 41 (1948), 175-79; K. L. Husbands and J. H. Shores, "Measurement of Reading for Problem Solving: A Critical Review of the Literature," *Journal of Educational Research*, 43 (1950), 453-65; H. C. Johnson, "Problem Solving in Arithmetic: A Review of the Literature," *Elementary School Journal*, 44 (1944), 396-403.

[7]At a later point in this chapter we will discuss the influence of previously learned methods of solution on the solution of new problems in more general terms (see p. 365).

inadequate for new problems. In other cases, the individual will revert to earlier modes of problem solution. Barker,[8] in an experiment with young children, found that when children were frustrated, their constructiveness of play decreased sharply. The children were placed in a room that had two parts. They played in one part: the other part contained toys known to be attractive to the children. A screen prevented the children from reaching the toys. The children's constructiveness of play dropped considerably, and they reacted as younger children would in an attempt to get to the toys.

An individual who is having difficulty solving a problem is probably motivated by several needs. Presumably he is motivated by the need that stimulated his goal-seeking behavior in the first place. When he is frustrated in his attempts to attain this goal, he probably is also motivated by a need to reduce the "painful" feelings associated with frustration. In this kind of situation, the individual may attempt to reduce his need—to avoid the painful effects of frustration—in such a way that his goal actually becomes the reduction of the tension associated with frustration. Persistence in making inappropriate responses, or reversion to earlier but currently maladaptive responses, may be effective in reducing this tension although ineffective in attaining the goal of the problem situation. The apparently inexplicable behavior of persisting in making inappropriate responses becomes intelligible if we find that the individual is satisfying some need by making these responses.

AGGRESSIVE REACTIONS. Another reaction to a frustrating situation is *aggression*, a hostile attack upon the problem situation or people in it.[9] Persons in the problem situation may be attacked verbally or physically; the person may throw down materials in anger, he may curse and swear or kick the nearest object. Whatever particular form the aggression takes, the individual is attempting to discharge his feelings of frustration and annoyance by directing them to some aspect of his environment. The aggression is usually maladaptive since it does not solve the problem: once the aggressive attack is over the person is still confronted with it. An aggressive response may be attempted because in the past such a response has removed obstacles to goals. A

---

[8]R. G. Barker, T. Dembo, and K. Lewin, "Frustration and Regression: An Experiment with Young Children," *University of Iowa Studies in Child Welfare*, 18 (1941), No. 1.

[9]For a discussion of the relationships between frustration and aggression, see J. Dollard *et al.*, *Frustration and Aggression*, New Haven, Yale University Press, 1939.

child may have learned that when he becomes angry he "gets his way." If such has been the case, an aggressive response may be an adaptive one in that it leads to goal attainment, though it may be socially undesirable or may prevent the child from attaining other goals such as friendship or approval.

In other cases, an aggressive response may be a way of reducing the tension associated with frustration. Since the aggressive response may not be effective in removing the source of frustration, we would predict that such a response would be only temporarily effective in reducing tension.

GOAL SUBSTITUTION. Still another reaction to frustration in attaining a goal is *substituting another goal for the desired one*.[10] Again, substituting one goal for another does not enable the person to solve his original problem. Frustration is reduced only if the substitute goal is capable of satisfying the needs and reducing the motivation that prompted the problem-solver to seek the original goal. The more closely the substitute goal resembles the original goal, the more likely it is to produce need-satisfaction. The student who wants to be an engineer but who does not have the necessary mathematical ability may find need-satisfaction by becoming a highly skilled technician in a field where advanced mathematical training is not required. If Allen has been unsuccessful in building a boat, he may attain need-satisfaction through other related activities, such as clay modeling or painting a picture, at which he may be more successful.

---

[10]For a review of experimental literature on substitute satisfaction, see S. Escalona, "Play and Substitute Satisfaction," in R. G. Barker, J. S. Kounin, and H. F. Wright, *Child Behavior and Development*, New York, McGraw-Hill Book Co., 1943, pp. 363-78.

Some individuals will attempt to attain the goal in *fantasy* by imagining that they are actually successful in attainment of the goal or by daydreaming about achieving the goal. The amount of need-satisfaction attained in this way is probably temporary and limited; however, some individuals will persist in fantasy solutions for relatively long periods of time. When an individual resorts to fantasy solutions for his problems, his mode of response is maladaptive even though it may be need-satisfying. Ordinarily we cannot determine whether the individual is satisfying the need which originated goal-seeking in the problem situation or whether he is satisfying a need to reduce the tension associated with attempts at problem solution. As long as the individual remains in the problem situation, the fantasy solution can provide only a temporary escape from the demands of this situation. The adolescent who dreams of being an engineer or a doctor must eventually face his own limitations; his dreams must be within reach of his ability if he is to adjust to his environment.

SUMMARY. The above modes of response to frustration in a problem situation are learned ways of responding to difficulties. These responses occur as ways of satisfying needs because they have produced need-satisfaction in the previous experience of the individual. The teacher who is analyzing the behavior of his students in a problem situation has two problems: (1) to determine the probability that any of these responses will occur; (2) to infer what need-systems could be satisfied through their behavior.

For either of these tasks, we ordinarily need considerable information about a student's approach to problems. We begin by attempting to answer the question: What has been this student's typical response when frustrated in a problem situation? Here it is appropriate to repeat our warning about the errors that can be made by making inferences from a few instances of behavior. The second task, that of determining the pattern of needs being satisfied by the behavior, also requires an inference which must be based on systematic observations. Recall also that such inferences need to be checked by repeated observation.

Analyses of this kind enable us to diagnose particular instances of student behavior; however, these do not give us information on how a particular mode of response has been learned. What factors in a person's experience stimulate the learning of these maladaptive responses in problem situations?

EFFECTS OF SUCCESS AND FAILURE
IN PROBLEM-SOLVING

Frequently the entire range of reactions discussed above will occur when a group of children is placed in a problem situation. Some children will succeed. Others will fail, and among those who fail, there will be those who attempt to withdraw from the problem situation by striving to attain substitute goals, by making aggressive and hostile reactions, or by persisting in inadequate responses. We have suggested that such modes of response are learned as ways of adapting to the tension associated with frustration. When a person cannot solve a problem, he has to adapt to the frustration produced by his unsuccessful attempts and to the fact of failure. We would predict that failure in problem situations will evoke maladaptive responses and will have a pervasive influence on the person's ability to cope with problems.

Lantz[11] studied the effects of success and failure in a problem-solving situation on children's intelligence test performance. In this experiment Lantz used a simple game problem. The children were placed within a barrier, and the problem was to reach a ball placed outside the barrier with the tools that were provided (see Figures 48 and 49). In the first two problems the children were able to reach the ball, but in the third problem the ball was placed at a distance beyond the farthest reach of each child. To motivate the children, the experimenter permitted them to pick prizes they would obtain if they reached the ball in the third problem. The third problem was of suffi-

---

[11]B. Lantz, "Some Dynamic Aspects of Success and Failure," *Psychological Monographs*, No. 271, 1945.

cient difficulty so that only half of the children could solve the problem.

Two groups were established by this procedure—a success group and a failure group. Before and after the problem situation the children were given intelligence tests and were rated on a wide variety of behavior characteristics. Lantz found:

1. Success significantly increased average scores on the intelligence tests, but failure depressed scores. The answers to questions requiring thought processes, rather than rote memory, were significantly improved by success; more errors were made on these questions under the failure condition.

2. The children who were successful were rated significantly higher on such characteristics as self-confidence, social-confidence, cooperation, alertness, friendliness, boldness, talkativeness, cheerfulness, quietness, persistence, and effort.

3. The success group spent less time working on the problems. The failure group took more time and gave more evidence of behavior indicating a desire to leave the problem-situation and reflecting tension.

4. The children made numerous comments in the problem-solving situation that indicated a departure from the realities of the situation. Superstitious and whimsical comments, such as "Wish I had a thinking cap," were made. Fantastic commands were directed at the tools, the child's hands, and the barrier. Some children held a rabbit's foot; others hit themselves with a stick before using it, spat on their thumbs and rubbed the palms of their hands before beginning the activity, crossed their fingers, crossed their legs, and evidenced other behaviors designed to improve performance by magic. While many of these behaviors were apparent in the behaviors of the children in both groups, a significantly greater number appeared in the failure group. In other words, the failure group engaged in more fantasy behavior and less realistic problem-solving behavior.

As the data in this study indicate, a person who is failing in a problem situation is affected in many ways. His general mental efficiency is depressed, and he engages in a variety of behaviors that, we infer, are attempts to escape from the problem situation and that actually interfere with his successful solution of the problem. That long-term success or failure has pervasive effects on personality was demonstrated in the experiment by Sears.[12]

Repeated attempts at problem-solving that are met with failure

---

[12] See the discussion in Chapter Four, pp. 108-12.

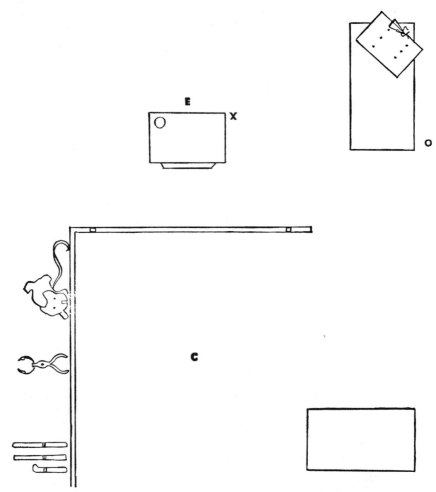

Ball Game situation for Problem I. Child (C) stands behind barrier with tools available behind barrier at his left. Examiner (E) back of chair. Ball (O) in rear corner of box on chair which is slightly wider than box. Leash (X) to be placed on ball for Problem I rests on right corner of back of chair. Folder with prizes on table within child's vision. Observer records at table (o). Examiner gives tests of Forms L & M, Stanford-Binet, at table indicated at lower right. (From Lantz)

FIGURE 48

are discouraging and frustrating for the student. He can adjust to failure in a variety of ways. He can lower his expectation for himself so that he will not strive and persist in his problem-solving attempts. He may systematically avoid problems or attempt only those which

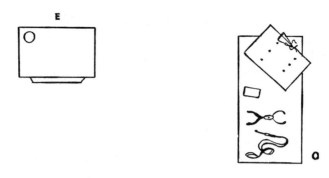

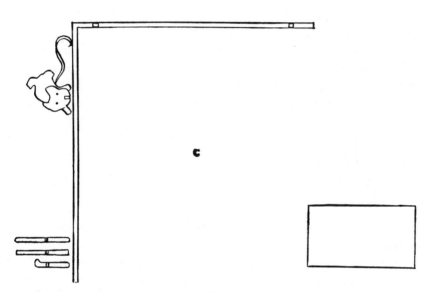

Ball Game situation for Problem III. Examiner, chair, and ball now four inches beyond child's farthest reach. Used tools in sight on table near O. Prize selected also in full view on table near prize folder. (From Lantz)

FIGURE 49

he knows he can easily solve. The poor problem solver has less confidence in his ability to meet problems, is less willing to attack problems, lacks persistence and self-confidence, and resorts to fantasy and superstitious behavior as a way of attacking problems.

ALLEVIATING THE EFFECTS OF FAILURE. Can these effects of failure in problem-solving be alleviated? Is it possible to arrange the problem-solving situation to provide children with enough success so that they will not lose confidence and will persist in attempting to solve problems? Keister[13] conducted an experiment in which children attempted problems at which they had initially failed. Some of the children were put through a training program designed to improve their ability to solve problems by encouraging them to persist in their problem-solving attempts. The training program was built on the principle that a child can meet failure in an acceptable and controlled manner if he has learned from experience the kinds of behavior likely to bring success or satisfaction to him. Specifically, the training program was designed to teach the child to persist even when the task was difficult, to depend less on help from adults, and to give fewer excuses for his failures. The training program began with a series of simple puzzles, similar to those on which the children had originally failed and on which they could work with a minimum of persistence. The puzzle series gradually became more difficult and, as the children worked on these puzzles, the experimenter encouraged them to keep trying and rewarded successful responses. The experimenter at no time helped the children solve the problems, but she did ask questions designed to suggest new ways of attacking the problem or new ways of handling the materials. Figure 50 compares the amount of time the children spent in various responses before and after training. Note the rise in the amount of time spent attempting to solve the problem alone, and the reduction in time spent asking somebody else to solve the problem and in rationalizing for failures. Interest in the problems also increased markedly.

To determine the long-term effectiveness of the program, Keister gave another set of puzzles four and one-half months after the original experimental period. In the original experiment one group of children had been retrained by the procedures outlined, and the other had not been trained. Figure 51 presents a comparison of the two groups after the four and one-half month interval. The trained group showed greater persistence, greater interest, and less rationalization than it had immediately after the training period, whereas the nontrained group performed about the same as it had during the original experiment.

---

[13]M. E. Keister, L. Heiliger, *et al.*, "The Behavior of Young Children in Failure," *Studies in Pre-School Education*, I, in *University of Iowa Studies in Child Welfare*, 14 (1937), 29-82. Also summarized in M. E. Keister, "The Behavior of Young Children in Failure," in R. G. Barker, J. S Kounin, and H. F. Wright, *Child Behavior and Development*, New York, McGraw-Hill Book Co., 1943, pp. 429-40.

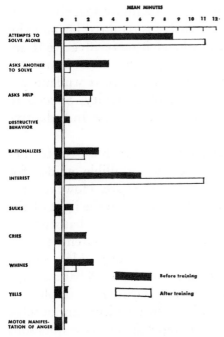

Responses of trained group on puzzle-box test before and after training. (After Keister)

FIGURE 50

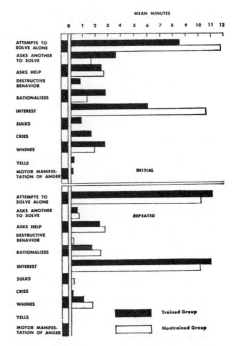

Responses of trained and nontrained subjects on initial and repeated tests. Interval between tests averaged four and one-half months. (After Keister)

FIGURE 51

While this experiment was conducted with young children and the results must be generalized with caution, the experimental procedures suggest a number of hypotheses on how to organize learning experiences in order to promote problem-solving behavior. The effects of failure are likely to be reduced if students work on problems within their capacities and for which they have appropriate information and skills. Here it is well to recall how the variable of familiarity is relevant to the learning of new material (see Chapter Six). A period of preparation in which relevant information and skills are acquired will probably facilitate attempts to solve problems for which students are not adequately prepared. The decision about how much information a student needs to work problems successfully is not easily made. Some teachers argue that such information is learned better if acquired while solving the problem. This issue has not been resolved experimentally. Some minimum level of knowledge is probably necessary, both to insure interest in the problem and to facilitate adaptive problem-solving behavior. How much knowledge is required beyond this minimum level, and whether such knowledge is more effective if acquired in the process of attempting to solve a problem is not known.

The effects of failure are likely to be minimized if students are presented with problems graded in terms of difficulty. Success in solving the easier problems probably encourages interest and adaptive behavior.

While these hypotheses provide the teacher with a basis for organizing learning experiences, they are not infallible guides for practice and the teacher cannot assume that they are. However, the teacher may analyze some commonly held opinions in the light of the evidence presented here. For example, some people argue that students should be presented with difficult problems; they contend that if students can solve these problems they will be better problem solvers But is such a procedure likely to work for all students? What assumptions about students' capacities and previous learning are implied in this hypothesis? What are we to conclude when a student cannot solve these problems? The teacher who has thought about these questions will recognize that in organizing learning experiences the focal questions are what kinds of problems, with what kinds of students, at what phase in the learning sequence.

As we have noted frequently throughout this text, a desired behavior is likely to be acquired if the behavior is need-satisfying. Reward should be provided for correct responses made in attempting to solve problems, and the child should be given maximum encouragement as he attempts to solve them. The teacher can probably facilitate appropriate problem-solving behavior by pointing out difficulties, indicating errors, and suggesting new ways of looking at the problem situation. Not every child is going to be able to solve every problem that he will meet in or out of the school situation. The capacities of children limit their ability to solve problems, but a child can be trained to be a more proficient problem solver within the range of his capacities by the manner in which the teacher presents problems to him and the procedures used to stimulate problem-solving behavior.

ANTICIPATING DIFFICULTIES IN PROBLEM-SOLVING. The experiments cited above also suggest some practical ways in which teachers may be alerted to poor problem-solving behavior. Frequently, teachers infer that a student is a poor problem solver from the effects or products of the problem-solving process. If a student has an incorrect answer, the teacher can say correctly that he has not solved the problem successfully. The teacher, however, can be alerted to poor problem-solving before the final stages are reached. He should be particularly sensitive to such behaviors as tendencies to give up without trying or without exploring the possibilities for solution, repeated requests for help, destructive behavior, excuses for failure, and such emotional responses as sulking, talking irrelevantly, crying, and sarcasm. From these behavior signs, the teacher can infer that the child is possibly experiencing failure and frustration in the problem situation and is meeting this failure by reactions which may lead to ultimate failure. By rearranging the problem sequence, by introducing less difficult problems, by encouragement, by careful supervision of the activities of the child, the teacher can facilitate the child's attempts to solve problems. Because of limitations in capacity, children cannot always be provided with success experiences, but they can be provided with enough success experiences to develop their problem-solving abilities to the limits of their capacities. The child who develops his ability to solve problems also develops his self-confidence and acquires a realistic conception of his own abilities and limitations. If a child must fail because of his limited capacity, failure ought to be a learning experience from which the child determines the extent and range of his ability. But failure should probably not occur until the child has approached the limit of his ability.

INFLUENCE OF EXPERIENCE ON PROBLEM-SOLVING BEHAVIOR

When a person meets a problem situation, he must rely on his previous experience to analyze the situation and determine probable solutions to the problem. Previous experience has both advantages and disadvantages for effective problem-solving.

THE MEANING OF "SET." The term "set" is used to denote a predisposition to view a problem-situation in a given way. While "set" may also refer to attitudes which predispose us to respond in a given way to a new situation, we will limit the meaning of the term to those cognitive processes that predispose us to organize new situations in ways in which we have organized other "similar" situations. For example, an individual who believes that government should play an important role in the management of the economy may see continued inflation essentially as the result of a failure on the part of the government to control wages and prices. Another person who believes the role of private management is an important factor in the health of the economy may see a cure for continued inflation in encouraging labor unions to moderate their wage demands. Each of these individuals analyzes the problem in terms of concepts and generalizations with which he is familiar and which he uses to analyze a wide variety of other problems. Obviously, the attitudes of these individuals are important determinants of the manner in which they will analyze the problem, and a separation of attitudes and "sets" in describing the behavior of these individuals is largely a logical distinction. Attitudes and "sets" interact in a complex process, but may be analyzed as if they were distinct processes. Hence, "set" refers to any aspect of this complex process which is cognitive in character.

A "set" factor which influences the adequacy of problem-solving behavior has been demonstrated experimentally. The experimental problems used by Luchins[14] will illustrate the influence of a "set" in solving problems. Luchins used a water jar problem. In this type of problem the experimental subject is presented with three jars of different capacities. The problem is to arrive at a specified amount of water by using the capacity of the jars available. Table XX lists the problem

Problem	Given the Following Empty Jars as Measures			Obtain the Required Amount of Water
1	29	3		20
2	21	127	3	100
3	14	163	25	99
4	18	43	10	5
5	9	42	6	21
6	20	59	4	31
7	23	49	3	20
8	15	39	3	18
9	28	76	3	25
10	18	48	4	22
11	14	36	8	6

(From Luchins)

TABLE XX

[14] A. S. Luchins, "Mechanization in Problem-Solving: The Effect of 'Einstellung'," *Psychological Monographs*, No. 248, 1942.

numbers, the capacities of the jars in each problem, and the required amount of water to be measured using the given jars.

In problem No. 1, twenty quarts can be obtained by filling the twenty-nine quart jar and then pouring from it into the three quart jar three times ($29-3-3-3 = 20$). In Luchins' experiment this problem was presented and explained to the experimental subject. Problem No. 2 was also explained. To solve the second problem the subject would need to fill the B jar, then pour off into the A jar, leaving 106 quarts; then by filling the C jar twice, the required number of quarts could be measured out (a simple formula represents a solution to this problem, $B-A-2C$). This problem and all of the following problems except No. 9 could be solved by this precedure. To solve No. 7, however, the subject had only to pour out from A jar into the three quart jar to obtain the required 20 quarts. No. 9 and No. 11 may also be solved by this simpler procedure. A different solution may be used for No. 8 and No. 10 (do you see it?).

Luchins administered this kind of problem to a large number of students ranging from grade school through the graduate school levels. In the majority of cases, the students used the three jar solution for all of the problems. This procedure was successful through the first six problems, and this success probably reinforced the response of using this procedure. Luchins, working with the same set of problems, divided the students up into two groups: one he allowed to work through the problems in the usual manner; to the other he gave the directions, "Don't be blind," after the sixth problem. The majority of the students who heard the instruction, "Don't be blind," shifted to the simpler solution.

This experiment illustrates the influence of *set* in a problem-solving situation. The students were able to work all but one of the problems by using the first method. The tendency to continue to use this method is a "set." The set was disadvantageous to the extent that it made the problem situation more complicated or prevented some solution.

In another experiment Luchins[15] attempted to make the problems more realistic by using cubic centimeters as units rather than quarts, as well as by providing small containers and water so that the subjects could manipulate the containers. The same effects were obtained; the students appeared to treat the problem essentially as an

---

[15] A. S. Luchins and E. H. Luchins, "New Experimental Attempts at Preventing Mechanization in Problem-Solving," *Journal of General Psychology*, 42 (1950), 279-97.

arithmetic problem to be solved by applying a rule. Apparently the problem appeared to them as similar to the kinds of problems in which solutions could be reduced to a rule, and once the rule was known additional problems could easily be solved. An overemphasis on solution of problems by formula probably produces a set to find the formula and to "stick to it" once it has been found. The larger the number of problems which can be solved by one procedure, the more likely it is that students will persist in using this procedure in attempting new problems.[16]

MINIMIZING THE UNDESIRABLE EFFECTS OF SET. A common teaching procedure is to explain a basic principle and then present students with a series of problems which require utilization of the principle. Frequently, exercises are arranged so that problems requiring the use of one principle are grouped together. If a student is working on a number of problems requiring the use of different principles for the solutions, a series of problems based on one principle will tend to produce a set which will interfere with the working of problems requiring another principle. The effects of set are reduced by arranging practice on the problems so that the student works one set of problems requiring one principle and then, after a period of time, works another group of problems requiring another principle.[17]

The influence of set in problem-solving is reduced by arranging problems so that fresh attacks are required for each problem. If the problems are arranged in such a way that the student achieves success using one method, he persists in using this method. The influence of this reinforcement on his problem-solving approach can be reduced by arranging problems so that he is continually required to vary his methods, and so that his expectancy for the success of a given method is not unduly strengthened. To develop facility in solving a given kind of problem, the student requires practice over a period of time; however, since the student is meeting many different kinds of problems, the problems should be continually varied to assure use of new methods in attempting solutions.

SET AS A FUNCTION OF FAMILIARITY. One of the effects of previous learning is the development of stabilized ways of perceiving

---

[16]R. P. Youtz, "The Relation Between Number of Confirmations of One Hypothesis and the Speed of Accepting a New and Incompatible Hypothesis," *American Psychologist*, 3 (1948), 248-49.

[17]H. H. Kendler, A. Greenberg, and H. Richmond, "The Influence of Massed and Distributed Practice on the Development of Mental Set," *Journal of Experimental Psychology*, 43 (1952), 21-25.

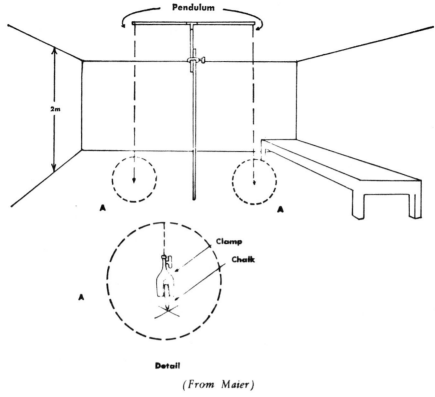

(From Maier)

FIGURE 52

objects in the environment. Learning experiences are designed to facilitate the development of these stable ways in order to prepare the learner to react to his environment with consistency. A small child is taught to identify objects. He is told that something with a flat surface and four legs is a table. He is also taught that tables have specific kinds of uses; one eats at tables and places objects on tables. The effect of this learning is that the child sees an object as having certain kinds of uses, and may not easily visualize other uses for it.

The development of these stable ways of perceiving objects may preclude problem solutions which require a new view of the situation. An experiment by Maier illustrates this phenomenon.

Maier[18] asked subjects to solve a problem that required new uses for objects. In this problem (see Figure 52) students were placed in

[18]N. R. F. Maier, "Reasoning in Humans: I, On Direction," *Journal of Comparative Psychology*, 10 (1930), 115-43.

a room in which were pieces of wood, clamps, wires, chalk, and a heavy table which was not to be moved. The problem was to construct two pendulums suspended so that, in swinging, they would make marks with the chalk on the floor. To solve the problem the student would have to attach the chalk to the clamp, and the clamp to a wire; he would have to develop a support by attaching two pieces of wood together; then he would have to wedge the piece supporting the pendulums against the ceiling. The problem apparently was extremely difficult for the college students attempting it, and they were able to solve it only when the experimenter gave a general hint that the problem could be solved if there were some nails in the ceiling. With this hint, a substantial proportion of the students were able to solve the problem, but almost no one could solve it without this suggestion. In this problem familiar objects, such as the table, could not be used, and the pendulum support was attached in an unusual way. The use of the wood to wedge a pendulum support against the ceiling is a sufficiently unique arrangement of materials that most students are not likely to see the uses to which the materials can be put. Familiarity in problem situations probably has both advantages and disadvantages.

A comparable kind of experiment demonstrates even more clearly that a tendency to use materials in a specific way inhibits adapting them to new situations. In this experiment[19] students were placed in a room which had two strings hanging from the ceiling. The problem was to tie the two strings together. The strings were placed sufficiently far apart so that both could not be held at the same time. The solution to the problem was to convert one of the strings into a swinging pendulum so that the subject could stand at the second string and grasp the first as it swung toward him. Two objects were available: an electric switch and a relay. Even if he recognized that swinging one of the strings would solve the problem, the subject still had to devise a way of weighting the string so that it would act as a pendulum. Although many subjects needed a hint to recognize that the key to the problem lay in constructing a pendulum, they did recognize that one of the heavy objects could be used to construct the pendulum. The purpose of this experiment, however, was to determine whether previous experience with the objects would influence a choice of object when the subject constructed the pendulum. Before

---

[19]H. G. Birch and H. S. Rabinowitz, "The Negative Effect of Previous Experience on Productive Thinking," *Journal of Experimental Psychology*, 41 (1951), 121-25.

the problem-solving part of the experiment, the subjects worked with either the switch or the relay in a simple wiring problem. The investigators found that seventeen out of nineteen subjects did not use the object they worked with in the wiring problem when they constructed the pendulum. Apparently these subjects saw an electrical switch or relay in terms of its proper use in wiring and could not make the shift to seeing these objects as potential pendulum bobs.

Although the experiments cited here are remote from many of the kinds of problems that are presented in classrooms, they illustrate an important principle of problem-solving. Problem-solving requires a fresh, direct attack on the problem at hand. Poor problem-solvers are limited in the kinds of analyses that they make of a problem situation. They rely too heavily on their old ways of looking at problem situations and tend to rely upon old habits, even if they are no longer appropriate. They see the elements in a problem situation in fixed, stable ways, and cannot view the elements in the problem in new ways.

One interesting aspect of these experiments is that when the experimenter made very simple suggestions, such as "Don't be blind," solutions quickly followed. If the emphasis in schools is on routine solutions of routine problems, students have little opportunity to test new ways of looking at problem-situations. To encourage a fresh approach to problems, the teacher should present students with problems that require new methods, new ideas, new concepts, new ways of using familiar materials, and should encourage students to be adaptive and creative in the problem-solving situation. One engineering professor, to encourage a creative approach to problems, requires his engineering students to solve the engineering problems of an imaginary planet on which the conditions are radically different from those of the earth. Working with these kinds of problems a student is forced to abandon the assumptions he has learned; he must work with new facts and find new ways of looking at what were familiar situations. As the Keister study[20] indicated, with sufficient encouragement and stimulation, students can develop persistence and the ability to work without help. The student finds that approaching problems in novel ways brings satisfaction in achieving solutions, and his behavior of taking a fresh approach is strongly reinforced. If the teacher is sensitive to the inhibiting effects of set and arranges problem situations so that students must utilize new methods of solution, he will encourage

---

[20]See p. 362.

habits of being persistent and of taking a fresh approach to problems.

The teacher will need to distinguish between adaptive and maladaptive persistence. Persistence is maladaptive when the problem solver continues to make responses which are not effective in attaining the goal of the problem situation. In some cases, persistence of this kind results from sets that prevent the problem solver from seeing the problem in a new way. In other cases, persistence may be a way of handling the tension associated with frustration in the problem situation. The first kind of persistence is likely to occur when there are a limited number of alternative methods of available solutions and when the probability of successful problem solution, as it is perceived by the problem solver, is small.[21] When students have been accustomed to only one or a few ways of attacking a problem, they are likely to depend on these methods. They also are more likely to "stick with" these methods when the problem appears to be difficult for them. We may hypothesize that any procedure which encourages routine or mechanical methods of problem solution is not likely to develop adequate problem-solving behavior; such a procedure is likely to induce sets which preclude novel approaches to new problems.

REALISTIC AND UNREALISTIC PROBLEMS

The recommendation is frequently made that if students are to become adequate problem solvers they must learn to cope with "life-like" problems. The problems used in the experiments discussed above were not "lifelike" problems. Few students would be able to lift a hundred and twenty-seven quart jar, and the problem of measuring out twenty quarts of water is not likely to occur in the form in which Luchins presented it. Do students become better problem solvers if they work with "realistic" rather than "unrealistic" problems?

MEANINGS OF REALISTIC AND UNREALISTIC. Before we attempt to answer this question, it is necessary to clarify what is meant by the terms *realistic* and *unrealistic*. There are two possible meanings for the latter term. Consider a problem such as the following:

> A captain with fifty men comes to the edge of a river and finds the only boat to be one in which two children are playing. The boat is so small that

---

[21]E. A. Robinson, "An Experimental Investigation of Two Factors Which Produce Stereotyped Behavior in Problem Situations," *Psychological Bulletin*, 27 (1940), 394-410.

it will hold only one man and not even a child in addition. How does the captain manage to get all his men ferried across?

This kind of a problem is little more than a puzzle. It is called "unrealistic" because it does not resemble the kinds of problems that people are likely to meet. Some problems are obviously artificial in this sense.

Students may be interested in such problems and enjoy attempting to solve them, but the evidence needed for assessing the educational value of this kind of problem is not available. One of the reasons that evidence may not be available is that we have not clarified what is to be learned by attempting to solve problems of this nature. Such problems frequently require the application of a generalization or a standard method of solution in order to solve them. The so-called "work problems" or "thought problems" in mathematics are occasionally of this kind. They may be useful in developing ability to translate into symbols a problem stated in words, or in reinforcing the learning of a method for solution; however, they may have relatively little utility in preparing a student to solve "life" or "real" problems.

Problems which resemble but do not duplicate "life" conditions are sometimes called "unrealistic" problems. Maier could have set up a miniature model of the materials in the room and asked students to attempt to solve the problem. The problem would have been unrealistic in that form, because it would not have duplicated the exact conditions of the situation in which the students were actually placed in a room with full-size materials.

Many of the experiences and problem situations provided for students are necessarily artificial or are models of the real life situation —with varying degrees of realism. The school is necessarily limited in the extent to which it can put students into real life situations. If we are teaching students the problems involved in the operations of the United Nations, we might set up a mock UN Assembly. In the sessions we would try to duplicate conditions as they exist in the UN Assembly. The students can only approximate the feelings and attitudes of the members whose roles they are imitating; the mock assembly is not the real life assembly. The students in the accounting or the typewriting class are solving problems similar to the problems they may later solve in business, but the problem conditions are not exactly duplicated. Moving model cars in a driver education class is not the same as actually driving a car down a crowded freeway, although such experiences may give preparation for solving "real life" problems by teaching students appropriate methods of analyzing problems and techniques for resolving them. A student participant in a mock UN Assembly may learn the importance of understanding other people's views on a problem situation and develop skills in arbitrating differences of opinion. The driver education class may prepare a student to anticipate the kinds of problems he may meet in driving and techniques for solving these problems.

LABORATORY VERSUS FIELD EXPERIENCES. Is there any evidence to suggest that problem-solving is improved by being attempted in the actual situation as contrasted with the laboratory or vicarious situation? Here again experimental evidence is limited, but the available evidence does not suggest that the realistic situation is necessarily or invariably superior in influencing the development of problem-solving behavior. Lorge[22] presented ROTC students with a field problem. He divided the students into two groups: one group was to solve the problem in a laboratory situation; the other, in a field situation. In the laboratory situation the students had a model of the field problem. Lorge found that the same kinds of solutions were developed in both the laboratory and the field settings. More new elements or new ideas appeared during problem-solving in the field setting, but these were not used in the final solutions.

The laboratory group did take longer to solve the problems than the field group. The field group may have solved the problems more rapidly because they were more interested or more involved in the problem, or perhaps because cues may be more readily available in a field situation than in a laboratory situation. Operating in a field situation, the students see things as they are typically accustomed to seeing them, whereas a laboratory group sees the problem in miniature. A laboratory group may need more time to become oriented to the problem situation.

This experiment does not settle the question of whether the degree of realism in a problem substantially improves problem-solving behavior in all respects. Problem-solving in realistic settings probably has some advantages, such as inducing greater interest. The more realistic the problem, the more similar conditions are to the actual

---

[22]I. Lorge et al., "Solutions by Teams and by Individuals to a Field Problem at Different Levels of Reality," *Journal of Educational Psychology*, 46 (1955), 17-24.

situation as the student may meet it. The student may solve many aspects of the problem in advance. The more lifelike kind of problem may have greater transfer value to "real life." On the other hand, a realistic problem situation can be so complicated that effective problem-solving behavior is inhibited. A student who is confronted with a complex situation may not be able to analyze it adequately. In the initial phases of solving a complex problem, refined and simplified problem settings will probably facilitate problem-solving. Mastery of important sub-problems within a complex problem probably promotes the solution of the total problem, but does not guarantee it. To encourage problem-solving behavior, the teacher should plan learning experiences designed to provide genuine problems which can be solved by the students within the limits of their experience. "Lifelike" situations may be more likely to be problem situations; however, the teacher must assess the student's readiness for handling particular problems and adjust the complexity of the problem-solving situation accordingly.

THE TRANSFER OF LEARNING IN PROBLEM-SOLVING

Problems rarely occur in identical form. The basic assumption in organizing a curriculum is that problem-solving in school will enable students to solve the problems they will meet when they have finished their schooling. When the child has gone through the experiences provided by a curriculum, he should be able to cope with problems in his society and culture and in his personal life. We teach children to read because reading will enable the child to continue to find new ways of interpreting and solving problems in his environment. A medical student enrolls in such subjects as chemistry, physics, and anatomy on the assumption that what he learns can be used in solving problems he will meet as a doctor. The engineering student studies mathematics because the problems treated will presumably enable him to solve engineering problems. One of the problems of curriculum construction is to keep the experiences up-to-date so that the child learns problem-solving behavior that will have value and meaning for him in later life. How may learning experiences be organized so that the problem-solving children do in school transfers to other problem situations both in and out of school?

STIMULUS SIMILARITY AND TRANSFER OF PROBLEM-SOLVING BEHAVIOR. Two problems—one a previously solved problem and the other a new problem—may have elements that are identical or similar. The new problem is likely to evoke the problem-solving behavior that was effective in solving the original problem.[23] For example, if a chemist is asked to determine the chemicals in a compound, he can solve this problem by using the methods of qualitative analysis. He proceeds by a process of making and testing hypotheses which eventually leads to the goal of isolating the constituents. The problem evokes behavior which has been effective in solving other problems of this kind. A solution will be achieved in such cases if the goal is attainable by this behavior.

Problem situations may be similar because the goals in the situations are similar. For example, Jane's goal in writing a feature article was to win the approval of her friends. Jane has probably attempted to achieve this goal in many different contexts. She has sought to win the approval of other people, such as her parents and teachers. We may assume that Jane has learned a category of behaviors, which we will call "approval-getting behaviors." These behaviors are likely to occur with varying degrees of probability in any situation in which Jane is striving to attain the goal of approval.

In other cases, the context of the problems will be similar. When Jane has decided to write a feature article to win approval, she is faced with a sub-problem or specific sub-goal, that of writing an interesting article. Jane has probably learned some behavior which has been effective in attaining this goal. She has had to write essays, book reports, and other newspaper articles. She may have given talks to her classes or clubs—situations which are relatively similar to that of writing an attention-attracting article. The problem situation of writing an interesting article is likely to evoke behavior that has proved effective in other contexts.

A reasonable inference from the preceding discussion is that transfer of problem-solving behavior learned in school experiences is likely to occur when the problems attempted in the school context are relatively similar to the kinds of problems students will eventually face. Problem-solving behavior learned in school is more likely to be effective in the future if such behavior has a wide adaptability to the

---

[23]This hypothesis is consistent with experimental work on concept formation. See A. H. Buss, "A Study of Concept Formation as a Function of Reinforcement and Stimulus Generalization," *Journal of Experimental Psychology*, 40 (1950), 494-503. For a general discussion of transfer and stimulus generalization, see C. I. Hovland, "Human Learning and Retention," in S. S. Stevens (ed.), *Handbook of Experimental Psychology*, New York, John Wiley & Sons, 1951, pp. 663-65.

many kinds of problems students are likely to meet.

Many recommendations for teaching problem-solving behavior are examples of specific ways in which the above principle can be implemented. One such suggestion is that students be taught appropriate methods for gathering information relevant to the problems they are solving.[24] Learning to use the library to gather appropriate information produces a set of behaviors that can be adapted to a wide variety of problem situations. Learning the operation of scientific instruments, such as the balance or the microscope, is another set of behaviors that has wide applicability to problems. Learning such procedures prepares students to solve problems for which these behaviors are relevant.

TRANSFER OF GENERALIZATIONS TO NEW PROBLEMS. Many problems cannot be solved by reducing them to problems similar to those with which the problem solver has had previous experience. Either the goals or the problem context is sufficiently different that appropriate behavior in one problem context is not directly transferable to a new problem. None the less, a principle or generalization learned in another problem context may be adapted to the new problem situation. Assume that Jane had to make a financial report to one of her clubs. Her goal may still be to win the approval of her club members, but the problem context has changed. Clarity and accuracy in the report are probably more important than interest-capturing details. To solve this problem, Jane may apply principles she has learned in solving other problems. She may have learned that clarity is achieved if the presentation is simplified and orderly. If she applies what she knows about organizing materials in a simplified and orderly fashion to the details of the financial report, she will probably solve the problem of achieving a clear presentation.

The development of understanding through the acquisition of principles and generalizations increases the probability of solving new problems to which the generalizations are relevant. Considerable experimental work by Katona and others supports this conclusion.[25]

---

[24]R. L. Thorndike, "How Children Learn the Principles and Techniques of Problem-Solving," *Forty-ninth Yearbook of the National Society for the Study of Education, Part I*, 1950, pp. 192-216.

[25]See G. Katona, *Organizing and Memorizing*, New York, Columbia University Press, 1940; also, E. R Hilgard, R. E. Irvine, and J. E. Whipple, "Rote Memorization, Understanding, and Transfer: An Extension of Katona's Card Trick Experiments," *Journal of Experimental Psychology*, 46 (1953), 288-92

In these experiments, subjects were given simplified problems that could be solved either by learning a principle that could be used to solve the problem or by memorizing a method of solution. The resulting data indicate that, once subjects have practiced a set of problems, the memorization group is quicker on new problems that are identical or highly similar to the problems on which they practiced; but when the groups are presented with new problems that are not highly similar to the original problems, the "understanding" group is much more successful than the memorization group. The general conclusion from this experimental work is that transfer of what has been learned in one problem situation to a new and relevant problem situation is more likely to occur when the original problem-solving has been achieved through understanding the principles of solution.

An experiment performed by Hendrickson and Schroeder[26] demonstrates how understanding a principle of solution facilitates solving other problems to which the principle of solution is applicable, even when the problems appear to be relatively similar. Hendrickson and Schroeder taught a group of eighth grade students how to hit a submerged target with an air rifle. Although this experiment appears to require learning of a motor skill, a problem is involved. Assume that the students practiced hitting a target submerged six inches below water level. Skill in aiming and controlling the gun are required to hit the target; however, since the target is submerged, the goal (hitting the target) cannot be attained by aiming as one would at a nonsubmerged target. Suppose that a student learns to hit the target at this depth, either by trial and error or by discovering that he must allow for the distortion of the image of the target. He will be faced with a new problem relatively similar to the original problem if we move the target up in the water. We assume that what has been learned in solving the original problem has transferred to the solution of the new problem if the student can solve this latter problem more quickly, that is, with fewer errors or with fewer unsuccessful attempts to hit the target.

We may also vary the degree of understanding of the principle of solution (the independent variable) by giving more complete explanations to some students than to others; this way we determine to

---

[26]G. Hendrickson and W. H. Schroeder, "Transfer of Training and Learning to Hit a Submerged Target," *Journal of Educational Psychology*, 32 (1941), 205-13. This experiment is a modification of an early experiment: see C. H. Judd, "The Relation of Special Training to General Intelligence," *Educational Review*, 36 (1908), 28-42.

what extent this variable influences transfer. In this experiment, for example, the boys were divided into three groups. The boys in the first group were given a gun with no instructions except that they should practice until they could perform the task successfully. Those in the second group were given instructions on the principles of refraction of light; they were shown that the target was not where it appeared to be (see Figure 53). The third group was given the same explanation, but was told that the deeper the lake, the farther the real rock would be from its image (see Figure 53). First, the students practiced hitting the target at a depth of six inches until they had

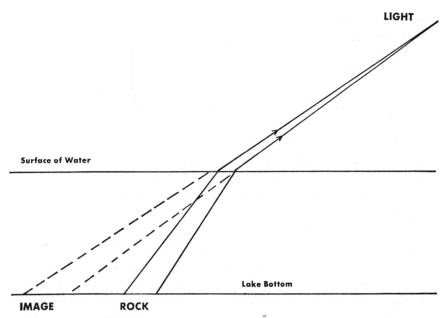

Diagram illustrating explanation of refraction. (After Hendrickson and Schroeder)

FIGURE 53

mastered the task; then the target was moved to a depth of two inches. The number of trials required to perform the task successfully was the measure used to compare the groups. As the data in Table XXI indicate, the two groups that had received instruction were both superior in performance; they required fewer trials to perform the task successfully. Furthermore, groups A and B were more successful than

Groups	Mean of Trials Required At 6″	Mean of Trials Required At 2″	Gain in Trials	Percentage of Improvement
Control	9.10	6.03	3.07	34.1
Experimental group A	8.50	5.37	3.13	36.5
Experimental group B	7.73	4.63	3.10	40.3

Summary Table Showing Improvement from First Problem to Second Problem (From Hendrickson and Schroeder)

TABLE XXI

the control group in transferring what they had learned in the first task to the second task. Not all the boys in groups A and B were equally successful, because the problem also involved the development of skill in aiming. The data from this experiment support the hypothesis that understanding the principles involved in the solution of problems facilitates the solution of new problems to which the principles are applicable.

Two levels of understanding were provided for in this experiment, but the difference did not affect the results. Apparently the students who were told the principles of refraction without being given a specific application to the problem at hand were able to derive this application for themselves. Other experimental work supports the idea that transfer effects are greater when subjects derive the principle for themselves. Haslerud gave subjects problems under two different experimental conditions.[27] For some kinds of problems both the principles of solution and their application were explained to the subjects. For other kinds of problems no directions relevant to solutions were given. The subjects were given a test that included both kinds of problems. A week later a similar test was given. On the second test, Haslerud found that his subjects did significantly better on the kinds of problems for which they had to derive the principle in order to work the problem.[28] Haslerud argues that a specific explanation blocks transfer because it prevents a subject from anticipating new applications of the principle.

This experimental evidence also supports the conclusion that

[27]G. M. Haslerud and S. Meyers, "The Transfer Value of Given and Individually Derived Principles," *Journal of Educational Psychology,* 49 (1958), 293-98.

[28]For a comparable discussion on the transfer of generalizations, see Chapter Six, p. 180. See also, pp. 171-74.

understanding is an important variable influencing the transfer of what is learned in one problem context to new problems. Problem situations are introduced into the curriculum on the assumption that what is learned in solving these problems will assist the student to solve the problems that he meets out of school or at later stages in his education. Such transfer of learning is likely to occur when the original problem-solving is accomplished through understanding of the principles involved in the solution. Such transfer also presupposes that a student understands that what he has learned in one problem context is applicable to other problems. Pointing out that a principle of solution is relevant to other problems and having students apply a principle of solution to a wide variety of problems probably facilitates this kind of transfer. We probably promote transfer by preparing students to recognize problems similar to those on which they have worked and to anticipate the usefulness of solution principles in solving new problems.

PROBLEM-SOLVING IN GROUPS

Many problem situations in which we place children in school may be resolved by either individual or group action. For example, the standard kinds of problems that children work on in an arithmetic class may be worked on by each child without assistance from his fellow students, or the teacher may organize the class into pairs or larger groups and ask the children to work on the problems together. A group discussion of the problems of inter-American cooperation is another example of cooperative problem-solving. The question of appropriate school dress may be treated as a problem to be solved by either individual or group action. In each of these cases, we assume that the stated problem is genuine—that it presents the student with goals that are not immediately and directly obtainable, although permitting solution by either individual or cooperative problem-solving.

THE TRANSFER VALUE OF GROUP PROBLEM-SOLVING. We expect our problem-solving activities in school to have "transfer value." Many of the problems that children in our society will eventually face require cooperative problem-solving. We may argue then that group problem-solving activities are appropriate learning experiences if such activities do prepare children for this kind of problem-solving. For example, we hypothesize that participating in student government activities prepares students for effective problem-solving in civic affairs. Such hypotheses, however, need to be tested if we wish to maintain that students are being prepared to solve problems requiring group action.

Some educators argue that participation in group activities promotes the learning of behavior required of individuals engaged in group problem-solving. The essence of this argument is that group activities are learning experiences in which the child acquires behavior patterns that prepare him or predispose him to participate effectively in group problem-solving. Listening attentively to other people's ideas, evaluating other people's ideas in terms of their worth rather than their source, and carrying one's share of a work load are examples of ways of acting presumably necessary for effective group problem-solving. We cannot assess directly the validity of so general a hypothesis until we specify both the particular behavior changes we desire to promote and the specific character of the group activities designed to promote them. Specific hypotheses—which are testable—may then be formulated.

For instance, we might hypothesize that when children participate cooperatively in planning the solution of a problem, they are more likely to "follow through" on carrying out the activities which will lead to its solution. In this hypothesis we have specified a group activity—cooperative planning—as the independent variable and we have related it to a specific kind of behavior change—the development of "follow through" behavior. Assume that the children are planning a field trip in conjunction with their study of local history. One of their problems is organizing transportation. They work out a transportation plan which involves assigning themselves places in the buses to be used. Each child knows in advance the bus on which he is to travel. If our hypothesis has considerable validity, the majority of the children should take their assigned places without direction from the teacher. If there is as much confusion in taking places as when the teacher assigns places, we question the validity of our hypothesis and consider other factors which may be related to the desired behavior, "follow through." In one study, the investigators questioned the generality of this hypothesis when they noted that some children did not "follow through" after cooperative problem solutions had been planned.[29] They studied the children who did not "follow through,"

---

[29] A. W. Foshay and K. D. Wann, *Children's Social Values*, New York, Bureau of Publications, Teachers College, Columbia University, 1954.

and on the basis of their observations of these children formulated the hypothesis that a child's feeling of being accepted by his group and his "follow through" were related. Further investigation suggested that children who felt more accepted by their group were more likely to follow through with group plans. At this point we hypothesize that, if we can increase a child's feeling of being accepted by his group, he is more likely to develop "follow through" behavior. In other words, other variables, as well as cooperative planning, influence "follow through."

The gist of the above discussion is simply that we may not assume that placing children in group problem-solving situations necessarily guarantees the development of behavior patterns requisite for effective participation in group problem-solving. The organization of group activities implies that we hold specific hypotheses about the relation of the activity to desired behavior changes. We are more likely to encourage these changes if we make the hypotheses explicit and if we revise them when we have evidence either that the desired changes are not occurring or that they are not occurring with any greater frequency than they did as the result of some other organization of the learning experience. We need to specify clearly the desired behavior change and then formulate and test hypotheses about the relation of this behavior to effective group problem-solving. We should also formulate and test hypotheses about the relation of specific activities to the promotion of the desired behavior change. Finally, we need to test our hypotheses about the relation between what is learned in one group problem-solving situation and what is effective in others. In the above example, we specified the desired behavior change as the development of "follow through." By its definition, this kind of behavior is related to effective group problem-solving, since the problem is not solved "completely" or "in reality" if the proposed solution is not carried out. We also hypothesize that cooperative planning promotes this kind of behavior change; furthermore, we hypothesize that the development of this behavior in the group activities planned will carry over to other problem situations. This example illustrates the many kinds of hypotheses we need to formulate and test before we can assume that participation in group problem-solving is preparing children to solve problems requiring cooperative action.

THE EFFECTIVENESS OF GROUP PROBLEM-SOLVING. It is a commonly held assumption that groups solve problems more effectively than do individuals. Some educators have argued from this assumption that we must train children to participate effectively in group problem-solving and to learn to value group problem-solving as a way of resolving important social problems. The complexity and character of many problems is such that they can be solved only by effective group action; furthermore, our system of values requires group action in the solution of many problems. None the less, we may question whether any problem may be solved more effectively by group action than by individual action.

Is a group more efficient than an individual in solving problems? This question has never been adequately answered. We cannot say that groups invariably produce better solutions than do individuals for all kinds of problems. Efficiency in problem-solving by groups depends on a variety of factors. A group will usually be superior to individuals when there is someone in the group who is both capable of solving the problem and of communicating this information to the rest of the group. Suppose we randomly divide a class into two parts: one set of children will work as individuals; the other, in pairs. Ordinarily, the pairs will come up with more correct solutions to a set of arithmetic problems than will the group of children working as individuals. However, when the data are examined, we usually find that there is someone in each pair who is capable of solving the problems and who transmits his answers to the other member of the pair. In other words, a pair has twice as many chances of coming up with a correct solution as does an individual. New statistical procedures are being developed to make allowance for this difference in the probability of achieving a correct solution.[30] But before we say more definitely that groups are more efficient in problem-solving than individuals, we will need to explore the influence of such variables as the kinds of problems being solved and factors related to the group's operation.

Teachers, however, are not merely concerned with improving the number of correct answers obtained on a set of problems. They also want to develop the problem-solving processes of children. What evidence is there to indicate that the child who works in a pair or a group is likely to do a better job than if he worked alone?

Bos,[31] in one experiment, worked with groups of children ranging

---

[30]I. Lorge and H. Solomon, "Two Models of Group Behavior in the Solution of Eureka-Type Problems," *Psychometrika*, 5 (1955), 139-48.

[31]M. C. Bos, "Experimental Study of Productive Collaboration," *Acta Psychologica*, 3 (1937), 315-426.

from eleven to thirteen years of age. One group originally worked problems individually. After some weeks this group repeated the same tasks in pairs. A second group began as individuals and was retested individually. A third group began work in pairs and later worked as individuals. The task required the children to identify, from a set of paintings, those paintings that had been done by the same painter. In another experiment, Bos modified this task and worked with younger children. In both experiments, children working in pairs were more accurate than when they worked as individuals. Bos explains the results by suggesting that the children were more careful in their work when they had to communicate about it to other children. In other words, one of the principal effects of working in a group may be increased motivation to think more carefully and to work more efficiently. These experiments do not duplicate the conditions of the classroom, in which the teacher is also a powerful social stimulus in motivating the child to work carefully. We have no data that compare the effects of working in a group with working under the close supervision of a teacher.

We would predict from what we know about group influences on individual behavior that one of the major effects of working in a group would be improvement in accuracy and the encouragement of careful thinking. Where the group is highly motivated to work towards a common goal and where success depends upon the efforts of all the group members, thoughtlessness and carelessness are likely to be punished by the group. The more strongly a child is identified with a group, the more likely he is to be sensitive to these group pressures.

Another factor that probably facilitates problem-solving in groups is the opportunity a group provides for *communication* among its members. A child attempting to solve a problem in a group can make a number of trial responses which, when made publicly in the group, can be criticized, analyzed, and evaluated. Since group members vary in their information and knowledge, a child can obtain information he does not have and can get clarification of concepts and generalizations that he does not adequately understand. Improved understanding would in turn facilitate problem-solving.

The effectiveness of groups in problem-solving appears to be related to the extent to which the group operation maximizes the factors that facilitate problem-solving. We may not assume that all the individuals in a group have become more proficient problem-solvers just because an adequate problem solution has been achieved. Neither may we assume that placing children in groups to solve common problems will guarantee either that the problems will be solved or that the children will become more effective problem-solvers.

FACTORS RELATED TO GROUP EFFECTIVENESS IN PROBLEM-SOLVING. Groups are not uniformly successful in solving problems because the group factors we have been discussing are not always maintained or maximized. A group of individuals working on a problem about which none of the individuals has adequate information is not likely to be superior to an individual who has considerable knowledge of the problem. If we put all the poorer students in the same group, the likelihood that they will solve problems quickly and efficiently is small. An individual student with adequate knowledge and information can solve the problem much more quickly and efficiently than a group of this kind.

One of the major advantages of a group is that a *division of labor for complex tasks is possible*. This arrangement usually results in quicker solutions because the work can be organized so that parts of it can be easily and quickly accomplished by an individual in the group. Groups are not invariably quicker, for the rapidity of solution depends in part upon whether the task can be divided up in such a way that the individuals in the group can work on parts of it. Husband[32] had forty subjects work alone and eighty subjects work in pairs on three types of problems: a word puzzle, a jigsaw puzzle, and five arithmetic problems. Paired subjects were faster than individual subjects, except on arithmetic problems. Klugman[33] also found that pairs of children working on arithmetic reasoning problems, while more accurate, needed significantly more time than did individuals. Pairing off children, or placing them into groups, will facilitate accuracy but not necessarily speed.

The larger the group, the more complicated is the process of generating adequate group communication. The members of the group must become familiar with one another and assess the amount of information that each has before a common solution can be achieved. This communication process encourages individuals to think

---

[32] R. W. Husband, "Cooperative versus Solitary Problem Solution," *Journal of Social Psychology*, 11 (1940), 405-409.

[33] S. F. Klugman, "Cooperative versus Individual Efficiency in Problem-Solving," *Journal of Educational Psychology*, 35 (1944), 91-100.

more carefully and to perform more accurately, but the communication process is so complicated that more time is required for achieving a complete solution.[34]

Another factor contributing directly to the success of groups in problem-solving is the quality of *leadership* provided in the group. Research evidence indicates that at least a minimum of leadership facilitates problem solution. Maier and Solem[35] used sixty-seven groups, each with five or six members, in a study of the effects of leadership on group problem-solving. Thirty-four of the groups were assigned a discussion leader, and the other thirty-three groups had a representative who acted as an observer. The tasks were mathematical problems and in neither kind of group was the discussion leader or the observer permitted to express an opinion about the problem; the discussion leader, however, was to facilitate discussion in the group by insuring that members had an opportunity to participate and by summarizing and clarifying. The group members were asked to record their answers to the problem before and after the discussion. Before the discussion, there was no significant difference in the number of correct solutions in the two kinds of groups. After the discussion, however, the leader-groups showed a significantly higher percentage of correct solutions.

When the data were analyzed, it was found that the major contribution of the discussion leader was that of protecting a correct minority opinion. In a leaderless group, the student with the correct answer can be overwhelmed by majority opinion. In a group that has at least a minimal kind of permissive leadership, the student is allowed to express his opinion on an answer and is partially protected from group pressures. As we suggested above, the efficiency of group problem-solving depends upon the knowledge of its members and the maximization of communication among them. In a leaderless group, the communication process is not maximized because deviant members—those who disagree with the majority opinion—are not given an opportunity to express their views or, if expressed, their opinions are rejected too quickly.

We have discussed the effects of frustration on problem-solving

---

[34]The following study provides evidence that under a time restriction larger groups reach consensus less frequently than do smaller groups: A. P. Hare, "Interaction and Consensus in Different Size Groups," *American Sociological Review*, 17 (1952), 261-67.

[35]N. R. F. Maier and A. R. Solem, "Contribution of a Discussion Leader to the Quality of Group Thinking," *Human Relations*, 5 (1952), 277-88.

behavior. One other advantage of the group situation for problem-solving is that in a tightly knit group the effects of frustration are minimized. Wright[36] paired children in a frustrating situation and found that pairs of good friends showed more cooperative behavior and less conflict than did other pairs. More effective problem-solving behavior is likely to occur when frustration is reduced. Group problem-solving may encourage the easily frustrated student to keep trying if he is strongly identified with the group.

At the present time we assume that as children learn to solve problems through group processes, they will participate more effectively in other group problem-solving situations. Group problem-solving procedures may encourage the development of more effective problem-solving behavior than individual procedures only when certain kinds of problems are attempted. By applying general principles of learning, we expect that effective problem-solving in group situations will promote the development of desirable kinds of problem-solving behavior in the individuals in the group. As in individual problem-solving, group achievement of a goal in the problem situation reinforces the behavior which promotes that achievement. The task for educators is to organize group learning experiences in such a way that effective problem-solving is likely to occur. The following generalizations relevant to this educational task are consistent with general principles of learning and experimental evidence on group processes.

1. The group must be motivated to attain the goal implicit in the problem situation.

2. The group must be composed of individuals who have sufficient information and knowledge to be able to attack the problem, or who can acquire this information while working on the problem. This principle is equally valid for an individual working in a problem situation.

3. There must be free and open communication between all members of the group, if all are to participate in the problem solution.[37]

[36]M. E. Wright, "The Influence of Frustration Upon Social Relations of Young Children," *Character and Personality*, 12 (1943), 111-22.

[37]A. Bavelas. "Communication Patterns in Task-Oriented Groups," in D. Cartwright and A. Zander, *Group Dynamics: Research and Theory*, Evanston, Illinois, Row, Peterson and Co., 1953, pp. 493-506.

4. A group leader who maximizes the communication between members is more likely to facilitate effective problem-solving.

5. Groups will solve problems quickly where the task permits a division of labor.

6. The larger the group, the less likely it is that all members in the group will participate actively in the group process.[38]

THE SCHOOL AND THE DEVELOPMENT OF PROBLEM-SOLVING BEHAVIOR

Problem-solving behavior begins with awareness of a problem, with the awareness of a desired goal that is not immediately and directly attainable. Problem-solving behavior may be encouraged in two ways: (1) by utilizing as the focus of learning experiences those problems of the child which arise from his own needs and goals, his interests and curiosity; (2) by stimulating his interest in problematic situations so that they become problems for him. In this sense, the school can create problems for children by placing them in situations which arouse their curiosity, provoke their interest, and require them to expend effort to attain desired goals. Learning situations may be organized so that they are genuinely problematic for the child.

The school prepares the child for problem-solving by encouraging the development of attitudes consistent with critical thinking, such as holding ideas tentatively and challenging assumptions and untested generalizations; presumably, these attitudes prepare the child for gaining the flexibility and adaptability necessary to effective problem-solving. Although problem-solving behavior provides its own reward by goal attainment, teachers may reward problem-seeking behavior by encouraging curiosity and thoughtful questioning.

Effective problem-solving requires adequate analysis of the goal to be attained and of the problem situation. The school provides the background of information and knowledge that prepares the child for this critical analysis and also teaches him ways of seeking out rele-

---

[38]For a discussion of group size in relation to group process, see R. F. Bales, F. L. Strodtbeck, T. M. Mills, and M. E. Roseborough, "Channels of Communication in Small Groups," *American Sociological Review,* 16 (1951), 461-68.

vant information. Information and skills in gathering relevant data are more likely to be retained when acquired in the context of problem-solving; they are also more likely to be used in new problem situations.

The school may also develop the child's ability to make and test hypotheses. Information and understanding are required to generate intelligent hypotheses. The understanding the child is developing provides a background of experience necessary for hypothesis-making. Furthermore, the act of hypothesis-making may be both encouraged and rewarded by the teacher.

The evaluation of hypotheses requires skill in gathering data relevant to the tests to be used. Here again the background of knowledge and technique the child is acquiring contributes to the development of his skill in hypothesis-testing. One important aspect of hypothesis-testing is the deduction of new hypotheses consistent with the hypotheses being tested, and the development of "if-then" kinds of relationships. The school is appropriately concerned with the development of the child's ability to reason inductively and deductively.

The above discussion suggests that practically the entire range of learning experiences in the school may contribute to the child's development as an effective problem solver. Unfortunately, information and skills relevant to problem-solving are often introduced to the child in self-contained packages, as if isolated from their relevance to problem-solving. Moreover, potentially problematic situations are sometimes presented as packages of questions that require the student to remember the answers. Such procedures minimize the many contributions that learning experiences can make to the development of effective problem-solving behavior.

Problem-solving is a complex process that requires an individual to integrate many aspects of his experience. Problem-solving cannot be taught as a simple unitary kind of skill, nor can it be learned in a single course. Problem-solving is learned when students have genuine problems that motivate flexible and adaptive goal-seeking behavior. Thorndike summarizes the school's contribution to this development of the child as follows:

> A wide range of interests and experiences, an organized and functional stock of background information, efficient skills for locating and organizing needed information, perseverance yet flexibility in attacking problem situations, a willingness to suspend judgment until the evidence is in, habits

of testing critically any proposed solution, attitudes of critical appraisal of the reliability and bias of sources, skill in 'if-then' thinking—these and many more are the qualities which a school must try to develop if it is to improve problem-solving abilities in its pupils.[39]

SUMMARY

In this chapter we have studied an important aspect of human behavior, problem-solving. Problem-solving behavior is no single kind of response but a complex integration of many different kinds of responses that vary from one problem situation to another. We infer that this complex process is influencing behavior from the behavior we observe in an individual who is confronted with a goal that is not immediately and directly attainable. We infer that an individual is problem-solving when he seeks new ways of attaining the goal, modifies previously learned patterns of goal-seeking responses, and acquires new patterns of responses to attain the goal.

Since problem-solving behavior is complex and varies from problem to problem, we do not observe highly specific patterns of response occurring in the behavior for all problem solvers. However, when problem-solving behavior has been analyzed, two general categories of response have been identified as essential to effective problem-solving:

1. *Responses related to analysis of the goal:* without a clear conconception of the character of the goal to be reached, the problem solver cannot select appropriate means to the attainment of the goal.

2. *Responses related to analysis of the problem situation:* by determining the conflicting elements in the problem situation, the problem solver can select appropriate means of resolving the conflict and attaining the goal.

When the problem solver cannot resolve the problem easily, he may experience frustration and annoyance while in the problem situation. A problem solver is behaving maladaptively when he makes responses which do not lead to the goal, which prevent goal attainment, or which keep him from attaining other goals even though they may

---

[39]R. L. Thorndike, "How Children Learn the Principles and Techniques of Problem-Solving," p. 215.

be temporarily successful in immediate goal attainment. Some characteristically maladaptive responses may be identified:

3. The problem solver may persist in making a response even though it does not lead to goal attainment. Such responses may have been effective in the past. Such persistency in response may occur because it is effective in reducing the tension and annoyance associated with difficulties in goal attainment.

4. The problem solver may react aggressively to objects or persons in the problem situation. Such a response may be effective in reducing frustration temporarily, or the problem solver may have learned from past experience that obstacles may be removed from the path to a goal by aggressive attacks.

5. The problem solver may substitute new goals and strive for attainment of these new goals. Such a response may be adaptive if the new goals will satisfy the needs that stimulated the original goal-seeking behavior. The response, however, is maladaptive if such satisfaction will not be achieved. Goal substitution is likely to be adaptive when the problem solver realistically evaluates his ability to attain the goal and chooses goals consistent with his capabilities.

Previous experience of the problem solver influences the kinds of responses that he is likely to make in a new problem situation. The problem solver has learned ways of viewing the elements in a problem situation and has also learned methods of attacking problems that have proved effective. These predispositions to respond in given ways in a new problem situation are called "sets." Sets inhibit problem-solving when the learned pattern of response is inappropriate or inefficient for the new problem situation. The effects of set can be minimized by arranging problem situations in such a way that new problem situations are sufficiently different from preceding ones that a fresh approach is required to solve the new problem.

Problem-solving behavior is fostered by the school on the assumption that the behavior taught in school will transfer to other problem situations. Some educators argue that this transfer will be promoted if students solve "realistic" problems in their learning experiences in school. Realistic problems are also used on the assumption that they develop more effective problem-solving; however, experimental evidence does not support these assumptions entirely. Realistic problems have not been found to induce more effective problem-solving, but the amount of experimental work on this problem is limited. Problem-solving in more realistic settings may have greater transfer value, but this hypothesis also needs to be tested more adequately.

Some problems may be solved either individually or by the cooperative efforts of a group working on the problem. One argument for using a group approach to problems is that children will need to learn to solve problems in groups since many important problems require cooperative effort for their solution. Two important questions are related to the decision to use group procedures in problem-solving:

6. Does problem-solving in groups produce more effective problem-solving by the members of the group? Groups are not necessarily more effective than individuals in solving problems; however, individuals may work more effectively in solving problems in group settings than they do when working on problems alone. This improved performance may result because the group setting maximizes some of the conditions for effective problem-solving. In a group setting, communication between individuals increases the opportunity for acquiring information and clarification of understanding relevant to problem-solving. Also, group pressures probably insure greater task-orientation.

7. Does problem-solving in groups promote learning relevant to participating in group problem-solving in other contexts? Children may learn behavior assumed to be relevant to effective participation in group problem-solving, but the extent to which such behavior is transferred to other contexts is not known.

Group problem-solving in school is not likely to encourage the development of behavior relevant to participation in groups if the group problem-solving is not effective. Problem-solving by groups is likely to be effective when:

8   The group has a genuine problem, that is, the members of the group are motivated to seek a goal.

9.   The group members have or can acquire the information, understanding, and skill necessary to problem-solution.

10   Communication within the group is maximized so that all members may participate in the solution. In some cases, a minimal kind of leadership is necessary to insure effective communication and task-orientation.

The school contributes to the development of problem-solving behavior of children in many ways. The school provides the background of information, understanding, and skill necessary to problem analysis and solution. The school "creates" problem situations by arousing the child's curiosity and then utilizing his interests and presently perceived problems to place him in situations likely to evoke problem-solving behavior. The school also prepares the child for problem-solving by encouraging him to make and test hypotheses, and by developing his skills in this respect. Problem-solving behavior is likely to be developed if "problems" are the central concern of the learning experiences provided in the school, and if the acquisition of information, understanding, and skill are made relevant to the solution of problems of genuine concern to the child.

STUDY AND DISCUSSION QUESTIONS

1. Describe each of the following situations as a problem-solving situation:

   a. Developing a concept of cooperation.

   b. Acquiring a favorable attitude toward athletics.

   c. Learning to play tennis.

2. Select a unit from some subject that you are teaching or plan to teach or from a section from this book. Describe the general kinds of problems that students would be expected to solve after participating in the learning experiences associated with these units. Be specific about the goals represented in the problem situations, the problem context, and the kinds of alternative solutions required for problem solution.

3. In each of the situations listed below, describe the goal or goals of the problem situation, the important elements in the problem context, and the kinds of alternative solutions available to a problem solver.

   a. Becoming an engineer.

   b. Entering college for the first time.

   c. Writing an essay on the role of public education in American life.

4. A teacher plans a unit on America's participation in World War II. Suggest some kinds of problem situations that could be organized in connection with the study of this particular unit. Be specific about the goals and problem context in these problem situations. How might students view the study of this unit in such a way that they are not motivated to solve the problems as they have been set by the teacher?

5 Analyze the following problem situation from the viewpoint of a teacher who wants to help the student, specifying the goals and the elements in the problem context relevant to problem solution. Suggest some alternative solutions and attempt to predict the consequences of utilizing these solutions:

> Molly is a bright and attractive-looking high school Junior. Molly is particularly uninterested in the study of American history. Her family is a typically upper middle-class family; her father, a lawyer. Molly plans to go to college and her primary interests seem to be mathematical in character. However, if she continues to perform at her present level, she may receive a failing grade in history. This low grade would jeopardize her college admission.

6. Suggest how Molly herself may view this problem situation and the ways in which she may attempt to solve the problem. Relate your solutions to this problem, as a teacher, to the kinds of solutions that the student may make of this problem.

7. Refer to the example of Cris and Allen and the discussion of persistence in problem-solving. How could you determine whether Allen was persisting in inappropriate responses because he felt secure or whether he was persisting in inappropriate responses because he did not have sufficient information to enable him to change his pattern of response?

8. Refer to the Lantz experiment discussed in this chapter. Assume that you are performing a similar experiment but that you arrange for an experimental group in which the children would fail at the first two problems. What hypotheses would you make about the effects of this failure experience on their intelligence test performances and other behavior patterns? What relationships do you perceive between the results obtained in this study and the discussion of success and failure in the Sears study presented in Chapter Four?

9. Review both the Lantz and Sears experiments. Assume that Lantz requested

the students to predict how they would do on a fourth problem. What effect would the success and failure experiences in this experiment probably have on students' levels of aspiration? Assume that you had a third experimental group that had failed on the first three problems, what predictions would you make about their level of aspiration with respect to a fourth problem?

10. Draw up a list of behaviors that you would expect to see when children are having difficulty solving a problem. Be specific about the kinds of behavior and suggest what needs the problem solver may be attempting to satisfy through such behavior. What variations in these behavior patterns would you expect with children of different ages? Are there some behavior patterns that you might expect to observe in both a young child and an adult?

11. Discuss the Keister experiment as an illustration of transfer of learning. Draw up a list of behavior patterns that would have applicability in a wide variety of problem situations.

12. How do you account for the fact that simple directions from an experimenter, such as "Don't be blind," appear to "break" a set which is inhibiting efficiency in problem-solving?

13. In what ways may a "set" in a problem situation be beneficial?

14. Some people argue that presenting students with realistic problems (that is, problems which are similar to problems students are likely to meet in their later lives) promotes better problem-solving. Discuss this argument in terms of both the motivational aspects of problem-solving and transfer of learning. In what ways may "lifelike" problems inhibit student interest? In what ways may "lifelike" problems inhibit transfer to other problem situations?

15. You are teaching a unit on the organization of local government. Describe some kinds of "laboratory" experiences which would facilitate the students' understanding of this organization. Also describe some "field" experiences which would contribute to the students' understanding of local government.

16. Assume that you took a class that is studying local government to a session of the city council. In what ways might this "field" experience interfere with the students' understanding of local organization? Assuming that this "field" trip occurs at the beginning of the learning experience, what benefits might it have in terms of enhancing greater understanding?

17. Assume that you are organizing a learning experience on the role of the railroad in American life. As a part of this experience, you take students to the local train depot where they visit the trains and talk with the trainmen. What aspects of understanding the role of the railroad in American life will probably not be acquired from this kind of an experience? What "laboratory" or classroom experiences may facilitate understanding the role of the railroad? Be as specific as you can about the kinds of understanding that you would hope stu-

dents would acquire from this learning experience, and suggest ways in which classroom and field experiences may contribute to the attainment of these objectives.

18. Some people argue that "group" activities in learning experiences actually interfere with the development of problem-solving behavior. Evaluate this argument, giving consideration to the kinds of behavior patterns that may and may not be learned in group problem-solving contexts.

19. A teacher is organizing a learning experience related to missiles and the space age. He divides the class up into two groups. One group is to do library reading and make reports on the various kinds of missiles. The other group is to construct models of the various kinds of missiles. In what ways may these organizations be appropriately thought of as "group" activities? How might the learning experiences be organized so that the use of groups contributes to problem solutions? May the activities of both of these kinds of groups be organized in such a way that they are working on common problems?

20. Teachers occasionally organize discussion groups on current social problems. Some people argue that this kind of learning experience is inefficient since in many cases the students who participate in these discussions are not particularly well informed about the problems. Evaluate this criticism and suggest how this kind of learning experience might be organized so that the criticism would not be appropriate.

21. Some people argue that discussions of the kind noted in the question above are beneficial, even though students are not particularly well informed, because they learn how to listen to other people's opinions. They argue that students learn how to interact with people in groups, and for this purpose the content of the group discussion is not important. Again, evaluate this argument, giving due consideration to the character of the objectives of this kind of learning experience and the organization of group activities designed to attain these objectives.

22. We noted that "follow through" behavior may be associated with a child's feeling of acceptance in a group. On the basis of this hypothesized relation, would you argue that children should be allowed to organize their own groups when attempting problem solutions? Assume that children were free to make choices in situations of this kind, what factors do you think would influence their choice of group members?

23. Below is a list of three different kinds of activities. What aspects of these activities may be thought of as "individual" problems? What aspects of these activities may be regarded as "group" problems?
    a. Producing a class play.
    b. Learning the plays for the next varsity football game.
    c. Working a series of algebra problems in the algebra class.

RECOMMENDED READINGS

The first reading is a general discussion of the principles of problem-solving with suggested applications to the organization of learning experiences. The second reading is a review of research on children's problem-solving. The third and fourth readings are critical reviews of the experimental literature on problem-solving. The fifth reading is an interesting analysis of general procedures in problem-solving; though the applications of these procedures refer to mathematical examples, the discussion is easily generalizable to other problem contexts. The sixth reading is a discussion of the use of group procedures in organizing learning experiences, with many useful applications of the principles discussed in this chapter.

1. R. L. Thorndike, "How Children Learn the Principles and Techniques of Problem Solving," *Forty-ninth Yearbook of the National Society for the Study of Education, Part I, Learning and Instruction,* Chicago, University of Chicago Press, 1950, pp. 192-216.

2. D. H. Russell, *Children's Thinking,* Boston, Ginn & Co., 1956, Chapters 9 and 13.

3. W. E. Vinacke, *The Psychology of Thinking,* New York, McGraw-Hill Book Co., 1952, Chapter 9.

4. H. H. Kelley and J. W. Thibaut, "Experimental Studies of Group Problem Solving and Process," in G. Lindzey (ed.), *Handbook of Social Psychology,* Vol. II, Cambridge, Mass., Addison-Wesley Publishing Co., 1954, Chapter 21.

5. G. Polya, *How to Solve It,* Princeton, Princeton University Press, 1945.

6. R. Strang, *Group Work in Education,* New York, Harper & Brothers, 1958.

PATTERNS OF DEVELOPMENT

In the last six chapters we discussed learning as a psychological process. Children are not born with concepts; they acquire them. Attitudes, values, and patterns of skill performance are also learned. These processes are not separate, discrete entities in personality, they are interrelated. At any stage of a child's life, the child is a unity—a personality. His personality changes as he acquires new concepts, attitudes, skills, and problem-solving facility. We say that he is developing, or that he is "maturing." Implicit in our concept of "mature" behavior are culturally-shared expectancies of what a child ought to be like at a given age. We do not expect a twelve-year-old child to whine and cry when he wants something. A ten-year-old, both literate and perceptive in his discussion of foreign policy, would surprise us. While a twelve-year-old and a ten-year-old might behave in these ways, such behavior does not accord with our general expectations for children at these ages.

The concept of "development" suggests that we may classify the behavior changes we observe in children at various ages. For example, we may describe progressive height and weight changes as functions of age. An important portion of psychological and educational research has been devoted to studying developmental behavior. This study is essentially descriptive in character; that is, it provides data on the relation between increases in age and changes in behavior. Besides revealing uniform patterns of change, such data make it possible for us to determine the variable factors in change. For example, knowing that ten-year-olds are not all of the same height, or weight, or mental age, we may describe these variations on the basis of the averages for a given age. With this kind of data, we may formulate a picture of the amount and kind of behavior change that may be expected over a period of time.

Behavior changes at given ages depend on changes in the growth functions of the organism and on changes that result from learning. The consequence of the interaction between growth and learning is a systematic development in many behavior patterns. Since our concept of this systematic development probably influences our expectations for children of a given age, it is important that the teacher understand the meaning and implications of the concept and its use in the analysis of behavior change. To understand a particular sequence of events in personality development, we need to be familiar with principles which describe general patterns of development and with the factors which influence variations in these patterns.

In this chapter we will explore the concept of development. We will be concerned only with general patterns of development, and not with details on the development of many specific functions.[1] Although we will also discuss the implications of this concept and the principles it affords for organizing learning experiences, our main emphasis will be on patterns of development in children and the factors upon which they depend.

How are the ideas to be developed here related to our model of personality and behavior analysis presented in Chapter Three? In this chapter we will analyze the development of the individual as a whole with respect to age. This developmental sequence is not represented in the model; it consists of changes in the structure and functions of personality (represented in the model) which occur over a long period of time. In analyzing development, we are studying

---

[1] A comprehensive survey of developmental studies of many different personality functions may be found in L. Carmichael (ed.), *Manual of Child Psychology*, 2nd ed., New York, John Wiley & Sons, 1954.

the dependent variable in the model, namely behavior, and classifying changes in behavior by age.

Still, two of the variables represented in the model are significantly related to the kinds of changes that we describe as developmental. Heredity, as an independent variable, may be related to behavior change and may determine in important respects the individual's potentialities for development. The capacities of the individual, which we have listed among the mediating variables, also influence potentialities for development and account in part for the observed differences in development. In this chapter we also will discuss general principles relevant to the influence of these variables on development.

THE PROCESS OF DEVELOPMENT

DIFFERENTIATION OF RESPONSES. *The process of development requires differentiation of responses.* At birth, the infant has a limited number of responses. As he grows, he acquires new responses and response systems. The process of development is not simply a process of acquiring responses. If we observe an infant we notice that he appears to be a mass of movement. Most of his movements are undifferentiated and undirected. The child simply moves. As the weeks and months pass, his movements become refined, and he acquires response patterns. The swinging of his arms and hands develops into a response of grasping. His kicking movements eventually change into pushing movements, and still later into the specific movements required for crawling and walking. In this pattern of change, finer responses are developed from the earlier gross movements.

This refinement of response also characterizes changes in other functions. The child's initial response to men may be to call them "Daddy," but he learns to differentiate his father from other men, and still later he learns how to call people by their names. He learns a complex set of familial relations which enables him to categorize people as mother, father, brother, sister, grandmother, and grandfather.[2] As the child's concepts become more differentiated, so do his attitudes, interests, and values. A child initially has a diffuse affectional tie with his parents and his family. He learns to react in a variety of emotional ways to other people. He may learn to love or hate his teacher, his

---

[2]See Chapter Five for a discussion of discrimination responses and concept formation.

schoolmates, and other adults whom he meets. *The mature person, or the relatively mature person, is capable of fine discriminations and refined and controlled responses to his environment.*

INTEGRATION OF RESPONSES. *The process of development also requires integration of responses.* To walk, a child must not only learn a number of specific responses, but he must also integrate them into response patterns. Grasping requires a complex coordination of hand and eye movements. Learning to read requires development of eye movements, association of words and sounds, acquisition of concepts and vocabulary, and the development of attitudes of interest and effort. The more proficient reader has smoother eye movements, a larger vocabulary, and a more extensive conceptual system, and because of these refinements, he can get more meaning out of his reading. Differences in ability to read are related to differences both in level of acquisition of particular response sets and in integration of these response sets. For example, a child who makes many eye movements may have difficulty in reading efficiently—although he may have acquired a high level of facility in such response patterns as sight recognition and phonetic analysis of words. Another child may read inefficiently because he has difficulty in relating these response patterns to one another in a continuous process of reading—even though he may perform any one set of responses quite well. Both of these children may be somewhat retarded in their development, but for different reasons.

The development of behavior patterns becomes progressively more complex and requires continual discrimination and the integration of new responses with previously learned responses. One of the consequences of this continual pattern of change is that the behavior patterns of the "mature" person, that is, the individual at an advanced stage of development, may be quite different in their totality from that of the beginner or relatively "immature" person. A "mature reader," for example, has greater and more diversified interests in reading, is able to get more and deeper meanings out of what he reads, and can read selectively to achieve many different kinds of purposes.[3] He is distinguished from the less mature reader in the specific kinds of responses he can make, as well as in the total pattern of his "reading behavior."

---

[3] W. S. Gray and B. Rogers, *Maturity in Reading*, Chicago, University of Chicago Press, 1956.

The two processes, discrimination and integration, describe but do not explain the course of development. In other words, any stage or sequence of behavior development may be described in terms of the response discriminations and integrations required to achieve a given level of development. A child learning to read begins by identifying the letters of the alphabet by sight and sound. He moves on to the sight recognition and phonetic analysis of familiar words. He learns to read words in sentences that he can understand. But as he acquires new responses, we may describe "stages" in his development in terms of the kinds of discriminations and integrations of responses he is making. The child who can recognize words by sight is further in the development of his ability to read than a child who can recognize only the letters of the alphabet. However, we have yet to account for his progression from one stage to another; we have merely described it.

FACTORS INFLUENCING DEVELOPMENT

A comprehensive discussion of the factors influencing development would take us well beyond the scope of this text and into a study of many sciences, such as genetics. None the less, a general discussion of these factors is relevant to the kinds of educational problems that we have been discussing throughout this book.

We have assumed that the purpose of the learning experiences we have provided for children is to encourage specified and desired behavior changes. Such a statement of purpose assumes that the behavior with which we are concerned is modifiable. We assume that we may influence the sequence of development in certain important respects; however, the extent to which behavior is modifiable depends on the kinds of factors that influence development. Behavior is not modifiable insofar as its course of development is controlled solely by hereditary factors. The pattern of development will emerge inevitably, or only those individuals with the appropriate heredity will profit from the learning experiences that we provide. For example, assume that the ability to read were inherited. Those with the appropriate heredity would inevitably learn to read, or only gifted people would profit from the learning experiences that we provide. In such a case of strict hereditary determination, experience would have as little influence as it does on eye color.

This discussion will describe the ways in which relevant factors are likely to influence development. A description of these influences on behavior development should improve our understanding of both the modifiability and the variability in behavior development that we may expect.

INFLUENCE OF HEREDITY. In Chapter Three we listed heredity as an independent variable that influences behavior development. How does heredity influence behavior? We may begin this discussion by indicating in what way heredity does not influence behavior. Behavior, or the psychological characteristics of the person, is not directly inherited. For example, behavior that we describe as relatively more or less intelligent is not inherited. We observe a child's responses on an "intelligence test," his ability to perform school tasks, his vocabulary development, and his ability to solve complex problems. We may compare his performance on these tasks to the performance of other children, and from this comparative data make inferences about his relative brightness. The "intelligent behavior" we have observed is not inherited as such, but some of the factors that influence the extent to which "intelligent behaviors" are acquired may be influenced by hereditary factors.

Popular thinking fails to make this distinction between inherited factors and behavior development that may be influenced by hereditary factors. For example, we observe that a child who is relatively more intelligent has parents who are apparently relatively more intelligent. Research studies have also demonstrated a substantial correlation between parent-child intelligence test scores.[4] From the available data we cannot conclude that heredity determines the development of intelligent behavior. Such an interpretation is consistent with the data, but other hypotheses are also consistent with the same data. Children of intelligent parents probably have superior environmental stimulation toward the development of intelligent behavior.[5] It is thus consistent with the data to hypothesize that the interaction between heredity and environmental opportunity influences the development of intelligent behavior.

Efforts to distinguish and isolate hereditary and environmental influences on behavior development have not been notably successful.

---

[4]H. S. Conrad and H. E. Jones, "A Second Study of Familial Resemblance in Intelligence: Environmental and Genetic Implications of Parent-Child and Sibling Correlations in the Total Sample," *Thirty-ninth Yearbook of the National Society for the Study of Education, Part II, Original Studies and Experiments,* 1940, pp. 97-141.

[5]E. A. Milner, "A Study of the Relationship between Reading Readiness in Grade One School Children and Patterns of Parent-Child Interaction," *Child Development,* 22 (1951), 95-112.

"How" either heredity or environment can influence behavior development is probably a more profitable inquiry.[6]

An individual's heredity consists of the specific "genes" that he receives from his parents at conception. Any behavioral characteristic that is hereditary must be linked to specific genes or gene combinations. However, the problem of determining the genetic base of some characteristics is complicated by the fact that genes combine in an infinite variety of ways, and the genetic influence on behavior may be more or less direct. Anastasi has pointed out four ways in which hereditary factors may influence behavior.[7]

1. A genetic deficiency may exist which precludes the possibility of normal development. For example, certain kinds of metabolic disorders are genetic in character and impair development to such an extent that environmental stimulations cannot compensate the deficiency.

2. A genetic defect may interfere with development by inhibiting the individual's ability to interact efficiently with his environment. Hereditary deafness, for example, interferes with normal social interaction and the individual's development is correspondingly affected. However, in these kinds of cases, appropriate training may compensate for the handicaps imposed by genetic deficiency. The genetic deficiency does not preclude "normal" development if appropriate training experiences can be developed.

3. Genetic deficiences may make an individual susceptible to certain kinds of physical diseases. In these cases the actual contraction of the disease is the determinant of the course of development. If the individual actually contracts the disease, development may be inhibited because he cannot attend school regularly or because he develops patterns of social interaction that interfere with his ability to profit from educational experiences. However, the individual may also compensate for the effects of illness, such as restricted social activity, by developing interests and abilities which enhance other aspects of his development. The genetic deficiency in these instances has a relatively less direct influence on behavior development since retardation in development depends on the contraction of the disease to which the individual is susceptible and his reaction to the effects of the disease.

4. Genetic factors determine many physical characteristics of the individual. Some physical characteristics influence the extent to which environmental

[6]A. Anastasi, "Heredity, Environment, and the Question 'How?'" *Psychological Review*, 65 (1958), 197-208.
[7]*Ibid.*

opportunities will be available to the individual. Sex, skin pigmentation, and body build, all of which have a hereditary base, are related in particular cultures to the kinds of environmental opportunities available to an individual. The boy whose body build is comparatively small may not be able to participate in athletics. Certain kinds of need-satisfactions and opportunities for development will not be available to him. He is not doomed to defective development, but his pattern of development will differ in some respects from that of a boy with a larger and more muscular body build.

These four examples illustrate only some of the ways in which genetic factors influence development. They point up the fact that the influence of heredity on development is relatively indirect, and that behavioral characteristics as such are not directly inherited. Genetic factors influence more or less directly the probabilities for what is called "normal" development.

The complexity of the relation of heredity to development suggests that we exercise considerable caution in making inferences about the "causes" of the particular patterns of development that we observe in children. The relatively indirect influence of heredity in many cases also suggests that appropriate environmental opportunities may compensate for some kinds of genetic deficiencies. We are also aware of the fact that some hereditary factors adversely affect development because of the cultural evaluations of their significance. In other words, many aspects of behavior development are modifiable even when they are influenced by hereditary factors.

Heredity sets the initial limits to the organic conditions under which behavior development occurs; however, the presence of requisite organic conditions does not guarantee behavior development. We have also seen that the absence of some organic conditions may influence behavior development, provided that the hereditary basis of the condition is more or less directly related to particular kinds of behavior development. As the above discussion has suggested, hereditary factors play an important role in development, despite the difficulty of isolating their effects from the effects of environmental factors.

THE INFLUENCE OF ENVIRONMENT. In the discussion of motivation and learning in the preceding seven chapters, we have assumed that variations in environment influence behavior change. If experimental evidence indicates that some variations are in fact related to specific kinds of behavior change, we have demonstrated ways in which environmental factors influence behavior change. In this section we will discuss the more general ways in which environmental influences affect the pattern of development.

By *environment* we mean all the stimuli that impinge on an individual from conception to death. Environment sometimes means the physical setting in which the individual lives. However, we will consider such a setting an environment—in the psychological sense— only if it is a stimulus which influences the kinds of responses an individual is likely to make. A child who is growing up in a lower socioeconomic class, whose parents are divorced and whose companions are mostly delinquents, is influenced only to the extent that these characteristics of the setting in which he lives are stimuli that are likely to evoke certain kinds of behavior. That such differences in physical and social settings are likely to be correlated with differences in psychological environment has been amply demonstrated.[8]

We may distinguish between two general classes of environmental influences that illustrate the complexity of the influence of environment on behavior. The first of these classes may be called *organic* environmental influences. Inadequate prenatal environment and birth injuries are examples of organic environmental factors that may influence development. Dietary deficiencies of pregnant women, for example, appear to be related to the intellectual development of their children.[9] Severe incapacitation from disease without accompanying injury to the higher neural centers is another example of an organic environmental influence which may have a bearing on development. In this case, however, the influence of the environmental factor is less direct. Incapacitation, either permanent or temporary, may inhibit the individual's interaction with the environmental influences likely to stimulate his development, but it does not necessarily doom him to complete or permanent retardation.

Other kinds of organic environmental influences may influence behavior development. A physically weak boy may take advantage of environmental opportunities to build up his body strength and ap-

[8] A. Davis and R. J. Havighurst, "Social Class and Color Differences in Child-Rearing," *American Sociological Review*, 11 (1946), 698-710; E. E. Maccoby and P. K. Gibbs, "Methods of Child-Rearing in Two Social Classes," in W. E. Martin and C. B. Stendler (eds.), *Readings in Child Development*, New York, Harcourt, Brace and Co., 1954, pp. 380-96; J. R. Williams and R B. Scott, "Growth and Development of Negro Infants: IV. Motor Development and Its Relationship to Child-Rearing Practices in Two Groups of Negro Infants," *Child Development*, 24 (1953), 103-121.

[9] R. F. Harrell, E. Woodyard, and A. I. Gates, *The Effect of Mothers' Diets on the Intelligence of the Offspring*, New York, Bureau of Publications, Teachers College, Columbia University, 1955.

parent muscular development. Within the limits of his structural characteristics, organic modifications have been made which are likely to influence the behavior of this boy. His associates will react differently to him now that he is stronger, and his own self-concept and subsequent behavior will probably change correspondingly. These examples illustrate that the influence of organic environmental factors on behavior may be more or less direct. They commonly reveal the way an environmental influence produces an organic change in the individual, which in turn has a more or less direct influence on subsequent behavior development.

The second class of major environmental influences is called *behavioral*, that is, environmental influences serving as direct stimuli to behavior change. The kinds of variables that we have been discussing in the preceding chapters are behavioral environmental influences. The expected effect of such environmental factors is some degree of behavior change. For example, a class discussion of the rise of dictatorships is designed to encourage increased understanding of certain historical events. The environmental influence is the class discussion, and its immediate effect is supposed to be the behavior change of increased understanding.

One may argue that such changes do not always follow immediately. The fact that they do not may reflect only our incomplete understanding of all of the environmental influences likely to evoke the desired changes. Recall that every environmental organization implies a hypothesis about the likelihood of such an arrangement evoking the desired change. Implicit in our thinking is the assumption that these environmental influences are likely to have a relatively immediate effect on behavior change. We abandon reorganizations of environmental influences only when we know that the behavior with which we are concerned cannot be modified by their direct influence.

While environmental influences are direct stimuli, the scope and permanence of their influence varies considerably. The socio-economic setting in which a child grows up has, typically, a pervasive influence on a child's development. An illustration of the effect of a restricted environment on development is provided in Table XXII.[10] The intelligence test scores of two groups of children living in somewhat different but generally restricted environments are given in this table. The

---

[10]M. Sherman and C. B. Key, "The Intelligence of Isolated Mountain Children," *Child Development*, 3 (1932), 279–90.

AGE	Pintner-Cunningham Test		National Intelligence Test		Goodenough Draw-A-Man Test		Pintner-Patterson Performance Tests	
	Mt.	Vill.	Mt.	Vill.	Mt.	Vill.	Mt.	Vill.
6- 8	84	94			80	93	89	
8-10	70	91		117	66	82	76	93
10-12	53	76	66	101	71	69	70	87
12-14			67	91	69	73	83	
14-16			52	87	49	70	73	

Mean IQ of Mountain and Village Children in Relation to Age
(From Sherman and Key)

TABLE XXII

mountain children lived in isolated valleys in the Blue Ridge Mountains; the village children lived at the foot of the mountains in a less isolated area. The mountain children also attended less adequate schools. In general, the environments of both of these groups were what are usually called "deprived" environments. The effect of these environments is reflected in the test scores of the children. Both groups scored, on the average, below 100, which is the average score usually obtained from an unselected group of children; however, the scores of the mountain children run lower than those of the village children. Successive decreases in score are also apparent through the older ages, but once again the decreases are smaller for the village children. The data illustrate only one aspect of retarded development, but intellectual retardation would have pervasive effects on other aspects of development. The gradual regression also suggests the pervasive influence of the total environment. Other studies of similar kinds of environments provide comparable data.[11]

Bilingualism in childhood is an environmental factor that may have a more or less pervasive influence on development depending on the accompanying circumstances. In some cases, bilingualism adversely affects personality development;[12] in others, it serves as a symbol of minority group status which in turn enhances emotional adjustment and personality development.[18]

---

[11]See, for example, H. M. Skeels and E. M. Fillmore, "Mental Development of Children from Underprivileged Homes," *Journal of Genetic Psychology*, 50 (1937), 427-39.

[12]N. T. Darcy, "A Review of the Literature on the Effects of Bilingualism upon the Measurement of Intelligence," *Journal of Genetic Psychology*, 82 (1953), 21-57.

[18]A. Anastasi and F. A. Cordova, "Some Effects of Bilingualism upon the Intelligence Test Performance of Puerto Rican Children in New York City," *Journal of Educational Psychology*, 44 (1953), 1-19.

The various kinds of environmental influences we have described suggest the variety of ways in which such factors are related to behavior development. Again, caution is recommended to the teacher who wishes to make inferences about the "causes" of a particular pattern of development he observes. Such inferences are hypotheses which must be tested. A wide variety of factors may have influenced the pattern of development we observe, and extensive knowledge of a child's genetic and environmental background, as well as of present influences on his development, are required before we can assess the relative influence of any of the factors.

INTERDEPENDENCE OF HEREDITY AND ENVIRONMENT. The above discussion should have illuminated one important fact: the influence of hereditary and environmental factors on behavior development is infinitely varied. While a number of theories have been offered to explain the relation of these factors to each other and to behavior development, a commonly-held theory is that these factors are mutually interdependent.[14] By mutual interdependence we mean that the contribution of either set of factors to behavior development is determined by the contribution of the other set. An environmental factor, such as an intellectually stimulating home environment, will have different influences on individuals with different genetic backgrounds since genetic background will influence the extent to which an individual is likely to profit from this environment. Similarly, two individuals of identical genetic background, such as identical twins, will develop differently if environmental influences on them are different.[15] Behavior development depends on the combination of hereditary and environmental influences.

The complexity of the relationships among factors influencing development is reflected in the many variations in the developmental patterns of children; however, we also find relative consistencies in these patterns. In the following section we will outline several principles that account for the variation in developmental patterns, and at a later point in the chapter we will discuss the factors that contribute to the relative consistencies we observe.

---

[14]For a critical analysis of these theories, see A. Anastasi, *Differential Psychology*, 3rd ed., New York, Macmillan Co., 1958, Chapter 3.

[15]H. H. Newman, F. N. Freeman, and K. J. Holzinger, *Twins: A Study of Heredity and Environment*, Chicago, University of Chicago Press, 1937.

GENERAL PRINCIPLES OF DEVELOPMENT

DIFFERENCES IN RATE OF DEVELOPMENT. *Children differ from one another in their rates of development.* The rate of development may be estimated by plotting behavior change against time. For example, suppose that we measure a child's height at successive ages. We may then estimate the changes in height for successive years by plotting the child's height at each age level. We obtain a picture of the child's rate of growth from this curve. If we obtain data on the growth of a large number of children and compute the average height of these children at each age level, we obtain a picture of "average" development at various ages. However, such "average" curves mask the range of variation in height at any age and the differences in rate of development for individual children.

In Figures 54 and 55 are plotted individual curves of development for two different kinds of behavior change.[16] Note the steady progression in development apparent in both sets of curves. Observe also the variation in attained level at any one age level. Compare also the amount of change per year for each of these curves. In Figure 54 we note that early superiority or inferiority is not necessarily maintained except for the most obviously superior or inferior children. Child 4F, for example, is eventually taller than child 5F, even though at age 12 their relative positions were reversed.

For all of these children the developmental pattern is relatively similar when plotted over a long period of time, though rates of development vary considerably. Development is also more or less rapid at different periods in each child's life.

The variations in the rate of development depend upon both physiological changes and the kinds of experiences that children are having. Included in these two broad categories are various specific factors that may affect development at any one time. The following research data illustrate the complexity of the interrelationships among factors which influence development and account for variations in developmental rates. Changes in physical structure will affect development, and these changes in turn may influence other aspects of development. The boy who is slow in developing physically may feel inferior because he is smaller and weaker than other boys of his age. The fact that he is not so strong or tall as other boys of his

---

[16]N Bayley, "Individual Patterns of Development," *Child Development,* 27 (1956), 45-74.

age may prevent him from participating in sports and receiving need-satisfactions that come from participating in these highly valued activities of boys. His feelings of inferiority may spread to other activities. He reacts to his experiential opportunities in a limited way, and his development is correspondingly affected.

In one extensive investigation of the relationship between motor performance behavior and general development, Jones compared the ten strongest and the ten weakest boys in a class on a variety of social and emotional factors at two different periods in their schooling.[17]

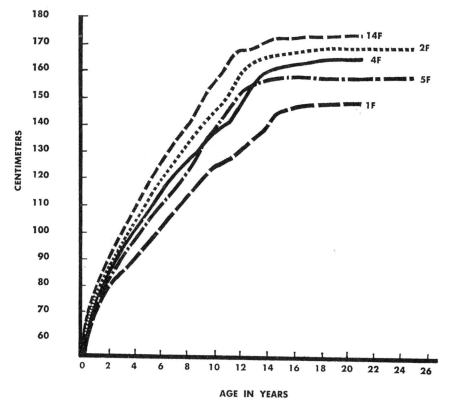

Curves of stature by age for five girls in the Berkeley Growth Study, including the tallest female in the group (14F), the shortest, and three girls of intermediate height. (From Bayley)

FIGURE 54

---

[17]H. E. Jones, *Motor Performance and Growth*, Berkeley, University of California Press, 1949.

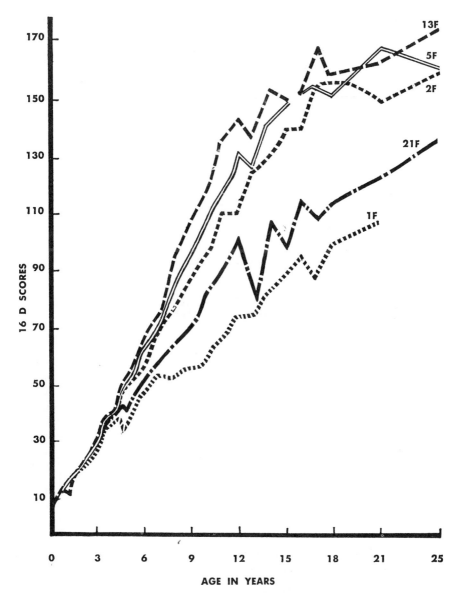

Individual curves of intelligence of 5 girls. (From Bayley)

FIGURE 55

The data are diagramed in Figure 56. In elementary school the two groups are comparatively similar, particularly on such traits as generalized tensions and popularity. However, by the senior year of high

413

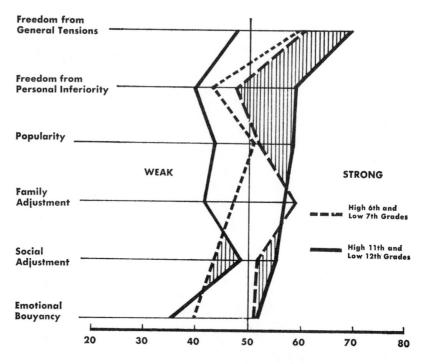

Contrasts between the 10 highest and the 10 lowest of 78 boys on total score on strength tests at 17.5 years. Popularity and emotional bouyancy as rated by staff observers during "free-play" activity; general tensions, personal inferiority, and adjustments as shown on a personal-social inventory filled out by the boys. The 10 strongest boys are shown to have been high on freedom from general tensions in grades 6-7 and higher yet in grades 11-12, but the 10 weakest were more inferior in this respect in grades 11-12 than earlier. (From Jones)

FIGURE 56

school the two groups are farther apart, the weaker group scoring lower and the stronger group scoring higher on these traits. In this period of the boys' schooling, the culture places great value on physical prowess and physical attributes. The child's physical appearance affects his social relations with other children and determines the extent to which he can participate in the highly valued athletic activities of the school. We are not surprised to find the weaker boys feeling more inferior and being less popular in their senior year than they were in grade school.

The teacher who sees a child for a relatively short period of his life must be careful in drawing conclusions about the child's rate of development. The more extreme the advancement or retardation of a child, the more likely it is that he will preserve his relatively high or low position over the span of life, but, within these extremes, variations in developmental rate lead to some changes in comparative developmental attainment with time.

DIFFERENCES IN RATE OF DEVELOPMENT IN EACH CHILD. *The psychological functions of each child vary in their rate of development.* In Figure 57, several different kinds of behavior change in one child are plotted.[18] Here, again, we see the same pattern as we observe when two children are compared. The various functions plotted in this diagram follow an over-all pattern of increasing development, but the rate at which any one function develops varies with time, and the pattern of variation is different for each function.

When we say that the child develops as a whole, we do not mean that every aspect of the child's personality is developing at the same rate or that, if we measure different functions of personality, we will find each of these functions at the same general developmental level. Some children will be comparatively advanced in all aspects of development, and others will be comparatively retarded. But the typical pattern, when the rates of development of the behavior patterns of an individual child are compared with each other, is a differential pattern of rate of development.

AGE-PATTERNING OF DEVELOPMENT. Parents and teachers continually observe the changes in children. The results of the extensive studies of child growth and development have been diffused throughout our society through the media of mass communication. One of the consequences of this widespread attention to child development has been that a set of cultural expectancies has developed which reflects the expected pattern of child development. For descriptive purposes, we divide the course of development up into periods, such as infancy, early childhood, late childhood, prepuberty, adolescence, and adulthood. Each of these periods is frequently defined in terms of an age span, and is understood to describe common levels of development in children who have reached these age levels.

Perhaps the most prevalent example of conceptualizing develop-

---

[18]W. C. Olson and B. O. Hughes, "Concepts of Growth: Their Significance for Teachers," *Childhood Education*, 21 (1944), 54.

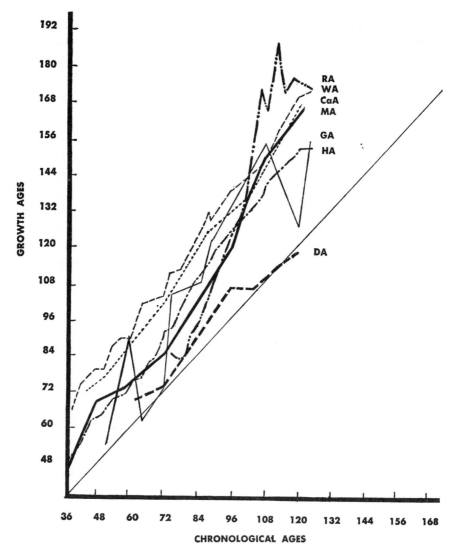

*Contrasted growth in reading age (RA), weight age (WA), carpal age (CaA), mental age (MA), grip age (GA), height age (HA), dental age (DA). * (From Olson and Hughes)*

FIGURE 57

*Both growth ages and chronological ages are given in months.

ment as a series of stages with given characteristics is reflected in the popular picture of the adolescent and the expectations associated with it. The adolescent is commonly expected to be moody, irresponsible, rebellious, a daydreamer, perhaps somewhat awkward, moon-struck, difficult to live with, and generally a remarkably different person from what he was five or ten years earlier in his life. This general cultural expectancy frequently predisposes us to see the adolescent in terms of this stereotype rather than in terms of his own unique patterns of behavior.

One of the major consequences of widely shared cultural expectancies for age groups is that children in these age groups are accorded differential treatment. We do not expect to treat the eight-year-old and the sixteen-year-old in identically the same way. However, not all eight-year-olds are alike. Some eight-year-olds are more like nine- or ten-year-olds than they are like eight-year-olds. Other eight-year-olds are not so well developed as the typical eight-year-old child. While children within any age span typically are more like other children within that age span than they are like children in other age groups, the range of variability within any age group is great.

This age-grouping conception of development ignores the interdependence of all phases of development and the complexity of the interrelationships among factors affecting behavior development. Until the child approaches the point of maximum development within the limits imposed by his native endowment and environmental opportunities, his pattern of development is essentially continuous. For example, a child's rate of development in height and weight gradually decreases, but the child is getting taller and heavier until he reaches his maximum development in these functions. At some periods in his development, he will appear to the casual observer not to be growing at all, but his growth is being maintained although it is less apparent. Such variations in rates of development may influence us to overlook the continuities in development. There are no sharp breaks in the pattern of development; an eight-year-old does not drop suddenly the behavior patterns of an eight-year-old and immediately take on the behavior patterns of a nine-year-old.

VARIABILITY IN DEVELOPMENT. In Figure 58 the mental ages of 167 girls at age eight, twelve, and sixteen are plotted.[19] The mental ages of some sixteen-year-old girls are below those of some eight-

---

[19] W. F. Dearborn and J. W. M. Rothney, *Predicting the Child's Development*, Cambridge, Mass., Sci-Art Publishers, 1941, p. 325.

year-old girls. Some of the twelve-year-old girls have higher mental ages than over half of the sixteen-year-old girls. However, a sixteen-year-old girl is different in many ways from an eight-year-old girl, even though the eight-year-old girl may be brighter than the sixteen-year-old. One of the explanations for these differences is that differential treatment is accorded to the two age groups. For example, in a

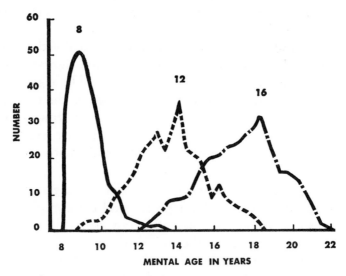

Distributions of mental ages of 167 girls at ages 8, 12, and 16. (After Dearborn and Rothney)

FIGURE 58

fifth grade class, we will typically find some fifth graders who are as bright as eighth graders, but these fifth graders are not treated in the same way as eighth graders. We do not expect as much of the fifth grader in terms of social responsibility as we do of the eighth grader. Parents typically supervise more of the younger child's activities. The younger child's present stage of development necessarily limits his opportunities for learning. He is not strong enough to participate extensively in body-contact sports as an older child is both permitted and frequently encouraged to do. Many of the environmental stimuli which evoke development in the older child are not provided for the younger child. In other words, the psychologically different environments of children of different ages result in substantial differences in development, even though a younger child may be more advanced developmentally in some respects.

· THE RANGE OF INDIVIDUAL DIFFERENCES

The discussion of development in the preceding two sections has emphasized the variation in patterns of development. The reader may have gained the impression that this variation is so great that developmental patterns cannot be ordered in any systematic way. We may

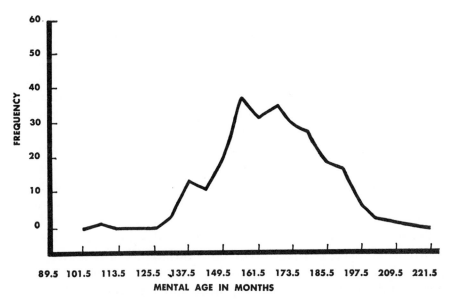

Distribution of mental ages of 256 girl subjects at age 12 in Harvard Growth Study. (After Dearborn and Rothney)

FIGURE 59

think that a teacher should expect infinitely varied patterns of development in his class. But data on differences in patterns of development may be organized in such a way that the range of variation in any behavior pattern for a group of children is predictable.

DISTRIBUTIONS OF INDIVIDUAL DIFFERENCES. We have noted that the complex interaction of hereditary and environmental influences results in considerable variation in behavior development. We expect

419

to find various levels of development for any behavior pattern in a group of children. We may order these differences in the following way. First, select a particular behavior pattern that we may wish to study, such as intellectual development. Second, choose a random sample of a group within which we wish to study variation, such as school-age children or sixteen-year-old girls. Third, obtain a measure of development status for each child in the sample by giving an intelligence test, for example. At this point we will have scores for each child in the group, and we may count how many children have obtained each score. These data may be conveniently plotted as in Figure 59.[20]

Note the clustering of frequencies around the average; the majority of children obtain scores at or near the average. We find decreasingly fewer students with progressively higher and lower scores. This ordering of the data gives us a picture of how variation in developmental status for one behavior pattern is distributed, and it enables us to make predictions about the variation in this kind of behavior to be expected in a random sample of children.

This kind of distribution of differences is obtained for many behavior patterns both over a wide age range and within specific age levels.[21] Such a distribution does not give us information on individual developmental rates, for which we would need plots of individual changes over time. Neither may we infer from these data the relative influence of particular factors affecting the development of a child. What we do have is a picture of how variation is distributed for a group. But other data are required before we can make judgments about individual rates of development and the factors influencing them.

THE RANGE OF INDIVIDUAL DIFFERENCES IN SCHOOL ACHIEVEMENT. This kind of distribution is obtained when we order differences in behavior patterns that are of immediate concern to the teacher. For example, within any class the achievement in school subjects may range anywhere from two to six or more grades above and below the grade at which the child is actually placed. Hildreth,[22] in sum-

---

[20]*Ibid.*, p. 175.

[21]Not all behavior patterns are distributed in this way. For an example of another kind of distribution likely to be obtained under certain conditions, see F. H. Allport, "The J-Curve Hypothesis of Conforming Behavior," *Journal of Social Psychology*, 5 (1934), 141-83.

[22]G. Hildreth, "Individual Differences," in W. S. Monroe (ed.), *Encyclopedia of Educational Research* (rev. ed.), New York, Macmillan Co., 1950.

marizing a series of studies on the range of achievement in classes, notes that in one group of seven-year-olds scores range from the first to the sixth grade level, and for a group of ten-year-olds the range was from the first to the ninth grade level.[23] Cook has pointed out:

> When a random group of six-year-olds enters the first grade, two percent of them will be below the average of four-year-olds in general mental development and two percent will be above the average of eight-year-olds. Disregarding the extreme two percent at either end, there is a four-year range in general intelligence. By the time this group has reached the age of twelve (sixth grade level) the range will have increased to almost eight years.[24]

REDUCING THE RANGE OF INDIVIDUAL DIFFERENCES. Most teachers are aware of the range of differences in their classes, and they have been concerned with providing learning experiences appropriate to the various levels of developmental status. One common assumption is that "good teaching" will reduce the range of individual differences or, in other words, that given appropriate learning experiences, all students can achieve the same level of development in school achievement. Such an assumption ignores the fact that differences among students result in part from the influence of factors over which the teacher has no or little control. None the less, the possibility remains that "good teaching" may reduce the range of individual differences in those behavior patterns in which development depends in some degree on the kinds of environmental stimulation the teacher can provide.

The evidence on this latter point is mixed. Some investigators have found increased variability after a specific learning experience, others have not.[25] This research does suggest that the assumed relationship between learning experience and reduction in range of individual differences is too broadly conceived to permit precise investigation. Note that we have not yet defined "good teaching"—having used only a vague and general conception as it is frequently stated. Consider

---

[23]See also W. W. Cook, "Individual Trait Differences in Public Schools with Implications for School Organization and Curriculum Development," *Teachers College Journal*, 19 (1947), 56-59, 67-70.

[24]W. W. Cook, "Individual Differences and Curriculum Practice," *Journal of Educational Psychology*, 39 (1948), 141.

[25]For a summary and analysis of this research, see L. E. Tyler, *The Psychology of Human Differences*, 2nd ed., New York, Appleton-Century-Crofts, Inc., 1956, pp. 466-72.

for a moment what might be meant by "good teaching." We are probably referring to a complex of variables, each of which in turn is complex. "Good teaching" probably presupposes that students are motivated to learn; we have already seen how complex is the variable called "motivation." In fact, every variable we have discussed in the preceding chapters is related in some way to "good teaching." To explore this problem adequately, we will have to investigate the influence of variation in each and all of these variables on individual differences. From this kind of research we could determine precisely which variables in a learning experience are likely to reduce the range of individual differences in a specific behavior pattern.

It is important for the teacher to understand the exact meaning of this discussion. We are not suggesting that appropriate learning experiences will not influence an individual child's developmental status; such experiences may radically influence the development of some children and will probably influence the development of all children in some way. However, the problem we are discussing here is whether learning experiences can be so organized that the *range* of differences within a group is substantially reduced. It is this question that we have said can be answered only by an extensive investigation of the influence of many specific variables.

At the present time the safest generalization we can make is this: the range of individual differences is not likely to be reduced by the learning experiences typically provided for children in a system of mass education. The range of individual differences is a fact with which every teacher must contend. There is no way to eradicate the differences among children. These differences originate because children have different capacities, have had different learning experiences, and are developing at different rates.

When a teacher meets a class he must be prepared to expect a range of differences. Such a range will typically be found at every age and grade level. We label children "third graders" and "fourth graders," but we cannot think of the children in the third grade class as identical units. The educational significance of this fact is that a uniform curricular experience cannot be provided for every child at a given age level. Learning experiences are more likely to be effective in promoting development when they are geared to individual levels of development.

PREDICTING DEVELOPMENTAL STATUS

Data on developmental patterns are gathered in two ways: by a *longitudinal* study, in which a group of children is tested or measured on a given behavior pattern over a period of time; or by a *cross-sectional* study, in which children at different age levels are measured on the behavior pattern. Using data from both kinds of study, we may compute the average of these measurements at each age level, and plot a continuous curve of averages. Figure 60 is an example of curves derived in this way. Such curves give us a picture of what, in the groups tested, is the typical pattern of development for specific kinds of behavior.[26] As we have already noted, these curves mask the range of variability about the average, but they are useful for depicting the general pattern of behavior development.

CONSISTENCIES IN DEVELOPMENT. These curves reflect relative consistencies in development for many children. The relative consistencies suggest that the factors influencing development affect large numbers of children in substantially the same ways. Environmental opportunities may be relatively constant within a culture or subculture, so that children in it tend to profit from the opportunities in substantially the same manner. As the data on the mountain children illustrate (see Table XXII), when the environmental opportunities are different from those in other parts of the culture, the pattern of development may be also different.

Another factor contributing to consistency in development among children is physical growth toward maturity, which provides the biological basis for behavior development. Again, when physical maturation is inhibited by some environmental influence, such as disease, or by hereditary deficiency, the pattern of development may be affected. The observed consistencies in development are the basis for the concept of "normal" development. The usual meaning associated with this concept is this: a child's development is "normal" when it approximates the average pattern of development for children of his age and with his environmental opportunities.

The term "normal" has unfortunate connotations. Its use by some people is meant to include the idea that marked deviations from the average are "abnormal." This usage may be criticized on the

---

[26]Dearborn and Rothney, *Predicting the Child's Development*, p. 312.

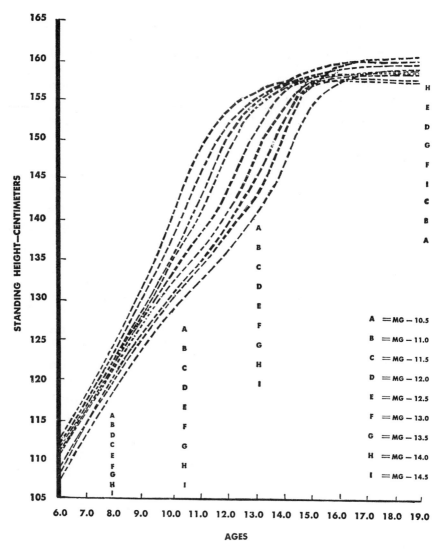

Growth trends in average standing height of nine groups of girls having different ages at maximum growth (MG). *(From Dearborn and Rothney)*

FIGURE 60

ground that it may imply more than the simple fact of marked deviation from an average. For example, an exceptionally bright child is markedly deviant from the average of his age group: he obtains high scores on intelligence tests, and he may perform in a superior fashion both academically and socially. But he is rarely "abnormal" in all the ways connoted by this term.[27] Some people also use the concept to mean that the pattern of average development is the "expected" pattern of development for all children. The use of the term "normal" to connote "expected" is inappropriate if we mean by "expected" that children should be like the "average." Our discussion of factors influencing development and the range of individual differences suggests that such a conception is naive. But a defensible meaning may be given to the term "expected" because we may use curves of average development to make predictions about children's development. If, for instance, a distribution of differences in developmental status is similar to that in Figure 59, we would predict that a majority of the children tested have attained a developmental status approximating the average. Less than half the children will be markedly different from the average of the group. In other words, "expectations" may be predictions about the developmental status of a group of children.

It is important that we distinguish between the data provided in developmental curves and the inferences we make from them. A developmental curve describes developmental status. We cannot infer from this curve what children ought to be like, although we may predict what a group of children will probably be like in terms of developmental status if they are similar to the children on whom the measurements were made.

THE CONCEPTS OF EARLY AND LATE MATURATION. The concept of "normal" development has limited usefulness, but it has been the basis for the development of the concepts of *early* and *late maturation.* A boy or girl who matures early reaches maximum development before the average age for attaining it. A boy who matures late is one who attains his maximum growth beyond the average age for reaching it. Figure 60 illustrates an application of these concepts to one aspect of physical growth. The girls who reached their maximum height at an earlier age are early maturing girls; as the curves indicate, these girls were consistently taller than the late maturing girls until all girls had reached their maximum growth. This fact illustrates another important principle. Since the curves indicate that the early

---

[27]L. M. Terman *et al., Mental and Physical Traits of a Thousand Gifted Children,* Stanford, California, Stanford University Press, 1925. See also L. M. Terman and M. H. Oden, *Genetic Studies of Genius,* V, Stanford, California, Stanford University Press, 1958.

maturing girls eventually fell below the average height for these groups, it is clear that early superiority or inferiority is not necessarily maintained over a long age span. We cannot predict on the basis of relatively early maturity in any one behavior pattern that the child will necessarily be superior in that pattern at a later date.

The concepts of early and late maturing may not be applied to all developmental patterns. They are most appropriately applied to behavior developments which are closely tied to physical maturation. Because early and late maturing are defined in terms of the average age of maximum growth, a pattern of development must reflect a point or period of maximum growth before the concepts may be used appropriately. Maximum growth cannot be defined for some behavior patterns because the pattern of development continues throughout the life span. For example, recent evidence suggests that intellectual development may continue through adult life, even though the rate of development is not as rapid as in the early years of life.[28] The concepts of early or late maturation have little meaning in relation to this kind of development.

We have pointed out that developmental rate varies for different psychological functions and that a behavior pattern may develop at different rates at different ages. Some people have argued that there are consistencies in over-all development: that, for example, a person who is developing rapidly in one respect is likely to be developing rapidly in all others. Here is another way of stating this hypothesis: the developmental rates among behavior patterns are positively correlated. Research evidence does not support this hypothesis. For example, rates of change in physical and intellectual functions are not highly correlated.[29] The relation between physical and mental development is probably indirect. A child who is experiencing rapid physical development is more likely to expand his environmental contacts, which in turn may facilitate his intellectual and social development.

THE RELIABILITY OF PREDICTIONS OF DEVELOPMENTAL STATUS. The teacher should be concerned with a child's probable pattern of development, as well as with his present status. Many decisions about appropriate learning experiences require predictions of future developmental status. At the end of the elementary school period a decision

---

[28]N. Bayley, "On the Growth of Intelligence," *The American Psychologist*, 10 (1955), 805-18.

[29]E. M. Abernethy, "Relationships between Mental and Physical Growth," *Monographs of the Society for Research in Child Development*, 1 (1936), No. 7.

is made about the kind of high school curriculum in which a child is most likely to succeed. A comparable kind of decision may be made by the elementary school teacher about the child who has demonstrated musical talent. Should this child be encouraged to develop his talent on the assumption that he may be able to succeed in a musical career? Implicit in both of these decisions is a prediction that on the basis of the child's present development he will or will not reach a level of development requisite for success in some activity.

How reliably can future status be predicted? Our discussion of the factors influencing variability in development suggests that such predictions are not likely to be perfectly reliable. Obviously, we cannot know all the factors which may influence development at some future date; we can only assess the probability that a person at a present level of development will be at a comparable level at some future time. We can ask this sort of question: What is the probability that a child who now demonstrates intellectual superiority will be intellectually superior in five years?

The general question whether future status can be reliably predicted cannot be answered until we ask a host of more specific questions—questions like the one posed about intellectual superiority. Still, some general principles have emerged from the extensive investigations of this question:

1. A long-term prediction is likely to be less reliable than a short-term prediction.[30] For example, we are more likely to be accurate in predicting a fifth grade child's sixth grade school achievement than in predicting his high school or college achievement.

2. The greater the superiority or inferiority in development, the more likely it is that this superiority or inferiority will be maintained. The child who is highly superior to his age-mates in intellectual development is likely to maintain his superiority.

Important qualifications of both these principles must be made. A long-term prediction is more likely to be reliable if it is made at

---

[30]R. L. Thorndike, "The Effect of Interval between Test and Retest on the Constancy of the IQ," *Journal of Educational Psychology*, 24 (1933), 543-49. Also by the same author, " 'Constancy' of the IQ," *Psychological Bulletin*, 37 (1940), 167-86, and "The Prediction of Intelligence at College Entrance from Earlier Test," *Journal of Educational Psychology*, 38 (1947), 129-48.

a later phase in the development of a behavior pattern. For example, predictions of a child's future intellectual status tend to be more reliable the older the child is at the time the prediction is made. There are important technical reasons for this greater reliability of prediction at later ages. For example, intelligence tests administered to younger children probably do not measure the same aspects of intellectual development that are measured by tests used with older children. Performance on early tests is not highly correlated with performance on tests administered to older children.[31] Still, the greater reliability of these predictions in later phases of development may also result from the cumulative effects of development. An older child may be reaching the point of maximum growth in the development of a behavior pattern, and the stabilization of development contributes to the improvement of prediction. In other aspects of development, previous learning influences the extent to which a child is likely to profit from new experience. Finally, development may have stabilized because environmental opportunities for additional development are not available. In all of these cases, our prediction of future status is more likely to be reliable because development has stabilized.

A qualification must also be made to the second principle. Recall the description of changes in height for early and late maturing girls (see Figure 60). Relative superiority in this kind of development was not uniformly associated with later superiority. The more direct the influence of native endowment on behavior development, the less reliable are our predictions of relative future status. In other words, early superiority is not highly correlated with final status in this development pattern. Again, if the prediction of future status is made near the time of maximum growth, it is more likely to be accurate.

Our predictions of future developmental status are probability statements made on the basis of present knowledge. Such statements are more or less reliable depending on the information available for making them. Many factors—the kinds of test instruments we use to assess developmental status, the stability of the environmental conditions in which the child is developing, and the time interval between present and predicted status—are related to the accuracy of our predictions.

---

[31]N. Bayley, "Consistency and Variability in the Growth of Intelligence from Birth to Eighteen Years," *Journal of Genetic Psychology, 75* (1949), 165-96.

The following example will illustrate the difficulties in making predictions of future developmental status.

Intensive study of life history data and intelligence test performance frequently reveals events in a child's life which have probably affected his general level of intellectual functioning.[32] Figure 61 shows the IQ performance and life events for three children. There is no proof that the life events listed in the figure caused the changes in

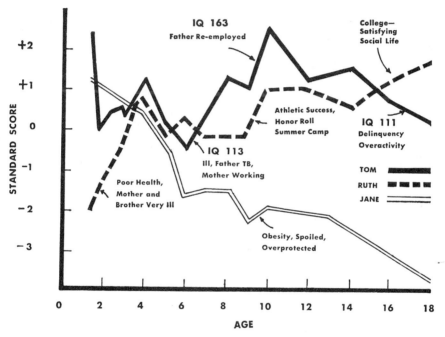

Three cases showing changes in general ability from 2-18 years (From Honzik, Macfarlane, and Allen)

FIGURE 61

IQ score. There is reason to believe, none the less, that events of this kind will affect intelligence test performance and general intellectual functioning. Compare the performance of Ruth and Jane. Ruth's initial performance is relatively low, but she gradually progresses: after a series of rewarding experiences, the curve continues on up

[32]See M. P. Honzik, J. W. Macfarlane, and L. Allen, "The Stability of Mental Test Performance between Two and Eighteen Years," *Journal of Experimental Education,* 17 (1948), 309-24.

through college. Jane, on the other hand, starts initially high and shows a progressive decline. Tom shows considerable variability, with his intelligence test scores ranging from very high points to much lower points. The teacher who had Tom in class at age ten may have thought that he was an exceptionally intelligent boy. If the teacher had been asked at that time to make a prediction about Tom's future status, he perhaps would have suggested that Tom ought to go on to college and enter one of the professions. If a teacher were studying Tom's intelligence test performance at age sixteen, he would predict that Tom's academic future was not a particularly bright one.

In this discussion we have emphasized two important principles: (1) the development of a child's psychological functions may vary considerably over a period of time; (2) predictions of future status may be more or less reliable, depending upon the time when the child is being studied and the stage of development of the particular functions being studied. The teacher's primary task is to test the child's present stage of development since learning experiences are planned for this stage of development. The relationship of present to future status is crucial when important decisions for the child's life must be based on predictions about his future. When such predictions must be made, they can probably be improved if we take into account the whole pattern of the child's previous development, the comparative development of the specific functions we are assessing, and the span of future time bridged by our prediction. If the child's pattern of development in any function has been irregular, if he is at a stage in which the function has not reached its maximum level of development, and if we are making a long-term prediction, then our predictions are likely to be less reliable. On the other hand, if the functions we are assessing are relatively stabilized, if there has been a relatively consistent pattern of development, and if our prediction is for a relatively short period of time, then the prediction is more likely to be reliable.

DEVELOPMENTAL TASKS

We have been emphasizing both the variability and the consistency in behavior development. Now we will discuss a theory which attempts to account for the consistencies in behavior development and relates development to effective socialization. This theory links two familiar ideas: (1) that similarities in behavior development result in part from common processes of maturing; (2) that similarities also result from the influence of common environmental opportunities. As we have seen, these two categories of influence on development are mutually interdependent. The theory of *developmental tasks* proposes that these two factors are interrelated in such a way that a pattern of expectations for development emerges. This pattern of expectation is reflected in the kinds of behavior patterns a child is expected to acquire and in the developmental goals he is expected to attain. In turn, socializing agents, such as parents and teachers, reward the child for attainments and punish him in some way for failures to achieve developmental expectations.

DEFINITION OF A DEVELOPMENTAL TASK. If we look over the entire span of development from infancy into adulthood we can conceive of this period as a series of tasks which the individual must perform successfully. Some of the tasks are closely related to bio-physical development: a child must learn to walk and to feed himself. Other tasks have been set by the society in which the child is growing up. In our society, for example, a child is expected to prepare himself for gainful employment. As a child masters the sequence of tasks set for him, he becomes an adjusted member of his society; that is, he acquires behavior that is rewarded and valued in his culture.

Havighurst, who introduced the concept of the developmental task into psychological and educational thinking, defines *a developmental task* as follows:

> . . . a task which arises at or about a certain period in the life of the individual, successful achievement of which leads to his happiness and to success with later tasks, while failure leads to unhappiness in the individual, disapproval by the society, and difficulty with later tasks.[33]

Note that the definition of a developmental task relates behavior development to social expectations for development. But, social expectations are not associated with every aspect of behavior development. Hobbies, for example, may have little if any direct social significance since there are no uniform and consistent social expectations that children develop hobbies. In other words, developmental

---

[33]R. J. Havighurst, *Developmental Tasks and Education*, New York, Longmans, Green & Co., 1952, p. 2.

tasks represent accomplishments expected of all children unless there are special incapacitating conditions, such as the effects of disease, that make them impossible. The definition also requires a systematic time sequence in the arrangement of these tasks. They do not occur at random, but instead, one accomplishment sets the stage for the next.

What are these developmental tasks? Empirical investigation is needed to identify the general social expectations for development, as well as to find the extent to which accomplishment of any one task affects the accomplishment of other tasks and general social adjustment. Lists of such tasks, at present, are based on inferences from sociological and psychological investigations. As might be expected, such lists vary with the preferences of different authors for classifying social expectations. These descriptions, however, have some common characteristics which suggest the general nature of developmental tasks.

CHARACTERISTICS OF DEVELOPMENTAL TASKS. Table XXIII gives a list—adapted from Havighurst—of developmental tasks that characterize American society. The following factors should be noted:

1. *Some of the tasks are common to all cultures and occur at about the same period of time in every culture.* The tasks are closely tied to the bio-physical structure and development of the child. In all cultures children learn to walk—and they learn to walk at about the same age.

2. *The character of some of the tasks is closely tied to specific cultures.* The age for choosing an occupation varies from culture to culture, as does the age for marriage. The kinds of occupations available in a society, the mores of courtship, the social customs associated with marriage, vary from one culture to another. While children in different cultures may be mastering the same general tasks, the specific behavior patterns differ and the ages at which the tasks are to be accomplished are different.

For culturally bound tasks, variations may take place even within a given culture over a period of time. The age of marriage is gradually changing in American society so that the average age of marriage is now a younger one than it was twenty or thirty years ago.

Age Span	Developmental Tasks
Infancy and Early Childhood	Learning to Walk Learning to Take Solid Foods Learning to Talk Learning to Control the Elimination of Body Wastes Learning Sex Differences and Sexual Modesty Achieving Physiological Stability Forming Simple Concepts of Social and Physical Reality Learning to Relate Oneself Emotionally to Parents, Siblings, and Other People Learning to Distinguish Right and Wrong and Developing a Conscience
Middle Childhood	Learning Physical Skills Necessary for Ordinary Games Building Wholesome Attitudes Toward Oneself as an Organism Learning to Get Along with Age-Mates Learning an Appropriate Masculine or Feminine Social Role Developing Fundamental Skills in Reading, Writing, and Calculating Developing Concepts Necessary for Everyday Living Developing Conscience, Morality, and a Scale of Values Achieving Personal Independence Developing Attitudes Toward Social Groups and Institutions
Adolescence	Achieving New and More Mature Relations with Age-Mates of Both Sexes Achieving a Masculine or Feminine Social Role Accepting One's Physique and Using the Body Effectively Achieving Emotional Independence of Parents and Other Adults Achieving Assurance of Economic Independence Selecting and Preparing for an Occupation Preparing for Marriage and Family Life Developing Intellectual Skills and Concepts Necessary for Civic Competence Desiring and Achieving Socially Responsible Behavior Acquiring a Set of Values and an Ethical System as a Guide to Behavior
Early Adulthood	Selecting a Mate Learning to Live with a Marriage Partner Starting a Family Rearing Children Managing a Home Getting Started in an Occupation Taking on Civic Responsibility Finding a Congenial Social Group
Middle Age	Achieving Adult Civic and Social Responsibility Establishing and Maintaining an Economic Standard of Living Assisting Teen-Age Children to Become Responsible and Happy Adults Developing Adult Leisure-Time Activities Relating Oneself to One's Spouse as a Person Accepting and Adjusting to the Physiological Changes of Middle Age Adjusting to Aging Parents
Later Maturity	Adjusting to Decreasing Physical Strength and Health Adjusting to Retirement and Reduced Income Adjusting to Death of Spouse Establishing an Explicit Affiliation with One's Age Group Meeting Social and Civic Obligations Establishing Satisfactory Physical Living Arrangements

A List of Developmental Tasks (From Havighurst)*

TABLE XXIII

*See Havighurst for a more detailed description of these tasks. Havighurst discusses the biological and cultural basis of these tasks, and variations in the tasks in different social classes in American society. He also explores the educational implications of these tasks.

433

3. *Some of the tasks need to be learned only once at a given period in life.* The child learns to walk, and, once he has mastered this task, he is never required to learn it again unless he is handicapped in some manner. A child learns to take solid foods and to feed himself, and, again, except in unusual circumstances, the essential features of development need not be relearned.

4. *Some tasks are recurrent and new aspects of the tasks must be learned at different ages.* The child's learning of his sex role is a continuous kind of task. The child begins to learn his sex role quite early in life and establishes his major expectations about how a boy or a girl is to behave. His conceptions of his sex role will vary with increasing experience and he will modify his behavior accordingly. The adolescent, for example, discovers a whole new dimension of his sex role with the advent of puberty.

5. *Some of the tasks occur at different ages or in different forms within a given society.* A child from a lower socio-economic group will probably make decisions about occupations and marriage earlier than the middle or upper class child who postpones marriage and career for more years of education. A child from the lower socio-economic class also learns different attitudes and values for some tasks. A middle- or upper-class child is taught to inhibit aggression or to express it in more subtle ways—restrictions not characteristically placed on the child in a lower social class environment. Sexual mores also vary with social classes.[34]

DEVELOPMENTAL TASKS AND ADJUSTMENT TO SOCIETY. The basic assumption in the theory of developmental tasks is that failure to meet developmental tasks successfully results in poor adjustment to society because failure in one task increases the probability of failure in others. This assumption appears to be reasonable. As the child develops, his needs are met through social interaction. His

---

[34]See A. C. Kinsey, W. B. Pomeroy, and C. E. Martin, *Sexual Behavior in The Human Male,* Philadelphia, W. B. Saunders Co., 1948.

needs for approval, affection, prestige, and status can be satisfied by acquiring behaviors that are socially valued. Society ties the satisfaction of needs to the achievement of developmental tasks, and it also fosters the development of needs which motivate the accomplishment of these tasks. Failure to master a task prevents need-satisfaction, and inadequate behavior development interferes with adaptive goal-seeking behavior. Inappropriate behavior development also evokes social punishment and exclusion.

Research evidence suggests that this assumption is tenable. Schoeppe and Havighurst[35] studied intensively the achievement of thirty adolescents on five developmental tasks: (1) learning an appropriate sex role; (2) achieving emotional independence of parents and other adults; (3) developing conscience, morality, and a set of values; (4) getting along with age mates; (5) developing intellectual skills. From their data the investigators concluded that the early period of adolescence is the crucial one in which changes in level of accomplishment take place, and that the level of achievement on these specific tasks is largely determined by age thirteen. (This and the other conclusions might be modified with an investigation of a larger number of students.) They also found that satisfactory relations with fellow students seemed to be closely linked to accomplishment of the other tasks, that achievement of the appropriate sex role was important, and that failure to accomplish one task adequately may be compensated by more successful accomplishment of another task.

The data also indicate that adolescents do not move through these developmental tasks in lock-step fashion. A variety of factors will determine whether a child will accomplish a particular task. A highly socialized adolescent is successful on most, if not all, of these tasks, whereas a child making a generally poor adjustment has failed at one or more of the tasks.

The differences in rate of accomplishment on the tasks results in part from the particular environmental influences that children meet. The influence of the culture is transmitted through significant individuals in the culture, such as parents and teachers. A study of the factors affecting success in the accomplishment of developmental tasks has revealed:

---

[35]A. Schoeppe and R. Havighurst, "A Validation of Developmental and Adjustment Hypotheses of Adolescence," *Journal of Educational Psychology*, 43 (1952), 339-53.

The fact that children whose parents exercise severe control in their formative years were hindered on accomplishment of the tasks. . . . Such severe parental control stifles the growth of emotional, personal security and results in the child's sensing himself as worthless as an individual; when he feels ego-impelled this inner feeling brings with it guilt feelings which he must repress.[36]

The social conditions under which children learn developmental tasks affect both the level of accomplishment and the manner in which they learn the tasks. A convenient way of conceptualizing the developmental tasks is to visualize them on a continuum of dependence-independence. As the child accomplishes each of the developmental tasks, he acquires greater personal autonomy and also greater social freedom. Each of the tasks requires some assumption of personal responsibility and initiative by the child. The successful accomplishment of a task is hampered if parents and teachers in his environment rigidly restrict freedom so that his learning opportunities are limited. Developmental tasks are essentially problems that the child must face and, as we noted when studying problem-solving, a problem cannot be solved unless the problem solver has freedom to explore his environment and to investigate alternatives for the solution of the problem. Freedom to explore and test alternative solutions to the problems posed by developmental tasks is a necessary condition for successful accomplishment of these tasks.

THE SCHOOL AND DEVELOPMENTAL TASKS. Havighurst is persuasive on the point that the theory of developmental tasks has important implications for the organization of learning experiences:

First, it helps in discovering and stating the purposes of education in the schools. Education may be conceived as the effort of the society, through the school, to help the individual achieve certain of his developmental tasks.

The second use of the concept is in the timing of educational efforts. When the body is ripe, and society requires, and the self is ready to achieve a certain task, the teachable moment has come. Efforts at teaching which would have been largely wasted if they had come earlier, give gratifying results when they come at the *teachable moment,* when the task should be learned.[37]

---

[36]A. Schoeppe, E. A. Haggard, and R. J. Havighurst, "Some Factors Affecting Sixteen-Year-Olds' Success in Five Developmental Tasks," *Journal of Abnormal and Social Psychology,* 48 (1953), 49.

[37]Havighurst, *Developmental Tasks and Education,* p. 5.

This point of view does not demand that the entire curriculum be organized around developmental tasks. However, the school assumes responsibility for the achievement of many of these tasks, while sharing the responsibility for some tasks with other social agencies. The essential point of this conception is that relating the learning experiences provided by the school to the accomplishment of developmental tasks would presumably insure consistency in the development of the child. Furthermore, the arrangement of learning experiences in terms of "teachable moments" is likely to increase the chance of a child profiting from the learning experiences provided by the school.

This theory suggests a way of relating the factors influencing development to the pattern of learning experiences which are provided to promote development. The theory calls our attention to the fact that social demands as well as maturational factors influence the course of development. Further, it relates development to the adjustment of the child as a member of society. In these respects, it is useful for clarifying our conception of the relation of development to the organization of learning experiences.

The theory does not solve all the problems associated with analyzing and predicting development that we have outlined in this chapter. All the concepts bearing on variability of development are also applicable to the accomplishment of developmental tasks. Individuals will vary in the rate at which they accomplish the tasks, but a general consistency in the total pattern of development will be apparent—largely because the opportunities for learning many of the tasks are age-graded. The probable relationship between accomplishment of developmental tasks and success in the many specific tasks the child must accomplish in school suggests the relevance of this theory. Radical or frequent failure in the major phases of development probably has a pervasive effect, spreading over the entire life of the child and affecting his performance in many particular learning activities.

SUMMARY

In this chapter we have studied how behavior patterns change with time. We have explored such questions as: Is there a consistent pattern of personality development? To what extent are there similarities in the personality development of individuals in the same culture? To what extent are there differences in development among individuals? What are the sources of both consistency and variability in personality development?

1. The consistency of personality development is reflected in the characteristics of the general process of development. Development may be described as a continual process of acquiring new responses and integrating them with previously acquired responses. The possibilities for future development are determined in part by the individual's present state of development; that is, the effects of development are cumulative. An individual's present state of development is the "equipment" with which he meets new opportunities for development. Present developmental status determines the likelihood of continued development—as well as the ways in which this development is likely to progress.

2. The pattern of personality development is influenced by hereditary and environmental factors. Behavior patterns as such are not directly inherited, but hereditary factors may have a more or less direct influence on behavior development. Some environmental factors have a relatively indirect influence on development; others are direct stimuli to behavior development.

3. Hereditary and environmental factors influence both the consistency and the variability of personality development. Hereditary and environmental influences form a pattern from which we can determine the probability of relatively consistent development. Varying combinations of hereditary and environmental influences account for the variations in behavior development among individuals.

4. Variations within general patterns of consistency characterize individual development. The behavior patterns of an individual vary in rate of development. When individuals are compared in terms of their developmental status within a specific behavior pattern, a wide range of variation in developmental status is typically found. This range of individual differences reveals the effect of the compound influence of hereditary and environmental factors.

5.   Teachers must frequently make, or help children to make, decisions based on predictions of future developmental status. Variations in the rates of individual development make such predictions difficult.

6.   Growth curves derived from measuring the developmental status of large groups of children provide us with a picture of average developmental change within a given group of children. However, individual development may vary considerably, although not necessarily from this "typical" pattern of development.

7,   Long-term predictions of developmental status tend to be less reliable than short-term predictions. Such long-term predictions are more likely to be reliable if the development of the behavior pattern being studied is relatively superior or inferior. In general, predictions of developmental status require adequate information on the genetic and environmental history of the child as well as on factors likely to influence present development. Caution is urged in making predictions about the developmental status of behavior patterns more directly influenced by maturational factors, for advanced or retarded status in these patterns is not highly correlated with final developmental status.

The theory of developmental tasks has been introduced to account for the relative consistencies in development among members of the same culture or subculture. Developmental tasks require the acquisition of behavior patterns and the attainment of goals which satisfy cultural expectations for development within a society. A major hypothesis in this theory is that successful accomplishment of developmental tasks increases the likelihood of progressive development and a correspondingly successful adjustment to and assimilation into society.

This conception of development as a succession of problems to be solved may be used to coordinate the efforts of the school and other social agencies in promoting the development of the child.

In this chapter we have been concerned with the patterns of development that characterize an individual and that are shared by members of a society. In the following chapter we will again explore the complex entity called *personality*. We will study personality as a unity and in terms of learned patterns of interaction with environmental influences, particularly other persons.

STUDY AND DISCUSSION QUESTIONS

1. Listed below are three broad categories of behavior patterns. Describe the kinds of expectations that adults hold for an eight-year-old, a fourteen-year-old, and an eighteen-year-old for each of these behavior patterns. Be specific about the kinds of behavior that are expected of children at each of these ages. Are there common expectations for all age levels for these behavior patterns?

   a. Table manners.

   b. Personal grooming.

   c. Friendship relations.

2. What kinds of experiences related to the age of a child might facilitate the learning of the expected behaviors, at each age level in the above behavior patterns?

3. Again, using the same behavior patterns as in Question No. 1, describe the response differentiations required as the child develops more complex patterns of behavior. What response integrations are required as the behavior patterns become more complex?

4. In what ways may a "mature" ten-year-old and a "mature" sixteen-year-old be alike? In what ways may these two children be different? What criteria are you using to evaluate maturity?

5. You may have heard some adults refer to a characteristic, such as becoming "easily angered," in the following way: "He gets that from his father's side of the family." Do such statements reflect an assumption that this kind of personality characteristic is inherited? Can you offer an account in terms of the kinds of experiences the child may have had which would explain the development of this particular characteristic? Is there any hereditary base for the development of a characteristic of this kind?

6. Describe some kinds of learning experiences that may be available to boys that are not available to girls. Describe some kinds of learning experiences for girls that may not be available to boys. In what ways will these different kinds of experiences influence development?

7. A teacher, in discussing a child with his mother, suggested that the child might be mentally retarded. The mother stated that she was not surprised since an older brother and sister had been slow in school. These children were first gen-

eration Mexican-American. How would you account for this child's apparently low level of achievement and intelligence test performance? (A study of Chapter Sixteen on intelligence tests may improve your answer to this question.)

8. Refer to the Kahl study presented in Chapter Four. Discuss the results obtained in this study in terms of the influences of hereditary and environmental factors on the college aspirations of the boys studied in this investigation.

9. Classify each of the following as an organic or behavioral environmental influence. Suggest some of the ways each of these environmental factors may influence behavior development.

   a. A poor diet.

   b. A nagging mother.

   c. A home in a "deprived" neighborhood.

   d. An older brother.

10. Review the data presented on the intelligence test performance of the mountain children. How might heredity have influenced the development of intelligence among these children? How might the interaction of heredity and environment account for the performance of these children on intelligence tests?

11. You observe a boy in your class who is somewhat smaller than the other boys in the class and who is also comparatively shy and quiet. Do you see any relationship between these two observations? Suggest some hypotheses that would relate physical size to personality traits, such as shyness or quietness. What other factors may account for the development of these traits?

12. Describe what seem to be the characteristics of adolescents as many adults expect to find them. Suggest factors in the experiences of children which may account for the development of these characteristics.

13. Many adults expect adolescents to have quite different value standards than adults do. For example, parents assume that children will have different value standards than parents for such things as dating, use of the family car, and the hour for returning home at night. Identify some value standards on which younger children may differ from their parents. What factors in the experiences of children and adolescents may account for the fact that they hold different value standards than their parents?

14. Recall the discussion of the identification process in Chapter Seven. By relating the identification process to acquisition of values, evaluate the parental point of view that adolescents are rebellious and have different value standards than adults.

15. A parent complains that his son is irresponsible in taking care of his personal property, such as his clothes and athletic equipment. The parent attributes this

irresponsibility to the fact that the boy is now an adolescent. Trace the kinds of experiences that this child may have had over a period of years that would account for his failing to learn responsible behavior.

16. Assume that you are counseling a high school sophomore who wants to become an engineer. What kinds of predictions about future developmental status will you have to make in order to counsel this pupil? What kinds of information do you need in order to make these predictions?

17. Assume that you are studying an eighth-grade student with a view to counseling him about his high school program. Which of the following kinds of predictions can you make more reliably?

    a. A prediction of his grades in senior English.

    b. A prediction of his probable performance in junior-year mathematics.

    c. A prediction about his height and weight when he is a junior.

    d. A prediction about his sociability when he is a junior.

What kinds of information would you need in order to make any of these predictions.

18. Refer to Figure 61. In what ways might the life-events listed in this figure account for the changes in intelligence test performance for each of the three children whose scores are reported in this figure?

19. Refer to Table XXIII. Note that Havighurst has listed "achieving a masculine or feminine social role" as a developmental task for middle childhood and adolescence. In what ways might the period of infancy and early childhood influence the learning of an appropriate sex role? Does the omission of this developmental task from later periods in life imply that the appropriate sex role is to have been learned by the end of the adolescent period?

20. Describe some ways in which a child in the period of middle childhood learns to "achieve personal independence." What kinds of experiences may contribute to successful accomplishment of this developmental task?

21. Select any one of the periods from infancy to adolescence and describe the kinds of learning experiences that the home, school, and other social institutions provide to facilitate the accomplishment of the developmental tasks listed for that period.

22. Suggest some ways in which failing to select and prepare for an occupation in adolescence may interfere with the total development of a child.

23. Describe the ways in which various aspects of the curriculum and extra-curriculum may contribute to the accomplishment of the developmental tasks of adolescence. In what ways do the experiences provided in the elementary school contribute to the accomplishment of the developmental tasks of middle childhood?

RECOMMENDED READINGS

The first reading is a more extended discussion of the concepts of heredity and environment. The second reading is a comprehensive work on child development and contains discussions and analyses of research on aspects of development. The third and fourth readings are general books on child development and provide additional information on the details of development. The fifth reading is an extended discussion of the concept of developmental tasks. The remaining readings are selections from authors whose theoretical positions on development differ in some respects from the point of view presented in this chapter, and provide many provocative ideas related to child development.

1. A. Anastasi, *Differential Psychology*, 3rd ed., New York, The Macmillan Co., 1958, Chapters 3 and 4.

2. L. Carmichael (ed.), *Manual of Child Psychology*, 2nd ed., New York, John Wiley & Sons, 1954.

3. S. Pressey and R. Kuhlen, *Psychological Development Through the Life Span*, New York, Harper & Brothers, 1957.

4. A. Baldwin, *Behavior and Development in Childhood*, New York, The Dryden Press, 1955.

5. R. Havighurst, *Developmental Tasks and Education*, 2nd ed., New York, Longmans, Green & Co., 1952.

6. J. Piaget, *The Language and Thought of the Child*, New York, Harcourt, Brace & Co., 1926.

7. J. Piaget, *Judgment and Reasoning in the Child*, New York, Harcourt, Brace & Co., 1948.

8. J. Piaget, *The Moral Judgment of the Child*, New York, Harcourt, Brace & Co., 1932.

9. H. Werner, *Comparative Psychology of Mental Development*, rev. ed., New York, International Universities Press, 1948.

PERSONALITY AND
THE SELF-CONCEPT

In the preceding chapters we have been discussing ways in which aspects of personality are acquired and how the general pattern of personality development is influenced by the capacities and experiences of a child. We have emphasized the relationships of the psychological processes to one another and to the development of the total personality, and we have conceptualized personality development as a process of behavior change.

The process of behavior change has two principal characteristics: (1) patterns of behavior become progressively differentiated through new discriminations; (2) the patterns become progressively integrated through a process of generalization. Thus, differentiation and generalization characterize the changes both in particular aspects of personality and in the development of personality as a whole.

In other words, personality structure becomes both more complex and unified. Personality structure is more complex in the sense that the individual is capable of responding to his environment in more diversified ways, but the pattern of re-

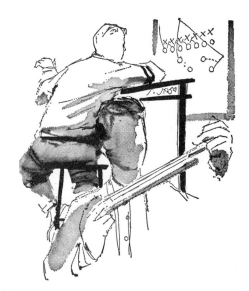

sponse tends to become more unified as response patterns are generalized to many particular situations.

Three major problems which are relevant to personality development remain to be discussed. First, we must amplify our understanding of the relative stability of personality development—particularly as reflected in patterns of social adaptation. Second, we need to discuss personality development and structure from the viewpoint of the person himself. Among the many concepts an individual acquires is his concept of himself as a person. How is this concept acquired and in what ways does it influence behavior change and social interaction? How is the consistency of personality development influenced by the person's concept of himself? Third, we need to explore the general characteristics of the socialization process as they influence the consistency and stability of personality development.

In this chapter we will be following two lines of thought. We will first study complex aspects of personality structure—specifically, the learning of role expectations and behaviors necessary for social interaction within a given culture and the development of a concept of self. With this analysis we will have completed our description of major components of personality. We will then relate the development of personality to the socialization process, an idea that we introduced in the first chapter. At that time we noted that personality development is continuous. An elaboration of the socialization process will help us account for the relative consistency, stability, and progressive unification in personality development.

This chapter may serve two purposes for the reader: (1) to complete his picture of the components of personality structure; (2) to clarify his understanding of the influence of social and cultural factors on personality development.

How are these factors related to the model of personality presented in Chapter Three? In the model the major aspects of personality are illustrated in a particular sequence of behavior change. In discussing this model, we have noted that it could be used to describe both personality as a whole and individual events of behavior change. We may analyze Jane's behavior at a more complex level in terms of categories represented in the model. For example, Jane is a student, and writing a feature article for the student newspaper is one behavior sequence in a complex series of activities she embraces by "being a student." Jane has learned a set of behaviors appropriate for students. Included in this comprehensive category of student behaviors are such activities as studying, attending class, choosing courses, speaking with teachers in a manner that is characteristic of a student in a situation of this kind, and many other actions we regard as appropriate to Jane's student status. This whole complex of behaviors, which we will refer to as a role, may be analyzed in the same way as the particular sequence of behavior change involved in writing a feature article. Analyses of complex behavior will illustrate the progressive integration of many aspects of personality and the generalization of behavior patterns from many specific environmental contexts.

In these analyses, we may conceive of Jane as acting within a particular context that we may call the "behavior space." Jane's conception of this context and of her relation to it will influence her actions in it. In analyzing the act of writing a feature article, we may describe the way Jane sees herself in relation to the context in which her action is carried out. The goals she believes she wants and her conception of her ability to attain them—these are aspects of her conception of herself in relation to this context of action.

We may also analyze Jane's total behavior as a student in the same way. This context is more comprehensive and the behavior patterns are more complex; but we may nevertheless conceptualize Jane as a behaving self within this larger context.

In either of these analyses we study a sample of Jane's behavior from which we make inferences about aspects of her personality, her conceptual development, her attitudes, her values, her concept of and behavior in the student role, her concept of herself as a personality. From many observations of this kind and with techniques that provide us with additional data, such as tests or interviews, we may form a picture of Jane's personality as a whole.

The description will be elaborate, complex, and detailed, but we can organize it on the basis of the categories provided in the model. Our discussions here will enable us to analyze the more complex units of behavior, which are integrations of many aspects of personality and which facilitate the individual's interactions in many contexts. We will also complete our description of the major components of personality structure.

ROLES AND ROLE BEHAVIOR

The concept of a role affords a convenient means of describing systematically the multitude of social interactions that occur within a social system such as a school, community, or level of society. Any social system may be described by listing the roles enacted within it.

The acquisition of role behaviors may also be conceptualized as an aspect of personality development. Role behaviors are complex units of behavior in which many different concepts, attitudes, values, and skilled responses are integrated into a generalized response pattern. In this section we will study roles from the viewpoint of persons learning them; that is, we will be concerned with roles as behavior patterns to be learned.

ROLES AS STABILIZED RESPONSE PATTERNS. Let us follow John as he comes to school in the morning and meets various people. As he enters the school he happens to meet the principal, whom he greets in a friendly manner. The principal asks him how he is doing in school, and John answers that he is doing "fine." After a brief chat during which the principal does more talking than John, John moves down the corridor and meets a group of his fellow students in front of the lockers. As they talk, John becomes a little more boisterous, speaks somewhat more frequently, tells Bill that he's a "stoop." In this brief meeting there is much good-natured "kidding" and jostling, an exchange of information about last night's dates, and expressions of hope that the day won't be "too tough." John then moves into his first period class. He takes a seat quietly and gets out his books and papers. As Mr. Henning, the teacher, begins the lesson, John follows attentively, asks questions, and participates in discussion. He carefully notes down the assignments. At the end of the class hour, John stops to ask Mr. Henning some questions that occurred to him during the lesson. They chat in a friendly way, and John listens attentively to the information and opinions offered by his teacher.

In this brief description, we see some rather obvious changes in John's behavior as he interacts with different people. We notice the respect and deference that he accords both the principal and the teacher. With them he is quiet and reserved, though with the teacher he does not hesitate to ask questions and exchange ideas. With his fellow classmates he is much less reserved, is freer in his comments, expresses his feelings about them as individuals, and puts up with some good-natured "ribbing" from them. If we observed John over a period of time, we would notice a general consistency in the ways in which he interacted specifically with the principal, his fellow classmates, and his teacher. We may observe some variations from day to day, but these variations in behavior will be within relatively well-defined limits. On one day he may be quieter with his fellow students and "kid" less with them, or on another he may be a little more forward with his teacher; but rarely, if ever, does he go beyond certain limits in his relations with these people. If John exceeds these limits, that is, if his behavior becomes inconsistent with what is expected of him as a student, his deviations may be explained in one of two ways: (1) that he has not learned what behavior is expected of students; (2) that his deviations from expected behavior give him need-satisfaction which cannot be gained by behaving consistently with expectations.[1] Except in such cases, John's behavior is consistent with a general set of expectations about what constitutes "appropriate" student behavior.

In each interpersonal situation, John is enacting a role. To enact this role, John has had to learn what behavior is expected of him and has had to learn what behavior to expect of his principal, his fellow students, and his teacher. He does not expect to be "kidded" by his teacher in the same way that his fellow students can "kid" him, and he would probably be horrified if the principal jostled him around in the same way that his classmates do. John also knows that he cannot treat the principal the same way that he would treat his fellow students, and he has learned that there are many things that he can do with his classmates that he cannot do with his teacher.

When we know an individual's relation to some members of a social system, we can predict the behavior patterns he will probably follow when he interacts with the others. These relatively predictable patterns of behavior vary with the relation of one person to another within a social system. The relation of one member to another is defined by their *positions* in the system.

THE CONCEPT OF POSITION IN A SOCIAL SYSTEM. A social system may be viewed as a complex organization of positions. The functions of individuals in achieving the common goals of a society define the system of positions in that society. For example, the common goal of the members of the school social system is the promotion of desirable behavior changes in certain members of this social system. Functions such as teaching and administering are carried on to achieve this

---

[1]"Deviation" as used here refers only to behavior patterns that are markedly different from those expected in a given social situation. It does not refer to "abnormal" personality patterns or "personality deviations" in the sense in which these terms are typically used.

goal; both of these functions define positions in the system, namely, those of the teacher and the principal. The position of student is defined by the function of being taught or of learning: a student is a person whose function in the school social system is to learn.

Positions in a social system are typically defined by the functions that may be carried out by many different individuals. The position of teacher is occupied by many persons, and though these individuals may vary in the way in which they carry out the functions of the position, we agree that the common function of the position "teacher" is to teach. In other words, positions tend to have stabilized conceptions of functions associated with them, even though the functions may change with time and although there may be disagreements about the specific characteristics of a function.

In any social system, the concept of the function of a position is shared by the members of the system. Positions in the system are interdependent and, in many cases, are reciprocal in character. The function of teaching cannot be carried out if the function of learning is not also carried out. In other words, the functioning of the system as a whole requires that the members occupying different positions perceive the relationship of their position to other positions in the system. The members of the system share common assumptions about who does what and for what purposes.[2]

An individual almost always belongs to more than one social system and, as a consequence, he occupies many different positions in various social systems. An adolescent, for example, occupies one position as a member of his family, another as a student, and perhaps still others as members of various school organizations. He also occupies the position of adolescent in the general structure of American society, within which he will also occupy a position as member of a particular social class.

Some positions are temporary in character, that is, individuals remain in these positions for only a portion of their lives. Other positions, such as male member of society, are occupied for an individual's entire life. Some positions may be occupied only once, such as the the position of marriage partner. Some kinds of positions will be occupied by all members in a society, such as those defined by age, sex,

---

[2] These assumptions need not be formalized or explicitly stated. It is sufficient that they be "understood" by the members of the social system and that they be communicated by the behavior of the members.

and social class. Other kinds of positions will be occupied by an individual only if he belongs to a particular social system.

The concept of position enables us to conduct two kinds of analysis: (1) of the structure of social systems and (2) of the influence of occupancy of positions on personality development. We are concerned with the second of these analyses in this chapter.[3] To analyze position occupancy further, we need to consider the concepts of role and role behavior.

DEFINITIONS OF ROLE AND ROLE BEHAVIOR. *A role is a set of expectations about how a person in a given position in a social system should act and about how the individuals in a reciprocal position should act. Role behavior* or *role action* is the observable behavior related to these sets of expectations. John's social position in the school is defined as that of a student, and the reciprocal positions are those of other students, teachers, and school administrators. *The student role* is the set of expectations that John has about how he should act in a social system in which he is called "student" and about how the teacher should act with respect to him as a student.

John has also learned specific ways of acting as a student. In relations with his teacher his behavior is respectful and perhaps even deferential. With his fellow students he is less deferential and indulges in such ritualized behavior as back-slapping and friendly pushing. John has learned standards of behavior for his role as a student, and these enable him to interact appropriately with other members of the school social system.

Role expectations are complex concepts acquired by an individual occupying a position in a social system. They are essentially shared conceptions of appropriate or desirable ways of behaving. These expected ways of behaving are assumed to be consistent with maintaining position functions so that group goals can be attained. For example, a child who is a "discipline" problem is behaving inconsistently with the role expectations for a student; for, although his behavior may attain need-satisfactions for him, it is regarded as inappropriate within the context of the class situation because it interferes with the attainment of the group goals. He will be urged to acquire the shared role concepts and behavior. Considerable social

---

[3]The study of social structures is the object of sociological investigation; however, in Chapter Seventeen we will discuss one such structure, the school, in order the explore its influence on personality development.

pressure may be brought to bear on him to understand and act in accord with these expectations.

An individual's adjustment to a social system is facilitated by his learning of role expectations and behaviors. In any social system, once an individual has identified his position with respect to the other members of the system, he knows how to act, provided that he has learned the role expectations for that position. If John meets someone in the corridor whom he has never met before, he knows how to act toward him as soon as he has identified him as another student.

TYPES OF ROLES. A complex society has many positions and many arrangements of positions within it. John is a student in the school social system and a child in the family social system. He may be a

member of school organizations, such as the athletic teams and clubs; he may belong to the Boy Scouts; he may be a member of the church choir; he may be a newsboy. Each of these memberships represents a different social position and each requires John to have certain role expectations and behaviors. John shifts roles as he moves from one social position to another. In his home he lives the role of a son and a brother; in school, the role of a student, a member of the football team, a member of the band, a member of the French club. In his neighborhood he may enact the roles of the boy next door and of the local newsboy. As John moves in and out of each of these social situations, his behavior changes in accordance with his expectations of how he and the other people should act in these situations.

If we look at societies or groups as a whole, we find this:

> All primary societies, irrespective of whether they stand alone or function as units of larger integrations, have certain features of organization in common. All of them divide their membership into various categories based on differences in age and sex. All of them differentiate certain individuals or groups of individuals from the rest of society on the basis of specialized occupations. All of them include within their organization smaller, internally organized units of two sorts: (1) family groups, membership in which is established on the basis of biological relationships, real or assumed, and (2) association groups, membership in which is established on the basis of congeniality and/or common interest.[4]

Role expectations and behavior are associated with the various memberships. Each individual in society is a member of one or more of these social systems. It is necessary that he learn the role expectations and behavior associated with these memberships if he is to interact successfully with other members of these groups. But no individual has to learn all the roles available in his society, and, as we have already indicated, many roles are *temporary* for the individual who performs them.

HOW ROLES ARE LEARNED. A child must be motivated to learn a role. The acquisition of role expectations and behavior is a way of attaining goals that will satisfy the child's needs. The five-year-old entering the kindergarten learns the role behaviors of a child in school,

---

[4] R. Linton, *The Cultural Background of Personality*, New York, Appleton-Century-Crofts, Inc., copyright 1945, pp. 61-62. Reprinted by permission of the publisher.

and as he does so, he receives approval from his parents and his teacher; this satisfies the child's need for approval. In a similar manner, the satisfaction of other needs—for affection, for achievement, for status—may be associated with acquiring appropriate role expectations and behavior.

Learning some roles requires abandoning others. This is likely to occur if the change is associated with need-satisfaction. A student may give up one role and learn another one because he thinks that the new role will produce more need-satisfaction. A senior will terminate his education at the end of high school because, by entering an occupation, he will achieve goals that will satisfy needs which cannot be satisfied by continuing to enact the role of a student. If he has a relatively strong need for independence, he may feel that by getting a job he will satisfy his need for independence. Other students will continue the student role through college because it is likely to lead to need-satisfaction for them.

The concepts, attitudes, and specific performances associated with role behavior are learned in the same way that any kind of concept, attitude, or performance is learned. John's concept of his masculine role can be learned if he sees instances or examples of masculine behavior. As he perceives examples of masculine behavior, he forms a concept of its characteristics. His attitudes about being a man are learned by identifying with male individuals. As John identifies with his father, he takes on his father's attitudes about being a man. Similarly he learns the performance requirements of the masculine role. He learns, for example, that men dress a certain way and have characteristic ways of talking, and he acquires these behaviors by imitating them.

Because a role involves many concepts, attitudes, and actions, the learning of a role is a complex and frequently time-consuming process. Some information about roles is acquired incidentally, and some of it is taught formally. However, it is usually communicated through socializing agents in a society who have themselves acquired relevant role behavior. John's father will comment to John on appropriate masculine behavior. He may provide need-satisfactions for appropriate masculine behavior and withhold satisfactions when the behavior is inappropriate. Boys are told "Don't act like a girl" or "Crying is for girls." A girl is told that "Ladies don't act that way." Through such communications, a child learns the behaviors expected of him in a given role. Many social systems have formalized training programs for teaching rituals associated with membership. When the initiate demonstrates that he has acquired the appropriate behavior for a role in the groups, he is given the privileges of full membership.

McClelland,[5] in discussing a case history, presents an analysis of how a child may have learned different role expectations and behaviors from his father (see Table XXIV). In the left-hand column of the table are classifications representing broad categories of roles that Karl will have to learn; in the middle column, some of the specific problems associated with the learning of these roles; in the right-hand column, Karl's statements about these particular problems and how they have been solved by his father. Karl, for example, has learned something about the control of children by observing the fairly strict discipline in his own home. He has learned something about work habits by observing the thoroughness of his father. From these interactions with his father, Karl learns how he can meet these

[5]D. C. McClelland, *Personality*, New York, The Dryden Press, 1951, pp. 299-300.

Status Classification	Associated problems	Role adjustments
I. *Family or kin*	*Problems facing a father*	
	1. Family support	"My father has always made a living for his family even during the depression."
	2. Nurturance of children	"My parents always took time to read us the funnies and play games with us . . . (they) love all their children."
	3. Control of children	"Our discipline at home was fairly strict."
II. *Age-sex*	*Problems facing an adult male*	
	1. Work habits	"My father is very thorough in all that he does . . ."
	2. Outlook on life	". . . but is excitable and constantly worried by everyone's troubles."
	3. Recreation	"His chief diversion is gardening."
III. *Occupation*	*Problems facing a skilled tradesman*	
	1. Job fluctuations	"My father is a skilled mechanic. During the depression he worked at everything."
	2. Job adjustment	". . . dislikes his present job to the point where he would like to quit and raise chickens "
IV. *Association*	*Problems facing a Christian*	
	1. Belief	"My father says very little though he claims Christianity as his faith."
	2. Church attendance	"Neither parent goes to church."
	3. Ethical dealings with others	"Nevertheless both parents are kind, rather generous, and have done quite a bit of community work in the past."

Role Adjustments Made by Karl's Father (From McClelland)

TABLE XXIV

same problems and also what to expect of men who occupy positions similar to those of his father. Out of these observations, Karl develops a conception of the masculine role, and the father-aspect of the masculine role. The fact that Karl has an opportunity to observe his father does not mean that he will necessarily think and act like his father, but if he identifies with his father, we would expect Karl to adopt some of his father's concepts, attitudes, and ways of acting.

In Chapter Seven we discussed the connection between a model and the acquisition of attitudes. There we stressed that the mere presence of a potential model does not guarantee that the person will take on the attitudes of that model. Similarly, for the learning of role behaviors, a role model will be imitated only if the child wants to learn the role, perceives the model as a representative of it, and identifies with the model.

To summarize, two general conditions facilitate role acquisition: (1) the learning of a role must be associated with need-satisfaction; (2) stimulus events must be available to the learner from which he may infer the relevant characteristics of the role. Role acquisition is a complex form of problem-solving in which the learner tries alternative ways of enacting a role. The likelihood that a person will acquire a role is influenced by the extent to which his attempts at role enactment lead to need-satisfaction.

To illustrate the principles that we have been discussing, consider the following example of a highly specialized role. One of the most important roles in Wabash School was the "queen role."[6] The complexity of that role is apparent in the following description:

> The queen's throne was a slippery place, made so by the intense competition for the office with accompanying risks in the social capital for any aspirant who chose to compete for the honor and failed.
>
> Functioning as a model for behavior among girls throughout the school, the office of queen was highly selective in the social type that achieved it. Its behavioral counterpart, the "queen role," integrated a complex set of expectations centered in the primary values of the adolescent female sex role: namely, beauty, approved dress, moral character, democratic personality, scholastic achievement, exercise of influence, and school service....
>
> As a type the queen had to be "sweet and natural in appearance," to have beauty, "prettiness," or at least "good looks." She must be physically attractive, but not "sexy"; careful in tasteful grooming and appearance; not "cheap in makeup"; well, but not expensively dressed according to the approved pattern and not "showy" nor a style setter in dress. Democratic behavior ranked high in the requirements for the queen; it was necessary for her to be "friendly to everyone and not snobbish," and equally popular with boys and girls. Clique membership was a liability, for many a girl had wrecked her hopes by exclusiveness in her associations.

---

[6]C. W. Gordon, *The Social System of the High School*, Glencoe, Ill., The Free Press, 1957, p. 57 ff.

The queen type had to be datable but usually did not "go steady" unless she dated a politically useful boy, who tended to be a casual or "nondater." A middle ground between too much and too little success with boys had to be maintained, or else she alienated both boys and girls. Better still, she had to lean in the direction of a "girl's girl," for queens were heavily supported by the Girls' Athletic Association . . . .

The moral character of the queen had to be above reproach. Drinking, smoking, and profanity were disapproved unless indulged with discretion. Virtue, and unquestioned virtue, was a major qualification. Girls who were "cheap" need not aspire.[7]

The expectations for the queen role are clearly defined and universally known among students. Previous queens serve as role models both for girls who aspire to the role and for students who vote for the queen in terms of the role expectations. The following quotation from an eleventh-grade girl who was not successful in the queen competition illustrates the process by which the students acquired the role expectations for the queen role:

In my Freshman year I attended Waterville High School, and I don't think I thought anything about being a queen. But in my Sophomore year when I came to Wabash, one of the first things that I noticed was the girls in my class and their desire to be on the court.

The first day at school I heard a discussion of who in 1951 would be on the coronation court. Various girls were named, so I thought I was as likely a candidate as any of them. So a girl friend and I set out to be popular.

This friend and I gave pajama parties to help make the girls like us. When the day was over, we would get together and add up our progress. Such things were included: what older boys had asked us for a date, or had talked to us? If any popular boy in our class talked to us or acted interested, what things could we do or say that would attract favorable attention from him?

When we did get dates, with older boys particularly, we tried in a subtle way to have them ask us to go steady. We also tried to be friends with the girls whom we heard would be 1951 Crest Court candidates. Then we tried to join every club we could, so it would look like we had done a lot for the school.[8]

---

[7]*Ibid.*, pp. 68-69.
[8]*Ibid.*, pp. 72-73

From this statement it is obvious that this girl has learned the significant characteristics of the queen role. The queen must be popular, she must be datable, and she must be of service to the school. The role expectations have been communicated and are widely shared, and the girls strive to acquire the appropriate behaviors for nomination for queen. That these expectations influence the selection of the queen is apparent in the following statement of one of the senior boys:

> We wanted someone we could be proud of. Even though Pritty Plenty was in our crowd, I voted for Violet. So did all the rest of the fellows in our bunch. Pritty had the looks but is less the queen type. We wanted someone who was sweet, who had contributed a lot to the school.[9]

The need-satisfactions associated with being queen were so great that girls strove for nomination and election to this position. A girl's need for approval, prestige, and status could be satisfied by acquiring the appropriate behavior and being elected to the queen role. For the girls, trying to be queen required problem-solving behavior. They brought to the solution of the problem all that they had learned from previous experience. The girls had learned something about being "feminine," and they used this learning in acquiring the behaviors of the queen role. They utilized their observations of the role models; they tried out appropriate role behaviors. Candidates for the role had been more successful in acquiring the requisite behavior. Though the "queen role" is temporary, the behavior patterns acquired by the candidates for it can be transferred to other roles; such transfer promotes continuity of personality development.

ROLE ACQUISITION AND THE DEVELOPMENT OF PERSONALITY. The development of a personality requires the learning of roles. The process of learning roles may be conceptualized as a series of developmental tasks which must be accomplished if an individual is to adjust to his society. Some roles have such great social utility that unless they are learned an individual cannot lead the normal life of a member of his society. A boy who does not acquire the masculine sex role has a difficult time with a wide variety of tasks in which successful performance is required by our society. He may have difficult occupational adjustments, and he may not be able to establish a satisfactory

---

[9]*Ibid.*, p. 69.

marital relationship. He is seen as a man, and he feels the social pressures reflected in the expectation that he enact the masculine role. Unless he can learn this role, he may find his adjustment to social interactions difficult and painful.

Is an individual who learns to enact a large number of roles a better adjusted member of his society? There is no simple answer to this question. Obviously, an individual must learn certain essential roles if he is to maintain his position in a social group. Once a child has learned the essential characteristics of the student role and has learned appropriate student behaviors, he can shift easily from one classroom to another and is prepared to maintain his position in almost any kind of a school environment. He may experience some difficulties in moving from one particular environment to another but, insofar as he has learned the essential characteristics of the role, his adjustment to these environments is facilitated. Some roles also require progressive adjustments at different ages, such as one's sex role, but learning the role at each stage prepares a person for these adjustments.

Since an individual will occupy positions in social systems at every stage in his life, he will need to acquire the appropriate role expectations and behaviors for many positions. Learning some of these roles is expected of all members of society; such learning is required for successful adaptation to society. The learning of other roles is not required for successful adaptation in society, but may contribute to successful adaptation because the behaviors acquired may be transferred to the learning of required roles. For example, we do not expect all children to learn the role of the local newsboy, but a child who learns this role may acquire behaviors—such as handling a job responsibly—that are relevant to other roles.

Role adjustment, defined as successful role enactment, depends on several factors.[10] We have already discussed two of these, namely, the association of role learning with need-satisfaction and the availability of appropriate information on expected role behavior. A third factor is related to the general problem of transfer of learning—namely, role expectations and behavior relevant to one learned role may be seen as applicable to other roles, and when such generalization occurs, role adjustment is facilitated. On the other hand, previous learning may inhibit new learning. For example, dependency behavior

---

[10]For a comprehensive discussion of variables influencing role enactment, see T. R. Sarbin, "Role Theory," in G. Lindzey (ed.), *Handbook of Social Psychology*, Vol. I, Cambridge, Mass., Addison-Wesley Publishing Co., 1954, pp. 223-58.

is consistent with the role expectations for younger children, but is inconsistent with the expectations for older children. An individual who has obtained need-satisfaction by acquiring a pattern of dependency behaviors may have difficulty in learning new roles because he transfers these behavior patterns to situations in which they are not appropriate.

Role adjustment is also difficult when the expectations are vaguely defined or when there is disagreement on the essential characteristics of the role. The role of the adolescent in our society may be such a role. This role typically contains expectations which are incompatible. The adolescent is expected to preserve some of the characteristics of a younger child—dependence on adults, for example. At the same time, he may be expected to demonstrate that he is capable of assuming some adult responsibilities. In such cases, the individual learning a role is likely to experience difficulty in determining the relevant role expectations and behavior.

DEVIANT SOCIAL BEHAVIOR. Roles, as we have defined them, are socially shared expectations for what constitutes appropriate behavior within a social system. Roles are institutionalized in the sense that the expectations associated with them apply to any individual occupying a position associated with a role. Deviant social behavior is behavior that is not consistent with expected role behavior.

Some individuals may not learn the expected role behavior for their position in a social system. They are considered socially deviant to the extent that their behavior is markedly different from that expected of individuals in their social position. In Chapter Seven, we pointed out that group members typically exert pressures to encourage conformity to the dominant group attitudes. Similarly, the members of a social system typically exert pressures to encourage conformity to role expectations.

In these cases the course of action taken by the individual whose role behavior is deviant depends on the likelihood that acquiring the appropriate role-behavior will lead to need-satisfaction for him. For example, the need-satisfaction associated with membership in a group may be such that the deviant individual will exert continued effort to acquire the expected behavior. In other cases, the individual may leave the social system and enter another in which the likelihood of obtaining need-satisfaction is greater; at the same time, he can preserve his present pattern of behavior. For example, a college student may join a fraternity expecting to attain the need-satisfactions associated with the social prestige of being a fraternity member. However, he may decide to leave the fraternity if he experiences difficulty in acquiring the appropriate role behavior, if he can obtain need-satisfaction in other ways, or if other need-satisfactions are more important to him.

Deviancy, as we have defined it here, is relative to particular social systems. A pattern of role behavior may be deviant in one social group but not in another; however, some patterns of behavior are regarded as deviant in practically all social groups within our society. Extremely hostile behavior, extreme physical aggression, lying, stealing, cheating are typically disapproved behaviors in most social groups. Nevertheless, there are some social groups in which these behaviors are "expected"; the delinquent group, for example, may value some or all of these behaviors.

As we have suggested at several points in this chapter, the learning of roles may be regarded as a problem to be solved. The successful solution of these problems contributes to the progressive and consistent development of personality. The learning of social roles is an essential aspect of the socialization of the child. Since the school is one of the agencies of socialization in our society, we may inquire in what ways the school contributes to the learning of social roles.

THE SCHOOL AND ROLE ACQUISITION. The school contributes to the learning of some roles because both teachers and students communicate the general social expectations for role behavior. The child learns the appropriate behaviors for his age and sex from teachers and students, as well as from his parents and other family or community members. The expectations for these roles are commonly shared, and teachers and fellow students participate in maintaining the appropriate role expectations.

The school assumes responsibility for communicating information on expectations for some roles for which society has provided no other systematic way of obtaining the role information. The school assumes this responsibility so that the majority of children will have an opportunity to acquire this information. For example, a course in vocational guidance is designed to give students role information even though some students may acquire this information in other ways. A course in home economics or family and marriage is designed to teach students role expectancies and to give them some preliminary practice in role actions, such as cooking and keeping house. The school also attempts to develop role expectancies related to the role of a citizen in a democracy.

The school alone is responsible for preliminary training for some roles. Initial role training for such occupational roles as that of engineer, doctor, lawyer, and teacher is provided by the school and specifically required by society.

In considering the contribution of the school to role acquisition, the reader will recognize that we meet again the problem of transfer of learning. Much of the training for a role occurs before the individual enacts it. An eventually successful role adjustment is the major criterion by which we evaluate the efficacy of these programs. We have explored this problem in other contexts (see Chapters Six, Eight, and Ten), and the reader may apply the principles discussed there to the particular problem of transfer of learned role expectations.

We have suggested that the role expectations conveyed in school reflect the pattern of role expectations shared by other groups and the larger society of which the school is a part. However, role expectations as conveyed in school may be overidealized, unrealistic, and inconsistent with the conception of the role as it is shared by the larger society.[11] For example, one of the ways in which children acquire role information is through reading. One study of readings used in the schools found marked differences in the portrayal of male and female roles.[12] Men were characterized as typically aggressive, achievement-oriented, and constructive, whereas women were portrayed as typically inactive, unambitious, uncreative, but sociable and kind. The extent to which such role portrayals affect role expectations and role adjustment is not known. If assimilated, such idealized role conceptions would probably affect role adjustment adversely in some respects. In any case, we need to determine the probable consequences of acquiring specific information on role adjustment and the relevancy of this information to society's conception of the role.

---

[11]For an interesting discussion of the discrepancies between role expectancies taught in some courses and the role as it is lived in the social system, see D. Lee, "Discrepancies in the Teaching of American Culture," in G. D. Spindler (ed.), *Education and Anthropology*, Stanford, Stanford University Press, 1955, pp. 163-76.

[12]I. L. Child, E. H. Potter, and E. M. Levine, "Children's Textbooks and Personality Development: An Exploration in the Social Psychology of Education," *Psychological Monographs*, No. 279, 1946.

THE SELF-CONCEPT

In our example above, John enacts different role behaviors as he moves from one situation to another. While John is in school, he enacts the role of a student, and his role as a member of the family is latent. When he leaves school, his role as a student is latent, and he begins to enact his role as a member of his family. In all of these situations he continues to enact the masculine role.

In the course of a day, a week, or over a period of time, John may enact many roles. Yet in each of the roles he sees himself as essentially the same person. Other individuals recognize him as the same person in many different situations. He is not usually referred to in one situation as "John the student" and in another as "John the child of the family next door." John and other persons see him as a unity, a totality, as being essentially the same person, though his behavior varies from one environmental context to another.

DEFINITION OF THE SELF-CONCEPT. John's conception of his integral unity as he moves from one role to another is his *self-concept*. His self-concept is the way he sees himself, the set of characteristics he associates with himself irrespective of the particular environment in which he may be at a given moment. An individual's self-concept is the set of inferences drawn from self-observation in many different situations. These inferences are descriptions of his characteristic behavior patterns.

VARIETIES OF SELF-DESCRIPTION. These self-descriptions may take many different forms if we ask a person to describe himself. John might say that he is five feet, ten inches tall and weighs one hundred and fifty pounds. He might state other physical characteristics, such as the color of his eyes and hair. He may also use descriptive trait names, such as "shy or open," "friendly or withdrawn," "talkative or quiet." He might say that he is interested in fishing and football, that he likes woodworking and mathematics. He may state why he wants to be an engineer or a doctor.

In Table XXIV, we presented a list of Karl's perceptions of his father's solutions to role adaptation problems. We suggested that these perceptions influenced Karl's conceptions of these roles. Here is Karl's picture of himself as an adolescent. What aspects of Karl's self-concept seem to have been influenced by his concepts of the roles outlined in the Table?

I was always cooperative and obedient, a good student, but influenced by others who sometimes led me into trouble. I was always sensitive and my feelings were and still are easily hurt.

I went to school, grammar school, at five, graduated at thirteen years of age. Very good marks, head of the class of eighteen. I always liked geography and history. Got the best marks in these courses. Liked math least of all although I received good marks in it. I had many friendships (got along alright with the teachers) and was regarded favorably by other boys and girls. I was always bashful around girls and was kidded a lot about it. I was very gregarious. In the younger days, third and fourth grade, I was occasionally picked on, but after a couple of fist fights I was goaded into I was left alone.

In high school my marks were excellent. I was at the head of the class, in many activities, president of the class for four years, on the football team, all-state guard, editor of the school paper. I worked well with all groups. My high school days were very happy and gratifying ones. I was very ambitious, wished to become a chemical engineer. I always did my work conscientiously and thoroughly and never wasted a minute. I always went to Sunday School, kept myself pure and led a model life. I graduated when seventeen years of age. I was confident working in groups when I knew the people, received cooperation and was usually chairman or a "wheel." I was very anxious to get ahead in the world and was very zealous toward going to college.

For amusement I played sports, went to the movie shows, etc., but not as much as the average. I was sometimes more content to sit home and read. I did a great deal of reading during my youth. I had no particular heroes. I always liked the cowboy heroes of the Westerns, Tarzan and others in the Saturday serials. I looked up to my football coach to an extent but not too greatly.[18]

In this description of himself, Karl gives us an abundance of factual data, as well as his impressions of himself. He says that he is sensitive and that his feelings are easily hurt; he also says that he was gregarious, although bashful around girls. He tells us what he wants to be—a chemical engineer. He gives us some conception of his values by telling us that he led a fairly model life.

Karl's self-concept was formed on the basis of his experiences with himself in a wide variety of situations over a long period of time. As Karl went through elementary and secondary schools, he formed impressions of what he was like. He found that he could get along with groups, that he was frequently elected chairman. He found that

---

[18]McClelland, *Personality*, p. 531.

he had no trouble in operating in a group situation. He then formed a picture of himself as an individual who is capable of working in a group and who has confidence that he can work in a group. He has a conception of himself as a successful student, based upon his experiences of successful achievement as he went through the grades. He knows what subjects he was good at and what subjects he liked and disliked.

Every individual has a concept of himself. The individual may not be aware of significant aspects of his personality, because it is too difficult for him to accept certain characteristics as being himself. Other people may see the individual quite differently from the way he sees himself. But regardless of how he is seen by others or how he describes and thinks of himself, his total picture of himself is his self-concept.

These self-descriptions may or may not embrace what we would regard as an objectively complete description of an individual's personality. In any case, the task of making a complete description either for the individual himself or for an observer would be an unending one. We do know that older and younger adults, men and women, apparently have characteristically different ways of describing themselves.[14] However, the more important task is explaining "why" an individual chooses to describe himself as he does. This question is partially answered when we understand what factors influence development of the self-concept.

THE DEVELOPMENT OF THE SELF-CONCEPT. From our definition of it, it is clear that the self-concept will change with an individual's experiences. An individual's concept of himself is necessarily limited at any stage in his life by what his experience has been. A pre-school child interacts with a limited number of people, mostly with his parents, brothers, and sisters. His picture of himself is determined by his experiences in these interactions. When he enters school he interacts with his teacher and with his classmates. New tasks are set for him, and as he is successful or unsuccessful in the accomplishment of these tasks, he makes inferences about himself. Even the children in the first grade learn quickly who is best at reading or art, even though the teacher may attempt to disguise these facts. As the child progresses

---

[14]J. F. T. Bugental and S. L. Zelen, "Investigations in the 'Self-Concept,' I. The W-A-Y Technique," *Journal of Personality*, 18 (1950), 483-98.

through school, he learns what his physical and mental capabilities are, he makes inferences about his ability to get along with other people, and he develops a pattern of likes and dislikes. During this process of assimilating new experiences, the child is continually revising his self-concept, trying to develop a fairly clear picture of himself. The self-concept probably changes throughout life.

Again, a self-concept is the set of inferences a person makes about himself on the basis of his experience. Some of these inferences may be tested in a relatively direct manner. A child's inference that he is stronger than other children may be tested in any task that requires strength for its performance. With repeated tests of this inference, the child may revise and refine his conception of his strength. He finds that he is stronger than most children his age but not as strong as most older children. In similar ways he may repeatedly check other inferences about himself. Karl, for example, checked his inferences that he could work well in groups by participating in group activities.

Since a person is interacting with other people at every stage in his life, he frequently receives descriptions of himself from other people. He may be told by his teacher, for instance, that "he isn't very good at mathematics" or that "he is bright"; his parents may tell him that "he is stubborn" or that "he is a friendly child." The child may accept these descriptions as reliable and may include these descriptions in his self-concept, saying about himself, "I'm not very good at mathematics" and "I'm stubborn."

In other cases, the child may make inferences about himself from the way in which he is treated by other people. He notes that few of his classmates choose him as a friend, and he infers that he is not likable.

That a person will accept other people's evaluations of himself should not surprise us. A parent or teacher or classmate may be an important source of need-satisfaction for a child. Accepting another person's evaluation of him may seem necessary to preserve the need-satisfaction that person provides. The child may also accept the evaluations because he has learned to trust his parents or teachers or even a classmate as a source of reliable information: "My mother says I'm stubborn; she should know."

In these ways a person's self-concept may be compounded from his own observations of himself and from other people's descriptions of him. Earlier we raised the question of why a person sees himself as he does. In general, the significant aspects of a person's self-description are the product of his inferences from self-observation and from others' descriptions of him that he has accepted. We can determine why a particular individual's self-description takes the form it does when we know what data he has used in forming his self-concept.

CONSISTENCY OF THE SELF-CONCEPT. One of the major problems in developing a self-concept is reconciling and integrating a wide variety of experiential data. To assimilate his experiences and to integrate them into a comparatively accurate picture of himself, the child learns mechanisms for interpreting what he knows and what he experiences about himself. These mechanisms for interpreting experiential data in relation to his self-concept involve complex interactions with his environment. For example, a child may have a picture of himself as friendly, warm, and agreeable. In school he attempts to make friends, but there is one student in the class who consistently rejects his overtures of friendship. The child can interpret this rejection in several ways, but he is most likely to interpret it so that his self-image will remain relatively unchanged. We are not now asking whether the child is seen by other people as friendly, warm, and agreeable; we are assuming only that the child sees himself as being like this. Our problem is to explain why he may continue to see himself in this way even though he has experiences from which he could infer that he is not friendly, warm, and agreeable.

One way of handling this inconsistent information is to explain it away or to _rationalize_. When the child rationalizes, he offers an explanation, more or less adequate, which enables him to reject the inconsistent information and maintain his original conception of himself. He says, for example, that the reason the other child does not respond to him is that the other child is really a very disagreeable kind of person or that the other child never gets along with anybody anyway. If he has found that other people see him as friendly, warm, and agreeable, his explanation may be a valid one. If his actions do not evoke friendly behavior from others, if he is not seen by other people as a warm and agreeable child, his explanation is probably a rationalization.

Another way of handling experiential data inconsistent with one's self-concept is to attribute to other people disagreeable qualities and traits which may be one's own. An individual who cannot accept the traits as his own may _project_ them, that is, he may see other people as having these traits. The child who is easily angered may see other people as easily angered, and himself as only responding to their hostility and aggressiveness. Posner[15] performed an experiment with eight-year-old children which illustrates this phenomenon. Posner divided the children up into two groups and gave them two toys to play with—one of which had previously been indicated by a child as a preferred toy and the other of which was a relatively nonpreferred toy. In one group the experimenter asked the children to give a toy to a friend. The child could give away either his preferred or nonpreferred toy. If a child gave away the toy that he did not like, he would presumably feel guilty—he had made a selfish choice. The child was then asked which toy the friend would have given away. If the child now says that he thinks the friend would give away the nonpreferred toy, we may assume the child is projecting his own feelings onto the friend. In other words, he sees the friend acting as he himself would act, and in this way relieves his guilt feelings. In the second group the children were not requested to give away toys. When the two groups were compared, much less projected selfishness was found in the second group than in the group requested to make choices. A child who wants to see himself as unselfish may maintain this concept of himself by attributing selfishness to other children.

Still another mechanism by which a person handles experiential data inconsistent with his self-concept is *denial* or *repression*. Some data that a child may receive about himself may be so threatening to his concept of himself that he cannot accept or tolerate it. A child who sees himself as a "good boy," but who lies or cheats on a test, may completely repress the memory of inconsistent behavior. He selectively remembers what has happened to him on the basis of what fits in with his concept of himself.[16] Some memories and feelings may be so denied by the individual that they can be recalled or re-experienced only in therapy, where the individual talks out his feelings and memories. Clinical experience attests to the fact that when a therapist establishes a relationship in which he accepts the patient, the patient can regain awareness of repressed memories and feelings, even though they may be painful. Repressions are largely unconscious and cannot ordinarily be recalled by the individual. In this manner, the individual

---

[15]B. A. Posner, "Selfishness, Guilt Feelings and Social Distance" (unpublished master's thesis), University of Iowa, 1940, cited in R. R. Sears, *Survey of Objective Studies of Psychoanalytic Concepts*, New York, Social Science Research Council, 1942, pp. 125-26.

[16]See Chapter Six on "Influence of Personal Factors on Forgetting," pp. 201-203, and Chapter Eight on "Influence of the Attitudinal-Evaluative Processes on the Cognitive Processes," pp. 286-293.

protects his image of himself and maintains a consistent concept of himself, even though it not be consonant with his experiences and feelings.

We have discussed three different mechanisms by which the individual handles data which are inconsistent with his concept of himself.[17] These mechanisms are complex processes of interpreting and evaluating experience. There is little experimental evidence on the factors which influence the learning of these mechanisms. An abundance of clinical evidence, and even common-sense observation, tends to support the hypothesis that they are fairly typical means by which individuals maintain a relatively consistent concept of themselves.

The consistency of the self-concept may also be maintained by self-selection of experiences likely to strengthen an individual's concept of himself. Individuals leave social systems in which the patterns of interpersonal relationships are markedly different from their preferred patterns.[18] There is some evidence to suggest similarities in personality types among the members of social systems.[19] The evidence does not prove that individuals select environments in which they are likely to have experiences compatible with their self-concepts, but this hypothesis is none the less consistent with this evidence. Again, clinical evidence and common-sense observation suggest that this hypothesis is tenable.

CONSISTENCY OF THE SELF-CONCEPT AND ANXIETY REDUCTION. The major hypothesis in this discussion has been that individuals learn ways of interacting with their environments and ways of interpreting their experience which tend to preserve a consistent image of themselves. This hypothesis appears reasonable if we make one further assumption, namely, that experience which is inconsistent with one's self-concept is anxiety-arousing. A person who sees himself as friendly but finds himself in a group that is unfriendly to him may infer that he is unfriendly and that the unfriendliness of the group is a response to his own disagreeableness. This new interpretation of himself may be anxiety-provoking. The person may then resort to one of the

---

[17]A detailed discussion of adjustment mechanisms may be found in P. M. Symonds, *The Dynamics of Human Adjustment*, New York, Appleton-Century-Crofts, Inc., 1946.

[18]See G. G. Stern, M. I. Stein, and B. S. Bloom, *Methods in Personality Assessment*, Glencoe, Ill., The Free Press, 1956.

[19]See A. Roe, *The Psychology of Occupations*, New York, John Wiley & Sons, 1956.

mechanisms discussed above to reject the inference and effectively reduce the anxiety provoked by this new interpretation of his behavior.

Why should interpretations of behavior which contradict his self-concept be threatening to an individual? This question may be answered if we recall the function of the self-concept as described in the model of personality in Chapter Three. The self-concept is inferred, that is, we infer that individuals act as if they maintained a consistent image of themselves. Within an individual personality, the self-image is a mediating variable between the experiences of the individual and the dependent variable of behavior. In other words, a person's behavior in a particular situation is a function both of independent variables, such as environmental stimuli, and the self-concept which mediates their influence. An individual interprets environmental influences in relation to his image of himself. He predicts the likelihood of environmental stimuli influencing his behavior from his own expected reactions to these stimuli. He may say, for example, "I will get along in this group because I like people."

The self-concept serves as a controlling or modulating influence on behavior in such a way that the individual obtains need-satisfaction: it develops in a way that increases the likelihood of obtaining need-satisfactions. If a child sees himself as friendly, he is likely to behave in ways consistent with this self-image. In so behaving, he obtains need-satisfactions, such as love and approval, from other people. But if experience tends to contradict his image of himself, anxiety is likely to be aroused because the whole behavior sequence which has led to need-satisfaction is threatened. The child perceives that the self-concept, which has been regulating behavior, may be influencing behavior so that need-satisfactions may not be obtained; this possibility is anxiety-provoking.

In the above discussion, we have been reading "thoughts" into people's adaptive processes, but it is important to remember that all we observe is behavior. We infer that anxiety is aroused, because that inference enables us to explain the behavior that we observe—such as that of rejecting interpretations of behavior that are inconsistent with the self-concept.

CONSISTENCY OF THE SELF-CONCEPT AND SELF-UNDERSTANDING. The self-concept is one of the orientation processes by which an individual is predisposed to interpret his environment in consistent ways. In this sense, the self-concept is an adaptive function of personality; however, the mechanisms for preserving the consistency of the self-image may interfere with successful adapting if the image that is preserved inhibits behavior change likely to lead to need-satisfaction. The following example illustrates the way in which these mechanisms might preserve a self-concept that is likely to lead to need-deprivation rather than need-satisfaction.

A high school student who wants to be an engineer, but has little mathematical ability, may persist in his efforts to become an engineer despite the fact that he is persistently failing in mathematics. He sees himself as having the abilities and qualities necessary to be an engineer. He also expects to achieve need-satisfaction by becoming an engineer, but he may infer from his failure in mathematics that he does not have the ability to become an engineer. To preserve his image of himself as a potential engineer, he may reject conflicting data about himself in several ways. He may have mechanical ability and, because he has, he may deprecate the importance of mathematical knowledge in engineering. He may attribute his failure in mathematics to poor teaching or poor texts or to the fact that he was doing too much other work to concentrate on mathematics. He may remember that he was quite good at arithmetic in the fourth grade and may completely ignore the fact that he failed mathematics in high school. Thus, he preserves the consistency of his self-concept; however, this self-concept may influence him to continue working for goals which are not attainable. He may want to enter an engineering school, so he takes the necessary high school courses. If he does poorly in them, he will probably not attain his goal. He is likely to be deprived of the need-satisfactions associated with becoming an engineer.

This student is probably obtaining some need-satisfaction by imagining himself as a potential engineer. He may associate with students whom he admires and win their approval by participating in their activities. He may receive parental approval because he has chosen an occupational goal that his parents regard as desirable. However, he lacks self-understanding to the extent that he does not perceive the discrepancy between what he thinks he can attain and what he is likely to attain. We say that he does not have *insight* because he does not understand the discrepancy between what he thinks he can or will do and what he is likely to be able to do.

Failures in self-understanding inevitably handicap a child since he will interact with his environment on the basis of his concept of himself. A child who sees himself as friendly, but who is not seen as friendly by his classmates and who by every objective criterion is not friendly, is not likely to change his behavior until he acquires some insight into the fact that he is, in effect, a hostile and aggressive child. The greater the discrepancy between an individual's experiences and his concept of himself, the more difficult it will be for him to adjust to his environment, particularly to the interpersonal relationships that his environment requires of him.

THE TEACHER AND THE CHILD'S SELF-CONCEPT. Throughout this book we have emphasized the importance of understanding the factors that may influence behavior change—self-concept being one of these factors. Unfortunately, in the present state of knowledge of this variable, we cannot spell out the many specific ways in which the self-concept may influence behavior change. None the less, the teacher will need to consider the influence of a child's self-concept in formulating hypotheses about behavior change.

Let us take a child who is not doing very well in arithmetic. One of our problems is to determine the factors likely to be influencing his performance. He may have inadequate mathematical concepts; he may not be interested in arithmetic; he may not be very intelligent. However, he may be doing poorly because he sees himself as poor in arithmetic and, consequently, does not select the means necessary to do reasonably good work. We formulate hypotheses that his poor performance may result from the influence of these factors. We may then proceed to check these hypotheses by gathering information on the child's previous performance in arithmetic, his intelligence level, and his self-concept.

These factors may be interrelated in complex ways. The child may have inadequate concepts and, as a consequence, has done poorly in arithmetic, and now sees himself as poor in arithmetic. In some cases, the child may be intelligent and may have done adequate work in arithmetic but, because of a few poor performances, concluded that he is not proficient. Or a child may have formed a conception of abilities from some remark made by an adult, such as "girls aren't good at arithmetic."

By making an analysis of this kind, the teacher may determine to what extent the child's self-concept is relevant to or an important determinant of his behavior.

In what ways can the teacher influence a child's self-concept?

As we have noted before, the teacher is one of many adults who describes and evaluates a child's behavior to him. The teacher may be an important source of the child's information about himself. The teacher, for example, is a major source of information about his ability to learn. It hardly seems necessary to stress that such information should be reliable if we want children to develop self-concepts consistent with their capabilities and present state of development. To facilitate self-understanding, we organize guidance programs in schools to help children clarify their self-concepts by providing them with reliable information about themselves. Both in these programs and in many less formalized ways the teacher may help children develop self-understanding.

Teachers, however, may not be able to help all children in achieving self-understanding. Some children lack self-understanding to such an extent that they require professional help before any pervasive change in their self-concepts is likely to occur. Teachers do not usually have the training to provide this kind of help, and will have to refer the child to trained therapists.

Assume that the child who is doing poorly in arithmetic is handicapped principally because of his conception of his abilities. Assume, also, that on the basis of his general level of intelligence and previous experience that we would predict that he should be doing reasonably well in arithmetic. Can we influence the child's self-concept so that he sees himself potentially as good in arithmetic? We might try several procedures, such as discussing his abilities with him. Or we might arrange his arithmetic experiences so that he is successful—in the hope that he will perceive himself differently afterwards. Here again, the teacher proceeds as a hypothesis-maker. Each alternative procedure is tried on the hypothesis that it is likely to promote a desirable change in the child's self-concept.

Our understanding of the variables which influence the development of a child's self-concept should improve the quality of our hypotheses. For example, if we know that a child has serious deficiencies in his previous training, we are not likely to hypothesize that encouragement alone will result in a change in his self-concept.

Teachers are frequently urged to help children accept themselves as they are and to respect their own intrinsic worth. This recommendation would be indefensible and naive if it meant that all patterns of personality development are in some vague sense "good." The recommendation is psychologically sound if it means that teachers may help a child to achieve a degree of self-understanding adequate for his age and developmental status, or that they may help a child use his conception of himself in obtaining need-satisfactions which are important to him. In these ways a child is helped "to accept himself." The child may be made aware of his "intrinsic worth" by being helped to achieve goals important to him in socially acceptable ways; he may then assume a place in a group which will value his contribution to the attainment of the group's goals. The child can develop a concept of his characteristics and capabilities that enables him to achieve need-satisfaction in ways that make him a valued member of a group. Presumably he will see himself as a "valuable" person because he can make a contribution that is valued by the group.

Personality development, as we have conceptualized it, is a process of progressive adaptation or adjustment. We have described each of the major aspects of personality as "orientation" processes, that is, processes which prepare an individual to interact with his environment in specific ways. However, we sometimes refer to a person as "adjusted" or "maladjusted," and, when we do, we are typically referring to his personality adaptation as a whole. "Personality adjustment" is another label for behavior change, which, however, frequently implies some criterion of "good" adjustment. In the following section, we will explore the meanings that may be associated with the concept of adjustment and their place in the total pattern of personality development.

THE MEANING OF ADJUSTMENT

Throughout the whole process of learning, a person learns many different kinds of responses or response systems—or, as we have called them, processes—which enable him to interact adaptively with his environment. Adaptation and adjustment are progressive processes. An individual may experience periods of temporary maladjustment, periods during which he has not yet learned the responses that will enable him to adapt to a particular situation. Entering school for the first time, taking on a new job, or moving into a new community, are experiences which may produce temporary maladjustment in the sense that the child has not acquired the responses necessary to interact successfully in the new environment.

DEFINITION OF ADJUSTMENT AND MALADJUSTMENT. We say that an individual is adjusted if he has learned responses that enable him to interact with his environment so that he obtains need-satisfactions while behaving in ways acceptable to the members of his society. An individual in a particular social situation can adapt or adjust to it in many different ways. In any classroom there are children with widely different personalities; yet the majority of the children have learned ways of interacting in this environment so that they obtain need-satisfactions and successfully enact the roles required of them.

We can see that there are at least two possible meanings that may be associated with the term "maladjustment." One meaning is basically a social concept: an individual is not adjusted if he has not developed a personality which enables him to interact appropriately in a given environment. The other meaning describes an individual as maladjusted if he is not obtaining need-satisfactions, even though his behavior may be appropriate for his society.

We have emphasized throughout this chapter that the two concepts of maladjustment are interrelated. A child who shouts out in class is not conforming to the standards of appropriate classroom behavior, but he may be satisfying his need for approval or prestige. Delinquent behavior may be a way of satisfying a need for aggression or prestige, but a delinquent is not an adjusted member of society. A child is motivated by certain needs and attempts to achieve goals that will satisfy them. Since the child is a social being, society attempts to develop needs that will motivate the child to seek goals and thereby acquire behavior consistent with the expectations for appropriate behavior in a given society.

In terms of our general conceptions of learning and the development of personality, poor adjustment—or maladjustment—results from inadequate or inappropriate learning.

DIFFICULTIES IN ADJUSTMENT. The learning process can break down at a number of points. The child may fail to acquire appropriate needs to motivate him toward desirable goals. In American society, for example, value is placed upon achievement. A child who does not develop some need for achievement will not seek goals and will not learn striving behaviors that are regarded as appropriate in some segments of society. Or a child may acquire behaviors in the process of satisfying his need for achievement that are not socially approved. We punish, in some way, a child who cheats on an examination; we do not encourage stealing or lying as ways of acquiring goals to satisfy achievement needs. We do not encourage a child to seek approval by acquiring dependent behavior; rather, we attempt to satisfy a child's need for approval by rewarding independent behavior.

Failures in adjustment may take place at all levels of personality. A child who is physically weak has difficulty in acquiring skills involving strength. The child who is not intellectually bright may have difficulty adjusting to the requirements of schooling. Inadequate concepts or inappropriate attitudes are potential sources of maladjustment. Failure to learn roles or being required to enact incompatible roles may result in maladjustment. Finally, a discrepancy between how one sees himself and how others see him is a potential source of maladjustment. The individual may have to learn new modes of responding to himself and to his environment. He may have to learn new concepts, attitudes, or roles, or he may have to revise his self-concept in order to obtain need-satisfaction in socially acceptable ways.

Persistent difficulty in obtaining need-satisfaction or inability to learn socially acceptable ways of obtaining need-satisfaction frequently results in the development of behavior patterns so maladaptive that the individual cannot adjust adequately in any situation. Such an individual requires special treatment to restore his ability for adapting successfully to his environment.

The adjusted person, according to our definition of adjustment, is the *socialized* person, that is, the person who obtains need-satisfactions by acquiring the behavior patterns expected from members of his society. The socialization processes in a society promote this development.

We may profitably conclude our discussion of the development of personality by studying the influence of the socialization process on the development of personality.

THE SOCIALIZATION PROCESS AND PERSONALITY

Society is not a disembodied entity, but a living complex of individuals. Within any society there are members who are already socialized, and these individuals, usually adults, communicate the values and standards of the society to the child.[20] A child learns the appro-

---

[20]For an interesting comparison of cultural differences in socialization processes, see M. Mead and M. Wolfenstein, *Childhood in Contemporary Cultures,* Chicago, University of Chicago Press, 1955.

priate behavior and develops the appropriate personality for his society largely through interaction with these socializing agents—in American society, principally parents and teachers. A child's peers, also, may influence his socialization insofar as they reflect cultural expectations in their interactions with him.

THE COMMUNICATION OF CULTURAL EXPECTATIONS. The socialization process has two aspects: (1) a set of tasks is provided for the child which must be mastered if he is to be a socialized or adjusted member of his society; (2) need-satisfactions are provided to facilitate the learning of behavior patterns required for mastery of these developmental tasks.

The environments in which a child moves are arranged to stimulate the learning of behavior patterns requisite for socialization. Responsibilities for organizing these environmental opportunities for learning are delegated to different social agencies, such as the home and the school. Socializing agents participate in the learning experiences provided and communicate the cultural expectations for relevant and appropriate learning. In these ways, the general pattern of behavior development is fostered in directions consistent with the cultural expectations.

The relation of particular learning experiences to socialization may be more or less direct. A course in advanced nuclear physics appears to be relatively remote from the socialization process, until we realize that a student may be taking such a course in preparation for a career of research in physics. The choice of a career and successful preparation for one are parts of the socialization process.

Other learning experiences may be more directly related to socialization. The study of American history may appear to be irrelevant to the socialization of the child, but a little thought will suggest its direct relevance. It is *American* history, and, in the study of American history, the school attempts to communicate to the child certain values and ideals that are directly relevant to his total development as an American citizen and as a personality who can adjust to American society. The child may also learn to value democracy and democratic processes. The high value that is placed on achievement-striving in American society may be communicated in the teaching of American history by the way emphasis is placed upon conquering the American frontier. We point out that America is a land of equal opportunity, the great "melting pot" of civilization. Through such a course, we attempt to communicate cultural attitudes and values.

Cultural expectations also are communicated in subtle ways in the multitude of interactions between the child and socializing agents, as the following example makes clear; the setting is a second grade classroom:

TEACHER: What would you think would be one of the first things to do for our play?

STUDENT: Get scenery and conversation. Get kids who can memorize it. Tell the name and speak with expression.
(Teacher nods head and replies affirmatively to each answer.)

TEACHER: But what is *the most important thing?*

STUDENT: The characters.

TEACHER: Name them.

STUDENT: Billy Goat, Gray Pony, Red Cow, Calf, Jolly Pig, Mrs. Pig.

TEACHER: What else?

STUDENT: Scenery.

TEACHER: Have you ever been in a play?

STUDENT: No, but I've seen one.

TEACHER: He's *using his head;* he's got *ideas.* Now what kind of scenery do we need?

STUDENT: Apple tree, pies, house, sky, fence, ground.

TEACHER: Would you have the outside and the inside of the house in one part? What do you call it when you divide a play?[21]

In this example of interaction between teacher and pupil, the children learn cultural values in addition to solving the particular problem of constructing a play. The teacher's emphasis on the "most important thing" reflects an important cultural value, namely, deciding what comes first. He is also emphasizing the importance of order and arrangement by discussing what is needed for the play and how it is to be arranged. Both of these values are reflected in common maxims, such as "first things first" and "everything in its place." Notice that the child who thinks receives special approval—"he's got *ideas.*"

The teacher may not even be aware that he is communicating

---

[21] J. Henry, "Culture, Education, and Communications Theory," in G. D. Spindler (ed.), *Education and Anthropology*, Stanford, Stanford University Press, 1955, p. 193.

these values. But as a socialized member of society himself, he has assimilated these values into his attitudinal and value system, and his behavior is influenced by these values. As a socializing agent, he is communicating the expectations of society to the children in his class.

VARIATIONS IN SOCIALIZATION PROCESSES. The socialization process in American society is not quite as uniform as the above discussion may suggest. In a comprehensive study of child-rearing practices, Sears found substantial differences in child-training practices between middle-class and working-class mothers.[22] In Table XXV are the data on these differences. A middle-class mother and a working-class mother do not raise their children in identically the same ways. A somewhat different system of rewards and punishments is used in the two kinds of homes. The middle-class mother, for example, apparently permits more dependent behavior than does the working-class mother, whereas the working-class mother punishes dependency more frequently than does the middle-class mother. The middle-class mother is somewhat permissive of mild sexual experimentation, whereas the working-class mother is not. A greater percentage of middle-class mothers expect their children to go to college.

The two kinds of mothers have different techniques for reward and punishment. The child of the working-class mother is praised more frequently for giving no trouble at the table than is the middle-class child. The working-class mother uses ridicule, deprivation of privileges, and physical punishment more frequently than the middle-class mother.[23]

The significance of these differences is that they foster the development of differential behavior patterns. The child of the middle-class mother has typically learned more aggression control, or at least has learned not to express his aggression in overt ways. The child of the working-class mother, though punished for aggressive activity, has a persistent model of aggression in his parents. He learns to use aggression in other interpersonal relationships, though he may learn to control his aggressive feelings within the home.

---

[22]R. Sears, E. E. Maccoby, and H. Levin, *Patterns of Child-Rearing*, Evanston, Ill., Row, Peterson & Co., copyright 1957, pp. 426-27. Reprinted by permission of the publisher.

[23]For other studies of social class differences in child-rearing practices, see A. Davis and R. J. Havighurst, "Social Class and Color Differences in Child Rearing," *American Sociological Review*, 11 (1946), 698-710; E. E. Maccoby, P. K. Gibbs, *et al.*, "Methods of Child Rearing in two Social Classes," in W. E. Martin and C. B. Stendler (eds.), *Readings in Child Development*, New York, Harcourt, Brace & Co., 1954, pp. 380-396.

Scales	Middle Class	Working Class
Median age at completion of bowel training	18.8 months	16.4 months
Percentage rated *high* on:		
Severity of toilet training	15%	26%
Permissiveness for dependency	42%	29%
Punishment, irritation, for dependency	44%	56%
Sex permissiveness (summary)	53%	22%
Permissiveness for aggression toward neighborhood children	38%	31%*
Permissiveness for aggression toward parents	19%	7%
Severity of punishment for aggression toward parents	36%	51%
Amount of restriction on the use of fingers for eating	66%	81%
Pressure for conformity with table standards and restrictions	23%	39%
Restrictions on care of house and furniture	65%	78%
Pressure for neatness and orderliness	43%	57%
Strictness about bedtime	28%	38%
Strictness about noise	28%	38%
Keeping track of child (frequency of checking whereabouts)	26%	33%*
Extent of father's demands for instant obedience	53%	67%
Importance of child's doing well at school	35%	50%
Percentage who expect child to go to college	70%	24%
Percentage rated *high* on:		
Use of praise if child gives no trouble at table	49%	63%
Use of ridicule	31%	47%
Deprivation of privileges	34%	42%*
Use of physical punishment	17%	33%
Amount of caretaking of infant by person other than mother or father	18%	11%*
Mother's warmth to child	51%	37%
Father's warmth to child	60%	56%*
Percentage showing some rejection of child	24%	40%
Percentage of mothers "delighted" over pregnancy	73%	65%
Percentage rated *high* on:		
Mother's esteem for father	54%	37%
Parents' disagreement on child-rearing policies	15%	19%*
Family authority exercised primarily by:		
Father	29%	25%*
Both equally	62%	59%*
Mother	9%	16%*

Differences in Child-Training Practices between Mothers of Two Social Classes (From Sears et al.)

TABLE XXV

*Differences between these percentages are not statistically significant.

481

Different values and needs are acquired by the children in these two kinds of homes. The middle-class child is typically achievement-oriented.[24] From early childhood he learns that his parents expect him to extend his schooling and probably to enter one of the professions or to aspire to the executive level in business. The working-class child learns that the "here and now" is important, that security is not to be sacrificed to striving for distant goals. He does not expect to go to college and does not learn to want to go to college.

Differences in specific aspects of the socialization process characterize the many social systems that are a part of our complex American society. Yet there is a pattern of socialization common to all aspects of this society. For example, a dominant cultural expectation is that children will prepare themselves to be self-supporting. Social classes, as well as ethnic and racial groups, may vary in the particular form that this cultural expectation takes. Since a child lives within a limited number of social systems, his pattern of development tends to be relatively consistent and reflects the cultural expectations for individuals in the groups to which he belongs.[25]

The effects of the socialization process are reflected in the systems of concepts, attitudes, values, skill performances, roles, and self-concepts that an individual acquires. The totality of these systems is what we call *personality*. The kinds of personalities that emerge in a society depend on the kinds of socialization processes that characterize it.

SUMMARY

In this chapter we have completed our discussion of the major components of personality, namely, roles and the self-concept. The process of personality development may be conceptualized as a process of progressive differentiation and integration of response systems. *Roles* are complex integrations of responses which are generalized to many different specific social contexts.

1.   A social system may be viewed as a matrix of positions. Posi-

---

[24]See B. C. Rosen, "The Achievement Syndrome: A Psycho-Cultural Dimension of Social Stratification," *American Sociological Review*, 21 (1956), 203-11.

[25]Students interested in the structure of American society and variations in cultural behavior patterns may find the following profitable reading: J. A. Kahl, *The American Class Structure*, New York, Rinehart & Co., 1957; R. Bendix and S. M. Lipset (eds.), *Class, Status and Power: A Reader in Social Stratification*, Glencoe, Ill., The Free Press, 1953.

tions are defined by the functions necessary to group operation and through whose maintenance group goals are attained.

2. A *role* is a set of expectations about the appropriate behavior
for individuals in a given position in a social system. Role behavior is behavior consistent with these expectations.

3. An individual needs to learn many different roles in order to
occupy positions in different social systems. Some roles, such
as age and sex roles, are expected learnings for all members
of a society. Other roles may be enacted by an individual for
periods of varying length; some roles may be enacted only
once in a lifetime; and some roles need to be learned only by
individuals belonging to particular social systems. Since an
individual occupies a position in some social system at every
stage of his life, role acquisitions are an important aspect of
the development of personality.

4. Social systems foster role learning by providing need-satisfactions for the learning and by communicating the social expectations for appropriate role behavior. Role learning may be
conveniently conceptualized as one kind of complex problem-
solving. Successful problem solution requires that the learner
attempt role behavior, making successive behavior changes
until the appropriate role behavior is acquired.

5. Successful role adjustment depends on (1) the extent to which
the learner is likely to obtain need-satisfactions by acquiring
role expectations and behavior; (2) the availability of relevant
information on role expectations; (3) the extent to which the
learner can transfer other learned response patterns to the
learning of the role. Role adjustment is particularly difficult
when role expectations are not clearly defined or when there
are conflicting conceptions of the role.

The school shares with other agencies the responsibility for encouraging role learning relevant to an individual's adjustment to society. The school communicates cultural expectations on appropriate
role behavior, though the kinds of role expectations communicated
through the school should be examined for their consistency with
general cultural expectations.

The other major component of personality discussed in this chapter was the *self-concept,* which is the set of characteristics that a person associates with himself.

6. The self-concept is formed by inferences from an individual's experiences. Such inferences may be made by inference from direct observations of one's own behavior or by assimilating other people's descriptions and evaluations of one's behavior.

7. Information about one's self that is inconsistent with his self-concept may be handled in three ways: (1) by rationalizing; (2) by projecting; (3) by denial or repression. Each of these mechanisms is essentially a way of dissociating from one's self characteristics inconsistent with the self-concept.

8. Information inconsistent with the self-concept is rejected because such information is anxiety-provoking. The self-concept presumably has been instrumental in acquiring behavior patterns that have obtained need-satisfaction. The sequence of behavior processes leading to need-satisfaction is threatened by information inconsistent with the self-concept, and this threat is anxiety-provoking.

9. An individual lacks self-understanding to the extent that there is a discrepancy between his self-concept and his experience. Lack of self-understanding handicaps an individual in his adjustment to his environment since the individual interprets his relation to his environment in part on the basis of his self-concept.

10. The teacher's understanding of a child's behavior may be improved by understanding the child's self-concept because this concept is one of the factors influencing the child's behavior. Teachers may improve children's self-understanding by providing them with reliable information about themselves. In some cases, teachers may also help a child to change his self-concept, but specific procedures for accomplishing this change cannot be given. Each procedure used by the teacher for this purpose embodies a hypothesis about the likelihood of the procedure producing changes in the self-concept.

The socialization process is the means used by society to foster the development of personality. The socialized person is adjusted to his society in the sense that he obtains need-satisfactions by acquiring socially acceptable behavior patterns.

11. The socialization process has two aspects: (1) it provides a series of developmental tasks that children master, and in the process of mastering these tasks they acquire the behavior patterns needed for adjustment to their society; (2) a system of need-satisfactions is provided to encourage the learning necessary for mastery of these developmental tasks.

12. The development of behavior patterns consistent with cultural expectations is accomplished through organized learning experiences, as in the school, and in the interactions of the child with socializing agents, such as parents and teachers.

13. Variations in specific socialization practices may be found in social systems, such as social classes, which are a part of the total society. These variations result in differences in personality development between members of these systems.

Personality is the complex integration of the components of personality that we have studied—the cognitive, attitudinal, and evaluative processes, patterns of skill performance, learned roles, and the self-concept. The development of specific behavior patterns in these components, as well as their integration into a personality, is fostered through the socialization process. Thus, personality development is a process of progressive socialization in which an individual develops the patterns of behavior which enable him to adapt successfully to his society.

STUDY AND DISCUSSION QUESTIONS

1. Using some social organization with which you are familiar, such as a club, describe the positions in the social system that comprise this organization. Identify the functions of each of these positions in relation to the achievement of the goals of the social system. What are the reciprocal positions in this system?

2. Using the same social system, describe the roles associated with each of the

positions you have identified. What are the role expectations and behaviors for each of these roles? How does an individual occupying a given position learn the role expectations for that position? In what ways do the members of the social system insure that the appropriate role expectations are learned? Are you familiar with any instances in which an individual deviated remarkably from the expected role behaviors? What were the consequences of his failure to enact the role in the expected way?

3. Describe the positions occupied by a ten-year-old child in his family, in his school, on his local baseball team, and in some club to which he might belong. What role expectations and behaviors are associated with each of these positions? What kinds of experiences are provided so that he may learn the appropriate role expectations and behaviors? What role expectations and behaviors learned in one social system may transfer to the learning of roles in the other social systems to which he belongs?

4 Describe some differences in role expectations for a student in elementary school, in high school, and in a college or university. Identify role expectations which are common to the student role in these three different social systems.

5. Refer to Table XXIII in Chapter Eleven. Analyze the set of developmental tasks outlined in that table in terms of the kinds of role expectations which are associated with the accomplishment of these developmental tasks.

6. Describe the principal concepts, attitudes, and role actions associated with each of the following roles:

   a. The role of son or daughter.

   b. The role of college student.

   c. The role of member of some club or social group to which you belong.

7. What kinds of need-satisfactions might a person obtain by learning the following roles?

   a. The student role in college.

   b. One's own sex role.

   c. An occupational role.

8. Identify several roles, the learning of which appears to be essential to successful adjustment in our society. Explain why you think that the learning of these roles is essential. By way of contrast, identify several roles which do not appear to be essential for successful adjustment in our society. Again, give your reasons for hypothesizing that the learning of these roles is not required for successful adjustment. How could you test your hypotheses in this respect?

9. What kinds of role expectations and behavior associated with the role of a high school student may interfere with successful learning of the role of a college

student? What aspects of the high school student role may be generalized to facilitate learning the role of a college student?

10. What learning experiences provided in the elementary and secondary schools contribute to learning the following roles?

   a. One's sex role.

   b. An occupational role.

   c. One's role as a citizen.

11. We have said that a person's self-concept is influenced by evaluations made of him by other people. Assume that an individual receives contradictory evaluations of himself from other people. What factors are likely to influence his acceptance of one of these evaluations?

12. In what sense is the self-concept a hypothesis about one's self? In what ways may an individual test these hypotheses about himself?

13. In each of the situations described below, explain how an individual might use one of the defense mechanisms, such as rationalization, to preserve the consistency of his self-concept. Also explain ways in which an individual may react to these situations without resorting to defense mechanisms.

   a. An average student is refused admission to a college which he wishes to enter.

   b. A muscular high school junior fails to make the varsity football team.

   c. An attractive girl is not invited to the class dance.

14. A student in your class tells you he would have done better in his last test if he had studied harder. How can you determine whether his explanation is or is not a rationalization? What kinds of information would you need in order to test the hypothesis that his explanation is, in fact, a rationalization?

15. Describe some ways in which an individual's self-concept may influence his behavior in each of the following situations:

   a. Choosing a career.

   b. Selecting a marriage partner.

   c. Selecting social organizations to join.

   d. Deciding whether or not to study a foreign language.

16. What kinds of behavior patterns are necessary for successful adjustment in each of the following situations:

   a. A child entering kindergarten.

   b. A high school graduate attending a residential college.

    c. A beginning teacher meeting his first class.

    d. A high school junior attending his first dance.

17. To what extent may the persons described in the above question be initially maladjusted in these situations? What are likely to be the consequences of failing to acquire the behavior patterns necessary to adapt to the situations described?

18. Referring to Table XXIII in Chapter Eleven, in what ways does the accomplishment of the developmental tasks described for the periods of middle childhood and adolescence contribute to the socialization of the child? What is the likelihood that failure to accomplish any one of these tasks may lead to maladjustment?

19. What kinds of cultural expectations may be learned in each of the following situations?

    a. In an American history class.

    b. In an algebra class.

    c. At a school dance.

    d. At a varsity football game.

20. Describe the kinds of social values that seem to have been emphasized in your own home. Describe incidents when emphasis was placed on the learning of these values. In what ways has the learning of these values enabled you to adapt successfully to other social situations?

RECOMMENDED READINGS

The first of the readings listed below presents an analysis of the concept of self and its relationship to motivation. The second and third readings present an extended discussion of personality in terms of the concepts that have been utilized in this chapter. The fourth reading is a review of research related to the social adjustment of children. The fifth reading is a discussion of general principles relevant to personal and social adjustment, with particular emphasis on the role of the school in facilitating adjustment.

1. E. Hilgard, "Human Motives and the Concept of the Self," *American Psychologist*, 4 (1949), 374-82.

2. T. M. Newcomb, *Social Psychology*, New York, The Dryden Press, 1950, Chapters 8-13.

3. D. C. McClelland, *Personality*, New York, The Dryden Press, 1951.

4. H. H. Anderson, "Social Development," in L. Carmichael (ed.), *Manual of Child Psychology*, 2nd ed., New York, John Wiley & Sons, 1954, Chapter 19.

5. C. Tryon and W. E. Henry, "How Children Learn Personal and Social Adjustment," *Forty-ninth Yearbook of the National Society for the Study of Education, Part I, Learning and Instruction*, Chicago, University of Chicago Press, 1950, pp. 156-82.

THE MANAGEMENT
OF LEARNING

In the preceding chapters we have considered the ways in which many different kinds of variables influence behavior change. Some of these variables were related to characteristics of the environments in which learning takes place. Others were related to characteristics of the individual learner. Still others—which we will discuss in this chapter—appear in the context of the teacher-student relationship.

At several places we have discussed variables over which the teacher has relatively direct control; among these were amount of guidance, arrangement of practice sessions, and provision of opportunities for need-satisfaction in learning experiences. We have assumed, in discussing these variables, that the teacher plays an important role in the organization of learning experiences. And, of course, the teacher's role is never confined to the impersonal; once he has arranged the environment, he is a major force in it. His own behavior is a stimulus event which influences pupil behavior, and many other features of the learning environment may be altered by the way he relates variables in order to promote changes in pupil behavior.

491

These functions may be illustrated in a hypothetical case. Mr. Johnson announces that he will deduct one point for every error in punctuation in the themes to be turned in by his senior English class. This announcement presumably follows some hypothesizing on Mr. Johnson's part about the probable influence of these penalties in reducing punctuation errors. The students in Mr. Johnson's class probably see this announcement as consistent with patterns of behavior they have come to expect from him: he is not likely to ignore errors; he expects careful work; he usually penalizes mistakes. He may also be friendly or unfriendly, kind or harsh, quick to praise good work or sparing in his praise. The students see relatively consistent patterns of behavior in Mr. Johnson's actions, and from these patterns they make inferences about the kind of person he is.

These patterns of expected behavior reflect the students' impressions of Mr. Johnson's personality. From your own experience as students, recall the descriptions that have been applied to teachers you have known: "rough," "demanding," "a nice guy," "tough but fair," "too easy on students," "a tough marker," and many others equally descriptive. Each of these terse phrases conveys an impression of a person. When we say someone is a "tough marker," we are led to expect that only a few "A" grades will be given to students in his class; we expect to meet a "no-nonsense" kind of person—a person who expects maximum effort and performance from students and one who will reward only markedly superior performances with high grades.

We would expect that the students' impressions of the teacher's personality influence their interactions with him. Mr. Johnson's announcement takes on additional meaning when seen in the light of the students' conceptions of him as a person. Assume for the moment that they know from previous experience that he is not likely to enforce his penalties. How would you expect his announcement to influence the punctuation of student themes? Conversely, suppose that the announcement is one of a long list of penalties that Mr. Johnson has been imposing and enforcing. Making any prediction is difficult without more information about the class, but we can imagine a number of possible reactions. This latest addition to the penalty list might be the "last straw" for the students; they might revolt, either openly or covertly. On the other hand, errors in punctuation might decline, but a marked decrease in creativity might appear in the themes; the students might be less willing to "let themselves go." And yet none of these unfortunate reactions might occur if the penalty is seen as a reasonable demand which Mr. Johnson tempers with understanding and encouragement. We cannot decide which of these alternatives is likely to occur until we know more about the students' conceptions of Mr. Johnson as a person. Note, however, that these alternative results appear to be reasonable possibilities when the meaning of the announcement is studied in the total context of teacher-pupil relations.

In other words, the patterns of teacher-pupil interaction are composed of variables which have considerable influence on behavior change. In this chapter we will consider those variables in the teacher-pupil relation that influence behavior change and the development of personality. We have already mentioned some effects of such variables. In discussing the teacher as an identification model, for instance, we were studying the influence of teacher behavior in changing pupil behavior.

In this chapter we will study the influence of the teacher's arrangement of learning experiences as another kind of variable. We know that behavior change results from the process of attaining goals that lead to need-satisfaction, and that the teacher controls to some extent the need-satisfactions available to students. If we ask, "What are the effects of *different patterns of control* of need-satisfactions?" we are asking a question about a variable that describes the teacher-pupil relation. We are asking this question, in a more concrete form, when we consider the probable differences in teacher-pupil relations between a teacher who seldom praises students and one who frequently does. We would expect different patterns of teacher-student relations to appear between these teachers and their respective students. As well as studying the effects of praise and blame on learning, we may study "praising and blaming" by teachers as variables in teacher-pupil relations which affect behavior change and the development of personality.

Some of the variables we will study here are classified as the "stimulus situation" in the model of personality presented in Chapter Three. We will conceptualize the teacher and his behavior toward students as stimuli likely to promote changes in student behavior.

The relations between a teacher and his class become a complex sequence of events. Arrangements of these events are designed to initiate and foster desired changes in behavior as students strive to attain goals which will presumably bring them need-satisfaction. The pattern of teacher-student relations influences both the available goals and the pattern of behaviors deemed desirable for attaining them. This complex pattern of behavior "control" is itself a variable influencing the patterns of behavior change. Insofar as it is influenced by the teacher's behavior, this pattern is itself a stimulus event that initiates and regulates pupil behavior.

We may also look at this pattern of relationships from the viewpoint of the student, again utilizing our model of personality for descriptive purposes. Many of the goals the student seeks may be mediated by the teacher. A student's need for approval, or affection, or achievement, may or may not be satisfied in particular cases because of the teacher's behavior. For example, a student with a strong need for approval is not likely to find his need satisfied in a classroom where the teacher rarely provides approval for changes in pupil behavior.

The teacher also controls to some extent the routes or means to goals. Recall that Jane's teacher encouraged her writing activities. In this way, he indicated to Jane that certain goals were available to her. He also acted on the acceptability of Jane's article; had the article been poorly written, he might have refused to accept it or he might have requested Jane to rewrite it. The stimulus situation to which Jane was responding as she sought need-satisfaction by writing a feature article included the teacher, as well as such other factors as her school, her classmates, and the availability of a teacher who had spent a year in Europe. In these ways the teacher's behavior influences, more or less directly, the development of a child's personality.

PERCEPTION OF ANOTHER
PERSON'S CHARACTERISTICS

In making judgments about the personality characteristics of other individuals, we frequently overlook the fact that our descriptions are really inferences from our observations of their behavior. At various points in this book we have noted that these inferences are influenced by the particular sample of behavior that we observe. The utility of these inferences for describing and explaining personality is also influenced by the kinds of descriptive categories that we employ in making them. For example, describing a child as a "bad actor" tells us very little about the child until we know what is meant or implied by the category, "bad actor." More impressive but equally vague categories such as "maladjusted," or "socially competent" tell us little about the kind of behavior that we might expect of an individual so described.

Our use of more or less vague descriptive categories or trait names should cause us to question the accuracy of our descriptions of other people.

SYSTEMS OF TRAIT ASSOCIATIONS. If you described a child as "intelligent," you would not also call him "stupid," unless you obtained information that required a revision of your judgment. While the meaning of these terms is not always perfectly clear, we do recognize that they cannot be applied to the same person at the same time. Similarly, a child who calls a teacher "cold" is not likely to describe him as also being "warm." Now ask yourself what traits you would expect to be associated with "intelligent." What descriptive terms occur to you immediately? You may say that a person described as "intelligent" could have almost any trait name applied to him, depending on his other characteristics. Agreed; but what traits do you *expect* to find associated with a person described as "intelligent"? If you are told that a child in your class is one of the brightest children in school, do you expect him to be "quiet," "bookish," "conceited," and "sure of himself"?

Of course, in describing anyone our descriptions will be influenced by the available information and by the extent to which we depend on direct observation of the individual in forming our judgment. But research evidence suggests that we tend to associate trait descriptions in related patterns. For example, if a group of people is asked about a set of traits they associate with "intelligent," the majority will say they expect a person so described to be "imaginative," "clever," "active," "conscientious," "deliberate," "independent," "reliable."[1] A group of people queried in this manner do not agree unanimously on all of the traits they associate with "intelligent." Greater agreement is apparent on such related traits as "reliable" and "responsible" than on such traits as "witty" and "practical." The amount of agreement on traits suggests the kinds of associations or expectations that people are likely to have about combinations of personality characteristics.

Some trait names apparently have greater influence in forming our impressions of a person than do others. Asch gave groups of stu-

---

[1] J S. Bruner, D. Shapiro, and R. Tagiuri, "The Meaning of Traits in Isolation and in Combination," in R. Tagiuri and L. Petrullo (eds.), *Person Perception and Interpersonal Behavior*, Stanford, Calif., Stanford University Press, 1958, pp. 277-88.

dents lists of trait descriptions; the lists were alike in all respects except one. The list received by one group included the trait "warm," whereas the list received by the other contained the trait "cold."[2] The students were asked to write a description of the person the traits seemed to suggest. Asch found remarkable differences between impressions of the "warm" and "cold" persons. Kelley used the trait lists to describe instructors whom students were to meet briefly.[3] Again, when the impressions of the students were collected, the marked difference in group impressions depended upon whether the instructor had been described as "warm" or "cold." Other research indicates that some trait names are less likely to produce differences of this kind and that the location of the trait name in the list also influences impressions.[4]

This research evidence suggests that we tend to form relatively consistent patterns of personality descriptions, so that we see certain traits as "going together." In other words, we acquire expectations about patterns of personality, as perhaps best exemplified in our tendency to describe individuals as "types."

The significance of this tendency is that it may operate independently of our observations of an individual, and in many cases may inhibit our observations. For example, a teacher who sees a child as "intelligent" may assume that he is "imaginative" or "reliable" without observing behavior from which he could appropriately infer either of these traits.

FACTORS INFLUENCING THE ACQUISITION OF TRAIT ASSOCIATIONS. Since comparatively little research evidence is available to suggest how trait associations are acquired, our discussion of these factors will be based primarily on deductions from generalizations we have considered in other connections.

In analyzing the concept of role expectations, we pointed out that individuals acquire a pattern of characteristics and behaviors that they associate with positions in social systems. Many role expectations are formulated in terms of the traits of individuals who occupy a given

---

[2] S. E. Asch, "Forming Impressions of Personality," *Journal of Abnormal and Social Psychology,* 41 (1946), 258-90.

[3] H. H. Kelley, "The Warm-Cold Variable in First Impressions of Persons," *Journal of Personality,* 18 (1950), 431-39.

[4] S. E. Asch, *Social Psychology,* New York, Prentice-Hall, Inc., 1952, pp. 205-21. See also M. Haire and W. F. Grunes, "Perceptual Defenses: Processes Protecting an Organized Perception of Another Personality," *Human Relations,* 3 (1950), 403-12.

position. For example, what traits do you expect in a football coach? Do you expect him to be "dynamic" and "energetic" or "shy" and "withdrawn"?

Sarbin played a variety of recorded statements to students and asked them to identify the role of the person making the statement.[5] One statement was, "All right, boys, get in there and fight!" and it was recorded in a shout by an actor described to the students as a middle-aged man. Ninety per cent of the students identified the actor as a coach. The students were responding to role behavior, but perceptions of role behavior may be and frequently are organized into conceptions of traits associated with the role. In this way we tend to assume that certain combinations of traits will characterize role occupants. In particular cases, we may assume that an individual has all the relevant role traits, or we may conclude that he has the pattern of traits from the fact that his behavior suggests one of the relevant role traits.

Some trait associations may be learned as significant ways of interpreting behavior within particular environments or in the context of pursuing particular goals. In studies of teacher characteristics valued by pupils, for instance, traits such as "kindliness," "patience," and "fairness" are chosen as traits characterizing teachers who were most helpful to students.[6] Such studies do not typically provide independent evidence of teacher behavior Still, the list of traits valued by students reflects characteristics of teacher behavior that assist pupils to succeed and to be reasonably satisfied in school. In other words, the pupils respond to characteristics most desirable to them as students.

A study of teachers' evaluations of pupil behavior suggests the same tendency: to note characteristics of pupil behavior directly related to the attainment of the teachers' goals. Schrupp and Gjerde prepared a list of traits and asked a group of teachers and a group of clinicians (mental hygienists) to rate these traits on a scale from "of no consequence" to "an extremely grave problem."[7] In Table XXVI is a list of traits rated by teachers and clinicians as most serious. In a list

[5]T. R. Sarbin and J. D. Williams, "Contributions to Role-Taking Theory: V. Role Perception on the Basis of Limited Auditory Stimuli," unpublished manuscript, cited in T. R. Sarbin, "Role Theory," in G. Lindzey (ed.), *Handbook of Social Psychology*, I, Cambridge, Mass., Addison-Wesley Publ. Co., 1954, p. 230.

[6]P. Witty, "An Analysis of the Personality Traits of the Effective Teacher," *Journal of Educational Research*, 40 (1947), 662-71.

[7]M. H. Schrupp and C. M. Gjerde, "Teacher Growth in Attitudes Toward Behavior Problems of Children," *Journal of Educational Psychology*, 44 (1953), 203-14.

Traits Rated More Serious by Teachers	Rank Difference	Traits Rated More Serious by Clinicians	Rank Difference
1. Impertinence, defiance	26.5	1. Shyness	31
2. Impudence, rudeness	26	2. Suspiciousness	27.5
3. Obscene notes, pictures, etc.	24	3. Dreaminess	25.5
4. Disobedience	24	4. Fearfulness	22
5. Disorderliness	24	5. Sensitiveness	20.5
6. Heterosexual activity	23	6. Overcritical of others	19
7. Masturbation	20	7. Imaginative lying	16
8. Untruthfulness	16	8. Nervousness	16

Traits on which Greatest Disagreement Appears when Rated by 1951 Teachers and Clinicians (From Schrupp and Gjerde)

TABLE XXVI

of fifty traits, there were only sixteen on which the rank difference (that is, the difference between the rank given by the clinicians and the teachers) was fifteen or greater. These differences between teachers and clinicians cannot be compared directly since the two groups were given different instructions for making their ratings: the teachers were asked to rate the problems *presently* serious, and the clinicians to rate those likely to indicate *future* difficulties in adjustment.

These differences are merely suggestive of the relative importance that teachers attach to various kinds of pupil behavior. The traits rated as more serious by teachers are overt demonstrations of behavior which usually interfere with classroom order; those rated more serious by clinicians are associated with symptoms of personality conflict and maladjustment. The two groups evaluated the seriousness of behavior in relation to two different contexts (induced at least in part by the differences in directions).[8] Fragmentary as this evidence may be, it is nevertheless consistent with the hypothesis that trait associations may be learned as ways of interpreting the significance of behavior within particular contexts.

An individual's self-perception, taken with his attitudes and values, appears to influence his perceptions of the characteristics of

---

[8]Studies of friendship or partner choices also indicate that the context of the choice is a relevant variable. This phenomenon appears to be similar to the one being discussed here. For data on this point see H. H. Jennings, "Sociometric Differentiation of the Psychegroup and the Sociogroup," *Sociometry*, 10 (1947), 71-9. See also H. H. Jennings, *Leadership and Isolation* (rev. ed.), New York, Longmans, Green & Co., 1950.

other people. Stagner determined the attitudes of students toward labor, and then asked the students to check traits characterizing factory workers and executives.[9] The students also checked the traits that they thought characterized themselves and rated the pleasantness and unpleasantness of all the traits in the list from which they worked. The results indicate the complexity of the relation between perceived traits, attitudes, and self-perceptions. Pro-labor students, for example, ascribed more traits to themselves that they had ascribed to factory workers and generally rated these traits more favorably. These data are consistent with the hypothesis that we are more sensitive to characteristics which we associate with ourselves.[10]

The above discussion suggests some of the ways in which an individual may acquire systematic conceptions of personality characteristics of which he is particularly aware. It follows from our previous analysis of cognitive processes as orientation processes that such predispositions to conceptualize personality characteristics in consistent ways are likely to influence teacher-pupil relations. These tendencies influence the expectations that teachers and pupils have of each other; we shall see that the character of these expectations influences teacher-pupil interaction in important ways.

TEACHERS' PERCEPTION OF PUPILS AND BEHAVIOR CHANGE. In the above discussion we have avoided the question of the "accuracy" of inferences that individuals make about other people. We would expect that if an individual is influenced more by his conception of trait consistencies than he is by his observations of behavior, his conception of the other person is not likely to be accurate. In this case inaccuracy means that the traits ascribed to a person have limited usefulness in predicting and explaining his behavior. If we assume that an "intelligent" student is also a "responsible" person, we are likely to err in our estimates of the responsibility traits of students. We can also hypothesize that such inaccuracies in our perception of pupils' personalities would affect their development adversely. Inaccurate perceptions would interfere with planning of appropriate learning experiences. We might be handicapped in our understanding of goals likely to motivate a particular student; we might also err in evaluating

---

[9] R. Stagner, "Psychological Aspects of Industrial Conflict. I. Perception," *Personnel Psychology,* 1 (1948), 131-44.

[10] See also, H. Fensterheim and M. E. Tresselt, "The Influence of Value Systems on the Perception of People," *Journal of Abnormal and Social Psychology,* 48 (1953), 93-98.

the factors likely to stimulate pupil change, or in our estimates of the factors inhibiting change.

Ojemann and Wilkinson studied the effects on pupil growth of providing teachers with more information about pupils.[11] The investigators set up two groups of students, an experimental and a control group. The teachers of the experimental group received detailed summaries and analyses of personality, as well as environmental data on the students in their classes. In personal interviews the teachers were given suggestions for improving their understanding of the children's behavior and for planning appropriate learning experiences. The investigators made periodic visits to these teachers' classes to discuss the pupils' progress. At the end of the year the investigators found significant differences in grade-point average, attitudes toward school, and personal adjustment—all in favor of the experimental group.

Many different procedures were used in this study, and care should be taken not to attribute the measured changes to any one of these procedures. We may not conclude from this study that providing teachers with more data about pupil behavior will necessarily improve their understanding of pupil behavior or will necessarily lead to marked changes in pupil progress; in addition to detailed information, the teachers were given interpretations of the data and suggestions about ways of interpreting and controlling pupil behavior. The teachers who participated in the experimental program commented that they felt they had greater understanding of pupil behavior. The experimental procedures used and the teachers' comments suggest that a reorganization of their perceptions was achieved. These changes may have made the teachers more amenable to suggestions which, if implemented, were likely to be effective in promoting behavior change.

The relationship between the teacher's understanding of pupil behavior and its changes is not a simple one; this is clearly indicated by the data from a study by Hoyt, who also studied the effects of teachers' knowledge of pupils on achievement of pupils and on their attitudes toward class work.[12] Hoyt established three levels of teachers'

---

[11] R. H. Ojemann and F. R. Wilkinson, "The Effect on Pupil Growth of an Increase in Teachers' Understanding of Pupil Behavior," *The Journal of Experimental Education*, 8 (1939), 143-47.

[12] K. B. Hoyt, "A Study of the Effects of Teacher Knowledge of Characteristics on Pupil Achievement and Attitudes Towards Class Work," *Journal of Educational Psychology*, 46 (1955), 302-10.

understanding of pupils. One group of teachers was urged to refrain from obtaining specific knowledge about individual pupils; a second group was asked to limit their study of their pupils, but was provided with copies of achievement and IQ scores for individual students in their classes, as well as distributions of the scores for the classes; the third group was given considerable information about individual pupils, and also participated in discussions about them. Subject content and the general approach in teaching methods were uniform for the three groups.

When pupil achievement and pupil attitudes were studied, however, no relationship between the teachers' knowledge of the pupils and pupil achievement was found. In other words, teachers who presumably knew more about their pupils did not produce greater pupil achievement (as measured by standardized achievement tests). However, the greater the teachers' knowledge of the pupils, the more favorable the pupils' attitudes towards teachers.

The negative evidence presented by the Hoyt study—that there is little relation between the information about pupils acquired by teachers and the achievement of their pupils—may serve to remind us that many variables influence behavior change. The teacher's perception of his pupils has been assumed to be one of these variables, but the evidence presented here suggests that the influence may be an indirect one.

Both the Hoyt and Ojemann studies treated the teacher's perception of his pupils as the independent variable and assumed that other factors influencing behavior change were relatively constant. This latter assumption probably is questionable. In the Ojemann study, for example, the teachers in the experimental group presumably individualized their instruction to a greater extent than did teachers in the control group; this effect illustrates the way in which a change in teachers' perceptions is likely to influence pupil change.

Both experiments produced attitude changes. This fact suggests the likelihood that changes in a teacher's understanding of pupils may influence some kinds of pupil change directly and other kinds indirectly. Attitudes toward school and toward the teacher changed in the favorable direction, presumably predisposing the students to be more interested in their work. Given other requisite conditions for behavior change, we would predict that pupil achievement would improve as it did in the Ojemann study, in which the pupils were studied over a longer period of time.

Devising ways of promoting behavior change is a problem for the teacher. The solutions he tries are likely to be influenced by his perception of the situation. The teacher's perception of the pupil's characteristics is one aspect of his total conception of the problem to be solved.[13] A reorientation in his picture of the student may thus stimulate new approaches to the problem. Reorganizing, expanding, modifying, or generally changing one's perception of a student is likely to be effective in promoting pupil change if these perceptual changes lead to more effective choices of ways to promote pupil growth.

TEACHER-PUPIL RELATIONS

"The educative act" is essentially a process organized to promote achievement of specified goals which represent desirable changes in pupil behavior. The educative act is directive in the general sense of being a goal-oriented process, and the specific activities that comprise the act regulate behavior in the sense that behavior is controlled in attaining the desired goals. For example, assume that a desired behavior change is that of having pupils understand the generalization: "The area of a rectangle is the product of its length and width." A complex set of activities will be initiated to foster this behavior change. In the process of carrying out the activities, certain kinds of pupil behavior will be regarded as facilitating goal attainment and other kinds as inhibiting it—the child who decides to read his history book may be reminded that this activity is now inappropriate.

MAINTENANCE OF GOAL ORIENTATION. The teacher's interactions with pupils may be conceptualized as ways of insuring goal orientation on the part of pupils, whatever the particular goal may be. The teacher establishes a pattern of relations with pupils designed to serve this general end. These patterns of interpersonal relations take many different forms and involve many different specific procedures. One teacher may be friendly and encouraging on the assumption that treating students in this way will facilitate their interest in and stimulate their activity toward goal attainment. Another teacher may remain relatively aloof from his students and have many rules designed

---

[13]For a discussion of the relation of problem-solving and perception of persons, see O. K. Moore, "Problem Solving and the Perception of Persons," in R. Tagiuri and L. Petrullo, *Person Perception and Interpersonal Behavior*, pp. 131-50.

to maintain "classroom order," again on the assumption that such procedures will facilitate goal attainment. Some teachers often praise students' efforts; others rarely praise them. Some use ridicule and sarcasm. Still other teachers feel that making classroom relations pleasant and interesting will guarantee goal orientation.

The kinds of teacher behaviors with which we are concerned in this section are those by which the teacher treats students as persons in order to facilitate their goal orientation. Again, we ask this general question: What are the effects of teacher behavior of this kind on change in pupil behavior?

THE TEACHER'S NEED-SATISFACTION IN INTERPERSONAL RELA-TIONS. Behavior used to facilitate pupil goal orientation is presumably need-satisfying for the teacher; organizing the educative act is related to the satisfaction of the teacher's needs. In this analysis, we conceptualize the teacher's interpersonal behaviors as ways of regulating pupil behavior. In some cases, a particular act of a teacher may be a way of satisfying his own needs, but it may inhibit goal attainment by a pupil. The pupil who is less than respectful in his relations with a teacher may evoke punitive behavior in some form from the teacher. The teacher's response may be directed toward satisfying his own needs rather than toward fostering desirable pupil change. We would predict that insofar as the student is aware of the intent behind his teacher's behavior, this behavior is not likely to be effective in promoting a reorientation of the student's behavior.

We may conceptualize the pattern of teacher-pupil relations as a way in which both teacher and pupils attempt to achieve need-satisfaction. The probability of changes in pupil behavior is maximized when teachers and pupils strive for mutually compatible goals that lead to need-satisfaction for both. Here we will study the factors in teacher-pupil relations that increase the likelihood of teachers and pupils working for mutually compatible and need-satisfying goals.

THE TEACHER'S CONTROL OF NEED-SATISFACTIONS. As we have seen, behavior change begins in a motivated state of the individual: the individual must want or need something. Energized by this need, he will seek goals to satisfy it. One of the ways in which the teacher controls learning is by controlling the need-satisfactions available to pupils. Some of these need-satisfactions will be intimately tied to the learning experience itself; others will be provided by the teacher in his interaction with the pupils and these may indirectly facilitate behavior change. A learning experience that does not provide need-satisfaction for the pupils is not likely to produce desired behavior changes.

One of the problems facing the teacher is that the means children have already learned for satisfying their needs are frequently incompatible with the goals of a learning situation. A child who continually requires the teacher's approval may be so preoccupied with securing approval that he does the class work inadequately. The following example illustrates a problem of this kind and demonstrates how the teacher attempted to solve it:

> Pat, a pampered first grader who lives with his grandparents, had a unique response to my suggestion that each time he required my attention without justifiable cause I would remember the times that I had to call his name before the class. (As, "Pat, get back to your seat—that is the fifth time that I have had to call your name this afternoon.") Pat loved every minute of this "game" and responded with "Mrs. S., watch me, that is number twenty-three."[14]

When the teacher first tried the technique of numbering the times Pat required her attention, the technique failed to reduce Pat's attention-seeking behavior. On analysis, an observer discovered that the teacher "lectured" Pat each time, in addition to indicating the number of times that Pat had tried to attract attention. The observer suggested that the teacher avoid "lecturing" and merely number the times Pat attempted to attract her attention. This technique proved successful, for Pat gradually abandoned his customary attention-getting devices.

This case illustrates the importance of recognizing the motives for a pupil's classroom behavior. These motives may be utilized to get the pupil involved in the learning experience and to seek satisfaction from it. While Pat was giving up his attention-getting behavior, he still needed the teacher's approval; at this point the teacher could help Pat learn that he would obtain approval by doing successful work rather than by causing disturbances in class.

ORIENTING STUDENTS' NEEDS TO GOAL ATTAINMENT. One of the teacher's more difficult problems is motivating students in a particular

---

[14] R. Dreikurs, *Psychology in the Classroom*, New York, Harper & Brothers, 1957, p. 115.

learning experience. Children in a classroom are always motivated in some way, but the problem is to help them seek the goals implicit in the learning situation and to obtain satisfaction from the attainment of these goals. The class "cut-up" is motivated and is obtaining need-satisfaction from the laughter and approval that he gets from his classmates. The problem is to utilize his need for approval or attention in constructive ways so that he can profit from the learning experience and obtain satisfactions from it. Al was a boy who continually argued with the teacher. When a paper was returned to him, he would argue with the teacher about the grade that he had received; he had learned to obtain satisfaction from getting into this kind of an argument with people. The teacher solved this problem of motivation in the following way:

> Recently I forgot to tell the boys and girls to look for the eclipse of the moon. I felt that here I had an opportunity to direct Al into a constructive channel. I called his home and told him to watch the eclipse and to report to the class the next day. I thought this would also give him a chance to contribute to the class on the useful side, thus giving him status within his group. He does not feel a part of his group; he complains that the children will not play with him.
>
> The next day Al was quite excited about giving his report to the class. He brought his source of information, a little bit about the solar system which he had in his collection of books. His report and his presentation were excellent. We decided to put Al's report in the newspaper which we publish monthly, and put his name under it.[15]

The teacher in this case was attempting to teach Al new ways of satisfying his needs. He was capitalizing on the boy's need for approval and status with his classmates by involving him in a learning experience that could satisfy these needs. If Al learned that he would obtain satisfaction of his needs for status and approval by participating intelligently and cooperatively in the class activities, he would be likely to abandon his attempts to obtain satisfaction by destructive means.

THE USE OF REWARD AND PUNISHMENT. From the viewpoint of the teacher, reward and punishment are incentives to induce and

---

[15]*Ibid.*, p. 124.

strengthen behavior change. An "A" grade may be an incentive of this kind. The teacher assumes that if a child wants a high grade he will work to achieve the goals of the learning experience. Subtracting points for errors may be a punishment; it may also be an incentive for inducing behavior change—in this case, the avoidance of errors.

What the teacher assumes to be rewards and punishments may not be so regarded by the students. Some children may not work for high marks because the attaining of a mark has little if any goal value for them; they may not see attaining a high mark as a way of obtaining need-satisfaction. A supposed punishment may actually provide a child with need-satisfaction, as in the case of the child who attracts the teacher's attention only when he talks out in class.

In general, if the rewards provided by the teacher are seen as potential sources of need-satisfaction, they are likely to induce and strengthen behavior change; however, before we can predict that certain students will work for particular rewards, we must consider another factor. A particular reward may be attractive to a child, but he may have little hope of attaining it. His past experience in working for such rewards and his estimates of his own ability to attain the reward influence his expectancy of attainment.[16] As a case in point, a child may have little expectancy for attaining high grades even though they represent highly desirable goals for him. Similarly, the child's understanding of a given punishment may determine whether or not he avoids the behavior for which it may be administered.

In general, the effects of punishment are more variable than the effects of reward. Sears, in a study on child-rearing, investigated the effectiveness of a wide variety of punishments, such as isolation of the child, spanking, withdrawing of love, deprivation of privileges. The investigators concluded:

> . . . punitiveness, in contrast with rewardingness, was a quite ineffectual quality for a mother to inject into her child training . . . our evaluation of punishment is that *it is ineffectual over the long term as a technique for eliminating the kind of behavior towards which it is directed.*

> The evidence for this conclusion is overwhelming. The unhappy effects of punishment have run like a dismal thread through our findings. Mothers who punish toilet accidents severely ended up with bed-wetting children.

---

[16]L. Worell, "The Effect of Goal Value Upon Expectancy," *Journal of Abnormal and Social Psychology,* 53 (1956), 48-53.

Mothers who punished dependency to get rid of it had more dependent children than mothers who did not punish. Mothers who punished aggressive behavior severely had more aggressive children than mothers who punished lightly. They also had more dependent children. Harsh physical punishment was associated with high childhood aggressiveness and with the development of feeding problems.[17]

In some cases, punishment is ineffective for producing avoidance of the behavior pattern it is designed to eliminate, as when a child punished for dependency behavior becomes more dependent: the punishment does not remove the child's need for dependency, and he continues to seek need-satisfaction by being dependent. In other cases, punishment of undesired behavior results in avoidance of that behavior, but a related and equally undesirable behavior pattern emerges, as in the case of the child who bed-wets even though he has been punished for toilet accidents. In still other cases, the child avoids the punished behavior in one context, but manifests it in another—as with the child who avoids being aggressive at home but who is highly aggressive in school.

Punishment may sometimes promote avoidance of an undesired behavior, but it does not necessarily stimulate the acquisition of a desired behavior pattern. A child may learn to control his aggressiveness without learning to become friendly; or he may learn to keep quiet in class without learning to ask appropriate questions.

Effects of the act of punishing are frequently undesirable. The threatening aspects of punishment may produce emotional tension in the child, and he may learn to hate the punisher because he fears the punishment. He may also acquire many undesirable behaviors in order to avoid being punished: he may lie or cheat in order to avoid it.

Teachers are frequently concerned with controlling classroom behavior that interferes with appropriate goal orientation. Teachers do not want pupils shouting out in the classroom, leaving their seats unnecessarily, talking to their companions, or practicing arithmetic when they should be doing reading assignments, and they frequently use punitive measures to eliminate these undesirable behaviors. A child may be put in the back of the classroom, he may be ridiculed, or he may be deprived of some privilege accorded the rest of the class. We would

---

[17]R. Sears, E. Maccoby, and H. Levin, *Patterns of Child-Rearing*, Evanston, Ill., Row, Peterson and Co., 1957, p. 484. Used by permission of the publisher.

expect that in a certain number of cases the child will stop doing these undesirable things in order to avoid punishment; but in other cases the child may not learn to take an interest in his class work, and, knowing no other ways, he may continue to seek need-satisfaction by talking with his companions or shouting out in the classroom.

INDIVIDUAL PERSONALITIES AND REWARD AND PUNISHMENT. Other factors also must be considered in using reward and punishment techniques. Thompson and Hunnicutt studied the effect of praise and blame on the work achievement of "introverts" and "extroverts."[18] In this experiment, fifth grade pupils from five classes were presented with a simple learning task. The experimenters gave a personality test to the children that classified them as "introverts" and "extroverts." Then the experimenters divided the children into five groups. Two groups were made up of extroverts, one of which was praised and the other blamed; two groups were made up of introverts, one of which was praised and the other blamed; and the fifth group received neither praise nor blame. It is important to know that in this study "praise" consisted in the teachers placing a mark of "G," meaning "Good," and that the "blame" consisted in the teacher placing a "P," meaning "Poor," on the pupil's test paper. The experimenters came to these conclusions:

1. If you put introverts and extroverts into one group with praise and blame distributed to both introverts and extroverts, the work output of this group is significantly higher than the control group, that is, the group that has not received rewards or punishments at all.

2. If repeated often enough, praise increases the work output of introverts until it is higher than that of extroverts who are praised or introverts who are blamed.

3. If repeated often enough, blame increases the work output of extroverts until it is higher than that of extroverts who are praised or introverts who are blamed.

These results are plotted in Figure 62. As the graph illustrates, the group showing the largest gains was the extrovert-blamed group,

---

[18]G. G. Thompson and C. W. Hunnicutt, "The Effect of Repeated Praise or Blame on the Work Achievement of 'Introverts' and 'Extroverts'," *Journal of Educational Psychology*, 35 (1944), 257-66.

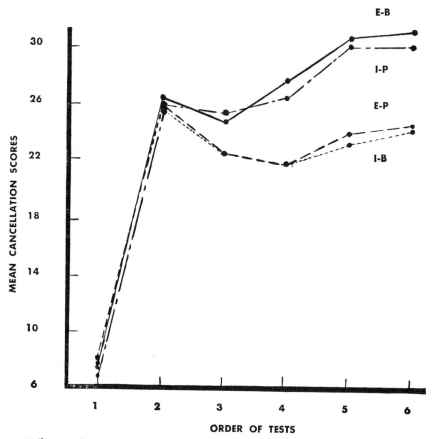

Effects of praise and blame on "introverts" and "extroverts."
(Thompson and Hunnicutt)

FIGURE 62

and the group showing the least improvement was the introvert-blamed group.

The conclusions from this study do not comprise rules for applying praise and blame to the behavior of students. The character of the "praise" and "blame" used in this experiment is limited and highly specific. All we know about the personality characteristics of these children is that they are introverts and extroverts as described by test scores on a personality test. However, the data do suggest that reward and punishment have different effects on individuals with different personality characteristics.

The experimental evidence from animal research, child-rearing practices research, and classroom investigations consistently suggests the superiority of rewarding over punishing in producing effective change in behavior.[19] Punishment has a limited usefulness as a control technique, but it may have real disadvantages in terms of the total learning of a child. From this evidence we would certainly be safe in concluding that a teacher whose interactions with pupils are largely characterized by punitive relationships is likely to be ineffective in promoting a wide range of desirable behavior changes.

THE TEACHER'S BEHAVIOR AS A STIMULUS EVENT. We pointed out earlier that the teacher's behavior was a stimulus likely to evoke certain kinds of responses from students. In the preceding sections, we discussed one way in which this stimulus behavior may be seen from the viewpoint of the student—namely, as a source of control over need-satisfactions. These stimulus events may also be considered as ways in which the teacher forces or leads a child toward goal attainments.

Anderson and his students investigated teacher-child relations to find whether teachers tended to dominate children or to work with them and to ascertain the effects of these two different patterns of teacher behavior.[20] In this investigation, domination was classified in three categories: domination with evidence of conflict; domination with no evidence of conflict; and domination in working together. In general, a "dominating" teacher sets the goals of a learning experience and uses some measure of direction to insure that students work for these goals. A teacher's behavior is classified as *domination with conflict* if the goals of the teacher and the pupil appear to be incompatible, and if the teacher is punitive in enforcing pupil goal-orientation. A teacher's behavior is classified as *domination in working together* if the teacher sets the goals and expected patterns of behavior but works cooperatively and nonpunitively with students to attain these goals. These categories represent points on an assumed continuum of "forcing."

Anderson classified "leading" behavior in two categories: *working together with conflict* and *working together without conflict*. A teacher's behavior was classified in the first of these two categories if

---

[19]See W. K. Estes, "An Experimental Study of Punishment," *Psychological Monographs*, No. 263, 1944; see also U. E. Whiteis, "Punishment's Influence on Fear and Avoidance," *Harvard Educational Review*, 26 (1956), 360-73.

[20]A summary with bibliography of these studies can be found in H. H. Anderson, "Domination and Socially Integrated Behavior," in R. G. Barker, J. S. Kounin, and H. F. Wright (eds.), *Child Behavior and Development*, New York, McGraw-Hill Book Co., 1943, pp. 459-83.

he allowed students to be more self-directive but did not succeed in producing goal-orientation. A teacher's behavior was classified in the second category if he encouraged self-directiveness that was effective in securing goal-orientation.

These classifications of teacher behavior are ways of describing different patterns of teacher-pupil interaction; essentially, they discriminate various degrees of what is sometimes called "teacher control." Anderson studied these patterns in terms of both teacher-child and teacher-class interactions.

What is the effect of these kinds of teacher behavior on the behavior of pupils? The major finding in this series of studies was that a particular kind of teacher behavior tended to evoke a similar kind of pupil behavior. Dominating behavior in a teacher tended to produce dominating behavior in his children. If a child is unable to dominate his teacher, he is likely to attempt to dominate fellow students. A teacher who worked with the pupils found that they tended to work with him. Such important characteristics of child behavior as spontaneity and participation in classroom activities decreased under the dominating behavior of a teacher.

In one of the studies in the Anderson series, the children were observed over a two-year period; for one year they had a teacher whose behavior was principally dominating; in the second year they had a teacher whose behavior was essentially that of working with them. The children's behavior was characteristically dominating and resisting under the dominating teacher, and cooperative and more spontaneous under the teacher who worked with them. These studies provide an analysis of some ways in which specific kinds of teacher behavior are likely to influence pupil behavior. We may not draw rules of action from them, but the data suggest some ways in which teacher behavior and pupil behavior are related.

THE PUPILS' PERCEPTION OF THE TEACHER'S BEHAVIOR. Common sense would suggest that the pupil's response to patterns of teacher behavior is likely to be influenced by other factors. A particular instance of teacher behavior may not be seen as harsh or punitive, or, if it is, the student may still regard it as justifiable. In these cases a dominating or resisting pupil response may not occur.

One factor that may influence students' perceptions of the teacher's behavior is their awareness of the status differential between teacher and pupil. To some extent, the teacher is regarded as having higher status. He is an authority on many matters for the students. Pepitone and Wallace found that individuals viewed the positive and negative actions of a higher status person as more justified if they were relevant to his status.[21] A teacher's actions may then be regarded as justifiable even though the students find them disagreeable. Students expect teachers to evaluate their work and to maintain "classroom order." The teacher's behavior is viewed as justified when he acts in ways consistent with these expectations.

As other studies indicate, students may not view all restrictions imposed by a teacher as justified simply because the teacher is a person of higher status. Such restrictions may be viewed by the students as arbitrary, and hence unjustified. Pastore conducted an experiment to study the relationship between hostility and the arbitrariness of a frustration.[22] He described a series of situations to his subjects and asked them to describe how they would feel in these situations. Each situation involved a frustration of some kind; for example, a date is broken or a bus does not stop. One set of these situations supplied reasons for the frustrations—for example, a date being broken because the girl was ill. The same situations were described to a second group in such a way as to indicate that the action was arbitrary. A significantly higher number of hostile responses were made by the subjects who received the arbitrary situations. In other words, if a disagreeable and frustrating situation is regarded as justifiable, people are less likely to respond to it in a hostile manner.

The above discussion suggests that an important determinant of one person's response to the behavior of another is his perception of the intent behind the behavior.[23] A reasonable hypothesis is that students will respond positively to a pattern of teacher behavior insofar as they trust the teacher's intention. If they believe that he is working for their best interests and is not arbitrary in his decisions, they are more likely to respond positively to him.

Dominating and punitive behavior is more likely to be interpreted as ill-intended or arbitrary. The teacher who hands out excessive punishments for mild digressions from acceptable classroom be-

---

[21]A. Pepitone and W. Wallace, "Experimental Studies on the Dynamics of Hostility," discussed in A. Pepitone, "Attributions of Causality, Social Attitudes, and Cognitive Matching Processes," in R. Tagiuri and L. Petrullo, *Person Perception and Interpersonal Behavior*, pp. 258-76.

[22]N. Pastore, "The Role of Arbitrariness in the Frustration-Aggression Hypothesis," *Journal of Abnormal and Social Psychology*, 47 (1952), 728-31.

[23]A. Pepitone and J. Sherberg, "Cognitive Factors in Interpersonal Attraction," *Journal of Personality*, 25 (1957), 257-66.

havior, or who makes unreasonable assignments, may be seen as hostile by his students. In such cases their responses are likely to be hostile and resisting.

CLASSROOM CLIMATE

The casual observer going from classroom to classroom will notice gross differences between the psychological "climates" of different classrooms. The term "climate" refers to the general pattern of social interaction observable in the relations of a group of individuals. These general patterns appear to be relatively consistent in a stable group, such as a class, and considerable variation in "climate" exists between the classes of different teachers.[24] In one classroom the students are working industriously and effectively; the teacher is a source of information and guidance; the teacher's and the pupils' goals do not appear to be incompatible. In another classroom a continual state of conflict exists between the teacher and the pupils; the teacher must use harsh and punitive methods to maintain minimum order; the pupils do not seem to be involved in the learning experience.

The psychological "climate" of a group is a pattern of forces on behavior that results from the social interactions characteristic of a group. Assume that you are in a class in which the teacher typically lets the students organize their own projects, provides guidance but counts on students to take responsibility for learning, and is supportive and encouraging. The behavior of the students in this class is likely to be quite different from that in a class where the teacher uses a radically different approach to his relations with the class. In other words, the patterns of teacher-pupil interaction in this class tend to determine the kinds of typical student behavior that may be observed in it.

These differences in classroom climate may be described on several dimensions. One such dimension is the method of behavior control typically used in the classroom. A "democratic" classroom, for instance, may be described as one in which there is a large degree of permissiveness in the teacher-pupil relationship: pupils are allowed selection of the work-projects, and they participate in decisions about the learning activities; they are not closely supervised, but are allowed

---

[24]J. Withall, "Assessment of the Social-Emotional Climates Experienced by a Group of Seventh-Graders as They Moved From Class to Class," *Educational and Psychological Measurement*, 12 (1952), 440-51.

to work independently. In contrast, an "autocratic" classroom may be described as one which is dominated by the teacher: the teacher decides on and attempts to impose the goals of learning activities; the pupils do not participate in either the selection of learning activities or the goals of these activities. These two descriptions of methods of behavior control represent end-points on a continuum of "self-directed"—"other-directed." There are many variations between the extreme of the "democratic" class and the extreme of the "autocratic" class. Also, while the definitions of the extremes are comparatively clear-cut, it is much more difficult to define the points between them. Some climates may be characterized by both "democratic" and "autocratic" procedures.

INFLUENCE OF CLASSROOM CLIMATE ON PUPIL BEHAVIOR. Do these differences in classroom climate produce differences in pupil behavior? Only a limited amount of experimental evidence is available in answer to this question. Lewin, Lippitt, and White conducted a series of experiments in which they tested the effects of three kinds of adult leadership on group behavior.[25] Table XXVII describes the characteristics of each of these kinds of leadership. The experimenters kept a complete record of the behavior of the boys under each kind of leadership. The following results were obtained:

1. Hostile and aggressive behavior occurred more frequently under autocratic leadership than under democratic leadership.

2. Aggressive behavior tended to generalize to other situations. There was a sharp rise in aggression when the autocratic leader left the room. The boys also became more aggressive when they moved to a freer atmosphere.

3. Two "wars," more or less playful, broke out between clubs meeting in the same room at the same time. These wars broke out either when there was no adult present or when a "hostile stranger" came into the room.

4. There were at least two striking instances of aggressive attacks on impersonal objects.

5. Under autocratic leadership "scapegoating" of some of the boys in the group occurred, a phenomenon that decreased under democratic leadership.

---

[25]K. Lewin, R. Lippitt, and R. K. White, "Patterns of Aggressive Behavior in Experimentally Created 'Social Climates'," *Journal of Social Psychology*, 10 (1939), 271-99. This report also contains information on other experiments performed by these investigators on this problem.

Authoritarian	Democratic	Laissez-faire
1. All determination of policy by the leader.	1. All policies a matter of group discussion and decision, encouraged and assisted by the leader.	1. Complete freedom for group or individual decision, without any leader participation.
2. Techniques and activity steps dictated by the authority, one at a time, so that future steps were always uncertain to a large degree.	2. Activity perspective gained during first discussion period. General steps to group goal sketched, and where technical advice was needed the leader suggested two or three alternative procedures from which choice could be made.	2. Various materials supplied by the leader, who made it clear that he would supply information when asked. He took no other part in work discussions.
3. The leader usually dictated the particular work task and work companions of each member.	3. The members were free to work with whomever they chose, and the division of tasks was left up to the group.	3. Complete nonparticipation by leader.
4. The dominator was "personal" in his praise and criticism of the work of each member, but remained aloof from active group participation except when demonstrating. He was friendly or impersonal rather than openly hostile.	4. The leader was "objective" or "fact-minded" in his praise and criticism and tried to be a regular group member in spirit without doing too much of the work.	4. Very infrequent comments on member activities unless questioned, and no attempt to participate or interfere with the course of events.

Characteristics of Authoritarian, Democratic, and Laissez-Faire Styles of Leadership (From Lewin, Lippitt, and White)

TABLE XXVII

6. The boys were almost unanimous in disliking the autocratic leader and practically unanimous in liking the democratic and even the laissez-faire leader.

The results of this experiment were clear-cut. Under autocratic leadership the children were frustrated, and they resolved their frustration problem by aggressive acts of one kind or another. They were also more apathetic and less personally involved in the work of their club. Control in the group and task-orientation disappeared when the autocratic leader was not present. The effects in the democratic group were just the opposite. Here, under democratic leadership, the children were responsive and spontaneous; they did not need the supervision of the leader to continue working, and they showed less evidence of aggression and hostility.

The above study is frequently cited as evidence that democratic leadership produces more task-orientation and more socially adaptable behavior than does autocratic leadership. However, the results of this study should not be overgeneralized. It is important to remember the following points: first, that the obtained effects of democratic and autocratic leadership reflect the manner in which democracy and autocracy were defined in this experiment; second, that the nature of the activities in which the boys were involved is limited. We do not know whether these same effects would be obtained for a wide range of activities, but they are consistent with the experimental data cited previously: an aggressive, hostile, punitive leader stimulates child behavior which is aggressive, punitive, and hostile. If the children cannot openly express their hostility and aggressiveness, they direct it toward impersonal objects or their companions and wait for a strategic moment in which to relieve their feelings. From the discussion of the Lewin experiment we may be tempted to conclude that a given set of procedures automatically produces the kinds of pupil behavior described in that experiment. But, we would also expect the pupils' expectations about or perceptions of the classroom climate to influence their behavior.

Recent experimental work suggests that both the students' perceptions of the typical pattern of control and the teacher's consistent maintenance of these patterns substantially influence pupil behavior.[26] In this experiment, two kinds of classroom climates were established: first, a "teacher-centered" one, in which the vote of the teacher on a problem of mutual interest counted twice as much as the votes of the students; second, a "student-centered" one, in which the teacher's vote on a common problem was given only one-fourth the weight of the student vote.

As part of the experimental procedure, both groups were required to vote on continuing the work in which they were involved.

---

[26]M. Horwitz, M. Goldman, and F. J. Lee, "A Further Study of the Effects of Power Reduction on Arousal of Hostility," *Office of Naval Research Technical Report,* 1956, discussed in M. Horwitz, "The Veridicality of Liking and Disliking," in R. Tagiuri and L. Petrullo, *op cit.,* 191-208.

The teachers in both groups overrode the students' decision. This behavior was consistent with the expectations of the students in the "teacher-centered" classroom where the teacher's vote counted twice as much; but it contradicted the expectations established in the "student-centered" classroom. Expressions of hostility and dislike were significantly greater in the "student-centered" classroom when the students were asked to rate the teacher.[27] When the teacher acted in a way consistent with the established expectations his behavior evoked less hostility than when he violated the established expectations, even though his behavior was disagreeable for the students.

How are the results of this experiment reconciled with those of the Lewin experiment? The student should note the ways in which the variables describing "climate" are defined in each of these experiments. In the "teacher-centered" classroom the rules of operation seemed generally understood, whereas in the autocratic group the "climate" was established primarily by the manner in which the leader treated the group. In the "teacher-centered" group the expectations were apparently "accepted." Another difference between the experiments is that the different effects obtained refer only to one behavior pattern, namely, expression of hostility.[28]

Despite these methodological differences, we may hypothesize that some patterns of classroom climate, such as the extreme form of "autocratic" control, are likely to be consistent in the effects they produce. But in many other cases, student behavior is more likely to be influenced by the expectations for control, assuming that such expectations are "accepted." In general, we would predict that the more extreme forms of autocratic control are less likely to be "accepted." We need not assume that the democratic pattern of control will necessarily be accepted. Although it is more likely to be accepted, its effectiveness depends upon the extent to which students "accept" it. In all cases the students' behavior will probably be influenced by the degree to which the teacher's behavior is consistent with established and accepted expectations.

---

[27]Additional confirmation of these results was obtained in other experimental work, see F. J. Lee, M. Horwitz, and M. Goldman, "Power Over Decision Making and the Response to Frustration in Group Members," *Office of Naval Research Technical Report*, 1954.

[28]Rate and retention of learning were investigated in the following experiment but the different experimental treatments did not produce significant differences between the groups in these two respects. See M. Horwitz and M. Goldman, "Veridicality of Attitudes Toward Authority and Effects on Rates of Learning and Psychological Oversatiation," *Office of Naval Research Technical Report*, in preparation—cited in M. Horwitz, "The Veridicality of Liking and Disliking," in R. Tagiuri and L. Petrullo, *op. cit.*, pp. 201-202.

From our review of the experimental evidence on the teacher-pupil relationship, it should be apparent that it is not possible to state conclusively just how the teacher should act or to prescribe all the operations most likely to be effective in producing desirable pupil behavior in all situations. One limitation of most of the experiments we have discussed is that they have investigated only a limited number of variables, or that they have studied variables so complex that it is not possible to determine to which particular set of procedures the experimental effects may be attributed. In the Lewin, Lippitt, and White study, for example, democratic leadership involved many specific operations, such as the manner in which the leader treated the boys, as well as the operations that were permitted in the group, such as participation in policy decisions. The obtained effects may have been due to one or both of these aspects of democratic leadership.

In studying relations of the teacher-pupil interaction to pupil achievement and pupil behavior, four important classes of variables need to be interrelated: (1) the personality of the student; (2) the personality of the teacher; (3) the character of the teacher-pupil interaction; (4) the nature of the learning experience. Each of these factors affects pupil change in varying degrees and more or less directly. The complexity of the relationships among these factors is obvious, but some understanding of this complexity may protect the teacher from making naive assumptions about the effects of his behavior on pupil change.

THE ORGANIZATION OF CLASSROOM GROUPS

Students are frequently placed in classes according to similarity of age, interest in a subject, preparation for study of a subject, or level of ability. A group formed on the basis of such general characteristics tends to be composed of children that are different in many other characteristics. Consider a few of the differences that might characterize any one of these collections of individuals. Students in a class organized by age may differ in terms of home backgrounds, previous academic achievement, interest in the subjects studied, and attitudes toward school and the teacher. Students in classes organized by interest in a subject may differ in terms of general level of ability, specific talents, and the kinds of need-satisfaction they hope to obtain by studying the subject. One student may be interested in algebra because he wants to be an engineer; another student because algebra is required for college admission; and still another simply because he likes mathematics. Typically, the students in any class are different in more ways than they are alike.

PUPIL CHARACTERISTICS AND GOAL ATTAINMENT. These differences among pupils are significant to the extent that any one dimension of difference is relevant to the achievement of the goals of learning experiences. The students who are interested in algebra for different reasons may still work effectively for the attainment of the goals involved in the learning of algebra. Other differences among them may be indirectly related or unrelated to the attainment of these particular goals. Still other differences, such as differences in ability or previous preparation, may be highly relevant to the attainment of the goals of the learning experience.

Two factors need to be considered in organizing students into groups for common learning experiences: (1) the particular goals to be attained and (2) the particular pupil characteristics relevant to the attainment of these goals.

THE INSTRUCTIONAL GROUP. We will call the group organized to work for a common goal in a learning experience the *instructional group.* The organization of such a group assumes that : (1) the attainment of the common goal represents the desired behavior changes attainable by the students in the group; (2) that the pupils in the group share to some extent those characteristics relevant to the attainment of the goal; and (3) that students in the group are motivated to work for the common goal.

Such groups will vary in size and composition as learning experiences are organized to attain different goals. For some goals and learning experiences, the instructional group may be the entire class. If a foreign visitor is invited to talk to the class on the customs of his country, the goal of the learning experience is probably the acquisition of certain basic facts and generalizations about his country. Assume, by way of contrast, that several students in the class are particularly interested in the customs of that country. They might be organized into a group to pursue the common goal of gaining greater understanding of the culture and life of that country. They may share such common learning experiences as a personal discussion with the speaker after his talk. In these two examples, note that the particular goals of the learning experiences and the character of the learning experiences themselves are different. The grouping of the students in each case is based on their motivation to work toward the common goal and other characteristics that are relevant to the attainment of these goals.[29]

GROUP AND INDIVIDUAL GOALS. Groups are typically organized to attain goals sought by the members of the group and more easily attained through common efforts. A distinction may be made between group goals defined in this way and common goals—goals shared by many individuals but attained principally by independent individual efforts. For example, a class of students may be working on a common set of problems where the goal of each student is to work the problems correctly. The goal in this case is shared, but it is not a group goal since a cooperative effort is not required or utilized to attain the goal.

Other goals may be individual goals in the sense that they are the goals of a particular student and are not shared by the other members of a class. Learning experiences may be organized to facilitate the achievement of these individual goals. The English teacher may organize a "free" reading period in which students pursue their own reading interests; the science teacher may encourage students to develop their own projects or experiments.

The organization of a class group implies the hypothesis that such an organization is more likely to lead to the behavior change involved in goal attainment than is some other organization. We may not assume that grouping procedures are necessarily more effective for all purposes than other arrangements; furthermore, the effectiveness of such groups depends on factors related to group organization and operation. These factors will be discussed in the following sections.

FACTORS AFFECTING GROUP EFFECTIVENESS. A group can be effective in attaining group goals only to the extent that the members of the group are committed to the achievement of the group goal. What factors influence the willingness of the members of a group to commit themselves to a group goal? One important factor appears to be the extent to which the members of the group have an opportunity to participate in deciding on the group goal and on procedures for attaining it. The evidence for this conclusion is derived from ex-

---

[29]For a discussion of a variety of ways to group students, see H. A. Thelen, "Classroom Grouping of Students," *The School Review*, 67 (1959), 60-78.

periments performed elsewhere than in the school.[30] The conclusions from these experiments, however, are clear-cut. When individuals have an opportunity to participate in the decision-making process, rather than being "lectured at" or told what to do, desired behavior changes are much more frequent.

What is the influence of varying degrees of commitment to group goals on individual behavior? An individual in a group is more or less committed to the attainment of the group goal. Individuals join groups for a variety of reasons; the need-satisfactions provided by achieving group goals may be only part of the need-satisfaction that a person obtains by being in a group. For example, the members of a class research committee may achieve need-satisfactions by carrying out their tasks successfully, but they may also achieve need-satisfaction from social interaction in the group. They may like to be with each other, they may like working together, and they obtain a certain amount of need-satisfaction from these relationships.

An individual's goals are not necessarily compatible with the group goals. One may be so preoccupied with preserving, maintaining, or improving his own status that he cannot work effectively for the group goal.

The individuals in a group who are primarily interested in satisfying their own needs may interfere with the effectiveness of the group —especially when their needs cannot be satisfied by attaining the group goal. A group of investigators studied the conflict between attempts to satisfy individual needs and attainment of the group goal. The investigators rated discussion groups on the extent to which the members apparently attempted to satisfy their individual needs even though their needs were incompatible with the attainment of the group goal.[31] When the observers rated the effectiveness of the groups, they found that the ones in which there was little common goal-orientation spent a longer period of time working on their agenda and completed fewer items on their agenda. The members of these groups were also more dissatisfied with the meetings as a whole and with the way in which the meetings were conducted.

Allowing group members to define their goals and procedures

---

[30]L. Coch and J. French, "Overcoming Resistance to Change," *Human Relations*, 1 (1948), 512-32; J. Levine, and J. Butler, "Lecture versus Group Discussion in Changing Behavior," *Journal of Applied Psychology*, 36 (1952), 29-33.

[31]N. T. Fouriezos, M. L. Hutt, and H. Guetzkow, "Measurement of Self-Oriented Needs in Discussion Groups," *Journal of Abnormal and Social Psychology*, 45 (1950), 682-90.

presumably permits an individual to relate his individual goals to those of other members. Commonality of purpose may be clarified and shared expectations developed. The development of common standards in turn increases the likelihood that pressures toward group attainment will be exerted on the individuals in the group.[32]

Group effectiveness also depends on the character of the leadership in the group. We have seen that at least a minimal kind of leadership is necessary.[33] However, leadership which interferes with the full participation of the group members tends to reduce individual need-satisfaction, although the group may still be effective in achieving its goal.[34] One of the major functions of leadership in the group is to preserve an open communication system so that members of the group can effectively exchange information and ideas.

There is probably a limit below which need-satisfaction may not drop without the group also becoming ineffective. A research committee may appoint a chairman whose job is to lead the discussions in which the group analyzes its research findings. If the leader controls the amount and kind of communication between the members in order to get a report prepared, he may be effective in getting the report prepared, but he may also have a committee that is less satisfied with the job it is doing. If the group members become too dissatisfied, they may relieve their frustration by activities which interfere with accomplishment of the group task. For a group to be successful, a balance probably needs to be maintained between effectiveness in achieving the group task and providing individual satisfactions for the members of the group. Compatibility between the goals that satisfy individual needs and the group goal is likely to facilitate both group effectiveness and individual need-satisfaction.

COOPERATION, COMPETITION, AND GROUP EFFECTIVENESS. The foregoing discussion stresses the importance of compatibility between group and individual goals. It is possible to organize a group in such a way that the group goal may be attained by either individual or cooperative effort. Such may be the case when a teacher organizes a

[32]S. Schachter, N Ellertson, D. McBride, and D. Gregory, "An Experimental Study of Cohesiveness and Productivity," *Human Relations*, 4 (1951), 229-38.

[33]N. Maier and A. R. Solem, "The Contribution of a Discussion Leader to the Quality of Group Thinking: The Effective Use of Minority Opinions," *Human Relations*, 5 (1952), 277-88.

[34]A. Bavelas, "Communication Patterns in Task-Oriented Groups," *Journal of The Acoustical Society of America*, 22 (1950), 725-30; also in D. Cartwright and A. Zander, *Group Dynamics: Research and Theory*, Evanston, Illinois, Row, Peterson and Co., 1953, pp. 493-506.

research committee to prepare reports for the social studies class, yet each student is to turn in an individual report for a grade. The students are to work together to prepare their reports, but the requirement of an individual report for which a grade will be given may encourage the group members to work for individual goals. The group goal in this case is largely a fiction; the group activity may be oriented to individual attainment.

An experiment conducted by Deutsch illustrates the kinds of effects that may occur in such situations.[35] Deutsch formed groups of students working in a problem-solving situation, using two kinds of groups. In one set of groups, the students had to work cooperatively in order to obtain the group goal; in the other group, the students could work together but each attained the group goal independently of the others. The students worked on two kinds of problems—puzzle problems and human relations problems. In the cooperative groups, the groups were rated as a whole on their performance on the problems, each person in the group receiving the group rating as his rating. In the competitive groups, while the individuals worked together by discussing the problem, each could present his own solution and was rated on this solution independently of the solution achieved by the others.

What were the effects of cooperation and competition? The following behavior patterns are some of the characteristics of cooperative groups as opposed to competitive groups: greater coordination of efforts, greater diversity in the amount of contributions, more subdividing of activity and responsibility, more achievement pressure, more attentiveness to fellow members, more common understanding of communication, more common evaluation of communication, more orientation and orderliness, more productivity per unit of time, better discussions, more friendliness during discussions, and more favorable evaluation of the group and its work. In short, the members of the cooperative group worked harder and accomplished more than did the members of the competitive groups. Some of the success in problem-solving in the cooperative groups occurs, of course, because there are individuals in the cooperative group who can solve the problems and communicate the solutions to other members.

Note that many of the behavior patterns that characterized the

[35]M. Deutsch, "The Effects of Cooperation and Competition on Group Process," summarized in Group Dynamics: Research and Theory, pp. 319-53.

cooperative groups are related to effective problem-solution (e.g., achievement pressure, problem orientation, and greater understanding and evaluation of communications). Others are related to behavior changes required for students to work effectively with other people, such as more attentiveness to fellow members, greater coordination of efforts, and more widespread division of activity and responsibility. Generalizing the results of this experiment to the classroom, we would say that a cooperative organization of group activities is more likely to promote widespread behavior changes than would be the case for a competitive organization. The successful accomplishment of a group task increases the cohesiveness and attractiveness of the group and tends to develop greater task-orientation and interest in the class work.

THE TEACHER'S USE OF GROUPING PROCEDURES. Classroom groups are organized to facilitate the attainment of certain goals. In using grouping procedures, two levels of hypothesis-making and hypothesis-evaluation are required of the teacher. In other words, the teacher is attempting to answer two questions: (1) Are grouping procedures likely to promote the desired behavior changes more effectively than some other arrangements? (2) Is this particular grouping arrangement with its relevant procedures likely to be effective in facilitating the attainment of specific group goals?

We may not assume that children naturally prefer to work in groups or that they necessarily learn better when working in groups.[36] Grouping procedures are not a panacea for the problems of classroom "discipline." Grouping of pupils is one of many general procedures a a teacher may use to foster behavior change.

SUMMARY

Patterns of teacher-pupil interaction comprise another set of variables which influence behavior change. The particular character of these interaction patterns develops in part as a function of the perceptions the teacher and the student have of each other.

1. Traits are descriptive classifications of perceived character-
    istics of another person. These categories may be more or less

[36]H. B. Gerard, "Some Factors Affecting an Individual's Estimate of His Probable Success in a Group Situation," *Journal of Abnormal and Social Psychology,* 52 (1956), 235-39.

precisely defined in terms of observable behavior and are based on inferences from these observations.

2. Individuals tend to develop systems of trait associations in which they see certain traits as necessarily or typically associated with other kinds of traits. In this way, individuals may be attributed traits they do not possess.

3. Perceptions of another individual's characteristics are frequently influenced by the relevance of these characteristics to environmental factors. This is seen in the way some teachers tend to perceive traits that interfere with classroom order as more serious than other characteristics. In other words, a teacher may be predisposed to attend to certain kinds of pupil behavior and to ignore other kinds. In this way the teacher's perceptions of a pupil's characteristics are limited to the kinds of behaviors that the teacher sees as desirable or undesirable in the classroom setting.

4. Some evidence is available to suggest that as teachers acquire more adequate information and greater understanding about their pupils, desired changes in pupil behavior are more likely to occur. The relationship between the teacher's perceptions of a pupil's behavior and the influence of these perceptions on pupil change is probably indirect. Changes in the teacher's perception of the pupil may sensitize the teacher to more alternatives for influencing pupil change, and in this way contribute indirectly to pupil change.

Teachers acquire ways of interacting with pupils which are presumably meant to promote pupils' attainment of the goals of learning experiences. In interacting with his pupils, the teacher attempts to maintain goal orientation and to eliminate behavior patterns which interfere with goal orientation.

5. One of the ways in which teachers maintain goal orientation is by controlling the need-satisfactions available to pupils. The teacher stimulates goal orientation by providing need-satisfactions which will be attained by goal achievement. One of

the major tasks in organizing learning experiences is to relate the kinds of need-satisfactions for which students have learned to strive with the particular goals of a learning experience.

6. Teachers use rewards and punishments as ways of maintaining goal orientation in learning experiences. The effectiveness of rewards and punishments depends on their relation to the kinds of goals that satisfy students' needs.

7. Rewards which provide need-satisfactions for students are likely to facilitate goal orientation. The effects of punishment are less predictable. Students may acquire many undesirable behaviors to avoid punishment. Punishment may be effective in teaching students to avoid undesirable behavior, but may be ineffective in stimulating them to acquire desired behavior. Punishment frequently fosters the kind of behavior that it is designed to eliminate.

8. The pupil's perception of the justifiability and the intent of the teacher's behavior influences his response to that behavior. Actions of the teacher which are seen by pupils as justifiable and well intended inspire less hostility from pupils, even though the teacher's behavior may be disagreeable to them. Some forms of teacher behavior are more likely to be viewed either as unjustified or as inspired by personal hostility to the student. Dominating behavior is probably seen in this way, and it is likely to evoke dominating and resisting behavior from the student.

Classroom climate is a typical and consistent pattern of teacher-pupil relations. This variable may be described on many different dimensions—in terms of variations in methods of teacher control of pupil behavior, for example.

9. Teacher control of pupil behavior is related to the kinds of expectations pupils have about the patterns of control. Pupils are less likely to be hostile and aggressive in their response to patterns of teacher control when the teacher acts consistently with established expectations. But some patterns of control are

more likely to evoke undesirable responses from students. Autocratic patterns of control are likely to evoke many undesirable kinds of pupil behavior, such as aggressiveness, unwillingness to assume responsibility without teacher direction, and lack of sustained interest in the learning experience.

Students may work either individually or cooperatively in groups to attain the goals of a learning experience. Group goals are more likely to be attained by cooperative efforts when the group is organized on the basis of pupil characteristics relevant to goal attainment.

10. A group is effective to the extent that group action leads to the attainment of the group goal. The effectiveness of groups depends upon the willingness of members in the group to work for the attainment of the group goal. Group members are likely to work cooperatively for the attainment of the group goal when their individual need-satisfactions and the satisfactions associated with goal achievement are compatible.

11. Individual group members may interfere with the attainment of the group goal by striving for personal need-satisfactions rather than striving for the attainment of the group goal. The procedures for attaining the group goal may be organized in such a way that individual need-satisfaction may be obtained only by attaining the group goal. Cooperative groups of this kind foster a wide range of behavior change in group members.

Particular patterns of teacher-pupil relations and the grouping of class members are based on hypotheses about the effects of such arrangements on changes in pupil behavior. The discussion in this chapter suggests the variables that the teacher needs to consider in formulating these kinds of hypotheses.

STUDY AND DISCUSSION QUESTIONS

1. Suggest some ways in which each of the following aspects of teacher behavior may influence teacher-pupil relations.

   a. The teacher's physical appearance and grooming.

    b. The quality of the teacher's voice.

    c. A teacher's posture habits.

2. For each of the above behavior patterns, suggest some kinds of variations in behavior that may be observed among teachers. What inferences may students be predisposed to make about the teacher's personality on the basis of the different behavior patterns apparent in the teacher's behavior?

3. List the principal kinds of need-satisfactions that may be provided in the typical classroom by the teacher. What kinds of teacher-pupil relations may develop if the teacher provides these kinds of need-satisfactions?

4. In what ways may the teacher be limited in providing satisfactions for student needs? Predict some effects that difficulty in providing these need-satisfactions may have on teacher-pupil relations.

5. What kinds of need-satisfactions may be provided by a teacher who is:

    a. Friendly but firm.

    b. Friendly but not firm.

    c. Strict and demanding.

Describe the behavior that you associate with each of the above traits, and predict the kinds of teacher-pupil relations that may result for teachers so characterized.

6. Recall your first day in some class. What kinds of impressions did you form of the teacher? What kinds of inferences did you make about his personality characteristics? What expectations did you have about teacher-pupil relations? Were your predictions in this respect confirmed?

7. What traits do you tend to associate with each of the following traits?

    a. Smart.

    b. Practical.

    c. Clever.

    d. Shy.

    e. Hard-working.

8. Analyze the associations that you have given to the traits listed in Question No. 7 in terms of the kinds of hypotheses you have about people who have these characteristics. What experiences have you had that lead you to expect that these traits are associated? Can you recall instances of people who may have the given traits but not the associated traits?

9. If you were told that an instructor whom you were to have in the near future

had a "warm personality," what other characteristics would you expect him to have? Explain why you think that these characteristics may be associated with the characteristics of "warmth."

10. For each of the statements listed below, describe the kinds of persons you think are likely to have made such a statement:

    a. It is essential that a study of science be included in a modern curriculum.

    b. Children do not mean to be malicious; this kind of behavior usually results when the child is frustrated.

    c. Studying history is a waste of time; it has no practical value.

11. Refer to the Schrupp and Gjerde study presented in this chapter. Assume that teachers had been asked to describe the traits they considered most serious for the future development of the child. Would you expect that the teachers would have given a different rank order to the traits that they considered most serious? Would you predict that there would have been greater agreement between teachers and clinicians? Explain the reasons for your predictions.

12. What kinds of characteristics would you expect a group of high school boys to value in a male teacher? What kinds of characteristics would a group of high school girls value in a female teacher? What variations would you expect to find in the kinds of characteristics that students value in their teachers? Relate the variations in characteristics among students to the kinds of characteristics they value in teachers.

13. Describe some of the ways in which a teacher may respond to a student whom he sees as:

    a. Friendly.

    b. Unfriendly.

    c. Intelligent.

    d. Not very bright.

14. Compare the Ojemann and Hoyt studies. What differences in procedures may have accounted for the differences in results obtained in these two investigations?

15. What kinds of need-satisfactions may a teacher be obtaining who is:

    a. Friendly with students.

    b. Firm with students.

    c. Strict with students.

    d. Unfriendly with students.

Define and describe the behavior that you associate with each of these terms and make your predictions in terms of the descriptions that you provide.

16. What kinds of motives may initiate the following instances of student behavior?

    a. A student regularly asks for extra work.

    b. A student offers answers to questions only when called on.

    c. A student regularly ignores assignments.

    d. A student appears to avoid any close relationship with the teacher.

17. In what ways may isolating a child in the back of a classroom provide the child with need-satisfaction? Are there any circumstances in which the use of this procedure may effectively eliminate undesirable classroom behavior?

18. Suggest some hypotheses to account for the relationship that Anderson found between dominating behavior of teachers and the frequency of dominating behavior in children. What kinds of need-satisfaction may a child be obtaining by responding in this way to the dominating behavior of a teacher?

19. Suggest some ways in which students might explain to themselves the following behaviors in teachers:

    a. Assigning extra homework.

    b. Requesting a student to leave class.

    c. Asking a student to have his parents visit the teacher.

    d. Organizing a class picnic.

20. For what kinds of learning experiences may students "expect" relatively more direction from teachers?

21. List a number of "teacher-controls" that students are likely to find disagreeable. Suggest the probable effects on pupil behavior of using these kinds of teacher-control procedures. What kinds of pupil behavior change would a teacher be attempting to achieve by using these procedures? What alternative forms of teacher-pupil relations may be available to achieve the same purposes?

22. Some people argue that students need to be placed in competitive situations in order to learn how to compete successfully. Evaluate this argument. Is the use of group procedures in the organization of learning experiences likely to inhibit the development of "competitive" behavior?

23. Some people argue that emphasis on the use of group procedures in the school tends to produce "conformity." They claim that this emphasis does not develop individuals who can think for themselves. Evaluate this argument in the light of the principles of group operation discussed in this chapter. Under what conditions might this criticism be justifiable?

24. In organizing project work, some teachers of social studies will assign the brighter students to a research committee and the other students to construction activities, such as painting a mural. Are such arrangements likely to lead to group effectiveness in problem-solving? What kinds of behavior changes might not be facilitated by these arrangements?

25. Assume that you mixed the students randomly on both committees. What effect would you predict that these arrangements would have on group effectiveness and satisfaction?

RECOMMENDED READINGS

The first reading is a report of an extensive investigation on teacher-pupil relations and contains many interesting case materials. The second reading is a critical analysis of research in the area of group dynamics. The third reading is a discussion of the implications of this research for the organization of learning experiences. The fourth reading contains extensive descriptions of the use of group procedures in the school. The fifth reading is an advanced theoretical analysis of person perception problems. The last reading contains research articles on various phases of group operation. The authors also provide summaries of the present state of research in many areas of group dynamics.

1. R. N. Bush, *The Teacher-Pupil Relationship,* New York, Prentice-Hall, Inc., 1954.

2. M. Horowitz, "The Conceptual Status of Group Dynamics," *Review of Educational Research,* 23 (1953), 309-28.

3. K. D. Benne and G. Levit, "The Nature of Groups and Helping Groups Improve Their Operation," *Review of Educational Research,* 23 (1953), 289-308.

4. R. Strang, *Group Work in Education,* New York, Harper & Brothers, 1958.

5. R. Tagiuri and L. Petrullo (eds.), *Person Perception and Interpersonal Behavior,* Stanford, Calif., Stanford University Press, 1958.

6. D. Cartwright and A. Zander, *Group Dynamics: Research and Theory,* Evanston, Ill., Row, Peterson, and Co., 1953.

PART THREE

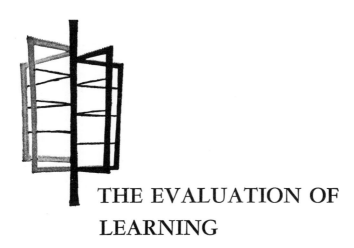

THE EVALUATION OF
LEARNING

THE EVALUATION OF BEHAVIOR CHANGE

In Chapter One we stated that the educative act had three aspects: (1) the formulation of a description of desirable behavior changes; (2) the organization of learning experiences designed to encourage these behavior changes; (3) the development of evaluation procedures for determining whether the desired behavior changes have occurred. There is a logical relationship between objectives, learning experiences, and evaluations, and it is important that the teacher remember this when considering any one of them. In this part of the book, we will focus our discussion primarily on the third aspect, with some necessary recourse to the first one.

In this chapter we will outline the basic principles of evaluation; in the following two chapters we will discuss the application of these principles, both in tests constructed by the teacher and in available standardized tests. The material presented in these three chapters is no more than an introduction to basic principles and procedures. The teacher who wishes to become thoroughly competent in developing and using evaluation procedures will want to pursue a more detailed study of this area.

WHAT IS AN EVALUATION PROCEDURE?

Consider the following example. A first grade teacher attempts to teach children the spelling of a list of words. Ordinarily, a child cannot spell when he enters the first grade. After presenting learning experiences designed to teach him how to spell, the teacher will make some determination of his present level of spelling performance. The teacher may ask, "How many words on this list can the child now spell correctly?" When the teacher has determined how many words the child can spell, he has a *measure of behavior change*. A child who could originally spell few if any words may now be able to spell fifty, seventy-five, or even a hundred words.

Once the teacher has determined the amount of behavior change, he must evaluate the extent of change by referring to some standard. Since any improvement in spelling ability is desirable, the question is this: Has the child changed as much as can be expected of him? Has he come up to some expected standard of performance? We probably want a child to be able to spell all of the words correctly.[1] Therefore, we *evaluate* the child's performance as "good" or "poor" by the degree to which he has approached this standard and by our estimate of his capacity to do so.

Again, if the teacher has organized a set of learning experiences designed to teach children cooperative behavior, he can determine the degree to which there has been an improvement in cooperative behavior by observing them during and after the learning experience. There will be varying degrees of improvement; the improvement of any one child must be evaluated by comparing his performance with our expectations for him. We evaluate his achievement on a dimension of "goodness," which is the degree in which he approaches the expectations. These expectations contain both a conception of what is an ideally or relatively good performance and an estimate of the pupil's basic ability to learn.

MAJOR PHASES OF EVALUATION. The task of evaluating behavior change has two aspects. First, a *measurement* must be made to determine whether a behavior change has occurred, and, if it has, in what

---

[1] The standard is the goal being worked for, not necessarily what the teacher expects each child will achieve. Furthermore, the expectation represents the teacher's standard and may not be the standard the child sets for himself.

degree.[2] Second, an evaluation must be made to determine the "acceptability" of the change. Below are some general concepts and principles relevant to evaluating a measured behavior change. Principles of measurement are discussed later in this chapter.

THE PROCESS OF EVALUATING A MEASURED BEHAVIOR CHANGE. Evaluating behavior change requires two kinds of judgments: (1) a judgment of what, in general, is a desirable behavior change; (2) a judgment of the "acceptability" or "goodness" of a particular behavior change. When a student has finished a course in American history, he has learned a number of facts and generalizations about American history; this change, we say, is desirable. But if he has responded to the learning situation by doing as little as he possibly can in order to "get by," we call this change undesirable. We base these decisions on our conceptions of what behavior changes are uniformly desirable.

Beyond this judgment we know that the performance of a student who does not know all the facts and generalizations to be learned in a history course is good or bad only in comparison with some standard of performance. To determine how "acceptable" his performance is, we make the second kind of judgment, a judgment based on our criteria of "acceptable" degrees or amounts of change.

CRITERIA FOR EVALUATION. In many cases the criteria of a "good" or "poor" performance are highly subjective. For example, a teacher who rates an English composition as "highly creative" is probably evaluating the writing in terms of his own conception of "creativity." His conceptions may or may not be shared by others. Objective criteria for behavior like "creativity" are difficult to determine, and standards tend to be influenced by uncriticized personal preferences. We are not implying that these subjective criteria are necessarily invalid or inappropriate. We would, however, expect considerable vari-

---

[2]Measurement is being used in this text in a comprehensive sense. We include under this heading categorization procedures, rank-ordering procedures, and scaling procedures. Some authors prefer to limit the concept of measurement to scaling procedures. The technicalities of these distinctions are beyond the scope of this book. An introduction to the characteristics of the above three procedures can be found in J. M. Bradfield and H. S. Moredock, *Measurement and Evaluation in Education*, New York, Macmillan Co., 1957. More technical discussions of this problem can be found in L. G. Thomas, "Mental Tests as Instruments of Science," *Psychological Monographs* No. 245, 1942, and in S. S. Stevens, "Mathematics, Measurement, and Psychophysics," Chapter I, in S. S. Stevens (ed.), *Handbook of Experimental Psychology*, New York, John Wiley & Sons, 1951.

ability in ratings of students' creativity when different teachers evaluate students' writing.

In other cases value standards may be more or less generally accepted. We would expect, for example, some general agreement among evaluations of children's cooperative behavior. This agreement is possible because people in our society have some common conceptions of what constitutes "acceptable" interpersonal relations.

In still other cases we use a prediction to evaluate performance. If a student's achievement in the fifth grade is very low, we may predict that he will do poorly in the sixth grade. We might then evaluate his fifth grade performance by calling it "unacceptable" as a basis for promotion to the sixth grade. Note that we may use the prediction to make a judgment. Our criterion may be that students who have not performed successfully should not be promoted. When we decide that the student will not be permitted to advance to the next level, we have made a *judgment* about the "acceptability" of the student's performance. The determination of the relationship between performance in one learning experience and that in another is a *measurement* problem. If judgments of acceptability are to be made in this way, the data necessary for making predictions must be gathered.

LIMITATIONS OF TYPICAL PERFORMANCE AS A CRITERION. The typical performance of students is frequently used as the basis for making an evaluation. For example, if we give a reading test to a group of fifth graders, we can arrive at an average score on the test for fifth grade children. We can also determine the range of performance or behavior change. We can determine the highest and lowest scores achieved by fifth graders. With this information, we can compare the performance of a student to the typical performances of fifth graders. We can say that he is performing as the average fifth grader performs, or above or below this average.

Such a description of the student's performance is the result of our *measurement procedures*. We have made an *evaluation* when we decide that the performance, as represented by the test scores, is or is not satisfactory. In this evaluation we have assumed that the criterion used represents a standard for·what fifth graders should be able to achieve. One must be careful about such an assumption. *The typical performance of a group of students does not necessarily set a standard for performance,* although teachers and administrators frequently assume so.

In principle, we cannot determine what "ought" to be from what "is." We cannot say that a student ought to read at a certain level because students typically read at this level. When we go beyond the descriptive data, we are adding some criterion of "acceptability."

PRINCIPLES FOR ESTABLISHING EVALUATIVE CRITERIA. The process of developing appropriate evaluative criteria is complex, and is a process in which the teacher is engaged continually. The following principles describe the characteristics that evaluative criteria ought to possess if they are to be useful:

1. The meaning of the value standard being applied should be precisely defined. The criteria of "acceptability" must be explicit and clearly defined if appropriate evaluative judgments are to be made. Applying the labels "good" or "poor" to a behavior change presupposes that we have defined exactly what is meant by each of these terms.

2. Since an evaluation determines the *degree* of "acceptability," the definition of the criteria must also define the levels or degrees of "acceptability." (See Table XXVIII).

3. The value standards embodied in the evaluative criteria should be relatively stable and should be applied consistently. Recall that evaluative criteria rest in part on a judgment of what constitutes a desirable behavior change. Students will have difficulty in clearly conceptualizing desirable goals if the evaluation of their changes in the directions of these goals is inconsistent or arbitrary.

4. Evaluative criteria should be consistent with the facts of child development. We have warned that typical performance does not set a standard for performance. But such typical performances do provide us with information on the range of pupil performance in relation to such variables as age, sex, grade in school, and intelligence level. With such data we can make an estimate of what a child might or might not be expected to achieve. For example, we will estimate that a child of below average intelligence will probably perform below the average

LEVEL	PERFORMANCE
I. Unsatisfactory	Cannot pronounce correctly the new words when seen written. Cannot answer questions about the most obvious facts contained in the story.
II. Fair	Can pronounce the new words correctly when seen written. Can answer questions about the most obvious facts contained in the story when the questions are phrased the same way as the statements in the story.
III. Good	Same as level II, and in addition: Can underline the new words from among other words when the new words are spoken. Also has a rough idea of the meaning of the new words. Can answer more subtle questions about the content of the story when the questions are phrased differently from the sentences in the story. Also can recall the sequence of the story.
IV. Excellent	Same as levels II and III, and in addition: Can correctly use new words in sentences of his own construction drawn from his own experience, and can identify when the new words are improperly used. Can relate the content of the story to his own experience and can give plausible explanations of the events in the story.

An Example of Definitions of Evaluative Criteria
(From Bradfield and Moredock)

TABLE XXVIII

of his class in many respects. We will not expect him to perform as well as the brightest child in the class.

Table XXVIII provides an example of a set of evaluative criteria that are consistent with the above principles. The development of this outline of evaluative criteria began with a conception of desired behavior change, a conception embracing two objectives: (1) to develop students' ability to remember and understand the factual content of a story and (2) to develop students' ability to recognize and use the new words presented in the story. The column labeled "Performance" describes the range of possible levels of achievement of these objectives. The column labeled "Level" represents the evaluation to be made of each of these levels of achievement. In this way degrees of achievement are related to degrees of "acceptability." Note also that the criteria are clearly defined.

The above discussion on evaluative criteria stresses that the operations of evaluating and of measuring can be thought of as logically distinct. In general, we assume that learning is acceptable when the desired behavior change has taken place; but since change is a matter of degree, we can make judgments on the relative "acceptability" of a performance only by referring to a standard more precise than that of "desirable."

A note of caution is appropriate here; it should be recalled in reading the remainder of this chapter. We have been using tests and testing situations as examples of the evaluation process; however, the teacher is continually evaluating his students' behavior changes. When a teacher asks a question in class, he makes an evaluative decision on the student's performance on the basis of the answer he receives. If the student does not know the answer to a question, the teacher has measured some aspect of the student's knowledge. But beyond this, the teacher will probably make an evaluation based on his assumption about whether the student ought to know the answer to this question. Formalized testing procedures are merely systematic ways of gathering data about changes in pupil behavior; evaluation procedures are not limited to these formalized testing methods.

EDUCATIONAL OBJECTIVES AND EVALUATION PROCEDURES

An educational objective is a statement about desired behavior change. Such a statement can be formulated at many different levels of abstraction. We can state that we want pupils to "have an appetite for learning," that we want a first grade child to "learn to share materials with his fellow students," or that we want a fifth grade child to "learn an appropriate concept of 'peninsula'." The first of these objectives is highly abstract and generalized. To acquire an "appetite for learning" requires many complex changes in the individual. The second objective is relatively less abstract; the third, fairly specific.

FORMULATING OBJECTIVES IN BEHAVIORAL TERMS. A clear conception of the desired behavior change is necessary if learning experiences are to be organized to produce these behavior changes and if evaluation procedures are to be established for assessing the extent of the behavior change. While we may agree that all students should have an "appetite for learning," such a statement does not tell us the behavior that characterizes an individual who *has* an "appetite for learning." We must know how such a person will act, think, and feel. We must be able to answer the question, "How can we recognize or identify a person who has an appetite for learning?"

Many educational objectives are stated at such a high level of abstraction that they have no utility for the organization of learning experiences or evaluation procedures. What behavior is implied in the phrase, "an appetite for learning"? What concepts, generalizations, attitudes, and values have been acquired by a person who has "an appetite for learning"? What behavior distinguishes this person from one who does not have "an appetite for learning"? These questions can also be raised about objectives such as, "The school should foster the development of intelligent participation in the processes of democratic government," or "The school should foster the development of cooperative behavior." Until we have defined these objectives in specific behavioral terms, we cannot organize a learning experience to foster these changes. Furthermore, we could not determine whether these desired changes had occurred since we have at best only a vague conception of the behavior to be observed or measured.

OBJECTIVES AS DESCRIPTIONS OF THE SCHOOL'S RESPONSIBILITIES. Statements of abstractly defined objectives are useful for describing the role of the school in society. Table XXIX lists objectives for the American school taken from a statement by the Educational Policies Commission of the National Education Association.[3] The Commission states that:

> The general end of education in America at the present time is the fullest possible development of the individual within the framework of our present industrialized democratic society. The attainment of this end is to be observed in individual behavior or conduct.[4]

---

[3]*The Purposes of Education in American Democracy*, Educational Policies Commission, National Education Association, 1938.

[4]*Ibid.*, p. 41.

THE OBJECTIVES OF SELF-REALIZATION

The Inquiring Mind. The educated person has an appetite for learning.

Speech. The educated person can speak the mother tongue clearly.

Reading. The educated person reads the mother tongue efficiently.

Writing. The educated person writes the mother tongue effectively.

Number. The educated person solves his problems of counting and calculating.

Sight and Hearing. The educated person is skilled in listening and observing.

Health Knowledge. The educated person understands the basic facts concerning health and disease.

Health Habits. The educated person protects his own health and that of his dependents.

Public Health. The educated person works to improve the health of the community.

Recreation. The educated person is participant and spectator in many sports and other pastimes.

Intellectual Interests. The educated person has mental resources for the use of leisure.

Esthetic Interests. The educated person appreciates beauty.

Character. The educated person gives responsible direction to his own life.

THE OBJECTIVES OF HUMAN RELATIONSHIP

Respect for Humanity. The educated person puts human relationships first.

Friendships. The educated person enjoys a rich, sincere, and varied social life.

Cooperation. The educated person can work and play with others.

Courtesy The educated person observes the amenities of social behavior.

Appreciation of the Home. The educated person appreciates the family as a social institution.

Conservation of the Home. The educated person conserves family ideals.

Homemaking. The educated person is skilled in homemaking.

Democracy in the Home. The educated person maintains democratic family relationships.

THE OBJECTIVES OF ECONOMIC EFFICIENCY

Work. The educated producer knows the satisfaction of good workmanship.

Occupational Information. The educated producer understands the requirements and opportunities for various jobs.

Occupational Choice. The educated producer has *selected* his occupation.

Occupational Efficiency. The educated producer succeeds in his chosen vocation.

Occupational Adjustment. The educated producer maintains and improves his efficiency.

Occupational Appreciation. The educated producer appreciates the social value of his work.

Personal Economics. The educated consumer plans the economics of his own life.

Consumer Judgment. The educated consumer develops standards for guiding his expenditures.

Efficiency in Buying. The educated consumer is an informed and skillful buyer.

Consumer Protection. The educated consumer takes appropriate measures to safeguard his interests.

THE OBJECTIVES OF CIVIC RESPONSIBILITY

Social Justice. The educated citizen is sensitive to the disparities of human circumstance.

Social Activity. The educated citizen acts to correct unsatisfactory conditions.

Social Understanding. The educated citizen seeks to understand social structures and social processes.

Critical Judgment. The educated citizen has defenses against propaganda.

Tolerance. The educated citizen respects honest differences of opinion.

Conservation. The educated citizen has a regard for the nation's resources.

Social Applications of Science. The educated citizen measures scientific advance by its contribution to the general welfare.

World Citizenship. The educated citizen is a cooperating member of the world community.

Law Observance. The educated citizen respects the law

Economic Literacy. The educated citizen is economically literate.

Political Citizenship. The educated citizen accepts his civic duties.

Devotion to Democracy. The educated citizen acts upon an unswerving loyalty to democratic ideals.

A Statement of Objectives for American Schools
(From Educational Policies Commission, National Education Association)

TABLE XXIX

The Commission identifies four aspects of educational objectives and outlines more specific statements in each of these categories (see Table XXIX). These statements define the responsibilities of the American school in the socialization of the child. These statements, however, must be refined by specifying the behaviors implied in the objectives as they are stated. Before we can hypothesize what curricula and what particular learning experiences will foster the attainment of these objectives, we must have a more complete statement, one that specifies the desired behavior changes more clearly.[5]

IMMEDIATE AND ULTIMATE OBJECTIVES. If we study closely the list of objectives outlined by the Educational Policies Commission, we will notice that these objectives represent end points to be reached. They are descriptions of what a person ought to be like when he has gone through a series of educational experiences. In the educational process as a whole, both immediate and ultimate objectives can be described. For example, the objective of the learning experience organized today may be the acquisition of information about the American Revolution, the development of the concept of a neutron, or facility in playing a musical score. In such cases the objective is immediate, and it is presumably attainable within a limited period of time.

But immediate objectives should be related to ultimate objectives. The child is acquiring a certain set of facts or a skill performance because such changes in behavior are consistent with becoming a person who has an appetite for learning, or who understands his society, or who appreciates beauty. In developing a statement of objectives we may proceed from generalized statements of ultimate objectives, such as those represented in the report of the Educational Policies Commission, to more immediate objectives which, when attained, are presumed to contribute to the attainment of the broader and more abstract objectives.

The teacher in a classroom situation is organizing learning experiences that do more than affect the child at this particular time in his life; they will have a permanent effect on him. The sequence of learning experiences is designed to provide for a systematic and orderly development of the child's personality. Table XXX shows teacher objectives for a kindergarten class and for a sixth grade class studying

---

[5]For more detailed suggestions for specifying objectives in behavioral terms, see Bradfield and Moredock, *Measurement and Evaluation in Education*, Chapter 2. Another discussion of the problem of specifying objectives can be found in B. S. Bloom (ed.), *Taxonomy of Education Objectives*, New York, Longmans, Green and Co., 1956.

KINDERGARTEN	SIXTH GRADE CLASS
I. TEACHER'S OBJECTIVE: To help the child learn to conform to the daily routine of the group. *Expected Behavior Changes:* 1. The child obeys school rules, which he has helped discuss and which he accepts. 2. He listens attentively, so that he carries out directions properly. 3. He willingly participates in art, music, and physical activities. II. TEACHER'S OBJECTIVE: To ease the child's adjustment to school situations. *Expected Behavior Changes:* 1. The child seeks answers to questions by making inquiries of the teacher and classmates. 2. He solves problems by himself. 3. He takes part in group play and activities. III. TEACHER'S OBJECTIVE: To teach the child to share with others. *Expected Behavior Changes:* 1. The child offers to share his toys with other children. 2. He waits in line to use play equipment, lavatory, and drinking fountain. 3. He is willing to share the place of prominence (first in line, holding the teacher's hand).	I. TEACHER'S OBJECTIVE: To help the child gain knowledge and understanding of the physical world of India. *Expected Behavior Changes:* 1. The child has a general idea of the physical features of India. 2. He knows what cholera is and how it is controlled. 3. He can explain some of the effects of altitude, temperature, and rainfall upon the economic and social conditions of India. II. TEACHER'S OBJECTIVE: To help the child gain skill and competence in using knowledge about the physical world of India. *Expected Behavior Changes:* 1. The child can make accurate measurements of physical phenomena such as rainfall, temperature, and wind speed. 2. He can interpret charts, maps, diagrams, and tables. 3. He can perform simple experiments in physical science. III. TEACHER'S OBJECTIVE: To help the child develop new attitudes and interests from his study of India. *Expected Behavior Changes:* 1. The child shows enthusiasm for movies and television programs with a scientific theme. 2. He is interested in new experiments in medicine. 3. He is interested in learning how men modify their environments.

*Teacher Objectives for a Kindergarten and Sixth Grade Class**

TABLE XXX

*These illustrative objectives were formulated by classroom teachers. Analyze them to determine whether they describe desired behavior changes in specific terms. Which of these objectives can be achieved while the child is in kindergarten or in the sixth grade? What is the relation of these objectives to the ultimate objectives of the school program?

India. Note the specificity of these objectives when compared to the statement of objectives by the Educational Policies Commission. The underlying assumption in the organization of the learning experiences in the kindergarten or sixth grade is that the attainment of these immediate objectives will contribute to the attainment of the ultimate objectives.

Ideally, the objectives of any particular learning experience ought to be derived from some conception of what the person is to be like when he has gone through a sequence of learning experiences. This ideal arrangement, however, is not always realized in practice. Lindquist made this point when he stated:

> Unfortunately, this ideal relationship among ultimate objectives, immediate objectives, and the content and methods of instruction has only rarely been approximated in actual practice. Some of the content of current instruction, if derived at all from sound and accepted ultimate objectives, has been derived from them by a process of faulty inference, and contributes much less to the realization of the objectives than other content which should be substituted for it. More unfortunately, a portion of the present content of school instruction is there only by reason of the organization of the curriculum by "subjects," and because of the practice of introducing new materials in intact subject units, or subject by subject, often without any careful selection for detailed content of those subjects. As a result of this practice many detailed elements which have no relationship whatever to any ultimate objectives have entered the curriculum simply because they "belong" in the same broad category of knowledge, or in the subject, with other content which could be readily justified, and because of which the subject as a whole was selected.[6]

This distinction between immediate and ultimate objectives has practical significance for the development of evaluation procedures. Since the objectives of the learning experience in a classroom are immediate, the evaluation procedures are of necessity designed to measure the attainment of the immediate objectives. We can measure what a student knows about American history, but we cannot measure what kind of a citizen he will be as an adult. We can determine the present reading level and interests of a fifth grade child, but we cannot measure what his reading level and interests will be ten years from now.

---

[6]E. F. Lindquist, "Preliminary Considerations in Objective Test Construction," in E. F. Lindquist (ed.), *Educational Measurement*, Washington, D.C., American Council on Education, 1951, p. 121.

RELATING THE ATTAINMENT OF IMMEDIATE OBJECTIVES TO ULTIMATE OBJECTIVES. In developing evaluation procedures, it is nonetheless possible to determine the relationship between the attainment of an immediate objective and some more comprehensive objective. We could, for example, study how students participate in student government, the extent to which they vote or do not vote in student elections. Then we could study the voting records of these children when they become adults and establish empirically the relationship between voting in student government elections and voting in municipal or national elections. With such data we could determine the likelihood that the attainment of an immediate objective will probably lead to the attainment of some more comprehensive one.

This kind of study is rarely carried out in our educational systems, or it is carried out in limited ways. We do have data on the relationship between success in high school and success in college. But we do not have anywhere near the information we need to assess the extent to which attainment of the immediate goals of a learning experience contributes to the attainment of more comprehensive goals.

By evaluating the degree of attainment of immediate objectives, we determine the value of a particular learning experience. By determining the relationship between the degree of attainment of immediate and ultimate objectives, we can also evaluate the learning experience in terms of its contribution to the attainment of the ultimate objectives. Suppose that we give a test in American history and find that the majority of students have profited from the learning experience as represented by their performance on the history test. The learning experience has apparently produced the results that it was designed to produce. But another evaluation of the relationship between learning American history and some more general objective, such as behavior at the polls, may suggest that the course in American history is making little contribution to the attainment of this objective. If the course is making little or no contribution to the attainment of the more comprehensive objectives, then the learning experiences provided in the course may need revising.[7]

---

[7]It should be noted that there are other criteria of value for the learning experience in American history courses. The learning experience provided in American history courses may contribute to ultimate objectives other than the one of voting in national elections. Other factors may also influence the frequency with which one votes in national elections.

TESTS AND EVALUATION PROCEDURES

An evaluation procedure begins in measurement. The function of a measurement process is to determine whether behavior change has occurred, and, if it has, to what extent. The measurement process itself begins with observations of behavior. We cannot determine whether a behavior change has occurred unless we observe behavior. We may determine the reading level of a student by observing, for instance, what kinds of material he can read. We may make an inference about a student's reading interests by observing the number and kind of books he reads.

TESTS AS SAMPLES OF BEHAVIOR. If we wish to measure the reading interests of students, we may gather data on the number and kinds of books they read, but we can rarely observe all of the behavior in which we are interested. Before we can determine a child's present reading interest, we must stop counting the number of books he reads. If we give a test in American history, we cannot ask every conceivable question that could be asked about American history. If we are observing children's cooperative behavior, we are ordinarily limited to observing this behavior at particular times and under particular circumstances. In other words, in making a measurement of behavior we obtain a *sample* of behavior.

A *test* is a sample of behavior, no matter what the form of the testing procedure may be. If the teacher tests the third grade class on a list of a hundred spelling words, he is obtaining a sample of the children's spelling performance. From a child's performance on these hundred words we may make an inference about what his performance would be like if we had given him all of the words that he has ever studied. If the teacher is measuring the cooperative behavior of his pupils, he may observe the number and kind of acts of cooperation among the children in a particular situation, such as when they are working in a committee or organizing a game. From this *sample* of a child's cooperative behavior, the teacher may make an inference about what the child's cooperative behavior is generally like.

NECESSARY CHARACTERISTICS OF A BEHAVIOR SAMPLE. The sample of behavior must be _representative_ of the total _population of behaviors_ that is being measured. By the *population of behaviors* we mean all of the behavior that could be observed if we had the time, means, and energy to observe this behavior. The population of potential behaviors in a course in American history includes the acquisition of all of the concepts, generalizations, solutions to problems, facts, attitudes, and values that the learning experience is designed to achieve. The sample of behavior that is observed in a test or test situation is only a portion of this population.

The sample of behavior observed is representative only if it is comprehensive enough and if it has the characteristics of the population of behaviors. While we cannot cover the entire range of behaviors, we must sample enough so that our conclusions about the child's behavior are reliable. We could not draw reliable conclusions about a child's knowledge of American history by his ability to answer the one question, "In what year did Columbus discover America?"

The behaviors that we sample must also be representative of the population of behaviors in the sense that they must be of the same kind as the behaviors in the population. If we wish to test a child's attitudes about American history, we must use procedures to determine what his attitudes are; we cannot come to conclusions about his attitudes by testing his ability to answer factual questions.[8] If we wish to test a child's ability to solve problems, we must place him in a test situation that requires problem-solving behavior; we cannot accurately estimate his ability to solve problems by testing his ability to produce facts. If we wish to draw conclusions about children's cooperative behavior, we must place them in situations in which cooperative behavior is likely to occur; we cannot infer from his reading habits the extent of a child's cooperative behavior. If we wish to test a child's understanding, we must have samples of the child's understanding behavior; if we wish to test a child's ability to solve problems, we must have instances of problem-solving behavior; if we wish to test a child's knowledge of facts, we must have instances of facts that the child remembers.

The basic assumption in any evaluation procedure is that the children being evaluated have had the opportunity to learn the desirable behavior changes the evaluation procedure is designed to measure. We patently violate this assumption if we define a sample situation, or

---

[8] It is conceivable that knowledge of some facts might be highly correlated with a given attitude. Even in this case, a test of facts enables us to make a prediction of what the attitude is likely to be, but is *not* a direct measure of the attitude itself. Furthermore, we must have empirical evidence that there is a relation between knowledge of facts and a given attitude; such a relationship cannot be assumed.

test, which gives us observations of behavior unrelated to the kind of behavior that was to be acquired in the learning experience. When teachers construct classroom examinations, they ordinarily sample subject content that could have been acquired in the learning experience. A fifth grade spelling test typically covers the words that were to have been learned by the fifth graders. But a test on subject content may not sample the behavior change specified as desirable. If a teacher gives a test on American history requiring only knowledge of facts, he can make inferences only about the children's knowledge of the facts of American history. He cannot make reliable inferences about the child's understanding of concepts and generalizations or about the development of the child's attitudes. The test sampled one aspect of the child's learning and, since it is representative of only this aspect, we can make inferences only about this kind of behavior change.

Another common error is testing for the attainment of objectives for which learning experiences have not been provided. If one of the important objectives of a learning experience is to develop concepts and understanding, but the whole emphasis in the learning experiences has been on the acquisition of facts, a testing procedure designed to test understanding is inappropriate. Many courses in social studies emphasize the development of social attitudes. A test on the content of social studies, as defined by the acquisition of facts, generalizations, and concepts, does not adequately sample the attitudinal changes in behavior.

Adequate evaluation procedures presuppose a consistency between objectives, learning experiences, and evaluation procedures. We are logically inconsistent if we attempt to evaluate a behavior change for which we have not provided adequate learning experiences. It is also inappropriate to make inferences about the attainment of all of the objectives of a learning experience from evaluation procedures which measure only some of these changes.[9] We would not attempt to determine a person's height by measuring his weight, unless there were some known and highly predictable relationship between height and weight. Neither would we attempt to make inferences about the height of ten-year-old boys by measuring the height of the first five ten-year-old boys whom we met. The principles of measurement suggested in these two examples are applicable to psychological and edu-

---

[9]Inferences of this kind are appropriate if there is a high correlation between the measured behavior and the behavior about which we are making inferences. This relationship must be demonstrated empirically.

cational measurement. A measurement is a sample of behavior that must be representative of a class or category, that is, a population of behaviors. We insure a representative sample by obtaining an adequate number of specific observations which are similar in kind to the behavior about which we are making judgments.

CHARACTERISTICS OF MEASUREMENT PROCEDURES

Every measurement procedure must have certain characteristics if we are to make accurate inferences about the behavior changes we are attempting to measure. The measurement procedures used in assessing behavior change also have certain characteristics which affect the kinds of inferences we may make from data gathered by using these procedures.

THE RELATIVE CHARACTER OF MEASUREMENT. If we are measuring height, we can make a statement about how tall a person is. We can also make statements about the height of the person in comparison with other people. We can say that he is taller or shorter than the average height of his group, or the height of some other individual.

Many behavior changes that we measure, however, cannot be broken up into units of amount. For example, we cannot break up changes in spelling behavior into units of spelling ability. If we are measuring how much American history has been learned, we cannot break up the behavior changes into units of knowledge of American history. We can, however, make inferences about the relative amount of behavior change that takes place. We can identify, in any class, the child who can spell the most words and the one who can spell the least. We can also identify the student who knows the most about American history and the student who knows the least.

Our measurement devices are essentially procedures for *categorizing people in terms of inferred amounts of behavior change*, rather than in terms of units of behavior change. This characteristic of educational measuring devices limits us to making statements of relative position or relative change. We can determine where a child stands in comparison with other children, and we can make simple categorical judgments about the presence or absence of change. But we have no devices for measuring the "absolute" amount of any behavior that we are measuring.

Teachers frequently make evaluative judgments based on a presumed measure of the absolute amount of a student's knowledge. A teacher may say, "This student knows nothing about spelling." A more precise statement would be, "This child knows less than children of his age and experience typically know." We may also make categorical judgments such as, "The child does not know the answer to this question." But we cannot infer from the failure to answer one question a complete absence of knowledge of the facts in a given subject. If a child does not know the answer to one question, we should not infer that he does not know the answer to other questions on the same topic. We may know that a child has not learned to spell all the words in a spelling list, but this measurement is only a relative measure of how much the child has changed.

THE RELIABILITY OF A MEASUREMENT PROCEDURE. Another important characteristic of every measurement procedure is that it must be *reliable*. When we say that a measurement must be reliable, we mean that it must be consistent; that is, repeated or comparable measures of a behavior change should place a child in relatively the same position on a scale of performance.[10] For example, if a teacher gives a child a spelling test, a second testing on the same or comparable words should place the child substantially in the same relative position, unless the child has been studying spelling between the testing sessions. An analogy from physical measurement will make this point clear. If we had a ruler that gave us differing measurements of height, assuming that we are taking the measurements one after the other or with comparable rulers, the measurement procedure would not be reliable.

FACTORS INFLUENCING RELIABILITY OF MEASUREMENT. Several factors influence the reliability of a measurement procedure. The measurement procedure must provide us with *enough instances* of the behavior that we are attempting to measure. Small samples of behavior are likely to yield relatively fewer reliable measurements. If we wish to draw conclusions about a child's ability to spell, we must give him enough words so that we can get a stable estimate of his spelling ability.

---

[10]There are several different ways in which reliability can be measured. A thorough discussion of these methods is beyond the scope of this book. The interested reader can find more information on this point in L. J. Cronbach, *Essentials of Psychological Testing*, New York, Harper & Brothers, 1949, pp. 59-73. See also A. Anastasi, *Psychological Testing*, New York, The Macmillan Co., 1954, Chapter 5.

We cannot reliably measure spelling ability by giving a child one word, nor can we measure a child's knowledge of social studies by asking him one question.

When we devise a measurement instrument, we also establish *optimal conditions* for measuring. We assume that a child is working at his maximum level of ability and that he is in good physical and emotional health. If a child is ill or emotionally disturbed, his perform-ance in a test situation will be affected.[11] Ordinarily, we want to know how a child can perform when he is functioning at his best, not how he is likely to perform when he is temporarily handicapped. Test scores may fluctuate when the optimal conditions for testing are not met. The most reliable score is likely to be the one obtained under optimum test conditions. When we say a measuring device must be accurate or reliable, we mean that it must be *reliable at the time of measurement and under the assumed conditions for measurement.*

THE VALIDITY OF A MEASUREMENT PROCEDURE. The most im-portant characteristic of a measurement device is that it must have relative *validity*. When we measure behavior change we want to be able to make inferences about a particular kind of behavior change. The measurement procedure is supposed to tell us something about this change. Insofar as the measurement procedure gives information on the behavior change we are studying, it is a relatively valid basis for making inferences about this behavior.

A test has relative validity only for specific purposes, that is, for measuring specific kinds of behavior change. The validity of a test is determined by the kinds of inferences that we want to make from our measurement. If we want to determine whether a child has learned the facts of American history, we must give him a test that is a valid measure of knowledge of facts. This test is relatively valid only for determining the extent of the child's knowledge of particular facts, and may have little or no validity for measuring his understanding of concepts and generalizations or for measuring his ability to solve problems.

The relative validity of a testing procedure must be determined for each kind of inference that we wish to make from the data the test provides. In this respect a word of warning is appropriate. Many

---

[11]M. L. Hutt, "A Clinical Study of 'Consecutive' and 'Adaptive' Testing with the Revised Stanford-Binet," *Journal of Consulting Psychology*, 11 (1947), 93-103. Also in A. P. Coladarci (ed.), *Educational Psychology: A Book of Readings*, New York, The Dryden Press, pp. 404-21.

published tests have descriptive titles which label the variables they purport to measure. A test may be called a test of "intelligence," or "mental maturity," or "social competence." A test user may assume that the test is measuring what he means by "intelligence," or "mental maturity," or "social competence," and may proceed to make inferences about these behavior patterns from students' test scores. But such a test is relatively valid only for the kind of intelligent behavior it measures. A given test may not measure, for example, the kind of intelligent behavior called "practical judgment," and inferences about students' "practical judgment" based on data from this test are not likely to be valid. Further discussions of this problem can be clarified by describing the general procedures that may be used to determine the relative validity of a test.

LOGICAL VALIDITY. Tests have two major uses in the evaluative phase of an educative act: (1) to determine the present status of performance; (2) to predict future performance on the basis of present performance. A test may be relatively valid for both or only one of these two purposes. The tests that teachers usually construct are relevant to the first of these purposes. If a teacher constructs a test that measures the behavior specified as desirable in a statement of educational objectives, and if the appropriate learning experiences have been provided, then the test is relatively valid for assessing the extent to which pupils have acquired the desirable behaviors. We say that such tests have "logical" or "face" validity. That is, "on the face of it," the test appears to be measuring what it is designed to measure or the tasks in the test are logically related to the kinds of behavior change specified as desirable. We have warned that we cannot too readily assume that the test actually does measure what it purports to measure. Teachers may assume that they are measuring a wide variety of behavior changes when, in effect, their tests are measuring only a limited number of such changes.

A distinction can be made between sampling behavior changes and sampling the content of a course of study. A test which asks questions on the facts, definitions, and principles of a subject may sample the students' knowledge of these aspects of the content of the subject. This test would have logical validity for measuring knowledge of the content, but it might not have logical validity for measuring specific kinds of behavior change. For example, a student may be able to work arithmetic problems which were part of the arithmetic content. Unless the test samples certain kinds of behavior, such as his ability to think quantitatively, to solve problems, or to reason logically, we have a measure only of what has been acquired of the content. In other words, we cannot assume that a measure of content acquisition is also a measure of the behavior changes that the learning experience was designed to foster. We are not suggesting that acquisition of content may not be important. We expect students to be able to remember facts and principles and to be able to perform routine operations. But these objectives are rarely our only objectives. In the next chapter we will discuss the problem of constructing tests that evoke the behavior we wish to measure. At this point, our discussion is sufficient if it has helped the teacher to be aware that a test on content may not always measure what he wants it to measure.

PREDICTIVE VALIDITY. A test has predictive validity in the degree to which we can use it to predict, from the test situation, performance in some other situation.[12] Here is one example of the way in which such a relationship could be established. A typing teacher dictates a business letter to his class and has the class transcribe the letter. When the teacher has graded the typed letters, he can make statements about the students' typing performance. He knows how many errors in transcription and typing the students have made. Assume that the letter he gave the students to type is similar to letters that they would have to type in business. Even so, the test has only logical or face validity because "on the face of it" the typing of this kind of business letter appears to be the kind of task that the student will eventually have to perform. This teacher could keep careful records of his students' performances on these exercises, and then obtain some rating of their performance on the job at a later date. If he then related performances on the test to those on the job, he could determine the predictive validity of his tests. If his typing tests had predictive validity, he would be able to say that a student who performed at a certain level on his typing test would be likely to perform successfully or unsuccessfully on the job. His tests would have both kinds of validity, logical and predictive. If a test has neither logical nor predictive

---

[12]There are several kinds of empirical validity, a technical discussion of which is beyond the scope of this book. A comprehensive discussion of this topic can be found in A. Anastasi, *Psychological Testing*, New York, The Macmillan Co., 1954, Chapter 6.

validity, we have no idea what it is measuring; it seems to be measuring some kind of behavior, but what kind we do not know.[13]

To establish predictive validity, it is necessary to have a *criterion performance* of what we are attempting to predict, that is, a standard to which we can relate present performance. For the typing class, the criterion performance was a specific performance on a job. If we relate performance in high school to performance in college in order to predict the latter, the criterion is college performance. A test of scholastic aptitude can be used to predict performance in a number of subject areas in both high school and college; in this case, performance in each of the areas is a separate criterion. Such a test has varying degrees of validity, since each of the predictions is based on a separate and distinct criterion performance.[14]

In saying that tests have relative validity for specific purposes, we mean this: predictions are probability statements about the relationship between performance on a specific test and a specific criterion performance. Consequently, it is important to determine the criterion performances that can be predicted from a test performance, and to know the relative validity of such predictions. At present, we do not have sufficient empirical data for judging many of the predictions implicit in the decisions of teachers. The predictive validity of almost all teacher-made tests is unknown, yet student performance on these tests affects many decisions made by teachers. A teacher who decides that a child should not be promoted to the sixth grade has decided, in one way or another, that performance in the fifth grade can be used to predict performance in the sixth grade. While we would assume that such a relationship exists, we may not know the relative validity of this prediction. Although tests which have logical validity may be used as the basis for inferences about the effects of a learning experience on behavior change, they should not be used to make predictions about future performance unless their predictive validity has been determined.

---

[13]A knowledge of statistical procedures is required to develop the kinds of predictive relationships that are being discussed here. Generally such predictive relationships are established by computing correlation coefficients, the significance of which can be used to determine the predictive validity of a measurement procedure.

[14]The following are examples of predictive studies: A. B. Crawford and P. S. Burnham, *Forecasting College Achievement*, New Haven, Yale University Press, 1946; G. K. Bennett, H. G. Seashore, and A. G. Wesman, *Differential Aptitude Tests: Manual*, New York, Psychological Corporation, 1959; E. F. Lindquist, *Iowa Tests of Educational Development: General Manual*, Chicago, Science Research Associates, 1957; H. T. Olander, M. J. Van Wagenen, and H. M. Bishop, "Predicting Arithmetic Achievement," *Journal of Educational Research*, 43 (1949), 66-73.

This same condition applies to making inferences about the relationship between attainment of immediate and ultimate objectives. Despite the difficulties in making valid predictions, the teacher's task frequently requires him to make judgments about future performance. And some kinds of validity can be attained; a teacher can make some general predictions from the level of a student's intelligence alone.[15] The lower the intelligence of the student, the less likely it is that he will succeed in the next learning situation. But it is important to realize that the teacher can make errors in inference when there are no reliable data on the relationship between performance in one learning situation and that in another. Such predictions should be made with caution and on the basis of as much relevant information as the teacher can gather.

OBSERVATION OF PUPIL BEHAVIOR
AS A MEASUREMENT PROCEDURE

The previous examples of test situations and measurement devices suggest neither the wide range of available measurement methods nor the broad area of behavior that can be measured. Here, we will indicate some of the major types of measurement methods that can be used in evaluation procedures. We will also point out some of the problems of measurement involved in using these methods.

A technique commonly used by teachers is that of observation of pupil behavior. As we observe the behavior of our students, we note important and distinguishing characteristics. We may say, "This child is aggressive and a bully," "This child is shy and quiet," or "This child does his homework." Statements of this kind are usually based upon *observations* of what pupils do in and out of the classroom. Since these judgments are frequently evaluative in character, the principles for evaluating behavior change (discussed earlier in this chapter) also apply to them. But we must not overlook the fact that these evaluations presuppose an adequate measurement of the behavior being evaluated. In the following sections we will discuss the method of observation as a technique for obtaining measurements of behavior change.

PROBLEMS IN USING THE OBSERVATIONAL METHOD. How ade-

---

[15] See studies cited in footnote 14 for data to support this statement

quate is the method of observation as a measurement procedure? Its relative value depends upon the extent to which it can give us reliable and valid information about pupil behavior. Three problems may arise when we attempt to obtain reliable and valid samples of pupil behavior by using the method of observation. When the precautions noted below are taken, however, such samples may be obtained.

The first problem in this method of measurement is obtaining a *representative sample* of behavior. Unless we use systematic procedures designed to obtain an adequate sample of observations, our measurement of pupil behavior may have less validity. Since the teacher cannot continually watch one pupil, but must interact with a comparatively large number of pupils, he usually obtains a limited and unsystematic set of observations. The sample of observations may also be biased because the teacher notes only unusual or deviant behavior. The teacher may be more likely to note and remember Johnny's speaking out of turn because this behavior disturbed "order."[16] Samples of behavior based on such unsystematic observations are likely to be unrepresentative of a child's *typical* behavior.

Another potential problem in using the observational method arises when the observations are not recorded until some time after they have been made. This *lapse in time* allows the influence of selective forgetting to affect the kinds of observations that are recorded. The teacher may remember and record only unusual and striking instances of behavior. The teacher filling out a rating scale on a pupil has the problem of remembering what this particular pupil is like. His ratings, which represent the summarizations of his observations, are probably biased both by the inadequacy and unsystematic order in which the observations have been gathered, and by the effects of selective forgetting.

A third potential problem in observation is that frequently the behavior to be observed is *not adequately defined*. For example, if we are to rate pupils on aggressive behavior, we must have a clear-cut definition of what we mean by aggressiveness. Two difficulties arise in attempting to define the kind of behavior to be observed. The first arises from the character of the language we use to describe behavior. We are frequently observing behaviors for which we have everyday descriptive terms. We want to observe behaviors that we call "aggressive," "selfish," "cooperative," or "friendly." Each of these terms,

---

[16]See Chapter Thirteen for a discussion on teachers' ratings of pupil behavior, pp. 497-98.

while it suggests a category of behavior, subsumes a wide variety of particular kinds of responses. Such words may have different connotations for each teacher who uses them. What behavior would you associate with each of the above adjectives? Before we can observe behaviors of this kind, we must specify the kinds of responses that will be called "aggressive," "friendly," or "selfish," and agree, at least for the purposes of observation, on the meanings to be associated with these terms.

The second difficulty associated with definition is *distinguishing between overt behavior and the inferred motive* for the behavior. If one child pushes another child, we may call this behavior "aggressive." On the other hand, we may decide not to call it "aggressive" because the child's *intent* was not to harm the other pupil. In defining the behavior that we are observing, we must decide whether we shall confine ourselves to describing overt responses or whether we shall also make inferences about the motive behind the behavior. For example, a teacher may describe a pupil as a "daydreamer." This inference may be based on the observation that the child is staring out the window frequently; however, a child may be "paying attention" while he is looking out the window. We can observe that "he is looking out the window"; we can only *infer* that "he is not paying attention."

IMPROVING THE TEACHER'S OBSERVATION OF PUPIL BEHAVIOR. We can devise observational procedures that minimize the possible errors in observation. If we carefully define the behavior to be observed, if our definitions comprise descriptions rather than inferences, if we set up a systematic observational schedule, and if we sample enough behavior over a long enough period of time, the disadvantages of the observational method tend to disappear. Many experimental investigations have used systematic observation of the kind described here.[17] When such methods are used, we find a relatively high degree of reliability in the observational method. As a matter of practical consequence, however, many of these precautions cannot be implemented in the classroom. A teacher in a classroom does not have time to make completely systematic observation of his pupils; he must also perform many other functions.

This discussion of the problems in observation should make the teacher aware of the possible errors that may occur when judgments are made on the basis of observed behavior. A comparatively casual observation in the classroom or on the playground is not a proper basis for making comprehensive judgments about students' behavior. The more extensive the evaluation of the pupils' behavior that is to be made, the more comprehensive and systematic must be the observations. And the teacher should recognize that he does have some opportunities for making systematic observations of pupil behavior. Teachers may use periods when they are not working directly with students to make systematic observations and records of these observations. Such observations can be made when students are working in committees or studying at their desks, or during an assignment to "yard duty."

The teacher also can check his inferences from observed behavior by making predictions from these inferences. These predictions in turn can be checked by new observations. For example, if a teacher has observed that a child becomes angry when he is frustrated, he might infer that this is the child's typical response to frustration. This inference can be checked by observing the child's reaction to other frustrating situations. How does he respond when he cannot work a

---

[17]See R. E. Arrington, "Time-Sampling Studies of Child Behavior," *Psychological Monographs*, No. 2, 1939; F. B. Newman, "The Adolescent in Social Groups," *Applied Psychology Monographs*, No. 9, 1946; P. S. Sears, "Doll Play Aggression in Normal Young Children," *Psychological Monographs*, No. 6, 1951; R. R. Sears, M. H. Pintler, and P. S. Sears, "Effect of Father Separation on Preschool Children's Doll Play Aggression," *Child Development*, 17 (1946), 219-43.

problem? What does he do if the teacher does not recognize his attempts to get attention? The teacher who checks inferences is likely to become increasingly sensitive to the distinction between what is observed and what is inferred.

Many of the above recommendations will not improve the use of observational methods if the teacher does not clarify his conceptions of the behavior categories that he uses to describe behavior. A teacher can think through what he means by such terms as "aggressive," "friendly," and "shy." Such clarification should be in the direction of defining these categories in terms of observable behavior. Increased clarification of descriptive categories is likely to improve the validity of inferences based on observations.

CHARACTERISTICS OF A TEST SITUATION

With observational methods, we can describe behavior as it occurs in typical situations in a classroom. However, it is sometimes necessary to arrange situations that will evoke the behavior change we wish to measure.

DEFINITION OF A TEST SITUATION. A *test* situation is a "contrived" experience to which the student is systematically exposed. As distinguished from a natural situation, it usually occurs at a specified time and in a specified place; the persons being tested are usually aware of the fact that they are being tested, and the test situation is, as far as possible, the same for each of the individuals involved in it. A test situation is not a measurement procedure itself, but rather a way of arranging situations so that measurements can be made. For example, if we want to study the cooperative behavior of children, we can organize a task and situation that should evoke cooperative behavior. Then by observation, we can measure the amount of cooperative behavior that occurs in this test situation.

ADVANTAGES OF A TEST SITUATION. One advantage of test situations is that they permit us to gather data about behavior in a more systematic manner than do natural situations. We also gather comparable kinds of data on each pupil from which we can make comparisons of relative achievement. Having students answer questions on a paper and pencil test, for example, enables us to gather data about all of the pupils in the class. Contrast this situation with one in which the teacher asks questions in class. As soon as the teacher obtains a correct answer to the question, he ordinarily moves on to the next question. He has no way of knowing whether any of the students who did not attempt answers could have answered the questions; he knows only which pupils answered correctly and which ones did not. He does not know how many other pupils could have answered the questions asked, or whether the pupils who did answer them could answer other questions. In other words, by using a comprehensive test, the teacher gathers a larger and a more representative sample of pupil behavior.

The measurement procedures used in test situations must have the characteristics required of any measurement procedure. Test situations usually provide more reliable and valid data since they afford more control over the behavior being studied.

CHOOSING APPROPRIATE TEST SITUATIONS AND MEASUREMENT PROCEDURES. The measurement procedure we use requires the student to use the kind of behavior we want to measure. If we have organized a learning experience designed to produce certain skill performances, we will want to use a measurement procedure relevant to these performance behaviors. For example, if we are teaching a course in driver education and one of the objectives is to develop skillful drivers, a paper and pencil test will measure *some* behaviors related to this objective. A driver must know the rules and laws of driving; a paper and pencil test will measure his knowledge of these rules. But his knowledge of the rules does not give us information about his skill in manipulating an automobile. If we wish to test how skillfully he drives an automobile, we must place him in an automobile and ask him to drive it under standardized conditions. The choice of a measurement procedure should be governed by the character of the learning experience itself and its objectives.

Procedures have been developed for measuring a wide variety of personality functions. We have tests of intelligence and aptitude, achievement and skill, attitudes and values, as well as tests of more complex aspects of personality, such as measurements of the need systems of an individual and his adaptive mechanisms.[18] Some of these tests can be used by teachers with some training. Other tests require extensive training before they can be used. Should the teacher want a more complete description of a pupil than the available test procedures can provide, he must refer the pupil to the school psychologist or psy-

---

[18]These various kinds of tests are discussed in Chapter Sixteen.

chometrist, who has been trained to make more comprehensive and thorough measurements and evaluations.

SUMMARY

Learning experiences are designed to foster desired behavior changes. Evaluation procedures are used to determine the effectiveness of the learning experience in fostering these changes. A logical continuity exists between the character of the desired changes, the learning experiences organized to foster these changes, and the procedures used to evaluate the extent of behavior change resulting from participation in the learning experiences. This chapter has presented some basic principles of measurement and evaluation. The following points were made:

1. A logical distinction can be made between *measurement* and *evaluation*. A measurement procedure is an arrangement for determining the amount of behavior change. We evaluate behavior change when we compare the measured change to some criterion of acceptable performance.

2. These criteria may be subjective and personal, or may be matters of agreement. Generally, teachers partially define their expectations in terms of pupil capacity. Empirical data on the relationship of one performance to another can also be used as a partial basis for establishing achievement criteria.

3. The first step in developing evaluation procedures is to define carefully the *objectives* of a learning experience. Many published statements of objectives are too abstract in character; they permit us neither to organize learning experiences that promote achievement of an objective nor to evaluate behavior change. The teacher will need to work out specific statements of objectives, that is, statements that describe desired changes in terms of observable behavior.

4. Broad statements of educational objectives are useful for defining the school's general responsibilities in the education of the child. We also assume a relationship between the attain-

ment of the immediate objectives of a particular learning experience and the attainment of the ultimate objectives described in these broader statements. At the present time, however, little empirical evidence is available to indicate the existence of such a relationship.

5. Measurement procedures can provide us with a sample of behavior. From this sample we can make inferences about the amount of change occurring in the population of behaviors from which the sample was taken. To make reliable inferences, we must obtain representative samples of behavior. These samples of behavior must contain an adequate number of instances of the measured behavior. The measured behavior must also have all the characteristics of the population of behaviors about which we are making inferences.

6. Any measurement procedure must have two characteristics: (1) it must be *reliable;* (2) it must be adequately *valid*. A measurement procedure is reliable in the degree to which it is consistent and stable. A measurement procedure is valid in the degree to which it provides us with a sample of the behavior that we wish to measure.

7. Measurement procedures will be reliable to the degree that we obtain a representative sample of behavior. Reliability also depends on the degree to which optimal testing conditions are maintained.

8. Measurement procedures are relatively valid for specific purposes. There are two major kinds of validity—logical and predictive. A measurement procedure has logical validity in the degree to which the sample of behavior is representative of the kind of behavior that we wish to measure. A measurement procedure has predictive validity in the degree to which we can use it to predict some future performance; it is valid if the predicted behavior — the criterion performance — actually occurs.

9. We have also analyzed the observational method as a measurement procedure. We have noted that there are three potential

problems associated with using observations as a method for gathering data about change in pupil behavior. First, since teacher observations are frequently informal and unsystematic, such observations may not give us a representative sample of pupil behavior. Second, the pupil behavior to be observed may be defined so vaguely that agreement on behavior change cannot be attained. A third problem in using the observational method arises when the recording of the observations occurs some time after the observations have been made. As a consequence, the report of the behavior may be affected by selective forgetting. We have also noted that, in defining the behavior to be observed, we must distinguish between observed behavior and inferred behavior. The observational method is likely to be useful if the behavior to be observed is carefully defined, and if systematic procedures are used to gather a representative sample of this behavior.

10. A test situation is an arrangement of a standardized task and of standardized conditions for performing it. Test situations differ from "natural situations," in which we observe behavior as it occurs. One of the advantages of using test situations is that we can use them to evoke the behavior we want to measure We can also make judgments of relative achievement in test situations since each person taking the test performs the same task under relatively similar conditions.

11. Finally, we have noted that the measurement procedure requires the student to use the kind of behavior we wish to evaluate. Irrespective of the particular form of measurement procedure used, the measurement device must provide a representative sample of the behavior to be measured and must be minimally reliable and valid.

The basic principles of measurement and evaluation will be applied in the next two chapters, in which we will discuss the principles of test construction and the use of standardized tests. The principles provided here are a starting point from which the teacher can begin to analyze his own evaluation procedures. The development of appropriate evaluation procedures is a necessary part of the teacher's task. The teacher cannot judge the value of learning experiences without using procedures which adequately measure the effects of these learning experiences on pupil behavior.

STUDY AND DISCUSSION QUESTIONS

1. Select a unit in some subject that you are teaching or may teach. Define the specific kinds of behavior changes that the learning experiences associated with this unit are intended to promote. Describe in detail the criteria that you would use for determining the extent to which the behavior changes that occurred were "satisfactory."

2. What hypotheses about child behavior have you used in establishing these criteria? In what ways can you determine whether the "acceptable" level of behavior change can be attained by the children in your class?

3. A school board member asked a sample of first grade children to identify the letters of the alphabet. He found that 12% made at least one error in identification and that 10% made at least two errors. He concluded that the schools were not doing a satisfactory job of teaching children the identification of the letters of the alphabet. What evaluative criteria are implicit in this person's criticism of these children's performance? What factors may be related to a first grade child's performance in identifying the letters of the alphabet? How would you account for the fact that 10% of the students made at least two errors in identification?

4. The same person asked a group of children to pronounce several words that he had selected and used a tape recorder to collect their responses. When he found several children who were unable to pronounce some of the words, he concluded that the teacher had not taught the children the use of phonetics. Evaluate his procedures and conclusion in terms of:

   a. The sample of behavior obtained from each child.

   b. The sample of the children studied.

   c. The criteria used to evaluate performance.

   d. The testing procedure.

5. You give a reading test to your sixth grade class and find that several students score considerably below grade level. What inferences would you make on the basis of these data? What information would you need to check your inferences? May you conclude that the learning experience was inappropriate for improving the performance of these children?

6. Some people argue that using the average test scores reported for large samples of students does not provide an accurate measure of what students can achieve.

These people argue that the average score tends to become the expected performance for students. Evaluate this argument and suggest some qualifications of this argument that need to be made.

7. Below are listed three general objectives. Describe each of these objectives in specific terms. Relate the attainment of these objectives to particular kinds of learning experiences at different levels of education. In what ways do the experiences in elementary school and high school contribute to the attainment of these objectives? What levels of behavior change may be expected at various points in the education of the child?

   a. The educated person writes the mother tongue effectively.

   b. The educated person can work and play with others.

   c. The educated citizen seeks to understand social structures and social processes.

8. Select the subject that you are or may be teaching and describe the ways in which the learning experiences you organize may or may not contribute to the attainment of each of the specific objectives you have listed. What kinds and amount of behavior change are to be expected as the result of the learning experiences organized in your class?

9. Given the objective: The educated citizen respects the law. In what ways do the home and school contribute to the attainment of this objective? What kinds of behavior change would you expect to observe if a child learns to respect the law? Be specific about the behavior expected and the context in which you expect to observe this behavior.

10. Assume that you have developed a testing procedure for determining the extent to which children have learned cooperative behavior. Essentially, your testing procedure consists in observing the frequency with which children share materials when working on a common project. What independent criteria could you use to determine the validity of your testing procedure? Does your testing procedure have logical validity?

11. A teacher has constructed a test on the content of Algebra I He finds, however, that he cannot predict how students will perform in Algebra II from the scores that they obtain on his test. How would you describe the validity of his test? For what purposes may the teacher utilize this test?

12. Assume that you wanted to measure the cooperative behavior of the students in your class. Describe the procedures that you would need to use in order to obtain a relatively reliable sample of pupil behavior. Be specific in your definition of cooperative behavior and in formulating the observational methods you will use to obtain samples of pupil behavior.

13. Some people argue that test situations are "artificial." They maintain that if we

want to understand pupils, we need to observe them under natural conditions. Evaluate this argument in the light of the principles of measurement discussed in this chapter.

14. Below are listed several traits on which teachers are frequently asked to rate pupils. Define each of these pupil characteristics in terms of observable behaviors. Suggest procedures by which teachers may make more reliable observations of these kinds of behavior.

   a. Courtesy.

   b. Application.

   c. Cooperation.

RECOMMENDED READINGS

Many excellent texts in measurement and evaluation are available; the readings listed below cite only a few of the references which will amplify an understanding of the topics discussed in this chapter. The first reading is particularly appropriate for students who are beginning their study of the principles of measurement. The second reading is a more advanced and technical discussion of the basic principles of measurement. The third reading is an excellent source book for an advanced discussion of basic principles of measurement.

1. R. Thorndike and E. Hagen, *Measurement and Evaluation in Psychology and Education,* New York, John Wiley & Sons, 1955, Chapters 6 and 13.

2. A. Anastasi, *Psychological Testing,* New York, The Macmillan Co., 1954, Chapters 2, 5, and 6.

3. E. Lindquist (ed.), *Educational Measurement,* Washington, D. C., American Council on Education, 1951, Chapters 5, 14, 15, 16.

CLASSROOM EVALUATION
PROCEDURES

In the preceding chapter we outlined some basic principles of measurement and evaluation. A teacher will also need to know some general principles of test construction if he is to develop adequate evaluative procedures. The formulation of a question, problem, or task may not serve to evoke the kind of behavior that we wish to measure and evaluate. A question asked in one form is likely to evoke one kind of behavior; asked in another form, it may evoke another kind of response. In this chapter we will discuss the relationship between the kinds of materials used in test situations and the kind of behavior we wish to measure and evaluate.

Evaluations can be made during any phase of a learning experience or prior to the initiation of a new experience. A "readiness" test, for example, measures the extent to which a student may be able to profit from a learning experience. We use this measurement to make an evaluation of his "readiness" for that new learning experience. A "diagnostic" test may be used to determine learning deficiencies either before or during a learning experience. Tests given at the end of a learning

experience may be used to measure achievement and to predict probable performance in a new situation. In each of these cases the function of the measurement procedure is to provide data for the evaluation of behavior change. To make these kinds of judgments, measurement procedures must be used which evoke the kind of behavior change we wish to evaluate.

WHAT IS TO BE EVALUATED?

A statement of the objectives of a course, a unit, or a learning experience determines what is to be evaluated. But even when they are fairly specific, these statements of objectives cover a wide range of psychological functions and behaviors. In most learning experiences the student acquires a wide variety of new concepts, attitudes, values, skill performances, and problem-solving techniques.

SPECIFIC DEFINITION OF EDUCATIONAL OBJECTIVES. The first step in devising evaluation procedures is to develop a systematic outline of the desired behavior changes in a form as specific as possible. Table XXXI gives a list of general objectives for a science course.[1]

---

1. Acquisition of Information.
2. Understanding of Important Technical Terminology and Symbols.
3. Ability to Identify Forms, Structures and Processes and to State Their Functions.
4. Familiarity with Reliable Sources of Information on Science Problems.
5. Ability to Recognize Unsolved Problems in Science.
6. Interest in Solving Science Problems for Which the Student Has No Present Solution.
7. Ability to Draw Reasonable Generalizations from Experimental Data New to the Students.
8. Ability to Plan Experiments and to Test Hypotheses.
9. Ability to Apply Scientific Generalizations to New Situations.
10. Skill in Laboratory Techniques.

General Objectives for a Science Course (From Hawkes et al.)

TABLE XXXI

---

[1] H. E. Hawkes, E. F. Lindquist, and C. R. Mann (eds.), *The Construction and Use of Achievement Examination*, Boston, Houghton Mifflin Co., 1936, Chapter V.

The statement of these objectives must be made more specific. For example, the teacher must determine what unsolved problems in science the students should be able to recognize when they have completed the course. They are not ordinarily required to be able to recognize all of the unsolved problems of science, nor are they even required to be able to recognize all of the unsolved problems in the special field of science being studied. What forms, structures, processes should the student be able to identify? What important technical terminology and symbols are to be learned? When the teacher has answered these questions, he will have an outline of the content of the unit or course and of the specific concepts, facts, generalizations, and attitudes that the student is expected to acquire.

Statements of objectives formulated as expected behavior changes are preferable to statements of objectives formulated as content to be acquired. One of the dangers in stating objectives as content to be acquired is that we may assume that content acquisition is correlative with other desired behavior changes. Wrinkle provides an example which makes this point:[2]

> Do you see why "knowing things" isn't a good objective unless something happens as a result of the learner's knowing the things that he knows? He can tell you that he should cross the street only at the intersections. He knows that is the correct answer. But what if he leaves the classroom and cuts across the street in the middle of the block? What if he knows that twenty-five miles an hour is the speed limit in the residential area in which he lives, but he drives thirty-five miles an hour?

In such cases facts have been remembered, but the desired behavior change has not occurred. Throughout this book we have emphasized that the educative act begins with a conception of desired behavior changes. Although the acquisition of knowledge is a behavior change, a statement of objectives in terms of content to be acquired may cause us to forget that we are often concerned primarily with other kinds of behavior change. The ideas, facts, and problems which constitute the content are the materials used to foster these behavior changes.

---

[2] W. L. Wrinkle, *Improving Marking and Reporting Practices*, New York, Rinehart and Company, 1947, p. 8. Used by permission of the author.

DETERMINATION OF RELATIVE IMPORTANCE OF OBJECTIVES. In preparing a statement of objectives, the teacher will need to determine the relative importance of each objective. Consider the objective of "understanding important technical terminology and symbols." Besides defining the number and kind of symbols or terms to be learned, the teacher will need to decide how these terms are to be understood and remembered. The definition of some terms must be memorized exactly because the terms are so important and are used so frequently that only precise definitions will clarify the meaning of the terms for the student. The student will need to define other terms only in his own words. Still other terms need only to be recognized, and we may not require the student to be able to define them exactly. These statements about how a term is to be understood and remembered indicate the relative emphasis placed on the specific performances to be acquired.

More comprehensive objectives will have varying degrees of importance attached to them. Some teachers will place major emphasis on recognizing unsolved problems in the science they are teaching. Other teachers will place a premium on the acquisition of factual information.[3] At this phase in the development of an evaluation procedure the teacher is answering the question, "How important is the attainment of each objective?"

The relative importance attached to the different objectives will determine the importance attached to the learning activities, as well as to the measurement procedures used to assess behavior change. Students usually do many things in a learning experience. In a social studies class the children read books for information and understanding, listen to the teacher's descriptions of events, participate in class discussion, write essays, make book reports, and organize into committees to carry out projects.[4] The amount of time planned for each of these activities should reflect the relative importance of the objectives of the course. If a teacher decides that what can be learned by independent research is more important than what can be learned by discussing a question in class, proportionately more time should be

---

[3] We are not suggesting that one of the objectives is inherently more valuable than the other. The decision about the importance of an objective is influenced by many factors, such as cultural and professional values, the nature of the material being studied, and the relationship of one unit or course to another.

[4] Note that either student behavior during these activities or the products of these activities themselves can be used to evaluate the influence of the learning experience. "Writing an essay" is a learning experience; the essay itself may be used to evaluate behavior change.

given for research. The teacher's evaluation of this independent research should be given correspondingly greater weight. If acquisition of information and concepts is the most important objective, then the testing procedures used to evaluate the learning experience should reflect proportionately more measurement of acquisition of information and concepts.

In Table XXXII is a list of concepts to be learned by sixth grade students during a unit on India. Some of these concepts must be

Culture	Irrigation	Mosque
Sari	Monsoon	Banyan
Turban	Millet	Universal
Caste	Maize	Fundamental
Desert	Bullocks	Optimistic
Mountains	Purification	Parable
Plateau	Ritual	Sorghum
Environment	Embroidery	Tamarind
Village	Shrine	Cobra
Population	Worship	Sacred
Tolerance	Scythe	Education
Brahmin	Mango	Self-confidence
Ceremonial	Bazaar	Beliefs
Betel nut	Charpoy	Resources
Chapatis	Koran	Homes
Peasant	Arable land	Diversity of beliefs
Manure	Pyre	Worth of individual
Deity	Imagination	

Concepts to be Acquired by Children Studying a Unit on India

TABLE XXXII

understood more clearly than others if the child is to attain the objectives of the unit. A test given to determine the extent to which children understand these concepts should reflect the relative emphasis the teacher has placed on the learning of these different concepts.

Logically, the systematic planning of objectives should precede organizing of the learning experience. Too frequently it is left until the time when the teacher evaluates behavior change. The teacher may revise his objectives in the light of pupil interest or pupil progress, but at the outset of a learning experience he needs to have some conception of why the children are participating in this particular experience. We have discussed this point at several places in the text, and repeat it here only to emphasize the relationship between the relative importance of specific objectives and the kinds of procedures used to measure behavior change leading toward achievement of these objectives.

SELECTING TEST EXERCISES

A test situation requires the person being tested to do something. We may ask the person to answer questions, supply meanings for words, perform a musical composition, write an essay, or operate a tool. We will use the term *test items* to refer to the *stimuli* designed to evoke the behavior we wish to measure. These stimuli may come in a variety of forms, requiring responses of many different kinds and of varying degrees of complexity.

TEST TASKS AS STIMULI. The test items must evoke the behavior we wish to measure. If we are testing a student's retention of a fact, we ask him a question that requires remembering the fact. For example, the question, "What year did Columbus discover America?" requires that the student recall the answer "1492." If we want to test a student's ability to add a column of figures, we present him with a column of figures to add. If we wish to test a student's ability to play a piece of music, we present him with a musical score to be played.

In the following sections, a set of examples of different item forms is given. These examples illustrate how the stimulus the item provides is likely to evoke different kinds of responses. The teacher will need additional study in the technique of item construction before he can become skillful in devising test items that will evoke the kind of behavior he wishes to measure. A number of books on this phase of test construction are listed at the end of the chapter.[5]

TEST STIMULI DESIGNED TO EVOKE RECALL RESPONSES. Below is an example of an item that tests the student's ability to recall information:

The primary colors are:
    (1)_____, (2)_____, (3)_____.

---

[5] A comprehensive collection of test items can be found in J. R. Gerberich, *Specimen Objective Test Items*, New York, Longmans, Green & Co., 1956.

To answer this question the student will have had to learn the names of the primary colors and be able to recall them.

Below is another example of a test item designed to test recall, but presented in a different form from that of the above item:[6]

Directions: One letter has been omitted from each of the words below. Write it in the blank space where it should be.
1. Priv_lege
2. Ne_essary
3. Mu_ilage
4. Cemet_ry
5. Per_eived

The following example is an item that tests acquisition of information, but requires the student only to recognize the correct answer, even though he might not have been able to recall it without this stimulus:[7]

Which one is not a lever?
1. Pencil sharpener
2. Seesaw
3. Derrick
4. Fishing rod
5. Scissors

Test items of this kind can be presented to students in a wide variety of forms, for example, as completion type, matching type, true-false, and multiple-choice types. To respond to each item, the student is required to recall or recognize something he should have learned previously.

Test items of this kind do not test understanding directly. If we wish to determine whether a student can use information, we must devise a test item or exercise that requires him to use information. In Figure 63 there is a test item of this kind.[8] The student has presumably

---

[6]C. W. Odell, *How to Improve Classroom Testing,* Dubuque, Iowa, William C. Brown Co., 1953, p. 54.
[7]From J. G. Read, *Read General Science Test, Form A,* Yonkers, New York, World Book Company, 1950.
[8]C. B. Arny, *Evaluation in Home Economics,* New York, Appleton-Century-Crofts, Inc., 1953, p. 143.

learned certain facts about choice of appropriate colors in clothing for men with different colors of hair, skin, and eyes. To answer this question he must remember these facts and then apply them to the particular type of man described in the test question.

Assume that the articles displayed on Screen I are to be worn with a suit of dark-value gray, a top coat of middle-value gray, and middle-value pigskin gloves. Choose the most becoming shirt, tie, handkerchief, and socks for each man to wear with the gray suit, coat, and gloves. Write the number corresponding to your choice in the blank at the left of each item, and list no article more than once.

ARTICLES OF CLOTHING	DESCRIPTIONS OF MEN
_____ 1. Shirt _____ 2. Tie _____ 3. Handkerchief _____ 4. Socks	A. Black hair, fair skin, and blue eyes
_____ 5. Shirt _____ 6. Tie _____ 7. Handkerchief _____ 8. Socks	B. Medium brown hair, blue eyes, and somewhat sallow skin
_____ 9. Shirt _____ 10. Tie _____ 11. Handkerchief _____ 12. Socks	C. Auburn (red) hair, brown eyes, and florid complexion

An item testing ability to apply information. (From Arny)

FIGURE 63

TEST STIMULI DESIGNED TO EVOKE CONCEPTUAL RESPONSES. Below is an item designed to test understanding of a concept:[9]

Directions: Some of the groups of words below are complete sentences and some of them are not. You are to read each group of words and ask yourself "Is this a sentence?" If you think the group of words is a sentence, you are to cross out the Y (Yes); if you think the group of words is not a sentence, you are to cross out the N (No).
1. To stand erect is good posture. N - Y
2. Run into the house and get your doll. N - Y

To respond to this question the student cannot call on his memory.

---

[9]R. V. Young and W. E. Pratt, *American School Achievement Tests*, Intermediate Form B, Test V, Language, Part 4, Sentence Recognition, Cincinnati, Ohio, Public School Publishing Company, 1943.

He has not memorized long lists of sentences among which are these particular sentences. The teacher has presented him with examples of sentences and with examples of non-sentences and has stressed the characteristics of the concept "sentence." If the student has acquired this concept, he will be able to recognize both examples and non-examples of the concept. This test item requires him to do just that. He must identify the examples and the non-examples of the concept, "sentence."

Figure 64 gives another example of a test item for determining concept development.[10] If the child has the concepts and the appro-

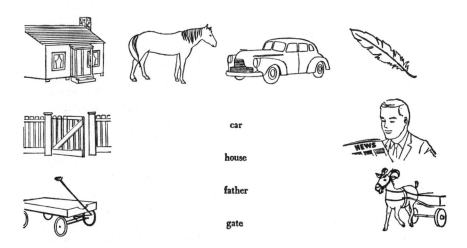

An item testing concept formation. The student is required to draw a line from the words to the appropriate picture. (After Hildreth)

FIGURE 64

priate word symbols for these concepts, he will be able to identify correctly each object in terms of its name. In this example the words are simple and familiar to most elementary school children. If they do not know what a car is, however, they cannot identify the correct

[10]G. H. Hildreth, *Metropolitan Achievement Tests*, Primary I, Form R, Test 1, Reading—Word Picture, Yonkers, N. Y., World Book Co., 1946, p. 3.

picture. From this we would infer that they have not yet acquired an adequate concept of "car."[11]

TEST STIMULI DESIGNED TO EVOKE GENERALIZING RESPONSES. The following is an example of a test item used to measure ability to draw reasonable generalizations from experimental data.[12]

Directions: In the following exercise, an experiment has been described. Below the description are some statements which have been suggested as interpretations of the experiment. Assume that the facts given in the description of the experiment and in the data obtained are correct; then on the basis of these facts only consider each statement. Mark with a figure 1 every statement which is a reasonable interpretation of the data obtained; mark with a 2 every statement which is most likely true but for which the given facts are insufficient to justify the interpretation; mark with a 3 every statement which cannot be judged as either true or false because of the insufficiency of the given facts; mark with a 4 every statement which cannot be true because it is contradicted by the data obtained in the experiment.

Nine hundred seeds of a certain plant were divided into nine groups of 100 seeds each. Each group of 100 seeds was placed in a germinator. The seeds in all the germinators were under the same conditions of air and moisture, and they were all kept in the dark. Each germinator, however, was kept at a different temperature. The various temperatures and the number of seeds which germinated within 30 days are shown in the table below.

Temperature in degrees Centigrade.....	6	8	11	13	18	25	30	35	39
Number of seeds which germinated.......	0	0	0	0	16	50	84	30	0

a. More seeds of this variety will germinate at 28° C. than at any other temperature ..... (3) a.___

b. None of the seeds germinated within 30 days

---

[11]The following book is recommended to the teacher who wishes to explore the problems of measuring understanding. This book discusses general principles and also provides applications of these principles to a wide variety of subject areas: N. B. Henry (ed.), *Forty-fifth Yearbook of the National Society for the Study of Education, Part I, The Measurement of Understanding*, Chicago, University of Chicago Press, 1946.

[12]Hawkes *et al., The Construction and Use of Achievement Examinations*, pp. 241-42.

at the temperatures in the experiment which
were below 18° C .... (1) b.___

c. The higher the temperature, the greater the
number of seeds which germinated .... (4) c.___

d. As far as the results of this experiment go,
30° C. is the optimum temperature for germinating these seeds .... (1) d.___

e. Some of the seeds of this variety will
germinate at 39° C. .... (2) e.___

f. The rate at which the seeds germinated was
affected by the temperature .... (2) f.___

g. Whenever seeds of this variety are germinated at 25° C., only one out of four seeds
will germinate .... (4) g.___

h. A decrease in moisture content reduces the
number of seeds germinating more than does a
decrease in temperature .... (3) h.___

i. Beginning at 30° C, an increase of 5° C. resulted in a much greater reduction in the
number of seeds germinating than did a
decrease of 5° C. .... (1) i.___

j. More seeds would have germinated at the lower temperatures if they had been left for a
longer time in the germinators .... (2) j.___

From the facts given, statements *b*, *d*, and *i* are reasonable interpretations. Statements *e*, *f*, and *j* are most likely true, although the facts are
not sufficient to justify them. Insufficient facts are given to decide whether
statements *a* and *h* are likely to be true or not, while statements *c* and *g* are
contradicted by the data obtained in the experiment.

The kinds of statements to be marked *2* or *3* are interpretations which
go beyond the data by extrapolation or interpolation. They are interpretations which include the whole population, whereas the experiment concerned
only a few individuals, and interpretations which include other kinds of
populations than those in the experiment.

TEST STIMULI DESIGNED TO EVOKE SKILL PERFORMANCES. If we want to measure a student's achievement of a performance skill, such as his ability to play a piece of music, operate a lathe, or hammer a nail in straight, we present him with the materials required for performance and then we observe the performance. To measure achievement in such situations, we must observe the performance and rate

(a) NAILS:

(1) Straightness 1 2 3 4 5 6 7 8 9 10
Are nails driven straight, heads square with wood, no evidence of bending?

(2) Hammer marks 1 2 3 4 5 6 7 8 9 10
Is wood free of hammer marks around nails?

(3) Splitting 1 2 3 4 5 6 7 8 9 10
Is wood free of splits radiating from nail holes?

(4) Depth 1 2 3 4 5 6 7 8 9 10
Are depths of nails uniform and of pleasing appearance?

(5) Spacing 1 2 3 4 5 6 7 8 9 10
Are nails spaced too close or too far apart?

(6) Utility 1 2 3 4 5 6 7 8 9 10
Will the nails hold?

(b) SCREWS:

(1) Slots 1 2 3 4 5 6 7 8 9 10
Are slots free of splitting and other evidence of driving strains?

(2) Straightness 1 2 3 4 5 6 7 8 9 10
Are screws straight, heads parallel with surface?

(3) Splitting 1 2 3 4 5 6 7 8 9 10
Is wood free of splits in the area of screws?

(4) Screwdriver marks 1 2 3 4 5 6 7 8 9 10
Is wood free of screwdriver marks near screws?

(5) Countersinking 1 2 3 4 5 6 7 8 9 10
Is countersinking neat and of satisfactory depth?

(6) Spacing 1 2 3 4 5 6 7 8 9 10
Are screws spaced too close or too far apart?

(7) Utility 1 2 3 4 5 6 7 8 9 10
Will the screws hold?

Example of a performance rating scale. (From Adkins et al.)

FIGURE 65

it. Figure 65 contains a performance rating scale.[13] The test requires the student to fasten pieces of wood in a woodworking project. In this case only one aspect of a complex performance is being measured:

---

[13] D. C. Adkins *et al.*, *Construction and Analysis of Achievement Tests*, Washington, D.C., Government Printing Office, 1948, p. 231.

how the fastenings are made. The kinds of fastenings are specified, and the characteristics of the fastenings are outlined in the column on the left. The questions in the right-hand column suggest the criteria of an acceptable performance. An observer would judge the extent to which the pupil approached perfect performance and rate him accordingly.

Skill performances also can be measured by rating the products of these performances. When we rate the product as such, we assume that better products are produced by individuals with more highly developed skills. For example, in the woodworking class we could rate the finished products of the students. Since a student may need to use many different skills in completing a project, a rating of the project as a whole tells us something about the student's ability to use all of these skills. The student may be more skillful in some respects than in others; if the teacher wishes to test particular skills, he must determine the desired behavior changes, the relative importance of each of them, and then select appropriate measurement procedures for rating skill performances. If an important objective is developing students' ability to construct a well-made product, then a rating of the product is probably an appropriate measure of the extent to which students have achieved this objective.[14]

These examples illustrate how the *item form* or *test stimuli* can evoke the particular kind of behavior we want to measure. The teacher should be aware of the particular kinds of behavior evoked by the test items he uses; and he should remember that only continual evaluation of the items themselves can assure that they provide the information necessary for making judgments about pupil progress.

ITEM FORM

There are many ways of asking a question. It can be stated directly: *In what year was the Colony at Jamestown founded?* It can require identification of the correct answer: *Jamestown was founded in (A) 1650; (B) 1607; (C) 1590; (D) 1603.* Or "Jamestown" could be listed among other colonies in one column, and the founding dates of each of these colonies in another; students could thus be asked to

---

[14]A comprehensive discussion of the problems of measurement involved in rating performances can be found in D. G Ryans and N. Fredericksen, "Performance Tests of Educational Achievement," in E. Lindquist (ed.), *Educational Measurement,* Washington, D. C., American Council on Education, 1951, Chap. 12.

match dates with colonies. Or we could write out the statement, "Jamestown was founded in 1607," and ask the students to identify this statement as *true* or *false*. Each of these item forms tests memory of a fact, although some of them test it as recall, whereas others test it by requiring the student to recognize the correct date.

CHOICE OF ITEM FORM. Any of the alternative item forms may be used so long as it evokes the behavior that we want to measure. But other considerations influence the selection of item forms. If we wish to test a wide range of factual knowledge, some parts of which we want the student to recall and other parts of which we want him only to recognize as being correct, we will probably find that using items that require the student to fill in a blank or to check the correct responses are more appropriate. A student can answer a large number of these questions in a comparatively short period of time.

APPROPRIATE USE OF SHORT-FORM QUESTIONS. Some forms of items can measure only a limited number of behaviors. For example, *the fill-in, the true-false, and the matching type items are most useful in testing acquisition of information.* If our purpose is to determine how much information students have acquired, using this kind of item allows quick and easy testing of a wide range of information. The short form of the questions makes it easy to identify errors. The disadvantage of this item form is that it places a premium on remembering information as isolated bits of fact.

A multiple-choice item can be designed to test remembrance of facts, knowledge of concepts and principles, or ability to draw generalizations and solve problems. We presented an item above in which the student had to draw inferences and generalizations from experimental data; that item illustrates one of the many uses of multiple-choice items. It is a common impression among many teachers that multiple-choice items can be used only to test factual information. This impression is probably the result of the way in which multiple-choice items are frequently used in teacher-constructed tests. An imaginative test constructor can use multiple-choice tems for testing a wide variety of behaviors.

APPROPRIATE USE OF ESSAY-TYPE QUESTIONS. Some questions require the student to respond at length; questions of this type are usually called *essay questions*. The *essay question* can be used to test some behaviors that cannot be or are not easily tested by other item forms. In Table XXXIII is a list of behaviors that can be tested by an essay question.[15] If we want to test a student's ability to organize information, to criticize and evaluate points of view and data, or to hypothesize about possible solutions to problems, we can most easily evoke these functions by presenting the student with questions to which he must respond extensively. We may also want to evaluate the student's ability to write clearly and correctly, and we may want to evaluate his style of writing. If these are the behaviors we want to measure, the essay question is probably the most appropriate form of question to use.

Some items often called "essay questions" do not evoke the behaviors most appropriately measured by this form. Because a student has to write out the answer to the question, *In what year was the Declaration of Independence signed?* the question does not become an essay question; yet some teachers refer to five or ten such questions which require remembering facts or generalizations as an "essay examination" simply because the student must write out the answers. The teacher could have obtained a more representative sample of behavior by using a short-form question, the answers to which allow a more reliable estimate of the student's knowledge of facts.

Some essay questions are too vague or too comprehensive to indicate to the student the kind of response desired. Since a properly constructed essay question tests at least one complex function, if not several, the question form should clearly indicate the kind of response that is desired. An essay question that states, *Discuss tariff regulations and American foreign relations,* does not clearly indicate what kind of response the student is expected to make. The meaning of "discuss" is not clear. As a consequence, the student does not know whether he is supposed to list specific instances of tariff regulations and their assumed effect on foreign relations, to criticize and evaluate the effects of the tariff regulations, or whether he is to suggest alternative regulations which could achieve the same effect. The student can respond at length, and frequently does, by attempting to cover as much ground as he thinks the question like this might require. Again, we emphasize that the teacher should clarify his understanding of the behavior changes he desires before designing procedures to measure

---

[15] W. S. Monroe and R. E. Carter, "The Use of Different Types of Thought Questions in Secondary Schools and Their Relative Difficulty for Students," *Bureau of Educational Research Bulletin,* No. 14, 1923.

1. *Selective recall—basis given.*
Name three important developments in measurement which occurred during the first decade of the twentieth century.

2. *Evaluating recall—basis given.*
Name the three persons who have had the greatest influence on the development of intelligence testing.

3. *Comparison of two things—on a single designated basis.*
Compare essay examinations and objective tests from the standpoint of their effect upon the study procedures used by the learner.

4. *Comparison of two things—in general.*
Compare standardized and non-standardized tests.

5. *Decision—for or against.*
In which, in your opinion, can you do better, oral or written examinations? Why?

6. *Cause or effects.*
How do you account for the great popularity of objective tests during the last thirty-five years?

7. *Explanation of the use or exact meaning of some phrase or statement in a passage.*
What is the meaning of "Delta" in the verse quoted on page 193?

8. *Summary of some unit of the text or some article read.*
Summarize in not more than one page the advantages and limitations of essay examinations.

9. *Analysis* (The word itself is seldom involved in the question).
Why are many so-called "progressive educators" suspicious of standardized tests?

10. *Statement of relationships.*
Why is it that nearly all essay examinations, regardless of the school subject, tend to be measures of the learner's mastery of English?

11. *Illustrations or examples (your own) of principles in science, construction in language, etc.*
Give two original examples of specific determiners in objective tests.

12. *Classification* (usually the converse of No. 11).
What type of error appears in this test item? "With what Balkan country did the Allies fight in World War I?"

13. *Application of rules or principles to new situations.*
In the light of China's experience with state examinations what would you expect to be the effect of the Regents' Examinations in New York?

14. *Discussion.*
Discuss the place of measurement in science.

15. *Statement of aim—author's purpose in his selection or organization of material.*
In view of the author's discussion on pages 19 and 20, why are so many authorities quoted in Chapter 1?

16. *Criticism—as to the adequacy, correctness, or relevancy of a printed statement, or a classmate's answer to a question on the lesson.*
Criticize or defend the statement, "The essay examination overrates the importance of knowing how to say a thing and underrates the importance of having something to say."

17. *Outline.*
Outline the principal steps in the construction of an informal teacher-made test.

18. *Reorganization of facts* (a good type of review question to give training in organization).
Name ten practical suggestions from Chapters 4, 5, and 6 that are particularly applicable to the subject you teach or plan to teach.

19. *Formulation of new questions—problems and questions raised.*
What are some problems relating to the use of essay examinations that require further study?

20. *New methods of procedure.*
Suggest a plan for proving the truth or falsity of the contention that exemption from examinations is a good policy in high school.

Responses that can be Tested with Essay Questions and Examples of Questions Likely to Evoke the Desired Response (From Monroe and Carter)

TABLE XXXIII

behavior change.[16] The problems which arise in scoring and grading essay examinations are discussed later in this chapter.

THE SCOPE OF EVALUATIVE PROCEDURES

The discussion of item forms and the range and function of measurement methods suggests the range of possible methods for evaluating behavior change. The teacher continually makes decisions about what and when to evaluate; although he may sometimes do this informally, he must often choose formal evaluative procedures and decide when to use them.

TEST FREQUENCY. One question that teachers often ask is, "How frequently shall I give tests?" The answer to this question varies with the kind of behavior being evaluated. Some kinds of behavior changes cannot be evaluated until the student has had time to integrate the effects of learning. For example, if we want to evaluate a student's ability to analyze a complex problem, we will have to wait until he has acquired the concepts, generalizations, and facts necessary to solve the problem. While we break up learning experiences into units, what is learned in one learning experience is frequently used in another unit of learning experience. A student who learns the symbols for chemical elements will use them throughout a chemistry course, even though he may have studied them originally in a unit on chemical symbols. If we want to test this student's knowledge of chemical equations, we must wait until he has learned all of the symbols required and until he has had sufficient experience in solving chemical equations.

We will want to measure some behavior changes at the time of the learning experience, and others at a later period in order to evaluate long-term change. To do this, a teacher may use a number of short tests or a series of long tests, and a comprehensive final examination. The final, comprehensive examination ordinarily measures long-term gains, whereas the periodic examination measures immediate mastery. The comprehensive examination can also be designed to measure the student's ability to integrate material he has learned over a long period of time. In other words, the timing of the examination serves different functions, as do the kinds of test situations that are provided.

---

[16]For a discussion of the many ways in which different item forms can be used, see Gerberich, *Specimen Objective Test Items*, Part III.

USE OF SHORT QUIZZES. Some teachers give short quizzes daily. Such quizzes may have two purposes: (1) to check on immediate mastery of what is being learned; (2) to serve as motivational devices that encourage students to keep up with their work. We should recall that the shorter the test, the less likely its reliability.[17] A short-question test of two or three items given daily is not usually a reliable test because it does not adequately sample what the student has learned. As a consequence, the teacher must be careful in drawing inferences about behavior change from the results of short tests, although the total of a series of short tests may yield a reliable measurement, even though any one of them is less reliable. And, as we have noted elsewhere, the use of tests for motivational purposes may result in rewarding inappropriate behavior.

Let us summarize here the basic concepts a teacher must use in setting up a testing program. In the first place, the teacher must have a clear conception of the behavior changes that are expected as the result of the learning experience, and he must design measurement devices to test changes in all of these behaviors. Second, the scope of the evaluation procedures must be as broad as the statement of desirable behavior changes. Third, the importance attached to attaining different behavior changes must be given corresponding emphasis in each of the evaluation procedures that the teacher uses. Fourth, the timing of evaluation procedures is determined by the kinds of judgments the teacher wishes to make.

AN EXAMPLE OF COMPREHENSIVE EVALUATION. Let us use an example to illustrate how these principles might be applied in a particular class. In a woodworking course, there are certain skill performances that we expect the students to learn. They also must acquire certain facts and concepts. Before we organize the learning experiences, we decide on the relative importance of facts and how they are to be remembered. We decide on the relative importance of learning concepts and generalizations and learning various skill performances. After doing this, we can organize a system of measurement procedures to determine the extent to which changes in these various behaviors have occurred.

One of our specific objectives may be to have the student learn

---

[17]For a discussion of this principle, see L. J. Cronbach, *Essentials of Psychological Testing*, New York, Harper & Brothers, 1949, pp. 60-61.

how to construct a table. This objective presupposes that he will first acquire the skills and knowledge necessary to constructing a table. The most appropriate evaluation procedure would be a performance test requiring the student to build a table.

At earlier points in the course we may test the student on specific skills, such as his skill in hammering nails correctly, his skill in making fastenings of one kind or another, or his skill in sanding and varnishing. We may give short-form questions to test his grasp of information and his understanding of concepts and generalizations. Some of these measurement procedures will be used to diagnose difficulties that the student is having in the learning experience, so that we can reorganize the learning experience for the student. Other measurement procedures will be used to make a final evaluation of the student's performance in this course. The measurement procedures used are chosen on the basis of the evaluation the teacher wishes to make and the purposes for which the evaluations will be used.

We have chosen the example of the woodworking class because in such a class we may use a variety of measurement procedures. In many other kinds of classes, an equally comprehensive set of measurement procedures is required if we are to determine the extent to which pupils have attained the objectives of the learning experience. No single procedure can be used to measure all of the behavior changes that are deemed desirable in any class.

We are limited in measuring some of these behavior changes by the lack of adequate measuring devices. When he lacks an adequate measuring device, the teacher should make only tentative judgments about behavior change, recognizing the very limited value of measurements which are unreliable.

Evaluating, like the organizing of learning experiences, is a process, not a single, static event. There are no simple, infallible rules for constructing and using appropriate measurement devices. In implementing evaluation procedures, the teacher is a hypothesis-maker. He may hypothesize about the appropriate time for a test, about appropriate item forms, and about the relation of test item responses to the kinds of behavior he wishes to measure. We have outlined some general principles from which the teacher should derive the innumerable specific hypotheses about the measurement procedures he will use in his classroom. Each of these hypotheses must be evaluated and revised if found to be relatively unsatisfactory.

SCORING AND GRADING

Ordinarily a student's performance in a test situation is summarized by a score. This score may be the number of problems worked correctly, the number of correct answers, or the number of errors made. These are called "raw scores." A raw score, such as the number of words spelled correctly in a test, tells us only what per cent of the student's responses were made in the appropriate manner. To gain a better understanding of the student's performance, we must translate raw scores into scores that indicate the student's relative position on a scale of performance. For example, we may arrange the scores by rank from highest to lowest, or we may group them in categories, such as "upper quarter," "middle half," and "lower quarter." Still another possible arrangement would be to group the scores by tenths —"top tenth," and on down to "lowest tenth." Each of these arrangements describes the student's status as it compares with that of other students in the class.[18]

GRADES AS EVALUATIVE SYMBOLS. When we have scored a test performance, we have quantified the learner's status or change, but we have not yet evaluated this change. Some criterion of acceptability must be established. That "70" shall be a passing grade is an example of such a criterion of acceptability. Another way of determining acceptability is to rank the students on their performance and assign letter grades, such as "A" or "B," to different levels of performance. An "A" grade ordinarily means an acceptable and superior performance; a "B" grade, an acceptable and good performance; a "C" grade, an average performance; and an "F" grade, an unacceptable performance. In using symbols of this kind, we are making evaluations on the basis of our measurements. Even when we use simpler systems of evaluating, such as labeling the student's performance "satisfactory" or "unsatisfactory," or "plus" or "minus," the symbol represents an evaluation of the performance based upon a measurement of it.

THE MEANING OF A GRADE. The major requirement for a system of symbols is that the meaning of the symbols be clear to those who

---

[18]The teacher will need to be familiar with several kinds of scores which indicate relative position. A fuller treatment of these scores is given in Chapter Sixteen. For a discussion of scores indicating relative position see R. Thorndike and E. Hagen, *Measurement and Evaluation in Psychology and Education*, New York, John Wiley & Sons, 1955, Chapter 7.

will use them. The grading systems used in schools are interpreted by pupils, teachers, administrators, and by such individuals outside the school system as employers or admission officers at more advanced schools.

It is a common assumption that grades represent the degree to which the student has attained the objectives of particular learning experiences. A letter grade of "A," or a mark of "100," usually represents a high degree of such attainment. However, some teachers maintain that a grade should also represent the amount of effort a student has expended in attempting to attain the objectives. We can judge this argument if we know the purposes for which the grades are going to be used. A teacher may want to convey to the student an evaluation of the progress that he is making. In such a case, the grade would represent the degree of progress achieved. In other cases, the teacher may want to inform the student of his position with respect to other students who have had comparable learning experiences. In this case, the grade would represent achievement relative to that of other students. Grades are also used by counselors for programing and by college admission officers for selecting students. When grades are used for these two purposes they should represent the relative achievement of the student.

The principle being applied here is that grades represent an evaluation of a student's performance. The criteria for this evaluation must be known, at least in a general way, by any one who will make judgments about a student on the basis of his grades. Since grades at some levels of education are commonly interpreted as measures of achievement relative to that of other students, they should probably represent no more than that. At any level, the decision about what a grade will represent should be determined by the uses that will probably be made of it.

GRADES AS SUMMARIES OF EVALUATIONS. One major difficulty in using a system of symbols is that a symbol summarizes a complex evaluation procedure. A grade of "A" or "F" is a summary of the evaluation of all of the changes that have been measured. As a consequence, the symbol system inadequately represents the extent of change in any student.

In discussing the construction of evaluation procedures, we suggested that the teacher weigh the relative importance of the objectives to be attained. We also said that the importance attached to the various evaluation procedures used should reflect the relative importance attached to the attainment of specific objectives. The grade or symbol used to summarize the results of evaluation should be similarly influenced by the relative weight assigned the various evaluations.

Suppose we have a class in which we have measured the students' performance by discussion, short quizzes, an essay, and a final comprehensive examination. We have four measurement procedures. From each of these procedures we draw some type of a score or grade which we must combine into a total summary grade. The weight we give each of the grades should reflect the relative importance of attaining the specific objectives. If we have decided that the most important objective of a course is gaining ability to criticize and evaluate a piece of literature, and if we have measured the attainment of this objective principally by using an essay test, then the grade on the essay should be given the greatest weight in determining the final grade.[19]

IMPROVING GRADING SYSTEMS. Since most marking systems use symbols which summarize a wide variety of behavior changes, attempts have been made to develop more comprehensive ways of reporting pupil change. Essentially, these systems require the teacher to rate the pupil on a wide variety of factors (see Figure 66).[20] While the attempt to evaluate students in terms of a wide variety of factors and to represent these evaluations in a comprehensive symbol system is desirable, there are both technical and practical difficulties associated with these systems.

The larger the number of factors on which a teacher must rate pupils, the more difficult it is to derive adequately reliable ratings. (Consider the list of behavioral traits in Figure 66.) A teacher with a class of thirty pupils would need adequately reliable and valid information on all of these behaviors for each student. However, he cannot systematically observe each child over a long period of time in order to evaluate behavior change in each of these respects, so he frequently relies on periodic observations and memory, with a resulting drop in the reliability and validity of his ratings. Practically, many teachers find these ratings difficult and tedious to make and, as a consequence, they tend to become careless in making the ratings. Such

---

[19]For a discussion of weighing different evaluation procedures in determining the final grade, see Thorndike and Hagen, *Measurement and Evaluation*, pp. 474-82.

[20]Wrinkle, *Improving Marking and Reporting Practices*, pp. 108-109.

Evaluation of Student Achievement

COLLEGE HIGH SCHOOL *of* COLORADO STATE COLLEGE OF EDUCATION
at GREELEY

	1 2 3 4 5 6	
Student	Secondary School Year	Date of This Report 194__
	6 8 12 36	2½ 5 10 15
Course or Activity	Weeks Enrolled	Regular Periods Each Week

GENERAL OBJECTIVES: The evaluation of the student's achievement of the twelve general objectives which follow is made in terms of what normally might be expected of students of similar age and school placement. O—OUTSTANDING. S—SATISFACTORY. N—NEEDS TO MAKE IMPROVEMENT. U—UNSATISFACTORY. X—INSUFFICIENT EVIDENCE OR DOES NOT APPLY. Specific Behaviors Especially Responsible for O, N, or U Evaluations Are Checked. Specific Comments Particularly with Reference to O, N, and U Evaluations Are Written on the Opposite Side of This Sheet.

——1. HE DIRECTS HIS INDIVIDUAL ACTIVITIES EFFECTIVELY ( ) begins work promptly ( ) makes good use of time ( ) requires minimum of supervision ( ) does more than the least that will be accepted ( ) meets responsibilities promptly

——2. HE FOLLOWS PLANS AND DIRECTIONS ( ) listens to and reads directions carefully ( ) follows and completes plans and directions which have been set up

——3. HE GETS ALONG WELL WITH OTHERS ( ) is considerate of rights and wishes of others ( ) is courteous and tolerant ( ) controls his temper ( ) conforms to reasonable social standards

——4. HE TAKES AN ACTIVE PART IN GROUP LIVING ( ) participates in group planning ( ) volunteers his services ( ) does his share in group activities

——5. HE SPEAKS CORRECTLY AND EFFECTIVELY ( ) speaks clearly ( ) adjusts his voice to the size of the group ( ) uses adequate vocabulary to express himself interestingly ( ) speaks with ease and confidence ( ) uses correct grammatical forms

——6. HE TAKES GOOD CARE OF PERSONAL AND SCHOOL MATERIALS AND EQUIPMENT ( ) shows respect for property ( ) does not waste or damage materials or equipment ( ) returns things when due ( ) reports breakage and loss

——7. HE OBSERVES ATTENDANCE REGULATIONS ( ) is regular and prompt in attendance except for approved cause ( ) arranges in advance for absence when possible ( ) takes initiative in making up work missed ( ) makes proper use of school health service

——8. HE READS WITH EASE AND UNDERSTANDING ( ) selects important ideas ( ) understands and evaluates what he reads ( ) reads with reasonable speed

——9. HE EXPRESSES HIMSELF CORRECTLY AND EFFECTIVELY IN WRITING ( ) expresses ideas clearly ( ) uses correct grammatical forms ( ) punctuates correctly ( ) spells correctly ( ) writes legibly

——10. HE UTILIZES AVAILABLE SOURCES OF LEARNING MATERIALS ( ) selects and uses appropriate sources of information ( ) uses library and library tools effectively ( ) effectively engages in interview and observation

——11. HE USES THE PROBLEM SOLVING METHOD ( ) recognizes problems ( ) states problems clearly ( ) collects and records appropriate information ( ) arrives at sound conclusions

——12. HE USES THE BASIC SKILLS IN MATHEMATICS ( ) uses accurately the simple fundamental combinations ( ) computes with reasonable speed ( ) uses fractions and per cents correctly ( ) selects correct processes

SPECIFIC OBJECTIVES: The specific objectives of each course and activity have been discussed with the student and used in classroom instruction and evaluation activities.

HIS ACHIEVEMENT OF THE SPECIFIC OBJECTIVES OF THIS COURSE OR ACTIVITY HAS BEEN:

☐ better than   ☐ consistent with   ☐ poorer than what reasonably might have been expected of him in terms of his background and ability.

☐ Such that full credit is not recommended on administrative records.

☐ Such that he cannot be recommended for admission to college courses or training programs to which this course is prerequisite.

Such as to justify encouraging him

to enroll in_____

not to enroll in_____

Supervising Teacher

This section is for record purposes and is to be detached before the report is issued to the student or his parents.

ACTUAL ACHIEVEMENT:	☐	☐	☐	☐	☐
	OUTSTANDING	ABOVE AVERAGE	AVERAGE	BELOW AVERAGE	VERY POOR*
EXPECTED ACHIEVEMENT:	☐	☐	☐	☐	☐

* Adjusted credit recommendation (in full year courses only): ¼ ½ ¾ regular credit should be allowed.

An example of a comprehensive report form. (From Wrinkle)

FIGURE 66

ratings are frequently characterized by the "halo effect," in which the teacher has a general impression of a student and consistently rates him on all of the traits in terms of this general impression.

When these more comprehensive reporting systems are used, parents, teachers, and students appear to find them more satisfactory. However, over a period of time, the practical difficulties of maintaining such a system seem to be too great.[21] Administrators and teachers are continuing to try to find a practical way to convey more information about the evaluation of pupil change. At present a system satisfactory from every point of view has yet to be developed.

It is important to remember that the assignment of grades is relatively arbitrary. The symbol systems and the meanings we give to them are matters of decision. What symbols we use and to what percentage of the class we assign various symbols cannot be determined by statistical means: we may determine the average of the class and the position of each student with respect to this average, but at what levels we establish the cutting scores for "A" grades, "B" grades, or "F" grades is basically a matter for the teacher to decide. "Marking on the curve" is an administrative policy and not something inherent in the nature of test scores. The decision to give a certain percentage of students "A's," "B's," and "F's" is made on the basis of the school's educational philosophy, the evaluative criteria used, and the functions the grades will serve. Whatever decision is made about the distribution of grades, the meaning of the grades in a particular class or school must be clear. All teachers do not have to give grades in identically the same way, but the grounds on which grades are assigned must be clear to students, teachers, and anybody else who will have occasion to use these grades in making decisions about the students.

OBJECTIVITY IN SCORING TEST PERFORMANCES

In the preceding chapter, we stated that an important characteristic of any measurement device is that it be highly reliable. The testing device or measurement procedure must be constructed in such a way that everyone who understands and uses the measurement procedure will obtain approximately the same score for a student's performance.

---

[21]For a discussion of one school's attempts to develop a comprehensive reporting system and the difficulties encountered, see Wrinkle, *ibid.*

A measurement of pupil performance, for instance, is unreliable if the scoring procedures tend to place the student in a different relative position each time the performance is scored independently. Falls[22] gave the same composition to one hundred English teachers, asking them to grade the composition on a percentage scale and to indicate the grade level at which they expected that quality of work to be done. The results of the grading are listed in Table XXXIV. Notice the range of grades assigned to the *same* composition. Obviously, these

Grade-Value	Percentage Mark								
	60-64	65-69	70-74	75-79	80-84	85-89	90-94	95-99	Total
XV								2	2
XIV									0
XIII							1	2	3
XII					1		2	3	6
XI			2			6	5	2	15
X			1	3	8	4	7	1	24
IX	1		1	1	8	4	4	3	22
VIII			2	2	2	3	4	3	16
VII				2	2	2	1		7
VI	1				1	1		1	4
V	1								1
Total	3		6	8	22	20	24	17	100

The Estimated Grade-Value and Percentage Marks Assigned to an English Composition by One Hundred Teachers (From Falls)

TABLE XXXIV

scores do not place the student in the same relative position each time the paper is scored independently.

The major advantage of the short-form question is that the *form* of the question makes scorer agreement easy to obtain. With only the the master answer sheet available, the scorer can obtain the same score for a student that any other scorer would.

IMPROVING RELIABILITY OF ESSAY EXAMINATION SCORES. One of the major disadvantages of essay examinations is that they are difficult to score reliably. In Table XXXV are data on the scores given by the

---

[22]J. D. Falls, "Research in Secondary Education," *Kentucky School Journal*, 6 (1928), 42-46.

same teacher to the same paper over a two-month interval.[23] Compare these data with that in the Falls study. There is an abundance of data to support the statement that two teachers grading the same set of essay examinations do not highly agree on the grade that they give, and that the same teacher grading the same set of examinations over a period of time does not assign the same grades to the students.[24]

This disadvantage of essay examinations can be remedied by a number of procedures. If the teacher defines in advance what it is that the essay question is to measure, and then grades on this and this

Pupil No.	First Marking	Second Marking
1	85	70
2	50	75
3	90	95
4	90	85
5	90	70
6	99	90
7	70	60
8	75	80
9	60	80
10	90	75

Remarking of Ten Examinations by Same Teacher after 2-Month Interval (From Tiegs)

TABLE XXXV

only, reliability probably will be improved. Another procedure that tends to improve reliability is to assign, in advance of the actual scoring, relative weights to every aspect of performance to be graded. For example, an English teacher may decide that greater weight is to be given to the theme of a composition than to correct grammar. The number of points or the letter grade to be assigned for each aspect of the composition could be allotted in advance and applied to each composition as it is graded. Figure 67 gives an example of directions to the

---

[23]E. W. Tiegs, "Educational Diagnosis," *Educational Bulletin No. 18*, California Test Bureau, 1952.

[24]See, for example, L. M. Childers, "Report of the Research Committee on Examinations," *Proceedings of the Sixtieth Annual Meeting*, National Association of Dental Examiners, 60 (1942), 77-106. C. E. Hulten, "The Personal Element in Teachers' Marks," *Journal of Educational Research*, 12 (1925), 49-55.

Purpose of the test

This part of the test is to obtain evidence of the student's acquisition of information. If you are able to identify the meaning of his statements, do not consider his spelling, handwriting, grammatical construction, or method of presentation in your evaluation. Judge only the accuracy and adequacy of the information he stated.

Values to be assigned to answers

Question 1a--How is the volume of a kilogram of air affected by changes in the pressure applied to it?

Allow 4 points credit for answers which indicate direction and nature of relation and constancy of temperature; for example, "Volume varies inversely as pressure if temperature remains constant."

Allow 3 points for answers which indicate direction and nature of relation but do not mention constancy of temperature; for example,

$$\frac{V_1}{V_2} = \frac{P_2}{P_1}$$

or an equivalent expression.

Allow 1 point for omissions, or "I don't know" statements. This assumes that the teacher considers it better for a student to recognize that he does not know than to be mistaken in the facts he thinks he knows.

Allow no credit for mistaken conceptions, such as "Pressure has no effect on volume," "Increasing pressure increases volume."

Question 1b--Upon what other gases do changes in pressure produce similar effects?

Allow 2 points credit for answers which indicate that all or nearly all gases are affected in similar fashion.

Allow 1 point credit for omission, or "I don't know" answers.

Allow no credit for mistaken conceptions, such as, "No other gases," "Gases which are lighter than air," "Gases where molecules are composed of only one atom."

Sample of directions for scoring essay questions.
(From Frutchey and Tyler)

FIGURE 67

scorer of an essay question.[25] Notice that the scorer is told what to grade and what credit to allow for each item he grades.

Using procedures such as these usually improves the reliability of grading essay questions or any type of performance in which the behavior to be measured is complex.[26] Where several teachers are to grade essay examinations on the same subject matter, the teachers should agree in advance on the criteria for grading. This principle also applies to the assignment of grades. In this way the grades or marks representing measurements of what are supposed to be the same kinds of performances have a consistency in their meaning, even though they may be given by different people to different students.

LIMITATIONS OF CLASSROOM EVALUATION PROCEDURES

One of the major limitations in classroom evaluation procedures is that there are many behaviors, particularly those of a complex nature, for which the teacher does not have adequate measuring instruments. In social studies courses we attempt to influence students' attitudes, but rarely do we have reliable and valid measuring devices for determining the extent to which pupils' attitudes have changed. We are also concerned with students' interests and values but, again, we do not have adequate measuring devices with which to measure them. Many teachers are annoyed, and rightly so, by the fact that their tests are limited to measuring knowledge of facts, concepts, generalizations, problem-solving ability, and performance processes. To measure many important behavior changes, the teacher must rely heavily upon his observations of pupil behavior. If the teacher is sensitive to the difficulties involved in making such observations, he can utilize data that he gathers in this way to make cautious inferences about pupil change.

The teacher can construct some instruments for measuring even complex changes for which tests may not be available. Figure 68 shows an example of an interest inventory test given to a group of bright

---

[25]F. P. Frutchey and R. W. Tyler, "Examinations in the Natural Sciences," in Hawkes *et al., The Construction and Use of Achievement Examinations,* pp. 218-19.

[26]For suggestions for improving essay examinations, see J. M. Stalnaker, "The Essay Type of Examination," in E. Lindquist, *Educational Measurement,* Chapter 13.

PUPIL INTEREST INVENTORY

1. What school subjects do you like the best? Number these school subjects from 1 to 10 to show the order in which you would choose them:

    (__) Reading   (__) Social Studies   (__) Language   (__) Music   (__) Art

    (__) Handwriting   (__) Arithmetic   (__) Science   (__) Spelling   (__) P.E.

2. Are there any school subjects not taught at your school that you wish were part of the school program? _____

3. Do you have a definite time to study at home? _____

4. How many books do you read in a week at home? _____

5. What are the names of some of the books you especially enjoyed reading in the last few years?

    _____

6. How often do you use the public library? Underline the answer that is right for you.

    Never   Once in a while   Every two weeks   Every week

7. How often do you read the newspaper?   Never   Once in a while   Regularly

8. Underline the parts of the paper that you read often:

    Local News   World News   Sports   Comics   Advertisements   Society Page

    Weather   Tides   Theatre, Radio, Television   Editorials

9. Do you like to read magazines? _____

    What magazines do you read often? _____

10. Do you often read comic books? _____ What comic books do you read? _____

    _____

11. Do you listen to the radio every day? _____ What kind of programs do you like best?

    _____

12. Do you have a television set in your home? _____ About how many hours do you spend watching tele-vision on a school day? _____ On a week end? _____ Please list your Five Favorite

    Television Programs: _____

13. How often do you go to the movies? Underline the best answer for you.

    Never   Two or three times a year   Two or three times a month

14. Underline the names of the places where you have been. Check the ones you would like to visit again.

    Natural History Museum   Airport   Ferry   Beach   Circus

    Ball Game   Art gallery   A park on the peninsula   Lighthouse

    Junior Museum   A dam   A broadcasting station   Opera

    Observatory   Planetarium   Symphony concert   Zoo   Aquarium

    A manufacturing plant   _____   _____

15. Have you ever visited any foreign countries? _____

    Name them. _____

16. Check any clubs or organizations to which you belong and add any which are not listed below:

    Boy or Girl Scouts   Cub Scouts   Brownies   Church Choir

    School Orchestra   Campfire Girls   Blue Birds   Gray Y

    Jr. Traffic Patrol   Student Council   School Chorus   Jr. Hi Y

    _____   _____   _____   _____

Comments: (If you have any)

FIGURE 68

students in an experimental program. The teacher wanted to know what the interests of these students were, both at the beginning and at the end of the experimental program. He constructed this test to measure interests; it asked students about books that they had read, the television programs that they had watched, and what subjects they liked and disliked in school. From these questions, gathered either formally through an interest inventory of this kind or informally through personal questioning, the teacher might collect data from which he could make inferences about the student's behavior. The advantage of the written interest inventory is that the teacher can gather the data in a systematic way for a large number of pupils. Every principle that we have stated about sampling behavior and about reliability and validity of measurement is applicable to the formal and informal procedures that the teacher may use to gather data on interests, attitudes, values, and even on the self-concept of the child. Until such time as tests are constructed to measure comprehensive behavior changes, the teacher will have to rely on procedures of unknown reliability and validity in gathering information from which to make inferences about pupil change. However, if the teacher is aware of the difficulty in making inferences with such procedures, and if he tests his inferences systematically, he is less likely to make serious errors in evaluating pupil change.

MEASUREMENT OF THE SOCIAL STRUCTURE OF A CLASS

Teachers frequently want to know the pattern of social relations in their classes. Data on these relations have important implications for the organization of learning experiences. It is important to know who is the least liked student in the class if we want to devise situations in which he will have an opportunity to interact more frequently with his fellow students and to become more accepted by them. The social structure of the class may also directly affect some kinds of learning experiences. If the teacher is organizing a committee to work on a project, placing on that committee a student who would not have been chosen by the other students may affect the amount and kind of work this committee will do.

SOCIOMETRIC MEASUREMENT TECHNIQUES. A number of simple techniques are available for making gross measurements of the social structure of a class. These are called *sociometric* devices because they measure the social structure of a group.[27] One of the simplest of such techniques is to ask each student to list the person he likes best and the person he likes least in the class. When the teacher obtains this information, he can rank all of the students by the number of times they were chosen as most liked and least liked. From the data we can also determine who chooses whom. An example of this technique is given in Figure 69, which tabulates the preferences of sixth-graders who were asked to list their first, second, and third choices of a person to sit by. Constructing a *sociogram* is another convenient way of plotting the same data; the sociogram in Figure 70 uses circles to represent the children, and arrows drawn between the circles to indicate choices (solid lines for boys, broken lines for girls).

There are many variations on the kind of question that can be asked to measure social interaction patterns. We can ask the students with whom they would like to work on a social studies committee, or with whom they would like to play on the same team in a game, or with whom they would like to walk home from school. Each of these questions yields different kinds of information about the pattern of social relations in a class. There may not be a high relationship between the children most frequently picked as work companions and those who are most frequently picked as play companions. The children in a class will evaluate their choices on the basis of utility for a particular activity. For example, children may most frequently pick the best athlete if they are choosing team members for a game, but they may frequently choose the brightest students in class to work on a committee with them. Moreover, the teacher can determine who is the best liked student and who is the least liked student for a variety of purposes or activities. He can ordinarily determine which student is rarely chosen for anything and which student is most frequently chosen. With this kind of information the teacher will be better able to understand pupil behavior, and he will also be able to use this information in planning group activities.[28]

Another variation on this technique is to disguise the purpose of the question. Instead of asking a child whom he likes, we ask him to

---

[27]Moreno first developed these techniques, and he has suggested possible uses for them. See J. L. Moreno, *Who Shall Survive?*, Washington, D. C., Nervous and Mental Diseases Publishing Company, 1934.

[28]For suggestions on such uses, see H. Jennings *et al.*, *Sociometry in Group Relations*, Washington, D. C., American Council on Education, 1948.

CHOOSERS \ CHOSEN	Pam	John	David	Steve	George	Brian G.	Paul	Scott J.	Scott K.	Jeff	Ruth	Marc	Libby	Sherman	Sharon	Tony	Judy	Alan	Brian S.	Jane	Wayne	Bill	Keith	Sandy	Lane
Pam													1		2		3								
John*																									
David			3	2												1									
Steve				1													3						2		
George							1									2					3				
Brian G.	1															2						3			
Paul							1					2									3				
Scott J.				2					1												3				
Scott K.							2									3						1			
Jeff			3														2					1			
Ruth												1									3				2
Marc							1									2	3								
Libby	3						2																1		
Sherman							2									1					3				
Sharon	3				1												2								
Tony		1																			3				
Judy	3														1										2
Alan							1										2				3				
Brian S.							2											1			3				
Jane			3						1			2													
Wayne							2					1				3									
Bill					3		2																1		
Keith		2	3																			1			
Sandy							2					1									3				
Lane							1								2								3		
CHOSEN 1.		1	1		1		2			1	3	4	2		1	2		1			3	1	1		
2.		1		2	7						1	1			1	2	2	1	2			1			2
3.	3		3	1			1									1	1	1	2	9	1		1		
TOTALS	3	2	1	3	1	3	9	0	1	1	3	5	3	0	2	5	3	3	4	0	9	4	2	2	2

* John absent

Chart of seating preferences in a sixth grade class.

FIGURE 69

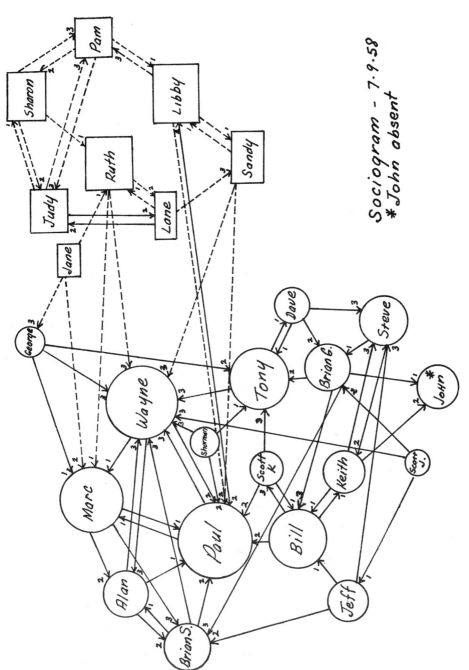

Sociogram – 7.9.58
*John absent

Sociogram based on seating preferences charted in Figure 69.

FIGURE 70

Name_____School_____Grade_____

THE CLASS PLAY

    Just imagine your class was going to put on a play and you are selected to direct it. Below you will see the kinds of parts that will be needed for this play. As director of the play, you have the responsibility of selecting any boy or girl in your class for any of the parts. Since many of the parts are very small, you may, if you wish, select the same boy or girl for more than one part.

    In order to make this play successful, and a lot of fun, you will need to choose boys and girls who you think would be most natural for the part. Make your choices carefully, and, if you have any questions about the meaning of a word or anything else, be sure to ask your teacher.

THESE ARE THE PARTS

Part 1 - The Hero -- someone who is good in sports and in school work. _____

Part 2 - Someone who is often mean and gets into fights a great deal (boy or girl). _____

Part 3 - The Heroine -- someone who gets along well with other boys and girls and with the teacher. _____

Part 4 - Someone who is always getting angry about little things. _____

Part 5 - Someone who could be the hero's friend - a kind, helpful boy or girl. _____

Part 6 - Someone who could play the part of a bully - picks on boys and girls smaller or weaker than himself. _____

Part 7 - Someone who has a good sense of humor but is always careful not to disturb the teacher or the class. _____

Part 8 - Someone who could play the part of a person who doesn't ever say anything. _____

Part 9 - Someone who is never mean and always friendly. _____

Part 10 - Someone who could act like the laziest person in the world--never does anything. _____

Part 11 - A boy or girl you would choose to be in charge when the teacher left the room. _____

Part 12 - This person knows all the answers and usually works alone. _____

Section II

A. Which part or parts would you like to play best? (Write number or numbers on line here.)_____

B. Which part or parts do you think you could play? (Write number or numbers on line here.)_____

C. Which part or parts do you think the teacher might ask you to play? (Write number or numbers on

line here.) _____

D. Which part or parts do you think most of the other kids would ask you to play? (Write number or

numbers on line here.)_____

(Compiled by California State Department of Education)

FIGURE 71

assign people to different roles. This is the "Guess Who" technique.[29] Essentially, it consists in asking the child to guess who is the most popular boy in class, who is the least popular, who is the brightest, and so on. In one variation of this technique the children are asked to assign parts in a play (see Figure 71). Again, from this kind of data the teacher can make inferences about the character of the social structure in the class.

Using this kind of a measurement device involves problems in reliability and validity. A sociometric device ordinarily has "face" validity only, and only for the kind of question that we ask. The teacher should not generalize about all of the various kinds of social relations of children from the answers to one question. Although we assume that the children are answering honestly, some children may be afraid to state what child they dislike, and may even refuse to answer such a question. Also, changes in the social structure take place as the children become better acquainted with each other or as the teacher manipulates their social relations. The basic assumption made in using a sociometric device is that the children know each other and have had some opportunity to interact. At best, a single use of this technique gives us a picture of the social structure of the class at that moment, insofar as the questions we ask can reveal social structure.

In this chapter we have discussed the evaluation procedures that the classroom teacher can construct and use; the principles outlined here can serve only as a starting point for a teacher's thinking about evaluation procedures. In the next chapter we will discuss standardized devices for measuring many aspects of personality; aspects of personality, such as intelligence, general pattern of interests, attitudes, and needs, cannot be assessed easily with measurement devices constructed by the teacher.

SUMMARY

We have presented some techniques of test construction that the teacher may use to measure pupil change, and we have discussed the relevance of the basic principles of measurement and evaluation to the use of these techniques. The evaluation procedure logically begins with a conception of the desired behavior change to be evaluated. Such a conception requires that the teacher:

---

[29]For examples of the use of this technique in studies of child behavior, see H. Hartshorne and M. A. May, *Studies in Service and Self-Control*, New York, The Macmillan Co., 1929.

1. Define the desired behavior carefully and precisely. This clarification is most likely to be achieved when the desired behavior is described in terms of observable responses.

2. Attach proper relative importance to the attainment of each objective, and specify what the importance is. This relative importance should be reflected in the kinds of learning experiences organized, the measurement procedures used to assess behavior change, and in the final summary evaluation of behavior change expressed in grades or marks.

Teachers frequently define the objectives of a course in terms of content to be acquired. While content acquisition is a behavior change, teachers are concerned with fostering other kinds of behavior changes as well. Measurement procedures used to assess content acquisition may not measure other kinds of behavior change.

When the statement of objectives has been clarified, evaluation procedures need to be devised which will evoke samples of the kind of behavior described in the objectives. A test item is a stimulus designed to evoke such behaviors. In this respect, we have noted that:

3. A primary consideration in devising test items is the character of the behavior likely to be evoked by them.

4. The same test stimuli may be arranged in a variety of forms. Item forms are chosen so that the total set of test items or questions will provide us with a representative sample of pupil behavior.

5. Many kinds of short-form questions, such as the completion, fill-in, true-false, and matching types, are most appropriately used in testing for recall and recognition of facts, generalizations, or principles. Multiple-choice items can be used for this and other purposes, such as testing for understanding of concepts, ability to apply generalizations, and ability to detect errors in inference. We recommend that the prospective teacher familiarize himself with specimens of these various kinds of items and the uses that have been made of them.

6. Essay questions are most appropriately used to test complex

functions that cannot be tested easily or efficiently with a short-form question. Essay questions should specify clearly the character of the response desired. Some teachers assume that if it requires an extensive written answer, the question is an essay-type question. Essay questions which test retention of facts could more appropriately be recast as short-form questions, which would obtain for the teacher a more representative sample of the pupil's behavior.

The results of a performance in a test situation are usually quantified in the form of a score. Such scores can be given meaning by translation into other scores describing the student's relative position on a scale of performance. Such scores are useful to the extent that they are objective. By *objectivity* of scoring, we mean that the procedures, if used by independent scorers, would place the student in the same relative position with respect to other students. The scoring of essay examinations tends to be relatively unreliable unless the responses to be graded are carefully defined and appropriate weightings are specified for different levels of performance.

Grades or marks are symbols used to summarize the results of evaluation procedures and to convey information about those results. One of the principal disadvantages of the commonly used symbol systems is that the letter or number grade used does not adequately convey all the available information about pupil status and change. Other systems have been adopted which give more information about pupil behavior, but these have frequently been abandoned because of practical difficulties in maintaining them. If grades or marks are to be used effectively, the criteria employed in determining the grade must be clear to the user of the grade. Consistency in grading can be improved by defining and agreeing on the evaluative criteria to be used in judging students' performances.

In the last section of this chapter we described measurement procedures that teachers may use to determine the pattern of social relations in their classes; these are called *sociometric* devices. In one simple form of a sociometric device, students are asked to list the fellow students with whom they would like to participate in some activity. By counting the frequency of choices, the teacher can determine which pupils were chosen the most and least frequently for this particular activity, the pattern of mutual choices, and even the hierarchy of leadership in the class. It is important to remember that such procedures describe the pattern of social relations only as it stands at the time of testing and only for the kind of activity tested by the stimulus question.

The teacher who wishes to become a skillful constructor of measurement devices will need additional training and experience. This chapter has suggested basic principles and techniques with which a teacher can begin to evaluate his own procedures. The process of measuring pupil status and change is a process of making inferences from data that are gathered about pupil behavior. The relative validity of the inferences depends on the relative validity and reliability of the data that the teacher gathers on pupil behavior. The teacher will need to check continually his inferences about pupil status and change.

STUDY AND DISCUSSION QUESTIONS

1. Select some unit of a subject that you are or may be teaching. Prepare a detailed list of behavior changes to be promoted by the learning experiences you will organize for this unit. Be as specific as possible in the statement of objectives. Indicate what aspects of each learning experience will facilitate the achievement of each objective. Indicate the relative importance of attaining each of these objectives. Specify the criteria for evaluating the behavior changes.

2. Describe the measurement procedures that you will use to evaluate the behavior changes specified in the statement of objectives. Construct test items, using any of the item forms discussed in this chapter. Explain the ways in which your item selection is appropriate for measuring the kinds of behavior change the item is designed to measure.

3. Now that you have constructed test items to measure the behavior changes, what procedures will be necessary to improve the test that you have developed? Be specific about the procedures you will use to determine whether the items are ambiguous and to determine the relative difficulty of the items.

4. Review your statement of objectives. Are there some behavior changes that cannot be measured, or measured only with difficulty, by using the test item forms discussed in this chapter? What procedures would you use to evaluate these kinds of behavior change? Specify the procedures that may be used to measure these behavior changes.

5. Describe the scoring procedures that you will use for evaluating behavior change. Also describe how you will use these measurements to determine grades. What may a person infer about pupil achievement in your class? What aspects of pupil achievement may be ignored by utilizing the grades that you provide?

6. Some people argue that distributing grades according to fixed percentages is an unfair and misleading procedure. Under what conditions would such a procedure be defensible? Under what circumstances might such a procedure be misleading?

7. A teacher constructs an essay examination with the following directions: "Select any five of the ten questions; each question has a value of 20 points." What difficulties in measurement and evaluation may result from the use of these directions?

8. A teacher indicates at the beginning of an essay examination that students will be penalized one point for every mistake in grammar. The essay examination covers the content of a history course. What difficulties in measurement and evaluation may result from using this procedure?

9. Some school systems use a grading system in which student achievement is reported in the following symbols: S (satisfactory), U (unsatisfactory), N (needs improvement). Some teachers argue that this kind of a grading system reduces students' motivation to work hard. Evaluate this argument. Under what conditions might this objection be valid?

10. Some parents feel that marks given on the basis of a child's ability give neither his parents nor the child a "true picture" of his achievement. How would you evaluate this argument? Under what conditions might the argument be valid? What assumptions seem to be implicit in this argument? Criticize these assumptions.

11. Some teachers feel that a grade should include some measure of the effort the student has made. What difficulties do you see in using such a procedure? Are there some conditions under which such a procedure may be defensible?

12. Refer to the sociometric diagram and data provided in this chapter. List the students who appear to be the most frequently chosen and the least frequently chosen. Can you identify any "cliques" from these data? What is the pattern of boy-girl choices? Do the most frequently chosen boy and girl select students who are also frequently chosen?

RECOMMENDED READINGS

The first reading contains a description of procedures for constructing the kinds of tests that teachers use in their classes. The second, third, and fourth readings contain an extended discussion of testing procedures, particularly in various subject areas. The fifth and sixth readings provide interesting examples of a wide variety of item forms. The seventh reading contains a discussion of basic principles relevant to the construction of tests.

1. R. Travers, *How to Make Achievement Tests*, New York, The Odyessy Press, 1950.

2. R. Thorndike and E. Hagen, *Measurement and Evaluation in Psychology and Education,* New York, John Wiley & Sons, 1955, Chapters 3 and 17.

3. T. Torgerson and G. Adams, *Measurement and Evaluation for the Elementary School Teacher,* New York, The Dryden Press, 1954.

4. G. Adams and T. Torgerson, *Measurement and Evaluation for the Secondary School Teacher,* New York, The Dryden Press, 1956.

5. J. R. Gerberich, *Specimen Objective Test Items,* New York, Longmans, Green & Co., 1956.

6. N. B. Henry (ed.), *Forty-fifth Yearbook of the National Society for the Study of Education, Part I, The Measurement of Understanding,* Chicago, University of Chicago Press, 1946.

7. E. Lindquist (ed.), *Educational Measurement,* Washington, D. C., American Council on Education, 1951, Chapters 6-13.

THE USE OF
STANDARDIZED TESTS

Measurement procedures, as we have seen, provide samples of pupil behavior. Before inferences may be made from such samples, the reliability and validity of the measurement procedure must be determined. Ordinarily, the teacher has neither the technical training nor the time for determining the reliability and validity of his own tests. He is also limited in the kinds of inferences he may make from his own tests. He may not, for example, compare the performance of his students with that of other students who have had comparable learning experiences.

Standardized tests have been developed to provide such comparisons. These tests have been administered to large groups of students to provide data on comparative performances, and their reliability and validity have been determined.

The kinds of standardized tests available to teachers may be divided into two categories: (1) those that may be used to measure the attainment of objectives of learning experiences; (2) those that measure pupil characteristics related to the attainment of these objectives.

Achievement tests are in the former category, and intelligence tests, tests of special aptitudes, and "personality" tests are in the latter category.

The discussion in this chapter is merely an introduction to the study of these tests. We will study the principal kinds of tests developed to measure some of the behavior patterns with which the teacher is concerned in making hypotheses about school learning. Some of these tests, such as intelligence tests, are used in practically all school systems, and the results of performance on these tests are available to teachers. The teacher needs to know what such tests measure, how to interpret the test scores, and the limitations of these measurement procedures. The administration of other kinds of tests, such as many personality tests, is reserved for individuals who have received special training in their use and interpretation. We will offer only a general discussion of the nature and uses of such tests.

One of the major advantages of the standardized test is that it provides comparative data on pupil performance; such data in turn provide additional information about the performances of students in a particular class. An understanding of the process of test standardization is required before these comparative data may be interpreted correctly.

THE PROCESS OF TEST STANDARDIZATION

In principle, a testing procedure is a controlled observation of behavior. To make this observation we obtain behavior samples that, presumably, are influenced only by the characteristic we are studying. Assume that we collect samples of "intelligent behavior" to make inferences about intellectual ability. We have an individual perform a series of tasks in such a way that his behavior is likely to be influenced only by his intellectual ability. We attempt to control all factors unrelated to intellectual ability that may influence his performance on these tasks.

STANDARDIZATION OF TEST CONDITIONS. One of the ways in which observations are controlled is to make the observation under a prescribed set of conditions. A standardized test typically provides directions about the way in which the test is to be given. Such directions usually prescribe the length of time to be allotted for the test and what directions are to be given to those being examined; they also usually describe the conditions that should be controlled to insure comparable performance. Maintaining these conditions does not guarantee that those being tested will work at maximum performance, but if the directions are followed the testing situation will not interfere with maximum performance and it will remain substantially the same for all groups to whom the test is administered. Standardized tests have been tried out on large numbers of subjects so that the conditions likely to facilitate maximum performance have been determined.

The administration of some group tests can be handled easily by classroom teachers. The administration of other kinds of tests, such as the Stanford-Binet Tests of Intelligence, require special training.[1] Standardized tests provide manuals with directions for test administration; these should be followed carefully if a controlled observation is to be made.

TEST NORMS. As we pointed out in Chapter Fourteen, psychological measurements are relative in character. We have no way of ascertaining the "goodness" of a student's test performance from the number of correct answers he gives. An estimate of his relative ability or achievement is made by comparing his test performance with that of other students.

Standardized tests have been given to large samples of subjects, and performance *norms* have been developed from the test performance data. These norms are scores which indicate an individual's relative performance—the position of his performance among those obtained by the group that has taken the test. A subject's test performance is initially described in terms of the number of correct answers, the time taken for task performance, the number of errors, or some other measure of performance. These scores are called *raw* scores. Norms enable us to translate these raw scores into scores that compare the subject's performance with that of others who have taken the test.

Teachers frequently use a simple process for obtaining norms for their own tests. Assume that we have administered an algebra test consisting of fifteen problems. We may construct the following frequency table after we have corrected the papers:

---

[1] See, for example, L. M. Terman and M. A. Merrill, *Directions for Administering Forms L and M: Revision of the Stanford-Binet Tests of Intelligence*, Boston, Houghton Mifflin Co., 1937.

No. of Correct Problems	No. of Students Getting This Many Problems Correct
15	1
14	2
13	0
12	4
11	4
10	5
9	6
8	4
7	4
6	3
5	2
4	0
3	0
2	1
1	0
0	0

From the table we see that approximately half the class worked nine or more problems correctly. Two students worked all but one of the problems correctly, and one had a perfect score. The student who worked only two problems correctly did quite poorly in comparison with the other students. We might compute each student's rank in class from these data. These ranks would provide us with a table of norms, that is, a set of scores from which we could determine a student's relative performance on the test. Many different kinds of scores may be used in tables of norms. We will discuss several kinds in this chapter. A teacher needs to know how to interpret some of these scores in order to interpret students' performances on standardized tests.

The group of subjects to whom a test is given so that norms may be developed is called the *standardization sample*. The characteristics of this sample are usually given in the manual accompanying the test. Before we may use norms meaningfully, we need to determine to what extent the group taking a test is like the standardization sample. If these two groups are not highly similar on the characteristics described in the manual, use of the test norms may lead to erroneous inferences about the performance of our students. Assume that the standardization sample was composed of students of lower intellectual ability than the group we are testing. A comparison of the performances of the tested group with those of the standardization sample will probably show the tested group to be relatively superior. We may reach the erroneous conclusion that our group has made greater gains in terms of their ability than may have been the case. A more meaningful comparison would relate the performance of our students to students of comparable ability.

One important caution should be emphasized concerning the use of norms: norms do not represent "ideal" performances; they are not measures of what a student "ought" to do. They represent only the actual performances of a specified group of subjects. Teachers have been criticized for a tendency to view the standardization group performance as a *criterion* against which to *evaluate* the performance of their own students. As we will point out later, the performance of the standardization sample may be used for making evaluations, but only under certain conditions and with considerable caution.

TEST RELIABILITY AND VALIDITY. Manuals accompanying standardized tests provide information on test reliability and validity.[2] This information is reported in the form of correlation coefficients. Numerically, correlation coefficients may range from minus 1 to plus 1. A high positive correlation, such as .90, probably indicates the test has sufficient reliability for the purpose for which it is intended. As a rule of thumb, the kinds of tests teachers are likely to use should probably have reliability coefficients of approximately .90.[3]

You will recall that a test may have logical or predictive validity. Tests on subject content typically have logical validity; that is, they test knowledge of the content of some subject previously studied. Standardized subject-matter tests typically have this kind of validity. We will make some qualifications concerning logical validity in the section on "Achievement Tests" later in this chapter.

The predictive validity of a test is determined by correlating test performance with a criterion performance, which is assumed or known to be an adequate measure of the behavior being studied. Information on predictive validity describes the criterion measure used and the correlation between test and criterion performance. High positive correlation indicates that the test is probably measuring the same kind of behavior measured in the criterion performance.

When such information is available, the predictive validity of a test is reported in the test manual. By studying the kinds of perform-

---

[2]See Chapter Fourteen for a discussion of the concepts of test reliability and validity.

[3]A more extended discussion of test reliability may be found in A. Anastasi, *Psychological Testing*, New York, Macmillan Co., 1954, Chapter 5.

ances that may be predicted from test performance, we obtain information on the kinds of behavior the test is measuring. An important caution is relevant here. Some test users make inferences from the test title about the kinds of behavior a test is measuring. Such inferences are likely to be valid only when the test measures knowledge of some content area. In general, what a test is measuring can best be determined from the kinds of performances that may be predicted from test performance.

Here we have outlined the principal kinds of hypotheses that are typically tested in relation to standardized tests. Such information about a standardized test enables us to use the test to make controlled observations of behavior. This kind of information is not available for most teacher-made tests. In the preceding chapters we pointed out cautions that should be observed in using one's own tests. A teacher who has advanced training in statistics and test construction may standardize his own tests. However, some standardized tests are suitable for use by most teachers, and are constructed to serve a wide variety of instructional purposes. In the following sections we will discuss some of the principal kinds of standardized tests a teacher is likely to use.

INTELLIGENCE TESTS

One kind of standardized test used in schools is the intelligence test. Basically, these tests are designed to measure the intellectual ability of a child. How is intelligence or general intellectual ability measured?

INFERRING INTELLECTUAL ABILITY FROM TEST PERFORMANCE. Assume that we ask children to add a column of numbers. We may arrange their performances on a scale in terms of the number of correct additions. A child who had never studied addition would probably be at the lowest point on this scale. But we may not immediately attribute his poorer performance to lack of intelligence. We know that ability to add a column of figures requires some experience in learning the meaning of numbers and how to add them. However, if the child had had the necessary learning experience but still could not add, we might infer that this child is not as intelligent as a child who can add these figures.

To measure intellectual ability, we present children with a series of tasks, the performance requirements of which have been equally available in the experiences of the children. If each of the children taking the test has had the experience necessary for learning the behavior required by these tasks, differences in performances may be attributed to differences in intellectual ability.

Many of the items in intelligence tests are tasks which a child may learn to perform at some level of his schooling. Other tasks represent what a child can probably learn on the basis of his general experience. We emphasize the importance of the assumption that the children have had an opportunity to learn the behavior required by the test tasks. When this assumption is in fact false, differences in performance on intelligence tests may not reflect differences in intellectual ability.

We cannot measure intellectual ability directly. We may make inferences about it from observations of what a person has learned.

INTELLIGENCE TESTS AS MEASURES OF RELATIVE BRIGHTNESS. Intelligence test performance, like performance on other psychological tests, cannot be interpreted directly. Performance on these tests is measured in terms of number of items answered correctly. Normative data permits us to determine a child's relative performance on these tests by comparing his performance to that of children in the standardization sample. We may say that a child is more or less bright when compared to other children. We cannot determine "how much" intellectual ability he has except in this sense.

Many people are familiar with the IQ score in which intelligence test performance is usually reported. Some people incorrectly assume that the IQ tells us "how much" intellectual ability a child has. The IQ is not a measure of some absolute amount of intelligence; neither is it, as we have seen, a direct measure of ability.

A brief consideration of the general character of intelligence tests and the arrangement of the tasks in them will suggest why we may not treat the IQ score as an absolute measure.

The tasks in an intelligence test are graded to approximate what a child should be able to do at a given age level. Intelligence tests used with younger children involve fairly simple kinds of tasks related to the kinds of learning experiences younger children typically have. An intelligence test given to an older child includes many items that are likely to have been learned only by a child at that age level. For example, an intelligence test for younger children may include a problem that requires a child to follow simple directions, such as, "Walk to the table, then pick up the book, and bring the book to me." Young children have usually had experiences requiring them to follow simple directions of this kind. Intelligence tests for older children may include arithmetic problems. In either case, the tasks can probably be accomplished by children at the respective age levels. But we may not compare test performances of children of different age levels unless they have attempted the same tasks. In other words, we are simply applying the principle that inferences about relative intellectual ability assume that the persons being compared have had comparable learning opportunities.

Of course, some younger children may be able to perform some of the tasks typically performed by older children. On intelligence tests including vocabulary items, a five-year-old may identify the meaning of some words that are known by ten-year-olds, and he may answer some questions not typically answered by five-year-olds. Our inference from this performance is that he is a bright five-year-old. We may not compare directly the intelligence test performances of a five-year-old child and a fifteen-year-old child. We may state how bright a five-year-old child is by comparing him to other five-year-old children. The performance of each child is compared to that of children likely to have had comparable kinds of experiences.

THE VALIDITY OF INTELLIGENCE TESTS. The constructor of an intelligence test has usually developed some conception of what is meant by intelligence; he constructs test items which he thinks will evoke responses reflecting differences in intelligence as he has conceptualized it. A test constructor may conceive of intelligence as the ability to do conceptual thinking.[4] He may then decide that verbal tasks, that is, tasks whose successful performance requires the ability to formulate ideas in verbal symbols, are the most appropriate kinds of tasks to measure this ability.

Such an intelligence test may be said to have some logical validity, since the test items are selected in terms of some conception of the meaning of intelligence. Vocabulary test items are included in many intelligence tests, because most definitions posit verbal ability as a part of general intelligence.

---

[4] See, for example, L. M. Terman, *The Measurement of Intelligence*, Boston, Houghton Mifflin Co., 1916.

As we have seen, we determine what a test is measuring from the kinds of predictive validity it has. Intelligence tests also have predictive validity. These tests have been given to large numbers of students and performance on these tests has been correlated with other performances, such as school achievement. Performance on intelligence tests correlates fairly highly with success in school.[5] These tests measure many of the abilities required for success in school.

Many of the intelligence tests are heavily loaded with verbal tasks, tasks requiring facility and knowledge of verbal concepts and symbols. As we would expect, such tests are more highly correlated with success in those aspects of schooling which require verbal ability than they are with learning that requires less verbal ability.

Performance on intelligence tests has also been correlated with the occupations of individuals. Figure 72 shows the average scores on a test of intellectual ability given to people in a number of occupations.[6] The greater the amount of verbal facility required in an occupation, the higher the average score for that profession or occupation. This relationship does not mean that everyone with a score above a certain level necessarily enters a particular profession. Note the range of scores in each of the occupations and the amount of overlap in scores between occupations.

Relationships of this kind enable us to make predictions about the likelihood of an individual succeeding in a given occupation when we know what his intelligence test score is. In some cases, the members of the occupation have set up minimum standards of performance on these tests, which must be met before an individual will be accepted into the training program for these occupations. Most medical schools require students to take an aptitude test, and those who score below a certain level are not granted admission. From some intelligence test scores we can determine the probability of a student being accepted into the training program of a given occupation; in other cases, we may use a test score as an index of the students' general aptitude for the work required in the occupation.

The relationship reflected in Figure 72 tells us nothing about the

---

[5]Q. McNemar, *The Revision of the Stanford-Binet Scale: An Analysis of the Standardization Data*, Boston, Houghton Mifflin Co., 1942, Chapter 3. A. Q. Sartain, "A Comparison of the New Revised Stanford-Binet, the Bellevue Scale, and Certain Group Tests of Intelligence," *Journal of Social Psychology*, 23 (1946), 237-39.

[6]In A. Anastasi, *Differential Psychology*, 3rd ed., New York, Macmillan Co., 1958, p. 516, based on the data from N. Stewart, "AGCT Scores of Army Personnel Grouped by Occupation," *Occupations*, 26 (1947), 5-41. Reprinted with permission of *Occupations*.

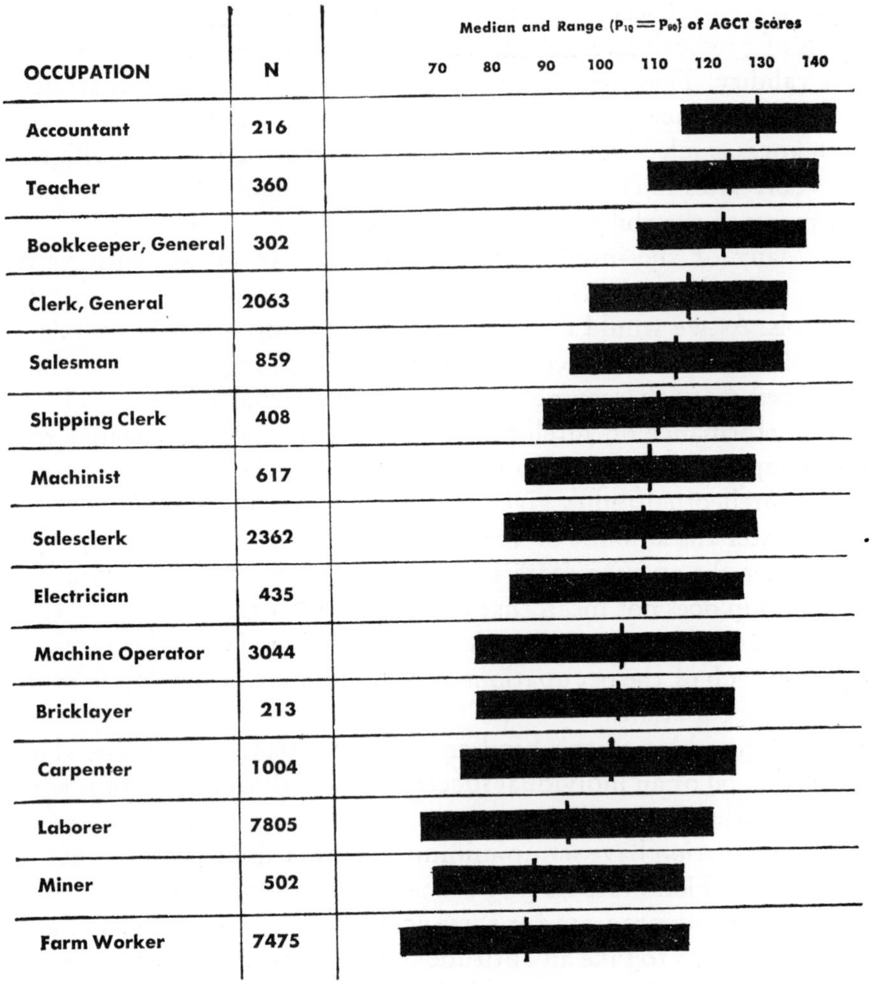

OCCUPATION	N	Median and Range (P₁₀ = P₉₀) of AGCT Scores

Army General Classification Test score in relation to civilian occupation. (From Anastasi based on data from Stewart)

FIGURE 72

relative success of individuals in these occupations. We may not assume that the brighter people within the occupation are the more successful members. Success in any occupation depends on a variety of factors, only one of which may be intellectual ability.

We note these qualifications to emphasize that permissible inferences are limited by the meaning of these established relationships.

Practically every teacher has met a student whose intelligence test score is high but who is not succeeding in school. One possible explanation for this discrepancy is that the intelligence test score is inaccurate. This hypothesis may be checked. But we also know that intellectual aptitude is only one factor that contributes to success in school. Even the brightest students may have difficulty in school if they are not appropriately motivated or have poor work habits. From what we know about what the test measures, we may make a prediction about the student's probable achievement, but our prediction may be in error because we failed to include data other than intellectual aptitude scores in making our prediction.

INTELLIGENCE TEST SCORES

Two kinds of scores are typically used to indicate a student's relative ability. One of these is the IQ score. Its meaning is more easily interpreted if we understand the concept of mental age.

THE MEANING OF MENTAL AGE. Suppose that on an intelligence test the average raw score for children of chronological age ten is forty-five correct answers out of a hundred items. A raw score of forty-five is equivalent to a mental age of ten. Not every ten-year-old will have a score of forty-five. Some will have answered more questions correctly; some, fewer questions correctly. But the average score of a ten-year-old is forty-five. The mental-age equivalents of raw scores are found by determining the average raw score obtained by each age group.

Now assume that the raw score performance of an eight-year-old is forty-five. This child is performing at the level of ten-year-olds. We say that he has a mental age of ten years. In other words, once we have given the test to a large number of students, we can establish the relationships between chronological age and raw scores; from these relationships we derive a scale of mental-age scores.

DEFINITION OF AN IQ SCORE. We can now define what is meant by the *intelligence quotient*, or IQ. The intelligence quotient is the ratio of mental age to chronological age:

$$\text{Intelligence Quotient} = \frac{\text{Mental Age}}{\text{Chronological Age}} \times 100$$

(Multiplication by 100 merely eliminates the decimal points)

619

From this formula we can see that if a child's mental age equals his chronological age, he will have an IQ of 100. The more advanced the child's mental age is in relation to his chronological age, the higher his intelligence quotient will be. Correspondingly, the lower his mental age with respect to his chronological age, the lower his intelligence quotient.

The intelligence quotient is a measure of relative brightness. If a child is bright for his age group, he obtains a correspondingly higher score on an intelligence test. In other words, he has profited from his experience to a greater extent than other children of his age. The IQ score is designed to show his relative superiority for a child of his age.[7]

PERCENTILE SCORES. The other form in which performance on intelligence tests is reported is the _percentile score_. Percentile scores range from 1 to 99. A percentile score tells us what percentage of students score above and below the student who obtains a given percentile score. For example, if a student's percentile score on a scholastic aptitude test is 97, we conclude that 3 per cent of students score above him. If a child has a percentile score of 15, we conclude that 85 per cent of the children score above him. The percentile score, like the IQ, establishes the relative position of a child with respect to a group of children who have taken a particular test. Percentile scores are used for reporting relative performance on many kinds of tests.

INTERPRETING INTELLIGENCE TEST SCORES. A high IQ score, as we have seen, enables us to make some predictions about what a child is capable of doing. What he actually will do, however, depends on many factors. The lower the child's IQ, the less likely he is to meet the school requirements for children his age. Below certain IQ levels a child is not likely to profit from the typical pattern of schooling and will require special instruction or care. To determine this kind of inadequacy requires the skills of a clinician who has the training required to identify and consider all factors that may be affecting a child's intelligence test performance.

All intelligence tests do not contain identically the same tasks. Furthermore, they may employ different scoring procedures and may

---

[7]Another form of IQ scores is the "Deviation IQ." Such scores are not based on mental ages, but they are measures of relative brightness. Essentially they represent the extent to which an individual's score "deviates" from the mean of the standardization group. Numerically they resemble IQ scores based on mental age.

be normed on quite different populations. Thus, a child may obtain different IQ's on two tests but maintain the same relative position in each case. On the other hand, a child may receive numerically the same score on two different tests, yet each score would represent a somewhat different relative position. Or, although he might perform in the same relative position on two tests, the tests might measure different abilities.

A comparatively easy way to decide on the meaning of an IQ score is to relate intelligence quotients to percentile scores. Table XXXVI lists IQ scores and the equivalent percentile ranks.[8] This table may be used as a rough guide for interpreting many intelligence

IQ	Per Cent of Cases	Per Cent of Cases Falling in and above Each Interval
150+	0.2	0.2
140-149	1.1	1.3
130-139	3.1	4.4
120-129	8.2	12.6
110-119	18.1	30.7
100-109	23.5	54.3
90- 99	23.0	77.3
80- 89	14.5	91.8
70- 79	5.6	97.4
60- 69	2.0	99.4
50- 59	0.4	99.8
Below 50	0.2	100.0

Percentage Distribution of IQ's in the Terman-Merrill Standardization Group (From Merrill)

TABLE XXXVI

quotients, although the teacher should refer to the test manual to learn the meaning of IQ's derived from the particular test he is using.

Teachers typically use intelligence test scores to make judgments about academic ability. The following brief discussion will illustrate the complexity of factors involved in making such judgments. Suppose that we were interested in making a judgment about a student's ability to do college work. In general, we can estimate the probability of a child succeeding in college from his intelligence test performance.

---

[8] M. Merrill, "Significance of IQ's on the Revised Stanford-Binet Scales," *Journal of Educational Psychology*, 29 (1938), 641-51.

But, since not all colleges maintain the same standards of admission, wide ranges of intelligence test scores may be found within colleges and from college to college. In two studies on the intellectual requirements at higher education levels, investigators found that the average Stanford-Binet IQ[9] required for college entrance was 118, for bachelor's degree recipients 123, for advanced degree recipients 126, and for persons receiving the Ph.D. 141.[10] In the colleges in which these studies were conducted the range of IQ scores was from 95 to 180. In some colleges the average IQ of students was as low as 100, and in others as high as 133. In Wrenn's study, 10 per cent of those who eventually received the Ph.D. scored below the average of the entering freshmen in the colleges they were attending. These facts, while startling, indicate that the standards for admission to different institutions vary considerably. While we have said that success in school may be predicted from intelligence quotients, we need to consider a variety of factors in making individual predictions. Among these factors are the particular school a student plans to enter and the particular course of study he will follow in that school.

THE INFLUENCE OF EXPERIENCE ON INTELLIGENCE TEST SCORES

In our preliminary discussion of the character of intelligence tests, we emphasized that these tests assume that the individual has had experiences from which he can learn the behaviors the tasks require. An abundance of evidence suggests that differences in environmental opportunity yield differences in intelligence test scores for children of comparable ages.

INTERPRETING SCORE DIFFERENCES RELATED TO ENVIRONMENTAL DIFFERENCES. If we test two groups of children from different environments and find differences in their intelligence test scores, three inferences are possible: (1) that differences in environment are responsible for the differences in test scores, or (2) that differences in heredity are responsible for the differences in test scores, or (3) that

---

[9]The Stanford-Binet IQ is an intelligence quotient score derived from the Stanford-Binet test —an individual intelligence test.

[10]R. B. Embree, "The Status of College Students in Terms of IQ's Determined During Childhood," *American Psychologist*, 3 (1948), 259. C. G. Wrenn, "Potential Research Talent in the Sciences Based on Intelligence Quotients of Ph.D.'s," *Educational Record*, 30 (1949), 5-22.

some interaction of environment and heredity accounts for the obtained differences. From many of the studies demonstrating the relationship of intelligence test score differences to environmental differences, the second and third inferences cannot be made because the relevant hereditary factors cannot be measured.

Still, a number of studies have been conducted in which the influence of heredity has been controlled. For example, differences in intelligence test performances between identical twins raised in different environments may be attributed to differences in environment since in this case heredity is identical. In Table XXXVII are data

Case No.	Sex	Age at Separation	Age at Testing	Environmental Differences				Twin Difference in IQ
				1. In Years of Schooling	2. In Estimated Educational Advantages†	3. In Estimated Social Advantages†	4. In Estimated Physical Advantages†	
11	F	18 mo.	35	14	37	25	22	24
2	F	18 mo.	27	10	32	14	9	12
18	M	1 yr	27	4	28	31	11	19
4	F	5 mo.	29	4	22	15	23	17
12	F	18 mo.	29	5	19	13	36	7
1	F	18 mo.	19	1	15	27	19	12
17	M	2 yr.	14	0	15	15	15	10
8	F	3 mo.	15	1	14	32	13	15
3	M	2 mo.	23	1	12	15	12	-2
14	F	6 mo.	39	0	12	15	9	-1
5	F	14 mo.	38	1	11	26	23	4
13	M	1 mo.	19	0	11	13	9	1
10	F	1 yr.	12	1	10	15	16	5
15	M	1 yr	26	2	9	7	8	1
7	M	1 mo	13	0	9	27	9	-1
19	F	6 yr.	41	0	9	14	22	-9
16	F	2 yr	11	0	8	12	14	2
6	F	3 yr	59	0	7	10	22	8
9	M	1 mo	19	0	7	14	10	6
20*	F	1 mo.	19	0	2	?	?	-3

Individual Data on Twins Reared Apart
(From Anastasi based on data from Woodworth, from Newman, Freeman, and Holzinger, and from Gardner and Newman)

TABLE XXXVII

*The first 19 cases are from Newman, Freeman, and Holzinger; case 20 was added later by Gardner and Newman.
†Ratings are on a scale of 50 points; the higher the rating, the greater the estimated environmental difference between the twins.

from a number of studies on identical twins who were reared in different environments.[11] The general finding in these studies was that the better educated twin had an IQ of 6 or more points higher than that of his less educated twin, and the greater the differences in opportunities for education, the greater the differences in IQ scores obtained. This kind of study clearly demonstrates the influence of environment on intelligence, although we may not conclude that education improves intellectual functioning.

SOCIAL CLASS AND INTELLIGENCE TEST PERFORMANCE. We find similar differences in average IQ's for children from different socioeconomic backgrounds. In Table XXXVIII are the average IQ's of children of fathers whose occupational level is indicated in the column on the left.[12] Notice that the difference in average IQ's between the highest and lowest classification levels is substantial. Relative superiority and inferiority may be maintained for a period of time. We should

Father's Occupational Classification	Chronological Ages			
	2-5½	6-9	10-14	15-18
I Professional	114.8	114.9	117.5	116.4
II Semiprofessional and Managerial	112.4	107.3	112.2	116.7
III Clerical, Skilled Trades, and Retail Business	108.0	104.9	107.4	109.6
IV Rural Owners	97.8	94.6	92.4	94.3
V Semiskilled, Minor Clerical, and Business	104.3	104.6	103.4	106.7
VI Slightly Skilled	97.2	100.0	100.6	96.2
VII Day Labor, Urban and Rural	93.8	96.0	97.2	97.6

Mean IQ's of Children According to Father's Occupations
(From McNemar)

TABLE XXXVIII

---

[11]In A. Anastasi, *Differential Psychology*, p. 299, based on data from the following studies: R. S. Woodworth, *Heredity and Environment: A Critical Survey of Recently Published Materials on Twins and Foster Children*, Social Science Research Council Bulletin, No. 47, 1941; H. H. Newman, F. N. Freeman, and K. J. Holzinger, *Twins: A Study of Heredity and Environment*, Chicago, University of Chicago Press, 1937; I. C. Gardner and H. H. Newman, "Mental and Physical Traits of Identical Twins Reared Apart," *Journal of Heredity*, 31 (1940), 119-26.

[12]Q. McNemar, *The Revision of the Stanford-Binet Scale*, p. 38.

remember that these are only average IQ's and that a wide range of scores may be found at any occupational level. Some children of professional men score as low or lower than many children of laborers.[13]

While we cannot attribute these differences conclusively to differences in environment, certainly we can make a strong case, particularly at the older age levels, for the influence of environmental factors on test performance. We know that home environments are not identical. We also know that differences in the financial returns yielded by various occupations probably create differences in the kinds of opportunities provided for the child's development. In the upper level occupations, we would expect to find a wider range of reading materials available and a greater emphasis on the advantages of schooling and achievement of school success. In general, these homes differ in the kind and amount of intellectual stimulation they provide—with consequent effects on the child's intellectual development.

Recall that comparisons of intelligence test performance assume that the individuals compared have had equal opportunities to learn. Analysis of intelligence tests indicates that they may contain items particularly related to the experiences of middle- and upper-class children.[14] In the studies reported by Eells *et al.*, a number of well-known intelligence tests were administered to a large sample of children between the ages of nine and fourteen. Children's test scores were divided into groups based on the socio-economic status of their fathers' occupation. The number of items passed or failed by children in these two groups was computed. Table XXXIX illustrates the percentage of items on which there was a reliable difference in the number of students who passed them from the two socio-economic groups. Davis attributes this differential performance to differences in the educational opportunities available to children in these two broad categories of socio-economic status.[15] (It should be noted that some of the items did not discriminate in this way.)

The wide variation in the amount of socio-economic difference found among items may be illustrated by citing two individual items. In the first

---

[13]For a comprehensive survey of studies of this kind, see J. Loevinger, "Intelligence as Related to Socio-Economic Factors," *Thirty-ninth Yearbook of the National Society for the Study of Education, Part I, Intelligence: Its Nature and Nurture,* 1940.

[14]K. Eells, A. Davis, R. Havighurst, V. Herrick, and R. Tyler, *Intelligence and Cultural Differences,* Chicago, University of Chicago Press, 1951.

[15]A. Davis, *Social Class Influences upon Learning,* Cambridge, Mass., Harvard University Press, copyright 1948 by the President and Fellows of Harvard College, p. 42. Reprinted by permission of the publisher.

Test	Number of Pupils High Socio-economic Group	Low Socio-economic Group	Proportion of Items Showing Socio-economic Differential
Tests given to nine-and ten-year-old pupils:			
Henmon-Nelson	226	322	93%
Otis Alpha (nonverbal)	223	316	46%
Otis Alpha (verbal)	223	326	70%
Kuhlmann-Anderson (Grade III)	225	327	56%
Kuhlmann-Anderson (Grade VI)	225	321	85%
Tests given to thirteen-and fourteen-year-old pupils:			
Terman-McNemar	233	361	100%
Otis Beta	235	364	91%
California Mental Maturity*	235	352	69%
Thurstone Spatial	235	352	84%
Thurstone Reasoning	232	358	100%

Item-Discrimination between Socio-economic Groups (From Davis)

TABLE XXXIX

*The figures for the California Mental Maturity test are based on only four of the six subtests. Two of the subtests were omitted because the test was too long to give in full in the time available.

case, 78% of the pupils in the high socio-economic group answered the item correctly, but only 28% of the pupils in the lower group did so—a difference of 46 percentage points. In the second case, the percentage answering correctly was practically identical for socio-economic groups, so that there was no statistically significant difference. The content of these two items suggests the reason for the great variation in their socio-economic differential. The first item requires the pupil to be familiar with the term 'sonata'—a word which will clearly be heard more often in a home in the high socio-economic bracket than in a family from the lower socio-economic group. The second item, on the contrary, requires the pupil to apply the concept of a "cutting tool" so as to distinguish between this type and several other types of implements. Both the tools and the other implements are common to all socio-economic groups.[16]

The data in these studies support the hypothesis that intelligence test performance is related to environmental factors. As the data

[16]*Ibid.*, p. 45.

indicate, performance on some test items is related to the socio-economic background of a child.

Further evidence of the influence of environment may be found in studies of the relationship between home atmosphere and intelligence test performance.[17] The atmospheres of a hundred and twenty-four homes were rated on such factors as warmth, indulgence, democracy, and activity. Children from these homes were given intelligence tests at two different ages, and the amount of change in intelligence test scores was determined. Children from homes described as "democratic-accepting" made substantially greater gains in intelligence test scores than did children from other kinds of homes. A "democratic-accepting" home is one in which the children are encouraged to express their preferences, which the parents consider in making decisions. Furthermore, children from such homes were consistently superior in originality, patience, curiosity, and planning—characteristics related to success in academic work and problem-solving.

For a final piece of evidence on the relationship of environment to intelligence test performance, see Table XL. In this table are listed the average IQ scores for children from urban, suburban, and rural regions.[18] The differences between suburban and urban children are

| Locality | Age Range in Years | | | | | |
| | 2-5½ | | 6-14 | | 15-18 | |
	N	Mean	N	Mean	N	Mean
Urban	354	106.3	864	105.8	204	107.9
Suburban	158	105.0	537	104.5	112	106.9
Rural	144	100.6	422	95.4	103	95.7

Mean Stanford-Binet IQ's of Urban, Suburban, and Rural Children (From McNemar)

TABLE XL

not significant. However, the differences between rural children and the other two groups run, on the average, about ten or eleven IQ points.

Certainly the evidence suggests that environmental factors have

---

[17] A. L. Baldwin, J. Kalhorn, and F. H. Breese, "Patterns of Parent Behavior," *Psychological Monographs*, No. 3, 1945.

[18] Q. McNemar, *The Revision of the Stanford-Binet Scale*, p. 37.

an important influence on intelligence test performance. This conclusion is of great practical significance for the classroom teacher who makes inferences about intellectual abilities from test data. If a child's family is from a cultural background other than the "American, white, urban" culture, his intelligence test performance is likely to be below that of the typical American child. Radical changes in IQ scores may also be apparent as the child spends more time in school and has the opportunity to assimilate the experience of the typical American child. However, such a change in IQ score will not necessarily follow, because the child's intellectual ability may actually be low.

An inference about a child's intellectual ability is a hypothesis based on an observation in which factors other than variations in intellectual ability have been controlled. Opportunity to learn may be an uncontrolled variable influencing this observation. Test manuals for intelligence tests describe the standardization sample, which should be considered in using the test. A test given to a child or group of children who do not have the characteristics of the standardization sample yields an uncontrolled observation from which valid inferences cannot be made.

CONTROLLING THE INFLUENCE OF ENVIRONMENT ON TEST PERFORMANCE. In an attempt to measure intellectual ability independently of the influence of environment, test constructors have attempted to construct what are called "culture-fair tests."[19] These tests present children with tasks likely to have been met in almost any culture. Whether such tests actually are culture-fair—that is, not reflecting the influence of particular environment—is a matter of empirical test.

Some test constructors argue that we will obtain a better estimate of a child's intellectual ability if we remove from intelligence tests the items that discriminate social and cultural differences. This argument is weakened by the fact that we have little data on the predictive validity of such tests. Although intelligence tests in their present form may be used to predict school success, the same environmental factors that influence differential test performances probably influence school achievement.

If a child's intelligence test performance is relatively poor, we

---

[19]A. Davis and K. Eells, *Davis-Eells Games: A Test of General Intelligence, or Problem-Solving Ability, Manual*, Yonkers, New York, World Book Co., 1953.

may predict that he is not likely to profit from the typical learning experiences provided by schools. We cannot infer that he does not have the intelligence to profit from this environment, but only that he is at least temporarily handicapped in doing so. Unfortunately, specific procedures for remedying this handicap are not easily determined.[20]

STABILITY OF INTELLIGENCE TEST SCORES

How consistent is a child's performance on intelligence tests? What is the likelihood that a child will obtain approximately the same score at age ten or age fifteen that he received at age seven? This kind of information is frequently needed when we have to make decisions about the kinds of educational programs that children will be permitted or encouraged to enter. Such information is also relevant to the decisions a child must make about entering an occupation.

FACTORS INFLUENCING VARIATIONS IN TEST PERFORMANCE. IQ scores do change over a period of time for a variety of reasons. The amount of change and the reasons for it are important considerations. Some changes reflect the effect of unreliable measurements. No intelligence test is absolutely reliable, although most of them are highly reliable. Some variations in a child's IQ score may be attributed to errors of measurement. Such variations are not usually large and they tend to occur at random. On the average, a child's intelligence test score may vary as much as plus or minus five points because of the unreliability of the measuring instrument itself.

Other variations in IQ will be due to changes in the child. Such variations reflect the effects of uncontrolled influences on test performance. Changes in motivation, as well as in health and emotional factors may influence his test performance.[21] When the factors influencing the test score are related to the child himself, the fluctuation in the test scores obtained may be large.

PREDICTING FUTURE TEST PERFORMANCE. Long-term predictions of intelligence test performance tend to be relatively unreliable. The

---

[20]See K. Eells, "Some Implications for School Practice of the Chicago Studies of Cultural Bias in Intelligence Tests," *Harvard Educational Review*, 23 (1953), 284-97.

[21]M. Hutt, "A Clinical Study of 'Consecutive' and 'Adaptive' Testing," *Journal of Consulting Psychology*, 11 (1947), 93-103.

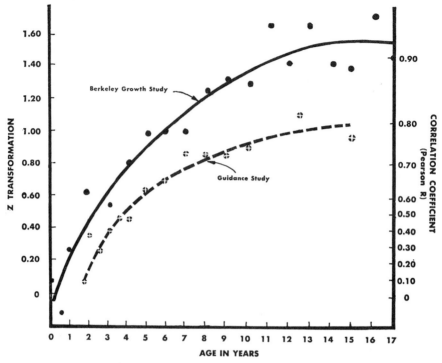

Correlation of intelligence scores at 18 years with scores at successive earlier ages. (From Jones based on data from Bayley and from Honzik, Macfarlane, and Allen)

FIGURE 73

curve plotted in Figure 73 shows the relationship between ages at which the tests are taken and the amount of correlation between test scores.[22] Select any age point along the bottom of the graph and erect a vertical line to one of the curves. Draw a horizontal line from the intersection point to the right side of the graph and read off the *correlation coefficient* (Pearson *r*) at that point. This is the correlation coefficient between scores at the age you selected and scores at age eighteen. Note that the correlations become increasingly higher as we make predictions at ages closer to age eighteen.

[22]Compiled by H. E. Jones, "The Environment and Mental Development," in L. Carmichael (ed.), *Manual of Child Development*, 2nd ed., New York, John Wiley & Sons, 1954, p. 639, based on data in the following studies: N. Bayley, "Consistency and Variability in the Growth of Intelligence from Birth to Eighteen Years," *Journal of Genetic Psychology*, 75 (1949), 165-96; M. P. Honzik, J. W Macfarlane, and L. Allen, "The Stability of Mental Test Performance between Two and Eighteen Years," *Journal of Experimental Education*, 18 (1949), 309-24.

One of the reasons that long-term predictions are less reliable is that the tests used at an earlier age frequently require different specific abilities than do the tests at a later date. A test of intelligence appropriate for very young children cannot utilize tasks requiring verbal facility because the child's language acquisition is limited. Because the later tests typically depend heavily on verbal materials, the earlier tests do not measure the same kinds of behavior that the later tests are measuring. We infer present learning ability, not some innate capacity, from intelligence test performance. Correlations between test performances are influenced both by the kinds of behavior tested and by the maintenance of the conditions required for a controlled observation.

INTERPRETING VARIATIONS IN TEST PERFORMANCE. A low test score should not be immediately attributed to unreliability of the measuring instrument or to unusual dispositions in the child. Before we may conclude that a test score does not represent a child's ability, we need some corroborating evidence to suggest other factors influencing his performance. We cannot say that he was not trying his best without some evidence. Nor may we attribute poor performance to illness or emotional maladjustment without supporting evidence.

When a test score is inaccurate, the amount of error is not usually large. It is not likely that we will identify a bright child as dull or a dull child as unusually bright. It is fortunate that such misidentifications, although possible, are not very likely, for they can promote tragic misunderstandings. Our judgment of the intelligence of a child does not depend exclusively on intelligence test scores. As teachers, we have intelligence test data available, but our judgments of a child's ability are also influenced by his achievement in school. If we find a child who has a high intelligence test score and consistently achieves above the average for his class, we are reasonably certain that he is a bright child. Correspondingly, a child whose intelligence test score is low and who does not achieve well in school is not likely to be a child of extremely high intelligence. If the teacher suspects that some factor may be influencing a child's test performance, he may refer the child to a clinical psychologist who can make an extensive analysis of the child's personality.

Practically speaking, the teacher is concerned with the child's present performance level. The question of long-term stability becomes important when we attempt to make predictions about future status. In all cases, our inferences about intellectual ability are hypotheses which need to be tested by gathering all relevant data on a child's learning ability.

ACHIEVEMENT TESTS

Standardized achievement tests are comparable to the kinds of tests teachers construct for their own use. We have achievement tests in reading, in arithmetic, and for almost every subject in the school curriculum.[23] Ordinarily, the achievement test is designed to measure the attainment of the objectives of a specific learning experience. Most of these tests have logical validity since they sample the typical content of school subjects. They have also been given to large numbers of students; therefore, norms of performance are available for them.

AGE AND GRADE SCORES. Achievement test scores may be reported as percentile scores, or as *age scores* or *grade scores*. An age score represents the performance of children of a given age; in an achievement area, it is determined in a similar way to that by which mental age scores are determined. Assume that we give a reading test to a large group of children and we compute the average raw score for each age level. If the average raw score is twenty-five for age ten, a child who obtains a raw score of twenty-five is given an age score of ten. A grade score represents the average performance of children at a given grade level. Grade scores are comparable to age scores, except that performances are averaged on the basis of grade rather than age level.

The grade score is one of the most common forms in which scores on achievement tests are reported. They are particularly useful for determining a student's achievement with respect to that of students who have had comparable learning experiences. A fifth-grade teacher may give a reading test to his class. When he has scored the test, he can convert the results into grade level scores. From these scores he can tell whether his children are reading at, above, or below grade level as it is measured by this achievement test.

A common error is frequently made in interpreting age or grade scores. We find that a child in the fifth grade is reading, according to

___
[23]Examples of such tests are: G. Hildreth, H. Bixler, *et al.*, *Metropolitan Achievement Tests, Manual*, Yonkers, New York, World Book Co., 1948; E. F. Lindquist, *Iowa Tests of Educational Development, Manual*, Chicago, Science Research Associates, 1948; E. W. Tiegs and W. W. Clark, *California Achievement Tests, Manual*, Los Angeles, California Test Bureau, 1951.

the norms, at the seventh grade reading level; his score is reported as grade seven in reading. This score represents the relative position of the child in reading achievement as compared to other fifth graders. He has answered more items correctly than the typical fifth grader. If this test is also used in measuring the achievement of seventh graders, he may have a score that is equal to the average score obtained by seventh graders. If the test is not usually taken by seventh graders, the symbol "seven" is being used to indicate how far above the fifth grade level his score is.

The score does not mean that this child reads like a typical seventh grader. He may or may not, but this is something that cannot be determined from the test score. The test score compares his reading performance to that of children at his own grade or age level who have taken the same test. In many cases a child will be reading well above the average for his grade level, but is not reading the same as, nor is he ready to read the same as, children at a higher grade level. He may not have the reading interests of children at a higher grade level, or his general background of experiences is not an adequate preparation for seventh grade reading experiences.

USING ACHIEVEMENT TEST NORMS. The published norms for most achievement tests have been obtained by giving the test to large samples of children. In using these norms, we assume that children taking the test are like the children in the sample from which the norms were developed. Real differences may exist between these two groups of children, either in the particular kinds of experiences that they are having in school or in their general background. We would not expect children from rural areas to perform in the same way on these achievement tests as children from urban areas. If the standardization sample has been composed of children from middle class urban areas, then test norms represent the average performances for children from that kind of an environment.

Ideally, local norms should be developed. With such norms, a child's achievement may be compared to that of children having comparable learning experiences. However, differences between local and national performances may be significant for reorganizing learning experiences. If we find, for example, that the children in our school system are below the national average, we may raise questions about the content of the experiences that they are having. Since such differences may also be related to differences in intellectual ability between the two groups or to differences in educational objectives, a great deal of caution must be exercised at this point.

ASSESSING THE CURRICULAR VALIDITY OF ACHIEVEMENT TESTS. When an achievement test is chosen to be used in a particular class we generally assume that it is measuring what the children have been learning in that class. This assumption may not be justified. Before a teacher uses an achievement test, he should examine it to determine to what extent the children in his class ought to be able to handle the items in the test. The standardized achievement test is a valid measure of the effects of a learning experience to the extent that it adequately samples the kinds of behavior change involved in the learning experience.

A particular standardized test may not measure all the objectives of a particular learning experience. Some achievement tests contain items that require only a knowledge of factual material. Such tests measure attainment of a limited number of objectives. Recall that an evaluation program is designed to measure attainment of all of the objectives of a learning experience. Standardized tests may not be available to measure all of these objectives. A common error is to assume that a test labeled "Reading Achievement" or "Arithmetic Achievement" is measuring all of the behavior changes desired in organizing learning experiences in reading or arithmetic.

If an achievement test has curricular validity for the courses in a school, it is useful for comparing the achievement of different classes, or schools within the same system. In using achievement tests in this manner, we may not necessarily assume that the average performance of any class must be at its grade level. There will be a range of performance on any achievement test, and the average performance of the class tends to be highly correlated with the general level of intellectual ability in the class. Brighter students have the ability to profit more from experience. When the brighter pupils are grouped in the same class, the teachers are likely to provide a wider and richer range of learning experiences. These differences in pupil ability and in the learning experiences provided are reflected in higher average performance scores.

PREDICTIVE VALIDITY OF ACHIEVEMENT TESTS. An achievement test may be used to predict future performance in the same or a related achievement area. Assume that we test students' achievement in

Freshman English, and that we want to use this test to predict achievement in Senior English. If the test is being used for the first time, such a prediction cannot be made since we do not know the predictive validity of the test. At some later date, however, we may obtain a measure of achievement in Senior English. Test scores may then be correlated with the measures of performance in Senior English. The achievement test has predictive validity to the extent that there is a substantial positive correlation between these two measures.

Test manuals for standardized achievement tests contain information on the predictive validity of these tests, when it has been determined. A relationship between achievement test performance and some future performance may not be assumed without such information even when achievement test performance appears to be logically related to the future performance.

MEASURES OF PERSONALITY CHARACTERISTICS

Teachers frequently make inferences about a wide variety of pupil characteristics. These inferences are usually based on observations of the pupil. We have repeatedly emphasized in this text that these observations must have certain characteristics if the inferences made from them are to be relatively reliable and valid. As we noted, the teacher faces many practical problems which make it difficult for him to obtain the kind of information that he needs.

Two problems in particular make it difficult for the teacher to obtain adequate information on pupils: (1) the demands on his time prevent the teacher from making systematic observations of pupil behavior; (2) observations tend to be biased because they are not based on representative samples of pupil behavior.

Another problem facing the teacher in this respect is that he observes the pupil almost exclusively in the school context. The kind of behavior the teacher observes is the kind likely to be evoked by the requirements of the learning experience. Even an elementary school teacher who sees the pupil for a major portion of the day observes mainly "school behavior." Pupils may and frequently do act quite differently in other contexts.

Still another obstacle to inferring from observations of students arises from the general problem of validity. Assume that a student requests a teacher's opinion on the advisability of preparing for a particular occupation. The teacher's advice will be based on his conception of the pupil's abilities, personality characteristics, and the requirements of the occupation. Even if the teacher has made reliable observations of the pupil's behavior, we may still question the relevance of these behavior samples to the kind of judgments the teacher is asked to make.

If a boy says that he is interested in engineering, for example, we may obtain information on his general intellectual ability which will help in making decisions about his general fitness for this occupation. In addition, we will need information on his special aptitudes, and we may question the strength and stability of his interest in engineering. What is the predictive validity of judgments based on the teacher's observations of the pupil?

A wide variety of tests have been developed to provide teachers with information on pupil characteristics. Special training is required to administer many of these tests. We will discuss some of these tests briefly to suggest their value as measuring instruments. Since many school systems use them, the data they provide on student performance are often available to teachers. We will offer some warnings on using them to make inferences about pupils. This discussion will also provide us with another opportunity to stress the importance of knowing the necessary characteristics of any measurement of behavior.

APTITUDE TESTS. We discussed one kind of aptitude test when we studied intelligence tests. An intelligence test measures a *general* ability. Psychologists differ on whether intellectual ability is in fact a general trait. Some psychologists argue that intelligence is a composite of many factors. Many common-sense conceptions of intelligence are factor theories of intelligence.

This issue is not easily resolved. A number of tests have been constructed which purport to measure factors of intelligence. The Differential Aptitude Test Battery is a test of this kind.[24] The percentile scores of a student on the factors of this test are plotted in Figure 74. The names of the factors or special aptitudes that this test measures are listed at the top of each column.

Tests of this kind are constructed in such a way that performances on parts of the test tend to correlate only in a low degree. But we may not conclude from this that intelligence is composed of inde-

---

[24]G. K. Bennett, H. G. Seashore, and A. G. Wesman, *Differential Aptitude Tests, Manual*, New York, Psychological Corporation, 1952.

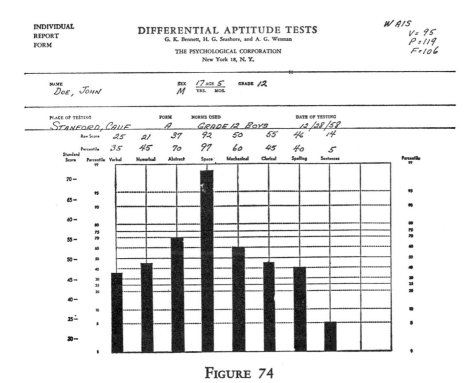

FIGURE 74

pendent factors. In other words, the "factors" measured express the way in which the test has been constructed. A general intelligence test is constructed in such a way that it measures principally one factor—"general intelligence." In these tests, performance on any one item tends to be highly correlated with total performance on the test. In a factored test, performances on some items tend to be correlated with each other, and these performances measure performance on a particular factor, such as "verbal reasoning." But performance on the items measuring one factor is not highly correlated with performance on the items measuring another factor.

Still another way of describing these relations is to say that we cannot predict a person's performance on one factor from his performance on another factor. Note that the student whose scores are plotted in Figure 74 has a superior performance on the spatial relations factor, but average or low average performances on other factors. A student may have high, low, or average scores on one, some, or all of the factors. The factored test is designed to make discriminations among abilities on the factors measured.

A test of special aptitude is so designated because performance on this test is not predictable from tests of general ability. We determine the extent to which a test measures a distinctive performance by the degree to which it correlates with other measures of aptitude. Test manuals provide data on the correlation of the tests with other measures of ability. If the test has a high correlation with other measures of aptitude, we infer that the test is probably not measuring an independent performance factor.

Aptitude tests have been constructed to improve predictions of future performance. Aptitude tests, like other tests, may have many predictive validities. In each case, performance on the test has been correlated with some criterion performance. From these correlations we may make inferences about the abilities that the test presumably measures.

Let us take this opportunity to warn that the test labels are frequently misleading. Some test users will select a test on the basis of the name, assuming that the test measures what its name suggests. The test user may assure himself by examination of the test manual that the test does measure an independent factor not measured by other tests. He may also derive the meanings to be associated with test performance by checking the predictive validities of the test.

One other kind of error may be made in using these tests. Aptitude tests are frequently used in making predictions about probable occupational success. A teacher may assume that the abilities a particular test purports to measure are required in a specific job. We may assume, for example, that the ability to visualize in space is required in engineering. The teacher may be tempted to make inferences about a student's probable success in engineering from his performance on a spatial relations test. As a matter of fact, performance on a particular test of spatial relations ability may not be correlated with success in engineering. The error the teacher makes is assuming that a test which purports to measure this ability must be measuring the abilities required in engineering. Again, this error may be avoided by checking the manual to determine whether the particular test of spatial relations being used does correlate with success in engineering. Some abilities, while they may be *necessary conditions* for occupational success, are not *sufficient causes* of it.

The correlation between performance on many aptitude tests and success on a job is not high, although it may be reasonably suggestive. This is not difficult to explain, since many aptitude tests are of a paper and pencil type and do not directly measure the performances required by a job. As we have noted before, job success depends upon a variety of factors—not just the ability to perform a specific task.

INTEREST TESTS. As we suggested in the previous chapter, one simple way to determine a person's interests is by asking him what he likes and what he does not like. An interest test consists of a series of questions in which a person is requested to express his likes or dislikes, or his preferences for various activities. While the method of determining interests is fairly simple, the problem of reliably measuring a person's interests depends in part on the kind of interest we attempt to measure. For example, if we ask a child what TV programs he likes, we probably will get an accurate estimate of his TV interests. If, however, we ask a child what occupations he is interested in, his answer may have no practical significance. He may have only the vaguest conception of a given occupation, and his "interest" may be based upon a superficial picture of what the occupation is like. A standard interest of high school boys is engineering, yet the interest is frequently unrealistic because the student is merely reflecting his conception of a glamorous male occupation. The interest may change as the boy develops a more realistic conception of what engineers do. Standardized interest tests have been developed to measure more complex kinds of interests.

Two of the best known interest inventories are the Kuder Preference Record and the Strong Vocational Interest Blank.[25] In each of these inventories the person taking the inventory is asked to check his preferences and his likes and dislikes. When the entire list of alternatives has been checked, the inventory is scored and a profile of relative strength of interests is obtained.

The differences between these two tests illustrate the kinds of information needed to use a test appropriately. The Kuder test, for example, reports interests in such broad categories as "scientific," "literary," and "mechanical." The question of the relation of these measured interest patterns to the interests of people in particular occupations is an empirical one. We may not assume that the "scientific" interest measured by the test is in fact the dominant interest of indi-

---

[25] G. F. Kuder, *Kuder Preference Record-Vocational, Manual,* Chicago, Science Research Associates, 1953; E. K. Strong, Jr., *Vocational Interest Blank for Men, Manual,* Stanford, California, Stanford University Press, 1951.

viduals in a particular job until we have determined how people in this job would respond on the test. The most recent test manual provides some data of this kind, although some of the occupational samples used are comparatively small.

The Strong test has been administered to successful people in a number of different occupations. The scores on the test compare the examinee's interests with those of successful people in these occupations. For example, an "A" score in an occupational category means that an individual has interests highly similar to those of successful people in that occupation. None the less, the character of these interests is not defined by the test score. A score indicating similarity of interests means that a person has checked alternatives in substantially the same way that successful people in a given occupation do.

Even after we have determined a student's pattern of interests, as measured by either of these two tests, we cannot conclude that he will succeed in the occupation of people whose interests are similar to his. A student must also have other personality characteristics and the ability required for an occupation. Still, both of these tests are useful for educational and vocational counseling. They are not useful for determining a wide variety of other kinds of interests, particularly the kinds of interests with which a teacher may be concerned in organizing a learning experience.

OTHER SELF-REPORT MEASURES. The person to whom an interest inventory is administered must give information about himself. Tests which require an individual to answer questions about himself are called self-report tests. A large number of such tests are available for measuring many different aspects of personality.

The Allport-Vernon-Lindzey Study of Values is an example of such a test. Here are two items from this test:[26]

> *Part 1.* The two alternatives are rated 3 and 0 if the subject agrees with one and disagrees with the other; if he has only a slight preference for one over the other, they are rated 2 and 1 respectively.
>
> *Example:*
> If you should see the following news items with headlines of equal size in your morning paper which would you read more attentively?

---

[26]G. W. Allport, P. E. Vernon, G. Lindzey, *Study of Values,* rev. ed., Boston, Houghton Mifflin Co., 1951, pp. 3 and 7.

(a) Protestant Leaders to Consult on Reconciliation; (b) Great Improvement in Market Conditions.

(a) ——————— (b) ———————

Part 2. The answers are rated in order of personal preference, giving 4 to the most attractive and 1 to the least attractive alternative.

Example:

In your opinion, can a man who works in business all the week best spend Sunday in—

    a. Trying to educate himself by reading serious books.

    b. Trying to win at golf, or racing.

    c. Going to an orchestral concert.

    d. Hearing a really good sermon.

This test is designed to measure the dominant value systems of an individual. In scoring the test, *a priori* assumptions are made about the values represented in each statement. We may infer that a person who is interested in the headline on church leaders rather than the headline on market conditions has major values which are religious in character. Obviously, this one item would not be conclusive evidence. The test presents a series of items in which the individual must make choices, or express preferences for one activity over another. In scoring the test, we determine what kinds of items the individual systematically prefers, and these preferences presumably reflect his dominant values.

The major advantage of these tests is that we obtain a comprehensive sample of an individual's behavior. Frequently, these tests give information about an individual that could be obtained only by an extended personal interview. The major disadvantage of such tests is that the information we obtain is based on a self-description. Previous warnings about assuming a meaning of what the test measures from the test label are appropriate here.

Because the individual's self-reporting may be unrealistic, or because the individual may consciously or unconsciously falsify descriptions of himself, personality tests have been developed using test situations in which it is difficult for the individual to know what might be a "good" response. Such tests are called *projective tests*. In a projective test an ambiguous stimulus situation is presented to the person taking the test, and he responds on the basis of his impressions. The Rorschach Inkblot Test is a well-known example of this kind of test. The complexities of the theory of scoring and interpreting such tests are beyond the scope of this book. The use of such tests requires special training, and they are not available to the classroom teacher unless the teacher has specialized training. The examples are presented here to suggest the wide range of tests designed to measure complex aspects of personality. These tests, as all other tests, are useful to the extent that they are reliable and valid measuring instruments and if a trained person administers and interprets them.

TESTS AND THE EVALUATION OF PUPIL BEHAVIOR. In the last three chapters we have reviewed the principles of test construction and the use of standardized tests. Recall that the function of an evaluation program is to assess behavior change in learning experiences. One phase of this program is concerned with the assessment of the student's personality, so that decisions about appropriate learning experiences may be made. Tests are ways of obtaining more adequate and reliable information about what pupils are like. The teacher should not lose sight of the fact that one test gives only a portion of the picture of a student's personality. If we are to make adequate and reliable determinations of the personality of a child, a comprehensive evaluation program is necessary.

It is important to remember that the child's total personality affects the whole course of his learning. Knowing a child's intelligence quotient gives us only a comparatively small piece of information. On the basis of it, we cannot tell how he will act in a variety of situations, or how he *typically acts*. Many of our measures of performance measure achievement or ability, but do not give us a picture of how the student usually acts. If we are to get a picture both of abilities and typical performances, we must utilize a wide range of evaluation procedures.

USING TEST INFORMATION

Test data gathered on pupils will be of value to teachers only if they preserve it systematically. Most schools maintain *cumulative records* on pupils. Into these records go the basic data about the child, such as his health record, his father's occupation, his test performance on intelligence and achievement tests, his academic record, and so on. In some schools teachers are requested to write up their observations about pupils and to place these in the cumulative record.

Cumulative records can be particularly useful to the teacher if certain precautions are observed in their use. The records must be kept up to date and the information in them must be correctly recorded. Many records are inadequate because they contain only a small amount of information about pupils.

ANECDOTAL RECORDS. The observations of pupils recorded by the teacher are valuable only if these have been gathered systematically and if the teacher has been careful in distinguishing what he has observed from what he infers from his observations. Many *anecdotal records,* as these observations are called, are gross, unsystematic observations of child behavior loaded with the teacher's inferences about what the pupil is like, rather than a careful description of the child's observed behavior.[27] Some teachers report only disagreeable aspects of pupil behavior in these records. Anecdotal records probably should not be used in the cumulative record unless teachers have systematic training in the observation of pupil behavior.

A major defect of many anecdotal records lies in the kinds of categories used to describe a pupil. The fifth grade teacher who picks up a cumulative folder and reads that Johnny is a "forward and pushy child," will interpret this record in terms of his own conception of "forward and pushy." Descriptive terms used in anecdotal records should be defined carefully. One way to improve these descriptions is to record the specific behavior observed. If the teacher records that Johnny is aggressive, the specific behavior that the teacher is labeling "aggressive" ought to be noted.

Another disadvantage of these anecdotal records is that they are frequently based on unsystematic observations. The teacher may record his observations when he has the time and opportunity to do so, and the record may be colored by the effects of selective memory. As a consequence, we obtain a biased picture of what the pupil's behavior is like. It is not necessary to repeat here all our previous suggestions about the limitations of and the possibilities for improving teachers' observations. The anecdotal record is simply a recording device; it is not in itself a measuring instrument. The anecdotal record is useful only insofar as it records reliable and valid observations.

ADVANTAGES OF THE CUMULATIVE RECORD. The principal ad-

---

[27]See A. E. Traxler, *The Nature and Use of Anecdotal Records,* New York, Educational Records Bureau, 1939.

vantage of the cumulative record, when it is properly maintained, is that it gives a picture of the child's development over a long period of time. Some teachers object that they prefer to make their own judgments of a pupil, and they do not want to be influenced by other teachers' conceptions of what the pupil is like. This objection has validity only when the cumulative record contains scanty or inaccurate information; it makes less sense if a systematic, comprehensive program of evaluation is maintained in the school, and if the teachers are trained to make systematic evaluations. The child's present behavior is a function of his past behavior and experiences. If we want to gain greater understanding of what a child is like, we need some conception of what has happened to him and how he has reacted over a period of time. We have noted, for example, that the IQ scores of an individual child may vary over a period of time. A teacher who uses only the child's most recent IQ score has no idea of whether this performance is consistent with the child's previous performances. The same may be said about consulting the results of achievement tests and other testing devices.

The first requirement for any attempt at gaining a comprehensive understanding of pupils is the development of adequate and appropriate procedures for measuring pupil behavior. A cumulative record is useful to the extent that it contains an accurate and comprehensive report of the results of evaluation procedures.

SUMMARY

Most teachers do not have the training or the time to carry out all the procedures necessary for determining the reliability and validity of their own tests. Standardized tests are available for measuring the attainment of many curricular objectives. They have also been administered to samples of children with known characteristics, and they provide data on the comparative performance of these groups. The process of test standardization involves:

1. *Determining the conditions under which the test is to be administered.* These conditions must be known if the test is to be administered so that it provides a controlled observation of behavior.

2. *Determining performance norms.* Norms are relative scores

which enable the test user to give meaning to the test performances. Norms of relative performance are derived by administering the test to a group of individuals of known characteristics; this group is called the *standardization sample*. The use of test norms to interpret test performance presupposes that the examinees have the characteristics of the persons in the standardization sample.

3. *Determining the reliability and validity of the test.* Knowing the predictive validities of a test enables us to specify more precisely what the test measures.

Standardized tests may be divided into two categories: (1) achievement tests, which measure the attainment of the objectives of learning experiences; (2) measures of pupil characteristics relevant to the attainment of these objectives. Intelligence tests are an example of tests of the latter kind.

4. An intelligence test is a measure of what a person has learned from his general experience. We infer intellectual ability from our observations of what the person has learned.

5. Intelligence tests provide a measure of relative brightness arrived at by comparing individuals who have had equal learning opportunities. IQ scores and percentile scores are used to provide estimates of relative brightness. These kinds of scores indicate a person's relative position in terms of intellectual ability within a group of people who have had comparable learning opportunities.

6. Intelligence test performance is influenced by environmental factors. Intelligence test performance has been found to vary with differences in socio-economic status, home atmosphere, and location in urban or rural communities.

7. Intelligence test scores of an individual may vary considerably over a period of time. In general, long-range predictions based on intelligence test performance tend to be less reliable than short-term predictions. This unreliability derives in part from the differences in content of tests used at various age levels and

in part from changes in the individual. Gross errors in prediction are not very probable and they occur in a relatively small number of cases. Inferences about pupils' intellectual ability may be made more reliably by considering more manifestations of intellectual ability than intelligence test scores.

A wide variety of achievement tests is available for use. Two considerations are relevant to the use of these tests:

8.   These tests may not have curricular validity for particular learning experiences. They may not sample the content included in a learning experience, or they may not sample all of the objectives of a learning experience. The usefulness of these tests is limited by the extent to which they have curricular validity.

9.   The norms provided for these tests are useful if the examinees have characteristics similar to those found in the standardization sample. Differences between the examinees and the standardization sample may lead to erroneous inferences about pupil achievement.

Other kinds of standardized tests are available for measuring pupil characteristics—such as special aptitude tests, interest tests, and "personality" tests. Many of these tests require special training before they may be used appropriately. However, two general principles are relevant to the use and interpretation of all of these tests:

10.   Most of these tests purport to measure special characteristics rather than general abilities. Independence of measurement in this respect may not be assumed. The extent to which any test measures factors measured by other tests may be determined from the correlations of the test with other tests.

11.   The meanings to be associated with performance on the test are determined from the kinds of predictive validities that have been determined for the test.

Test information about pupil performance and pupil characteristics is most useful when it is recorded and maintained systematically. Cumulative records are one means for maintaining a file of information on pupil behavior. The cumulative record, however, is merely a device for recording information, and the usefulness of the information in the record depends on the kinds of measurement procedures that have been used to obtain this information.

12.   Anecdotal records of pupil behavior are frequently included in these cumulative records. Anecdotal records are useful when systematic observations of pupil behavior have been made and the behavior itself carefully recorded. Anecdotes are misleading when they reflect biased observations and faulty inferences.

Three principles have been stressed throughout this chapter: (1) curricular objectives determine to some extent the usefulness of particular kinds of standardized tests, such as achievement tests; (2) the usefulness of the norms of any standardized test depends on the extent to which examinees possess the characteristics of the standardization sample; (3) the interpretation of a test score depends on the predictive validities of the test.

A test provides a limited sample of pupil behavior. A comprehensive evaluation of pupil characteristics and behavior change requires a comprehensive measurement program. Standardized tests may provide important information about pupils, but they should not be regarded as the only source of information about pupil behavior.

STUDY AND DISCUSSION QUESTIONS

1. Select any intelligence, achievement or aptitude test in which you are particularly interested or which your school may use. Use the references at the end of this chapter or the test manual if it is available, and gather information on the following points:

     a. Reliability of the test.

     b. Validity of the test.

     c. The kinds of scores in which test performance is reported.

     d. Characteristics of the standardization sample.

2. What kinds of predictions about pupil behavior could you make from data on

student performance on the test you have selected? What kinds of predictions could not be made from these data? Describe some student populations for which using information on this test might lead to unreliable inferences about pupil behavior.

3. You have extensive intelligence test data on a high school freshman. You note that his test scores fluctuate considerably. His most recent score would place him in the upper fourth of high school students in terms of intellectual ability. What inferences would you make about his intellectual ability? What information would you need in order to test your inferences? What inferences would you make about the fluctuations in test performance, and how would you gather data to test these inferences?

4. Below are the percentile scores received by three high school students on a scholastic aptitude test. The test items are largely verbal in character. The test has been given to a large sample of high school students. Describe these students' performances. What kinds of predictions would you make about their ability to do college work? Do you have sufficient information to make these predictions?

   a. Eighty-fifth percentile.

   b. Forty-fifth percentile.

   c. Twentieth percentile.

5. What assumptions underlie the development of age and grade norms?

6. A sixth-grade student in your class receives a reading grade score of 8.2. What inferences would you make about this pupil's ability in reading? Would you recommend that he read eighth-grade reading materials?

7. A Mexican-American child receives a low score on an intelligence test that is given to your sixth-grade class. What inferences would you make about his intellectual ability? What data do you need to check these inferences?

8. A student has received an average score on an intelligence test, but his achievement in your class is above average. What conclusions would you draw from these data? How may you test your inferences?

9. You are told that 75% of the sixth-grade students in your school score above the national average on a reading test. What conclusions would you draw from these data? What additional information would you want?

RECOMMENDED READINGS

The first two books on the recommended list contain critical analyses and discussions of the kinds of tests described in this chapter. The third reading contains critical reviews of a large number of tests; this book is particularly valuable for obtaining the basic information a teacher needs about a test. The fourth reading is a comprehensive discussion of the use of tests in education.

1. R. Thorndike and E. Hagen, *Measurement and Evaluation in Psychology and Education,* New York, John Wiley & Sons, 1955.

2. A. Anastasi, *Psychological Testing,* New York, Macmillan Co., 1954.

3. O. K. Buros, *The Fourth Mental Measurements Yearbook,* Highland Park, N. J., Gryphon Press, 1953. Earlier editions of this book are available, and it is periodically revised and brought up to date.

4. E. Lindquist (ed.), *Educational Measurement,* Washington, D. C., American Council on Education, 1951, Chapters 1-4.

PART FOUR

THE SCHOOL AS A
SOCIAL SYSTEM

THE SCHOOL AS A
SOCIAL SYSTEM

In Chapter Thirteen we discussed a social system as an arrangement of positions with associated roles. Social systems may be distinguished from each other by differences in the arrangement of these positions and their various roles. The family may be viewed as a three-position system, the positions being those of mother, father, and child. The system increases in complexity with additional children, who will have positions with respect to each other. Contrast this social system with that of a small town, which is characterized by a more complex organization of social positions. The number and kinds of positions in these two systems and their relationship to each other influence the kinds of interactions that are likely to occur among the members. These differences in patterns of interaction create differences in role expectations and behavior. The character of a social system influences the behavior of its members by stimulating the learning of the behavior patterns requisite to membership.

The school may be described as a social system because it is an organization of social positions. Three principal kinds of positions charac-

terize this system—administrator, teacher, and student.[1] These positions describe one aspect of the formal organization of the school as a social system. The school also embraces the complex of social positions derived from the formal and informal organization of student activities. A child located in the social position of "student" may also occupy positions based on his membership in such organizations as the athletic team or the band, and may have other positions in the informal groupings of friends and associates.

An understanding of this system is necessary in order to recognize many of the variables that influence behavior change. Formally organized learning experiences embrace only some of the variables influencing learning. A child's attitude toward "school achievement," for example, may be influenced more by the attitudes of his friends than by his teacher's conception of what constitutes desirable achievement. Many aspects of a child's personality development may be influenced by the specific experiences likely to be associated with the positions he occupies in the social system of the school.

In the model of personality in Chapter Three, the social system of the school is classified as a "stimulus situation" variable. An analysis of the influence of these stimulus variables on behavior constitutes the subject matter of this chapter.

SOCIAL POSITION AND SOCIAL STATUS

A status system based on prestige is typically associated with the arrangements of positions in a social system. The status associated with a position may derive from the character of the formal organization. The higher status of some positions is based on the greater responsibilities and privileges associated with their occupancy. The positions of principal and teacher may be viewed in this way; both involve responsibilities not required of students, and they have some privileges associated with them that are not accorded to students. The presidency of a school club is another example of this kind of status associated with a position.

In other cases the status associated with a position reflects the dominant values of the members of a system. In a school the members

---

[1] The three roles named here refer to roles in a school. Such roles as that of school superintendent and board member may also be considered as relevant to a discussion of the school as a social system. The roles of teacher, student, and principal have been arbitrarily selected as focal to the study of personality development.

of the varsity football team may have high status associated with their position as team members. This status is based on some generally shared values about the importance of the activities of the football team.

The status of a position may vary depending on the particular social system we are studying. The presidency of a club may have high status within the social system of the club, but relatively low status in the system of clubs in the school. A position may also be regarded as having high status by some members of a system but not by others. However, we are concerned here only with the relatively stable aspects of status in relation to positions in the school's social system.

FORMAL AND INFORMAL ORGANIZATIONS AND STATUS. The school's social system may be described in terms of its formal and informal organizations. The positions in the formal organization may be represented along several status dimensions. One dimension of status includes all of the individuals within the school, and the major positions on this status dimension are principal, teacher, student. The formal organization of classes also defines students' status positions with respect to each other. Seniors generally have higher status than do the Juniors, and Juniors have higher status than Sophomores and Freshmen. In most schools, varieties of activities or clubs—with varying degrees of prestige—define another status dimension.

Within the formal organization in the school, many informal groupings develop through associations of students for which the school system as such does not systematically provide. In Wabash School, for example, we saw that there were a number of cliques, and that the group with the highest status was the "athletic crowd."[2]

INDIVIDUAL SOCIAL STATUS IN THE SCHOOL. In general, the social status of an individual student in the school depends on the prestige of the positions he occupies within both the formal and the informal organizations of the school. A student who is a Senior is assured of a relatively high prestige position within one aspect of the formal organization of the school. But if he is not a member of one of the informal organizations with high status, his general social status will probably be lower than that of another Senior who belongs to a high prestige organization.

Variations arise from school to school in the importance of posi-

---

[2] C. W. Gordon, *The Social System of the High School*, Glencoe, Illinois, The Free Press, 1957.

tions in both the formal and the informal social systems. The student's position in the formal organization may be more influential in determining his general social status if his school places little emphasis on participation in clubs and activities so that most of his personal associations exist outside the school. The informal organization may be more influential in determining a student's general social status if most of his personal associations are with other students in school activities. In most schools, the student's status in the social system is a complex combination of his status in both the formal and informal organizations.

INFLUENCE OF FORMAL ORGANIZATIONS OF STUDENTS ON STATUS. At the student level, three kinds of formal school organization may be identified: (1) grade-sex groups; (2) class groups; (3) classroom groups. A *grade-sex group* would be, for example, all the eighth-grade boys, or all the eighth-grade girls. It is an association based upon sex and common grade in school. The members of the Freshman class would constitute a *class group*. A *classroom group* would be the students in Mr. Day's class. These groups are the principal organizational units in a school, and the principal roles within these organizational units are teacher and student roles.

The formal organizations are typically controlled by the administration and the teachers in the school, and they tend to be "achievement-oriented." The major goal of these systems is likely to be "success in school." "Success in school" frequently means success in achieving grades, which are the principal goals linking the striving for need-satisfaction with achievement. "Success in school," as measured by grades attained, may embrace more than academic achievement; although the grades a student receives may be principally determined by his academic performance, other factors may also be considered in determining his grades. The following statement from the grading policy of Wabash School indicates the factors which are implicit in some systems of grading:

E and S indicate that the pupil is above the class in school average and that superior work is done. F indicates that the pupil is failing and will not pass the course unless improvement is made. An I is unsatisfactory. Absence or tardiness without a good reason is inexcusable. *Grades are not determined by knowledge of subject matter alone.* Other extremely important factors are regularity, punctuality of attendance, attitude, effort, and contribution to class discussion.[3] (Italics added.)

The probable result of a policy of this kind is that students develop expectations about standards of achievement and appropriate classroom social behavior. A student acquires the relevant role expectations for a position within these formal organizations by learning the expectations for appropriate "school behavior." The expectations for achievement and classroom social behavior define the major characteristics of the roles in these systems. Status within these systems depends on the extent to which a student's behavior accords with the pattern of expectations.

To what extent does status in these formal systems influence the general social status of pupils? The influence of status within the formal administrative organizations of the school will vary both from school to school and at different levels of the educational system. In other words, the extent to which achievement in the formal structures is valued is one factor that may distinguish the social system of one school from that of another. We would hypothesize that a student's social status will be influenced by the status of his position in these formal structures to the extent that such achievement is generally valued in a particular school.

One factor that may influence the value placed on such achievement is the extent to which need-satisfactions are provided through other organizations in the school. Prestige may be thought of as an index of the degree to which a position in a social system provides highly desired need-satisfactions. Occupancy of certain positions is valued because attainment of need-satisfactions is associated with the position, and the higher value placed on the position is reflected in the symbols of prestige accorded it. Following this line of thought, we may hypothesize that a variety of other kinds of organizations in the school may influence the extent to which achievement in the formal structures tends to be valued. In "street-car universities" where students have few associations other than class associations, we would expect social status to be determined mainly by achievement within the formal department structures. In elementary schools and high schools where there are usually large numbers of clubs and activities, as well as many informal student groups, social status is more

---

[3]*Ibid.*, p. 34.

likely to be influenced by the student's prestige within the informal system.

Within any one school, the status associated with achievement in the formal structures appears to have varying degrees of importance. Occupancy of some social positions is clearly related to achievement in these structures; in other cases, status in the formal structures may have a negative correlation with general social status. The queen role was a high prestige position in Wabash School. The girl who hoped to obtain the position of queen had to have prestige within both the formal and informal organizations of the school. Among the boys at Wabash School, the students with the most prestige were accorded the title "big wheel." The "big wheel" status, as distinct from the queen role, depended heavily on participation in school activities. A student could not become a "big wheel" unless he belonged to a wide variety of important activities. One essential criterion was that of being a member of the "athletic crowd," one of the informal organizations. It was impossible for a non-athlete to attain full "big wheel" status.

Activity	No. of Members Possible	Grades in Which Allowed				Criteria of Eligibility											
		3	4	5	6	Sponsor Appt.	Prin. Appt.	Elected	Indiv. Choice	Talent	Scholarship	Dependability	Leadership	Grade	Sex*	Initiative	Pupil Need
Safety Squad	85				✓	✓						✓	✓	✓			
Color Guard	7				✓	✓						✓		✓	b✓		✓
Art Club	18		✓	✓	✓						✓	✓				✓	
Office assistant	5				✓		✓					✓		✓	g✓		
Glee Club	64		✓	✓	✓					✓	✓	✓					
Gym captains	56	✓	✓	✓	✓				✓			✓	✓				
Stage crew	1				✓	✓						✓		✓	b✓		✓
Upper Student Council	24		✓	✓	✓				✓			✓				✓	
Orchestra	29	✓	✓	✓	✓	✓				✓		✓					
Waitresses	6		✓	✓	✓	✓						✓					✓
Library	3				✓	✓						✓					
Piano	75	✓							✓	✓				✓			
Ushers	6			✓	✓	✓						✓		✓	b✓		✓
Cafeteria helper	2			✓	✓	✓								✓	b✓		
School Patrol	9							✓				✓		✓	b✓		
Milk girls	6		✓					✓			✓	✓		✓	g✓		✓
Cot girls	2		✓					✓			✓	✓		✓	g✓	✓	
Violin	35	✓	✓	✓	✓					✓	✓			✓	g✓		
Lower Student Council	24	✓							✓								
Primary Chorus	58	✓									✓						
Instrumental ensemble	5	✓			✓	✓					✓						
Total	520	7	7	10	15	11	3	4	2	7	3	15	2	9	8	3	6

Requirements for Participation in Social Activities (From Taba)

TABLE XLI

These formal organizations influence social status in another important way. The membership in particular grade-sex or class group organizations appears to be related to opportunities for participation in other organizations in the school. Table XLI indicates the criteria for eligibility in the school organizations in an elementary school.[4] As is apparent, almost all of the organizations set a grade standard for membership, and some of them also set a sex standard for membership. Belonging to the Color Guard was possible only for a sixth grade boy, whereas only third-graders were excluded from the Art Club, which both boys and girls were allowed to join.

INFLUENCE OF THE FORMAL ORGANIZATION OF CLUBS AND AC-TIVITIES ON STUDENT STATUS. In addition to class associations, schools usually provide clubs or organized activities—varsity athletic teams, foreign language clubs, musical groups. These organizations are typically thought of as having varying degrees of status in the social system of the school. In Table XLII is a list of clubs and activities at Wabash School ranked according to their prestige in the eyes of the students.[5] These clubs and activities usually maintain both formal and informal standards of membership. The extent to which students generally participate in them depends in part on the exclusiveness of their criteria for membership.

In a comparative study of the social systems of schools the investigators found that one school, which they called "Old School," had the lowest level of student participation in clubs of all the schools studied. The investigators attributed this low level of participation to the exclusive standards of the clubs at "Old School." They stated:

> Perhaps the chief factor in this pattern was the tradition of exclusiveness in all school clubs sponsored by a few "old clubs." The barriers to admission were, therefore, many and high. In a school with a heterogeneous population, grade requirements usually work especially against the lower economic group and racial or ethnic minorities. Because these conditions usually magnify the cleavages already inherent in such schools, a considerable proportion of students become inactive, indifferent, and even hostile to group activities. In Old School . . . the club program was such as to interest only a minority of students. School clubs had either social exclusiveness or academic pretensions as their main focus.[6]

---

[4]H. Taba, *School Culture: Studies in Participation and Leadership,* Washington, D. C., American Council on Education, 1955, p. 70.

[5]C. W. Gordon, *op. cit.,* p. 61.

[6]H. Taba, *op. cit.,* p. 96.

Organization	Girls' Rank	Boys' Rank	Combined Rank
Student Assembly (Student Governing Body)	1	2	1
Varsity Basketball	3	1	2
Varsity Football	5	3	3
National Honor Society	4	8	4
Cheerleaders	2	9	5
Crest Coronation (Yearbook Queen's Court)	6	7	6
Varsity Baseball	11	4	7
Crest Staff (Yearbook Staff)	9	5	8
Varsity Track	14	6	9
Senior Play Cast	7	13	10
Junior Prom Committee	8	12	11
Scoop Staff (School Newspaper)	17	11	12
Mixed Chorus	10	14	13
Varsity Wrestling	20	10	14
Girls' Athletic Association	12	19	15
Senior Dramatics Club	16	15	16
School Band	15	18	17
"B" Basketball	18	16	18
School Orchestra	13	23	19
Quill & Scroll (Honorary Publications)	19	21	20
Junior Ring Committee	22	17	21
"B" Football	21	22	22
Varsity Tennis	28	20	23
"T-13" (Honorary Girls' Athletic)	23	26	24
Pep Club	27	24	25
Junior Dramatics	25	28	26
Junior Rotarians	24	33	27
Junior Town Meeting	26	32	28
Bowling Club	30	27	29
Rifle Club	29	30	30
Projection Staff	31	29	31
Varsity Golf	37	25	32
Intramural Basketball	40	31	33
Drum Majorettes	34	35	34
Stage Crew	33	37	35
Gym Assistants	32	42	36
Office Assistants	35	41	37
Chess Club	49	48	38
Art Club	39	39	39
Intramural Volleyball	41	36	40
Diversified Occupations (Vocational Club)	43	38	41
Student World Federalist	36	45	42
Intramural Tennis	44	40	43
Library Club	42	44	44
Junior Red Cross	38	46	45
Roller Skating Club	45	43	46
Outdoor Club	50	34	47
Pencil Pushers (Creative Writing)	47	47	48
Riding Club (Horseback Riding)	46	49	49
Knitting Club	48	50	50

Prestige Ranks of Activities in a High School (From Gordon)

TABLE XLII

Many of the clubs had been established at Old School by the mothers of the present generation of children. The children of these mothers were encouraged to join the same clubs to which their mothers had belonged. The status of these clubs was supported in part by the activities of the parents who encouraged the maintenance of this particular organization of activities.

The extent of participation in clubs and activities is one measure of differences between the social systems of schools. In Table XLIII is a list of schools and the percentages of students participating in activities at each grade level.[7] Although wide variation in the extent of

No. of Activities Participated In	Upper Grades		Primary Grades	
	No. of Participants	% of Upper-Grade Students	No. of Participants	% of Primary-Grade Students
6	1	0.3	------	--------
5	------	--------	------	--------
4	7	2.4	------	--------
3	26	8.8	7	2.0
2	68	22.9	20	6.0
1	84	28.3	107	31.9
Total	186	62.7	134	40.0
0	111	37.4	201	60.0
Total	297	100.1	335	100.0

Student Participation in School-Wide Activities of an Elementary School (From Taba)

TABLE XLIII

student participation is apparent, the reasons for this vary: in a school like Old School, the reason for a low level of participation might be the exclusiveness of clubs and activities; in another school, it might be emphasis on participation in community activities rather than in school activities. Participation in school activities appears to depend upon general community expectation for such participation; these differences in expectation reflect local cultural values.

The hypothesis relating membership in these organizations to social status is that a student's social status will be positively correlated

[7] *Ibid.*, p. 68.

with the status of the activities in which he participates. This relation assumes that social positions may be maintained both in the formal administrative organizations of students and in the activity organizations. Some students may experience difficulties in achieving or maintaining status in both systems, but the above hypothesis assumes that the membership demands of the two systems are not in serious conflict with each other.

One characteristic by which the social systems of schools may be distinguished is the relative amounts of prestige that may be achieved in them. The extent to which a student achieves relatively high social status is in turn influenced by the value placed on membership in the formal structures.

INFORMAL ORGANIZATIONS AND SOCIAL STATUS. Informal associations or "cliques" of students may be found in every school. These groups are formed and maintained, at least in part, by the choices of students. Some of these associations will constitute major groupings of students whose membership will carry some degree of prestige. Membership in prestige groups provides such need-satisfactions as approval from classmates, special privileges, and control over the behavior of other people. The following statement from one of the "big wheels" at Wabash School reflects the privileged status accorded to a "big wheel":

> Everyone enjoys privileges but no one intends to take advantage of them, although I feel that sometimes I do. I am a necessary member of the choir, and I am afraid that I take advantage most of the time. I am constantly absent or late to class.

> Today was a typical example. At 1:07 I stole into class and took my seat. I thought that Andrews (the teacher) wouldn't say anything, but he stopped and asked me for an excuse. I gave my usual simple answer of, "Why, am I late?" He says, "Are you late? Seven minutes!" To this I just said, "Oh, do you want me to get an excuse?" He gives up and we go on singing without my giving any sort of reason for being late.

> If I am just a minute or less after the bell, I just nod to him as I go in and he lets me go. What are the kids' reactions? They all think it's a big joke. Some girls come out with, "big wheel," so I may hear it. This annoys me to be called "big wheel"![8]

---

[8] C. W. Gordon, *op. cit.*, p. 63.

EFFECTS OF SOCIAL POSITION AND
STATUS ON PUPIL BEHAVIOR

As we have seen, a student's general social position and status depend on his position and status in both the formal and informal organizations of the school system. A student does not move from the formal organization to the informal organization; he is a member of both at the same time. He has a social position within each and a corresponding amount of status or prestige. For example, if a child is achieving high grades in school, if he belongs to the most important clubs in school, and if he belongs to the cliques which have high prestige, his general social status in the school is likely to be high. In other words, he meets all the criteria, both formal and informal, for high social status. Failure to meet some or all of these requirements would place him in a different social status.

The "outsider" in any school may be so for a variety of reasons. He may not be reaching an adequate achievement level in school and, as a consequence, he may be recognized as not meeting the standards of the formal organizations. He may be a member of low status organizations, or he may not be a member of any group of students. Another child may be achieving well within the formal system, but he may have relatively low social status because he does not take part in any of the important activities, or because he has not been accepted as a member of an important clique.

It is important to remember that an individual's social status reflects a complex interaction of factors. Although knowledge of the social positions occupied by an individual enables us to predict his probable social status, it does not enable us to determine directly why he occupies any position. A child may have relatively low social status because he is not a member of any of the important cliques in a school. Why he is not a member is another problem.

Another important consideration is related to the way in which we visualize social status as influencing behavior change. Social status, as we have described it, is an index reflecting the prestige of the positions occupied by an individual. To what extent does occupancy of relatively high or low status positions influence behavior?

SOCIAL STATUS AND NEED-SATISFACTION. An individual's social status is a measure of the associations he is likely to have. A student with relatively low social status in the school may be an individual who is not a member of important prestige groups. From this fact we might infer that the need-satisfactions available to these group members may not be available to this student. We might also infer that the student may be obtaining these need-satisfactions in other ways; or he may not be motivated by the needs that membership in these groups satisfies; or that, in fact, his needs may not be satisfied. Each of these inferences is a hypothesis that may be tested by gathering appropriate data about the student.

A social system provides means for attaining desirable ends or objects by cooperation among the members. For example, the control that a clique exercises over the dating behavior of its members may be accompanied by provisions for guaranteeing that its members will be able to date. The prestige of the clique may attract the opposite sex to its members. Membership in these and other groups provides a way of obtaining a wide variety of need-satisfactions. For this reason, a student's social positions in the school affect the kinds of need-satisfactions available to him.

In some cases, a group in the school may provide a certain need-satisfaction that compensates for failure to achieve another need-satisfaction in another group. A clique that emphasizes popularity and participation in student activities while devaluating academic achievement may provide prestige and approval for members who could not gain these satisfactions by academic achievements. As we have seen, striving for need-satisfaction is the motivational force behind behavior change. Since the kinds of need-satisfaction available to a student depend on his position in the school's social system, his social position influences the kinds of goals he may seek to achieve need-satisfaction.

SOCIAL STATUS AND GROUP INFLUENCES ON BEHAVIOR CHANGE

Knowing a student's positions in a social system enables us to predict the kinds of behavior patterns he is likely to learn. Both the formally organized clubs and the informal associations of students are likely to be reference groups for their members. These groups set standards of appropriate behavior for their members. An individual's awareness of his group identifications increases the probability of his conforming to the group attitudes and behavior patterns.

Charters and Newcomb performed an experiment to determine

the effects on behavior of informing students that they were in a group with which they were likely to be identified.[9] They formed several groups of students on the basis of religious background. In some groups—the control groups—the students were not aware that all of the members of the group were of the same religious faith. In the experimental groups, the leader of the group made clear to the members that they were all of the same faith. The problem that the groups were to work on was the construction of a questionnaire on religious beliefs. In the experimental groups, the leader conducted a discussion on the basic and commonly shared religious beliefs of the particular religious group to which the members belonged.

Before the discussion periods, the experimenters had the students answer an attitude questionnaire on a variety of topics related to religious principles. After the discussions, the students were requested to take the same attitude questionnaire. Table XLIV lists the average scores of the experimental and control groups on items related to their respective religious positions. A Catholic item, for example,

Type of item	Theoretical orthodoxy	Experimental group	Both control groups	University norms
Catholic	1.00	2.09*	2.36	2.73*
General religious	1.00	2.04*	2.41	2.77*
Church	1.00	1.50*	1.80	2.15*
Protestant	1.00	2.56	2.67	2.60
Jewish	1.00	2.36	2.38	2.23
Feminist	1.00	1.76	1.78	1.65
Political	1.00	1.95	2.07	2.17

Mean Scores of Catholic Students, Classified by Type of Item
(From Charters and Newcomb)

TABLE XLIV

*Difference between mean scores of control subjects and experimental subjects or university norms is at or beyond the .01 level of significance.

was, "Birth-control information should be provided to all married individuals who desire it." Catholic students would be expected to

---

[9] W. W. Charters, Jr., and T. M. Newcomb, "Some Attitudinal Effects of Experimentally Increased Salience of a Membership Group," in E. E. Maccoby, T. M. Newcomb, and E. L. Hartley, *Readings in Social Psychology* (3rd. ed.), New York, Henry Holt & Co., 1958, pp. 276-81.

take a definite position on this item since their religious faith generally takes a negative position on birth control. A Jewish item was, "Under no conditions is there any justification for quotas limiting admission to schools and colleges on a racial or religious basis." The general Jewish position on racial or religious prejudice should influence a Jewish student's response to this item. If the scores in the table are examined, it is apparent that the scores of the experimental groups

Religious group	Control	Experimental
Catholic	24	8
Jewish	3	6
Protestant	9	16

Percentage of Subjects in Each Religious Group with High Deviation Scores* (From Charters and Newcomb)

TABLE XLV

*Figures entered in this table represent the proportion of subjects in the respective categories with high deviation scores. Total number of subjects in each category is:

Catholic "auditorium" control	58
Catholic experimental	46
Jewish control	92
Jewish experimental	58
Protestant control	45
Protestant experimental	33

are much closer to "orthodoxy" on items that tested attitudes likely to be influenced by religious beliefs. In general, fewer Catholics in the experimental groups gave deviant responses than did Catholics in the control group (see Table XLV).[10] This experiment illustrates the effect that awareness of group membership may have on change in attitudes. We may not conclude from this experiment that such changes are permanent, since they may be an expression of public conformity.

Dittes and Kelley explored the relationship between social acceptance and conformity, and their work sheds some light on the

---

[10] As the Table indicates, this relationship was found for Catholic groups but not for Protestant and Jewish groups. The experimenters suggest that the reason for this may be that the Protestant and Jewish faiths are not reference groups for these students, or may even be negative reference groups. The attitudes of the Protestant group were similar to those of a general student group, whereas the attitudes of Catholic students were considerably more religious.

relationship of social status to behavior change.[11] These investigators systematically manipulated experimental conditions so that group members were accorded two levels of acceptance by their respective groups. In each group, some members were given less than complete acceptance but were allowed to see the possibility of obtaining such acceptance. Other group members were accorded little acceptance and given no hope of gaining acceptance. The experimental tasks required group discussions and decisions, and the group members were given opportunities and incentives to deviate from the common judgments of their groups. Two patterns of conformity appeared in this situation: (1) a high degree of genuine adherence to group judgments among group members who had hopes of attaining complete acceptance; (2) high public conformity to group judgments, but private rejection among group members who had little hope of complete acceptance.

On the basis of this experimental data, we would expect that the extent to which a student genuinely accepts the attitudes, values, and behavior patterns of a group will be related to his status in the group and his hopes for improving his status.

The behavior patterns of students are acquired in part from the kinds of associations they have developed in the school. Some of these associations accrue as a result of sex, age, and grade in school. Some of them result from membership in activities, and others from friendship relations and common interests.

A student's position in these social systems influences his status in the school; both his social position and its status influence the kinds of experiences that he is likely to have. Thus, the social system of the school shapes and diversifies the kinds of experiences available to a student. The character of these patterns of experience serves as a stimulus to behavior change.

THE TEACHER'S ROLE IN THE
SCHOOL'S SOCIAL SYSTEM

The school is a social institution and the teacher's role implements its functions. The school as an institution defines the directions of desirable behavior changes to be expected of students; these changes

---

[11]J. E. Dittes and H. H. Kelley, "Effects of Different Conditions of Acceptance upon Conformity to Group Norms," *Journal of Abnormal and Social Psychology*, 53 (1956), 100-107.

667

represent the goals to be attained through the functioning of the school. The teacher's task is to promote these behavior changes.

VARIATIONS IN TEACHER ROLE EXPECTATIONS. The role of the teacher is seen by students, administrators, and parents as essentially that of organizing learning experiences to facilitate desired behavior changes. This expectation is the essential characteristic of the institutionalized role of the teacher; however, role expectations are also determined within a school by the fact that the role is being enacted within a particular social context. In this particular context, the teacher interacts with individuals in reciprocal roles. These roles also are defined both institutionally and by the informal social system of the school. A student has an institutionalized role related to the goals of the school as a social institution, but his role is also defined by the expectations set for it by the informal organization of the school. The teacher's role is defined in relationship to this institutionalized student role, but the role of a teacher in a given school is also defined by its relationship to the student's role as it is defined locally. The role expectations for Mr. Day are determined by the institutionalized conception of this role and by the expectations for the way Mr. Day will enact this role as a teacher in a particular school.

Because the role of the teacher is institutionalized, general expectations for what a teacher may and should do are shared by many different social groups and individuals, and characterize the role of the teacher in many different schools. But the variations in the role should also be expected because the role is being enacted in a particular social system, the local school. The following statement suggests the factors influencing these variations:

> In Wabash the teacher role was conditioned by the fact that he faced in the classroom a system of student organization which was differentiated by *grade rank, grade achievement, sex, social class,* and *prestige cliques* which were value differentiated by their participation in both the formally organized and the informal student culture. . . .
>
> The teacher's perspective of the classroom was one in which behavior was defined according to an ideally conceived classroom situation in which performances approximated the ability and knowledge of the students. . . . Teachers accepted the personal limitations of pupils as part of the educational situation. Students understood the teacher's perception of the situation and the rules of its operation. However, the students calculated their

relation to two sets of status positions, those of students of variously rated performance and those of the informal groups; namely, an adolescent in relation to same sex and opposite sex, "dater-nondater," "athlete-nonathlete," "brain," "big wheel" or "non-wheels" and "fruits" (derogated group), clique member, and isolate. Each of the above labels defines roles which incorporates expectations counter to those of the teacher. Teacher-defined roles which were not accepted resulted in strain in the role of the teacher.[12]

RECONCILING VARYING CONCEPTIONS OF THE TEACHER'S ROLE. In Wabash School, as in other schools, the differing value systems of the formal and informal organizations result in differing role expectations for the teacher role. The extent to which a teacher will enact a teacher role successfully within the social system of the school appears to be related to his ability to reconcile conflicting role expectations. The extent of conflict in role expectations varies from school to school. As we have noted above, the student role is defined both by the formal and informal organizations. Student expectations for the teacher role need not be completely incompatible with those defined by the formal organization and shared by the teacher himself.

One of the apparent effects of trying to resolve the conflict between the institutionalized conception of the role and the expectations for the role within a particular social system is that teacher behavior tends to be influenced by the generalized social status system within the school.[13] This tendency to be influenced by the status system of the school is sometimes reflected even in the evaluation of students, an aspect of the institutionalized role of the teacher. The teacher may give higher grades to a student whose achievement does not merit them, but who has considerable prestige within the school.[14] The following excerpt from a teacher's report suggests how such decisions might be made:

Art was the top student in his class, a member of the football team, and in the school play. Near the end of the school year he fell in love and his performance in class dropped considerably. When we came to the end of the marking period, on the basis of Art's performance on tests he should have been graded C or less in practically all of his subjects. Another teacher and I discussed Art and felt that his drop in performance was understandable.

---

[12]C. W. Gordon, op. cit., pp. 45-46.
[13]See ibid., pp. 40-49.
[14]A. B. Hollingshead, Elmtown's Youth, New York, John Wiley & Sons, 1949.

> We did not want his record to carry a lot of low grades, because this might influence his admission to college and his ranking for scholastic honors in the school. As a consequence we graded him much higher than he deserved and not really on the basis of his present performance.

In this case the teachers consciously and systematically evaluated a pupil on the basis of their general perception of his status in the school. Teachers do not invariably accept the status system of the school and grade pupils accordingly. But if the teacher insists on the achievement values of the formal system when the informal system is not achievement-oriented, he runs the risk of incurring the disapproval or hostility of students.

THE TEACHER'S ROLE IN RELATION TO THE PRINCIPAL. Conceptions of the teacher's role in a particular school may be influenced by the principal's expectations of how this role should be enacted. For example, one expectation of the teacher's role is that the teacher maintain control and have authority within his own classroom; in a given school, however, the range of problems to be handled by the teacher might be defined by the principal.

One important question that faces every classroom teacher confronted with disorderly classroom behavior is, "Shall I send this pupil to the principal?" While the role expectation for the teacher seems to be that he will handle problems of disorder or control within his own classroom, each school may define the extent to which these problems may be handled exclusively by the teacher. A policy statement may represent a role expectation or define the role of the teacher in this particular area. More data from the Wabash School study will illustrate this point.

> The number of classroom evictions over a three-year period was for successive years respectively 160, 81, and 50. Reduction in the number of evictions was related to the dissemination of a rumor among teachers that the principal kept a *mythical little "black book"* in which he records the number of students which teachers send to the office. "When he gets ready to rate your teaching he looks in the little black book and decides your salary increase for next year." It appeared that the greater the support the principal gave the teacher's authority, the more likely the formal *institutional role* of the teacher was utilized to coordinate the classroom. The less willing the principal was to support the teacher's institutional authority, the more likely was the teacher to absorb conflict in his classroom, and the

more likely he was to resort to *personalized* leadership and faced a situation of endemic conflict.[15]

In conceptualizing his role, the teacher will need to interrelate the expectations of the informal social system among students and the expectations of the administration of his own school. The following example, again from Wabash School, illustrates how these varying role expectations influence a teacher's behavior:

> Mr. Spears' class is often a topic of discussion. There is constant fun-making by the most organized group in school: Rudy, Milton, Myers, Hack, Vance, Moon, and Ash as they are all in one class. The only person who could complete this group to make it the rest home for Spears would be Arnold. Spears realized at the beginning of the second semester when Myers, Hack and I joined the rest that it would be constant conflict. We all enjoy hearing him blow up unless it happens to be directed at one of us individually. The tendency is to bother Spears as a group; secondly, to get him to bawl someone else out.
>
> Many a time I have given myself a pat on the back for getting my trouble-making buddy, Vance, in "dutch." But today he evened up all those times by getting Spears mad enough to throw me out of class. What happened?
>
> Vance tore the name paper off the inside cover of my book and was proceeding to stick it into Ash's shirt when I discovered my loss and in a loud voice so all the other fellows could get the full benefit of the trouble I was to cause Vance, I started saying, "What the heck are you doing, Vance, just what are you doing to my book?" Mr. Spears having been disturbed once too often this day, instead of finding out what Vance was doing, just beat on the desk and screamed as loud as he could for me to get out. All he could say was: "Moon, get out, get out, just get out."
>
> I realized the harder the storm the sooner it's over, so I just sat there ignoring the outburst for I had no intention of leaving. I could say nothing and didn't try to. I looked him in the eye and he'd holler, "Get out." So I would just disgustedly look away, feeling he would cool off and go on, realizing that I wouldn't be giving him any more trouble for the day. Finally, he went on reading. I remained silently in class, and the class also stayed quiet for about five minutes.[16]

The teacher in this example may have acted consistently with

[15]C. W. Gordon, *op. cit.*, pp. 44-45.
[16]*Ibid.*, pp. 43-44.

the institutionalized concept of the teacher role: if the student's behavior is a clear violation of the teacher's authority, the teacher is empowered to act by evicting the student. On the other hand, the way a teacher treats a particular student is determined in part by the local concept of how he can treat students in this school. This set of particularized expectations is influenced both by the student's expectations and the principal's. If the teacher had evicted Moon, as he apparently wanted to do, he would have had to face the principal's expectation that teachers should handle such problems themselves. In evicting Moon, he would have run the additional risk of creating disapproval and resentment in the informal student system. Eviction is serious even to the members of a fun-loving group; the consequences are serious for maintaining their positions within the school. The teacher in this conflict situation was apparently immobilized: his personal frustration is apparent in his outburst; the fact that he did not adequately resolve his conflict is shown by his failure to insist that Moon leave the class.

Concepts of the roles of teacher and administrator may vary from school to school, within the general limits set for these expectations by the institutionalized concept of the roles. Some evidence is available to suggest that if the role expectations of the administrator are relatively clearly defined and known by the teachers, there is greater satisfaction among teachers.[17] That this clarification is not the only requisite for reducing conflict among role expectations should be apparent from our discussion above. In general, when role expectations are clearly defined and widely shared within a social system, personal conflict (conflict in the individual about expected behaviors) is likely to be reduced. But an understanding of the institutional roles of students, teachers, and principals, although helpful, cannot always account for the various and conflicting role expectations that may exist in a given community.

ROLE CONFLICT AND THE TEACHER'S ROLE. *Role conflict* may be defined as a clash of incompatible expectations about the desirable characteristics of a role. Consider again the question of the teacher's

---

[17]See C. E. Bidwell, "The Administrative Role and Satisfaction in Teaching," *Journal of Educational Sociology*, 29 (1955), 41-47. Evidence that similarities in personality characteristics between leaders and group members increase group effectiveness may be found in W. Haythorn, A. Couch, D. Haefner, P. Langhan, and L. Carter, "The Effects of Varying Combinations of Authoritarian and Equalitarian Leaders and Followers," *Journal of Abnormal and Social Psychology*, 53 (1956), 210-19.

authority in the classroom. Parents have certain expectations about the teacher's role in this respect. They expect the teacher to maintain at least enough control to insure desirable behavior changes in the pupils. The principal and the teachers themselves also share this expectation. But when a problem situation arises, differences between the expectations are all too frequently apparent. The principal, as we noted above, may expect the teacher to keep the problem in the classroom. Assume that the teacher does, and in solving the problem of disorderly conduct uses physical punishment on the child. The parents' expectation may be that the teacher will exercise as much control as is necessary without using physical punishment, and as a consequence a disagreeable situation arises. The teacher's behavior here has been influenced by the role expectation as it has been defined both institutionally and by the principal and students. Also influencing the role expectations are the expectations of parents and other members of the community about how a teacher ought to act. Communities and parents frequently set standards for the behavior of teachers. In some communities, for example, teachers may not smoke, and may not date in the community. The concept of the teacher's role is defined by the expectations for it in a particular social context.

The teacher has a socio-economic role; he is a citizen-teacher, a professional person, and a teacher within a particular school. All of the sub-roles of his role as a teacher are influenced by community and school expectations. A teacher will have difficulty in adjusting to his role when there are conflicting expectations about the character of it within a particular social context. This difficulty in adjustment will probably be accompanied by heightened anxiety; if the teacher cannot adequately resolve the conflicting expectations, his anxiety may become so acute that he may be forced to leave the teaching profession.

Role conflict is sufficiently pervasive in the teaching profession to constitute a serious problem. Probably only certain kinds of personalities can tolerate this role conflict over a long period of time. We do not know whether teachers' personalities are radically different from those of other people, although some evidence suggests that there is a characteristic pattern of needs among teachers who have remained in the profession for a comparatively long period of time.[18]

---

[18]P. W. Jackson and E. G. Guba, "The Need Structure of In-Service Teachers: An Occupational Analysis," *School Review*, 65 (1957), 176-92; E. W. Guba, P. W. Jackson, and C. E. Bidwell, "Occupational Choice and the Teaching Career," *Educational Research Bulletin*, The Ohio State University, 38 (1959), 1-12, 27-28.

However, the evidence suggests that these personality characteristics may be related to tolerance of role conflict.

At present, the research available on the role conflict of teachers is limited.[19] Getzels and Guba found a variety of significantly different personal reactions to role conflicts in teaching.[20] These investigators found that this conflict springs from the teaching situation in general, as well as from particular schools and communities. They noted that many expectations for the teacher role are inconsistent with the expectations attached to other roles the teacher typically occupies. For example, because teaching is a respected profession, the teacher may be expected to maintain a social status within the community which the salary provided him will not allow. They also found that certain characteristics of teachers were related to reactions toward role conflict. Male teachers felt significantly more role conflict than female teachers. Teachers with one dependent, as compared to teachers with no dependent, also felt significantly more role conflict, as did teachers who had part-time jobs instead of full-time positions.[21] That a male teacher would feel more role conflict than a female teacher should not surprise us, since the teaching role in the elementary and secondary schools has typically been seen as a female role. Neither should we be surprised that teachers who have part-time jobs feel more role conflict than full-time teachers. The teacher who needs additional income to maintain a social position in the community may need to reconcile what is expected of him as a teacher and the expectation reflected in the salary paid him.

While we have emphasized throughout this discussion the complex character of the expectations for the teacher's role, we do not wish to convey the impression that enacting this role is impossible. We have discussed the complexity of the social system in the school because the roles of the teacher and the student are frequently discussed in highly simplified terms. Both in Chapter Thirteen, where we discussed teacher-pupil interactions, and in this chapter, we have emphasized the complexity of the teacher-pupil relationship. This relationship is not a single, isolated, person-to-person kind of relationship. The social system of the school has a complex structure of

---

[19]For a review of research on the role of the teacher see W. B. Brookover, "Research on Teacher and Administrative Roles," *Journal of Educational Sociology*, 29 (1955), 2-13.

[20]J. W. Getzels and E. G. Guba, "The Structure of Roles and Role Conflict in the Teaching Situation," *Journal of Educational Sociology*, 29 (1955), 30-40.

[21]*Ibid.*, p. 38.

penalties and rewards and, as a social system, it demands a certain amount of behavior conformity from its members. This conformity does not require all students or teachers to be alike. A highly unique personality is not required for membership in the social system; but, on the other hand, neither is the social system so simple that we can lay down neat, well-defined rules for teacher-pupil or teacher-principal interactions. The teacher should be sensitive to the varying demands placed upon him by this social system, and be able to work out an adjustment in which he fulfills to a considerable degree the expectations of both the formal and informal organizations. Considerable flexibility, awareness of the social system, and sensitivity to the expectations and demands of this complex system are probably required to effect such an adjustment. The teacher who is at least aware of the complexities of the social relationships within a school is more likely to make adjustments than the teacher who sees the role of the teacher in its institutionalized aspects as fixed and immutable in all social contexts.

SUMMARY

In this chapter we have discussed the social system of the school as a complex of stimulus variables which influence behavior change. A social system is an arrangement of social positions. Status relations are typically correlated with this matrix of social positions; status relations reflect the prestige and social acceptability associated with the various positions.

The social system of the school may be described by the position arrangement involved in the formal organizations of the school. These formal organizations are of two kinds:

1. The formal organization of pupils in administrative units, such as class groups, classroom groups, and age-sex groups.

2. The formal organization of clubs and activities provided for students.

The social system of the school may also be described on the basis of the informal organization of associations of students.

3. A student occupies positions in each of these aspects of the social system of the school. A student's general status in the school depends in part on his status in each of these organizations. A student's position in the social system and the prestige associated with that position influence behavior in several ways.

4. Social status influences the kinds of need-satisfactions available to an individual. Since the individual's status depends on his positions in the formal and informal organizations of the school, his status is an index of his associations. Many need-satisfactions are mediated through the associations available in a school. Striving for need-satisfaction is the motivational force in behavior change; hence, social status is likely to influence behavior change by influencing the kinds of need-satisfactions available to motivate behavior.

5. Social status and positions are measures of the kinds of group influences on behavior change. An individual's social status is an index of his group membership. This group membership influences his behavior to the extent that the group is a reference group for the individual. Social status may be related to conformity to group standards to the extent that an individual hopes to improve his status by meeting group standards.

The teacher role is another major role in the social system of the school. The teacher's role is an institutional role in the sense that its characteristics are defined in relation to the attainment of the goals of the social institution. In this respect the teacher's role is conceptualized in terms of expectations associated with the organization of learning experiences.

6. Such expectations are influenced, however, by the expectations characteristic of local schools.

7. These variations in role expectations arise from expectations of students and the administration with respect to the teacher's role.

8. These expectations may be at variance with the expectations associated with the institutionalized conception of the role.

9.   Other variations in expectations in the role concept of a teacher arise from the conceptions of appropriate teacher role behavior held by parents and other community members.

10.   These variations in role expectations may be incompatible and result in role conflict.

11.   Role conflicts may be reduced in part when teachers and administrators share similar expectations for their respective roles. Role clarification may tend to reduce some aspects of role conflict. However, since role expectations are frequently influenced by local values, role conflict in particular social contexts is not unlikely.

A conception of the complexity of the social system of the school may make the teacher aware of the many influences on student behavior change. Expectations for both the teacher and student roles are shared in many different schools, but the role expectations also tend to be influenced by the social system of a particular school. Sensitivity to such variations may prepare the teacher to make the adjustments required for successful role enactment in a particular school.

STUDY AND DISCUSSION QUESTIONS

1. Select some organization with which you are familiar, preferably one of which you are a member. Describe the arrangement of social positions within this organization. What functions are associated with each position? What is the relative status of the various positions in this organization?

2. For the same organization, describe the criteria for membership in this organization. What are the criteria for the various positions in this organization? Who may not be a member of this social system?

3. Describe the system of formal student organizations in the school in which you are now either a student or a teacher. Describe the criteria for membership in these organizations.

4. Describe the informal organizations in the school in which you are now a student or a teacher as you see them. Check your descriptions with those of a fellow student or teacher. What are the criteria for membership in these informal organizations?

5. Select some student whom you know well and describe his or her social status in the school. To what organizations does this student belong? Of what organizations is this student not likely to become a member? How has his position in these various organizations of the school influenced his prestige with fellow students?

6. What organizations of the school use the sex of the student as a criterion for membership? What organizations in your school set grade level or department association as a criterion for membership?

7. Identify a student who appears to have relatively low prestige or social status in the school. To what organizations, if any, does he belong? How do you account for his relatively low social status in the school?

8. What personality characteristics are used as criteria for membership in the various school organizations with which you are familiar? How do the members of these organizations determine whether a prospective member has the requisite personality characteristics? What observable behaviors define or describe the personality characteristics that are used as criteria for membership?

9. Identify the club or activity which has the highest prestige in your school. What appear to be the dominant value standards of this organization? In what ways are the value standards of this organization consistent or inconsistent with achievement in school? How do the members of this organization appear to perceive the role of the teacher in your school?

10. Identify the informal organization in your school which seems to have the highest social status. What value patterns appear to be shared by the members of this organization? In what ways are these value patterns consistent or inconsistent with achievement in school?

11. Again, using the formal and informal organization with the highest prestige in your school, describe the ways in which these organizations provide need-satisfactions for their members. What need-satisfactions do these organizations provide that are not likely to be obtained by membership in any other organization in the school? In what ways do they provide need-satisfactions that are not likely to be obtained in the typical classroom activities?

12. Refer to the Charters and Newcomb experiment described in this chapter. Assume that the investigators had used students of different political persuasions instead of members of religious groups. The experimental procedures would be substantially the same, except that the items in the questionnaire would refer to matters on which political parties have taken a position. Would you expect the results to be comparable to those obtained when students of different religious faiths were used?

13. Assume that you were trying to influence a student who is a member of a group whose attitudes are "anti-school" in character to change his attitudes toward

school. What factors will affect your success in influencing this student? What is the relationship between his position in this group and the extent to which your persuasion is likely to be effective?

14. Describe the principal role expectations associated with the role of the teacher in your school.

15. Compare the general role expectations for the role of a high school teacher and a university professor. In what ways are the role expectations similar? In what ways are they different? In what ways are the role expectations for the teacher role related to the expectations for the student role?

16. Describe the different kinds of role expectations that parents, teachers, and the principal and students may have in relation to the following:

   a. Grading students.

   b. Managing "discipline" problems.

   c. The teacher's position on religious matters.

   d. The teacher's position on local political activities.

17. Are there some personality characteristics that may make it difficult for a teacher to resolve role conflicts associated with teaching? If you think so, suggest what these characteristics might be, and describe the ways in which they would be related to a failure to resolve role conflicts adequately.

RECOMMENDED READINGS

The first reading contains an extended discussion of many of the ideas developed in this chapter. The second reading is a description of the social system of a particular school frequently referred to throughout this text. The third reading is a comparative study of the social systems of several schools. The fourth reading presents a discussion which correlates the principal ideas presented in this chapter.

1. T. M. Newcomb, *Social Psychology*, New York, The Dryden Press, 1950, Chapters 13, 14, and 15.

2. C. W. Gordon, *The Social System of the High School*, Glencoe, Ill., The Free Press, 1957.

3. H. Taba, *School Culture*, Washington, D. C., American Council on Education, 1955.

4. R. Havighurst and B. Neugarten, *Society and Education*, Boston, Allyn and Bacon, 1957, Chapters 8 and 17.

THE TEACHER AND THE IMPROVEMENT OF EDUCATIONAL PRACTICE

In this book we have conceptualized the teacher's function as being essentially that of a creator of learning environments. The school, as a social institution, is formally constituted by society to foster the development of specifiable and desirable behavior changes in children. The teacher is an agent of society who assumes responsibility for creating the situations in which these desired changes can most likely be developed.

As a creator of learning situations, the teacher must "do something." Educational practice is a series of operations, created in the light of specified behavior changes, which are designed to foster the development of behavior change in desirable directions.

Logically, educational practice begins in a series of decisions—decisions about what to do, when to do it, for what kinds of pupils, and in the light of what goals. We have stressed that there are no general, immutable, or even highly valid specific *rules* on the basis of which the teacher can make decisions about the potential value of learning experiences. The basic conception of

educational practice presented in this book is that any procedural decision is based on a hypothesis about behavior change. This book has been written to help teachers become more intelligent hypothesizers, and to encourage them to analyze critically the bases for the decisions they make.

We have previously analyzed some concepts and generalizations that teachers may use in formulating hypotheses relevant to educational practice; if the preceding chapters have been effective, the reader will have some conception of what is meant by hypothesis-making.

In the present chapter we will discuss in greater detail the concept of critical inquiry into the validity of educational practices. A teacher is not born a critical inquirer; he becomes one. A course in educational psychology contributes in part to his development in this respect by clarifying both the general characteristics of the learning situation and the more specific nature of the tasks to which inquiry is directed.

As a concluding statement, this chapter will support many of the propositions outlined in preceding chapters; it should also serve as an introduction to a way of thinking useful both for further study in education and for analyzing the classroom teaching experience.

THE IMPROVEMENT OF EDUCATIONAL PRACTICE

The concept of critical inquiry is related to another concept— the improvement of educational practice. Why are we concerned with "the improvement of educational practice?" The use of this terminology suggests that educational practice in its present state may leave something to be desired.

THE RELATIVE VALIDITY OF GENERALIZATIONS ABOUT PRACTICE. The assumption that educational practice can be improved is implicit in our conception of the character of empirical knowledge. We assume that knowledge about observable events and knowledge of propositions which describe and explain these events is essentially *probabilistic* in character. Therefore, since any statement about educational practice is a statement about observable events, it can be only *probably* true.

Suppose, for example, that a teacher uses a film on India as part of a unit on "understanding other cultures." He may find that students are interested in the film and acquire considerable information from it and that they ask intelligent questions about the customs of the Indian culture and show an increased sensitivity to cultural differences. For this teacher, this film "works." That is, when he used the film in a learning experience, behavior changes occurred in the directions he had specified as desirable. Has this teacher invented an educational practice which cannot be questioned, cannot be improved upon, or should not be changed?

THE FRAME OF REFERENCE OF A GENERALIZATION. These questions can be answered intelligently if we view the propositions about the use of this film as being only *probably* true. Why are they only *probably* true? In the first place, because the film was used within a framework of environmental variables. The teacher may not have analyzed these environmental variables, or even identified them. We can suggest what some of these variables might be. Some might be related to the particular sample of pupils who saw the film; although these children have many characteristics in common with other children, they may systematically differ from other children on the variables relevant to their ability to learn from the film being used. The intelligence levels of the children, their ages, social class backgrounds, and previous learning experiences are some of the variables which may be relevant to the fact that the film "worked."

There are other contextual variables which might have been relevant to the success of the film, such as the content communicated, the manner of content presentation within the film itself, the presence or absence of emotional appeals in the film, the prestige of a communicator in the film (if one is used), or the manner in which the teacher related the film to other activities. We have not specified all of the possibly influential variables, nor is it necessary to do so for our purpose. The point here is that this film was used in a particular set of conditions, and the validity of the proposition about the success of the film is *probably* high if the film is to be shown only within the context of the same conditions.

The analysis of any set of empirical events is essentially a finite process; that is, the analysis is carried out within specific contexts. Propositions about these sets of empirical events assume, as a necessary condition, the contextual conditions that were present when the proposition was originally derived. The proposition that the film "works" is true only for a specific film used in a specified way under certain given conditions.

DECISION-MAKING AND THE RELATIVE VALIDITY OF GENERALI-
ZATIONS. Certainly no one will argue seriously that we should not
make the best decisions that can be made about educational practice
on the basis of our present knowledge of it. Our explicit assumption
that educational practice should be improved is a statement that we
need to make better decisions—decisions with greater probability of
being valid. You will notice that we have not adduced horrendous
examples of poor educational practices as evidence that educational
practice needs to be improved. We did not do so precisely because we
are attempting to point out that decisions about the validity of an
educational practice can be made only after critical inquiry which
takes account of the changes in behavior specified as desired. An educational practice is not "poor" because it did not "work" nor "good"
because it did. Until we have specified what we mean by saying that
a practice "works," and until we specify under what conditions and
for what purposes a practice is likely to be effective, we are not in a
position to label any practice as generally "good" or "poor."

The author recalls being told by an older teacher, at the beginning
of his first year of teaching, "Don't smile for the first six months."
Some readers may be amused by this suggestion, but the author must
confess that he accepted it with some seriousness. For the purposes of
our discussion, notice the character of this proposition. It is a statement about what to do in a classroom setting. In context, it is a suggestion about how to act in order to achieve "pupil control." Implicit
in this statement is the hypothesis that if a teacher does not smile
during the first six months of school he will be more likely to achieve
"pupil control." This proposition could be buttressed with deductions
from propositions about the role of the teacher in relation to his
pupils, the pupils' perceptions of a young teacher, and other generalizations about teacher-pupil relations. Is the suggested educational
practice a "good" or a "poor" practice? Assume that the author had
followed this suggestion (which he did not) and found that he was
able to maintain an unspecified state of affairs called "pupil control."
Could we say that he had discovered a practice that guarantees success
in "maintaining order"?

Formally, this proposition is a statement about a set of observable
events and, in principle, it can be only probably true. We would not
contest the fact that a given teacher did not smile for six months nor
that he maintained "pupil control." Our proposition is drawn from
two specific sets of events, stating a relation between them; as a gen-

eralization, however, it is meant to be applied to a wide variety of comparable situations. Furthermore, there may be other generalizations which are more probably valid than this one. Educational practice can be improved if we obtain these more valid generalizations because decisions for practice based on them are more likely to be valid.

DECISION-MAKING AND IMPROVED
PREDICTION OF BEHAVIOR CHANGE

We can summarize the above ideas while introducing a new conception. Educational practices are based on propositions about sets of observable events, propositions which describe or explain the relations between learning experiences and pupil change; they can be used as bases for the decisions required to create learning environments. The use of more valid generalizations in the decision-making process improves educational practice by strengthening our ability to predict and control the events with which we are concerned.

Assume that we find that a more valid statement about the relationship between teacher behavior and pupil behavior to be this: "Pupil interest in classroom activity is related to the degree in which teachers manifest a personal interest in their pupils." This generalization enables us to improve our predictions about the relationship between teacher behavior and pupil behavior. It suggests that if a teacher takes a personal interest in his pupils, the students will probably show increased interest in class activities. It directs us toward more valid information about the variables related to pupil interest in class activities.

We have noted two characteristics of propositions that describe educational practices: (1) they are generalizations about relationships between sets of events; and (2) as generalizations, they are inferences from observations made within specific contexts. The validity of these propositions depends in part upon the context of conditions within which the observations were made. Implicit in any proposition describing educational practice is a set of conditions upon which its validity depends. These sets of conditions specify a frame of reference within which the generalization is said to be probably valid.

APPLYING GENERALIZATIONS IN MAKING SPECIFIC DECISIONS. The importance of the conditions on which the validity of a generalization depends is apparent when we analyze the requirements for making decisions about specific educational practices. Assume that the teacher has formed a generalization about the relationship between his behavior and the behavior of his pupils. He now wishes to "apply" this generalization in making decisions about specific practices in his classroom. Before he can "apply" this generalization to his own practice, he must assess the probability that the defining conditions of the generalization are present in his classroom. The generalization was derived from the experiences of a particular sample of pupils (with all their individual characteristics) and a particular teacher (with his own individual characteristics). Furthermore, the generalization probably applies only to certain kinds of teacher and pupil behavior.

You will recall that we analyzed the generalization "Praise improves pupil performance." This generalization was derived from data obtained in an experimental situation; this situation defined the conditions under which the generalization would probably be true. The teacher will have to assess the extent to which these conditions are present in his classroom before applying this generalization in the context of the learning environments he is creating.

Before making this application, the teacher should formulate a second level of hypotheses. These hypotheses are more specific than the generalization and apply to the context of the particular learning experience. One such hypothesis might be: "If I praise the pupils in my class for correct answers when they are working on arithmetic problems, performance in arithmetic is likely to improve." The validity of this derived hypothesis is unknown. We predict that it is likely to be valid insofar as the conditions in this classroom are similar to the conditions under which the original generalization was derived. Coladarci makes this distinction between levels of hypotheses in the following way:

> If we knew for certain what the correct manipulations were [manipulations of the learning environment to produce behavior change], we would have an easy solution to questions about educational procedure—we could have valid "rules" to follow. We frequently do not have such knowledge. Even our most rigorous and competent research provides conclusions that are properly stated only as probabilities.[1]

---

[1] A. P. Coladarci, "Research in a Local District," in *Educational Research in Local School Districts*, Research Resume No. 3, San Francisco, State Advisory Council on Educational Research, California Teachers Association, 1957, p. 28.

The practitioner must translate these probabilities into a secondary set of probabilities about what would happen in the case of his purposes and his pupils. He must make inferences about the application of these probabilities to his teaching methods, curriculum, organization, and so on. The educator's operations are best thought of as hypotheses and, like any hypotheses, they must be tested.

The teacher's operations, as an educational practitioner, are analogous to those of a medical practitioner. In the course of his training the medical practitioner has learned certain generalizations about practices likely to cure illnesses; but he must also make second-order hypotheses about the applicability of these generalizations to specific patients. For example, he may have learned a generalization about the likelihood of sulfa drugs curing certain kinds of infections. When he is treating a patient with an infection, he does not act on the generalization until he makes a hypothesis that the use of a certain sulfa drug will cure this particular infection in this individual patient. If it does not, the practitioner need not assume that the generalization was necessarily incorrect, but rather that the conditions under which it is correct were not fulfilled in this particular case. The teacher, like any practitioner, operates within a specific context and with specific people.

THE TEACHER AND THE VALIDATION OF HYPOTHESES. This discussion should suggest to the reader that two levels of critical inquiry are necessary for the improvement of educational practice: at one level, we should test generalizations that are applicable to a wide variety of particular events; at the other, we should test each specific hypothesis derived from a comprehensive generalization.

The first of these tasks is properly the work of trained investigators. Comprehensive generalizations can be developed from data gathered according to careful experimental designs; this kind of systematic research requires skills which most classroom teachers do not have. But critical inquiry into the validity of hypotheses derived from these generalizations is a task for the classroom teacher. Thousands of teachers in thousands of classrooms make numerous decisions each day about the effects of learning experiences on pupil behavior. The likelihood is small that each of these hypotheses will be investigated with formal experimental procedures. But if teachers do not assume the responsibility for a critical evaluation of their own procedures, it is not likely that educational practice will be improved—they will remain mystified as to why what "worked" yesterday does not "work" today. Without such critical evaluations, teachers will be unable to support or defend their methods, and hunches, guesses, and recipes of unknown validity will continue to be the sources of decisions about educational practice.

ATTITUDES APPROPRIATE TO CRITICAL INQUIRY INTO THE VALIDITY OF EDUCATIONAL PRACTICES

The process of critical inquiry into the validity of educational practices is essentially a process of hypothesis-making and hypothesis-testing. We have noted that making and testing hypotheses requires training which most teachers do not have. Nevertheless, we have urged that teachers critically evaluate their procedures. If teachers do not have all the requisite skills for critical evaluation of their hypotheses, how can they engage in this process of evaluating educational procedures? A partial answer to this is that they can develop attitudes appropriate to critical inquiry and gain some understanding of the requirements of critical evaluation. In this section we will discuss both the attitude of critical inquiry and some of the basic principles relevant to making appropriate evaluations of educational practice.

ATTITUDES TOWARD CRITICAL INQUIRY. What kind of an attitude does a trained investigator have toward the generalizations he is attempting to develop about any phenomenon that he studies? The basic attitude in this respect is one of *holding propositions tentatively;* the investigator recognizes that his propositions are only probably true and must therefore be held tentatively. New investigations may indicate that the generalizations were invalid, or new generalizations which are more probably valid may be developed.

The teacher can adopt this scientific attitude toward the validity of statements about educational practice, and toward the hypotheses that he derives from these generalizations. Assume that a teacher formulates the following hypothesis: "If I teach subtraction at the same time that I am teaching addition, my students will probably understand better the processes involved in both of these operations." This proposition is a hypothesis about specific learning experiences for particular pupils. The teacher may have derived it from a generalization about this method based upon an experimental study of these processes. Both the generalization from which this hypothesis was derived and the specific hypothesis itself must be held tentatively. In either case, they are only probably true.

If the teacher is a critical inquirer, he will be willing to regard these propositions as tentative. He is prepared to find out at some future date that the original generalization may not be valid, or that there may be more comprehensive generalizations which are more valid. He will also be prepared to discover that his application of this generalization in a derived hypothesis may not hold true. With this attitude toward the body of knowledge presently available about educational practice, a teacher is more likely to consider alternatives to his present practices. Being more disposed to see himself as a generator of hypotheses, he is not likely to assume that present knowledge about educational practice is definitive and fixed for all time.

CHALLENGING THE OBVIOUS. Another attitude involved in the habit of critical inquiry is the willingness to challenge the obvious. The obvious is frequently the creature of our own habits of thinking. We have a way of looking at events, and we may assume that this is the only way they can be viewed. Even generalizations which have no experimental support are treated by some people as if they were obvious and necessary conclusions.

To many people it is obvious that a good teacher must know subject matter. But ask yourself, "Why is this obvious?" We are not implying that good teachers do not need to know the subject they are teaching; we would agree that a person cannot teach another person something he knows nothing about. But does this proposition cover the case in which the teacher is "keeping one page ahead of the students"? We do demand that teachers be well informed in the subjects they are to teach, but this "obvious" generalization is frequently the basis for unsupportable statements about how to train teachers. We cannot demonstrate that teachers need to know only subject matter in order to be effective, nor that the only requirement for effective teaching is knowledge of subject matter.

When we claim that a generalization is obvious, we are appealing to some implicit validity criterion. Until this criterion is made clear, we cannot determine whether the proposition is valid or invalid. "Obviousness" is not a criterion for validity. The history of science is replete with examples of successful challenges of the obvious.

We are not recommending that teachers hold a negative attitude toward every suggestion for the improvement of educational practice.

Many of us are familiar with the sophomoric attitude of criticizing anything and everything. Rather, we are urging that teachers adopt an attitude of "tentativeness" toward propositions about educational practice: a willingness to look for and consider alternatives, to reserve judgment in the absence of evidence, and to revise one's ideas if subsequent data suggest the need for change.

Many people seem to be afraid to encourage teachers to think in this way. A young teacher has reported that he was told, when he assumed a position in a teacher-training institution, to "forget the theories; tell them what to do." Such a recommendation reflects an attitude inconsistent with the one advocated here. Sponsors of such recommendations apparently assume that there are specific prescriptions applicable to any and all educational contexts; they are not sufficiently sensitive to the implications of the probabilistic character of our knowledge.

PROCEDURES FOR CRITICAL EVALUATION OF EDUCATIONAL PRACTICE

As we noted above, the systematic investigation of educational practice requires a knowledge of formal experimental procedures. While teachers may not be able to evaluate their derived hypotheses in the systematic manner that characterizes formal research, certain principles of research are relevant to the informal evaluations that the teacher can make of his hypotheses. In the following sections we will outline some basic principles of critical inquiry that may be useful to the teacher in analyzing his own educational practices.

DEVELOPING TESTABLE HYPOTHESES. Propositions about educational practice are, in principle, hypotheses about conditions likely to produce behavior change. If these hypotheses are to be evaluated, they must be stated in a testable form. Recall the generalization that we used as an example of a proposition assumed to be obvious. This proposition is essentially untestable in the form in which it was stated. If we gave tests to determine how much teachers knew about the subjects they were teaching and determined that they had limited knowledge of them, we still would not have tested the hypothesis. We would have obtained information about their knowledge of subject matter, but we would not have determined the effectiveness of their instruction.

A hypothesis relates two variables—in this case, "good teaching" and "knowledge of subject matter." Until we have measured both of these variables and determined the relationship between them, we have not tested the hypothesis. Before doing this, we must define "good teaching" and "knowledge of subject matter." Once we have formulated these definitions, it may be possible to develop measurement procedures for discerning degrees of "good teaching" and "knowledge of subject matter." At this point it is possible to test the relationship between the two variables.

Some hypotheses are untestable because they relate variables which are outside the domain of empirical events. For example, the hypothesis that pupil misbehavior is caused by "devils" is untestable in principle. Only one of the variables in this proposition is measurable—namely, the extent to which pupils misbehave. The other variable, "infestation with devils," cannot be defined in empirical terms and, consequently, cannot be measured in any way.

A less absurd example, but one representing an equally untestable hypothesis, would be the following: "Inspiration promotes creativity." We can define "creativity" in empirical terms, difficult as this may be, but "inspiration" is such a vague concept that we cannot tell whether there are any empirical referents for it. Indeed, we probably cannot observe the variable called "inspiration" without confounding it with the variable "creativity." We cannot test such hypotheses.

THE FORMULATION OF HYPOTHESES. There are two general processes by which hypotheses are developed: induction and deduction. An *inductive* hypothesis is formulated as a generalization from observed relationships. Teachers who have noticed that students are restless during a rainy season might make this inductive hypothesis: "Rainy weather produces restlessness in children." Using the process of induction does not guarantee the validity of the generalization. As we have noted consistently throughout this book, inferences must be checked, and inductive hypotheses are inferences.

The hypothesis about restlessness could also be tested by making deductions from it and then testing these deductions as minor hypotheses. From our original hypothesis we might deduce that students would be less restless during other seasons of the year. If this deductive hypothesis has validity, we infer that the general hypothesis from which it was deduced also has some validity. However, before we can determine the validity of the more general hypothesis, we must de-

DEFINITIONS

1. *Reading* is defined as a controlled form of talking in which the words that are said are controlled by the nature of the written symbols presented.
2. *A correct reading response* is defined as the act of saying the agreed-upon interpretation of the written symbol presented.
3. *Accuracy of response* to a word is defined as the percentage of attempts to say the words that are correct.
4. *The perception of learning to read as a goal* is evidenced by such behavior as the pupil asking the teacher for reading activities, participating voluntarily in reading activities, choosing reading activities rather than others.

POSTULATES

1. When reading is learned by means of the sequence: written word presentation, vocal response by the teacher, vocal response by the pupil, the frequency of occurrence of this sequence is related to the accuracy of response of the pupil. (Reader, note that this method of learning to read is commonly referred to as the "look-and-say method" and will be so referred to here.)
2. The effectiveness of the look-and-say method in generating correct reading responses in the pupil is related to the ability of the pupil to discriminate form and shape. Pupils must have a minimum of the latter ability if the method is to produce learning. Additional increments of the ability beyond the minimum result in increased rates of learning.
3. The effectiveness of the look-and-say method in producing correct reading responses is related to the extent to which the pupil perceives the learning of reading as a desirable goal and is motivated to achieve that goal.

DEDUCTIONS

1. Measures of motivation to read will be correlated with accuracy of response in the early stages of reading in the case of those pupils who perceive reading as a desirable goal.
2. Failure to discriminate two words is a function of the similarity of the shape of the two words.
3. The look-and-say method produces greater accuracy of response when it is supplemented by procedures that emphasize the discrimination of the form of one word and the form of another than it does when such methods are not used.

A Theory of the Early Stages of Learning Reading
(From Travers)

TABLE XLVI

velop a whole series of deductive hypotheses, each of which must be tested.

As the preceding example has shown, a deductive hypothesis is drawn from, and is consistent with, some more comprehensive generalization or proposition. Travers has provided an interesting example of deductive hypotheses from more comprehensive statements of relationships (see Table XLVI).[2]

Note that the deductions do not follow directly from the more comprehensive propositions. For example, the second deduction, while generally related to the second proposition, is also related to hypotheses about the relationship between similarity of forms and difficulty in discrimination. This deductive hypothesis, as stated, is consistent with the second proposition only if we also assume as relatively valid a generalization about the relationship between similarity and discrimination. This hypothesis is deductive because it can be deduced (with additional premises) from the original proposition.

DEDUCTIVE HYPOTHESES AND THE SYSTEMATIC DEVELOPMENT OF KNOWLEDGE. A little thought will suggest that deductive hypotheses can be particularly useful if we have adequate generalizations from which to make them. One of the purposes of studying educational psychology is to acquire generalizations about human behavior which have relative validity. While a study of educational psychology does not supply all the generalizations needed for developing a complete set of deductive hypotheses about educational practice, it can supply knowledge sufficient for the development of a good many specific hypotheses.

Corey reports an investigation conducted by a group of social studies teachers, which we can use t illustrate the point that generalizations are available that can serve as a starting point for developing specific hypotheses.[3] This group of teachers was interested in determining to what extent a study of biographies of famous figures in American history influences student behavior. The teachers formulated the following hypotheses: (1) that a relationship would be found between the amount of pupil information about these famous Americans and the extent to which they were admired by the pupils; (2) that the degree of admiration for these famous Americans would be increased by one semester of instruction in American history; (3) that a relationship would appear between the traits pupils admired in these historical persons and the reputation that pupils gained for behaving in a manner consistent with the traits they admired.

---

[2] R. W. Travers, *An Introduction to Educational Research,* New York, Macmillan Co., 1958, pp. 28-29.

[3] See S. M. Corey, *Action Research to Improve School Practices,* New York, Teachers College, Columbia University Press, 1953, pp. 61-70.

Our discussion of the acquisition of attitudes should have suggested that the first hypothesis is not likely to be valid. When we analyzed the processes that influence attitude acquisition, we hypothesized that the identification process was crucial in attitude formation. In noting that identification relations probably were not likely if an individual did not know something about the person with whom he might identify, we observed that the process of identification did not depend entirely upon accurate and reliable information about the identification figure.

Should these teachers have formulated this hypothesis? Probably not, unless they were interested in demonstrating again that amount or correctness of information, as such, is not highly correlated with degree of admiration.

The second hypothesis can be criticized on similar grounds. We discussed the influence of courses of instruction on attitude change. We cited data suggesting that participation in a course does not necessarily guarantee changes in attitudes. Since this hypothesis ignored the important variables in attitude formation, the teachers again embarked upon a task that was probably a waste of time.

The origins of the third hypothesis are obscure, but the reasoning seems to run something like this: (1) Famous Americans have admirable qualities; (2) if students admire a famous person, they are likely to have traits similar to that person; (3) since these students have admirable traits, they will have a reputation among their fellow students for possessing these traits. Note that each of these premises is in itself a hypothesis in need of testing. The second premise is the only one of the three that bears some relationship to known psychological generalizations. This principle would be consistent with generalizations about the identification process.

These hypotheses are consistent with a common-sense kind of psychology. In the early stages of development of any science, it is customary to test such common-sense propositions, and in this process of analyzing the obvious, more comprehensive kinds of generalizations are usually developed. But considering the present state of psychological knowledge the three hypotheses above are somewhat naive.

THEORY AND PRACTICE IN THE DEVELOPMENT OF SYSTEMATIC KNOWLEDGE. There appears to be a tendency in educational research repeatedly to evaluate common-sense propositions of this variety. One of the functions of a course in educational psychology is to provide the teacher with information sufficient for making critical analyses of such obvious generalizations. We hope that after completing this course a student will be able to formulate more sophisticated hypotheses about personality and behavior change than the ones mentioned above.

On the other hand, we do not wish to suggest that the present body of psychological knowledge provides generalizations applicable to each and every educational practice with which teachers are concerned. Many psychological generalizations have been developed in laboratory situations which do not entirely duplicate classroom conditions; they may even have been developed from experimentation with lower animals. One of the functions of educational research is to test the validity of these generalizations in the educational context. Even if psychological science were more completely developed than it is at the present time, we would still need to evaluate generalizations and their derivations continually.

In many cases, teachers can participate in the development of systematic knowledge by active cooperation in research programs and by suggesting hypotheses which, from their own experience, need testing. In short, we are proposing a more intimate relation between theory and practice. When suggestions for practice are developed from comprehensive generalizations, they need to be tested in classroom situations. Similarly, suggestions for fruitful hypotheses can be arrived at by careful, critical evaluations of classroom experience. In this way theory is nourished by two roots: (1) by new derivations from known generalizations and (2) by the more comprehensive generalizations which can be made by induction from specific practices.

DEFINING VARIABLES TO BE TESTED. Since a hypothesis relates two variables, it cannot be tested until its variables are precisely defined in terms of observable behavior. Many variables in hypotheses are formulated at such a high level of abstraction that the hypotheses cannot be directly tested. We have noted this earlier, but it bears repeating. Consider the hypothesis: "Effective leadership enhances group morale." Before this can be tested, we must define "effective leadership." And since the process of definition requires a restatement of the variable in terms of observable behaviors, we must answer the question, "How can we recognize 'effective leadership'?"

The same problem exists for the variable "morale." Think of a class of students for the moment. What would we mean if we said that a class had "morale"? Would we mean that the students will do what the teacher tells them? Or would we mean that the members of the class like each other? Would we mean that the members will work together to attain common goals? Even after choosing any one of these as definitions for the variable, we would still need to define the behaviors we recognize as "working for a common goal," "liking each other," and "doing what the teacher tells them."

From the viewpoint of the formulator of a hypothesis, a variable is a concept for discriminating aspects of observable events. In the first place, the concept of the variable must be clearly defined. Moreover, adequate terminology needs to be developed which conveys the concept in the meaning that the hypothesis-maker intends.

One of the problems in developing hypotheses in professional education is that the concepts and variables we discuss have not been adequately defined. Indeed, we do not have an appropriate technical language for describing concepts. We tend, rather, to use everyday language, with the result that our concepts frequently connote more than we intend. Consider, for example, the variable called "permissiveness." Every teacher has heard a wide variety of generalizations about the relationship of permissiveness to changes in student behavior. But what is "permissiveness"? The concept of the variable itself has not been adequately defined in terms of observable behavior; accordingly, we seldom find a detailed and specific description of a "permissive teacher," or a "permissive classroom climate." Furthermore, the word "permissiveness" itself probably has more connotations than were originally intended for it; this being so, teachers can fill the vacant, undefined concept of the variable with their own individual understandings of the term "permissiveness."

Some terms may actually encourage false interpretation. Coladarci and Getzels have noted this danger in the use of metaphorical language:

> A word should be said about the metaphoric flavor of pedagogical language. Metaphors and similes are useful devices in communication. They may become dangerous, however, when the analog unconsciously is translated into a reality. It may have been useful, for instance, for a resident of early Salem to note that "Dame Robinson acts like a witch"—if we assume that what is meant is that the behavior of Dame Robinson resembles that represented in the stereotype of fictional witches. It becomes dangerous only when one is led to think of Dame Robinson *as* a witch and to treat her

accordingly—when actually the treatment for Dame Robinson should be quite different from the treatment of witches. That is, one may be led to talking about witches rather than about Dame Robinson. . . . We must be sensitive to the possibility that such language will lead to asking the wrong questions and defining the wrong problems.[4]

Even some terms which have precise denotations in the social sciences carry with them the more vague connotations they have in common, everyday usage. For example, a teacher may describe a child as one who is "maladjusted." What does the teacher mean by the term "maladjusted"? The teacher may be using the word in the general sense, and the content of his communication about the child will be less clear since he has not precisely defined what he means by "maladjusted." We have discussed this problem in other contexts throughout this book; here we are mainly concerned with pointing out that only clear definitions of variables can enable us to formulate testable hypotheses.

In the last several sections, we have outlined principles for formulating testable hypotheses. These principles can be used by any classroom teacher; any teacher should be able to ask clear questions and make meaningful statements about educational practice—indeed, the purpose of this book is to help him do so.

TESTING HYPOTHESES. Hypotheses must be tested as well as formulated. As we have suggested, the formal testing of a hypothesis requires a knowledge of experimental design and technical skills that classroom teachers seldom have. We hope that some teachers will be stimulated to acquire these technical skills. But even if a substantial number of teachers did learn the procedures of experimental research, most of them would not have time to conduct formal research. Does this mean that teachers are unable to evaluate their hypotheses about educational practice?

Some hypotheses may be simple enough for the teacher to conduct comparatively systematic evaluations of them. Others may be more complex, requiring the use of more formal procedures. Even in the latter case, however, teachers can begin the evaluation process by observing effects. Suppose, for example, that a teacher predicts that a new spelling method will work more effectively. A strict test of this hypothesis would require that we set up two comparable

[4]A. P. Coladarci and J. W. Getzels, *The Use of Theory in Educational Administration*, Educational Administration Monograph No. 5, Stanford, California, Stanford University Press, 1955, p. 13.

groups of students, one of which learns by the new spelling method and the other by the old method; we would first test the spelling performance of both groups under the old method, and then, after a period of time during which one group is taught by the old method and the other by the new one, we would compare the performance of the two groups. This design would provide a reasonably careful test of the hypothesis.

Although the teacher may not be able to implement such a design, he can observe the effects of using a new method. While using a new method, he can ask: Have the pupils improved? Are they learning to spell quickly and easily? Do they seem to be interested in spelling?

We are not suggesting simply that teachers try something "to see if it works." We are suggesting that teachers attempt to gather data systematically *to find out if predicted effects do occur.* Gathering and using factual data on behavior change eliminates some of the inaccuracies inherent in general impressions of student performance. A teacher can keep a record of the "successes" and "failures" of an educational practice. With such a record, he is better equipped to ferret out possible reasons for the relative success or failure of his procedures, and to revise and retest them accordingly.[5]

MEASUREMENT PROCEDURES IN HYPOTHESIS-TESTING. In the third section of this book we discussed the basic principles of measurement as they apply to gathering data on behavior change of pupils. These principles are also applicable to the measurement procedures used in testing hypotheses.

Reliability and validity must characterize the measurement procedures used in systematic tests of hypotheses about educational practice. In testing some hypotheses, the teacher can use standardized tests to gather reliable and valid data on pupil change in behavior. In testing others, the teacher will need to construct his own measurement devices; in such cases, the reliability and validity of these devices must be determined. Unfortunately, the literature of educational research is replete with examples of studies utilizing measurement devices of unknown reliability and validity. Obviously, the validity of a generalization depends upon the kinds of data gathered to test it. We cannot draw conclusions about the validity of a gen-

---

[5]A comprehensive discussion of the relation of individual predictions of this character to the more formal procedures of scientific investigation can be found in P. E. Meehl, *Clinical versus Statistical Prediction*, Minneapolis, University of Minnesota Press, 1954.

eralization if we have used unreliable or invalid measuring instruments to gather the basic data.

The process of data gathering may not be as complex as some teachers assume. Many kinds of data about pupil change can be gathered reliably and validly. In the study conducted by the social studies teachers referred to above, for example, the teachers used relatively simple devices for gathering data upon which to test their hypotheses. Using a list containing the names of many historically famous Americans, they asked students to indicate the men they admired by using numbers to express their degree of admiration. This procedure has "logical" validity in that it appears to be sampling the behavior to be studied. Its reliability could easily be estimated by asking the students to repeat the test a short time after its original use. If there occurred a high positive relationship between rankings on these two occasions, we could infer that the phenomenon of "admiration" was fairly stable and that our instrument was providing us with consistent information about student behavior in this respect.

The same teachers also used two other comparatively simple measurement devices: a test for measuring student information on these famous Americans, and a test asking the students to rate each other on traits characterizing the historical figures. Each of these measurement procedures could easily be checked for reliability, and both of them appear to have logical validity.

The final measurement problem in evaluating hypotheses is determining the relationship between variables. This relationship is usually determined by using statistical procedures. Some knowledge and skill is needed to choose and apply a statistical procedure appropriate for testing the significance of a relationship between given variables. These statistical procedures are not so complex that they cannot be learned by teachers. And while we do not expect teachers at the present time to develop a wide range of skills in this respect, many of these skills would enhance the teacher's ability to analyze data on behavior change. For some analyses, comparatively simple statistical procedures can be used. Many school systems employ research personnel who can assist in making elementary kinds of analyses of the data that the teacher has gathered.

It is beyond the pale of our discussion here to do more than urge teachers to study such procedures, with the suggestion that the fears they may have associated with learning them are perhaps unfounded. In any case, the requirement that data must eventually be analyzed should not deter the teacher from making careful formulations of hypotheses and systematic attempts to gather data about change in pupil behavior.

FALLACIES IN INFERENCE. Testing hypotheses can yield information on the extent to which a predicted effect occurs, but not explain *why* the effect occurred. Unless adequate control of variables has been provided for in the measuring procedure, we cannot make valid inferences about relationships among variables. Using a new spelling method is a complex process involving many variables, each of which may have some influence on pupil change. Without adequate control of these variables, inferences about the effect of particular variables cannot be made. We can only discover that when a given method was used, a change in performance was obtained. Without additional experimentation, we cannot attribute the change in performance to the new spelling method.

OBSTACLES TO CRITICAL INQUIRY

Although some aspects of critical inquiry require the acquisition of technical skills, the attitude of critical inquiry can be shared by all teachers, and all of them can make some systematic approaches to critical inquiry. Many of the obstacles to critical inquiry are emotional or attitudinal rather than rational. In the following sections we will discuss some of the emotional attitudes that interfere with developing the habit of inquiring critically into the validity of educational practices.

FEAR OF THEORIZING. Many educators seem afraid to hypothesize about educational practices. Teaching is often thought of as a practical art, and the relationship of practice to more fundamental considerations is often ignored. Some teachers will say "that theory is impractical." It is a continuing criticism of courses in professional education that they are too theoretical and too remote from the classroom.

This conception of the relationship of theory to practice is not defensible if we analyze critically what is meant by theory and practice. We have suggested that a teacher makes many decisions about specific procedures for use in promoting certain changes in pupil behavior These decisions are not made at random; they usually arise out of some conception of what procedures are likely to be effective. In principle, therefore, a theory or hypothesis underlies every decision—as we have emphasized throughout this chapter. Teachers are using theories and hypotheses even when they are not aware of them:

> We make decisions on the basis of generalizations and assumptions (hidden or explicit) and, in so doing, we act in terms of a theory. If this is done without full awareness, we run the risk of making poor decisions and are not able to see that the difficulty is not so much with the decision as with the basis for it (the theory). . . . Everyone who makes choices and judgments implies a theory in the sense that there are reasons for his actions. . . . Those who learn from their experience in ways which mean revising their judgments and decisions (hypotheses) are modifying their theories in a never-ending process of self-correction. Such people are theorizing—it may be poor theorizing, but it is theorizing nonetheless.[6]

We frequently hear theories for educational practice prefaced by the phrase "on the basis of my experience." When such a recommendation is made the recommender is explicitly formulating a generalization which he has induced from his observations. He himself may think of this generalization as a simple statement of fact, but in principle it is a hypothesis for which he has some evidence, but one which needs to be tested systematically. For the purposes of discussion here, we note that this person has, in effect, participated in the process of hypothesis-making, irrespective of the validity of the hypothesis that he supports.

A strong argument can be made for the idea that nothing is more practical than a theory or hypothesis. An observer must conceptualize the kinds of phenomena that he wishes to observe. He uses one concept to observe and gather one set of facts, and other concepts for gathering other kinds of facts. For example, the teachers who were interested in studying the relationship between information about famous Americans and student admiration of them gathered different kinds of data for measuring each variable. "Admiration" can be defined in many ways, and the kind of "facts" gathered about this variable will depend upon our definition of it. To illustrate: We could say that a student admires a famous American if he reads biographies of that person; using this definition, the facts that we would gather to measure the extent of his admiration would be facts about his

---

[6] Coladarci and Getzels, *op. cit.*, p. 5.

reading habits. The teachers whose experiment we studied, however, chose to measure admiration by the extent to which students said they admired these famous persons; they chose a different set of facts or behaviors by which to measure the extent of admiration. Larrabee[7] has made clear this point about the relationship of observation to concepts in the following statement:

> The advice "to get the facts" is not a blanket injunction to expose one's self to anything in the way of experience that may come along. It leads one to the query: "But what facts?" Certainly, if facts and theories are to be fitted together in such a way as to yield reliable knowledge, "just any old facts" will not do, nor will "any old theory" do either. Relevant facts do not label themselves as relevant. That is an element which must be added by the knower. Unless he is a mere random collector of odds and ends the seeker of knowledge cannot go through life merely looking *at* things; he must be looking *for* something; that means active inquiry with some directing factor in control.

As the above arguments imply, a necessary relationship exists between theoretical considerations and practical procedures. We have been arguing that the teacher is continually theorizing and hypothesizing. An emotional predisposition to reject the value of hypothesis-making probably leads to poor hypothesis-making and a tendency to assume as obvious and "factual" relationships which, in effect, are not.

UNWARRANTED RESPECT FOR "AUTHORITY." In an earlier chapter on the study of attitudes we noted that the prestige of a communicator can influence attitudes and opinion changes. Teachers, like almost all human beings, are susceptible to this influence. In education, unfortunately there appears to be a tendency to rely heavily on the opinions of "experts" and "authorities." Even a casual reading of educational literature will suggest how frequently the opinion of experts is used as a criterion of value. Teachers' meetings regularly feature educational experts whose apparent function is to give teachers the "truth."

We are not suggesting that some individuals are not better informed than are others, nor that we should reject out-of-hand another's opinion about the value of an educational practice. What we do advocate is a critical analysis of opinions and the rejection of *un-*

---

[7]H. A. Larrabee, *Reliable Knowledge*, Boston, Houghton Mifflin Co., 1945, p. 167.

warranted reliance upon the opinions of either actual or assumed experts. The validity of generalizations about educational practice does not depend upon the prestige of believers in these generalizations. Teachers and educational "experts" are as susceptible as anyone else to overgeneralizing conclusions and to speculating without reliable evidence. We have tried to emphasize throughout this chapter the probabilistic character of empirical knowledge. Some of the principles and generalizations that we have discussed in this book may be rejected at some future date, when better and more comprehensive generalizations are developed. If the teacher recalls the probabilistic character of knowledge, he will be protected against the tendency to accept uncritically the opinions of other individuals, no matter what their prestige.

As we noted above, some individuals will attempt to support their hypotheses about educational practice by citing their long experience in the classroom. The comment of a cynical observer is appropriate here. As this observer noted, some teachers who appeal to their "twenty years of teaching experience" are, in fact, appealing to one year of experience repeated twenty times.

EMOTIONAL IDENTIFICATION WITH PERSONAL VIEWS. Teachers are not above having emotional attachments to their own opinions. The tendency to regard our own opinions as valuable simply because they are ours, or because they are important to us, can be a genuine obstacle. If we hold a hypothesis about educational practice because it appeals to us on some emotional grounds, we should recognize that it is not being held on the grounds of its empirical validity. Holding opinions and hypotheses on emotional grounds precludes the intelligent consideration of alternative points of view. Our "common sense" will suggest that we have not yet reached, nor are we ever likely to, a state of affairs in which ideas are always held on rational grounds and propositions objectively evaluated. But the tendency to support opinions chiefly by emotions is nonetheless undesirable: the more widespread this tendency among professional educators, the more likely it is that knowledge in this field will develop only slowly.

Developing the habit of critical inquiry is not easy. Unless each teacher assumes personal responsibility for developing this approach to educational problems, the profession as a whole will continue to be guided by preferences and opinions based on uncriticized and unanalyzed personal experiences.

The point of view advocated throughout this book, and especially in this chapter, is clearly presented in the following quotation from John Dewey:[8]

> Facts which are . . . interrelated form a system, a science. The practitioner who knows a system . . . is evidently in possession of a powerful instrument for observing and interpreting what goes on before him. This intellectual tool affects his attitudes and modes of response in what he does. Because the range of understanding is deepened and widened, he can take into account remote consequences which were originally hidden from view and hence were ignored in his action. Greater continuity is introduced; he does not isolate situations and view them in separation as he was compelled to do when ignorant of connecting principles. At the same time, his practical dealings become more flexible. Seeing more relations he sees more possibilities, more opportunities. He is emancipated from the need of following tradition and special precedents. The ability to judge being enriched, he has a wider range of alternatives to select from in dealing with individual situations.

As Dewey suggests, and as this text has argued consistently, the improvement of educational practice requires teachers who can think critically about the processes of education. Such an approach promises much for the teacher himself. Educational activity conceptualized in this way can be a challenging enterprise. No longer will we view the teacher as a simple craftsman who has learned the "tools of his trade." Rather, we will see him as immersed in a potentially creative and imaginative task in which he can find intellectual stimulation by the continual analysis of the educational process.

SUMMARY

This chapter has presented a plea for a systematic, critical approach to educational practice. This plea is grounded on the following observations and conclusions:

1. Statements about educational practice are, in principle, hypotheses about relationships between teaching procedures and changes in pupil behavior, although teachers do not always

---

[8] J. Dewey, *Sources of a Science of Education*, New York, Liveright Publishing Corp., 1929, pp. 20-21.

conceptualize such statements as hypotheses. Rather, we have argued that educational practice can be improved by explicitly formulating these statements about educational practice as hypotheses.

2. Generalizations about educational practice are statements about relationships between observable events, and as such they can have only a *probable* validity; consequently, any practice must be held tentatively and critically evaluated. We have related the probabilistic character of empirical knowledge to the idea of improving educational practice. In principle, educational practice improves as we generate hypotheses of greater validity. The teacher, as a practitioner, continually makes decisions. These decisions are based upon some conception of the relationships among variables. Since the decision-making processes depend upon generalizations of this character, decisions can presumably be improved by developing generalizations of greater validity. To improve educational practice thus requires that we improve our ability to predict the relationship between teaching procedures and a set of events called "changes in pupil behavior."

Critical inquiry into the validity of educational procedures requires that teachers hold certain attitudes. Chief among these attitudes are:

3. The willingness to hold hypotheses and generalizations tentatively. Such an attitude is consistent with our conception of these generalizations as being relatively valid.

4. The willingness to challenge the obvious. Although many generalizations have an "obvious" and "common-sense" note to them, we cannot assume that an obvious generalization is also a valid one.

In connection with our discussion of hypotheses, we noted that:

5. A hypothesis is a statement of a relationship between variables; it must be stated in a testable form. This relationship cannot

be tested if the variables do not refer to empirical events, or if the variables are so vaguely defined that these empirical events are unknown.

6. A hypothesis can be developed either by induction from observable events or by deduction from more comprehensive generalizations. In either case, the hypothesis arrived at must be tested.

7. Fruitful hypotheses can be developed by deduction from generalizations derived from careful experimentation. Considerable effort can be wasted in testing hypotheses that are likely to be invalid because the generalizations from which they are developed have little validity. Unfortunately, too much educational research is devoted to testing relationships which appear to be obvious, even though they are often inconsistent with generalizations of known validity.

We have warned that reliable and valid measuring instruments must be used in the data-gathering stage of hypothesis-testing. The validity of a generalization cannot be determined if the data gathered are unreliable or irrelevant.

We have also noted that generalizations derived from experimental studies cannot be applied immediately to specific educational situations. A second order of hypotheses, derived from these broader generalizations, must be developed by the teacher. These hypotheses also must be critically evaluated. One common error in making deductions from comprehensive generalizations is forgetting that the behavior sample from which the more comprehensive generalization was developed should be substantially similar to the sample to which the particular hypothesis is meant to apply; the less similarity between samples, the less validity in the hypothesis.

Finally, we have pointed out that certain attitudes militate against adopting an attitude of critical inquiry into the validity of educational practices. The following are some of these negative attitudes:

8. The tendency to regard theorizing and hypothesis-making as impractical. We have pointed out that in making decisions,

teachers are continually using theoretical conceptions—they are, in fact, formulating hypotheses. The tendency to reject hypothesis-making as impractical is likely to interfere with clear thinking and the willingness to evaluate generalizations critically.

9. Uncritical acceptance of the opinions of experts and authorities. Such opinions are to be held tentatively, as are any other generalizations; the prestige of a communicator does not lend any inherent validity to his generalizations.

10. Emotional attachment to one's personal views or opinions. Such attachment inhibits willingness to consider alternative propositions and to evaluate critically one's own preferences.

The teacher who adopts an attitude of critical inquiry toward the educational enterprise is likely to see it as intellectually stimulating and challenging. It is this attitude that makes the teacher a professional person; it is his practice of responsible critical inquiry that lifts teaching above the realm of the skilled trades and into the company of the professions. Finding improved educational procedures is a great and ever-present challenge. Our greatest hope for meeting it successfully rests on the classroom teacher who sees the practice of his art as a profession. It must be chiefly through the work of such teachers that greater opportunities for personal development will be given the children who pass through our schools.

STUDY AND DISCUSSION QUESTIONS

1. A sixth grade teacher of social studies organizes a learning experience on the transportation system of the local community. As part of this learning experience, he takes the children on trips on the buses which are part of this transportation system. He finds that the pupils ask many more questions about the operation of the transportation system and seem to have a clearer understanding of its purposes and functions. The teacher hypothesizes that this procedure is effective in producing greater understanding of the complexities of the transportation system. What variables associated with the character of this experience and the children who participated in it may be related to the extent to which the teacher's hypothesis can be generalized to other classes and to similar kinds of experiences?

2. Assume that this same teacher is organizing a learning experience related to the operation of city government. He hypothesizes that a visit to the city council will increase the pupils' understanding of the functions of city government. He feels reasonably certain that the predicted behavior changes will occur because of his experience with the field trip in the study of the transportation system of the city. What variables in these situations may limit the extent to which the teacher may generalize results from the first experience to the second? What assumptions is the teacher making about relationships among these variables when he generalizes from his previous experiences? What factors in the second experience that may not have been present in the first experience might limit the effectiveness of this procedure?

3. Suggest ways in which the following hypotheses need to be clarified before they can be tested and before conclusions can be drawn about their generality.

   a. The use of films in social studies classes improves the students' grasp of concepts.

   b The use of films in social studies classes improves the students' ability to understand cultural differences.

   c. Field trips make the isolated and abstract facts of the text come to life.

   d. Effective problem-solving behavior results when students work on problems that have meaning for them.

4. How would you respond to the statement that a teacher's experience is the best basis for deciding what are appropriate educational procedures? In what sense is this statement defensible? What assumptions are implicit in it? How would you qualify it?

5 Some people claim that a concern for predicting and controlling the events of a classroom situation is a mechanistic approach to education. In what respects may this argument be valid? What assumptions are implicit in it? In what respects is an attempt to predict and control the events of the educative act a defensible description of the process of organizing learning experiences?

6. You will recall that a hypothesis suggested as tenable was: Pupil satisfaction is related to the extent to which teachers behave consistently with the pupils' expectations for teacher behavior. Review the experimental situations in which this hypothesis was tested (see Chapter Thirteen). To what extent are the defining conditions described in these experiments reproduced in the classroom situation? What differences may there be between the classroom situation and the experimental situation which may limit the extent to which this hypothesis can be generalized?

7. Recall, if you can, some situations in which this hypothesis appeared to be invalidated. What factors in these situations may have accounted for the fact

that the proposed relationship between teacher and pupil behavior did not seem to hold? What qualifications or sub-hypotheses would you offer to account for these variations?

8. Recall the general hypothesis that praise improves performance. Recall also the data which indicate that praise is not uniformly beneficial for all students. Suggest some other hypotheses relating differences among pupils and variations in praise and blame given them. What concepts in these hypotheses need clarification and precise definition? Select some student with whom you are well acquainted and make a specific hypothesis about the effect of praise and blame on his performance.

9. Some people argue that the teacher is too busy and the classroom situation too complicated to permit systematic critical inquiry into the validity of educational procedures. How would you respond to this argument?

10. Consider the following hypothesis: "A good teacher understands his students." Is this hypothesis stated in a testable form? What modifications would have to be made in the form of the hypothesis before it could be tested? Suggest some clarifications of meaning that are necessary before the hypothesis may be tested.

11. Recall our discussion of pupil-teacher relations and suggest some generalizations which may indicate that the above hypothesis is not likely to be highly valid.

12. Some educators have argued that, since educational theory is not highly developed at the present time, the safest procedure to use in improving educational practice is to develop educational practice by a process of trial and error. How would you respond to this argument?

13. Consider the following hypothesis: An authoritarian teacher is less likely to effect significant pupil changes than a democratic one. Identify and define in precise terms the variables and relationships suggested in the above hypothesis. Attempt to develop more specific hypotheses when you have clarified the meaning of the concepts and relationships included in this hypothesis.

14. Assume that you had a film on the role of transportation in the development of the American economy and that the content of the film was also covered in the text you were using. How could you determine whether the use of the film alone, the text alone, or the use of both is more likely to be an effective procedure for improving students' understanding of this topic? Describe how you could arrange learning experiences to derive data from which you could draw conclusions in this respect. What kinds of pupil change would you predict would be effected by the film that may not be effected by reading the text? What kinds of changes is reading the text more likely to produce than seeing the film? What kinds of pupil behavior would you observe or test in order to gather data to validate your hypotheses?

15. What hypotheses would you offer to account for the fact that some educators appear to fear or mistrust a theorizing approach to educational practice?

16 Assume that you wish to test the hypothesis that permitting students to select the goals of a learning experience improves student performance. What kinds of "facts," that is, behavioral observations, are relevant to testing this hypothesis? Describe specifically the kinds of behavior which appear to be more relevant to the test of this hypothesis.

17. A recent study provided teachers with a series of statements about educational practice. Some of these were identified as the most recent and modern opinions on what constitutes "good" educational practice. Others were not so identified. The investigator found that teachers more consistently chose, as a practice that they regarded desirable, those practices which were labeled "modern." What hypotheses would you offer to explain these data?

RECOMMENDED READINGS

The first reading is a discussion of the problem of developing a science of education. The second reading is a comprehensive discussion of methods and procedures for developing reliable knowledge concerning empirical events. The third reading is a description of some procedures teachers may use in a critical inquiry into the validity of their educational practices. The fourth reading is an example of the way in which theory may be related to one aspect of educational practice.

1. J. Dewey, *The Sources of a Science of Education*, New York, Liveright Publishing Corp., 1929.

2. H. Larrabee, *Reliable Knowledge*, Boston, Houghton Mifflin Co., 1945.

3. S. Corey, *Action Research to Improve School Practices*, New York, Teachers College, Columbia University Press, 1953.

4. A. P. Coladarci and J. W. Getzels, *The Use of Theory in Educational Administration*, Educational Administration Monograph No. 5, Stanford, Calif., Stanford University Press, 1955.

AUTHOR INDEX[1]

---

[1]Italicized numbers indicate references found on recommended reading lists at the end of chapters; the symbol q indicates that a quoted passage from the author's work is included on the page(s) cited.

SUBJECT INDEX

100-06 (figs., tab.)
Civic responsibility
Objectives of, 543 (tab.)
Class, social
 See Social class
Class groups, 656, 659, 675
Classroom
 As an environment, 15
 Problems in failure experiences, 116-17
 Use of incentives, 119-20
 Use of "exploratory periods" in 176-77
 Climate of, 513-18 (tab.), 526-27
 See also School
Classroom evaluation procedures, Ch. XV
 Scope of, 585-87
 Limitations of, 596-98 (fig.)
 Summary, 603-06
Classroom groups
 Organization of, 518-24, 656, 675
 See also Ability groupings
Climate, meaning as applied to classrooms, 513-18 (tab.), 526-27
Cliques, 237-39, 662-64
Clubs, school
 Influence of, on student status, 655-62 (tabs.), 675-76
Cognitive-attitudinal-value system, 59, 61 (fig.)
 Defined, 131
 Relation to stimulus situation, 63-64
 Relation to need system, 64
 And behavioral perception, 64-66
 Influence on conception of self, 67
 And behavior changes, 68
Cognitive processes
 Defined, 160
 Personality development and, 132-33
 Use of, in critical thinking, 178-79
 Described and analyzed, Chs. V and VI
 Influence of attitudinal-evaluative processes on, 286-93 (tab., figs.)
 Influence on teacher-pupil relations, 499
 Kinds of
  See Associative thinking; Critical thinking; Generalizations; Logical reasoning
  See also Concept formation; Concepts; Set
Cognizance, need for (Murray), 86 (tab.)
Commonality

In personality development, 8-9 (tab.)
Of needs, 85, 88
Possible errors in inferences regarding, 91
Of attitudes, interests and values in groups, 235
Common goals
 Distinguished from group goals, 520, 527
 Value of active participation in attaining, 520-21
Common sense
 In classroom problems, 116-17
 And building from simple to complex concepts, 149-50
 And retention, 195
 Ideas on logical argument, 261
Common-sense explanations of behavior, 42-43
 Inferences regarding motivation, 76
Common-sense psychology, 694, 705
 Relation to scientific psychology, 48-49
Communication
 Patterns of, and conformity pressures, 243-44
 Significance in attitude acquisition, 249, 293
 And identification process, 270-72
 As provided by groups in problem-solving, 385-89, 393-94, 523-24
 Responsibility of leader to maintain in groups, 387-89, 394, 522
 Of cultural expectations, 478-80, 485
Communicator
 Influence of prestige and credibility of, in attitude change, 254-58 (tabs.), 702, 707
Competition
 And group effectiveness, 522-24, 527
Concept
 Defined, 134-35
 Nature of, 133-36
Concept formation
 Process of, 132-33, 136-43
 Discrimination in, 134-35, 137-38, 146, 159-60
 Contrasted with memorization, 134, 143, 155, 162
 And the inferential process, 137-38
 And the character of experience, 138-40

Individual personalities and, 508-10
(fig.)
  As incentive for behavior change,
14, 99, 102, 104, 185, 281, 283,
505-08, 526
    In stabilization of imitative be-
havior, 225-27, 229, 235
    For acquisition of skills, 307, 321-
23 (fig.), 337
    For correct problem-solving, 364,
389
  Provided by groups, 238-39, 266-67
    As pressure to group conformity,
240, 243-44
  Provided by school environment,
117-20, 234
    Use in learning process, 46-47
    Not all controlled by teacher, 265
    Teachers as sources of, 285-86
    In social system of, 675
  In acquisition of attitudes, 222, 244-
45, 250, 277, 278, 280
    Example of effectiveness in pro-
ducing attitude change, 272
    See also Incentives; Prestige;
Status
Role
  Defined, 451-52
  Explained, 482-83
Role acquisition
  And personality development, 448,
459-61
  As a complex form of problem-solv-
ing, 457-59, 462, 483
  School and, 462-63, 483
Role behavior
  Defined, 448, 451-52
  And roles, 447-63 (tab.), 482-83
  Successful problem-solving by means
of, 483
  Effect on trait associations, 497
    See also Roles
Role conflict
  Defined, 672
  And the teacher's role, 672-75, 677
Role expectations, 451-52
  Problems in, for adolescents, 461
  Relation to trait associations, 496-
99 (fig.)
  For pupils, 668, 677
  Variations for teacher, 668-70, 676
  For teachers, by parents, 673, 677
  For teachers, by communities, 673,
677
Role model, 457

Role-playing
  Device for producing attitude
change, 268-70 (tab.)
  Effectiveness in attitude change,
273, 294
Roles
  And role behavior, 447-63 (tab.),
482-83
  Types of, 452-53
  How learned, 453-59 (tab.)
  Concepts involved in, 454-59
  Transfer of learning in, 460-61, 463,
483
  And adjustment to environment,
476-77
  Effects of socialization process re-
flected in, 482, 485
  In school organizational units, 656,
657
  Institutionalized, for teachers and
students, 668-70, 676-77
    See also Role behavior
Rorschach Inkblot Test, 641-42
"Rote" learning
  Relation to "meaningful" learning,
170, 171-72, 192-94 (tabs.), 203
  Does not include deductive learning,
171

Safety, need for
(Maslow), 87 (tab.)
School
  As an environment, 15-17, 18
  Behavior change brought about by,
16-17, 18
  And the cognitive processes, 132
  Responsibility in developing concep-
tual system, 159-60, 161-62
  And development of critical think-
ing, 184-85
  Function in attitude formation, 211-
12, 245, 273-80, 295
  And the identification process, 228-
35
  Influence of, on development of val-
ue system, 285-86
  And development of problem-solving
behavior, 346-47, 389-91, 394
  Need to encourage a fresh approach
to problems, 371-72
  Assumptions on problem-solving in,
375-77, 381
  And development of ability to make
hypotheses, 390, 394